Exploring Human Sexuality

Donn Byrne
and Lois A. Byrne
Purdue University

Thomas Y. Crowell
HARPER & ROW, PUBLISHERS
New York   Hagerstown   San Francisco   London

301.417
Ex7
11/522
Oct.1979

EXPLORING HUMAN SEXUALITY

Copyright © 1977 by Thomas Y. Crowell Company, Inc.

Library of Congress Cataloging in Publication Data

Main entry under title:
Exploring human sexuality.
    Includes bibliographies and index.
    1. Sex. 2. Sex customs. 3. Sex—Psychology.
I. Byrne, Donn Erwin. II. Byrne, Lois.
HQ16.E96   1977   301.41'7   77-664
ISBN 0-690-00882-1

This book is
lovingly dedicated to
our 2.0 children,

Keven Singleton Byrne
Robin Lynn Byrne

Contents

Contributors

Elizabeth Rice Allgeier
  New York State University College, Fredonia
Ben N. Ard, Jr.
  California State University, San Francisco
Arthur P. Aron
  University of British Columbia
Robert A. Baron
  Purdue University
Gilbert D. Bartell
  Northern Illinois University
Hugo G. Beigel
  Journal of Sex Research, New York
Paul A. Bell
  Colorado State University
Leonard Berkowitz
  University of Wisconsin
Ellen Berscheid
  University of Minnesota
G. N. Bianchi
  University of New South Wales
Ann Bjorseth
  Western Washington State College
Edward M. Brecher
  West Cornwall, Connecticut
Clifton D. Bryant
  Virginia Polytechnic Institute and State University
Vern L. Bullough
  California State University, Northridge
Donn Byrne
  Purdue University

J. E. Cawte
  University of New South Wales
Cornelia V. Christenson
  Indiana University
Helen Colton
  Family Forum, New York
Herbert J. Cross
  University of Connecticut
James P. Curran
  Purdue University
George Cvetkovich
  Western Washington State College
John A. DeNinno
  University of Washington
Donald G. Dutton
  University of British Columbia
Charles R. Ervin
  Cremona, Italy
J. Erwin
  University of California at Davis
Jeffrey D. Fisher
  University of Connecticut
William A. Fisher
  Purdue University
Robert Fuhr
  State University of New York at Stony Brook
John Gagnon
  State University of New York at Stony Brook
Paul H. Gebhard
  Indiana University
James H. Geer
  State University of New York at Stony Brook

Robert H. Glass
University of San Francisco
Annette G. Godow
Illinois State University
Michael Goldstein
University of California at Los Angeles
Richard Green
State University of New York at Stony Brook
Barbara Grote
Western Washington State College
Harry F. Harlow
University of Wisconsin
Hans Hessellund
University of Aalborg (Denmark)
Barbara Hogan
Cornell University Medical College
Morton Hunt
East Hampton, New York
Christine Jazwinski
Purdue University
Virginia E. Johnson
Reproductive Biology Research Foundation, St. Louis
Lewis Judd
University of California at San Diego
Harold Kant
The Legal and Behavior Institute, Los Angeles
Helen S. Kaplan
Cornell University Medical College
Nathan G. Kase
New Haven, Connecticut
Richard N. Kohl
Cornell University Medical College
John Lamberth
Temple University
Leslie Lo Piccolo
State University of New York at Stony Brook

Joseph Lo Piccolo
State University of New York at Stony Brook
Mary McIntosh
University of Leicester (England)
Jay Mann
University of California Medical Center
William H. Masters
Reproductive Biology Research Foundation, St. Louis
John C. Messenger
Indiana University
G. Mitchell
University of California at Davis
Herman E. Mitchell
University of Washington
John Money
Johns Hopkins University
Donald L. Mosher
University of Connecticut
Avodah K. Offit
Cornell University Medical College
George Orwell
Deceased
C. Eddie Palmer
Virginia Polytechnic Institute and State University
Ollie Pocs
Illinois State University
Wardell B. Pomeroy
Cornell University Medical College
Clinton Rice
The Community Skills Center, Los Angeles
Julia Sarkissian
Western Washington State College
Siegrid Schafer
University of Hamburg
Gunter Schmidt
University of Hamburg
David F. Shope
Pennsylvania State University

Jack Sidman
University of California at Santa Cruz
Volkmar Sigusch
University of Hamburg
William Simon
Institute for Juvenile Research, Chicago
Arden Snyder
Linn County Mental Health Program, Albany, Oregon
Robert Staples
Howard University
Sheldon Starr
Veterans Administration Hospi-

tal, Palo Alto
Ellen Belle Vance
University of Washington
Nathaniel N. Wagner
University of Washington
Douglas H. Wallace
Virginia Commonwealth University
Elaine Walster
University of Wisconsin
Gerald Wehmer
Salvation Army Harbor Light Center, Detroit
Stephen West
Florida State University

Preface

There is in our society a pervasive aura of explicit sexuality ranging from television situation comedies dealing with hitherto taboo topics to hard-core pornographic movies in which one can view all possible combinations of nude males and females engaging in every conceivable sexual act. *Time* magazine worries about "the plague of pornography" in a cover story, and other magazines run advertisements for sensuous condoms. In the midst of these profound changes in our culture, an increasing number of behavioral scientists have become interested in studying human sexuality, and an increasing number of college undergraduates have been enrolling in courses that deal with this aspect of behavior. One reason for the research and the courses is that there is much that we each need to learn about sex and perhaps more that we need to unlearn. Scientists and nonscientists alike find themselves asking new questions about human sexuality and reformulating old questions that we had once assumed were already resolved.

What sort of inquiries are now being made in sexual research? The following are some examples: Has there really been a change in sexual attitudes and sexual behavior in recent years? Is the mind the ultimate erogenous zone? Why do some people respond to erotic material with anxiety and disgust while others eagerly seek out the same material for their personal enjoyment? Do men and women actually differ in their sexual responsiveness? Are sexual attraction and love the same thing? Is sexual adjustment crucial to a happy marriage? Why do teen-agers often avoid using any form of contraception? What are the effects of pornography on behavior? What sexual behaviors should be considered to be abnormal? Is there a relationship between totalitarianism and sexual repression?

These and similar issues are the focus of the material presented in this book. Because new sexual knowledge is accumulating at a rapid pace, we have chosen articles primarily from among those published in the 1970s. The area of sexuality is a broad one and "belongs" to no single field; our selections, therefore, have been drawn from sociology, anthropology, medicine, and history as well as from our own field of interest—personality and social psychology. There is also a subjective dimension of sexuality and we have tried to make contact with this aspect of sexual experience by including occasional fictional quotations and excerpts. Thus, the present book tries for a comprehensive view of sexuality, which includes the anatomical, physiological, cognitive, emotional, behavioral, interpersonal, and political spheres. A broad collection of topics has been organized into four primary parts: Introduction; A Theoretical Perspective; Sexuality, Love, Marriage, and Conception; and Society and Sexuality. Each of these parts is introduced by an Overview which serves to integrate this diverse material.

The primary reason for assembling readings into a book such as this is the desire to bring students directly in contact with those conducting research. Research is not necessarily mysterious, and it would be ideal if all individuals could examine primary sources of information for themselves rather than having to rely on secondary descriptions and on conclusions drawn by others. It is our experience, however, that the average person who examines an article in a scientific journal must overcome some very difficult obstacles. When confronted by statistical symbols, parenthetical citations of names and dates, and unfamiliar terminology, even the most interested student is likely to feel dismayed. Even when research articles are carefully selected and reprinted in book form, the elements that mystify and alienate students tend to be retained. In the present volume, we have tried to overcome this problem and to bridge the gap between student and research by an extensive editing process. We have tried to separate the basic student-relevant content of each article from the content relevant primarily to the professional. When the technical details are eliminated, what remains are the ideas, the procedures, the findings, and the speculations in a form that an undergraduate can easily comprehend. Specifically, statistical notations have been eliminated, the tables and figures that are retained are simplified and explained, and references appear only at the end of each article. Introductory material has been written for every selection in order to place it in context, to tie it in with other sections of the book, and to anticipate student questions about unfamiliar concepts. The goal is to communicate to the nonprofessional without distorting the basic content of the professional's contribution. It might be noted that technical details and statistical analyses are extremely important to the advanced student, the researcher, and the professional reader; they will want to examine the original articles as well as the present edited versions. Another aid to understanding is the glossary of terms which appears at the end of the book. It should also be noted that much of the material is interesting, enlightening, and entertaining. Sometimes the "scientific study of sex" can sound terribly somber and ponderous, but it is possible to approach such research in a relaxed fashion. Most people are already aware that sex can be fun, but we would like to suggest that sex research also can be fun.

The study of sexual behavior is still something of a pioneering enterprise with more questions than answers. Those who read this book can be expected to discover some things that they did not know previously, to accept some of the ideas presented here and to reject others, and, most importantly, to raise questions that can only be answered by future research. This discovery, controversy, and curiosity represent the heart of the scientific process, and human sexuality is an intriguing arena in which to become acquainted with that process. A few readers will become intrigued enough to enter one of the scientific fields represented among our selections. Further, if any of our readers should find that some of their ideas about sexual behavior have been altered in a more realistic, less anxious, and more joyful direction, that would be a very welcome extra dividend.

PART ONE

Introduction

An Overview:
The Study of Sexual Behavior

In an undergraduate personality course at Purdue, sexual behavior is one of the topics ordinarily covered. Recently, at the beginning of this portion of the course, index cards were distributed; the students were invited to write any question they might like to have answered or discussed. As you might expect, there were dozens of questions covering most aspects of sexuality from anatomy to love. A male asked, "Is sex related to aggression?" A female asked, "How widespread is the practice of group sex among supposedly happily married adults?" A male asked, "Why, approximately a minute after orgasm, do males lose all interest completely? Personally, I would just as soon play football or eat a pizza as continue." A female asked, "Are there any differences in how males and females respond to skin flicks?" A male asked, "Why does our society teach kids to fear sex?" You may wonder about some of the same things, and an attempt is made to answer these and other questions throughout this book. In the class, one female student asked a more general question, however, when she wrote, "Are all the studies done on sex really necessary?"

Well, why *would* anyone find it necessary to study sexual behavior? Why all the surveys, the experiments, and the observations? We will first try to suggest some of the reasons for research on human sexuality, and then we will briefly describe some of the difficulties involved in conducting that research.

WHY STUDY HUMAN SEXUAL BEHAVIOR?

In one sense, the easiest and probably least satisfactory answer is that the sciences are dedicated to the search for knowledge for its own sake. The ordinary citizen wonders how grown people can go around studying dead languages, unreachable stars, and the mating call of the bullfrog. Congressmen complain that tax money is being squandered on inquiries into the kinship patterns among Australian aborigines, cell division in the amoeba, and why college students fall in love. Those engaged in research know and try not very successfully to explain that the undirected search for knowledge and understanding underlies all scholarship, all science, and ultimately all advances in our civilization. True, much of the effort is "wasted" in the sense that it neither leads us to greater understanding nor to any practical applications. The catch is that there is no way to know in advance whether either type of payoff will occur. To borrow a basketball metaphor suggested by Weinberg[3] the game plan is simply for scientists to keep the ball moving, and every now and then an Einstein, a Darwin, a Freud, or an Oppenheimer breaks through to make a basket.

All that is well and good, of course, but still we might ask, "why sex?" Since there are countless aspects of the universe that remain to be investigated and understood, why are an increasing number of individuals in many different fields turning their attention to sexual concerns, especially to the study of human sexual behavior? Asked in this way, the question becomes one of values and perhaps should be answered individually by each person engaged in sexual research. As a general answer, it may be noted that sexual needs and their satisfaction are crucial components of human behavior. Sexuality can be the basis of our most intense pleasures and our most agonizing miseries. Sexual expression can involve the closest and most intimate expression of love between two human beings or the most cruel and degrading exploitation of one person by another. One's own sexual desires can be a source of joy and delight or the basis of guilt and self-hatred. Surely, each increase in our knowledge about this powerful need and its positive and negative consequences increases the possibility that our society can progress toward a more positive and better adjusted sexual orientation than has been true in the past.

There is another aspect of sexuality that provides an additional imperative reason for expanding our knowledge base. Obviously, the biological or evolutionary "reason" for sex is procreation—the continuation of the species. While the details of conception, gestation, and birth are important areas of ongoing research, there is now a special interest in this topic from the viewpoint of limiting the number of people living on our planet. Overpopulation is a controversial public issue having political, economic, and theological overtones. Nevertheless, the actual decisions about conception and contraception are made by individuals in the privacy of their own sexual lives. For this reason, the study of human sexuality has become of vital concern in part because of the way in which it directly affects problems as seemingly remote as those involved in population planning.

An additional factor contributing to the growth of sex research is that people in general are very much interested in almost anything that is discovered by those working in this field. Even research books as respectable and difficult to read as those by Kinsey and his colleagues[5,6] and by Masters and Johnson[7,8] quickly became best sellers to the surprise and delight of their publishers. This type of public response is not simply based on prurient curiosity. There is clearly much that people feel they do not know and wish that they did know about sexual behavior. Even in this final quarter of the twentieth century, there is widespread misinformation about sexual matters. For example, country and western singer Loretta Lynn has written that, when she married at the age of 13, she was not only uninformed as to the details of sexual intercourse but was unaware of the relationship between intercourse and conception. To a less extreme degree, many more individuals possess bits and pieces of misinformation. Surveys show that substantial numbers of people incorrectly believe, among other things, that it is impossible to become pregnant during one's initial act of intercourse, that masturbation causes or contributes to the development of acne, that females ejaculate a fluid when they experience orgasm, and that sexual functioning ceases by age 60 or earlier. At a different level, there is much misinformation among scientists as well. To take just one example—prior to 1970, it was generally believed that only men became sexually aroused by erotica whereas women almost never respond to such stimulation. As we shall see in Chapter 6, new findings have led to very different ideas about male and female responsiveness.

Besides the need to obtain factual information about sexual matters, there is an additional reason for public interest in the findings of such research. Festinger's[2] theory of social comparison proposes that human beings have the need to compare themselves with others with respect to opinions, values, abilities, and all other characteristics. We want to know where we stand, whether we are like others or different, whether we are better or worse than those around us. Such comparisons go on continuously as we observe what others do and say, what they wear and what they eat, how fast they run and what movies they enjoy, and so forth. Until recent decades, however, sexual attitudes and sexual behavior were largely cut off from the social comparison process. Because it was taboo to talk about or write about sexual activity in any detail, because sexual activity was not depicted in our plays or books or movies, and because sexual interactions rarely occur in public, how was anyone to evaluate his or her sexual attitudes and activities? There was a great, and until recent years unsatisfied, need to know with respect to sexuality: what do others think and do and how frequently? Now, for perhaps the first time in recorded history, people are able to compare themselves to others with respect to their sexual orientations and activities as easily as they compare every other behavior.

So, in partial answer to the student's question as to the reason for sexual research, several possibilities have been suggested. (1) Knowledge about sex, as about everything else, is sought for its own sake. (2) Sex is an important physiological need which often affects human happiness and well-being. (3) Effective contraception and family planning may be critical necessities in determining the future of our species. (4) There is still much that is not known about sexuality, and the social comparison process impels us to learn about how others are like ourselves and how they are different. Perhaps as you read this book still other reasons for the study of sex will suggest themselves to you.

CONDUCTING RESEARCH ON HUMAN SEXUAL BEHAVIOR

There are two basic types of sexual research, and each is represented in this book. We will now describe some of the special characteristics and some of the common problems connected with *survey research* and with *laboratory experimentation*.

Survey Research

In survey research on sexuality, individuals are presented with questions about their attitudes and activities to which they give some form of verbal response. Such research ranges from the case history material gathered by clinicians in the course of therapeutic interactions with their patients to nationwide sampling of the population with standardized questionnaires and interviews. People are asked about their experiences with masturbation, intercourse, or homosexual activities. They are asked about the frequency of sexual acts, the number of sexual partners they have had, and about their emotional reactions to various activities. Sometimes the questions deal with sexual fantasies and dreams, with memories of childhood behavior, and with reactions to erotic stimulation. In survey research, background information about the respondents also is obtained so that comparisons can be made with respect to such characteristics as sex, age, race, social class, educational background, and religious preference.

The primary advantage of this type of research is that, in a relatively painless and efficient way, the otherwise private and unobservable experiences of a great many individuals become publicly available. Beginning in the latter part of the nineteenth century, these clinical and sociological studies have provided voluminous statistics on topics about which each person's knowledge would otherwise be limited to his or her own personal experiences. We now know how frequently married couples in their 20s have intercourse—and in what positions. We know what proportion of college males and females masturbate—and what fantasies they have as part of the process. We know the differences between white-collar males and blue-collar males in their feelings about cunnilingus—and how these differences are rapidly disappearing. Despite the utility and intrinsic interest of this growing array of data, there are two major problems with survey research, and you should be aware of these drawbacks.

One problem is basic to all types of sexual research. In any such endeavor, a relatively small sample of the total population serves as subjects; on the basis of their responses, generalizations are made about the population as a whole. In order to make valid generalizations, we must assume that the sample consists of randomly selected representatives of the total population. While that assumption is probably never precisely true, we know with respect to sex research that it is almost certainly untrue. The reason is that a great many people are unwilling to provide information, even anonymously, about their sexual lives. Some are fearful and anxious, some feel that it is no one's business, some are embarrassed to reveal what they believe to be abnormal or unacceptable facts about themselves, and some are suspicious that the investigator has ulterior motives for violating their privacy. Not only are many individuals reluctant to participate, but it has been found that those who volunteer for sexual research are different in systematic ways from those who refuse to volunteer; the participants are more sexually liberal, have had more sexual experience, and are more self-confident than nonparticipants.[4,9] There is evidence, however, that if subjects are truly convinced that their responses are genuinely confidential, volunteers for sex research do not differ markedly from nonvolunteers.[1]

A second difficulty with survey research is that it is dependent on what the subjects are willing and able to report about themselves. With respect to any topic, but especially with respect to sex, anxieties can lead to distortions in what subjects report about themselves. If a married individual believes that masturbation is only for kids, he or she may deny ever masturbating as an adult or may inaccurately minimize the frequency of such acts. If a female believes that nice women are repelled by pornography, she may report having no desire to see such material and having no sexual response to it. If a male believes that any interest in nude men is indicative of homosexuality, he may report that he is disgusted by the sight of male centerfolds in magazines. If an unmarried virginal male believes that everyone else is engaging in nightly sex with a succession of partners, he may describe his own sex life as an equally active one. The general point is that it is difficult to be completely candid in describing one's sexual "secrets."

In addition, even if subjects are totally honest and totally unaffected by the social desirability of their responses, accuracy still may suffer as the result of simple forgetting. If you were asked to report the date on which you first engaged in any type of masturbatory activity, the number of sexual dreams you had last month, or the average duration of intercourse, could you do so? Probably not. In studies in which there is some way to assess the accuracy of responses, it is shown that many errors inevitably creep into the self-reports. For example, when husbands and wives are asked independently about the frequency with which they engage in intercourse with one another, they tend to give somewhat different answers.[10]

In general, then, these considerations suggest that you might be at least mildly cautious in evaluating the results of survey research. These studies are valuable, and the resulting data tell us a great deal about sexuality in our society and about changes in sexuality over the years. Remember, though, that the precise figures or percentages you encounter may only apply to the liberal, experienced, confident people who volunteer to serve as subjects and that the figures may not therefore reflect what the other segments of the population do or feel. Remember also that the responses are affected to an unknown degree by what people are willing and able to verbalize about themselves.

Laboratory Experimentation

Except for studies of animal behavior, the laboratory study of sex has a much shorter history than is true for survey research. The major advantages of the experimental approach are that behavior can be manipulated and observed rather than just reported in retrospect and that the effects of specific influences can be determined while the effects of other influences are held constant or controlled. Thus, instead of asking males and females how they have responded in the past to erotic pictures, an experimenter can present each subject with the same display of pictures and ask him or her to report their immediate emotional reactions. Here, one can compare the two sexes with respect to exactly the same stimulus experience and not with respect to different experiences they might recall from the past. Instead of asking people whether sexual arousal ever leads to aggression on their part, it is possible to arouse some of the subjects and afterward provide them with the opportunity to behave aggressively. If the level of aggression is different from that of subjects who were not aroused sexually, the question has been answered directly.

Despite the very definite advantages of experimentation, there are nevertheless some difficulties with this type of research. Just as with survey research, sampling remains a problem. In fact, it seems likely that a more selective process operates in obtaining experimental subjects than is true for other types of research. That is, interviewers typically try to get a cross section of the population, but experimenters usually are forced to rely on subjects from some "semicaptive" group such as college students, hospital patients, or prisoners. Less frequently, experimental subjects are obtained by means of advertisements offering payment to those who participate. In effect, a smaller and less heterogeneous segment of the population is asked to serve in experimental studies than in survey studies. Further, they are asked to do something potentially more anxiety evoking and more time consuming than responding to a questionnaire. Experimental activities range from filling out rating scales after exposure to hard-core pornography to the direct measurement of genital changes by means of physiological recording devices. Perhaps the ultimate and least common laboratory experience is that of engaging in masturbation or intercourse under controlled and observed conditions. Ethical considerations obviously demand that any subject in any such experiment be fully informed beforehand of all details so that the individual can freely consent to take part in the study or to refuse. Most experimenters would also feel that it is important that any subjects be able to terminate participation at any time during the course of the experiment if they wish to do so. All of these factors should lead to more selective and less representative volunteers for experiments than for surveys.

The other major concern about experimentation is that of artificiality. By definition, experimental conditions are not precisely like those of the nonlaboratory world outside. Experimenters purposely create a situation at least somewhat unlike the real world so that it is possible to manipulate certain selected variables while controlling others. In all such investigations, not just sexual ones, there is the attempt to make conditions enough like the real world to permit generalization of the findings beyond the laboratory. In each instance, however, we never know for certain how accurate the generalization may be until later research demonstrates its applicability. We might guess that watching *Deep Throat* in a laboratory and then filling out a rating scale is not precisely the same as seeing the same movie at a drive-in theater with a member of the opposite sex. We might guess that having intercourse in a laboratory while attached by wires to various recording devices is not the same as having intercourse in the honeymoon suite of the Bide-A-Wee Motel. The hope, nevertheless, is that there are a sufficient number of common elements across such divergent situations to permit extrapolation from one to the other.

This brief description of the problems and pitfalls of sexual research is not meant to disparage its value but rather to suggest the reasons for caution in interpreting research findings. Science provides the best way for expanding knowledge yet devised, and there is currently a welcome explosion of what is known about human sexuality. There is no better source of information about human sexual behavior than that provided by scientific research. As a consumer of such information, you should simply keep your eyes open and remember to read the label on each research can before swallowing the contents uncritically.

REFERENCES

1. Barker, W. J., & Perlman, D. Volunteer bias and personality traits in sexual standards research. *Archives of Sexual Behavior*, 1975, **4**, 161–171.

2. Festinger, L. A theory of social comparison processes. *Human Relations*, 1954, **7**, 117–140.

3. Greenberg, D. S. Biomedical policy: LBJ's query leads to an illuminating conference. *Science*, 1966, **154**, 618–620.

4. Kaats, G. R., & Davis, K. E. Effects of volunteer biases in studies of sexual behavior and attitudes. *Journal of Sex Research*, 1971, **7**, 26–34.

5. Kinsey, A. C., Pomeroy, W., & Martin, C. *Sexual behavior in the human male*. Philadelphia: Saunders, 1948.

6. Kinsey, A. C., Pomeroy, W., Martin, C., & Gebhard, P. *Sexual behavior in the human female*. Philadelphia: Saunders, 1953.

7. Masters, W., & Johnson, V. *Human sexual response*. Boston: Little, Brown, 1966.

8. Masters, W., & Johnson, V. *Human sexual inadequacy*. Boston: Little, Brown, 1970.

9. Rosenthal, R., & Rosnow, R. L. *The volunteer subject*. New York: Wiley-Interscience, 1975.

10. Wallin, P., & Clark, A. Cultural norms and husbands' and wives' reports of their marital partner's preferred frequency of coitus relative to their own. *Sociometry*, 1958, **21**, 247–254.

CHAPTER ONE

Current Sexual Attitudes and Behavior

Sexual Changes in Society and in Science

We tend not to think much about alterations in the world around us unless they occur very suddenly or unless we deliberately pause and take the time to compare past and present. We seem to adjust or adapt fairly easily to new circumstances, especially if they develop gradually over a period of time. Experiences that would have been surprising 10 years ago, amazing 20 years ago, and unthinkable 30 years ago, become commonplace or even expected. This kind of adaptation to our modified world takes place whether the event in question is color television, environmental pollution, space exploration, or sexual expressiveness.

It can be useful to focus on change for a variety of reasons. First, different changes occur in different generations, and it is difficult to communicate beyond our own age group unless we understand the differences in the experiences of our children, ourselves, our parents, and our grandparents. Second, a realistic appraisal of the present is possible only by examining it side by side with the past. It is much easier to convince ourselves that whatever we currently do, feel, or experience is simply "human nature" if we remain ignorant of what we and others have previously done, felt, and experienced. Third, the emphasis on historical changes reminds us that the future need not necessarily be like today or yesterday. Obtaining an historical perspective will not tell us what the future will or should be, but it does give us the basis on which to attempt to make deliberate decisions about what we think the future should be.

In the following article, changes in several aspects of sexuality are discussed. The increasing sexual explicitness and permissiveness in books, magazines, and movies is paralleled by analogous changes in scientific research on human sexuality. Investigators can and do study sexual behavior today in ways which would have been impossible in past decades. Whether these changes in society and in research represent a step forward or a step backward for our civilization is, of course, a matter you must decide for yourself.

Sexual Changes in Society and in Science

Donn Byrne

Sexuality plays a curious role in human behavior. There is obviously a physiological need for sexual gratification which becomes especially intense after we have reached puberty, and yet many individuals have lived a lifetime without engaging in sexual intercourse. Sexual activity is an obvious source of human pleasure, and yet societies have consistently created barriers to sexual expression in the form of laws, customs, and taboos which are incorporated by individuals as fears, shame, and guilt about forbidden thoughts or practices. Sexual curiosity is surely a powerful motivating force beginning in early childhood; studies of both human infants and the young of other primate species show this clearly.[12] Nevertheless, it has traditionally been extremely difficult to obtain accurate information on this topic from parents, teachers, ministers, or even physicians.

Now, it seems, the times they are changing. Not only are there very few advocates of lifelong chastity, we are currently propagandized from all sides about the joys of sex, the importance of being sensuous, and the physical and psychological benefits of frequent, creative, and explosive orgasms. Today, we are finally able to learn everything that we always wanted to know about sex and more besides.

Though it is not possible to draw any firm conclusions about causes and effects, there have been changes over the last couple of decades in society's tolerance of sexual expression, in the way in which scientists investigate sexual behavior, and in both sexual attitudes and sexual behavior. In this and the following two articles in Chapter 1, some of these changes will be described.

A thorough study and documentation of societal changes is beyond the scope of the present book. Rather, what follows is an impressionistic sampling of some of the more dramatic changes in public tolerance for the depiction of sexual behavior. These observations are primarily limited to North America and to portions of Western Europe, because there are vast cross-cultural differences in societal permissiveness regarding all aspects of sexuality.

CHANGES IN FICTION:
FROM **** TO THE BLOW-BY-BLOW DESCRIPTION

Writing about sexual behavior in an explicit manner was not an invention of the late twentieth century. From the *Kamasutra* through the underground writings of Victorian England up to this morning's hastily scribbled rest room graffiti, men and women have been writing in various degrees of explicit detail about the intricacies of obtaining sexual pleasure. The notion of employing legal sanctions against such writing first arose in England in 1708 when there was an attempt to censor *The Fifteen Plagues of Maidenhead*. Surprisingly, the judge ruled in favor of the author and noted that punishment of such "bawdy stuff" was a spiritual rather than a legal matter. The forces of law and order soon rallied from this initial defeat, however, and strict antipornography statutes were enacted throughout the world. In the first half of this century, the groundwork for artistic sexual candor was laid (no pun intended) when James Joyce published *Ulysses* in 1914 and D. H. Lawrence published *Lady Chatterley's Lover* in 1928. Both books were the objects of censorship and court battles in more than one nation. Free speech eventually triumphed, and the final outcome of such struggles may be seen today in what is legally permissible and readily available to the general reading public. The language and the graphic detail that were long characteristic of underground hard-core pornography gradually worked their way into the socially acceptable fiction on the best-seller charts.

One way to illustrate these changes is by means of a few personal observations. In the early 1940s when I was of junior high school age, there was a great furor about the sexual content of Betty Smith's *A Tree Grows in Brooklyn*. Being inquisitive and having tolerant parents, I obtained a copy and avidly read this widely banned book with lascivious intent. To my disappointment, the scorching sexual revelations were limited to such material as the mention of condoms brought home from the rubber factory where a female character was employed and a scene in which a derelict exposed himself to the young heroine as she climbed the stairs to her family's apartment. Neither my sex education nor my erotic fantasies were notably enriched.

Near the end of World War II, Kathleen Winsor[19] went several steps further when *Forever Amber* was published. This novel contained much more sex than the one about the Brooklyn family. Amber rose from poverty to success by means of her sexual talents, but the reader had to infer these rather than learn of them directly. Even a supposedly explicit sexual scene was astonishingly circumspect from today's perspective:

> Their mouths came together with sudden devouring violence. Unexpectedly she began to cry and her fists beat against him, passionate, demanding. Swiftly he pushed her back upon the bed and her arms strained him to her. When the storm was spent, he lay with his head on her breast, relaxed against her. Now their faces were still and peaceful, content. Tenderly her fingers stroked through his course black hair [p. 719].

In reading such scenes, it is interesting to speculate as to what they would convey to a Martian anthropologist who was attempting to understand human behavior by reading novels. He might well remain unenlightened as to how we reproduce our species. This was also the period during which sex was often indicated by having a male and a female enter a boudoir near the end of a chapter only to find the chapter quickly concluded by****. The next chapter would then open on the following morning when one of the characters would awaken, stretch languorously, and smile in response to fond but unspoken memories of the previous night.

In the postwar novels, sex began to be treated much more openly but still with caution as to sexually explicit details and even words. In *From Here to Eternity*, James Jones took us with his soldiers to a house of ill repute in Honolulu, but he did not provide explicit details as to what they did there. In *The Naked and the Dead*, Norman Mailer[16] had to settle for having his servicemen continually say "Fug you" or "Fug the sonofabitchin' mud" in place of a similar word that everyone knew they actually would have said. He also described a few bits of almost explicit sexual interaction as in this flashback to prewar petting in Willie's car:

> God, I love you, Beverly.
> I do too, Willie. (The car radio is playing when it rains it rains . . . Pennies from Heaven. Her hair has a clean root smell, and her nipple is delicately fragrant against his mouth. He feels her writhing in his grasp, sobbing-panting.)
> Oh, kid.
> I can't, Willie, I love you so much please I can't [p. 551].

By the mid-1950s barriers to the spoken word were crumbling rapidly. Novelists were somewhat more free in naming and describing bodily parts and functions than the public had previously experienced, at least in respectable books. Nevertheless, a book such as Vladimir Nabokov's *Lolita* in 1955 was more notable for the age discrepancy between the nymphet title character and the middle-aged Humbert Humbert than for any painstaking descriptions of their sexual activities.

By the 1960s there were almost no limitations on what authors wrote, and the reading public was exposed to ever more explicit descriptions of increasingly varied sexual activities. An interesting example is Norman Mailer's *An American Dream*. The same author who was forced to create "fug" to protect the sensibilities of the public in 1948 was able in 1964 to cover six pages with the details of what happens after Rojack finds the maid masturbating while looking at an erotic magazine. The hero proceeds to take off his clothes and to engage, in alternating minutes, in both anal and vaginal intercourse. After some indecision as to which orifice should be the scene of his ejaculation, "I chose her cunt." Two years later, Jacqueline Susann wrote the first of her sexual novels, *Valley of the Dolls*, in which a large cast of characters provided multiple variations in sexual couplings. By 1967, the last barrier was broken by Philip Roth in *Portnoy's Complaint* when the joys and guilts of male masturbation were repeatedly chronicled. This particular sex act apparently shocked Ms. Susann who remarked on a talk show that she wouldn't mind meeting Mr. Roth, but she would not like "to shake his hand." Though less startling at the time, *Portnoy's Complaint* also deals with fellatio, cunnilingus, and group sex. Among these relatively current books, however, there is still a lingering tendency to defuse the sexual content by avoiding the more shocking sexual words, leaving many of the actual details to the reader's imagination, and/or interlacing the sexuality with humor. Authors and publishers seemed to be trying to adhere to Judge Woolsey's 1933 court decision under which *Ulysses* was finally admitted into the United States. In that landmark ruling, the favorable outcome rested not only on the literary merit of the total book but also on the crucial point that *Ulysses* was not obscene because it "did not tend to excite sexual impulses or lustful thoughts" and did not "tend to be an aphrodisiac." The general point was that sexual content was acceptable so long as it did not elicit sexual arousal.

The trend toward greater and greater permissiveness in this regard continues into the 1970s, and there now seems to be little possibility of additional increases in sexual candor, because all restraints have been abandoned. Apparently it is now possible not only to be explicit but also to excite sexual impulses and lustful thoughts with literary aphrodisiacs. It seems safe to predict that the days of euphemisms and asterisks are forever behind us. In 1973, in *Fear of Flying*, Erica Jong describes her heroine in bed for the first time with her lover, Adrian. She notes that the best thing about making love with a new man is being able to rediscover a man's body because her husband's body is too familiar. She describes the taste and feel of his "pink penis" and "hairy balls."

One last example from the 1970s demonstrates an explicit description of petting which is not at all like Mailer's sparse description of the activities of Willie and Beverly written 25 years earlier. In *Final Analysis*, Lois Gould[10] thinks back to her experiences with a boy when she was 16:

> He was the first person even to insert a fingertip in any orifice of mine. I had never until then believed I actually had an orifice that would be of any use to anyone. I certainly did not think I had one of a size suitable for insertion of anything, not even a Junior Tampax, much less a sophomore cock.
>
> By the time we drifted apart, this dumb Adonis and I, he had put a finger all the way up inside me, and I had held his entire cock in my hand, and I was more firmly convinced than ever that nothing like that would ever make it where his finger had gone. He ejaculated once onto a plaid skirt I had . . . [p. 31].

In summary, the sexual content of our fiction has undergone dramatic and far-reaching changes during the last four decades.

CHANGES IN MAGAZINE PHOTOGRAPHS: FROM NUDIST VOLLEYBALL TO MASTURBATORY MODELS

Almost as soon as the camera was invented, enterprising pornographers began taking photographs of individuals, couples, and groups engaging in the full array of possible sexual acts. These early productions were, by the way, often sad and dreary scenes in which not very attractive individuals struck their poses, tried to hide their faces, and mysteriously left their socks on. Again, our interest here is not in these underground photographs but in what could be freely and legally obtained at the corner newsstand or drug store. Falling somewhere in between furtive underground pornography and cocktail table respectability are such publications as *SCREW*; when the pictorial content of *SCREW* becomes as socially acceptable as that of *Newsweek*, magazine sexuality will equal novelistic sexuality in its candor. Not surprisingly, photographic sex has consistently lagged behind the written word over the years in terms of permissiveness. Even today, the U.S. Customs will allow any and all written material to be brought into this country without question whereas "obscene" photographic depictions of sexual acts are routinely confiscated.

Prior to the publication of the first issue of *Playboy* in the early 1950s, sexual photographs were essentially nonexistent in widely circulated publications. The major exceptions were *National Geographic* featuring bare-breasted women and the nudist magazines such as *Sunshine and Health* which featured nude males and females playing endless games of volleyball or smiling healthfully beside a swimming pool. The poses of the nudists were carefully chosen so that nets, trees, or diving boards prevented lapses into total frontal nudity. Other exceptions were the crime magazines in which partial nudity was most likely to appear if a female had been brutally murdered and left in a provocatively disheveled condition. Changes in magazine pictorials can perhaps best be documented in the girly publications. We will consider only the photographs printed first in *Playboy* and then in more recent competitors such as *Penthouse*. The changes between 1954 and today are as great as the changes in novels.

In its earliest years, *Playboy* depicted nude females in much the style of calendars traditionally hung on the walls of car repair shops. In such photographs it was possible to reveal breasts but with enough airbrushing about the nipples to soften any unseemly erotic details. The genital area was not usually shown because only the girl's back or side was facing the camera, or she was holding a strategically placed pillow or telephone. Bubble baths were also used to achieve the same modest purposes. The closest these early efforts came to baser sexuality was when the model utilized a small cat to obscure her lower abdomen, thus allowing the leering viewers to create their own puns.

These pictorial representations grew slowly but steadily bolder through the 1960s, and frontal nudity became commonplace. Nevertheless, there was a curious aspect to these photographs. No one had pubic hair. In fact, the airbrush was used heavily to blot any trace of genital detail. Our Martian anthropologist whose observations were limited to such pictures would be forced to assume that earth females are as genitally blank as Barbie dolls and that they are afflicted with a cloudy mist floating about their thighs. Depictions of breasts became bolder, however, and the photographers began to furnish ice cubes so that the models could rub themselves just before the shutter snapped in order to ensure erect nipples.

The mild changes in photographs of female nudes escalated rather rapidly in the 1970s. Though there are journalistic disputes about the claim, *Penthouse* is said to be the first magazine to have shown pubic hair. Then, *Cosmopolitan* introduced a nude male centerfold with much of actor Burt Reynolds on display. Because both of these innovations brought only increased sales rather than legal sanctions, there have been efforts to go one step further almost every month in *Playboy*, *Penthouse*, *Oui*, *Viva*, *Playgirl*, and other pictorial magazines of this type. In successive issues, the female models began gazing toward their breasts, then touching them, then gazing toward their genitalia, then placing their hands suggestively near this bodily region, and finally engaging in increasingly explicit masturbation. Pictures began showing multiple models, with two females and then both sexes—kissing, touching, embracing. Males at first were usually fully or partially clothed, but gradually they, too, were photographed in the nude in flaccid poses.

At the present time magazine photographs seem to be at a stage analogous to that of fiction in the late 1940s and early 1950s. That is, there is now some simulated or suggested intercourse and other sexual acts that escape the status of hard-core pornography by the absence of erect penises and the failure to show the penetration of any bodily orifice. Despite the differences between novels and magazines, the direction of change is very much the same in both media, and the changes have taken place over the same general period of time.

CHANGES IN MOVIES:
FROM TWIN BEDS TO SPLASH SHOTS

Once again, it must be stressed that explicit sexuality in the movies is not a new phenomenon. Whenever appropriate, our technological advances are quickly applied to the sexual field. There are pornographic movies stretching back to the turn of the century and they include such American classics as *The Casting Couch* (an early black-and-white sound production), *Smart Alec* (starring the Texas stripper Candy Barr, who was the well-publicized girl friend of a mobster), and *The Nun* (starring a young Ava Gardner look-alike). In such movies, sexual acts were clearly depicted, and care was taken to demonstrate in close-ups that the actors and actresses were actually performing these exploits and not simulating them.

For the respectable movie-going public, film content was very different. After some early flirtation with nudity, Hollywood adopted a production code of ethics in 1934 which spelled out a restrictive and detailed list of just what could and could not be said and done on the silver screen. Generations of us grew up in the 1930s and 1940s being shown that all married couples sleep separately and presumably chastely in twin beds, that kisses involve only lip contact which was never prolonged, that one foot always remains on the floor when two people even talk to each other in the same bed, and that those reckless or immoral enough to engage in (unseen) nonmarital sexual intercourse would (1) most certainly become parents and (2) suffer for their misdeeds with countless well-deserved physical and psychological miseries. Nudity, even partial nudity, was unthinkable. Teen-age sexuality was exemplified by Andy Hardy whose goal was to obtain permission to kiss a girl lightly on the lips as the climax to several dates after a suitable show of reluctance on the girl's part. After such a kiss, a happy Mickey Rooney would shout "Wow!" and run home, jumping over several fences and hedges.

By the end of the 1940s and early 1950s, various producers began to rebel at the restrictions of the code. Two notable examples were the *The Outlaw* in which Jane Russell exposed more than the approved amount of cleavage and *The Moon Is Blue* in which the word "virgin" was actually spoken aloud. The box office success of such code breakers led to the weakening of the restrictions on movie content and a gradual increase in the boldness of what was said and done on the screen.

During the 1960s, the language of the films became much more realistic; the sexual scenes became gradually more explicit; partial or total nudity was not uncommon; and themes of premarital sex, rape, and adultery were treated with varying degrees of openness. The nude backside of a stand-in for Elizabeth Taylor in *Reflections in a Golden Eye* is one example. A number of foreign films went beyond the limits of those made in the United States, and their success probably hastened the changes in this country.

Stretching the limits of respectability in those years were the "sexploitation" films typified by *The Immoral Mr. Teas* or any of the Russ Meyer productions in which female nudity was the most important element along with simulated indications of sexual acts. During that decade, there were numerous almost explicit soft-core sexual movies featuring the perpetually aroused stewardesses, nurses, and schoolgirls of male fantasies.

The proliferation of sex and, to some degree, violence in the movies of this period led to the death of the production code in 1968 and the establishment of the rating system which serves primarily to restrict film content on the basis of the age of the viewer. An implicit, though possibly unintended, implication of this system was that *anything* could be shown in an X-rated movie. This message plus ambiguously permissive Supreme Court decisions soon led to the big-screen hard-core sexual movies of the 1970s. The surprise of such landmark movies as *Deep Throat* and *Behind the Green Door* was not only in the amount of money they earned in return for modest investments, but in the acceptance of this new film genre by the middle-class public. Porno-chic was born. The result was a flood of such movies with gradually improved acting, writing, and direction, and the creation of a galaxy of sex film stars on both the East and West Coasts of the United States. After both Marilyn Chambers and Linda Lovelace had appeared on the Phil Donahue television show to chat with an audience of housewives, it became evident that a new era of film permissiveness was firmly upon us. In the films themselves, the typical content, regardless of the story line, included a series of explicit sexual acts such as masturbation, cunnilingus, fellatio, and intercourse in a variety of positions. In the tradition of the old stag films, the latter two acts usually involve withdrawal of the penis at the climactic moment so that the male's ejaculation can be verified as genuine (in the industry, such scenes are known as wet shots or splash shots). It might be noted that while lesbian scenes occur frequently in these movies, male homosexual encounters tend to be found only in films made exclusively for showing in gay theaters to a gay audience. Perhaps because of the relative impact of the big screen productions in sound and color, changes in movies seem even more dramatic than the analogous changes in books and magazines.

This brief summary of the increased acceptability of sexual material in our society is only part of the story, of course. Beyond books, magazines, and movies, there are many other ways in which sexuality has become more and more explicit. Topless, and sometimes bottomless, go-go dancers, waitresses, and now waiters have been with us since Carole Doda first made national news exposing her siliconed breasts as she danced in San Francisco in the early 1960s. Some late-night radio talk shows are devoted solely to discussions of sexual issues. Nudity in the theater became respectable after the launching of *Hair* and *Oh! Calcutta!* The advertising industry has moved gingerly from displays in which an attractive, clothed female was draped over the hood of a new car to provocative wording and nudity that is used to sell stereo equipment, blue jeans, after-shave lotion and perfume, cameras, and perhaps most surprising of all—condoms in varying styles and colors by mail. Even television stations have turned to explicit sex in after-midnight X-rated movies and erotic cable TV presentations. In an even greater departure from the past, in 1975 the first TV commercial for contraceptives was broadcast in San Jose, California: "The makers of Trojans condoms believe there is a time for children . . . the right time . . . when they are wanted." The general point is clear—our society has undergone massive changes in the last few decades, and especially in the last few years, with respect to its tolerance for sexuality. There are some signs of reversal in this trend (such as the conspiracy trial of *Deep Throat* in Memphis) but it would be difficult to turn back the clock permanently.

CHANGES IN SEXUAL RESEARCH: FROM SURVEYS TO LABORATORY INTERCOURSE

Though no one can convincingly document cause and effect, it will soon be seen that the changes in what the general public reads and views are paralleled by actual changes in sexual attitudes and behavior. There is another set of changes that is perhaps less well known—the way that sexual behavior is studied by scientists and the public acceptance of such research.

At the turn of the century when Sigmund Freud[5,6] first began to report on and theorize about the sexual aspects of his patients' lives, much of the scientific community was as scandalized as was the general public. Notions of child sexuality, castration fears, penis envy, and incestuous desires were rejected as being totally unacceptable. During this era, people were equally astounded by the writings of Richard von Krafft-Ebing[15] and Havelock Ellis.[4] Much of this work was clinical in tone and dealt with abnormal functioning, however, so it would be dissociated from the everyday concerns of most people. Survey studies of normal individuals were potentially more upsetting.

Even though earlier pioneers such as Lewis Terman,[18] Katherine Davis,[3] and George V. Hamilton[11] had conducted surveys of sexual behavior in the 1920s and 1930s, it was the work of Alfred Kinsey,[14] first published in the late 1940s, which burst into national prominence. People were interested in, embarrassed by, comforted with, and incredulous about the carefully compiled data on the frequency of intercourse, masturbation, homosexuality, oral sex, and other unmentionable activities contained in the interview schedules. Kinsey and his co-workers were greeted by some of the same condemnation that Freud met half a century earlier, but the sales of each volume of the "Kinsey Report" suggested strongly that more people wanted to read such books than to burn them.

The experimental study of human sexual behavior was necessarily slower to develop than the survey or interview studies. In the psychological literature, a few tentative studies began to appear in the 1950s. A typical experiment was one by Clark[2] in which only male subjects were used, the stimulus material consisted of "cheesecake" photos, and the response measure was the Thematic Apperception Test in which the subjects were asked to write stories to describe a series of pictures.

Experimental studies in the laboratory became gradually more common and less cautious by the late 1960s and into the 1970s as we shall see in subsequent parts of this book. Among the changes were the increased use of female subjects, the increased use of stimulus materials that could be characterized as explicit hard-core erotica, and the use of response measures that ask subjects about physiological changes in their genitals as well as about the details of their sexual behavior outside of the laboratory.[1]

Some of these investigations go beyond verbal reports; experimenters directly assess the excitement of males by measuring erections with a penile plethysmograph[7] and the arousal of females by recording vaginal contractions, temperature, and blood volume.[9,13] Most dramatic of all have been the investigations of Masters and Johnson[17] which first were widely published in the late 1960s, in which individuals and couples were observed as they engaged in various sexual acts while their physiological responses were simultaneously monitored.

Because of the intense popular interest in sexual matters, research on sexual behavior tends to be communicated quickly to the general public by ways of mass media magazines, advice columns, articles dealing with popularized science, and textbooks in psychology, sociology, physiology, and home economics.[8] In a similar way, the cultural mores as to what is acceptable to read, view, talk about, or do are translated quickly into the experimental procedures and questionnaires of those conducting sexual research. The societal and scientific changes with respect to sexuality have been of major proportions, and we can only begin to speculate about the meaning of these changes for each of us. For good or ill, these changes are occurring; they are among the most challenging and intriguing aspects of life in the final quarter of this century.

REFERENCES

1. Byrne, D. Sexual imagery. In J. Money & H. Musaph (Eds.), *Handbook of sexology*. Amsterdam: Excerpta Medica, 1976.

2. Clark, R. A. The projective measurement of experimentally induced levels of sexual motivation. *Journal of Experimental Psychology*, 1952, **44**, 391–399.

3. Davis, K. B. *Factors in the sex life of 2,200 women*. New York: Harper & Row, 1929.

4. Ellis, H. *Studies in the psychology of sex* (1899). New York: Random House, 1936.

5. Freud, S. *Three contributions to the theory of sex* (1905). New York: Dutton, 1962.

6. Freud, S. *The sexual enlightenment of children*. New York: Collier, 1963.

7. Freund, D., Sedlacek, F., & Knob, K. A simple transducer for

mechanical plethysmography of the male genital. *Journal of the Experimental Analysis of Behavior*, 1965, **8**, 169–170.

8. Gagnon, J. H. Sex research and social change. *Archives of Sexual Behavior*, 1975, **4**, 111–141.

9. Geer, J. H., Morokoff, P., & Greenwood, P. Sexual arousal in women: The development of a measurement device for vaginal blood volume. *Archives of Sexual Behavior*, 1974, **3**, 559–564.

10. Gould, L. *Final analysis.* New York: Random House, 1974.

11. Hamilton, G. V. *A study in marriage.* New York: Boni, 1929.

12. Harlow, H. F. Lust, latency, and love: Simian secrets of successful sex. *Journal of Sex Research*, 1975, **11**, 79–90.

13. Jovanovic, U. J. The recording of physiological evidence of genital arousal in human males and females. *Archives of Sexual Behavior*, 1971, **1**, 309–320.

14. Kinsey, A. C., Pomeroy, W., & Martin, C. *Sexual behavior in the human male.* Philadelphia: Saunders, 1948.

15. Krafft-Ebing, R. von. *Psychopathia sexualis* (1886). Philadelphia: F. A. Davis, 1894.

16. Mailer, N. *The naked and the dead.* New York: Holt, Rinehart & Winston, 1948.

17. Masters, W., & Johnson, V. *Human sexual response.* Boston: Little, Brown, 1966.

18. Terman, L. M., Buttenwieser, P., Ferguson, L. W., Johnson, W. B., & Wilson, D. P. *Psychological factors in marital happiness.* New York: McGraw-Hill, 1938.

19. Winsor, K. *Forever Amber.* New York: Macmillan, 1944.

Changes in Sexual Attitudes in the
Past Generation

Most observers agree that sexual attitudes are changing rapidly in the direction of increased tolerance and permissiveness. It is obvious that the depiction of sexual activities and concerns that would have been unthinkable a few years ago is now accepted as a matter of course in movies that children may attend and in family programs shown on television during "prime time." As has been discussed, with respect to publications and films restricted to adult audiences, there is literally no sexual activity which is not now being written about or photographed. Such changes in public offerings suggest that there must also have been changes in private sentiments. How can we verify these impressions? Beyond our own circle of friends and relatives, can we find out what people in general feel about the acceptability of masturbation, premarital intercourse, oral sex, or anything else?

In 1972, the Playboy Foundation sponsored a nationwide investigation of the sexual attitudes and behavior of over 2000 adults in various parts of the United States. There was an effort to represent the total population as closely as possible with respect to sex, age, race, marital status, education, occupation, and rural versus urban backgrounds. The findings of this study serve to bring those of Kinsey "up-to-date," and they are presented in detail by Morton Hunt in his book, *Sexual Behavior in the 1970s.*

A portion of that book dealing with sexual attitudes, which is presented here, verifies what many of us have guessed, except perhaps that the general attitudes are a bit more liberal and permissive than might have been anticipated. That is, attitudes about sex education, females initiating sexual advances, premarital intercourse, homosexuality, masturbation, mate swapping, oral sex, anal intercourse, and pornography all seem to be more positive than anyone would have predicted as recently as 10 years ago. Whether this increased tolerance is an indication of a more relaxed and less maladjusted sexual outlook, as we believe, or whether it represents the final evidence of our culture's decadence and decay, as some may fear, it is important that we know what our fellow citizens actually do feel and how they evaluate various aspects of sexuality.

Changes in Sexual Attitudes in the Past Generation

Morton Hunt

We sought to examine sexual attitudes before investigating overt behavior. The Kinsey team did so, too, but attached little value to the answers and reported very little attitudinal material except in the form

Reprinted in an edited version from: Hunt, M. *Sexual behavior in the 1970s.* Chicago: Playboy Press, 1974. Pp. 19–24.

of broad, impressionistic comments. They reasoned that an individual's acts show what his attitudes really are, while the things he says are "little more than reflections of the attitudes which prevail in the particular culture in which he was raised."[3] Kinsey himself had originally been a biologist dealing with infrahuman creatures—wasps, in fact—which may account for his antiverbal bias. It is not, however, shared by most sociologists or psychologists. For one thing, sociologist Ira Reiss, a leading investigator of contemporary sexual mores, compared the expressed standards of a group of 248 unmarried college students with their own actual behavior and concluded that "in the great majority of cases belief and action do coincide."[6] But even when what a person says is not the same as what he does, his expressed attitudes indicate some of his feelings about his own behavior, sometimes revealing self-disapproval, wishful thinking, unsatisfied hungers, and so on. And even if what he says sometimes reflects not his own feelings but the views that he thinks of as socially acceptable, this yields important information as to the probable direction of behavioral change in the future, for it is well established that when attitudes change, behavioral change follows suit.

Because attitudes were so sparsely reported in the first and second Kinsey volumes, we could make only a few direct comparisons to those works. But even without a firm statistical base line, it is abundantly clear to anyone who is reasonably acquainted with the state of sexual attitudes a generation ago that in many particulars our data show a dramatic shift toward permissiveness (by which we mean tolerant or liberal attitudes toward sexual ideas and acts, especially those held and practiced by other people), and more generally toward sexual liberalism (by which we mean both attitudinal permissiveness and freedom to include certain formerly forbidden acts in one's own behavioral repertoire). The new permissiveness and liberalism are not, of course, homogeneously distributed throughout the population. But even taking the sample as a whole, and assuming it to be reasonably indicative of the society as a whole, we find a remarkably large proportion holding far more permissive attitudes than those which were dominant a generation ago. The following are a few examples:

Three-quarters of all males and more than three-quarters of all females feel that schools should teach sex education, and by far the largest number of these feel strongly about the matter.

Should the man always be the one to initiate sexual intercourse? Over four-fifths of all males and females said no, and most of them took the strong position on the matter. Only 1 out of every 20 males and 1 out of every 40 females took a strong position against female initiative. There is nothing comparable in Kinsey, but it is worth pointing out that in marriage manuals written or still being sold as late as the 1940s, authors carefully assured their readers that it was permissible and even desirable for the woman to initiate sexual activity on occasion, a reassurance that would hardly have been necessary if this were not a point on which most men and women needed education.[2,7]

Attitudes toward premarital intercourse have definitely swung strongly toward the permissive and approving end of the spectrum. While Kinsey offers nothing directly useful concerning attitudes in this area, the Roper polling agency asked national samples, in 1937 and again in 1959, "Do you think it is all right for either or both parties to a marriage to have had previous sexual intercourse?" There was virtually no change over that long span of years: Both in 1937 and 1959, 22% said it was all right for both men and women, 8% said it was all right for men only, and somewhat over 50% said it was all right for neither.[8] But samples taken in the 1960s by various sociologists, including Ira Reiss, Harold Christensen, and Robert Bell, suggested that attitudes on this issue were changing markedly, particularly among the younger part of the population.[6] Our own survey provides evidence of a very considerable shift toward permissiveness: Depending on the degree of affection or emotional involvement between the partners, anywhere from 60 to 84% of our males felt that premarital sex was acceptable for men, and anywhere from 44 to 81% felt it was acceptable for women. The females in our sample were somewhat less permissive, but even so, anywhere from 37 to 73% felt that it was all right for men, and anywhere from 20 to 68% felt that it was acceptable for women. Similarly, when we asked our respondents what they thought of the statement "People who have sex before marriage are more likely to have happy and stable marriages later on," 59% of the males and 43% of all females agreed with the statement, a definite indication of a major shift in the direction of permissiveness. A 1973 Gallup poll, made after our own survey, showed a quite comparable shift over a very short period. In 1969, 68% of a national sample had said premarital sex was wrong, but in 1973 only 48% said so. While older persons were more conservative than younger ones, the shift was as great among them as among the young.[5] And one more indication: In the early 1940s, the Roper agency found that from 64 to 72% of a national sample, depending on social class, felt that men should require virginity in a girl for marriage.[8] We did not ask this, but did offer the statement "Most men want to marry a virgin" —and found that only half of our total sample agreed, a sharp drop from the Roper figures. Moreover, well over two-thirds of the women and three-quarters of the men did not agree that a women who goes to bed with a man before marriage loses his respect.

Our questionnaire offered the simplistic proposition "Homosexuality is wrong," representing the unequivocal moral norm on this matter that has existed in our culture since early Christian times. But over half of all women and close to half of all men in our survey disagreed. Nearly half of all men and women, in fact, indicated in response to another item that homosexuality should be legal; slightly smaller proportions felt it should not; and the rest had no opinion.

We asked respondents for their reactions to the statement "Masturbation is wrong." Fewer than 8% of the men and a little over 8% of the women agreed strongly, while roughly five times as many of each sex disagreed strongly. Even lumping together the "strongly" and "somewhat" responses, we find only one-fifth of all men and women viewing masturbation as wrong, and well over two-thirds viewing it as not wrong. The general population has evidently adopted an attitude toward masturbation held only by the enlightened and psychologically sophisticated a generation or so ago.

On a number of issues that have long been thought to run counter to majority opinion, we found near-majorities or even large majorities of our total sample taking the supposedly unpopular or avant-garde view. We had distinct majorities, for instance, favoring the legalization of prostitution, the legalization of abortion and the adoption of divorce laws that eliminate the need to offer reasons to the court.

Mate swapping, virtually unmentionable until recently, and violative of our most deeply entrenched ideas about sex and marriage, is wrong in the eyes of a majority—but, surprisingly, not an overwhelming one. Only 62% of men and 75% of women agreed that it was wrong, while a sizable minority—nearly one-third of the men and one-fifth of the women—felt that it was not.

Although no specific data on attitudes toward the use of the mouth upon the sexual organs exist in Kinsey, we can judge the attitudes of a generation ago by the circumspection with which both fellatio and cunnilingus were treated even in so daring a marriage manual as that of Van de Velde. (Most other authors of mariage manuals at that time either avoided the subject altogether or mentioned it only in passing, noncommittally observing that psychiatrists and other experts did not necessarily consider these acts perversions, if used occasionally and only as foreplay.) But when we offered the statement "It is wrong for a man to stimulate a woman's genitals with his lips or tongue," three-quarters of all men and four-fifths of all women disagreed, most of them strongly. An even larger majority of men and very nearly as large a majority of women, also refused to characterize as wrong the woman's stimulating of the male genitals with her lips or tongue.

In contrast to the ancient Greeks and Romans, and to many other peoples, Christian civilization has always held anal intercourse to be among the vilest of perversions and the blackest of sins. We expected to find some measure of tolerance for it appearing as part of the general liberal trend, but were unprepared for the results that came out of the computer. Only a little over one-quarter of all men and women agreed with the statement "Anal intercourse between a man and a woman is wrong," while well over half of each sex disagreed. The data are so remarkable that it is worth giving them here in detail. The explicit permissiveness of the "Disagree" replies is, if anything, understated by Table 1-1, since the unusually large proportion of "No opinion" replies may represent noncriticism of the practice. This is not to say that the majority of our sample considers anal intercourse appealing, exciting or mutually satisfying, but the majority clearly no longer accepts the historical evaluation of the act.

Both the Gallup and the Harris polls have reported in recent years that very large majorities of Americans want pornography to be controlled by stricter laws, or even outlawed.[1] But the congressionally authorized Commission on Obscenity and Pornography sponsored its own rather deeper-probing survey and concluded that while only one-third of all Americans feel that adults should be allowed to read or see any sexual material they wish, over half indicated that they would feel this way if it were proven that such material does no harm.[1] Our own data indicate a similar admixture of restrictive and permissive feelings, and of traditional and liberal responses to encounters with erotic materials. Four-tenths of all men and women reported that pictures, drawings, movies, and writings showing or describing sexual acts either disgust them or cause a mixture of disgust and delight; yet anywhere from one-half to over nine-tenths also admit to being sexually aroused by various material of this sort. The latter figures are up to four times as large as the comparable figures reported for women by Kinsey, and up to twice as large as his figures for men.[4] In some part, the greater arousability probably has to do with greater opportunity; undoubtedly, a larger number of women today see erotic materials with some frequency than they did a generation ago. But apart from opportunity, it is obvious that a substantially larger part of the population than formerly, especially the female population, not only sees erotic materials any-

Table 1-1
"Anal Intercourse between a Man and a Woman Is Wrong"

	Percentage Giving Each Response	
	Males	Females
Agree strongly	17	18
Agree somewhat	10	9
Disagree somewhat	26	25
Disagree strongly	33	32
No opinion	14	16

More than half of the subjects disagreed with the statement, "Anal intercourse between a man and a woman is wrong." Only 27% of the subjects expressed agreement.

where from occasionally to often but has become sufficiently uninhibited to be aroused by it, even though continuing to feel an admixture of revulsion or guilt due to cultural conditioning.

Thus, taking the sample as a whole, there is ample evidence of a marked shift toward permissiveness in sexual attitudes. Putting it another way, the average American now holds many opinions about sex that a generation ago were rarely held by any but highly educated urban sophisticates and bohemians.

REFERENCES

1. Commission on Obscenity and Pornography. *The report of the Commission on Obscenity and Pornography.* Washington, D.C.: U.S. Government Printing Office, 1970.

2. Davis, M. *The sexual responsibility of woman.* New York: Permabooks, 1959.

3. Kinsey, A., Pomeroy, W. B., & Martin, C. E. *Sexual behavior in the human male.* Philadelphia: Saunders, 1948.

4. Kinsey, A., Pomeroy, W. B., Martin, C. E., & Gebhard, P. H. *Sexual behavior in the human female.* Philadelphia: Saunders, 1953.

5. *The New York Times,* August 12, 1973.

6. Reiss, I. L. How and why America's sex standards are changing. *Transaction,* 1968, **5**, 26–32.

7. Stone, H., & Stone, A. *A marriage manual.* New York: Simon & Schuster, 1952.

8. Wheeler, S. Sex offenses: A sociological critique. In J. Gagnon & W. Simon (Eds.), *Sexual deviance.* New York: Harper & Row, 1967.

Changes in Sexual Behavior in the Past Generation

One of the familiar catch phrases of recent years has been "the sexual revolution." The existence and extent of such a revolution have been debated, and numerous research projects have attempted to determine precisely what behavioral changes may have taken place in our culture, especially among adolescents and young adults. Speculation has varied widely. Some have suggested that sexual behavior has remained much the same over the years and that the only change is a verbal one. That is, people are no more sexually active now than in grandma's day, but currently they *do* feel free to talk about it. The opposite view is that sexual freedom is sweeping the country and that touchy-feely encounter groups, swinging suburban orgies, and bisexuality have replaced canasta, television, and bowling as leisure time activities. Again, how do we find out?

In the same *Playboy* investigation described previously, Morton Hunt gathered information about contemporary sexual behavior and, whenever possible, compared these findings with those of Kinsey. It is a general rule that attitude change is followed by behavioral change, but the magnitude of change is likely to be greater for attitudes than for behavior. Thus, we would expect the shift toward increasingly permissive and tolerant sexual attitudes to be followed by similar, though less extreme, shifts in sexual behavior. That is precisely what Hunt discovered among his subjects.

Between the 1940s and the 1970s, there have apparently been increases in the frequency of many types of sexual behavior, including masturbation (among both married and unmarried individuals) and premarital intercourse. There are also marked increases in sexual activities such as cunnilingus, fellatio, and anal erotic acts. Interestingly, homosexuality seems to be no more common now than in Kinsey's day, acts of sadism and masochism occur as rarely today as ever, and bestiality even appears to have decreased in frequency. Such popularly discussed activities as mate swapping and group sex undoubtedly occur more frequently than before, but they are still restricted to a very small proportion of the population. Adultery does not appear to be increasing in popularity and neither does prostitution. Most of the subjects in this survey agree that the most satisfying sex is that which occurs in an affectionate relationship between emotionally involved partners. Purely recreational sex has not become an integral part of our culture.

There is, of course, no final answer to the question of whether the kinds of behavioral changes documented by Hunt constitute a sexual revolution. It is clear, however, that Americans are engaging in more varied sexual activities more frequently than ever before. It is also clear that, for most people, this new sexuality takes place within the confines of a loving two-person relationship.

Changes in Sexual Behavior in the Past Generation

Morton Hunt

We have seen that during the past generation the sexual attitudes of Americans in general have shifted considerably in the direction of permissiveness, and among younger adults this shift has been so pronounced as to markedly diminish the attitudinal dissimilarities previously associated with differences in social class, educational attainments, religious feelings, and political orientation.

But have there also been corresponding changes in overt behavior? Have most people merely become more tolerant of sexual liberation in others, or have they themselves become more liberated in their own actions? An uncritical reading of the more lurid accounts of contemporary sexual behavior would lead one to imagine that young Americans have no hesitancy about doing virtually anything to be found in the lexicon of sexual behavior, and that the casting off of all restraints, internal as well as external, is the true meaning of sexual liberation. Indeed, we found some advocates of sexual liberation who were embarrassed by their own inability to enjoy every activity suggested to them. As one young divorcee said, "I feel so silly—this fellow I'm seeing is keen on rimming [performing analingus on her], but I always get embarrassed and turned off by it. I guess I'm not as loose as I'd like to be." And a young man said, "Some of my friends tell me I'm still hung-up because I can't bring myself to try sex with guys. Maybe they're right— I mean, what difference does it really make? But I'm chicken, or something; I just can't do it."

But most people read a different meaning into sexual liberation. They regard it not as an obligation to do anything and everything but as a freedom within which they have the right to remain highly selective, choosing only those sexual acts that meet their emotional needs. It is true that a number of practices that were proscribed and avoided by all but the sophisticates a generation or so ago have now been adopted, or at least tried out on occasion, by many people in various parts of American society; but a number of other practices have remained generally unacceptable and uncommon. While many Americans now use forms of foreplay and coital variations that were shunned by the previous generation, and while they take a somewhat more unfettered enjoyment in their own sensations, by and large they have added to their repertoire only acts that are biologically and psychologically free from pathology, they have remained highly discriminating in the choice of their sexual partners, and they have continued to regard their sexual

Reprinted in an edited version from: Hunt, M. *Sexual behavior in the 1970s.* Chicago: Playboy Press, 1974. Pp. 31–38.

acts as having deep emotional significance rather than as merely providing uncomplicated sensuous gratification.

Even masturbation continues to be linked to sexual acts of emotional significance; a large majority of men and women in every age group say that while masturbating they most commonly fantasize having intercourse with someone they love. But they do feel notably freer than formerly to administer such sexual relief to themselves in times of tension or deprivation. While we found only small increases in the percentages of all males and all females who have ever masturbated (over nine-tenths of our males and over six-tenths of our females have done so at some time in the course of their lives), we did find that girls are far more likely today to start masturbating early in adolescence, and that even boys begin somewhat earlier.[1,2] Moreover, as young adults, single males and single females masturbate considerably more frequently than formerly.[1,2] Both of these trends, we feel, indicate the lessening of guilt feelings. (They might also indicate increased sexual frustration, but since the very same single men and women are also having more intercourse, this possibility can be ruled out.)

What is even more indicative of lessened guilt feelings is the increase we found in masturbation among the married. It was surprising, in 1948 and 1953, to learn that any married people masturbated at all; today it may be equally surprising to learn that many more of them are doing so, and that the males are doing so far more often. Kinsey's data showed, for instance, that in the 1940s more than 4 out of 10 married men between the ages of 26 and 35 still masturbated,[1] while today, according to our own data, more than 7 out of 10 married men in approximately the same age range do so. Moreover, the frequency with which married men masturbate has increased considerably: The median (the typical, or midpoint) individual, among married males who still masturbated in that age group in Kinsey's sample, did so about 6 times a year,[1] as compared with 24 times a year in our own. Among married women in the same age range, Kinsey found one-third masturbating, the median frequency of those who did so being about 10 times a year,[2] we found no increase in frequency among our own comparable married women, but more than twice as large a proportion of the women were involved.

Even allowing for any differences between Kinsey's survey methods and ours which might have slightly overstated—or, for that matter, understated—the change, the increases are remarkable. What can they signify? They might, of course, mean that the marital sex relations of young people today are inferior to those of a generation ago, but other data from our survey effectively eliminate this possibility. Alternatively, and more probably, the figures indicate that whenever sexual frustration does occur within marriage, caused by sexual or emotional conflict, unavoidable separation, or abstinence due to illness, pregnancy, and other extrinsic factors, young husbands and wives feel freer than their counterparts of a generation ago to turn to masturbation. That they do so without any residual feelings of guilt or self-contempt seems doubtful. We do feel, however, that such feelings must at least be far weaker in the young today than they were in the young a generation ago.

In the area of premarital intercourse, our figures confirm the popular impression: It will come as no surprise to anyone to learn that it is a good deal more acceptable and more common today than a generation ago. This applies to men as well as women. In Kinsey's study, well over one-quarter of unmarried American males (excluding those with only grade-school education) had not yet experienced intercourse by age 25[1]; in our own 1972 sample, the comparable figure is about 3%. The more significant increase in premarital intercourse has, however, taken place among females: One-third of the females (single and married combined) in Kinsey's sample had had premarital intercourse by the age of 25,[2] as compared with more than two-thirds in our sample. Of his women who were married before or by 25, between 42 and 47% had had premarital intercourse,[2] as compared with 81% of ours. The double standard, it would appear, has been relegated to the scrap heap of history.

But if young women are much more likely than their mothers were to feel that they have a right to a complete sexual life before marriage, they do not exercise that right in a lighthearted and purely physical way; the inhibitions of the *demi-vierge* of the 1940s have been replaced not by free-and-easy swinging but by sexual freedom within the confines of emotional involvement, the new norm being, in sociologist Reiss' words, "permissiveness with affection." In Kinsey's study, 46% of all married women who had premarital intercourse had had it only with their fiances,[2] in our sample, while twice as many had had premarital intercourse, an even larger proportion—slightly over half—had limited it to their fiances, and among the youngest women in our sample the figure was still higher. It is very likely that in absolute terms there are more single young women today than formerly who are willing to have intercourse without any emotional ties, but in relative terms it remains true that most sexually liberated single girls feel liberated only within the context of affectionate or loving relationships.

The repertoire of sexual variations used by both unmarried and married people seems to have broadened considerably since Kinsey's time. Many younger Americans have now adopted, or at least occasionally experiment with, variations which only the sexually sophisticated used to employ. In the 1940s, for instance, only 4 out of 10 of Kinsey's married males said they had ever kissed or tongued their own wives' genitals[1]; in contrast, 63% of all our males say they have done so in just the past year. Only about 4 out of 10 married males in Kinsey's sample said they had ever been fellated by their wives[1]; 58% in our sample say they have been in just the past year. A remarkable aspect of this change is that it has taken place in all age groups, though to the greatest extent among the young.*

As we expected, college-educated, nondevout, politically liberal, and white-collar people feel freer to use these and other advanced techniques of foreplay than do noncollege, devout, politically conservative, and blue-collar people. Yet here, too, as with sexual attitudes, the shift toward liberalism among the young is generally narrowing the gap and tending to bring about something close to a consensus or dominant sexual ethic among the young, despite the diversity of their life styles. As an example, consider cunnilingus once more: In Kinsey's time about one-sixth of all males with only high school education ever performed this act on any female, while nearly half of all males with at least some college education did so.[1] In our own sample not only have more men in each category done so, but among younger men the gap has vanished —in fact, there now seems to be a gap in the opposite direction. But one need not suppose that cunnilingus has, in reality, become more popular with the lower-educated men than college men; the fact is that noncollege men start active heterosexual lives earlier and marry earlier than college men, and thus get around to cunnilingual activity sooner. In any event, it is apparent that lower-educated men no longer view the practice as unnatural, unmanly, and disgusting but have adopted the college-educated men's view that it is natural, manly, and aesthetically pleasing.

Still more remarkable is our evidence that the buttocks, and even the anus—regarded as erogenous and sexually attractive areas by many other cultures—are gaining some measure of acceptance among Americans. We do not see an increase in pathology in this trend, for there were few responses in our survey or our interviews indicative of obses-

---

Table 1-2
"Have You Ever Performed Cunnilingus?"

	Percentage Replying "Yes"	
	Some college	No college
35 and over	68	50
Under 35	75	83

More males indicate that they have performed cunnilingus than was true in Kinsey's time, and the percentages are greatest for the younger males. In addition, Kinsey's data indicating the greater frequency of cunnilingus among college-educated males than among noncollege males has disappeared (or even reversed) among the younger males in the 1970s.

---

* Even among married men 45 and over in our sample, nearly one-third had been fellated by their wives in just the past year (that is, with some regularity); in Kinsey's sample, only about one-third of college-educated men of 46 and over had had the experience, even once, in their married lives.

sive anality, or of coprophilia and coprophagia (fecal fetishism). We do, however, find that rather large minorities of men and women have had at least some experience of nonpathological forms of anal stimulation. Kinsey,[1] as mentioned earlier, offered no data on these matters and even noted, in his volume on the male, "Anal activity in the heterosexual is not frequent enough to make it possible to determine the incidence of individuals who are specifically responsive to such stimulation [p. 579]." While we do not know how many people respond strongly to such stimulation or employ anal foreplay regularly, we did find that such techniques as fingering, kissing, and even tonguing of the anus have been used, at least experimentally, by anywhere from a sizable minority to a majority of younger Americans and by a small but measurable minority of older ones, and that about one-quarter of married couples under 35 use anal intercourse at least now and then. Once again, not only do the young employ these practices more readily than older people, but among the young the factors of devoutness, occupational level, education, and political orientation make relatively little difference. Liberation to regard the buttocks and anus as sexual objects is not yet general throughout our culture, but is becoming so.

The new freedom, in short, extends primarily to acts which are not pathological, which do not jeopardize the basic conception of marriage, and which do not disjoin sexuality from affection or love. Major change has thus occurred within a framework of cultural continuity. A genuine overthrowing of the past and of all cultural values concerning sexual behavior would be evidenced by such things as (1) the displacement of vaginal coitus by nonvaginal sex acts *substituting* for it rather than *preliminary* to it, or by sex acts violating biological and/or psychological criteria of normality, such as sexual connection with animals, sadomasochistic acts, and homosexuality; or (2) a major increase in sexual acts that fundamentally alter the connection between sex and marriage, such as mutually sanctioned extramarital affairs, mate swapping, and marital swinging; or (3) a growing preference for sex acts devoid of emotional significance or performed with strangers.

As nearly as we can tell—many of these practices not having been surveyed a generation ago—there is no evidence that any such radical change or violent discontinuity with the past has occurred.

To generalize, we find, as to point 1, that sex acts with animals are actually less common than when Kinsey was taking histories; homosexuality is not measurably more common than in his time (though there are, to be sure, difficulties in comparing our data to his on this issue); sadomasochistic acts, for all their popularity in humor and pornography, are very uncommon (less than 2½% of our sample had had any sadistic sexual experience in the past year, a similar percentage had had any masochistic sexual experience in the past year, and for most of these people such experiences had been very few in number); and oral, anal, and masturbatory methods of gratification have not been substituted, in any systematic or significant way, for vaginal intercourse.

As to point 2, we find that those much publicized sexual practices that greatly alter the relationship between sex and marriage are far less common than they are generally alleged to be. Granted that our survey methods may have missed some fraction of the most unconventional persons in the country, we think it significant that in our total sample, which closely parallels the national population in most ways, only 2% of our married males and less than 2% of our married females have ever participated in mate swapping with their spouses, and most of them on very few occasions. As for covert extramarital intercourse, despite the popular impression that it is virtually universal, its overall incidence has not changed for either sex; the only changes we do find are a moderate increase among men under 25, and a considerable one for women under 25—but even the latter increase only brings these young females close to, but not up to, the male level of activity. It is also worthy of note that the great majority of married people—including the youngest group— are not at all inclined to grant their mates permission for overt extra-marital sex acts.

As to point 3—sex devoid of emotional significance, or sex with strangers—a trend in this direction should go hand in hand with an increase in prostitution (there is no such increase), in group sex, especially with multiple partners (only 16% of all our males and 3% of all our females had ever had the latter kind of experience, and most of them rarely or only once), and in a considerable increase in premarital coitus of a purely physical or sensual sort (but this, as we saw a moment ago, is not what most young unmarried people desire). Finally, in an attitude section of the questionnaire we offered the statement, "Sex cannot be very satisfying without some emotional involvement between the partners." There was very little difference in the reactions of the various age groups; large or very large majorities of all of them agreed with the statement—most of them strongly.

To the majority of Americans, sexual liberation thus means the right to enjoy all the parts of the body, the right to employ caresses previously forbidden by civil or religious edict and social tradition, and the right to be sensuous and exuberant rather than perfunctory and solemn—but all within the framework of meaningful relationships. Sex, for the great majority of Americans—including the liberated—continues to express loving feelings or to engender them, or both. It has not been successfully disjoined from love and remade into a simple appetite, except by a tiny minority of swingers.

This ought not surprise us, after all, for there is a wealth of evidence in the literature of psychology to show that the physical care and love given the child by the mother and the father promote digestion and other autonomic functions, create a sense of health and well-being, and thus build into the nervous system a deep, abiding linkage between sensuous well-being and the state of loving. And being laid down in our nervous structure so early in life, this synthesis of sex and affection is not likely to be dissolved by the liberation of American sexuality from its heritage of guilt and shame.

REFERENCES

1. Kinsey, A., Pomeroy, W. B., & Martin, C. E. *Sexual behavior in the human male*. Philadelphia: Saunders, 1948.
2. Kinsey, A., Pomeroy, W. B., Martin, C. E., & Gebhard, P. H. *Sexual behavior in the human female*. Philadelphia: Saunders, 1953.

PART TWO

A
Theoretical Perspective

An Overview:
Four Aspects of Human Sexuality

No one has yet constructed a theory which encompasses all of the details of sexual behavior. Mostly, investigators working in this field have been interested in a specific problem and how it might be explained. We think it could be useful, however, to present a rough conceptual framework in an attempt to bring some of this material together. We will briefly consider four aspects of human sexuality. These aspects correspond in part to mankind's developmental history. The earliest sexuality involved simply a biological process that resulted in *reproduction*. With human beings, sex eventually became more complicated as people acquired *learned variations* with respect to what stimulus conditions created sexual arousal and what behaviors could be sexually satisfying. The intellectual ability of our species also has enabled us to create *imaginative fantasies* and to utilize these to control our sexual activities. Finally, for a great many reasons, sexual behavior began to be regulated and these efforts to control sex resulted in negative as well as positive *emotions* becoming associated with sex and sexuality.

In outlining each of these four aspects of sexuality, we will consider three phases of the sexual act as adapted from Masters and Johnson.[10] First, there is *stimulation* of the sexual drive which leads to characteristic bodily changes, especially in the genitals. Second, this aroused state leads to *sexual behavior* of various kinds. Third, sexual behavior ordinarily results in *orgasm*. We will describe the variations in these three phases in conjunction with the four aspects of human sexuality.

REPRODUCTION

The biological function of sexual behavior is to maintain the species. All living organisms must reproduce in some fashion, and this most often involves the production of sperm by the male and of ova by the female plus some mechanism to bring these microscopic elements together in order to create a new member of the parents' species. The process of conception need not involve any direct physical contact between the two sexes. For example, many female fish deposit their ova in the mud, and the male afterward deposits his sperm in the same location; many plants depend on mobile insects to complete their reproductive cycle by tramping about from blossom to blossom with pollen on their feet. There is no necessary reason for such activities to be enjoyable, and we could have evolved in such a way that the sexual act was something to do automatically (as when we grow fingernails) or something to do to avoid pain (as when we breathe). Neither fingernail growing or breathing is especially fun or something we ordinarily think much about. As it happens, we mammals developed in such a way that reproduction involves a pleasurable interaction between two individuals. What are the basic details of reproductive sexual behavior?

Stimulation Phase

Sexual arousal occurs in response to internal cues that are regulated by hormones and external cues that involve a member of the opposite sex. Hormone level is crucial to sexual arousal among lower animals, and they mate only when their sexual glands produce the appropriate substances. Thus, sex often occurs only at specific periods or during specific seasons. Among the higher species such as human beings, there is little or no direct relationship between hormonal state and the sexual responsiveness of either males[13] or females.[7]

If an animal is physiologically primed for sexual stimulation by his or her glands, arousal will occur if the appropriate external cues are encountered. Such cues can involve any of the senses, but the most common one is smell. Females produce a sexual attractant in their vaginal secretions called pheromones. These substances are very powerful in other species—male monkeys without the sense of smell will not mate,[11] and pheromones placed on a male rat cause other males to attempt to mount him and engage in intercourse.[5] Though human females produce similar substances, there is no evidence that males are sexually aroused by their odor.[6] It might be noted that in the world of commercials we are taught that some odors (bad breath, underarm wetness, smelly feet) will drive the opposite sex away while other odors (perfume, after-shave lotion, soap) will attract eager partners from miles around. There is little scientific evidence to support either claim.

Visual cues are also important among many species, and our closest primate relatives become aroused when they see the sexual organs of a potential sexual partner. Stimulation among male chimpanzees, for example, occurs whenever females bend over and display their genitals. All such sexual cues serve to arouse the individual, to bring about the appropriate physiological changes in the penis and vagina, and to motivate the two sexual partners to approach one another closely.

Behavioral Phase

The behavioral phase begins when the male and female interact by touching, biting, and licking one another as they progress to intercourse in which the penis is inserted in the vagina. Each species has a characteristic pattern of coitus that includes the single thrust of the bull into the cow, the series of mountings and withdrawals practiced by the male rat, and the vigorous and increasingly rapid thrusting of the monkey. One commonality among all mammals except ourselves is that intercourse takes place from a rear entry position with the male standing behind the crouching female, clutching her with his two front paws. Only very rarely, and then only in captivity, has a pair of mating animals been observed to engage in any variant of this position.

No one knows the sexual practices of the earliest human beings, of course, but it seems likely that their behavior would not have been very different from that of our primate relatives. By the time that our ancestors developed to the point at which they could create pictures portraying sexual behavior and words to describe it, they had also created new sexual positions and activities.

Orgasm Phase

In each species, the sexual act ends with the ejaculation of the male, depositing sperm in the female's vaginal cavity. Intercourse is clearly rewarding to both sexes, but there is no evidence that females below the human level experience orgasm. Males do, and each species behaves in a characteristic way with respect to the vocalizations, the facial expressions, and the bodily movements that occur when the climax is reached.[4]

LEARNED VARIATIONS

All animals have the ability to learn—to alter their behavior as a function of experience. Organisms as highly developed as mammals are able to learn very well. In nature, this learning ability is obviously an asset to survival. In captivity, animals have been taught to do an amazing variety of "unnatural" things, with food as the most common reward. Thus, at circuses or on television we can marvel at dancing elephants, performing dogs, and motorcycling chimpanzees. Sexual gratification is a powerful reward, and it could lead to equally remarkable learning. Animal trainers find food more convenient, however, and the satisfaction of sexual needs does not ordinarily involve the learning of new responses. Only when animals are deprived of their usual sexual outlets (as sometimes happens in captivity) are they motivated to learn alternative sexual behaviors such as masturbation or homosexual acts. Human beings, however, began spontaneously to learn sexual variations at least many thousands of years ago, and this learning has brought us very different types of sexuality beyond that of simple intercourse between a male and a female.

Stimulation Phase

By the classical conditioning process, any stimulus can become associated with sexual arousal and hence become arousing itself. Thus, any visual stimulus, any smell, any sound, any taste, any bodily sensation can become a sexual cue. For example, there is nothing naturally arousing about a motel room, a bed, or underclothing, but we can easily learn to associate them with sexual desire and to become aroused in response to them.

We each know in our own lives that we have had experiences which created links between particular stimuli and sexuality. If you read the advertisements in sexual publications, the letters written to sexual magazines, or case history material, you can quickly discover that at least some human beings have learned to be stimulated by almost everything imaginable. Probably through accidental conditioning experiences, individuals have learned to be excited by articles of clothing, portions of the body of the opposite sex and/or of the same sex, the stump of an amputee, being bound and dominated, binding others and dominating them, receiving pain, giving pain, taking an enema, drinking champagne, entering a rest room at a bus station, smelling a bouquet of roses, listening to the Rolling Stones, seeing a "Do Not Disturb" sign on a hotel door, and much else you might name. For human beings, stimulation is by no means limited to a partner of the opposite sex.

Behavioral Phase

An infinite variety of behaviors may be learned if the activity leads to reward, and this is as true of sexual behavior as any other. Over the centuries, members of our species have discovered multiple ways to engage in sexual acts.

For example, intercourse can occur in many different positions, and ancient drawings and carvings from Greece, Rome, China, Japan, India, Africa, and the Americas show graphically that people have long approached mating from every conceivable angle. In addition, people learned to masturbate and to stimulate one another manually, to use orifices such as the mouth and anus for sexual pleasure, to interact with multiple partners of either sex, to seek gratification with members of other species, to use fruits and vegetables to stimulate their genitals, and to utilize inanimate objects ranging from bicycle seats to battery-powered vibrators.

Thus, people have discovered multiple ways to experience genital friction beyond that of contact between penis and vagina in an unvarying position.

Orgasm Phase

The ability to learn also affects the orgasm phase of sexual behavior. For example, individuals have discovered ways to delay orgasm and hence to prolong sexual activity, to have multiple orgasms (at least among females), and to intensify orgasms by simultaneously stimulating other parts of the body or through the use of drugs. More important, perhaps, is the fact that varied stimulation and varied behavior lead to orgasms that preclude the possibility of reproduction. As we shall see, the fact that sex involves both procreation and recreation has raised issues and provided problems which no society has ever completely resolved in a satisfactory way.

IMAGINATIVE FANTASIES

Though there is no way to document the existence of imagination in other animals, we know that our fellow human beings easily and frequently create pictures and stories both while they are asleep and while awake. Some of these fantasies involve sex, and that adds still another dimension to human sexuality.

Stimulation Phase

As we progress up the evolutionary scale, there is an increase in the complexity of the brain, especially of the cerebral cortex. One result is that, in the higher mammals, behaviors such as sex are controlled less by built-in physiological mechanisms such as hormones and reflexes and more by thought processes.[1] Among the consequences of this development is that the "sex drive" tends to be based in large part on self-stimulation by means of fantasies rather than on hormonal production and external cues.

People are able to create sexual scenes in their minds, and these scenes are sexually arousing.[3] The power of erotic imagination is such that human sexual activity need not be adversely affected by nonfunctioning sex glands. Neither the removal of ovaries or testes nor their gradual decline in the aging process necessarily decreases sexual desire or impairs sexual functioning.

It may even be that differences in the level of sexual activity among individuals or across cultures lies not in biological differences but in the extent to which people learn to stimulate themselves with sexual fantasies. It should be noted that such fantasies may be created by the individual, may consist of memories of past experiences, or may be adapted from stories and pictures created by others. Surely one of the functions of erotica is to add to the storehouse of sexual fantasies that individuals utilize when they wish to become aroused.

Behavioral Phase

Though it seems not to have been widely acknowledged or discussed until recent years, most people utilize sexual fantasies to maintain or increase their excitement during sexual acts such as masturbation and intercourse. It thus appears that human sexuality is often far more than a biological need. Rather, it is often a self-created motive that is satisfied in the context of an imaginative scene in which the individual plays a starring role.

Presumably, the fantasies accompanying sexual behavior not only increase the individual's pleasure but they also counteract the effects of boredom or monotony that can arise with overfamiliarity. For example, happily married couples can engage in a limited number of physical acts with the same partner in the same bed for several decades while imagining a limitless variety of activities, partners, and settings.

Orgasm Phase

It also seems that the pleasure accompanying orgasms can be enhanced by the fantasies that go along with the sexual act. Further, individuals who find it difficult to achieve orgasm can often be helped when they are taught to utilize fantasies.[8] It can be seen, then, that imagination may make a marked difference in one's desire for sex, enjoyment of sexual activity, and ability to reach a climax.

EMOTIONS ASSOCIATED WITH SEX

It is obvious that sex is naturally pleasurable. Unless there were interference, sex would be experienced as something good, happy, fun, entertaining—in short, as something totally positive. We know, of course, that this is very often not so. Sex can be the source of anxiety, guilt, fear, anger, and disgust. Think of the words commonly used to describe sex and sexuality—dirty, smutty, filthy, nasty. Sex is all too often seen as somehow unclean and embarrassing. How did such feelings come to be and what effect do they have on human sexuality?

Sex as a Source of Problems

Among the earliest human beings, it is likely that intercourse was as natural and as simple and as entertaining as eating food. Either act was a source of discomfort only when there was an obstacle preventing gratification. Thus, the primary factors regulating early sexuality were the availability of partners and the strength to win out over rivals. Three elements gradually arose which complicated sexuality—the knowledge that intercourse leads to pregnancy, the learning of diverse sexual practices, and the tendency of each society to regulate the sexual behavior of its members.

The connection between the sex act and the creation of babies is not as obvious as you may think. Both tended to occur frequently along with a lot of other activities, and it actually is rather amazing that intercourse *is* in fact responsible for the creation of new individuals. Even in the present century, primitive tribes have been found in which that link was not yet perceived. Once people grasped the cause of conception, however, they began to formulate rules concerning who was permitted to have intercourse with whom. Therefore, ideas about incest, about the value of premarital chastity, and about the complications of adultery began to arise in various social groups as they developed ideas concerning who was responsible for whom and about the duties and privileges of a permanent mate. As other sexual activities developed, the very existence of the group could be threatened by any nonprocreational activities such as masturbation, oral and anal intercourse, homosexuality, and bestiality. Because of the high death rate, a tribe or other group could increase in size and strength only if sperm were regularly being deposited in vaginas and not elsewhere.

These concerns and the rules that evolved to solve them became translated into customs, religious taboos, and laws. People were ridiculed, exiled, imprisoned, tortured, and killed for violating the sexual codes. It became an important aspect of socialization for each generation to instill ideas in the next about good sex and bad sex. Bad sex was anything that did not conform to the rules and good sex generally became limited to marital sex. The teaching process most often has involved strong emotional overtones in which the forbidden activities or even thoughts become associated with feelings of shame. Not surprisingly, emotional responses to bad sex often were generalized to all sex. It is fairly easy, for example, to teach a young person that the body is something to hide, that the genitals are especially shameful, that masturbation is wicked and dangerous, that lustful thoughts are harmful to body and soul, and that premarital sex is to be avoided at all costs. It is not easy, however, to teach the same person to relax at the conclusion of the wedding ceremony and to enjoy marital sex happily ever after.

Even when the rules or the reasons for them change, we are all stuck to some degree with our heritage of sexual anxieties. For example, we no longer believe that masturbation has dire physical consequences; most individuals of both sexes now realize that masturbation is natural and most report that they masturbate. Despite all this, how comfortable are *you* in openly discussing your masturbatory practices with your friends and family? Though there are vast individual differences in the degree to which sexuality has negative connotations, few people are completely free to enjoy sex as easily as they enjoy eating hamburgers.

Emotions and the Three Phases of Sexuality

Most of the research on the emotional aspects of sexuality has dealt with differences among individuals and the way in which sexual anxiety and sexual guilt affect reactions to sexual stimulation, sexual behavior, and the attainment of orgasm.

Some of this research will be presented in the following chapters.

Briefly, it has been found that sexual excitement may be perceived as an entertaining and pleasurable state or as a cause for negative feelings; similarly, erotic stimuli may be viewed as something to be sought for pleasure or as disgusting pornography to be censored.[2] When negative feelings predominate, various sexual acts are likely to be viewed as obscene,[2] and there is a relatively low frequency of sexual activity.[12] Finally, negative emotions lead to decreased enjoyment of the sexual act and to an interference with the ability to have an orgasm.[9] The effect of emotions on all phases of sexuality is great, and much of the research in this area deals with attempts first to discover the way in which these feelings are learned and then to develop procedures to reduce negative feelings.

We will next turn to a more detailed examination of these four aspects of human sexuality: reproduction, learned variations, imaginative fantasies, and the emotions associated with sex.

REFERENCES

1. Beach, F. A. It's all in your mind. *Psychology Today*, 1969, **3** (2), 33–35, 60.

2. Byrne, D., Fisher, J. D., Lamberth, J., & Mitchell, H. E. Evaluations of erotica: Facts or feelings? *Journal of Personality and Social Psychology*, 1974, **29**, 111–116.

3. Byrne, D., & Lamberth, J. The effect of erotic stimuli on sex arousal, evaluative responses, and subsequent behavior. In *Technical report of the Commission on Obscenity and Pornography*. Vol. VIII. Washington, D. C.: U. S. Government Printing Office, 1971.

4. Chevalier-Skolnikoff, S. Heterosexual copulatory patterns in stumptail macaques (*Macaca arctoides*) and in other macaque species. *Archives of Sexual Behavior*, 1975, **4**, 199–220.

5. Connor, J. Olfactory control of aggressive and sexual behavior in the mouse (*Mus musclus L.*). *Psychonomic Science*, 1972, **27**, 1–3.

6. Doty, R. L., Ford, M., Preti, G., & Huggins, G. R. Changes in the intensity and pleasantness of human vaginal odors during the menstrual cycle. *Science*, 1975, **190**, 1316–1318.

7. Griffith, M., & Walker, C. E. Menstrual cycle phases and personality variables as related to response to erotic stimuli. *Archives of Sexual Behavior*, 1975, **4**, 599–603.

8. Hartman, W. E., & Fithian, M. A. *Treatment of sexual dysfunction.* New York: Aronson, 1974.

9. Kutner, S. J. Sex guilt and the sexual behavior sequence. *Journal of Sex Research*, 1971, **7**, 107–115.

10. Masters, W. H., & Johnson, V. E. *Human sexual response.* Boston: Little, Brown, 1966.

11. Michael, R. P., Keverne, E. B., & Bonsall, R. W. Pheromones: Isolation of male sex attractants from a female primate. *Science*, 1971, **172**, 964–966.

12. Mosher, D. L., & Cross, H. J. Sex guilt and premarital sexual experiences of college students. *Journal of Consulting and Clinical Psychology*, 1971, **36**, 27–32.

13. Raboch, J., & Starka, L. Coital activity of men and the levels of plasmatic testosterone. *Journal of Sex Research*, 1972, **8**, 219–224.

CHAPTER TWO

Reproduction: Anatomy, Physiology, Intercourse

Anatomy and Physiology

Though the major emphasis of the present book is on the personal and social aspects of sexuality, it is nevertheless important to be aware of the anatomical details of the sexual organs and the way in which they function.

One reason for paying some attention to these biological underpinnings is that many individuals in our culture have gaps in their knowledge of this area of the body. While parents are eager to teach their young children the names for most parts of the body, they tend to ignore the area between the navel and the knees or to pass it off with some vague term such as "the place where you make wee-wee" or even simply "down there." Children quickly learn that this is not a bodily area to be discussed or exposed. Otherwise realistic dolls mysteriously eliminate the genitals in favor of an expanse of smooth plastic. With this much reluctance to deal with the simple descriptive details of the external genitalia, it is not surprising that many people have learned to feel uncomfortable with respect to their sexual organs and to believe that this portion of the body is somehow different from all the rest—a region of unclean ugliness. Also, many people feel that they are somehow unique, and they worry about the size, shape, color, or odor of their genitalia.

Often, knowledge about internal structures and functioning is even more sketchy. We have personally talked to college students in the 1970s who believed that the testicles swell up with semen if a male becomes too excited, that the most sensitive area of a female's anatomy is the tip of the uterus (thus, a long penis is required to excite a woman), that the penis contains two tubes (one for urine and one for semen), and that diaphragms are dangerous as contraceptives because they may be sucked into the uterus and lost there.

In the following article, Shope presents a brief factual description of the male and female genital systems plus some general summary statements about several aspects of sexual functioning.

Anatomy and Physiology

David F. Shope

This brief review of gross sexual anatomy and physiology is intended to give the reader only a glimpse of the most elementary aspects of sex organ structure and function.

MALE ANATOMY

Gross male sexual anatomy comprises the penis, testicles, scrotum, vas deferens, seminal vesicles, and prostate gland. Their respective locations can be found by referring to Figure 2-1.

Reprinted in an edited version from: Shope, D. F. *Interpersonal sexuality*. Philadelphia: Saunders, 1975. Pp. 297–303.

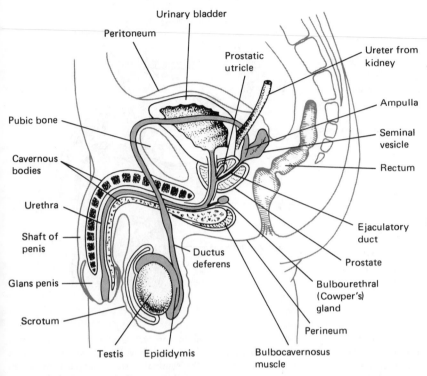

Figure 2-1. This drawing of the male reproductive system shows the location of the major structures and the way in which they are interrelaed.

The penis consists of the shaft and glans or head. Tumescence (erection) occurs when hollow spaces within the shaft fill with blood, and detumescence takes place when blood flows from these spaces faster than it flows in. The glans, especially the undersurface, is highly sensitive and quite responsive to stimulation. Smegma, a smelly, cheeselike substance, is produced by the small Tyson's glands located on the undersurface of the glans.

Sperm and testosterone, an androgen partly responsible for erotic sensitivity in both sexes, are produced by the testicles. Sperm are transported by ciliary action through the sperm duct (vas deferens) to the seminal vesicles. Here they are stored until ejaculation. At this stage the matured sperm, only about $\frac{1}{500}$-in. long, are quite lethargic.

Semen, the male ejaculate, is manufactured primarily by the seminal vesicles and the prostate. On the average, 3.5 cc of semen are produced by the healthy male between the ages of 20 and 50 after 2 or 3 days of continence. The buffered semen and a fluid—the small amount of clear liquid that can be seen oozing from the penis during sexual excitement —provide the alkaline environment essential to the life of sperm.

Ejaculation occurs in two steps (Figure 2-2). During the first phase the seminal fluid is forced from the prostate and other accessory organs

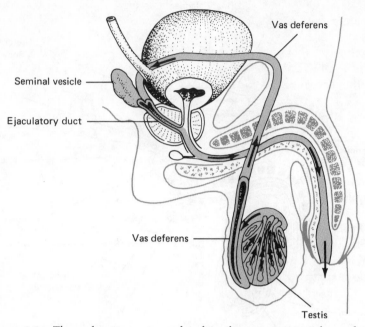

Figure 2-2. The male sperm are produced in the testes or testicles and travel through the vas deferens to the seminal vesicles where they are stored. When ejaculation occurs, these sperm are expelled from the seminal vesicles, mixed with semen and other fluids, and ejected from the body through the urethra and out of the penis.

into the urethra. The impending ejaculation can be felt at this time, and for 2 or 3 sec the male can sense the process before the second stage begins. During the second stage semen is propelled through the urethra by a series of muscular contractions. In the adult male, orgasm and ejaculation usually occur together, although some males experience orgasm without ejaculation from time to time. Younger males may experience orgasms before they have developed the capacity to ejaculate. It should also be pointed out that it is possible to ejaculate without having achieved an erection.

Here are a few facts about male anatomy and physiology:

1. There is no reliable relationship between body dimension and penis size.
2. Except for the possible psychological effects, penis size makes no difference in how effectively a woman will be stimulated by penetration, except in cases of unusual vaginal or penile hypertrophy.
3. Erections can occur from causes other than sexual arousal. A few of these are penile irritation, heavy lifting or other stressing of muscles in the perineum, and unusual emotionality.
4. Once the period of normal growth is past, nothing is likely to increase the size of the penis. If treated with hormones early enough,

male children with unusually small penises may be assisted toward normal growth.

5. Sexually active persons are believed to have less loss of size due to the atrophy of aging than those less active. In this way regular sexual indulgence helps prevent loss of size.

6. Men do not undergo a change of life similar to that of women. There may be a few men who experience a male climacteric owing to hormone deficiency, but such changes can hardly be equated with menopause, which is a normal physiological event. Some middle-aged men go through an "emotional change of life" during which they try to regain their youthful vigor. This, if severe, may call for psychological counseling or at least reassurance, support, and understanding from their wives.

7. The majority of young men experience nocturnal emission (wet dreams), and some do so fairly frequently. Lowered inhibitions during sleep are usually considered the important cause.

8. Castration does not necessarily destroy the sex drive. Once a male has matured, his sex drive is related to many factors, such as good health and proper nutrition, the kind of learning he has had, the availability of erotic stimuli, and so forth. Since the male's sex drive is not entirely dependent upon the testicles, it is no surprise to find that their removal will not necessarily destroy it, especially if hormones (androgen) are regularly administered. Younger castrates may demonstrate signs of lack of sexual interest, such as the inability to achieve an erection, but this does not mean that they will not show a psychological interest in sex, although the lower the age at which an individual is castrated, the more likely he is to be disinterested. Castration, in brief, does not dispel the need for sensual expression.

FEMALE ANATOMY

The gross sexual anatomy of the human female may be divided into sexual (Figure 2-3) and reproductive (Figure 2-4) aspects. Most of the parts we will label as sexual are also involved in reproductive functions, but these are secondary to the erotic sphere. The reproductive organs are only secondarily involved in sexual relations.

The major female organs are the mons pubis, major and minor labia, vestibule, and clitoris, which collectively make up the vulva or external sex organs. The organs of the vulva along with the vagina have been termed "sexual organs" because they serve most importantly in erotic arousal and responsiveness, regardless of whether pregnancy ensues. The uterus (womb), fallopian tubes, and ovaries are more strictly reproductive in function.

The mons pubis (also called mons veneris) is the rise caused by the female pubic bone. Because it is erotically and aesthetically pleasing, it is also known as the "fount of love" or the "mount of Venus." The

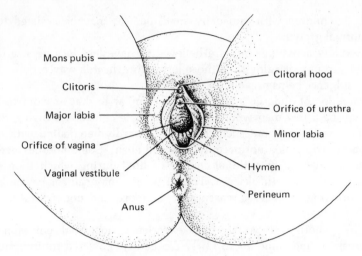

Figure 2-3. This drawing of the external genital system of the female shows the location of the primary anatomical features.

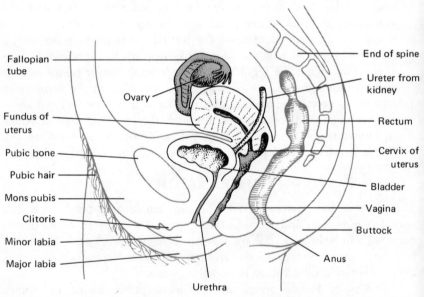

Figure 2-4. This is a side view of the internal reproductive system of the female. Ova are produced by the ovaries and pass into the fallopian tubes. If there has been intercourse, sperm deposited in the vagina travel through the uterus and up the fallopian tubes where conception occurs if a sperm and an ovum unite.

major and minor labia serve to protect the entrance to the vagina. In addition, the minor labia are quite erotically sensitive and may change in color from bright red to burgundy for the woman who is about to reach climax.

The clitoris, the homologue of the penis, is the major organ of female sexual responsiveness and has no other known function than to serve as the seat of erotic sensitivity. It too engorges with blood upon excitement and the shaft increases in diameter. Although clitoral erection does not occur, a tumescent glans may leave this impression. During periods of high sexual excitement, the clitoris withdraws into the labial hood, making direct contact with it virtually impossible.

A nontraditional way of conceptualizing the clitoris has been suggested.[1] The clitoris comprises not only the organ we have labeled as such but internal sections of the "clitoral system" as well. These unseen aspects have their counterparts in the penis, including nerve and blood supplies and hollow areas that fill with blood, simulating erection. The inward extension of the clitoris is continuous with the part that protrudes and may provide the basis for so-called vaginal orgasms.

The vagina is lined with a membrane famous for its accordionlike capacity to expand. The vagina produces the sticky fluid that serves to lubricate its surface during periods of sexual arousal. Since there are very few sensory cells within the vagina itself, it cannot be a major source of physical arousal, although it is often of considerable psychological importance.

The area between the edge of the vagina and the beginning of the anus is known as the perineum. It is composed of several underlying structures, but from the standpoint of sexual stimulation, the muscles seem most important. When the perineum of either sex is appropriately stimulated, these muscles can be felt as stiff and rigid, and the entire area can be a source of considerable eroticism. The perineum is important in childbirth, as it can be severely stretched or torn.

The uterus or womb is about 3 in. long and 2 in. wide and is divided into the fundus and cervix. The uterine blood supply is especially rich and the entire area is laden with blood vessels and nerves. The body or fundus is intertwined with many heavy muscles that contract to expel the child during the birth process, and the outside is covered with peritoneum. The structure of the endometrium or lining of the uterus varies with the time of life, day of the month, whether or not one is using oral contraceptives, and whether or not one is pregnant. The major function of the uterus is to house and protect the unborn child.

The cervix, or neck of the uterus, extends partially into the vagina. It is rounded or conical in shape and has a central canal through which the fetus and menstrual flow may pass. Normally it is held tightly closed by strong muscles. During sexual intercourse, however, the cervix withdraws into the pelvic cavity; consequently, it is no longer regarded as a major source of sexual excitement.

The fallopian tubes lead from the fundus to the ovaries but have no direct connection with the latter. The ends closest to the ovaries have fimbria that assist in capturing the ovum. It is through the fallopian tubes that the sperm must make their way, and it is within them that conception occurs.

In addition to ova production, the ovaries excrete the hormones responsible for the appearance of female secondary sexual characteristics.

Menstruation

Follicle stimulating hormone (FSH) incites the ovaries to begin ova production within the small sacs in which each ovum is contained. These sacs, the Graafian follicles, also grow under the influence of FSH. Simultaneously, estrogen is produced from cells within the Graafian follicles. This initiates the build-up of this important female hormone in the bloodstream. When an ovum has matured and ruptured its Graafian follicle, the estrogen level is at its peak and inhibits further production of FSH, but the pituitary gland begins secretion of the luteinizing hormone (LH), whose function is to bring about the development of the corpus luteum. The corpus luteum is formed in the crater left by the rupture of the Graafian follicle. The corpus luteum produces a little estrogen but mainly progesterone, another important female hormone. Progesterone causes the 'endometrium to thicken and increase in vascularity. If the ovum is impregnated, the corpus luteum continues to produce progesterone, as does a new source of this hormone, the endometrium.

If the ovum is not fertilized, the progesterone level falls owing to regression of the corpus luteum. This lowering of the progesterone level begins on approximately the twenty-second day after the beginning of the last menstrual period, and by the twenty-eighth day progesterone is below the level needed to keep the endometrium intact. Menstruation, the shedding of the lining of the uterus, begins. Although the 28-day cycle is typical, it is well known that normal variations range from 22 to 35 days, and that whatever its duration, the cycle is brought about by the same hormonal physiology.

At some point the lowered level of estrogen and progesterone induces renewed production of FSH, and the process of ovulation begins anew. Usually the ovaries alternate monthly in ovum production, and within 12 to 14 days after the beginning of the last period, a new ovum will be released. Although it is possible to menstruate without the ovulatory process, such anovulatory cycles are unusual.

The following are a few facts about female anatomy and physiology:

1. During sexual arousal, the cervix draws well up into the false pelvis and discharges nothing even remotely resembling ejaculate, nor does it "suck" sperm into itself.
2. Masturbation does not produce acne or smaller breasts, nor does it

"show up" in one's facial expression nor have any other known relationship to body size or functioning.

3. There is no known relationship between the size of any normal anatomical part and sexual responsiveness. The ability to become passionate is shaped largely by learning.

4. Orgasm is believed to occur only rarely or not at all among female animals. Some 10 to 15% of American women never reach it, and it has been shown that among women rate of orgasm varies in response to cultural conditioning.

5. Menopause does not engender severe physical or psychological stress in most women. There may be slight distress for many women and considerable discomfort for a few, but the stories surrounding menopause often are exaggerated.

REFERENCE

1. Sherfey, M. The evolution and nature of female sexuality in relation to psychoanalytic theory. *Journal of the American Psychoanalytic Association*, 1966, **14**, 28–128.

The Sexual Response Cycle

Beginning late in the 1950s and continuing into the 1960s, Masters and Johnson instituted an unusual research program at Washington University in St. Louis that was designed first to learn as much as possible about the physiological details of the human sexual response and then to utilize this knowledge in the treatment of sexual dysfunctions such as impotence, premature ejaculation, and frigidity. Their procedure was to bring volunteer subjects of both sexes into a laboratory setting where they engaged in intercourse or masturbated while every detail of their bodily responses was being observed and recorded. Their findings were first publishd quietly in such professional journals as the *Annals of the New York Academy of Science* and the *Western Journal of Surgery, Obstetrics, and Gynecology.* The general public first became aware of this research in 1966 when their book *Human Sexual Response* was published.

It was easy enough to express shock at this work or to be amused by the idea of white-coated researchers peering eagerly at their busy subjects. One scene in the play *Oh! Calcutta!* makes fun of such a situation: the male and female subjects engage in intercourse while attached to electrodes as the doctor and nurse sing a love song. Despite such satire and a good many angry condemnations, the findings of Masters and Johnson have had a tremendous influence both on sexual therapy and on the average person's understanding of sex. The parallels between males and females in their phases of excitement, plateau, orgasm, and resolution constituted impressive evidence of their sexual similarity. Perhaps more surprising was the discovery that females could be *more* sexually responsive than males in their capacity to have multiple orgasms while males were stuck with the refractory period. Their emphasis on the sensitivity of the clitoris and its importance in female arousal was a revelation to many females who had previously felt guilty about experiencing more pleasure in masturbation with clitoral stimulation than in intercourse with vaginal stimulation. This was also a revelation to many males who were not even aware of the existence of the clitoris. One might suggest with tongue in cheek the installation of an historical plaque on the outskirts of St. Louis enscribed, "Site at which the clitoris was discovered—1966."

The Sexual Response Cycle

William H. Masters and Virginia E. Johnson

The techniques of defining and describing the gross physical changes which develop during the human being's sexual response cycles have

Reprinted in an edited version from: Masters, W. H., & Johnson, V. E. *Human sexual response.* Boston: Little, Brown, 1966. Pp. 3–8.

been primarily those of direct observation and physical measurement. Since the integrity of human observation for specific detail varies significantly, regardless of the observer's training and considered objectivity, reliability of reporting has been supported by many of the accepted techniques of physiologic measurement and the frequent use of color cinematographic recording in all phases of the sexual response cycle.

A more concise picture of physiologic reaction to sexual stimuli may be presented by dividing the human being's cycles of sexual response into four separate phases. Progressively, the four phases are: (1) the excitement phase; (2) the plateau phase; (3) the orgasmic phase; and (4) the resolution phase. This arbitrary four-part division of the sexual response cycle provides an effective framework for detailed description of physiologic variants in sexual reaction, some of which are frequently so transient in character as to appear in only one phase of the total orgasmic cycle.

Only one sexual response pattern has been diagrammed for the human male (Figure 2-5). Admittedly, there are many identifiable variations in the male sexual reaction. However, since these variants usually are related to duration rather than intensity of response, multiple diagrams would be more repetitive than informative. Comparably, three different sexual response patterns have been diagramed for the human female

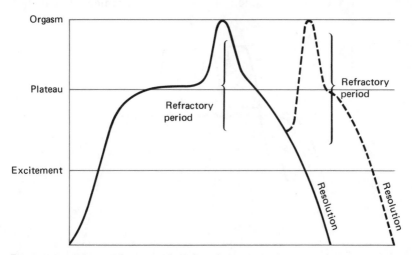

Figure 2-5. Most males were found to have a single type of sexual response cycle in which excitement built rapidly, entered a relatively brief plateau stage, peaked at orgasm, and then returned rather rapidly to the preexcitement state in the resolution phase. Right after orgasm, males tend not to be responsive to continued stimulation, and this is called the refractory period. When that period is over, further stimulation can lead to a second orgasm (shown in dotted lines) followed by an even longer refractory period.

(Figure 2-6). It should be emphasized that these patterns are simplifications of those most frequently observed and are only representative of the infinite variety in female sexual response. Here, intensity as well as duration of response is a factor that must be considered when evaluating sexual reaction in the human female.

The first or excitement phase of the human cycle of sexual response develops from any source of somatogenic or psychogenic stimulation. The stimulative factor is of major importance in establishing sufficient increment of sexual tension to extend the cycle. If the stimulation remains adequate to individual demand, the intensity of response usually increases rapidly. In this manner the excitement phase is accelerated or shortened. If the stimulative approach is physically or psychologically objectionable, or is interrupted, the excitement phase may be prolonged greatly or even aborted. The first segment and the final segment (resolution phase) consume most of the time expended in the complete cycle of human sexual response.

From excitement phase the human male or female enters the second or plateau phase of the sexual cycle, if effective sexual stimulation is continued. In this phase sexual tensions are intensified and subsequently reach the extreme level from which the individual ultimately may move to orgasm. The duration of the plateau phase is largely dependent upon the effectiveness of the stimuli employed, combined with the factor of individual drive for culmination of sex tension increment. If either the

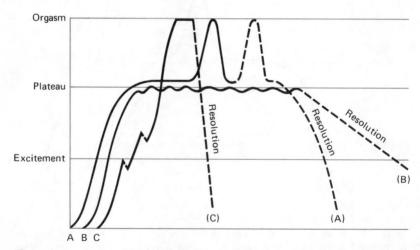

Figure 2-6. Among females, three basic types of sexual response cycles were found. Type (A) depicts an excitement, plateau, and orgasm pattern much like males except followed quickly by a second orgasm without a refractory period. Type (B) shows a plateau phase characterized by a long series of small orgasmic responses and a very slow resolution phase. Type (C) shows a somewhat slower and irregular excitement phase that bypasses the plateau phase and reaches a quick, extended orgasm followed by a very rapid resolution phase.

stimuli or the drive is inadequate or if all stimuli are withdrawn, the individual will not achieve orgasmic release and will drop slowly from plateau-phase tension levels into an excessively prolonged resolution phase.

The orgasmic phase is limited to those few seconds during which the vasoconcentration and myotonia developed from sexual stimuli are released. This involuntary climax is reached at any level that represents maximum sexual tension increment for the particular occasion. Subjective (sensual) awareness of orgasm is pelvic in focus, specifically concentrated in the clitoral body, vagina, and uterus of the female and in the penis, prostate, and seminal vesicles of the male. Total body involvement in the response to sexual tensions, although physiologically well defined, is experienced subjectively on the basis of individual reaction patterns. There is great variation in both the intensity and the duration of female orgasmic experience, while the male tends to follow standard patterns of ejaculatory reaction with less individual variation.

The human male and female resolve from the height of their orgasmic expressions into the last or resolution phase of the sexual cycle. This involutionary period of tension loss develops as a reverse reaction pattern that returns the individual through plateau and excitement levels to an unstimulated state. Women have the response potential of returning to another orgasmic experience from any point in the resolution phase if they submit to the reapplication of effective stimulation. This facility for multiple orgasmic expression is evident particularly if reversal is instituted at plateau tension level. For the man the resolution phase includes a superimposed refractory period which may extend during the involutionary phase as far as a lower excitement level of response. Effective restimulation to higher levels of sexual tension is possible only upon termination of this refractory period. With few exceptions, the physiologic ability of the male to respond to restimulation is much slower than that of the female.

Physiologic residuals of sexual tension usually are dissipated slowly in both the male and female unless an overwhelming orgasmic release has been experienced. Total involution is completed only after all manner of sexual stimuli have been withdrawn.

It always should be borne in mind that there is wide individual variation in the duration and intensity of every specific physiologic response to sexual stimulation. Those that occur early in the response cycle and continue without interruption during several phases are obvious (penile erection or vaginal lubrication). However, some physiologic reactions are fleeting in character and may be confined to one particular phase of the cycle. Examples are the plateau-phase color changes of the minor labia in the female and the coronal engorgement of the penis in the male.

In brief, the division of the human male or female's cycle of sexual

response into four specific phases admittedly is inadequate for evaluation of finite psychogenic aspects of elevated sexual tensions. However,
the establishment of this purely arbitrary design provides anatomic
structuring and assures inclusion and correct placement of specifics of
physiologic response within the sequential continuum of human response to effective sexual stimulation.

Initial Heterosexual Behavior of Adolescent Rhesus Monkeys (*Macaca Mulatta*)

There is no way to determine what human sexual behavior was like in pre-historic times and there is no ethical way to determine what today's human sexual behavior would be like without the "contaminating" influences of what is learned in each culture. Thus, we cannot know which sexual acts are natural parts of our animal heritage and which are a result of the good and bad effects of the complex heritage provided by our civilization. Would a sexually mature couple who had never seen nor heard nor read about sex begin having intercourse when they first met? What sexual position would they assume? Would they pet, engage in oral sex, or discover any other sexual variations for themselves? Would the male and the female be equally receptive to sexual activity? Unfortunately, without a time machine, we will never be able to discover the details of unadulterated human sexuality.

An indirect approach to such knowledge *is* possible, however, as animal behaviorists Erwin and Mitchell demonstrate in the following article. Observations of the sexual behavior of animals, especially those that are related most closely to ourselves, provide useful clues as to the basic elements of sexual behavior among human beings. For one thing, it is clear that as more complex species developed, sex became less instinctively controlled by physiological factors and more controlled by the central nervous system; thus, the sexual behavior of the higher mammals is dependent on early experience, it varies considerably from couple to couple, and it can be greatly altered by learning. By way of contrast to primate behavior, consider the stereotyped sexual pattern of some lower animals such as the salmon that blindly go through intricate mating behavior involving migration and spawning, each individual in a fixed, biologically controlled fashion.

In the following study, rhesus monkeys were provided with the necessary early social experience with their mothers and later with peers, and, at sexual maturity, placed with a member of the opposite sex. They quickly, though at times clumsily, began interacting sexually in the typical way with males entering the females from the rear and thrusting to climax. Equally interesting are the individual differences that were observed among these subjects. Some were eagerly sexual and some reluctant. Some fought and some embraced face to face. Some engaged in oral sex and others did not. In short, except for intercourse position, our monkey cousins do not seem to be terribly different in their initial sexual activities from a comparable group of highly developed, sophisticated, twentieth-century human adolescents.

Initial Heterosexual Behavior of Adolescent Rhesus Monkeys (*Macaca Mulatta*)

J. Erwin and G. Mitchell

Relationships between early social experience and later social adequacy, particularly in the realm of heterosexual activity, have been investigated using nonhuman primates as subjects.[7,13,17] Such studies have clearly indicated that nonhuman primates reared in social isolation exhibit deficits in sociosexual behavior as adults. Research has also shown that neither social experience *only* with the mother nor experience *only* with peers can guarantee completely adequate sociosexual development, although social experience with either the mother or peers is clearly superior to rearing in social isolation.[12] Even combined mother and peer experience does not appear to be sufficient to produce appropriate adult male copulatory behavior if the maternal experience is limited to the first 3 months of life.[1] In free-ranging groups of rhesus monkeys, the normal pattern of social development involves a waning of the infant's tie to his mother during the infant's second half-year of life and an increasing preoccupation with peer interactions, particularly with peers of the same sex.[16] Peer interactions are especially frequent during the second year of life,[8] and the importance of peer interactions during this developmental phase is, consequently, likely to be especially great. While there are overlaps between developmental phases, the sequence (under normal conditions) always progresses, as Harlow and Harlow[6] have suggested, from the mother-infant affectional system, which develops first, to the peer affectional system, and, eventually, to the mature heterosexual affectional system. Under normal group-living conditions, of course, it is most difficult to distinguish between cross-sexed *peer* affectional interactions and immature *heterosexual* interactions, and it is virtually impossible to determine if a specific sexual interaction is the first for an animal.

This report describes the initial heterosexual responses of young rhesus monkeys who had received sequential social experience with mothers and like-sexed peers in a laboratory setting. We were interested in evaluating the effects of this sequential pattern of rearing experience on heterosexual social behavior, and were particularly interested in the initial sociosexual reponses of these animals to other-sexed peers.

Reprinted in an edited version from: Erwin, J., & Mitchell, G. Initial heterosexual behavior of adolescent rhesus monkeys (*Macaca mulatta*). *Archives of Sexual Behavior*, 1975, 4, 97–104.

METHOD

Subjects

The subjects for this study were 12 young rhesus monkeys (*Macaca mulatta*), 6 males and 6 females. All of the subjects were laboratory-born and had been reared in wire cages accompanied only by their mothers. No peer contact was allowed until after weaning, which took place at about 8 months of age. At an average age of 9 months, each subject was paired with another of the same age and sex. When the subjects were a little over 2 years old, the members of each dyad were separated from one another.[5] Shortly after their separation from like-sexed peers, eight of these animals were paired with 6-month-old infants[2] from which they were separated after 3 months.[9] The infants involved in these pairings were divided evenly across sex and rearing experience (mother-only and social isolation). Half the pairings were same-sex and half were other-sex. Thus two male and two female subjects employed in the present study received experience with other-sexed infants. About 3 months after the separation from infants, these animals were selected for the cross-sex pairings reported here. The mean age of the subjects at the time of this study was 3.15 years for the males (range: 3.10–3.24 years) and 2.98 years for the females (range: 2.94–3.03 years).

Procedure

Each pairing was accomplished by introducing one male and one female into a 3-by-3-by-3-ft cage identical to the cages in which the subjects had been previously housed. The cages were constructed of wire mesh except for the front wall, which was made of $3/8$-in. thick acrylite. The cages were all in the same room. All subjects were in auditory, and to some extent, visual contact.

Responses to pairing were recorded by two observers, one observing each subject, for a period of 30 min. The initial 3 min of each pairing, as well as some other portions of the observation period, were recorded cinematographically. All pairs were also observed twice each week for 6 weeks, during which each pair experienced a 2-day separation.[3] They were occasionally observed during the following 6-month period as well. This report focuses primarily on the initial 30 min during which these heterosexually naive animals were exposed to one another.

RESULTS

While there was much variability in the subjects' responses to pairing, there were also some consistencies. The initial responses of most of the pairs were awkward and uncoordinated. The behavior of each pair will be described separately in order to facilitate appreciation of the individual differences displayed in the interactions.

Pair 1

At the introduction of the first pair, the male immediately attempted to mount the female but the female did not assume the appropriate receptive sexual-present posture. Instead she sat, crouched, or collapsed. The male repeatedly attempted to mount, and thrusted against whatever portion of his partner was proximal. Eventually he bit the female's neck and dragged her about the cage. During the initial observation period, the female presented once, and then only briefly. This pair was later observed to copulate normally, but the rate of copulation remained low throughout the entire period during which they were together.

Pair 2

By contrast with the female of Pair 1, the female of the second dyad presented fully within the first minute of pairing. The male mounted immediately, but ejaculated without achieving intromission. During the rest of the second pair's initial 30 min together, the male ignored the female despite her attempts to attract his attention with full and enduring sexual presents. This pattern of interaction continued to be typical of Pair 2. Copulation occurred infrequently, but the female was almost perpetually solicitous. She sometimes hung upside down from the top of the cage shaking her head from side to side. This activity was interrupted only by long gazes in the direction of the male or by sexual presents. She often initiated contact with the male, but the male usually ignored or actively avoided her advances. However, the pattern of copulation in this pair was sufficient for the female to conceive within the first month of pairing. The male was allowed to remain with the female during the entire term of her pregnancy, and he was present during the birth of a healthy female infant. Copulation was observed during the time when the female was pregnant, and attempted mounting was observed immediately prior to, during, and following parturition.

Pair 3

In the third dyad, the male mounted the female immediately on introduction, but the female did not present. The male persisted in mounting, but each time he did so the female sat down or collapsed under his weight. After about 8 min of pairing, the female presented adequately and within the next 5 min the male had achieved several intromissions and had ejaculated. This pattern was repeated, and before the initial observation period had expired the sexual behavior of this pair closely resembled the pattern typical of experienced adult consort pairs. The female presented, the male mounted (with species-typical ankle clasp), the female turned her face toward that of the male, both lip smacked at one another, and the female reached back with one hand to grasp the thigh of the male. This pair exhibited very little social contact or sexual activity during later periods of observation, aside from their reunion after a 2-day separation. The separation took place after they had been paired for 2 weeks.

Pair 4

The fourth dyad displayed the most unusual response to pairing. The female immediately presented to the male. The male mounted several times with adequate posture and apparent intromission, but began to bite the female's neck (normal copulating males sometimes do this). Immediately following these bites, she turned on him and attacked him repeatedly, biting his neck, face, back, and tail. The male crouched, grimaced, and screeched, but the female continued her attacks. When the female finally presented to him, the male did not mount but instead presented. The female responded by mounting the male several times, complete with extended bouts of pelvic thrusting. Toward the end of the initial 30-min observation period, the male alternately groomed and mounted the female. The female was observed to mount the male at other times, particularly during periods of excitement, but this pair did display adequate heterosexual behavior as well.

Pair 5

The animals in the fifth dyad established contact immediately, when they were paired, by embracing ventroventrally. They maintained contact for the first few minutes, spending most of the time huddled together with the male embracing the female. After nearly 6 min of contact, the male attempted to mount. First, he clutched the female about the chest with both arms, then he oriented appropriately, and thrusted rapidly against the female's posterior. He failed, however, to clasp her ankles with his feet. She did not present, but sat down. There were no successful copulations by Pair 5 during the initial observation period. These animals copulated adequately but not frequently during the remaining 6 months. They did, however, exhibit an unusually high degree of social proximity and contact, including frequent and enduring bouts of grooming. Fellatio was observed only in this pair, and was initiated during extended grooming bouts by the female. The duration of fellatio was generally brief. The male usually swatted the female away shortly before ejaculation, and completed arousal to ejaculation by masturbation. The ejaculate was usually eaten by *both* members of the dyad. Another idiosyncratic pattern of sexual behavior emerged from extended grooming by the female. The male often stretched out flat on his back as the female groomed his chest and abdomen. Occasionally the female straddled the male as he lay on his back and thrusted rapidly against his ventrum.

Pair 6

The sixth pair was the most sexually active. When they were first introduced, the male immediately established contact by mounting, thrusting, and neck biting. The male alternately groomed and mounted. Initially the mounts were unsuccessful, largely as a result of the female's response (she sat down, backed into a corner, or collapsed). After only 2½ min, however, this pair executed a fully coordinated present-mount-intromission sequence which lasted for more than 30 sec. Much awkward mounting occurred during the initial observation period. Some of this was the result of poor orientation on the part of the male and some resulted from inappropriate female posturing. Eight complete present-mount sequences (with intromission but without evidence of ejaculation) were observed during the first 30 min. The male bit the female's back and neck repeatedly, pulling out mouthfuls of hair, but she responded with neither avoidance nor grimacing. This pair continued to be sexually active throughout most of the period during which they were paired, even though the female conceived shortly after the two animals were paired. The male was present at the birth of this pair's healthy female offspring. The members of Pair 6 also groomed one another frequently, although not as often as did Pair 5.

DISCUSSION

The results of this study demonstrated that rhesus monkeys which receive maternal care (during the period in which mother-infant interaction is normally most intense), supplemented by experience with one same-sexed peer (during the period when peer interaction is normally highest), are capable of establishing qualitatively species-typical patterns of sociosexual behavior. While most initial attempts at copulation in our subjects were clumsy and uncoordinated, the animals adapted very quickly. All six pairs copulated in species-typical fashion within the first 3 weeks they were together, and three pairs did so within their first 30 min of social access. Apparently practice was needed by the members of some pairs before coordinated copulation was possible. It should be noted, however, that the males had some prior practice at mounting, since each had been observed to mount the like-sexed animal with which he had been paired for his second year of life. The earlier practice may have also played an important role in the development of adequate sexual posturing.

The copulatory facility of the males in this study was particularly remarkable because of their young age.[10,14] Although they occasionally displayed bizarre behaviors—e.g., self-biting, self-clasping, and eye poking ("salute")—which are commonly associated with restricted early social experience, they did so very seldom, and only under such conditions of intense stimulation as have been observed to elicit similar responses from caged feral-reared animals.[4] While the occurrence of such behaviors *may* reflect residual effects of early deprivation, the degree of social deprivation which these subjects experienced was not sufficiently severe to suppress sexual competence.

While all males attempted to mount their female partners during the first 30 min, not all females were receptive to these attempts. The mean number of mounts by males (including attempted mounts) during the initial 30 min of pairing was 15.5, while the mean number of presents by females was only 3.8. One factor which may have contributed to the lack of receptivity on the part of some females may have been their stage of sexual cycle. However, rhesus monkeys, unlike many mammals, do not have a well-defined estrus period.[15] They instead have a menstrual cycle which resembles that of the human, and they display a pattern of receptivity which is remarkably similar to the human pattern,[11] i.e., they are receptive throughout the cycle, although in general there is greater receptivity during the follicular phase than during the luteal phase. Individual differences in receptivity are great, however, both for humans and for rhesus monkeys, with some females being almost constantly solicitous of sexual activity and others being rarely receptive. The sexual cyclicity of our females was not directly monitored, but inspection of the data acquired over the 6-week period following pairing revealed no marked cyclical fluctuations in sexual activity. Thus the stage of female sexual cycles was not responsible for a major proportion of the individual differences observed in the initial responses of these animals to their first heterosexual encounters. Other "personality" factors (such as aggressiveness, submissiveness, irritability, and attractiveness), all of which have complex developmental-psychobiological bases, probably contributed greatly to the variability observed between pairs.

REFERENCES

1. Anonymous. Male monkeys raised only with peers likely to show sex deficits at maturity. *Primate Record*, 1972, **3** (2), 12–13.

2. Brandt, E. M., & Mitchell, G. Pairing pre-adolescents with infants (*Macaca mulatta*). *Developmental Psychology*, 1973, **8**, 222–228.

3. Erwin, J., Brandt, E. M., & Mitchell, G. Attachment formation and separation in heterosexually naive pre-adult rhesus monkeys. *Developmental Psychobiology*, 1973, **6**, 531–538.

4. Erwin, J., Mitchell, G., & Maple, T. Abnormal behavior in non-

isolate-reared rhesus monkeys. *Psychological Reports*, 1973, **33**, 515–523.

5. Erwin, J., Mobaldi, J., & Mitchell, G. Separation of rhesus monkey juveniles of the same sex. *Journal of Abnormal Psychology*, 1971, **78**, 134–139.

6. Harlow, H. F., & Harlow, M. K. The affectional systems. In A. M. Schrier, H. F. Harlow, & F. Stollnitz (Eds.), *Behavior of nonhuman primates*. Vol. II. New York: Academic Press, 1965.

7. Harlow, H. F., Harlow, M. K., Hansen, E. W., & Soumi, S. J. Infantile sexuality in monkeys. *Archives of Sexual Behavior*, 1972, **2**, 1–7.

8. Lindburg, D. G. The rhesus monkey in northern India: An ecological and behavioral study. In L. A. Rosenblum (Ed.), *Primate behavior: Developments in laboratory and field research*. Vol. II. New York: Academic Press, 1971.

9. Maple, T., Brandt, E. M., & Mitchell, G. Separation of preadolescents from infants (*Macaca mulatta*). Paper presented at the meeting of the Western Psychological Association, Anaheim, Calif., 1973.

10. Maple, T., Erwin, J., & Mitchell, G. Age of sexual maturity in laboratory born pairs of rhesus monkeys (*Macaca mulatta*). *Primates*, 1973, **14**, 427–428.

11. Michael, R. P., & Zumpe, D. Rhythmic changes in the copulatory frequency of rhesus monkeys (*Macaca mulatta*) in relation to the menstrual cycle, and a comparison with the human cycle. *Journal of Reproduction and Fertility*, 1970, **21**, 199–201.

12. Mitchell, G. Abnormal behavior in primates. In L. A. Rosenblum (Ed.), *Primate behavior: Developments in field and laboratory research*. Vol. 1. New York: Academic Press, 1970.

13. Mitchell, G., Raymond, E. J., Ruppenthal, G. C., & Harlow, H. F. Long-term effects of total social isolation upon behavior of rhesus monkeys. *Psychological Reports*, 1966, **18**, 567–580.

14. Napier, J. R., & Napier, P. H. *A handbook of living primates*. New York: Academic Press, 1967.

15. Rowell, T. E. Behavior and female reproductive cycles of rhesus macaques. *Journal of Reproduction and Fertility*, 1963, **6**, 193–203.

16. Sade, D. S. Ontogeny of social relations in a group of free-ranging rhesus monkeys (*Macaca mulatta*). Unpublished doctoral dissertation, University of California, Berkeley, Calif., 1966.

17. Senko, M. G. The effects of early, intermediate, and late experience upon adult macaque sexual behavior. Master's thesis, University of Wisconsin, Madison, Wis., 1966.

Chapter Three

Learned Variations

Sexual Repression: Its Manifestations

It was pointed out earlier that human beings can and do learn a remarkably varied array of sexual practices. These vast differences in sexual behavior and sexual outlook can perhaps be seen best in the reports of anthropologists who have studied diverse cultures. On the basis of such studies, we know that individuals can be taught to behave in quite different ways sexually. Members of a given society may engage in intercourse several times a day or only a few times a year, masturbation may be rare or commonplace, oral sex may be practiced by almost everyone or it may be unknown, premarital intercourse may be encouraged or condemned, intercourse positions may be limited to a single one or may include a variety of possibilities, and female orgasm may be virtually universal or totally absent within the group. To sample such cultural variations, we will present descriptions of two very different island communities, one in Europe and one in the South Pacific.

The first of these is a sexually repressive community, called Inis Beag, that is located on a small island off the Irish coast. Anthropologist John Messenger and his wife studied these islanders over a period of 19 months between 1958 and 1966. This settlement of 350 persons has been a stable one for at least 200 years. The individuals who live there seldom visit the Irish mainland, and the rare tourist can reach Inis Beag only by transferring from a ship to a small boat and then being rowed ashore. In this relatively isolated setting, these islanders have learned their own characteristic set of negative sexual attitudes and limited practices.

Sexual Repression: Its Manifestations

John C. Messenger

Both lack of sexual knowledge and misconceptions about sex among adults combine to brand Inis Beag as one of the most sexually naive of the world's societies. Sex never is discussed in the home when children are about; only three mothers admitted giving advice, briefly and incompletely, to their daughters. We were told that boys are better advised than girls, but that the former learn about sex informally from older boys and men and from observing animals. Most respondents who were questioned about sexual instructions given to youths expressed the belief that "after marriage nature takes its course," thus negating the need for anxiety-creating and embarrassing personal confrontation of parents and offspring. We were unable to discover any cases of childlessness based on sexual ignorance of spouses, as reported from other

Reprinted in an edited version from: Marshall, D. S., & Suggs, R. C. (Eds.) *Human sexual behavior.* Englewood Cliffs, N. J.: Prentice-Hall, 1971. Pp. 14–20.

regions of peasant Ireland. Also, we were unable to discover knowledge of the sexual categories utilized by researchers in sex: insertion of tongue while kissing, male mouth on female breast, female hand on penis, cunnilingus, fellatio, femoral coitus, anal coitus, extramarital coitus, manifest homosexuality, sexual contact with animals, fetishism, and sadomasochistic behavior. Some of these activities may be practiced by particular individuals and couples; however, without a doubt they are deviant forms in Inis Beag. Thus it is difficult to obtain information about these sexual activities.

Menstruation and menopause arouse profound misgivings among women of the island, because few of them comprehend their physiological significance. My wife was called on to explain these processes more than any other phenomena related to sex. When they reach puberty, most girls are unprepared for the first menstrual flow and find the experience a traumatic one—especially when their mothers are unable to provide a satisfactory explanation for it. And it is commonly believed that the menopause can induce "madness"; in order to ward off this condition, some women have retired from life in their mid-40s, and, in a few cases, have confined themselves to bed until death, years later. Others have so retired as a result of depressive and masochistic states. Yet the harbingers of "insanity" are simply the physical symptoms announcing the onset of menopause. In Inis Beag, these include severe headaches, hot flashes, faintness in crowds and enclosed places, and severe anxiety. Mental illness is also held to be inherited or caused by inbreeding (or by the Devil, by God punishing a sinner, or by malignant pagan beings) and stigmatizes the family of the afflicted. One old man came close to revealing what is probably the major cause of neuroses and psychoses in Ireland, when he explained the incarceration of an Inis Beag curate in a mental institution for clerics as being caused by his constant association with a pretty housekeeper, who "drove him mad from frustration." This elder advocated that only plain-appearing older women (who would not "gab" to "our man") be chosen for the task. Earlier, according to island opinion, the same priest had caused to be committed to the "madhouse" a local man who publicly challenged certain of his actions. The unfortunate man was released 6 months later, according to the law, since he was not mentally ill.

Sexual misconceptions are myriad in Inis Beag. The islanders share with most Western peoples the belief that men by nature are far more libidinous than women. The latter have been taught by some curates and in the home that sexual relations with their husbands are a "duty" which must be "endured," for to refuse coitus is a mortal sin. A frequently encountered assertion affixes the guilt for male sexual strivings on the enormous intake of potatoes of the Inis Beag male. Asked to compare the sexual proclivities of Inis Beag men and women, one mother of nine said, "Men can wait a long time before wanting it, but we can wait a lot longer." There is much evidence to indicate that the female orgasm is unknown—or at least doubted, or considered a deviant response. One middle-aged bachelor, who considers himself wise in the ways of the outside world and has a reputation for making love to willing tourists, described one girl's violent bodily reactions to his fondling and asked for an explanation; when told the "facts of life" of what obviously was an orgasm, he admitted not realizing that women also could achieve a climax, although he was aware that some of them apparently enjoyed kissing and being handled.

Inis Beag men feel that sexual intercourse is debilitating, a common belief in primitive and folk societies. They will desist from sex the night before they are to perform a job which will require the expenditure of great energy. Women are not approached sexually during menstruation or for months after childbirth, since they are considered "dangerous" to the male at these times. Returned "Yanks" have been denounced from the pulpit for describing American sexual practices to island youths, and such "pornographic" magazines as *Time* and *Life*, mailed by kin from abroad, have aroused curates to spirited sermon and instruction.

The separation of the sexes, started within the family, is augmented by separation in almost all segments of adolescent and adult activity. Boys and girls are separated to some extent in classrooms, and completely in recess play and movement to and from school. During church services, there is a further separation of adult men and women, as well as boys and girls, and each of the four groups leaves the chapel in its turn. The pubs are frequented only by men or by women tourists and female teachers who have spent several years on the mainland while training and thus are "set apart" (and, of course, by inquisitive female ethnographers). Women occasionally visit the shops to procure groceries, but it is more common for them to send their children to do so, since supplies and drinks are proffered across the same counter, and men are usually to be found on the premises. Even on the strand during summer months, male tourists tend to bathe at one end and women at the other. Some swimmers "daringly" change into bathing suits there, under towels and dresses—a custom practiced elsewhere in Ireland which has overtones of sexual catharsis.

It is often asserted that the major "escape valve" of sexual frustration among single persons in Ireland is masturbation; frustration-aggression theorists, however, would stress the ubiquity of drinking, alcoholism, disputes, and pugnacity as alternative outlets. Pugnacity can also be linked to the widespread problem of male identity. Our study revealed that male masturbation in Inis Beag seems to be common, premarital coitus unknown, and marital copulation limited as to foreplay and the manner of consummation. My wife and I never witnessed courting—"walking out"—in the island. Elders proudly insist that it does not occur, but male youths admit to it in rumor. The claims of young men focus on "petting" with tourists and a few local girls, whom the "bolder" of them kiss and fondle outside of their clothing. Island girls, it is held by their "lovers," do not confess these sins because they fail to experience pleasure from the contact. The male perpetrators also shun the confessional because of their fear of the priest.

We were unable to determine the frequency of marital coitus. A considerable amount of evidence indicates that privacy in the act is stressed and that foreplay is limited to kissing and rough fondling of the lower body, especially the buttocks. Sexual activity invariably is initiated by the husband. Only the male superior position is employed; intercourse takes place without removing underclothes; and orgasm, for the man, is achieved quickly. Almost immediately after intercourse the man falls asleep. (I must stress the provisional nature of these data, for they are based on a limited sample of respondents and relate to that area of sexual behavior least freely discussed.)

Many kinds of behavior disassociated from sex in other societies, such as nudity and physiological evacuation, are considered sexual in Inis Beag. Nudity is abhorred by the islanders, and the consequences of this attitude are numerous and significant for health and survival. Only infants have their entire bodies sponged once a week, on Saturday night; children, adolescents, and adults, on the same night, wash only their faces, necks, lower arms, hands, lower legs, and feet. Several times my wife and I created intense embarrassment by entering a room in which a man had just finished his weekly ablutions and was barefooted; once when this occurred, the man hurriedly pulled on his stockings and said with obvious relief, "Sure, it's good to get your clothes on again." Clothing always is changed in private, sometimes within the secrecy of the bedcovers, and it is usual for the islanders to sleep in their under-clothes.

Despite the fact that Inis Beag men spend much of their time at sea in their canoes, as far as we could determine none of them can swim. Four rationales are given for this deficiency: the men are confident that nothing will happen to them, because they are excellent seamen and weather forecasters; a man who cannot swim will be more careful; it is best to drown immediately when a canoe capsizes far out in the ocean than swim futilely for minutes or even hours, thus prolonging the agony; and finally, "When death is on a man, he can't be saved." The truth of the matter is that they never dared to bare their bodies in order to learn the skill. Some women claim to have "bathed" at the back of the island during the heat of summer, but this means wading in small pools with skirts held knee high, in complete privacy. Even the nudity of house-hold pets can cause anxiety, particularly when they are sexually aroused during time of heat. In some homes, dogs are whipped for licking their genitals and soon learn to indulge in this practice outdoors. My wife, who can perform Irish step-dances and sing many of the popular folk songs, was once requested to sing a seldom-heard American western ballad; she chose "The Lavender Cowboy," who "had only two hairs on his chest." The audience response was perfunctory and needless to say, she never again was "called out" to sing that particular song.

The drowning of seamen, who might have saved themselves had they been able to swim, is not the only result of the sexual symbolism of nudity; men who were unwilling to face the nurse when ill, because it might have meant baring their bodies to her, were beyond help when finally treated. While my wife and I were on the island, a nurse was assaulted by the mother of a young man for diagnosing his illness and bathing his chest in the mother's absence. (In this case, Oedipal and sexual attitudes probably were at work in tandem.)

It must be pointed out that nudity is also shunned for "health" reasons, for another obtusive Inis Beag character trait is hypochondria. In some cases, however, it is hard to determine whether concern with modesty or health is dominant in a particular behavioral response. Fear of colds and influenza is foremost among health concerns; rheumatism and related muscular joint ailments, migraine headaches and other psychosomatic disorders, tooth decay, indigestion ("nervous stomach"), and hypermetropia are other widespread pathologies which cause worry among the folk—not to mention those of supernatural origin.

Secrecy surrounds the acts of urination and defecation. The evacuation of infants before siblings and strangers is discouraged, and animals that discharge in the house are driven out. Chickens that habitually "dirty" their nests while setting are soon killed and eaten. Although some women drink spirits privately, they seldom do so at parties. In part, this is because of the embarrassment involved in visiting the outside toilet with men in the "street" looking on. One of the most carefully guarded secrets of Inis Beag, unreported in the many works describing island culture, is the use of human manure mixed with sand as a fertilizer. We were on the island 8 months before we discovered that compost is not "street drippings" and "scraw," but decomposed feces. With "turf" becoming more difficult to procure from the mainland, some islanders have taken to importing coal and processed peat and burning cattle dung. The dung is prepared for use in difficult-to-reach plots at the back of the island when tourists are few in number; it is burned covertly because of the overtones of sex and poverty. Another custom that my wife and I learned of late in our research, due to the secrecy surrounding it, concerns the thickening of wool; men are required to urinate in a container and tread the wool therein with their bare feet.

Other major manifestations of sexual repression in Inis Beag are the lack of a "dirty joke" tradition (at least as the term is understood by ethnologists and folklorists) and the style of dancing, which allows little bodily contact among participants. I have heard men use various verbal devices—innuendos, puns, and asides—that they believed bore sexual connotations; relatively speaking, they were pallid. In the song that I composed, one line of a verse refers to an island bachelor arising late in the day after "dreaming perhaps of a beautiful mate"; this is regarded as a highly suggestive phrase, and I have seen it redden cheeks and lower glances in a pub. Both step- and set-dancing are practiced in Inis Beag, although the former type is dying out. This rigid-body dancing, from which sex is removed by shifting attention below the hips, appears to have originated in Ireland during the early nineteenth century. The set patterns keep partners separated most of the time; but, even so, some girls refuse to dance, because it involves touching a boy. Inis Beag men, while watching a woman step-dance, stare fixedly at her feet, and they take pains to appear indifferent when crowding at a party necessitates holding women on their laps and rubbing against them when moving from room to room. But they are extremely sensitive, nevertheless, to the entire body of the dancer and to these casual contacts, as are the women. Their covert emotional reactions (which become overt as much drink is taken) are a form of catharsis.

Sex Training and Traditions
in Arnhem Land

At the opposite extreme of the geographic and sexual world from Inis Beag is Elcho Island off of the coast of Australia's Northern Territory, part of the area known as Arnhem Land. The aborigines who live there have a very different cultural history from that of the repressed Irish community and their sexual attitudes and behavior present a startling contrast to those just described.

John Money and his colleagues were especially interested in this Australian group, called the Yolngu, because it is a culture in which small children are permitted to play games imitating sexual intercourse and are actually expected to play in this fashion. Since infantile sex play is practiced among all primates except ourselves, the investigators wanted to determine the effect of such experiences on other aspects of sexuality among the Yolngu. It might be thought that our own culture is rather odd with respect to attitudes about childhood sex play in that we encourage our offspring to rehearse every other type of adult behavior. They drive toy cars, bake in toy ovens, prescribe toy pills from a toy doctor's satchel, and "kill" their playmates with toy guns. Playing at intercourse, however, is likely to evoke shock, concern, and a letter to Ann Landers. As we shall see, the Yolngu think such behavior is amusing.

Sex Training and Traditions
in Arnhem Land

John Money, J. E. Cawte, G. N. Bianchi, and B. Nurcombe

The group at the back of the room laughed with that peculiar squeal characteristic of Yolngu aboriginal children when something is funny and playfully dangerous or risky. The stir in the classroom was in response to the report of an 8-year-old that two 6-year-old relatives at the campfire the previous night had given a demonstration of nigi nigi,* to the accompaniment of everyone's hilarity.

Reprinted in an edited version from: Money, J., Cawte, J. E., Bianchi, G. N., & Nurcombe, B. Sex training and traditions in Arnhem Land. *British Journal of Medical Psychology*, 1970, **43**, 383–399.
* Nigi nigi (pronounced "niggi niggi") means sexual intercourse. It also appears in an Australian student song which goes as follows:
> With my hand on myself
> What have I here
> This is my joymaker
> My mother dear
> Joymaker, joymaker
> Niggi niggi naggi nool
> That's what they taught me
> When I went to school.

INFANTILE COITAL PLAY

Among the Yolngu children of Arnhem Land it is not peculiar that school-aged boys or girls should consider it funny, but not wrong, to tell of other children playing at sexual intercourse. They are simply expressing the attitude of their elders and their culture. To the casual white observer, biased by a prudish morality, it may seem that the Yolngu are careless, indifferent, or promiscuous in matters of sex, but that is not so. Their standards differ from our own, but they are to be adhered to nonetheless. One such standard, very surprising to middle-class Australians and Americans, is that children may play at making the movements of sexual intercourse. They know that they are playing at what older people do to reproduce the species. It is much the same as a kitten playing at hunting, but using only a dry leaf or seed pod, in preparation for the real thing later. Probably all children are meant by nature to play sexually. Monkeys, and in fact all the primates in their native habitat, rehearse in the playfulness of infancy various movements and postures that will later be used in earnest in reproducing the species.

Yolngu children are not instructed by their parents or elders about sexual intercourse, nor do they learn from observing adults, unless by accident. Parents do not give sex instruction to the young, and normally they seek privacy or darkness when they themselves copulate with their respective partners. Little children do, however, learn by what they see. What they see may be the play of other children scarcely older than themselves or the more serious play and sexual activity of older children and teen-agers on whom they are spying, "in the bush."

CIRCUMCISION CEREMONY

The timing and arrangement of the dhapi ceremony are made by the mother's brother, a man who is as important in a boy's life as his father. If several boys are of suitable age, a joint ceremony may be arranged, so that a large part of the community becomes intimately involved. In any case, the occasion is one for public rejoicing. The history of the people is celebrated in mimetic dance and chanting to the accompaniment of the rhythmic drone pipe, or didgeridoo, and clapsticks. The evening ceremony continues until the morning star rises. After daylight it continues until the climactic moment when the ceremonial initiates among the elders carry the boy off, safe from the view of girls and women, encircling him in close formation. One of them lies on his back on the ground, the boy lying face upward upon him and pinioned in a locked embrace. Another man holds down the boy's legs. A third does the actual cutting. In ancient times a stone knife was used. Today the instrument is a razor blade. The cutting is more likely to be a series of dissection movements than swift incision. The boy may cry out with the pain. Immediately the foreskin is removed, the men in charge carry the boy into the bush nearby where he is passed through the smoke of a fire for spiritual cleansing. The bleeding of his penis is stopped by cauterizing with a piece of hot charcoal and the application of hot, wet leaves. He returns to his home camp fire and there rests and recuperates for about a week.

Today the young boy about to undergo his dhapi is given no specific instruction in advance. He may have learned something by witnessing another ceremony and he may have had information passed on by older boys. He does not know exactly what will be done to him, nor when, nor how much pain there will be. The experience becomes, therefore, part of a training in stoicism, resignation to suffering and indifference to wounding or killing others, if tradition demands it. The tradition of blood revenge is now all but extinct, but stoicism when in pain still is an aboriginal trait. In an earlier era a male's stoicism would be put to the test by more than circumcision, for eventually the septum of his nose would be pierced so as to hold a bone ornament, and the skin of his chest, shoulders, and arms would be incised so as to raise decorative scars.

However much the aboriginal boy fears his initiation rite of dhapi, he invariably says that he wants it or is glad that he had it. Different boys have different rationalizations as to why it is necessary. One said that the penis would get to be like a hook, another that he would get a sickness, and another that without dhapi "we don't get married." Socially, the ceremony gives status to a boy as a member of the masculine sect, so to speak. It officially sanctions his right to the ceremonial knowledge and ritual which is the exclusive prerogative of men. It gives him access to his father's inherited right to reproduce ancestral totemic rituals, dances, chants, designs, and sacred objects. The ceremony also places on him the obligation to obey the complicated totemic rules of social permissions and avoidances, especially as they apply to one's promised partners in marriage. One obligation imposed by these totemic rules is linguistic. The partner whom one may marry should belong to a linguistic and tribal-totemic or clan group different from one's own.

CLOTHING AND NUDITY

The onset of sex education of the Yolngu may be traced to the ancient tradition of soothing fretful infants by stroking their sex organs. This tradition implies a lack of prurience or guilt regarding the genitals which is evident also in the relaxed attitude toward infantile nudity. An ancient custom of the Yolngu, surviving into the present century, was to wear no clothes at all, even at night when they might feel too cold after the campfire had burned to ashes. There was one aged man who refused in 1968 to relinquish his lifelong custom of defeating the midday heat by resting naked under a makeshift canopy. The children in the preschool, adjacent, would point him out to their teacher as an oddity. At the same time of day, many mothers rest with their infants, in the shade of their living quarters, wearing only a skirt. If whites approach, they usually contrive to put on a top. Children under school age unself-consciously wear nothing at all. They enter preschool at the age of 4. Some of them insist on wearing clothes to school—cotton shorts for the boys, pants and skirts or dresses for the girls—in order to conform to the model of their older brothers and sisters in primary school. Some might come to preschool naked. Before the indoor activities begin, and before they are given something to eat, all the children, boys and girls together, are soaped under a shower and dressed in clothing issued and laundered by the school. Now that they have adopted clothing, Yolngu children, and many adults too, wear it as they used to wear their naked skin, and are reluctant to remove it. They have always lived in close symbiosis with the earth, unoffended by what Westerners recoil from as mud, dirt, and grime, and do not feel compelled to remove clothing to prevent its becoming soiled. Nor is it removed if they go in the sea to swim, which they do relatively little. We found that the boys would make no compromise with nudity in order to go swimming, at least in front of white men, and were embarrassed and amazed that we would dry off in their presence. Men once did their ceremonial dances with their bodies covered only with body paint. Now they wear baggy cotton-print diapers of early nineteenth-century missionary design, and respect them as traditional!

Despite the shame of nakedness they will eventually acquire, it is obvious that Yolngu children grow up completely well informed of the external anatomical differences between the sexes. They take elimination for granted and in infancy do it wherever the need dictates. Because it is permitted in their play, they take for granted the bodily contact of the sexes in copulation. Whether their playing at sexual intercourse with pelvic thrusts is a spontaneous emergence—as apparently it is in lower primates—or whether it is a sequel to copying other children, is an issue still to be decided. Though this form of playfulness in infants and young children is publicly acceptable to Yolngu adults, it is tacitly understood throughout the culture that, by middle childhood, it will be kept respectfully out of sight.

SEXUAL PLAY OF CHILDHOOD

By the letter of the law, heterosexual play after middle childhood, even though covert, should be only between a boy and a potential promise girl of like age—or at least a girl from the correct totemic or clan group. By this time, a boy has had his dhapi ceremony and is supposed to conform to the ways of men. Therefore he ought not to participate in sexual play with a girl who is promised to someone else.

A Yolngu couple who ought not to be pairing off together do not easily have privacy or secrecy available to them for sexual play. Ahead of time it is common, therefore, for them to use sign language to declare their intentions and lay their plans for where and when to meet. Signals in eye talk and finger talk can be made to appear as inadvertent movements to onlookers. Yolngu sign language is so highly developed that people were able to communicate back and forth with two deaf mutes in the village with apparently uninterrupted fluency.

Though we had no way of taking a census or other tally, we have the impression that boy-girl agreements to meet were not very common in the prepubertal years as compared with later.

GIRLS' SEXUAL PLAY

Children have another more direct way of circumventing the restrictions on childhood sexual play secondary to totemic avoidancy taboos. Two or more girls together, for example, might decide to play house. One would take the role of the father. When the time comes for sexual intercourse, the "father" might simulate the coital motions of the male, possibly using a finger or stick to insert into the partner's vagina. So far as could be ascertained, the counterpart in boys' games, wherein a younger boy would impersonate a female's sexual position for an older partner, is uncommon and seems to have been associated with delinquency in puberty, i.e., from around age 13 to the middle teens. In the case of girls, there has been no known association of their coital play with delinquency, nor with subsequent lesbian interests which are apparently unheard of in adulthood. Coital play also does not appear to be associated with undue emphasis on masturbation in girls. Female masturbation has the status of a childhood activity—a diluted form of coital play when no partner is present. In the context of the moral teaching of the mission, some Yolngu girls and women officially frown upon stimulation of the vagina, alone or in unmarried pairs. It qualifies as adultery, according to their usage of biblical terminology. The Yolngu use of the vagina in girls' coital play may also, however, be interpreted as a childhood rehearsal phenomenon of the same order as playing mother to a doll improvised from a stone or branch of leaves.

For Yolngu girls, even more than boys, it is probably essential to the maintenance of the polygamous promise system that their childhood experience with sex allows coitus to be emotionally uncomplicated, like killing birds or lizards to eat, or watching a baby breast feeding. By the time she goes to her promise man, a girl must have been prepared to perform sexually with him, even though she may not be in love with him or may even feel repelled by his appearance and age.

EDUCATION FOR MENSTRUATION AND CHILDBIRTH

The unmarried adolescent girls who recorded interviews had been prepared for menstruation a year or two ahead of time by their mothers, and they also knew something from the talk of other girls. In an earlier era, the first menses would have been negotiated with ceremonial body painting and chants which today have fallen by the wayside of cultural change. A girl is still expected, however, to pay lip service at least to the ancient custom of menstrual isolation. Formerly she was isolated under a woven conical mat where she rested and slept. She conformed to dietary restrictions, notably the avoidance of fish and shellfish. Educated girls today, away in the city at school, still are likely to obey the dietary rule, so as to play safe and avoid the risk of falling sick. There is no further adherence, however, to the old custom of concluding menstruation with a spiritual cleansing by being passed through the fumes of a smoky fire.

Boys and young adolescent males, at least those who talked to us, had negligible or inadequate knowledge of menstrual bleeding in girls. They confused it with bleeding resulting from early or initial intercourse with a boy.

When a girl goes to her early marriage, she knows about getting pregnant, but is, according to present custom, given no systematic preparation for childbirth until she experiences it at first hand. It is probable she will know that, whereas today the majority of women deliver in the hospital, in former times a woman in labor went in the bush with several older women, one of whom would get in front, the other in back, to hold and help her have the baby, delivered from a squatting position.

The squatting position is the one traditionally favored also for sexual intercourse. The man sits on the ground, legs outstretched, and the woman squats on his erect penis. This positioning was nicely illustrated, unrequested, when a young man elected to include a sexual theme as one in a series of drawings (Figure 3-1). Preliminary love play, especially manual, may precede coitus itself, but the information available on this topic was meager and difficult to obtain because of the language barrier in talking with older, experienced males. There is at present no problem of venereal disease in the community, though gonorrhea did once put in an appearance, returning with a man who had been visiting in Darwin.

Among teen-aged boys and young men today there is a good deal of joking talk about the possibility of sexual relations with a white girl. There is in this talk the implication not only of status and prestige, but also that white girls, not being subject to the restrictions of the promise system, are more free to choose and more sexually proficient. Adolescent boys and young men assume that girls have a corresponding interest in white boys, but the girls do not reveal their secrets directly in the presence of males. In the presence of white men, the women scrupulously follow the avoidancy rules. They averted their gaze when meeting us. The younger generation of aboriginal males expressed no misgivings about interracial marriage, which has been recorded at other missions and settlements, albeit infrequently.

Figure 3-1. A young Yolngu man drew this picture to illustrate the usual way in which couples engage in intercourse in this culture.

PERFUNCTORY SEXUALITY IN WOMEN

Systems of human behavior, as already indicated, must be self-sustaining, otherwise they disappear. Obviously then, the Yolngu polygamous promise system has so far been successful in the sense that a girl adjusts to copulating and breeding within it. Exactly how well she adjusts to it is difficult for a male investigator to ascertain, for the system imposes a taboo on a woman's talking about her sex life to a man. Most older women are bound by the taboo, some younger educated ones less so. There are some women who have a joyous sex life with their husbands. But not all the evidence is positive. There are today some young women who balk at the promise system and hold out in favor of a boy friend. There are a few also whose elderly husbands have died and who categorically have refused to be claimed by the deceased husband's brother, as the system prescribes. At least one of these women has, by her own admission, said good-bye to sexual intercourse forever. She wants no more than the four children she has. She professed no interest in contraception, should it become available at the local hospital, since she has decided on celibacy. Though she obeyed the taboo against talking of her sex life, there was not much doubt that it had been a joyless, perfunctory affair, with no experience of sexual climax ever.

This particular woman is not unique. Several others from among a group with chronic complaints of minor ailments[1] were reported to have said that they had abandoned sexual intercourse permanently, glad perhaps that a new and younger wife could take on the duties of satisfying the husband and bearing the children.

Until fairly recently, a girl who did not adjust to her marriage partner might look forward to the one great episodic outlet or escape, the kunapipi. A major ceremony of song and dance celebrating a cycle of the mythical history of the people, rather like carnival or mardi gras, kunapipi was an acknowledged and customary time for the free exchange of sexual partners. Secret lovers could meet openly, and men without promise partners could have sex without fear of reprisals.

For a woman with a permanent grudge against the marriage system there was also, in times past, another outlet for her emotions. She could, especially as she got older, retaliate by railing at the younger men of her family group for their lack of manhood in not being diligent enough in the pursuit of a blood feud. Taunted into action, the men would take up the challenge and spear an alleged opponent, perhaps on the basis of no more evidence than the divinations of a witch-doctor. Thereby they became next on the cycle of retribution and would be speared themselves. This type of incitement to ritual murder nowadays seldom ends in actual killing. The most recent attempt was to kill a man at Yirrkala, because he in turn had been a killer. This socially disruptive feud remains still unresolved.

In a closed community as that of the Yolngu at Elcho, there is little anonymity. Everyone has something known about him. This information by hearsay extends the range of data from detailed sex-history interviews, obtained only from those who spoke English fluently enough. Combining these two sources of information, one has the impression that the sexual problems of Yolngu women were essentially the problems of sexual apathy, frigidity, or joylessness, and of despair at having more children than their health, often chronically impaired by anemia caused by untreated hookworm, permitted them to cope with. There were no other ascertained instances of psychosexual pathology or sexual behavior disorders in females.

MEN'S SEXUALITY

The male counterpart of sexual apathy and frigidity in the female, namely apathy, impotence, and/or premature ejaculation, did not present itself as a problem. To all intents and purposes, these complaints do not exist among Yolngu men, unless in association with pathological depression in rare cases. The men also did not complain about the burden of too many children. On the contrary, they were buoyantly aware of the fact that, thanks to the high birth rate and low mortality rate of life on the mission station, the Yolngu are no longer doomed to the threat of extinction that before World War II seemed so imminent. Men have no direct responsibility for child care. They spear large game, fish, and birds for food, but most of what children eat today is either gathered by the women or supplied by the community kitchen of the mission. Fathers permit babies an indulgent amount of physical proximity when they are resting together with their infants, and they are solicitously attentive to them.

Among young teen-aged boys there was some reported admission of masturbation, and some evasive evidence of talking and joking about it. Boys and young adolescents joked about using the glutinous sap from chewed leaf stalks of the malwun tree as a masturbatory lubricant. There was no overt evidence of masturbation among young men segregated from women on fishing trips or in lumber camps. White supervisors who knew the language reported overhearing no sexual bragging of the locker-room type and seeing no sexual horseplay.

Among adult men the reported incidence of any form of sexual behavior pathology was extremely rare. There were stories of one man, now deceased, from an adjacent settlement who buffooned at being a dog having intercourse with an actual dog. He was universally known as being a person who did not respond appropriately when spoken to: the same word is used for a deaf mute as for a person who is out of his mind. This man had no wife and no promise girl. His public display with the dog might be interpreted, therefore, both as a reproach to his people and a symptom of insanity.

Among adult men there was also a report of behavior that at first glance, though not when subject to closer scrutiny, might appear to be the psychopathology of transvestism. This behavior was considered to be prankish by those reporting it, especially insofar as a young man not only put on a woman's dress, but also filled out the breasts with wads of clothing. The prankster's purpose was to be able to rendezvous with his girl friend, and perhaps her female accomplices, after nightfall, according to a prearranged plan. From a distance and through the darkness, other people would see only a group of females together, and nothing more would be thought of it. The wolf in woman's clothing meanwhile had the perfect opportunity to sneak off into the shadows illicitly, with the lover otherwise forbidden to him.

There was no reported or observable incidence of effeminate homosexuality among grown men, nor of homosexual preference of partners among noneffeminate men. Sexual activity between two males was reported only in connection with prepuberty and adolescence. Young male informants had no more inhibition or shame in reporting this activity than any other play activity. Their game was one in which a partner, usually a younger boy, would acquiesce to taking a feminine coital position in interfemoral, but probably not anal or oral intercourse, for the reward of nothing more than being accepted by the older boys who held prestige in his eyes.

TO EVADE PSYCHOSEXUAL PATHOLOGY

In the next generation or two, as the new tradition becomes consolidated in a more and more operational and viable compromise with the old, one of the many challenges for the Yolngu people will be to find a way of preserving their remarkable freedom from most of the psychopathologies of sexual behavior, and their virtually complete freedom from homosexuality and related disorders of gender identity. To this end, it will be almost essential for them to preserve, among other things, their present unprudish attitude to the normalcy of nudity and sexual play of young children. They will need preschool teachers, like the wise woman they have at present, who at rest periods remains unfazed when a small boy lying in proximity to a small girl unself-consciously begins to make pelvic thrusting movements. This teacher can approach this behavior with the same equanimity as when a child wets his pants or sucks his thumb too much, making it neither an offense nor a display. That, by the standards extant in the United States and in most of Australia today, is no mean accomplishment.

The straightforward attitude of the Yolngu toward nudity and sex play in young children allows these children to grow up with a straightforward attitude toward sex differences, toward the proper meaning and eventual significance of the sex organs, and toward their own reproductive destiny and sense of identity as male or female. It is here that one may look for an explanation for the relative freedom, in Yolngu society, from sexual behavior disorders.

From the point of view of psychosexual theory, it does not so much matter what is considered masculine and what feminine in the Yolngu social order: what does matter is that the two are quite clearly differentiated. Children can easily grow up to develop a gender identity without any confusion as to their proper gender role, present or future. The restrictions and taboos they will encounter do not refer to the practice of their masculinity or femininity, but to the eligibility of the partner with whom they may practice it. In our own society we have both types of taboos. The Yolngu, especially the women, are not completely free of sexual "hang-ups." The "hang-ups" affect the frequency of sexuality, but not the way of expressing it (sexual intercourse) nor the sex of the partner (heterosexual) with whom to express it.

CONCLUSION

At the outset of my Arnhem Land experience I had, with my colleagues, asked two questions. The first we could answer affirmatively: yes, the infants do play at the movement of sexual intercourse without taboo or secrecy. The second question, regarding the effect in adulthood of this lack of prudery or taboo on infantile sex play, could not be answered so simply. The effect of sexual frankness in infancy is masked by the imposition, after the age of 8, of a complicated set of social rules that require a boy or a girl to set up avoidancy relationships with certain other boys or girls. These same rules also specify who might marry whom, and dictate that a girl must share her "promise man" with other wives who usually are her sisters. Thus the aboriginal society imposes limits, regulations or taboos on sexual expression that are as stringent as our own, if not more so—but they are different restrictions and are imposed at a different age in a child's development. These restrictions seem to have more of an adverse effect on a woman's sex life than on a man's in today's aboriginal world, since many wives have joyless and perfunctory sexual relations with their husbands.

In the aboriginal system it is not sex itself that is taboo, but certain selections of the person with whom one may have it. This may be the key to the finding that there is very little or nothing at all in the way of abnormal sexual behavior, like homosexuality, and the other paraphilias, among the Arnhem Land people.

REFERENCE

1.   Bianchi, G. N., McElwain, D. W., & Cawte, J. E. The dispensary syndrome in Australian Aborigines: Origins of their bodily preoccupation and sick role behaviour. *British Journal of Medical Psychology*, 1970, **43**, 375–382.

CHAPTER FOUR

Imaginative Fantasies

Sexual Imagery

Traditionally, there have been two approaches to erotica—those sexual fantasies that are communicated in words and pictures. On the one hand, such material has been sought eagerly, primarily by males, at every age from childhood to senility. Pictures, magazines, and books are examined with prurient interest, furtively shared with close friends, and then hidden in drawers, on closet shelves, and under mattresses. On the other hand, erotic material has been denounced as worthless pornography and its corrupting influence fought from the pulpit, in courts of law, and in the streets where indignant citizens march in protest against adult book stores and movie theaters. Both the consumers and the castigators have agreed, however, that there is something shameful, or at least not respectable, about an interest in erotica.

When the great legal battles over sexually explicit novels were fought in the first half of this century, a crucial distinction was made between a work of literature that happened to contain erotic scenes and a work of pornography which was designed with the sole purpose of bringing about sexual excitement. Both the conservatives in favor of censorship and the liberals in favor of artistic freedom could agree that it was proper to ban pure pornography. Thus, if one became aroused while reading *Lady Chatterley's Lover* or *Ulysses*, it was an unintentional side effect of a particular type of literary creation. If an individual read a tattered paperback copy of *Hannah Had Hot Pants* with the express purpose of becoming sexually excited, both sides of the censorship question could agree in their negative reactions to the reader, the pornographer who wrote it, and the smut peddler who profited from such human weakness.

In recent years, these issues have been viewed from a quite different perspective. It is now recognized that fantasies are an integral part of human sexual expression for both males and females. Since that is so, it becomes difficult to defend the position that these self-created sex fantasies are normal and useful while commercial sex fantasies are somehow perverted and harmful. A more reasonable approach, as in the following article, is to attempt to understand the role that both types of imaginative creations play in our sexual lives.

Sexual Imagery

Donn Byrne

One of mankind's more intriguing attributes is the ability to generate internal imaginative experiences that can re-create past events, anticipate future occurrences, or create novel scenes which bear no relationship to

Reprinted in an edited version from: Money, J., & Musaph, H. (Eds.) *Handbook of sexology*. Amsterdam: Excerpta Medica, 1976.

reality. This capacity for imagery serves numerous functions ranging from simple amusement to contingency planning. One of the more curious aspects of imaginative activity, however, is the effect it has on the motivational-emotional responses of the individual who generates the fantasy *and* of anyone to whom the fantasy is communicated.

The self-arousal properties of imagination can be easily demonstrated for oneself by recalling or anticipating specific interpersonal situations appropriate to anger, depression, fear, or joy. If they are sufficiently vivid, such imaginative activities can evoke the appropriate physiological and psychological accompaniments. Similarly, external cues such as words, drawings, photographs, or motion pictures are able to elicit the same kinds of responses, and it is logical to assume that imaginative processes serve as mediators. For example, a magazine photograph of a rich, moist chocolate cake plus a succulent description of its taste and texture can elicit images of cakes which, in turn, evoke the salivary response and the desire to eat. Because of these arousal effects of internal and external imaginative cues, human beings are not dependent on the occurrence of actual interpersonal interactions to evoke such emotions as anger nor on internal physiological deficits to evoke such motives as hunger. In the realm of sexual activity, it should not be surprising to find that precisely the same mechanisms are operative. We can be sexually aroused by our fantasies whether these are self-generated or triggered by the externalized fantasies of others.

EROTIC FANTASIES AND HUMAN SEXUALITY

Erotica as a uniquely human enterprise

Not only can human beings become aroused in response to internal and external sexual images, they apparently have sought to do so throughout recorded history. The prehistoric origins of erotic fantasies are obviously not available to us, but it can be noted that some of the earliest drawings and carvings include depictions of genitalia and of sexual acts. In fact, it seems accurate to assert that progressive developments in art, technology, and communication skills are almost immediately put to use in depicting and communicating sexual images. There are countless examples of our species' long-standing interest in representing and communicating erotic images and of our ingenuity in utilizing all available artistic and technological skills in this enterprise. Prior to the twentieth century, erotic creations included Latin American clay figures, African phallic statues, bas-relief sculptures in Indian temples, Pompeian frescoes, sexual paintings by artists such as Rembrandt, the underground erotic stories and novels of Victorian England, and the photographic postcards from nineteenth-century France. In the current century, advancing technology has given us the stag movie and multitudes of sexually explicit 8-mm loops suitable for home viewing, the rampant sexuality of familiar comic strip characters in "Tijuana bibles," humor-oriented erotic "party records," audio tapes of sexual encounters complete with sound effects, the big-budget full-color sex movies of the 1970s, and the videotaped erotica currently available in certain motels.

Why are erotic images created and communicated?

We have seen that our species has the ability to create sexual images, the tendency to be aroused by them, and the apparent desire to spend time and effort in this pursuit. Though it may seem a naive question, not much effort has been devoted to explaining *why* such behavior occurs. Among the few answers that have been offered is the suggestion that all such erotic activities are evidence of perversity and moral depravity or that they represent conspiratorial efforts to subvert and debauch others. A letter to *Playboy* magazine suggests that pornography is inherently evil. A letter to the Norman, Oklahoma, *Transcript* expresses the belief that erotica is a menace to humanity. A letter to the St. Louis, Missouri, *Globe-Democrat* sees pornography as a poison to body and soul. If erotica is seen as evil and threatening, it is not surprising that its presence is attributed to a sinister plot on the part of Communists to brutalize Americans (according to a former Indiana congressman) or on the part of capitalists to distract Czechoslovakians from political concerns (according to the Soviet Young Communist League). A more all-purpose explanation was provided in medieval Europe when Satan was seen as the perpetrator of sexual fantasies; sexual dreams and nocturnal orgasms, for example, were believed to be caused by the stealthy ministrations of succubi and incubi.

While it is not possible in the present context to ascertain or evaluate the activities of Communists, capitalists, or Satan, it *is* possible to suggest four primary reasons that may help to explain the human propensity for exposing ourselves to internal and external erotic images.

Erotica as a source of knowledge When individuals are asked to specify the primary source of their knowledge about sex, very few name their parents, schools, or churches. Instead, the most important sex educators seem to be friends of the same age with pornography as supplementary source material.

Though very little research has been directed at this question, retrospective accounts by adults suggest that the details of sexual anatomy and the complexities of copulation often are communicated most clearly and most specifically by erotic stories and pictures. In the movie, *Summer of '42*, there was an excellent portrayal of the eager curiosity of adolescent boys examining an illustrated medical text. Though our laws and mores prohibit this, it seems likely that the exposure of youngsters to erotica could be an effective and economical teaching device. Unselected erotica unfortunately can also be a source of misinformation about sex, and hence its potential value is usually mitigated by society's refusal to acknowledge its pedagogical role.

Once the basic anatomical aspects of genitalia are understood and their interactive properties mastered, there are still two major ways in which erotic images continue to be educational and informative. First, there are all the myriad variations in intercourse positions, paragenital sexual acts, and multiparticipant sexuality. In effect, educational erotica can progress from introductory to intermediate and advanced sexual behavior. Second, there is a different type of knowledge imparted by sexual fantasies, one which touches on very important psychological concerns. According to Festinger,[1] human beings have a need for social comparison. We constantly seek information as to where we stand in reference to others with respect to ability, skills, opinions, and so forth. Such comparison processes provide us with a sense of who we are and inform us of areas in which change would be desirable. The one aspect of human behavior which historically has been the least open to direct social comparison is that of sexuality. It was noted earlier that sex research is one way in which such needs are satisfied. Through erotica, sexual behavior is actually put on public display and thus it becomes possible for the viewer to assess his or her abilities and proclivities, at least in comparison with the depicted individuals. Of course, any distortions of reality in erotica unfortunately lead to erroneous bases for social comparison.

Erotic images as aphrodisiacs   Because sexual activity in our species is largely under cognitive control, it follows that we can, to a surprising degree, regulate our sexual behavior by creating erotic fantasies or sharing the fantasies of others. In effect, we can become excited whenever we wish to do so. Though much time, effort, money, and wishful thinking have been directed toward the search for an effective aphrodisiac, many individuals have learned that they are carrying one of the most powerful instruments for stimulation right inside their own heads. The arousal properties sought in ginseng roots, antelope antlers, or cantharides can be obtained much more easily and reliably by exposure to stories, pictures, and thoughts involving sexual activity.

Not only are sexual images utilized to obtain self-arousal, but their motivating properties have long been utilized in attempts to manipulate the arousal of others—most often by males attempting to arouse females. There are numerous historical and literary references to such uses of erotica. The anonymous author of *My Secret Life* in the early 1800s in England recounts several examples of seduction aided by erotic books, pictures, and conversations. On the basis of his laboratory findings, Griffitt[2] notes, "If, in fact, males attempt to arouse female partners sexually by exposing them to erotica, the present data suggest that their efforts would be generally successful. . . ."

Erotic images, arousal, and pleasure Many drive-arousal theories suggest that motivation is based primarily on unpleasant physiological states of either deprivation or painful stimulation. When such states become sufficiently noxious, the organism behaves in such a way as to reduce the drive. Drive reduction is reinforcing, and, with human beings at least, the accompanying emotional state is described as one of pleasure. It also follows that the stronger the drive, the greater the drive reduction when the appropriate goal is achieved. Common experience tells us that the greater the drive reduction, the more intense the accompanying pleasure. It is a truism that food tastes best when one's mealtime is delayed, that great thirst enhances the pleasurable qualities of even a glass of water, that sleep deprivation makes it all the more delightful to lie down in a comfortable bed, and so forth.

When the relationships outlined above are extrapolated to the area of sexuality, it seems plausible to suggest that erotic images act to increase drive level and that any subsequent orgasm would involve increased drive reduction and hence intensified pleasure. If this analysis is correct, it means that imaginative fantasies can serve to enhance sexual gratification. There is some research evidence indicating that fantasy is widely used for this purpose. For example, Hariton and Singer[3] found that the majority of their sample of married women regularly have sexual fantasies during intercourse. These fantasies are not associated with sexual or marital difficulty but simply serve to increase desire and to heighten pleasure.

Imagination versus reality Reality is restrictive for a variety of reasons. One advantage of imaginative activities is that they can go beyond the confines of reality in allowing one to engage vicariously in activities which are legally and/or morally condemned, which are physically impossible, or which might be intriguing at the level of fantasy but acutely unpleasant in actual fact.

Both in commercially distributed erotica and in self-reports of fantasies, sexual behavior frequently involves taboo or illegal activities. Though the taboos and the laws change over time and though they vary across localities, it is clear that rape, adultery, prostitution, homosexuality, anal sex, and sadism, for example, have played a much larger role in our public and private fantasies than has, say, the heterosexual intercourse of spouses in the dorsal-ventral position, female supine. It also seems safe to assume that more individuals have thought about and become aroused by the idea of quasi-illicit activities such as group sex, for example, than actually had the opportunity or the willingness to engage in the activity.

In addition, realistic obstacles can be overcome by imagination. Anyone can dream the impossible dream and engage in whatever sexual acts with whatever person or persons one chooses. The most unattractive female can be the lust object of Robert Redford and Paul McCartney. An equally unattractive male can make easy conquests of Jane Fonda and Linda Lovelace. In imagination, no one need worry about the size or shape of any anatomical feature, there is no frigidity or impotence, and unrequited desire is unknown. Even at a more mundane level, sexual fantasies are much simpler than the real world in which individuals must deal with the details of steering wheels, motel clerks, brassiere hooks, shoes and socks, etc. The idea is described well by Erica Jong in *Fear of Flying*[4] when she presents her fantasy of the "zipless fuck" which was "more than a fuck. It was a platonic ideal. Zipless because when you came together zippers fell away like rose petals, underwear blew off in one breath like dandelion fluff. Tongues intertwined and turned liquid [pp. 11–12]."

Finally, many exciting imagined activities would be much less exciting and much less pleasant if they actually occurred. Perhaps a prime example is rape. Females may report rape fantasies as arousing and pleasurable, but actual rape, in contrast, involves fear, pain, and humiliation. Similarly, many individuals who are turned on by sadomasochistic themes in fantasy would be repelled by the stark reality of administering or receiving pain. It is suggested, then, that sexual imagery can sometimes be preferable to its real-life counterparts.

REFERENCES

1. Festinger, L. A theory of social comparison processes. *Human Relations*, 1954, **7**, 117–140.

2. Griffitt, W. Response to erotica and the projection of response to erotica in the opposite sex. *Journal of Experimental Research in Personality*, 1973, **6**, 330–338.

3. Hariton, E. B., & Singer, J. L. Women's fantasies during sexual intercourse: Normative and theoretical implications. *Journal of Consulting and Clinical Psychology*, 1974, **42**, 313–322.

4. Jong, E. *Fear of flying*. New York: Holt, Rinehart, & Winston, 1973.

Cognitive Factors in Sexual Arousal:
The Role of Distraction

A number of experimenters have been able to demonstrate that both male and female subjects can easily follow instructions to imagine a sexual scene. This imaginative activity results in arousal both as reported by the subjects themselves and as indicated by physiological measuring devices attached to the penis or inserted in the vagina.

In the following experiment, psychologists James Geer and Robert Fuhr suggest that our responses to erotic stimuli also involve such fantasy activity. That is, there is probably no automatic sexual response to words and pictures that portray erotic activity. Rather, such material stimulates thought processes, and it is this cognitive activity that brings about arousal. They tested this hypothesis in an ingenious experiment in which subjects were exposed to a sexually explicit recording in one of several conditions involving varying degrees of cognitive interference. The prediction was that as subjects spent an increased amount of cognitive effort on a nonsexual task, they would be less aroused by the erotic story. The results strongly support the notion that, to a large extent, human sexuality is based on our ability to use our imaginations.

In this article, the authors also make the more general point that the study of sexual behavior will benefit from the application of the research methodologies and strategies of other areas of psychology. As they suggest, these bridges between the study of sex and the study of other types of behavior help, at long last, to bring sex research "in out of the cold."

Cognitive Factors in Sexual Arousal:
The Role of Distraction

James H. Geer and Robert Fuhr

Clinical observation has long noted that the introduction of asexual stimuli into an erotic situation often reduces sexual arousal. Masters and Johnson[6] noted such a phenomenon when they said that "Penile erection may be impaired easily by the introduction of asexual stimuli, even though sexual stimulation is continued simultaneously [p. 183]." The present study investigated the suggestion that the effect may be produced, in some instances, by distraction or interference with the cognitive processing of erotic material. It is suggested here that sexual arousal produced by other than direct physical manipulation of the genitals requires that either the individual attends to and thus processes erotic

Reprinted in an edited version from: Geer, J. H., & Fuhr, R. Cognitive factors in sexual arousal: The role of distraction. *Journal of Consulting and Clinical Psychology*, 1976, 44, 238–243.

stimuli or is engaging in erotic thoughts. If a distracting nonerotic stimulus or thought occurs, arousal will be reduced in direct relation to the degree or amount of distraction from or interference with processing of the erotic stimulus or thought. The present study was designed to systematically and empirically evaluate that suggestion.

The phenomenon of decreased arousal via distraction has implications for at least two sexual dysfunctions. One is premature ejaculation; the other is impotence. In premature ejaculation, clinical approaches have often focused on strategies that distract the premature ejaculator from erotic stimuli, presumably thus reducing arousal and delaying ejaculation. Although clinical techniques such as "pause" and "squeeze" are not necessarily conceived of as distraction devices, it is possible that they operate via distraction. More direct distraction is evident when the premature ejaculator deliberately thinks of or attends to something nonsexual, such as mental arithmetic. Such distraction procedures have been applied to premature ejaculation unsystematically with varying degrees of reported effectiveness. We recognize that alternative theories of premature ejaculation suggest different strategies. Kaplan[4] believes that "premature ejaculators do not clearly perceive the sensations premonitory to orgasm, which in turn, deprives them of the regulatory power of the higher nervous influences [p. 301]." Tuthill[9] and Hastings[3] proposed that premature ejaculation results from too infrequent sex. Each of these formulations would suggest alternative strategies to distraction for the treatment of premature ejaculation. At this point in time, there are no controlled data that can be brought to bear on determining which, if any, of the theories concerning premature ejaculation is correct. Therefore, our study will be relevant to the treatment of premature ejaculation if in the final analysis cognitive factors producing too rapid arousal contribute to the phenomena.

Impotence has been seen as the obverse of premature ejaculation. Masters and Johnson[7] have suggested that the impotent male often fails to maintain his erection because he concentrates too much on sexual performance. The concentration on performance, to the extent that such thoughts are nonerotic, would act as a distraction or interference reducing arousal and the resultant erection. Thus, we are suggesting that distraction or interference with cognitive processing of erotic material may play a role in the development of impotence and the treatment of premature ejaculation.

Related to the concept of distraction is the concept of attention. To the degree that an individual is distracted from a stimulus, the less he or she can attend to that stimulus. Experimental cognitive psychology has used the concept of attention as an important feature in theory construction. It is generally assumed that complex cognitive processes require that the individual be attending to or focusing on the material being processed. Therefore, distraction or interference with such processing will reduce the effects of the material. There are various explanations for this effect. One suggests that since individuals must have limited capacities for information processing, partial or complete use of such capacity will reduce the likelihood of processing additional information. We assume that in order for sexual arousal to occur to nongenital stimuli (i.e., visual or auditory) complex processing must occur. Thus, we expect that by using significant portions of the processing capacity we will interfere with sexual arousal. The present experiment was designed to test the above proposition through systematic distraction from or interference with processing of the erotic material by providing the subject with nonerotic cognitive processing tasks and then studying the effect on sexual arousal. It was predicted that as subjects were involved in increasingly complex processing of nonerotic stimuli the arousal produced by the erotic stimuli would be reduced.

One paradigm used by cognitive psychologists to study attention and/or distraction, among other phenomena, is dichotic listening. In this procedure, subjects are presented with two oral messages, one in each ear. The subject is instructed to attend to one message or stimulus and to ignore or disregard the other. The experimenter then examines the effect of the nonattended message on the attended. The general finding is that when the subject is "busy" with processing on the attended channel very little of the nonattended message is perceived; however, see Lewis[5] and Corteen and Wood[1] for exceptions. In the present experiment, a variant of dichotic listening was employed in which subjects were presented single digits every 3 sec on the attended channel. Using a procedure developed by Posner and Rossman,[8] subjects were assigned tasks to be performed on those digits. The tasks varied dramatically in the amount of cognitive processing required to perform the operations. Thus, given that their attention was focused to varying degrees on the attended channel, subjects were distracted from the second channel. On the second channel, subjects were presented with an erotic tape recording describing a sexual encounter. Although subjects were not instructed to ignore the second channel, and although they knew that it contained erotic material, they had different amounts of time or processing capacity available to process the erotic material. The experimental hypothesis was that physiological measures of sexual arousal elicited by the erotic tape would vary inversely with the amount of cognitive processing required by the nonerotic task.

METHOD

Subjects

There were 31 male undergraduates who served as volunteer subjects. They were randomly assigned to one of four conditions.

Equipment

A polygraph was used to record changes in penile tumescence, our measure of sexual arousal. A mercury strain gauge was used to detect changes in tumescence. Tape recordings were played on a stereo tape recorder through stereo headphones.

Procedure

Subjects came to the laboratory to participate in a study of "sexual responses to erotic stimuli." They were participating as part of their requirement in introductory psychology. Upon arrival at the laboratory, all details of the experiment were explained to the subjects, and they were invited to participate. Care was taken to ensure voluntary participation, and there were no negative consequences for declining to participate. All subjects who came to the laboratory volunteered to continue in the experiment following its description.

Following the briefing, subjects were instructed in the placement of the mercury-filled rubber tube that was the penile strain gauge. These instructions included both a verbal description by the experimenter and a mimeographed illustration that showed the subject that he was to place the gauge just behind the coronal ridge. The wires from the strain gauge were to be led out through the fly or over the edge of the pants. Prior to placement of the strain gauge, the experimenter left the room. All subsequent communication with the subject was conducted over an intercom between the subject's room and the equipment room next door. Thus, complete privacy was assured.

After seating himself in a comfortable armchair, the subject indicated over the intercom when he was ready. The experimenter then adjusted the recording equipment, and when clear recordings were obtained, a 75-sec rest period commenced before giving instructions. The instructions, taken from Posner and Rossman,[8] were delivered over the intercom. The subject was told those operations, if any, he was to perform on the single digits that were about to be presented. In the "listening only" control group, subjects were informed that they would be hearing digits along with an erotic tape; however, they were given no instructions as to what they were to do with the stimuli. The "copy only" group was told to write down the digits as they were presented. The "add pairs" group was instructed to add together successive pairs of digits and to write down the result. Thus, if they heard 5, 7, 8, 3, they were to write down 12, 11. The "classify" group was the final condition. Subjects in this group were instructed to listen to successive pairs of digits and classify them according to the following instructions. If the pair formed by the two-digit number was above 50 and odd (e.g., 71), the subject wrote "A." If it was above 50 and even (e.g., 88), the subject wrote "B." If below 50 and even (e.g., 22), he was to write "a"; and if below 50 and odd (e.g., 21), he was to write "b." As can be readily appreciated, this classification task required all or most of the subjects' attention or processing capacity and, in fact, yields many errors when performed in a cognitive study[8] without erotic stimuli to distract. The important point to note is that all subjects, regardless of group assignment, received identical auditory stimuli; they differed only on the operations they were to perform on those stimuli. The order of groups from least to most cognitive processing performed on the digits is listening only, copy only, add pairs, and classify.

When the subject indicated that he understood the instructions, a 125-sec warm-up period followed during which the subjects performed their assigned tasks while hearing the number alone. This warm-up period also was used as the baseline condition for determining criteria for measurements of penile responses. At the end of this period, the erotic message was presented to the unattended ear while the numbers continued. The numbers and the erotic message were equated for peak volume. The erotic tape with the accompanying numbers lasted for 5 min, 50 sec. It contained a woman's voice describing her participation in a sexual experience. The sexual encounter consisted of extensive foreplay, oral-genital contact, and coitus—all described in explicit terms. Prior research in our laboratory has demonstrated that these types of erotic stimuli reliably produce high levels of sexual arousal. The ear in which the erotic tape was presented was varied randomly across subjects to control for possible effects of hemispheric localization of emotional responding. Following the presentation of the auditory stimuli, subjects removed the strain gauge and indicated over the intercom that they were finished. The experimenter then went to the experimental chamber and accompanied the subject to the equipment room where the subject was shown the apparatus, all questions were answered, and an informal debriefing occurred.

RESULTS

The dependent variable used to assess sexual arousal was the measure of penile tumescence. The amplitude measure was the mean amplitude of tumescence changes. To calculate the dependent variable, all changes in tumescence were measured in millimeters of increase above the greatest change that occurred during the baseline condition. Since the mean baseline change was zero for all subjects, the mean increase in tumescence during the erotic tape presentation became the dependent variable used in the subsequent statistical analyses. Figure 4-1 displays a plot of the mean amplitude for the four conditions.

The most direct test of the experimental hypothesis was the correlation between group assignment, ordered with respect to the complexity

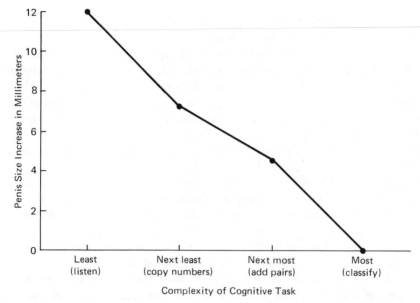

Figure 4-1. Male subjects listened to an erotic story while carrying out one of four types of complex cognitive tasks. The more complex the task, the less sexually aroused the subjects were.

of the cognitive task, and the individual's mean amplitude. The correlation was .76, which was highly significant.

DISCUSSION

The results of this experiment strongly support the hypothesis that in the human male sexual arousal is powerfully influenced by the amount of distraction from or interference with cognitive processing of erotic stimuli. The greater the distraction or interference, the less the arousal. Although the same may be true for women, the present study does not address itself to that question. Further, we can only speculate that the same effect would be found if the modality of erotic input were visual or tactile.

Our results fit well with clinical observation and anecdotal evidence and for the first time provide clear empirical evidence for the effect of distraction in sexual arousal. Reference to the figure reveals the strength of the effect. In the classify condition, during which distraction is maximal, there was virtually no sexual arousal produced by the erotic tape. Yet during listening only control, arousal occurred at a very high level. Inspection of the individual records was even more persuasive in that it revealed that six of seven subjects in the control group showed arousal for more than 75% of the erotic tape, whereas six of seven classify subjects showed virtually no arousal at any time. It is possible that such powerful effects would be even greater in real-life situations such as may be found in erectile dysfunctions.

We have no data on which we can draw to clarify the exact experiences of our subjects. Nonsystematic interviews indicated that subjects in the classify condition reported not hearing the erotic message, which parallels much of the work in cognitive psychology which reports that subjects do not perceive nonattended messages. A study by Corteen and Wood[1] is of particular interest in that they reported galvanic skin responses (GSRs) to previously shocked words when those words were presented on a nonattended channel. Further, they noted that subjects reported the GSR-eliciting words as not being perceived. Our findings differed in that the nonperceived stimuli did not have much, if any, effect on a physiological measure. One could speculate that sexual arousal from nontactile stimuli requires cognitive processing at a level that includes awareness. Why awareness seems necessary for genital responses, but not GSRs as in Corteen and Wood, is not clear.

The present study does directly support the clinical and anecdotal reports of reduced sexual arousal resulting from distraction. The results suggest that various strategies of distraction would be effective in reducing unwanted arousal such as occurs in the premature ejaculator. Empirical evidence could be obtained to devise optimal strategies for arousal reduction; the present study only indicates that increased distraction yields greater amounts of arousal reduction. It may turn out that the content of the interfering cognitions may be of importance. If, for example, we learn that cognitions accompanied by anxiety or cognitions concerning performance demands are particularly interfering with sexual arousal, this information would be of value in clinical applications. These considerations make clear the necessity for using caution in directly applying laboratory data to the "natural" setting in which many additional and often unknown variables operate.

It should be made clear that if the thoughts that occur during a sexual interaction are erotic, even though not directly relevant to the occurring situation, one would not expect decreased arousal. One might, for example, view Ellis'[2] therapeutic strategy of thinking or fantasizing about whatever one finds erotic as an aid to increasing arousal within a sexual interaction as reflecting in part the role of attention. In that instance, erotic thoughts, though not of the immediate situation, may result in increased sexual arousal.

As a final point, this study demonstrates the utility of applying concepts and paradigms from experimental cognitive psychology to the study of human sexuality. This application has several advantages. First, it helps bring sex in from the cold. For too long much of the research on human sexuality has proceeded on its own, divorced from the mainstream of behavioral science. Deliberate ties to other areas should result in advantages to all involved. The second obvious advantage of the application of cognitive psychology is the potential for exploration of relevant phenomena in an objective manner. Although many recognize that much of human sexuality may be described as reflecting cognitive processes, there has been essentially no attempt to study those processes in any detail. It is our hope that research such as that described in the present study will be part of a growing trend. Science has often shown major strides when concepts and models from one field have been applied to another. It is our hope that the study of human sexuality will be advanced by its association with experimental cognitive psychology.

REFERENCES

1. Corteen, R. S., & Wood, B. Autonomic responses to shock-associated words in an unattended channel. *Journal of Experimental Psychology*, 1972, **94**, 308–313.

2. Ellis, A. *Sex without guilt.* New York: Lyle Stuart, 1965.

3. Hastings, D. W. *Impotence and frigidity.* Boston: Little, Brown, 1963.

4. Kaplan, H. *The new sex therapy: Active treatment of sexual dysfunctions.* New York: Brunner-Mazel, 1974.

5. Lewis, J. L. Semantic processing of unattended messages using dichotic listening. *Journal of Experimental Psychology*, 1970, **85**, 225–228.

6. Masters, W. H., & Johnson, V. E. *Human sexual response.* Boston: Little, Brown, 1966.

7. Masters, W. H., & Johnson, V. E. *Human sexual inadequacy.* Boston: Little, Brown, 1970.

8. Posner, M. I., & Rossman, E. Effect of size and location of informational transforms upon short-term retention. *Journal of Experimental Psychology*, 1965, **70**, 496–505.

9. Tuthill, J. F. Impotence. *The Lancet*, 1955, **1**, 124–128.

Masturbation and Sexual Fantasies in Married Couples

In a number of current research reports, including the following one, the sexual fantasies of both males and females have been presented. Beyond the details of the fantasies themselves, an additional point is worth noting. When individuals are asked to describe their sexual fantasies, most are able to do so without hesitation. That is, it seems that members of each sex, those who are sexually experienced and those who are not, and both married and unmarried individuals regularly have sexual fantasies and are willing to share them with experimenters. It is commonly reported that these fantasies occur when the individual is alone and masturbating and also when the individual is with a partner and engaging in various sexual activities. Most of these studies have involved college students or relatively well-educated adults in the United States. Additional research must be conducted in order to determine whether fantasy activity is equally common among less verbal and less educated persons in our society and whether there are cultural differences in either the frequency or the content of erotic imaginings.

In the next article, one such cross-cultural study is reported with a sample of married couples in Denmark. This particular investigation deals with two topics that were at one time taboo—masturbation within marriage and sexual fantasies. By now it is clear that both activities are a natural part of human sexual expression.

As in other studies of sexual imagination, males and females are found to differ somewhat in the content of their fantasies. In this group of subjects, males reported more thoughts of group sexual experiences while females were more inclined to think of a single partner, especially someone other than their spouse. One striking difference between these fantasies and those reported in a number of recent American studies is the absence of the rape theme among the Danish couples. Systematic research on such cultural differences is needed in order to identify the origins of the specific themes we each find exciting and to determine the part that such themes play in other aspects of our lives.

Masturbation and Sexual Fantasies in Married Couples

Hans Hessellund

Masturbation or autosexuality as a way of obtaining sexual release has been and still is widespread. As a sexual practice it has a long history of general condemnation.[2,6,7] Masturbation is not an exclusively human

Reprinted in an edited version from: Hessellund, H. Masturbation and sexual fantasies in married couples. *Archives of Sexual Behavior*, 1976, 5, 133–147.

activity but occurs regularly among other mammalian species, even with willing partners available.[3] In a cross-cultural and a cross-species perspective, autosexuality is more common among males than females. These facts considered, masturbation should be conceptualized as a normal or natural pattern of behavior, originating in built-in biological mammalian systems.

Although masturbation is universal in occurrence, attitudes toward it are extremely varied.[3] However, the main effect of masturbatory taboos seems to be masturbation in secret rather than a reduction in occurrence. Viewed more generally, there has been a progressive liberalization in the attitudes toward masturbation, especially among the more affluent classes. Masturbatory techniques are, for instance, now used in the treatment of psychosexual problems such as impotence and frigidity.[8,9] Another aspect of the more permissive attitude toward masturbation finds expression in sex education texts for young people, especially in Scandinavia. While formerly much energy was invested in the prevention of masturbation in the young,[10] autosexuality is currently considered not only a harmless but even a useful way of obtaining sexual release. It is recommended for young people who have no current sexual partner.

Although masturbation is in theory considered to be without harmful effects, less is known about some psychological aspects, for instance, the significance of masturbation for male and female self-esteem. Abramson[1] found that masturbation was a greater psychological threat for males than for females, and, further, that there was no connection between frequency of masturbation and intercourse. Greenberg and Archambault[5] found that guilt feelings connected with masturbation occurred in 40% of men and 48% of women in a sample of university students. In agreement with the Kinsey findings, our data show that males masturbate more than the females and that the unmarried masturbate more than the married. While there was a significant difference in intercourse frequency among married and unmarried subjects, there were no significant differences in frequency of masturbation between married and unmarried subjects. If masturbation is considered a substitute for intercourse, one would expect that the frequency of masturbation would be greater among unmarried subjects than among subjects with daily sexual access to a partner. This hypothesis was not borne out. Greenberg and Archambault[5] did not find significant differences between frequencies of masturbation and intercourse.

MASTURBATION

Sample

A small part of an intensive study on the sexual behavior, attitudes, and knowledge in 38 married couples with children is reported. The sample was drawn from the general population, through the public files, with the following criteria: the age of the husband was between 34 and 39 years, and each couple had at least one child.

The couples had been married between 1 and 19 years, with a mean of 10.7 years. The majority of the subjects were content with their marriage, loved their spouses, and had never seriously regretted the union. The mean age of the husbands was about 37 years and of the wives, 34 years. The mean number of children was 2.3. Couples of all social classes were represented, as well as urban and provincial locales. None had consulted doctors, clergymen, psychologists, marriage counselors, or other professional people with problems of a sexual or marital nature.

Occurrence and frequency of masturbation

Of the couples, 15 men (39.5%) and 24 women (63.2%) never masturbate. Among 12 couples (31.6%), both partners independently stated that they never masturbate. Twelve women have husbands who masturbate from "seldom" (once or twice per year) to daily. Where both spouses masturbate, the husband masturbates more frequently than his wife.

Significant sex differences exist. Of the 15 men who do not masturbate, only 3 state that they have never done so. Among the 24 women who do not masturbate, 18 state that they have never done so. The figures for experience with masturbation (males 92.1%, females 52.6%) correspond with the Kinsey figures for experiences with masturbation (males 94%, females 58%). Subjects who no longer masturbate state that they did so when young and until married.

I don't masturbate any longer. I did when young, but after getting to know girls I stopped. (male)

I never masturbated after I got married. (male)

I masturbated before I got married. (female)

Masturbation as secret from spouse

Among 11 couples where both husband and wife masturbate, only 3 husbands and wives know of this. Five husbands and wives stated that they do not think their spouses know. Among those 11 couples where only the husband masturbates, 5 husbands feel certain that their wives know, while among 4 couples where only the wife masturbates, only 1 wife states that her husband knows. Only 1 husband who masturbates felt that it was a problem for his wife. This subject masturbates from three times a day to twice per week: "I told her in one of those periods when she was not interested in intercourse. She got very unhappy, so it was lucky that I did. She has not complained about it." The wife stated that she masturbates "once in a while" and further that her husband knows about it, since he encouraged her masturbating: "He has even given me a vibrator."

When it is possible to hide masturbation from a person as close as a husband or wife this is connected with time and place for masturbatory behavior. More than half of the husbands and more than three-fourths of the wives masturbate in bed when the spouse has fallen asleep.

The main difference between men and women here is that about 40% of the men always masturbate in the bathroom, either morning or night when they prepare for going to work or bed. Those men masturbate as a matter of routine before brushing their teeth and washing their hands. None of the wives states that this only takes place in the bathroom, but that it might happen.

Husband: I do it rather often. Every second day or so. At night in bed, when my wife is asleep. She never wakes up.

Wife: Twice a week. In the evening, when my husband is away or in the afternoon. When I feel like it. Often in bed or in the bathroom.

Husband: Normally twice a month, but it varies rather much. It depends on the total sexual activity and the emotional climate. But it is seldom now. I masturbated a lot when I prepared for my examinations—by God, I did it all day long. If I didn't eat or smoke, I masturbated—and then I could go on studying. (The wife knows, but it has not caused any problem.) If it happens now it is especially when we are on bad terms. It happens in bad periods. It indicates that we are not getting along very well together.

Wife: Twice a week. It is periodical, but normally every third day, even if we are together. It can be any time during the day and often in bed. (The husband knows about it, and it has not caused any problems.) Well, I tell him about it and say it is sad that it has to be like that. But it is as if he doesn't realize that I want to be with him more often.

Husband: Twice a week. In the morning, before I milk the cows.

Wife: It is very seldom, at most a couple of times a year. Normally at the afterdinner nap, when my husband is asleep.

Husband: Twice a month. In the bathroom, before we go to sleep. (Wife does not know.)

Wife: Twice a month. Mostly just before my periods. I am most prurient, then. It is when I feel like it and I'm alone and a little sad. (Husband does not know.)

Husband: Twice a week. Either in the morning or in the evening. It's a bloody mess, so in the end I go out in the bathroom. (Wife does not know.)

Husband: Four to five times a month, when my wife has her periods. (The wife knows about it, and it has not caused any problem.) Our relationship is so good that she also helps me sometimes.

As indicated by some of the above quotations, the reason why men, much more than women, masturbate in the bathroom might be to dispose of the ejaculate expediently—partly for hygienic/aesthetic reasons and partly to prevent disclosing stains on bedclothes.

Masturbation has, among other things, been described as a substitute for intercourse. The masturbation frequency of both men and women is generally lower than the stated intercourse frequency. Six men and two women report the same frequency for the two types of outlet, and six men and one woman state that their masturbation frequency exceeds their intercourse frequency. For these seven, their intercourse frequency is one or two times per week.

The conclusion of these analyses is that the norm of intercourse frequency in the marriage is defined by the woman and is generally one or two times per week. It can also be tentatively concluded that for men masturbation functions more as a supplement to the sexual life, while for women it is to a greater extent a substitute for intercourse. The women more than men were satisfied with intercourse frequency, and the women masturbate less.

Attitude toward masturbation

Having described behavior and experience with respect to masturbation, we turn to the relation between behavior and attitude toward masturbation and a comparison between husband and wife. Contrary to expectation, persons who masturbate do not have a more positive attitude toward masturbation than persons who either no longer masturbate or never masturbated. There is an indication that men and women who masturbate have a somewhat more negative view of masturbation than those who do not.

With respect to the attitudes of husband and wife, for 11 couples (28.9%) the husband and wife have the same attitude. For 16 couples (42.1%), the husband has a more positive view of masturbation than his wife, and for 11 couples the wife has a more positive view of masturbation. None of these differences is statistically significant. The men as a group show a very positive or a positively charged attitude toward masturbation, while the women are scattered equally over the attitude categories. Further statistical analyses show no significant differences between attitude toward masturbation and social status or education.

A number of the persons stating that they masturbate have at the same time a distinctly negative attitude toward this kind of sexual outlet. Thematically, this negative attitude toward masturbation is marked by a formulated view of it as wrong, unnatural, repelling, and morbid. Masturbation is looked upon as an unnatural substitute, which the performer experiences as wrong. The action is described as impersonal and cold and causing a sense of guilt and shame.

SEXUAL FANTASIES

Men as a group report a higher occurrence of sexual fantasies than women. This corresponds with other research.[4]

Content of sexual fantasies

In Table 4-1 is a summary of the sexual fantasies reported by the subjects. Men appear more inclined to fantasies involving several persons. For both men and women, in about half the cases the spouse never appears. Five women (42.8%) have sexual fantasies only about sexual intercourse with their husband. This theme is seen with six men (27.3%). Five men (22.7%) have sexual fantasies about either their wife or another woman.

Table 4-2 gives a survey of times and situations where sexual fantasies may occur. The category "unspecified" refers to the fact that it may happen anytime and anywhere: at work, during sexual intercourse, by masturbation.

Table 4-1
Types of Sexual Fantasies
Reported by Danish Married Couples

Fantasy Content	Percentage of Men Reporting This Fantasy	Percentage of Women Reporting This Fantasy
Harem—a bunch of beautiful girls swarming around the man, who can pick and choose	22.7	0
Sexual intercourse, either with the spouse or with some other attractive woman you have seen	22.7	0
Sexual intercourse with spouse	27.3	35.7
Group sex—several men and one girl	4.5	7.1
Group sex—several girls and one man	4.5	0
Other partners than the spouse, but only one at a time	13.6	57.1
Other	4.5	0

In the sexual fantasies reported by a sample of Danish couples, those of males and females tended to be somewhat different in content. Both sexes indicated that intercourse with the spouse was one common theme, but males were more likely in addition to imagine scenes of group sex while females imagined intercourse with a man other than their spouse.

Table 4-2
When and Where Sexual Fantasies Occur

Time or Place	Percentage of Men Reporting	Percentage of Women Reporting
During intercourse	0	21.4
Masturbation, when you are about to fall asleep or before you get up	41.7	21.4
When separated	8.3	14.3
At work	12.5	0
When the relationship is bad	4.2	0
Unspecified	33.3	42.9

Sexual fantasies seem to be most likely to occur during masturbation or intercourse, though they are obviously not limited to those times.

EXAMPLES

Husband: I'd like to be a sheik with a harem of fancy birds. To have a lot of nice girls swarming about you, so that you can choose a partner for each day, and the others lend a hand by serving champagne and such. It happens in the morning when you lie half asleep or when you see a sweet girl in the street and think: "Gosh, wasn't that something."

Husband: A wonderful sexual intercourse. Either with my wife or with a nice girl I've seen.

Wife: That can be very different. I can very well think of myself making love to someone else, or that my husband is together with someone else, or that five men are tackling me at the same time. Everything you can't do in reality. You must use your fantasy for that.

Husband: Sexual intercourse with a woman. It may be my wife or women I've seen.

Wife: I may have it during sexual intercourse. But not otherwise. But I can't dish up any stories like those by Inge and Sten Hegeler [two Danish sexologists]. Only about how I look. But I don't really know what it is I'm thinking, but something is spinning around in my head during sexual intercourse.

Husband: Mature women, perhaps 45–50. I imagine intercourse with them. They are well developed in every way, well upholstered. This thing with several women at the same time does not attract me.

Wife: Such as a weekend or week alone with my husband. I may think of that. You don't have much time for each other when you have children. I think of it on ordinary days. You can have a feeling of drifting apart when you have children.

Husband: I may sit at my office and work and then suddenly imagine my wife without clothes, and also other women. Yes, I dream a lot also about sexual intercourse. That can happen all the 24 hours.

Husband: You can sit and think of something happening. I only imagine sexual intercourse. It happens at vacant hours, at work, on weekends. You may very well sit in the daily jog-trot and think that it would be nice to come down to your wife.

Husband: It is only in periods with a bad relation to my wife. I think that some girls come and make love to me heartily (madly) and, you know, admire me a little. They are just crazy about me, and then one of them gets an orgasm and then the next and it is simply marvelous.

Husband: It's mostly my wife. But now and then it's other girls. But I don't know where I get it from. I have never seen them. Sometimes it's a whole bunch of girls.

Husband: I'd like a few—two or three—it might very well be two men and one girl.

Wife: What the man does and how he treats you. Affectionate. My own husband is. It's mostly when I'm cleaning. You know, when I'm alone. It has also happened while I'm looking at my husband when we are just about to fall asleep.

Wife: I think of other men. I don't think of my husband. I may sometimes think of being unfaithful to him. That I find exciting. It's not at all something special. It's something nice and warm and affectionate. I can't say anything special. It sometimes happens during sexual intercourse. If it's hard for me to be aroused then I force myself to think of something exciting in order to come along.

Husband: It does happen sometimes. I don't think about it very much. You do that more when you're young. I only think of my wife. When I masturbate.

Husband: That I'm making love with a girl. It's not one I know. There may also be more people—e.g., a whole group. You know such a group thing, where they are lying all around.

Husband: When I'm sailing, I imagine how nice it would be if my wife were there. When I get really turned on. When I have a night watch on the ship. I have written to my wife about it. And she writes about the same things to me.

Wife: I think about my husband and otherwise only about my own satisfaction. When I write letters and have to find something nice to say, and when I masturbate. I write about it in my letters to him—he finds it exciting.

Wife: I think of the one I'm interested in for the moment. Never my husband, that is.

Wife: It's especially when long time has gone. Then you imagine things. I don't know quite what I'm imagining but it's something about sexual intercourse, and I have a feeling of desire. But it's never my husband.

Husband: It ranges from my wife to female acquaintances to a whole harem. But there are never men involved. If there is another man, then it's never in relation to my person.

Wife: I imagine being with the other man. Something sexual and tender.

Husband: Something with a triangle. Me and two other girls, and else about all the fancy girls you meet. I told my wife about the triangle. It was completely out of the question.

The above quotations document to a certain extent qualitatively different ways of thinking of sex. The men demonstrate an action and achievement orientation. The themes show further that these fantasies also serve to maintain a masculine self-image with the power to satisfy women as a criterion of one's own sexual satisfaction. The women stress the tender, emotional aspects of sexuality and appear more person oriented in the content of their fantasies.

DISCUSSION

Masturbation and sexual fantasies appear to have different functions for men and women independently of common social background variables. As far as men are concerned, masturbation appears to be a supplement to coital behavior, while for women it seems to be a compensation. These functions appear independently of the frequency of sexual intercourse. The function of masturbation as a supplement for men is probably due to the fact that the wife is the one to decide the matrimonial standard of sexual intercourse.

Feelings of guilt in connection with masturbation appear in some subjects. The guilt feelings apparently make subjects who masturbate more likely to express negative attitudes toward masturbation than nonmasturbating subjects. From a qualitative analysis, however, there is reason to expect that the attitude toward masturbation is strongly dependent on whether one regards masturbation as a natural or an unnatural action. The aspect of naturalness appears related to whether one feels that sexual intercourse is the natural way to get satisfaction. A sense of guilt arises partly because one feels engaged in an unnatural action and partly because one feels that in this unnatural action something is taken away from the spouse.

The other view of masturbation is that it is a quite legitimate physical action just like washing hands and brushing teeth. In terms of behavior and attitudes, men are as a group considerably more positively inclined toward masturbation than are women. This again appears relative to the existence of sexual fantasies. However, women who masturbate also generally report sexual fantasies.

REFERENCES

1. Abramson, P. R. The relationship of the frequency of masturbation to several aspects of personality and behavior. *Journal of Sex Research*, 1973, *9*, 132–142.

2. Dearborn, L. W. Autoeroticism. In A. Ellis & A. Abarbanel (Eds.), *The encyclopedia of sexual behavior*. New York: Hawthorn, 1967.

3. Ford, C. S., & Beach, F. A. *Patterns of sexual behavior*. New York: Harper & Row, 1951.

4. Gagnon, S., & Simon, W. *Sexual conduct*. Chicago: Aldine, 1973.

5. Greenberg, J. S., & Archambault, F. X. Masturbation, self-esteem and other variables. *Journal of Sex Research*, 1973, *9*, 41–51.

6. Kinsey, A. C., Pomeroy, W. B., & Martin, C. E. *Sexual behavior in the human male*. Philadelphia: Saunders, 1948.

7. Kinsey, A. C., Pomeroy, W. B., Martin, C. E., & Gebhard, P. H. *Sexual behavior in the human female*. Philadelphia: Saunders, 1953.

8. Lo Piccolo, J., & Lobitz, W. C. The role of masturbation in the treatment of orgasmic dysfunction. *Archives of Sexual Behavior*, 1972, *2*, 163–171.

9. Masters, W. H., & Johnson, V. E. *Human sexual inadequacy*. Boston: Little, Brown, 1970.

10. Platen, M. *Den naturlige laegemetode* (The natural method of healing), Selskabet til udbredelse af litteraere vaerker, Copenhagen, 1914.

Chapter Five

Emotions Associated with Sex

Psychosexual Development

We learn to attach emotional significance to sexual cues because of countless learning experiences throughout our lives, especially during childhood and adolescence. Some of the positive associations to sex are shared by males and females. For example, it feels good to touch one's genital area, and even very small children can be observed to respond to this sort of friction with signs of pleasure. It's more fun than rubbing your elbow. Both boys and girls also share some negative associations. Children quickly learn that certain parts of the body are mysteriously special, these parts tend to have unusual names (often in a code known only to one's family), and genitals are not to be discussed in public. Such body parts must be covered by clothing except when changing one's attire, taking a bath, or visiting a doctor; guests may exclaim over a child's pretty hair, strong muscles, or note how his or her nose resembles that of a relative, but similar notice of the youngster's penis or vulva would be unthinkable. Both sexes also learn, in time, that masturbatory activity is to be practiced only secretively and in private, and eventually they are warned about the many dangers lurking in interpersonal sex, including the all-purpose concept of sin as well as the practical dangers of disease and parenthood.

There are several emotional learning experiences that differ for males and females, as sexologists William Simon and John Gagnon point out in the following article. Males tend to learn that it is good to seek sexual gratification, and there is even subtle and not so subtle parental encouragement for male sexuality. In addition, there is enthusiastic support from a peer group that provides praise for anatomical development, for verbal expressions of sexual terms and descriptions, for becoming interested in erotica, and for lust-oriented heterosexual encounters in which a much admired "stud" is one who "makes" multiple girls, each one counting as an additional "score." Though there is evidence of cultural changes beginning to occur, as we shall discuss in a later chapter, females are still more likely to learn much that is negative about sex. For example, many girls learn, and some never unlearn, that the female genitalia are visually unattractive and an unclean source of offensive odors. They may learn to be ashamed of menstrual functions, and they are taught of the special dangers of pregnancy for them and of the hazards of being "an easy lay," of being "used" and "exploited," and of acquiring the reputation of being "cheap." Such different cultural influences on the two sexes not surprisingly result in some long-lasting male-female differences in emotional reactions to sex.

Psychosexual Development

William Simon and John Gagnon

Erik Erikson has observed that, prior to Sigmund Freud, "sexologists" tended to believe that sexual capacities appeared suddenly with the onset of adolescence. Sexuality followed those external evidences of physiological change that occurred concurrent with or just after puberty. Psychoanalysis changed all that. In Freud's view, libido—the generation of psychosexual energies—should be viewed as a fundamental element of human experience at least beginning with birth, and possibly before that. Libido, therefore, is essentially a biological constant to be coped with at all levels of individual, social, and cultural development. The truth of this received wisdom—that is, that sexual development is a continuous contest between biological drive and cultural restraint—should be seriously questioned. Obviously sexuality has roots in biological processes, but so do many other capacities, including many that involve physical and mental competence and vigor. There is, however, abundant evidence that the final states which these capacities attain escape the rigid impress of biology. This independence of biological constraint is rarely claimed for the area of sexuality, but we would like to argue that the sexual is precisely that realm where the sociocultural forms most completely dominate biological influences.

It is difficult to get data that might shed much light on the earliest aspects of these questions: Adults are hardly equipped with total recall and the preverbal or primitively verbal child does not have ability to report accurately on his own internal state. But it seems obvious—and it is a basic assumption of this article—that with the beginnings of adolescence many new factors come into play, and to emphasize a straight-line developmental continuity with infant and childhood experiences may be seriously misleading. In particular, it is dangerous to assume that because some childhood behavior appears sexual to adults, it must be sexual. An infant or a child engaged in genital play (even if orgasm is observed) can in no sense be seen as experiencing the complex set of feelings that accompanies adult or even adolescent masturbation.

Therefore, the authors reject the unproven assumption that "powerful" psychosexual drives are fixed biological attributes. More important, we reject the even more dubious assumption that sexual capacities or experiences tend to translate immediately into a kind of universal "knowing" or innate wisdom—that sexuality has a magical ability, possessed by no other capacity, that allows biological drives to be expressed directly in psychosocial and social behaviors.

Reprinted in an edited version from: Simon, W., & Gagnon, J. Psychosexual development. *Transaction*, 1969, *6*, No. 5.

The prevailing image of sexuality—particularly in the Freudian tradition—is that of an intense, high-pressure drive that forces a person to seek physical sexual gratification, a drive that expresses itself indirectly if it cannot be expressed directly. The available data suggest to us a different picture, one that shows either lower levels of intensity, or, at least, greater variability. We find that there are many social situations or life-roles in which reduced sex activity or even deliberate celibacy is undertaken with little evidence that the libido has shifted in compensation to some other sphere.

A part of the legacy of Freud is that we have all become remarkably adept at discovering "sexual" elements in nonsexual behavior and symbolism. What we suggest instead (following Kenneth Burke's 3-decade-old insight) is the reverse: sexual behavior can often express and serve nonsexual motives.

NO PLAY WITHOUT A SCRIPT

We see sexual behavior therefore as *scripted* behavior, not the masked expression of a primordial drive. The individual can learn sexual behavior as he or she learns other behavior—through scripts that in this case give the self, other persons, and situations erotic abilities or content. Desire, privacy, opportunity, and proximity to an attractive member of the opposite sex are not, in themselves, enough; in ordinary circumstances, nothing sexual will occur unless one or both actors organize these elements into an appropriate script. The very concern with foreplay in sex suggests this. From one point of view, foreplay may be defined as merely progressive physical excitement generated by touching naturally erogenous zones. The authors have referred to this conception elsewhere as the "rubbing of two sticks together to make a fire" model. It would seem to be more valuable to see this activity as symbolically invested behavior through which the body is eroticized and through which mute, inarticulate motions and gestures are translated into a sociosexual drama.

A belief in the sociocultural dominance of sexual behavior finds support in cross-cultural research as well as in data restricted to the United States. Psychosexual development is universal, but it takes many forms and tempos. People in different cultures construct their scripts differently; and in our own society, different segments of the population act out different psychosexual dramas—something much less likely to occur if they were all reacting more or less blindly to the same superordinate urge. The most marked differences occur, of course, between male and female patterns of sexual behavior. Obviously, some of this is due to biological differences, including differences in hormonal functions at different ages. But the significance of social scripts predominate; the recent work of Masters and Johnson, for example, clearly points to far greater orgasmic capacities on the part of females than our culture would lead us to suspect. And within each sex, especially among men, different social and economic groups have different patterns. Let us examine some of these variations, and see if we can decipher the scripts.

CHILDHOOD

Whether one agrees with Freud or not, it is obvious that we do not become sexual all at once. There is continuity with the past. Even infant experiences can strongly influence later sexual development.

But continuity is not causality. Childhood experiences (even those that appear sexual) will in all likelihood be influential not because they are intrinsically sexual, but because they can affect a number of developmental trends, *including* the sexual. What situations in infancy, or even in early childhood, can be called psychosexual in any sense other than that of creating potentials?

The key term must remain "potentiation." In infancy, we can locate some of the experiences (or sensations) that will bring about a sense of the body and its capacities for pleasure and discomfort and those that will influence the child's ability to relate to others. It is possible, of course, that through these primitive experiences, ranges are being established—but they are very broad and overlapping. Moreover, if these are profound experiences to the child, and they may well be that, they are not expressions of biological necessity, but of the earliest forms of social learning.

In childhood, after infancy there is what appears to be some real sex play. About half of all adults report that they did engage in some form of sex play as children and the total who actually did may be half again as many. But however the adult interprets it later, what did it mean to the child at the time? One suspects that, as in much of childhood role playing, their sense of the adult meanings attributed to the behavior is fragmentary and ill-formed. Many of the adults recall that, at the time, they were concerned with being found out. But here, too, were they concerned because of the real content of sex play, or because of the mystery and the lure of the forbidden that so often enchant the child? The child may be assimilating outside information about sex for which, at the time, he has no real internal correlate or understanding.

A small number of persons do have sociosexual activity during preadolescence—most of it initiated by adults. But for the majority of these, little apparently follows from it. Without appropriate sexual scripts, the experience remains unassimilated, at least in adult terms. For some, it is clear, a severe reaction may follow from falling "victim" to the sexuality of an adult; but, again, does this reaction come from the sexual act itself or from the social response, the strong reactions of others? (There is some evidence that early sexual activity of this sort is associated with deviant adjustments in later life. But this, too, may not be the result of sexual experiences in themselves so much as the consequence of having fallen out of the social mainstream and, therefore, of running greater risks of isolation and alienation.)

In short, relatively few children become truly active sexually before adolescence. And when they do (for girls more often than boys), it is seldom immediately related to sexual feelings or gratifications but is a use of sex for nonsexual goals and purposes. The "seductive" Lolita is rare but she is significant: she illustrates a more general pattern of psychosexual development—a commitment to the social relationships linked to sex before one can really grasp the social meaning of the physical relationships.

Of great importance are the values (or feelings, or images) that children pick up as being related to sex. Although we talk a lot about sexuality, as though trying to exorcise the demon of shame, learning about sex in our society is in large part learning about guilt; and learning how to manage sexuality commonly involves learning how to manage guilt. An important source of guilt in children comes from the imputation to them by adults of sexual appetites or abilities that they may not have but that they learn, however imperfectly, to pretend they have. The gestural concomitants of sexual modesty are learned early. For instance, when do girls learn to sit or pick up objects with their knees together? When do they learn that the bust must be covered? And, since this behavior is learned unlinked to later adult sexual performances, what children make of all this is very mysterious.

The learning of sex roles, or sex identities, involves many things that are remote from actual sexual experience, or that become involved with sexuality only after puberty. Masculinity or femininity, their meaning and postures, are rehearsed before adolescence in many nonsexual ways.

A number of scholars have pointed, for instance, to the importance of aggressive, deference, dependency, and dominance behavior in childhood. Jerome Kagan and Howard Moss have found that aggressive behavior in males and dependency in females are relatively stable aspects of development. But what is social role, and what is biology? They found that when aggressive behavior occurred among girls, it tended to appear most often among those from well-educated families that were more tolerant of deviation. Curiously, they also reported that "it was impossible to predict the character of adult sexuality in women from their preadolescent and early adolescent behavior," and that "erotic activity is more anxiety-arousing for females than males" because "the traditional ego ideal for women dictates inhibition of sexual impulses."

The belief in the importance of early sex-role learning for boys can be viewed in two ways. First, it may directly indicate an early sexual capacity in male children. Or, second, early masculine identification may merely be an appropriate framework within which the sexual impulse (salient with puberty) and the socially available sexual scripts (or accepted patterns of sexual behavior) can most conveniently find expression. Our bias, of course, is toward the second.

But, as Kagan and Moss also noted, the sex role learned by the child does not reliably predict how he or she will act sexually as an adult. This finding also can be interpreted in the same two alternative ways. Where sexuality is viewed as a biological constant that struggles to express itself, the female sex role learning can be interpreted as the successful repression of sexual impulses. The other interpretation suggests that the difference lies not in learning how to handle a preexistent sexuality but in learning how to *be* sexual. Differences between men and women, therefore, will have consequences both for *what* is done sexually, as well as *when*.

Once again, we prefer the latter interpretation, and some recent work that we have done with lesbians supports it. We observed that many of the major elements of their sex lives—the start of actual genital sexual behavior, the onset and frequency of masturbation, the time of entry in sociosexual patterns, the number of partners, and the reports of feelings of sexual deprivation—were for these homosexual women almost identical with those of ordinary women. Since sexuality would seem to be more important for lesbians—after all, they sacrifice much in order to follow their own sexual pathways—this is surprising. We concluded that the primary factor was something both categories of women share: the sex-role learning that occurs before sexuality itself becomes significant.

Social class also appears significant, more for boys than girls. Sex-role learning may vary by class; lower-class boys are supposed to be more aggressive and put much greater emphasis on early heterosexuality. The middle and upper classes tend to tolerate more deviance from traditional attitudes regarding appropriate male sex-role performances.

Given all these circumstances, it seems rather naive to think of sexuality as a constant pressure, with a peculiar necessity all its own. For us, the crucial period of childhood has significance not because of sexual occurrences but because of nonsexual developments that will provide the names and judgments for later encounters with sexuality.

ADOLESCENCE

The actual beginnings and endings of adolescence are vague. Generally, the beginning marks the first time society, as such, acknowledges that the individual has sexual capacity. Training in the postures and rhetoric of the sexual experience is now accelerated. Most important, the adolescent begins to regard others (particularly one's peers, but also adults) as sexual actors and finds confirmation from others for this view.

For some, as noted, adolescent sexual experience begins before they are considered adolescents. Kinsey reports that one-tenth of his female sample and one-fifth of his male sample had experienced orgasm through masturbation by age 12. But still, for the vast majority, despite some casual play and exploration that post-Freudians might view as masked sexuality, sexual experience begins with adolescence. Even those who have had prior experience find that it acquires new meanings with adolescence. They now relate such meanings to both larger spheres of social life and greater senses of self. For example, it is not uncommon during the transition between childhood and adolescence for boys and, more rarely, girls to report arousal and orgasm while doing things not manifestly sexual—climbing trees, sliding down bannisters, or performing other activities that involve genital contact—without defining them as sexual. Often they do not even take it seriously enough to try to explore or repeat what was, in all likelihood, a pleasurable experience.

Adolescent sexual development, therefore, really represents the beginning of adult sexuality. It marks a definite break with what went on before. Not only will future experiences occur in new and more complex contexts, but they will be conceived of as explicitly sexual and thereby will begin to complicate social relationships. The need to manage sexuality will rise not only from physical needs and desires but also from the new implications of personal relationships. Playing or associating with members of the opposite sex now acquires different meanings.

At adolescence, changes in the development of boys and girls diverge and must be considered separately. The one thing both share at this point is a reinforcement of their new status by a dramatic biological event—for girls, menstruation, and for boys, the discovery of the ability to ejaculate. But here they part. For boys, the beginning of a commitment to sexuality is primarily genital; within 2 years of puberty all but a relatively few have had the experience of orgasm, almost universally brought about by masturbation. The corresponding organizing event for girls is not genitally sexual but social: they have arrived at an age where they will learn role performances linked with proximity to marriage. In contrast to boys, only two-thirds of girls will report ever having masturbated (and characteristically, the frequency is much less). For women, it is not until the late 20s that the incidence of orgasm from any source reaches that of boys at age 16. In fact, significantly, about half of the females who masturbate do so only after having experienced orgasm in some situation involving others. This contrast points to a basic distinction between the developmental processes for males and females: males move from privatized personal sexuality to sociosexuality; females do the reverse and at a later stage in the life cycle.

THE TURNED-ON BOYS

We have worked hard to demonstrate the dominance of social, psychological, and cultural influences over the biological; now, dealing with adolescent boys, we must briefly reverse course. There is much evidence that the early male sexual impulses—again, initially through masturbation—are linked to physiological changes, to high hormonal inputs during puberty. This produces an organism that, to put it simply, is more easily turned on. Male adolescents report frequent erections, often without apparent stimulation of any kind. Even so, though there is greater biological sensitization and hence masturbation is more likely, the meaning, organization, and continuance of this activity still tends to be subordinate to social and psychological factors.

Masturbation provokes guilt and anxiety among most adolescent boys. This is not likely to change in spite of more "enlightened" rhetoric and discourse on the subject (generally, we have shifted from stark warnings of mental, moral, and physical damage to vague counsels against nonsocial or "inappropriate" behavior). However, it may be that this very guilt and anxiety give the sexual experience an intensity of feeling that often is attributed to sex itself.

Such guilt and anxiety do not follow simply from social disapproval. Rather, they seem to come from several sources, including the difficulty the boy has in presenting himself as a sexual being to his immediate family, particularly his parents. Another source is the fantasies or plans associated with masturbation—fantasies about doing sexual "things" to others or having others do sexual "things" to oneself; or having to learn and rehearse available but proscribed sexual scripts or patterns of behavior. And, of course, some guilt and anxiety center around the general disapproval of masturbation. After the early period of adolescence, in fact, most youths will not admit to their peers that they did or do it.

Nevertheless, masturbation is for most adolescent boys the major sexual activity, and they engage in it fairly frequently. It is an extremely positive and gratifying experience to them. Such an introduction to sexuality can lead to a capacity for detached sex activity—activity whose only sustaining motive is sexual. This may be the hallmark of male sexuality in our society.

Of the three sources of guilt and anxiety mentioned, the first—how to manage both sexuality and an attachment to family members—probably cuts across class lines. But the others should show remarkable class differences. The second one—how to manage a fairly elaborate and exotic fantasy life during masturbation—should be confined most typically to the higher classes, who are more experienced and adept at dealing with symbols. (It is possible, in fact, that this behavior, in which girls rarely engage, plays a role in the processes by which middle-class boys catch up with girls in measures of achievement and creativity and, by the end of adolescence, move out in front. However, this is only a hypothesis.)

The ability to fantasize during masturbation implies certain broad consequences. One is a tendency to see large parts of the environment in an erotic light, as well as the ability to respond, sexually and perhaps poetically, to many visual and auditory stimuli. We might also expect both a capacity and need for fairly elaborate forms of sexual activity. Further, since masturbatory fantasies generally deal with relationships and acts leading to coitus, they should also reinforce a developing capacity for heterosociality.

The third source of guilt and anxiety—the alleged "unmanliness" of masturbation—should more directly concern the lower-class male adolescent. ("Manliness" has always been an important value for lower-class males.) In this group, social life is more often segregated by sex, and there are, generally, fewer rewarding social experiences from other sources. The adolescent therefore moves into heterosexual, if not heterosocial, relationships sooner than his middle-class counterparts. Sexual segregation makes it easier for him than for the middle-class boy to learn that he does not have to love everything he desires and therefore to come more naturally to casual, if not exploitative, relationships. The second condition—fewer social rewards that his fellows would respect—should lead to an exaggerated concern for proving masculinity by direct displays of physical prowess, aggression, and visible sexual success. And these three, of course, may be mutually reinforcing.

In a sense, the lower-class male is the first to reach "sexual maturity" as defined by the Freudians. That is, he is generally the first to become aggressively heterosexual and exclusively genital. This characteristic, in fact, is a distinguishing difference between lower-class males and those above them socially.

But one consequence is that although their sex lives are almost exclusively heterosexual, they remain homosocial. They have intercourse with females, but the standards and the audience they refer to are those of their male fellows. Middle-class boys shift predominantly to coitus at a significantly later time. They, too, need and tend to have homosocial elements in their sexual lives. But their fantasies, their ability to symbolize, and their social training in a world in which distinctions between masculinity and femininity are less sharply drawn, allow them to withdraw more easily from an all-male world. The difference between social classes obviously has important consequences for stable adult relationships.

One thing common in male experience during adolescence is that while it provides much opportunity for sexual commitment in one form or another, there is little training in how to handle emotional relations with girls. The imagery and rhetoric of romantic love is all around us; we are immersed in it. But whereas much is undoubtedly absorbed by the adolescent, he is not likely to tie it closely to his sexuality. In fact, such a connection might be inhibiting, as indicated by the survival of the "bad-girl-who-does" and "good-girl-who-doesn't" distinction. This is important to keep in mind as we turn to the female side of the story.

WITH THE GIRLS

In contrast to males, female sexual development during adolescence is so similar in all classes that it is easy to suspect that it is solely determined by biology. But, while girls do not have the same level of hormonal sensitization to sexuality at puberty as adolescent boys, there is little evidence of a biological or social inhibitor either. The "equipment" for sexual pleasure is clearly present by puberty but tends not to be used by many females of any class. Masturbation rates are fairly low and, among those who do masturbate, fairly infrequent. Arousal from "sexual" materials or situations happens seldom, and exceedingly few girls report feeling sexually deprived during adolescence.

Basically, girls in our society are not encouraged to be sexual, and may be strongly discouraged from being so. Most of us accept the fact that while "bad boy" can mean many things, "bad girl" almost exclusively implies sexual delinquency. It is both difficult and dangerous for an adolescent girl to become too active sexually. As Joseph Rheingold puts it, where men need only fear sexual failure, women must fear both success and failure.

Does this long period of relative sexual inactivity among girls come from repression of an elemental drive or merely from a failure to learn how to be sexual? The answers have important implications for their later sexual development. If it is repression, the path to a fuller sexuality must pass through processes of loss of inhibitions, during which the girl unlearns, in varying degrees, attitudes and values that block the expression of natural internal feelings. It also implies that the quest for ways to express directly sexual behavior and feelings that had been expressed nonsexually is secondary and of considerably less significance.

On the other hand, the "learning" answer suggests that women create or invent a capacity for sexual behavior, learning how and when to be aroused and how and when to respond. This approach implies greater flexibility: unlike the repression view, it makes sexuality both more and less than a basic force that may break loose at any time in strange or costly ways. The learning approach also lessens the power of sexuality altogether; all at once, particular kinds of sex activities need no longer be defined as either "healthy" or "sick." Subjectively, this approach appeals to the authors because it describes female sexuality in terms that seem less like a mere projection of male sexuality.

If sexual activity by adolescent girls assumes less specific forms than with boys, that does not mean that sexual learning and training do not occur. Curiously, though girls are, as a group, far less sexually active than boys, they receive much more training in self-consciously viewing themselves—and in viewing boys—as desirable mates. This is particularly true in recent years. Females begin early in adolescence to define attractiveness, at least partially, in sexual terms. We suspect that the use of sexual attractiveness for nonsexual purposes that marked our preadolescent "seductress" now begins to characterize many girls. Talcott Parsons' description of how the wife "uses" sex to bind the husband to the family, although harsh, may be quite accurate. More generally, in keeping with the childbearing and child-raising function of women, the development of a sexual role seems to involve a need to include in that role more than pleasure.

To round out the picture of the difference between the sexes, girls appear to be well-trained precisely in that area in which boys are poorly trained—that is, a belief in and a capacity for intense, emotionally charged relationships and the language of romantic love. When girls during this period describe having been aroused sexually, they more often report it as a response to romantic, rather than erotic, words and actions.

In later adolescence, as dates, parties, and other sociosexual activities increase, boys—committed to sexuality and relatively untrained in the language and actions of romantic love—interact with girls committed to romantic love and relatively untrained in sexuality. Dating and courtship may well be considered processes in which each sex trains the other in what each wants and expects. What data are available suggest that this exchange system does not always work very smoothly. Thus, ironically, it is not uncommon to find that the boy becomes emotionally involved with his partner and therefore lets up on trying to seduce her, at the same time that the girl comes to feel that the boy's affection is genuine and therefore that sexual intimacy is more permissible.

In our recent study of college students, we found that boys typically had intercourse with their first coital partners 1 to 3 times, while with girls it was 10 or more. Clearly, for the majority of females first intercourse becomes possible only in stable relationships or in those with strong bonds.

"WOMAN, WHAT DOES SHE WANT?"

The male experience does conform to the general Freudian expectation that there is a developmental movement from a predominantly genital sexual commitment to a loving relationship with another person. But this movement is, in effect, reversed for females, with love or affection often a necessary precondition for intercourse. No wonder, therefore, that Freud had great difficulty understanding female sexuality—recall the concluding line in his great essay on women: "Woman, what does she want?" This "error"—the assumption that female sexuality is similar to or a mirror image of that of the male—may come from the fact that so many of those who constructed the theory were men. With Freud, in addition, we must remember the very concept of sexuality essential to most of nineteenth-century Europe: it was an elemental beast that had to be curbed.

It has been noted that there are very few class differences in sexuality among females, far fewer than among males. One difference, however, is very relevant to this discussion: the age of first intercourse. This varies inversely with social class; that is, the higher the class, the later the age of first intercourse—a relationship that is also true of first marriage. The correlation between these two ages suggests the necessary social and emotional linkage between courtship and the entrance into sexual activity on the part of women. A second difference, perhaps only indirectly related to social class, has to do with educational achievement: here, a sharp borderline seems to separate from all other women those who have or have had graduate or professional work. If sexual success may be measured by the percentage of sex acts that culminate in orgasm, graduate and professional women are the most sexually successful women in the nation.

Why? One possible interpretation derives from the work of Abraham Maslow: Women who get so far in higher education are more likely to be more aggressive and perhaps to have strong needs to dominate; both these characteristics are associated with heightened sexuality. Another, more general interpretation would be that in a society in which girls are expected primarily to become wives and mothers, going on to graduate school represents a kind of deviancy—a failure of, or alienation from, normal female social adjustment. In effect, then, it would be this flawed socialization, not biology, that produced both commitment toward advanced training and toward heightened sexuality.

For both males and females, increasingly greater involvement in the social aspects of sexuality—"socializing" with the opposite sex—may be one factor that marks the end of adolescence. We know little about this transition, especially among noncollege boys and girls, but our present feeling is that sexuality plays an important role in it. First, sociosexuality is important in family formation and also in learning the roles and obligations involved in being an adult. Second, and more fundamental, late adolescence is when a youth is seeking, and experimenting toward finding, his identity—who and what he is and will be; and sociosexual activity is the one aspect of this exploration that we associate particularly with late adolescence.

Young people are particularly vulnerable at this time. This may be partly due to the fact that society has difficulty protecting the adolescent from the consequences of sexual behavior in which it pretends he is not engaged. But, more important, it may be because, at all ages, we all have great problems in discussing our sexual feelings and experiences in personal terms. These, in turn, make it extremely difficult to get support from others for an adolescent's experiments toward trying to invent his sexual self. We suspect that success or failure in the discovery or management of sexual identity may have consequences in personal development far beyond merely the sexual sphere—perhaps in confidence and feelings of self-worth, belonging, competence, guilt, force of personality, and so on.

ADULTHOOD

In our society, all but a few ultimately marry. Handling sexual commitments inside marriage makes up the larger part of adult experience. Again, we have too little data for firm findings. The data we do have come largely from studies of broken and troubled marriages, and we do not know to what extent sexual problems in such marriages exceed those of intact marriages. It is possible that, because we have assumed that sex is important in most people's lives, we have exaggerated its importance in holding marriages together. Also, it is possible that, once people are married, sexuality declines relatively, becoming less important than other gratifications (such as domesticity or parenthood); or it may be that these other gratifications can minimize the effect of sexual dissatisfaction. Further, it may be possible that individuals learn to get sexual gratification, or an equivalent, from activities that are nonsexual or only partially sexual.

The sexual desires and commitments of males are the main determinants of the rate of sexual activity in our society. Men are most interested in intercourse in the early years of marriage—women's interest peaks much later; nonetheless, coital rates decline steadily throughout marriage. This decline derives from many things, only one of which is decline in biological capacity. With many men, it is more difficult to relate sexually to a wife who is pregnant or a mother. Lower-class adult men receive less support and plaudits from their male friends for married sexual performance than they did as single adolescents; and we might also add the lower-class disadvantage of less training in the use of auxiliary or symbolic sexually stimulating materials. For middle-class men, the decline is not as steep, owing perhaps to their greater ability to find stimulation from auxiliary sources, such as literature, movies, music, and romantic or erotic conversation. It should further be noted that for about 30% of college-educated men, masturbation continues regularly during marriage, even when the wife is available. An additional (if unknown) proportion do not physically masturbate but derive additional excitement from the fantasies that accompany intercourse.

But even middle-class sexual activity declines more rapidly than does bodily change. Perhaps the ways males learn to be sexual in our society make it very difficult to keep it up at a high level with the same woman for a long time. However, this may not be vital in maintaining the family, or even in the man's personal sense of well-being, because, as previously suggested, sexual dissatisfaction may become less important as other satisfactions increase. Therefore, it need seldom result in crisis.

About half of all married men and a quarter of all married women will have intercourse outside of marriage at one time or another. For women, infidelity seems to have been on the increase since the turn of the century, at the same time that their rates of orgasm have been increasing. It is possible that the very nature of female sexuality is changing. Work being done now may give us a new light on this. For men, there are strong social-class differences; the lower class accounts for most extramarital activity, especially during the early years of marriage. We have observed that it is difficult for a lower-class man to acquire the appreciation of his fellows for married intercourse; extramarital sex, of course, is another matter.

In general, we feel that far from sexual needs affecting other adult concerns, the reverse may be true: adult sexual activity may become that aspect of a person's life most often used to act out other needs. There are some data that suggest this. Men who have trouble handling authority relationships at work more often have dreams about homosexuality: some others, under heavy stress on the job, have been shown to have more frequent episodic homosexual experiences. Such phenomena as the rise of sadomasochistic practices and experiments in group sex may also be tied to nonsexual tensions—the use of sex for nonsexual purposes.

It is only fairly recently in the history of humankind that people have been able to begin to understand that their own time and place do not embody some eternal principle or necessity but are only dots on a continuum. It is difficult for many to believe that people can change, and are changing, in important ways. This conservative view is evident even in contemporary behavioral science; and a conception of humans as having relatively constant sexual needs has become part of it. In an ever-changing world, it is perhaps comforting to think that human sexuality does not change very much and therefore is relatively easily explained. We cannot accept this. Instead, we have attempted to offer a description of sexual development as a variable social invention—an invention that in itself explains little and requires much continuing explanation.

Sex Guilt and Premarital Sexual Experiences of College Students

In examining the emotions associated with sex, most investigators have concentrated on negative reactions. It is assumed that sexual activity is naturally pleasurable and that individuals have to be taught to respond negatively. Donald Mosher proposes the concept of sex guilt as the culmination of all of the negative learning about sex. That is, a person may be taught that certain sexual acts are morally wrong, that sex may lead to pregnancy or disease, that premarital sex leads to loss of respect, or whatever. The end result of such learning is sex guilt which consists of a generalized anxiety about violating one's standards of proper behavior. If these feelings of guilt are sufficiently strong, they presumably will prevent the individual from engaging in the forbidden behavior. Thus, conscience acts to control what the person does sexually.

In the following article, it is reported that sex guilt is related to sexual behavior, sexual standards, and the individual's stated reasons for not engaging in certain behaviors. Theoretically, a particular cause-and-effect sequence follows from childhood learning. In the early part of their lives, some people learn to think of various kinds of sexual activity as morally wrong, dangerous in practical terms, or just vaguely unacceptable. These negative feelings eventually become translated into the person's moral code or set of ethical standards. The combination of the emotional reactions and the verbalized rules of conduct act to prevent the person from entering situations that are likely to involve the forbidden activities. As the authors point out, the type of research data available at present does not allow us to conclude with certainty that such a causal sequence operates in that way. We *do* know, however, that negative reactions to sex are related to what individuals do sexually and to how they feel about such activity.

Sex Guilt and Premarital Sexual Experiences of College Students

Donald L. Mosher and Herbert J. Cross

It is useful to distinguish between the concept of guilt as a personality disposition and as an episodic affective state. As a personality disposition, sex guilt is acquired or learned in a series of situations related to sex and conscience development. Sex guilt as a disposition may influence the way in which situations are perceived or the reaction tendencies of individuals in specific situations. A preliminary definition of sex guilt as a personality disposition might define sex guilt as a generalized expec-

Reprinted in an edited version from: Mosher, D. L., & Cross, H. J. Sex guilt and premarital sexual experiences of college students. *Journal of Consulting and Clinical Psychology*, 1971, **36**, 27–32.

tancy of self-mediated punishment for violating or for anticipating violating standards of proper sexual conduct. Such a disposition might be manifested by resistance to sexual temptation, by inhibited sexual behavior, or by the disruption of cognitive processes in sex-related situations. Following a moral transgression, report of an affective state of guilt, self-punishment, confession of wrongdoing, or expiatory behavior would suggest the presence of sex guilt. The affective state of guilt is a transient episode which is only one of several potential referents for the personality disposition of guilt.

To measure sex guilt as a personality disposition, Mosher[8,10,11] developed both male and female versions of sentence completion, true-false, and forced-choice inventories which measure sex guilt, hostility guilt, and morality conscience. Mosher[10,11] demonstrated convergence between the different measures of the same aspect of guilt and differentiation from such variables as anxiety and social desirability. The construct validity of the measure of sex guilt is supported by data from several investigations. In a perceptual defense task, high-sex-guilt males were less influenced by situational cues relevant to the probability of censure from the experimenter than were low-sex-guilt subjects.[9] High-sex-guilt males gave fewer sexual responses to double-entendre word-association stimuli such as "screw" or "rubber" than did less guilty males.[3,4] Lamb[6] found that following sexual arousal, high-guilt subjects reduced their discomfort by rating sexual cartoons as humorous and enjoyable. Galbraith[2] investigated correlates of sex guilt with Thorne's[15] Sex Inventory and found sex guilt positively correlated with repression of sexuality, and negatively correlated with sex drive and interest and negatively correlated with promiscuity and sociopathy. Mosher and Greenberg[12] observed the relationship of the disposition of sex guilt to the occurrence of affective states in females after reading an erotic literary passage. High-sex-guilt females reported an increase in the episodic state of guilt compared to their prereading state and to the postreading state of low-sex-guilt females.

Past investigations of the relationship between guilt and premarital sexual experience have used retrospective reports of guilty feelings as their index of guilt. Kinsey, Pomeroy, Martin, and Gebhard,[5] in their study of sexual behavior in the human female, pointed out, contrary to common beliefs, that their female subjects experienced little guilt or regret following premarital intercourse. Reiss[13,14] has argued that guilt feelings do not generally inhibit sexual behavior, since his subjects eventually came to accept sexual behavior that had once made them feel guilty. Reiss argued that as a person continues to engage in sexual behavior which violates his current standard, feelings of guilt diminish and the standard is liable to revision toward greater sexual permissiveness.

The purpose of the present study was to investigate the relationship of sex guilt as a personality disposition to reports of sexual experiences, sexual standards, feelings about sexual behavior, and reasons for nonparticipation in certain forms of sexual activity. It was expected that subjects who were disposed to sex guilt would restrict their range of sexual experiences, have less permissive sexual standards, report negative feelings following more intimate sexual involvement, and give moral reasons for not engaging in more intimate forms of premarital sexual behavior.

METHOD

Subjects

The subjects were 136 never-married college students, of whom 60 males and 46 females were undergraduates at the University of Connecticut, and 30 females were undergraduates at Emmanuel College.

Procedure

All of the female subjects were secured from dormitories and tested in groups of five or less by an undergraduate female. The women were not told the nature of the task until they were ready to begin and were permitted to remain anonymous. There were almost no refusals to participate. The women first completed the Sexual Experiences Inventory and then completed the Mosher Forced-Choice Guilt Inventory. The University of Connecticut women completed the female version of the Mosher Forced-Choice Guilt Inventory,[11] while the Emmanuel College women completed only the Sex-Guilt Subscale of the original Forced-Choice Guilt Inventory.[10]

The male subjects were tested in a large group. They had volunteered to participate in a study of prohibited behaviors to meet the experimental requirements of their introductory psychology course. They were permitted to remain anonymous, and none refused participation. The men completed a number of inventories related to perceived parental-rearing practices and drug use in addition to completing the Sexual Experiences Inventory and the Sex-Guilt Subscale of the Mosher[10] Forced-Choice Guilt Inventory which are the two measures relevant to the present study.

Measures

Sexual experiences inventory The sexual experiences inventory was constructed by preparing a list of sexual experiences that had been found by Brady and Levitt[1] to form a Guttman Scale for men. The sexual experiences were the following:

1. Kissing
2. Kissing with tongue contact
3. Manual manipulation of clad female breast by a male

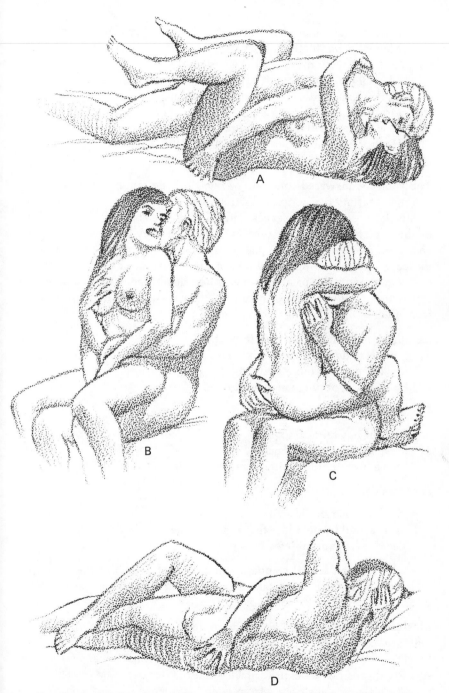

Four basic variations in coital position. (A) Ventral-ventral position, man superior. (B) Ventral-dorsal position. (C) Ventral-ventral position, woman superior. (D) Ventral-ventral position, side entry.

4. Manual manipulation of unclad female breast by a male
5. Manual manipulation of female genitalia by a male
6. Oral contact with female breast by a male
7. Manual manipulation of male genitalia by a female
8. Heterosexual intercourse: ventral-ventral
9. Oral contact with male genitalia by a female
10. Oral contact with female genitalia by a male
11. Heterosexual intercourse: ventral-dorsal
12. Homosexual relations

The subjects answered four sets of questions pertaining to experiences, feelings, reasons for nonparticipation, and sexual standards, in relation to this list of sexual experiences. The questions relating to the occurrence of the experience required subjects to check if they had had the experience with a loved one in the past year, or with a loved one sometime in the past, and with a nonloved one in the last year, or with a nonloved one sometime in the past. If subjects had never had a particular sexual experience, they were asked to indicate their reasons for nonparticipation from among the following alternatives:

1. I have never had the desire to do it.
2. I was afraid people would find out.
3. I believed it was morally wrong.
4. I was afraid of pregnancy or disease.

For males:

5. The girl has refused to do it.
6. I respect the girl too much.
7. I have been timid in initiating or suggesting it to the girl.

For females:

5. The boy has refused to do it.
6. I was afraid I would lose the respect of the boy.
7. The boy has not initiated or suggested it.

The questions on sexual standards inquired as to whether they believed each item in the list of sexual experiences was acceptable premarital or postmarital behavior for males or for females.

Mosher Forced-Choice Guilt Inventory Mosher [8,10,11] has constructed sentence completion, true-false, and forced-choice measures of three aspects (sex guilt, hostility guilt, and morality conscience) of the personality disposition of guilt for males and for females. The forced-choice inventories were constructed from male[10] and from female[11] completions given to sentence completion stems. An internal consistency item analysis was used to select forced-choice alternatives. The following are examples of sex-guilt items:

As a child, sex play
    a.   was a big taboo and I was deathly afraid of it.
    b.   was common without guilt feelings.
When I have sexual desires
    a.   they are quite strong.
    b.   I attempt to repress them.

RESULTS AND DISCUSSION

Examination of the data revealed that both the males and females approximated the Guttman ordering reported by Brady and Levitt.[1] A score for cumulative sexual experience was determined by giving 1 point for each of the 12 possible sexual experiences in which a subject had ever participated. In a similar fashion, scores were determined for sexual experiences with loved and unloved partners in the last year or in the past, and for premarital and postmarital standards for males and females. Means of these scores are presented in Table 5-1.

Table 5-1 provides a rough summary of the standing of the groups in terms of participation in sexual experiences. For example, the mean of 7.60 for the University of Connecticut males on cumulative sexual experience indicates, when referred to the numbers of the list of sexual experiences, that slightly more than half of them have engaged in ventral-ventral heterosexual intercourse. While the samples were not selected with the intention of making between-samples comparisons, some generalizations about the sexual experiences and standards will provide a useful framework for the consideration of later results. It is not surprising that University of Connecticut males, then University of Connecticut females, and finally Emmanuel College females order from most to least sexually experienced. Emmanuel College is a small Roman Catholic college for women. For males, sexual experience with loved and nonloved partners within the last year and in the past are all approximately similar. For females, sexual experience is much more likely to have progressed to heavy petting only with loved partners and often only within the last year. Both men and women tend to endorse more liberal premarital standards for men than for women, and the premarital standards of men are more permissive than are those of women. Postmarital standards are more similar for both sexes, although men still tend to retain a more liberal outlook in regard to oral-genital relations.

The intercorrelations between sex guilt and sexual experiences and sexual standards for the three samples of subjects provide support for the prediction that the personality disposition of sex guilt is negatively correlated with the occurrence of premarital sexual experiences. College men and women who are predisposed to respond with guilt over sex were less likely to engage in the more intimate forms of sexual contact. The size of the negative correlations was in part a function of the range

Table 5-1
Mean Number of Different Sexual Experiences of Undergraduate Males and Females

	Total Number of Different Sexual Experiences	Number of Recent Sexual Experiences with a Loved One	Number of Past Sexual Experiences with a Loved One	Number of Recent Sexual Experiences with a Nonloved One	Number of Past Sexual Experiences with a Nonloved One
University of Connecticut					
Males	7.60	5.22	5.44	5.20	5.62
Females	6.43	5.67	4.52	2.57	2.80
Emmanuel College					
Females	5.80	4.83	3.87	2.63	2.37

Undergraduates were given a list of 12 sexual activities ranging from kissing to petting to oral and genital sex, and they indicated which ones they had experienced and with whom. It may be seen that males are more likely than females to report engaging in sexual activities with someone they do not love. Also, females at the state university are somewhat more sexually active than females at the Catholic college.

of sexual experiences engaged in, but most were moderately large as well as clearly significant. For the University of Connecticut samples, the distribution of guilt scores was divided at the median, and analyses were conducted for participation-nonparticipation in each of the 12 sexual experiences. Low-guilt males, significantly more often than high-guilt males, had manually manipulated the female genitalia, had oral contact with the female breast, had been masturbated by a female, had engaged in cunnilingus, had ventral-dorsal intercourse, and had experienced homosexual relations. Low-guilt females, significantly more often than high-guilt females, had their unclad breast manually manipulated, had been manually masturbated by a male, had masturbated a male, had ventral-ventral intercourse, and had experienced cunnilingus.

The negative correlations between sex guilt and permissive premarital sexual standards were moderately high. Guilty subjects had less permissive premarital standards. Only in the sample of University of Connecticut females was sex guilt significantly related to postmarital sexual standards. Many behaviors that are not open to the unmarried become acceptable with marriage in our culture, and the relation of postmarital standards to sex guilt tends to diminish. Among the University of Connecticut females, there were significant differences between the high-guilt and low-guilt females in regard to postmarital oral-genital contact. Low-guilt females believed fellatio and cunnilingus to be more acceptable as postmarital sexual behavior than did high-guilt females.

The analysis of reasons for nonparticipation in the various sexual behaviors was fruitful, since many of the subjects had not participated in the more intimate forms of sexual behavior. For the University of Connecticut males, high-guilt males significantly endorsed the following reasons more often than low-guilt males for not engaging in ventral-ventral intercourse: believed it was morally wrong; afraid of pregnancy or disease; respect the girl too much. High-guilt males in comparison to low-guilt males gave the following reasons for not participating in fellatio: afraid of pregnancy or disease; respect the girl too much. For not participating in cunnilingus, high-guilt males in comparison to low-guilt men stated they were afraid of pregnancy or disease. The high-guilt males gave as their reasons for not participating in ventral-dorsal intercourse the belief that it was morally wrong and fear of pregnancy or disease. For the University of Connecticut females, the only reason for nonparticipation which differentiated between high- and low-sex-guilt females was the belief that the sexual behavior was morally wrong. High-guilt females endorsed this belief significantly more often than low-guilt females for the following sexual behaviors: oral contact with the female breast; fellatio; cunnilingus, ventral-dorsal intercourse; and homosexual relations. For females, the discrimination between high- and low-sex-guilt subjects in terms of their differing only in the endorsement of the belief that a behavior is immoral could not have been more clear. However, males who score high on sex guilt are differentiated from low-guilt males in their reasons for nonparticipation in intercourse or oral-genital relations, not only in terms of moral beliefs, but also in terms of respect for the girls and most strongly in terms of fear of pregnancy or disease. This may reflect some lack of discriminant validity in the sex-guilt measure, or it may reflect a transformation of internal guilt by the male into an external fear of pregnancy or disease. It should be noted that fear of other people finding out (shame?) did not differentiate the high- and low-guilt subjects.

In conclusion, the data have generally supported the construct validity of the Mosher measure of sex guilt. College men and women who are predisposed to responding with guilt over sex reported limiting their sexual participation to the less intimate forms of sexual behavior. The premarital sexual standards that the guilty subjects endorsed were less permissive. Postmarital sexual standards were less related to the disposition of sex guilt. However, for the University of Connecticut females, there was a significant negative correlation with sex guilt, and the data revealed a less permissive attitude toward postmarital oral-genital relations. Finally, the reasons for nonparticipation in the intimate forms of sexual behavior which discriminated high- and low-sex-guilt subjects were, exclusively, moral belief for the females; and moral belief, respect, and most consistently, fear of pregnancy or disease for the males.

Two potential limitations of the present study deserve comment. First, the data on sexual experiences rest on the willingness of the subject to report accurately past sexual behavior. The precautions of anonymity, no pressure to participate, and the wording of the instructions, which stressed that results of the research were dependent on the cooperation, honesty, and integrity to report truthfully and fully past sexual behavior, were undertaken to increase the probable accuracy of the self-reports. Second, the correlational nature of the study does not delineate cause-and-effect sequences precisely. As with all research, greater confidence in these findings will be forthcoming as converging data increase confidence in method and findings. Certainly a study which related previously collected measures of sex guilt to sexual behavior in the laboratory à la Masters and Johnson[7] would stand more strongly on its own results.

REFERENCES

1. Brady, J. P., & Levitt, E. E. The scalability of sexual experiences. *Psychological Record*, 1965, 15, 377–384.
2. Galbraith, G. G. The Mosher Sex-Guilt Scale and the Thorne Sex

Inventory: Intercorrelations. *Journal of Clinical Psychology*, 1969, **24**, 292–294.

3. Galbraith, G. G., Hahn, K., & Lieberman, H. Personality correlates of free-associative sex responses to double-entendre words. *Journal of Consulting and Clinical Psychology*, 1968, **32**, 193–197.

4. Galbraith, G. G., & Mosher, D. L. Associative sexual responses in relation to sexual arousal, guilt, and external approval contingencies. *Journal of Personality and Social Psychology*, 1968, **10**, 142–147.

5. Kinsey, A. C., Pomeroy, W. B., Martin, C. E., & Gebhard, P. H. *Sexual behavior in the human female.* New York: Saunders, 1953.

6. Lamb, C. Personality correlates of humor enjoyment following motivational arousal. *Journal of Personality and Social Psychology*, 1968, **9**, 237–241.

7. Masters, W. H., & Johnson, V. E. *Human sexual response.* Boston: Little, Brown, 1966.

8. Mosher, D. L. The development and validation of a sentence completion measure of guilt. Unpublished doctoral dissertation, Ohio State University, 1961.

9. Mosher, D. L. Interaction of fear and guilt in inhibiting unacceptable behavior. *Journal of Consulting Psychology*, 1965, **29**, 161–167.

10. Mosher, D. L. The development and multitrait-multimethod matrix analysis of three measures of three aspects of guilt. *Journal of Consulting Psychology*, 1966, **30**, 25–29.

11. Mosher, D. L. Measurement of guilt in females by self-report inventories. *Journal of Consulting and Clinical Psychology*, 1968, **32**, 690–695.

12. Mosher, D. L., & Greenberg, I. Female's affective reactions to reading erotic literature. *Journal of Consulting and Clinical Psychology*, 1969, **33**, 472–477.

13. Reiss, I. L. *The social context of premarital permissiveness.* New York: Holt, Rinehart & Winston, 1967.

14. Reiss, I. L. How and why America's sex habits are changing. *Transaction*, March 1968.

15. Thorne, F. C. The sex inventory. *Journal of Clinical Psychology*, 1966, **22**, 367–374.

Evaluations of Erotica: Facts or Feelings?

The emphasis of the previous study was on sex guilt and its presumed power to cause people to avoid certain sexual activities. In the next article, the focus is on the feelings that are aroused when an individual is exposed to erotic stimuli. It seems likely that those high in guilt would respond with negative emotions while those low in guilt would respond positively. As we shall see, however, the feelings aroused by sexual cues involve more than a simple positive-negative dimension.

The main theme of the following article is the importance of emotions (affective responses) in determining the kind of judgments we make. In essence, we like whatever makes us feel good and dislike whatever makes us feel bad. The conditioning model outlined in this article suggests that we, like Pavlov's dogs, also learn to make positive and negative emotional responses to any stimulus associated with the original feelings. Because people have had many different learning experiences with erotic material, any pictures or stories that deal with nudity, masturbation, intercourse, oral sex, etc., can bring forth either pleasant emotions (arousal, enjoyment, curiosity) or negative emotions (disgust, nausea, depression) or both. Individual differences in such affective reactions to erotica presumably depend on the kinds of positive and negative learning experiences each of us has had throughout our lives. Though the present research did not investigate the child-rearing experiences of the subjects, the findings dealing with authoritarianism and with religious behavior at least suggest that individuals' negative reactions to erotic stimuli are likely to occur within a somewhat traditional and restrictive family background in contrast to individuals responding positively to erotica.

This article also points out that people do not usually say simply that something makes them feel good and hence they like it or that it makes them feel bad and hence they dislike it. Rather, most people attempt to justify their reactions. For example, those who are made uncomfortable by erotic stimuli tend to label such material as pornographic and to favor censorship and other legal restrictions on it. It seems to be difficult to separate one's personal and quite legitimate emotions from the seemingly intellectual judgments and decisions that may interfere with the preferences of others.

Evaluations of Erotica: Facts or Feelings?

Donn Byrne, Jeffrey D. Fisher, John Lamberth,
and Herman E. Mitchell

In determining that an erotic stimulus is pornographic and that it should therefore be subject to legal restrictions or other societal sanctions, an individual is making an evaluative response that can have

Reprinted in an edited version from: Byrne, D., Fisher, J. D., Lamberth, J., & Mitchell, H. E. Evaluations of erotica: Facts or feelings? *Journal of Personality and Social Psychology*, 1974, **29**, 111–116.

widespread consequences. Although research relating exposure to erotica with behavioral effects has consistently refuted the popular belief that deviant acts are elicited by sexual pictures and stories,[7] large segments of the population are either unaware of such findings or remain unconvinced by them. In fact, the relatively mild recommendations of the Commission on Obscenity and Pornography were rejected by the president and by an overwhelming majority of the Senate of the United States. One approach to understanding this discrepancy between the available research data and politically acceptable public opinion is provided by a general theory of evaluational behavior.

A reinforcement-affect model of evaluative responses has been formulated in the context of research on interpersonal attraction.[2,3,6] Evaluation is assumed to be mediated by positive and negative affect. Stimuli with reinforcing properties serve as unconditioned stimuli for implicit affective responses. These affective responses fall along a subjective continuum from pleasant to unpleasant. Any discriminable stimulus paired with an unconditioned stimulus becomes a conditioned stimulus and is subsequently able to elicit affective responses. The individual's evaluation of the conditioned stimulus varies with the magnitude of positive and negative affect conditioned to it. Evaluative responses include attraction, approach and avoidance behavior, and a variety of evaluative judgments. Most of the research testing hypotheses derived from the model has been in the area of interpersonal attraction, and substantive links have been shown among reinforcement, affect, and evaluation.

Further generality for the model should be provided by its extension to the study of erotica. Several investigators have shown that erotic stimuli elicit various affective responses,[18] but the theoretical role of such responses as mediational variables has not been systematically examined. It follows from the model that evaluations of erotica are based on the relative intensities of elicited positive and negative affect. Specifically, it is hypothesized that judgments about the pornographic quality of erotic stimuli and opinions about the value of imposing legal restrictions on them are a function of the affect elicited by such material.

The conceptualization of individual differences in response to erotica is also facilitated by an affective interpretation. It should be possible to identify those individuals for whom particular kinds of erotic stimuli elicit positive or negative affect and then to investigate both the antecedents and the consequents of such responses. To date, individual differences in sexual responses have been examined with respect to relatively general dimensions such as authoritarianism,[8,9,17] liberalism-conservatism,[19] and repression-sensitization,[5,16] and with respect to relatively specific dimensions such as sexual guilt[12-15] and sexual liberalism-conservatism.[20] In the present context, all such variables are seen as useful to the extent that they are predictive of affective responses.

METHOD

Thirty-two married couples (at least one member of each pair was a Purdue University student) volunteered to serve as subjects in response to a bulletin describing the study as one dealing with opinions about pornography. The subjects were run in small groups of couples in a classroom setting at night. Complete subject anonymity was maintained by the use of code numbers.

The subjects first completed a feelings scale[5] that required self-ratings of affect on 11 dimensions, each represented by a 5-point rating scale: sexually aroused, disgusted, entertained, anxious, bored, angry, afraid, curious, nauseated, depressed, and excited. In addition, each subject filled out a 22-item version of the California F-Scale, balanced to control for acquiescent response set.[11]

The experimental stimuli were 19 themes of heterosexual, homosexual, and autosexual acts presented in either pictorial or verbal form. For subjects in the pictorial condition, 19 slides were shown for 20 sec each.[10] For those in the verbal condition, 19 short mimeographed passages selected to match the slides were given to the subjects for 1 min and 15 sec each.

Following the presentation of each theme, the subjects indicated how arousing they found it to be on a 0–5 scale. All of the themes were presented a second time and were evaluated as to whether each was perceived as pornographic or nonpornographic. A dictionary definition of pornography as "obscene or licentious; foul, disgusting, or offensive; tending to produce lewd emotions" was provided. The number of themes judged pornographic could range from 0 to 19. Then, the feelings scale was readministered to assess each subject's affective response to the stimuli. Finally, an opinion questionnaire was given to ascertain the subject's support of restrictive legal measures concerning the dissemination of erotica. The subjects were asked whether the majority of the items they had seen should be forbidden entirely, forbidden in public display and advertising, or forbidden to unmarried individuals, to teenagers, and/or to children. Total restrictiveness scores could range from 0 to 5. Demographic information on each subject was also obtained.

RESULTS

Factor analysis of feelings scale

In order to determine the most meaningful clustering of the items on the feelings scale, the subjects' responses to the postexperimental scale were factor analyzed. Rather than a single affective dimension ranging from positive to negative, two independent affective dimensions were found. The first factor was labeled positive affect and consisted of the items excited, entertained, sexually aroused, anxious, curious, and not bored. The second factor was labeled negative affect and consisted of the items disgusted, nauseated, angry, and depressed. A cross-validation of these factors has been provided by William Griffitt with a sample of undergraduates at Kansas State University who were presented with the same stimuli used in the present investigation. These same two factors were found in the Kansas State sample as in the Purdue sample.

Affect and evaluative responses

Male and female subjects were separately divided into four affective arousal subgroups: high or low positive affect and high or low negative affect. Tentatively, the responses of the individuals in the subgroups were categorized as affectively prosex (high positive, low negative), affectively antisex (high negative, low positive), ambivalent (high on both dimensions), and affectively indifferent (low on both dimensions). Affective subgroup frequencies for the pictorial and verbal conditions did not differ for either males or females, so the data were combined across conditions. As hypothesized, self-reported affect on the feelings scale was found to be associated with evaluative responses, as shown in Tables 5-2 and 5-3.

Table 5-2
Number of the 19 Themes Judged To Be Pornographic by Individuals High and Low in Positive and Negative Affect

| | Negative Affect | | | |
| | Males | | Females | |
Positive Affect	Low	High	Low	High
High	6.60	5.70	4.28	9.00
Low	1.38	10.50	3.42	9.66

For males, the number of the themes rated as pornographic was a function of how negatively *and* how positively such stimuli made them feel. For females, the pornography ratings were simply a function of how negatively the stimuli made them feel.

Table 5-3
Restrictiveness[a] toward Erotic Stimuli by Individuals High and Low in Positive and Negative Affect

| | Negative Affect | | | |
| | Males | | Females | |
Positive Affect	Low	High	Low	High
High	2.00	1.40	1.42	2.83
Low	.63	3.38	2.14	3.16

[a] Possible range is 0 (not at all restrictive) to 5 (extremely restrictive).

For males, restrictiveness about the production and sale of erotica was a function of how positively *and* how negatively such stimuli made them feel. For females, restrictiveness was simply a function of how negatively the stimuli made them feel.

For females, degree of negative affect was the only predictor of evaluative responses. The total number of themes judged pornographic and the total number of restrictiveness judgments were each associated with the degree of negative affect.

For males, both the degree of negative affect and the interaction of positive and negative affect were associated with evaluative responses. This held true both for the total number of pornography judgments and for total restrictiveness scores.

The overall pattern seems to suggest that only those males high in negative affect who were also low in positive affect rendered negative evaluative judgments; females high in negative affect evaluated erotica negatively regardless of level of positive affect.

For females, total sexual arousal correlated positively with pornography judgments and with restrictiveness opinions; for males, neither relationship was significant.

The preexperimental feelings scale was subjected to the kinds of analysis described for the postexperimental scale. Preexperimental level of affect was unrelated to evaluative responses, thus indicating that it was only the experimentally aroused affect that was responsible for the reported relationships.

Authoritarianism and demographic variables

As the authoritarianism of a subject increased, there was an increase in the number of stimuli judged pornographic and in restrictiveness. It was also found that both religious preferences and frequency of church attendance predicted pornography judgments and restrictiveness opinions; these data are summarized in Table 5-4. As might be anticipated from these interrelationships, authoritarianism was found to be associated with religious preference and church attendance.

The effects of one other demographic variable, political preference, were also explored. Of the 64 subjects, only 22 identified themselves as Democrats and 16 as Republicans. The mean authoritarianism score of the Republicans ($M = 72.81$) was significantly higher than that of Democrats ($M = 56.36$). Members of the two parties were not significantly different in pornography or restrictiveness responses.

DISCUSSION

The relationship between affective responses and evaluative responses in the present study provides support for the applicability of the Byrne-Clore model in conceptualizing various reactions to erotica. The subjects exposed to erotic stimuli reacted with quite diverse positive and negative affective responses, and this experimentally induced affect showed a systematic relationship with judgments about pornography and opinions about restrictiveness. It would appear that affect is a general predictor

Table 5-4
Religious Preference and Church Attendance as Predictors of Authoritarianism and Evaluative Responses to Erotica

Variable	Authoritarianism[a]	Number of Themes Judged To Be Pornographic	Restrictiveness toward Erotic Stimuli
Religious preference			
Agnostic	52.82	4.70	1.53
Protestant	62.94	5.62	2.25
Catholic	72.69	10.62	3.25
Church attendance			
Never	49.77	4.86	1.50
Seldom	57.95	5.00	1.85
Weekly	78.42	12.25	3.92

[a] Possible range is 22 (least authoritarian) to 154 (most authoritarian).
Authoritarianism, pornography ratings, and restrictiveness were highest among Catholics and lowest among agnostics. All three variables were also highest among those who attend church weekly and lowest among those who never attend.

of evaluative responses to erotica. In the absence of empirical evidence indicating negative behavioral effects from exposure to erotic stimuli, decisions about pornography and censorship probably are made simply on the basis of how such stimuli make one feel.

Presumably, the affect an individual experiences when exposed to sexual content is the end product of numerous affect-eliciting rewards and punishments that were associated with sexual matters during the socialization process. It is this previously conditioned positive or negative affect that becomes paired with the otherwise neutral pictures and words presented in the laboratory and that mediates evaluations of those words and pictures. The reinforcements associated with sex come not only from one's own sexual sensations but also from parents, religious dogma, peers, and the mass media. Very likely, variables such as authoritarianism, religious preference, and frequency of church attendance act as predictors primarily because they are associated with differential past and present sexual reinforcements.

There appear to be sex differences in the way in which affective responses influence evaluations of erotica. For females, evaluative responses are determined on the basis of level of negative affect, but for males it is the interaction of positive and negative affect that is the crucial determinant. Also, for females, sexual arousal is positively associated with pornography and restrictiveness responses, but this is not true for males. It seems possible that for females in our culture there is basically an association of varying degrees of negative affect with explicitly presented sexual content, while for males both positive affect and negative affect become associated with erotic depictions. Much more so than is true for females, males learn that it is acceptable to obtain pornography, share it with same-sex members of their peer group, and use it as a stimulus for masturbation fantasies.[1] Thus, males can have various positive experiences with pornography as well as degrees of negative affect supplied by societal repressiveness.

In addition to the proposed influence of affective responses on subsequent evaluative judgments, additional processes may be operative. Positive and negative feelings about a stimulus influence one's general evaluation of the stimulus; moreover, there is a tendency to attempt to justify such feelings and evaluations in more general terms. For example, in research on interpersonal attraction, when the attitudes of a stranger arouse negative affect, that stranger is evaluated negatively with respect to such attributes as intelligence, morality, and adjustment, and he is judged to be a source of unpleasant future experiences.[2] It seems difficult for most people to indicate that someone or something makes them feel good or bad and hence that they simply respond with like or dislike. Instead, the individual's own reactions are attributed to the object itself in terms of its intrinsic qualities. Thus, an erotic depiction is not just pleasing or displeasing to oneself; the depiction itself is good or bad. Next, there is an attempt to justify such judgments and to vindicate them by attributing a general benefit or harm to the object. Thus, erotica has been characterized as a liberating and healthful influence and as a poison to men's souls, as man's great hope in the fight against tyranny and a communist plot to weaken our society.[4] It can be seen that what begins as a personal affective response can end as an elaborate belief system. If so, it is not surprising that research data which are relevant to such systems tend to be accepted or rejected not on their own merits but on the basis of the justification or vindication that they provide. It may well be that attempts to alter judgments and beliefs succeed only when it is possible to alter the underlying affective responses from which they derive.

This general orientation suggests the possible efficacy of focusing on the affective quality of such enterprises as formal or informal sex education, sexual therapy, and marital counseling. What is taught about anatomical structures, physiological processes, and techniques of the sexual act may not be as important as what is intentionally or unintentionally conveyed affectively.

REFERENCES

1. Athanasiou, R., & Shaver, P. Correlates of heterosexuals' reactions to pornography. *Journal of Sex Research,* 1971, *7*, 298–311.

2. Byrne, D. *The attraction paradigm.* New York: Academic Press, 1971.

3. Byrne, D., & Clore, G. L. A reinforcement model of evaluative responses. *Personality,* 1970, **1**, 103–128.

4. Byrne, D., & Lamberth, J. The effect of erotic stimuli on sex arousal, evaluative responses, and subsequent behavior. In *Technical report of the Commission on Obscenity and Pornography.* Vol. 8. Washington, D. C.: U. S. Government Printing Office, 1971.

5. Byrne, D., & Sheffield, J. Response to sexually arousing stimuli as a function of repressing and sensitizing defenses. *Journal of Abnormal Psychology,* 1965, **70**, 114–118.

6. Clore, G. L., & Byrne, D. A reinforcement-affect model of attraction. In T. L. Huston (Ed.), *Foundations of interpersonal attraction.* New York: Academic Press, 1974.

7. Commission on Obscenity and Pornography. *The report of the Commission on Obscenity and Pornography.* Washington, D. C.: U. S. Government Printing Office, 1970.

8. Eliasberg, W. G., & Stuart, I. R. Authoritarian personality and the obscenity threshold. *Journal of Social Psychology,* 1961, **55**, 143–151.

9. Kogan, N. Authoritarianism and repression. *Journal of Abnormal and Social Psychology,* 1956, **53**, 34–37.

10. Levitt, E. E., & Brady, J. P. Sexual preferences in young adult males and some correlates. *Journal of Clinical Psychology,* 1965, **21**, 347–354.

11. Mitchell, H. E., & Byrne, D. The defendant's dilemma: Effects of jurors' attitudes and authoritarianism on judicial decisions. *Journal of Personality and Social Psychology,* 1973, **25**, 123–129.

12. Mosher, D. L. The development and multitrait-multimethod matrix analysis of three measures of three aspects of guilt. *Journal of Consulting Psychology,* 1966, **30**, 25–29.

13. Mosher, D. L. Measurement of guilt in females by self-report inventories. *Journal of Consulting and Clinical Psychology,* 1968, **32**, 690–695.

14. Mosher, D. L. Psychological reactions to pornographic films. In *Technical report of the Commission on Obscenity and Pornography.* Vol. 8. Washington, D. C.: U. S. Government Printing Office, 1971.

15. Mosher, D. L., & Cross, H. J. Sex guilt and premarital sexual experiences of college students. *Journal of Consulting and Clinical Psychology,* 1971, **36**, 27–32.

16. Paris, J., & Goodstein, L. D. Responses to death and sex stimulus

materials as a function of repression-sensitization. *Psychological Reports*, 1966, **19**, 1283–1291.

17. Rothstein, R. Authoritarianism and men's reactions to sexuality and affection in women. *Journal of Abnormal and Social Psychology*, 1960, **61**, 329–334.

18. Schmidt, G., & Sigusch, V. Sex differences in responses to psychosexual stimulation by films and slides. *Journal of Sex Research*, 1970, **6**, 268–283.

19. Schmidt, G., Sigusch, V., & Meyberg, U. Psychosexual stimulation in men: Emotional reactions, changes of sex behavior, and measures of conservative attitudes. *Journal of Sex Research*, 1969, **5**, 199–217.

20. Wallace, D. H., & Wehmer, G. Evaluation of visual erotica by sexual liberals and conservatives. *Journal of Sex Research*, 1972, **8**, 147–153.

PART THREE

Sexuality, Love, Marriage, and Conception

An Overview:
Establishing Sexual Behavior Patterns

Though sexuality can be a very private and individual aspect of one's life, much of it is also interpersonal and involves the most intimate social interaction in which human beings can engage. Thus, in addition to one's sexual anatomy, physiology, learned responses, fantasies, and feelings, it is necessary to consider what sexuality means with respect to the relationship between males and females.

Specifically, we should examine the possible similarities and differences between men and women, identify the variables that determine whether a particular male and female will join together as mates, and consider the personal and social consequences of conception.

THE SEXES

It is unfortunate, but nonetheless true, that males and females in our society frequently cast themselves as somewhat antagonistic subgroups who merely tolerate one another for sexual and economic reasons. There are widely held stereotypes that characterize females as gentle, quiet, tender, artistic, passive individuals who need security and a strong mate to lead them; males are rough, loud, aggressive individuals who are ambitious and comfortable in assuming the leadership role.[7] In trying to understand the sexes, Sigmund Freud once confessed that he could not figure out what it is that women want. In *My Fair Lady,* Professor Henry Higgins asks in frustration, "Why can't a woman be more like a man?" On the other side, women sometimes have great difficulty in tolerating males. Have you ever heard anyone express such sentiments as "Isn't that just like a man?" or "Boys will be boys" or "Men are all alike—they're just after one thing"?

Given these stereotypes, frustrations, and hostilities between males and females, it is not at all surprising that their sexual desires and sexual activities would be a focal point of misunderstanding. We will briefly describe the traditional views of the presumed differences between the sexes and then we will look at some of the reasons for the current changes in these views.

Traditional Views: Men Want It
and Women Put Up with It

Generally, males and females have been viewed as very different in their sexuality. Men are presumably in a state of continual arousability and are willing to seek satisfaction with whatever partner is available—"If I'm not near the girl that I love, I love the girl I'm near" or "Turn 'em upside down and they're all the same." Women, in contrast, are said to have little interest in sex except that it is a way of expressing affection and a means to obtain children and the security of a protective mate. The traditional role of the female in the sexual act is as a passive participant. Victorian women were told to close their eyes and think of England. Eleanor Roosevelt advised her daughter that sex is something that a woman must endure. Wives, of course, could try to minimize their discomfort by finding reasons to avoid intercourse. There is a joke about a married couple visiting the zoo. At the gorilla cage they stop, and the gorilla waves at the woman. "What shall I do?" The husband says, "Wave back." The gorilla motions her over to the side of the cage. "What shall I do?" "Go over to him." The wife then asks, "What if he tries to get romantic?" The husband replies, "Tell him about your headache." It seems to be widely assumed, even in marriage manuals,[20] in books about joyful sex,[15] and among college coeds[23, 28] that males are more interested in sex and more easily aroused than females. Syndicated columnist George Crane periodically states that men need more "erotic calories" than women, and he advises wives to pretend to be interested in sex, serving "boudoir cheesecake" to their mates. "Even if you are tired and sleepy, at least turn on a seductive act for 10 minutes, since most divorces start in the bedroom" (March 29, 1976).

Interestingly enough, these views of the relatively disinterested female have existed side by side with the image of another kind of woman. It was unthinkable to apply to one's mother or sister or wife or daughter, but nevertheless men knew there were *some* women who actually liked sex. Our language contains many terms, mostly derogatory, to describe them—nymphos, whores, tramps, chippies, and all the rest. Perhaps the saddest aspect of this conceptualization is that countless women who found themselves enjoying sex to the fullest worried that such pleasure was an indication of latent "nymphomania." Similarly, countless men who had a sexually liberated mate became concerned as to how their wives learned "to behave like a whore." We can only hope that these worries and concerns will disappear from future case histories and letters to advice columns, because some very different facts are now available about female sexuality.

Current Views: Sex Is for Both Sexes

Prior to the mid-1960s, evidence about the sexual behavior of females in our culture was quite consistent with the traditional views just outlined. Contradictory evidence was available, and the implications for ourselves were not widely recognized. Studies of animal behavior revealed that males were almost always more sexually aggressive than females; in fact, there is no evidence that females of other species even experience orgasm. Female animals do, however, have strong sex drives; they will learn responses that are reinforced only by intercourse, and they will risk leaving a safe hiding place in order to mate.[4, 32] In addition, cross-cultural studies[31] have informed us for some time that human beings of both sexes can learn to be much more and much less sexually active than ourselves.

The real turning point in our knowledge came with a series of very different events in the late 1960s and early 1970s. The work of Masters and Johnson has been cited many times, but their description of females as physiologically similar to males in sexual responsiveness and their documentation of the females' capacity for multiple orgasms were enormously significant research findings. Partly as a function of these laboratory data, there was a sudden reversal in the way in which male and female sexuality was discussed by some commentators. Males were now characterized as rather fragile sexual performers who, if they could get beyond the problems of impotence or premature ejaculation, might be able to attain one or sometimes two climaxes per session. Females, in contrast, were now seen as sexual superwomen who could achieve a series of orgasms by manipulating their clitorises, using a vibrator, or exhausting a platoon of male partners. Though this complete reversal of roles is a bit overstated, its general message was congruent with the increased awareness among females of their right to be liberated human beings rather than second-class citizens.

Other data also began to demonstrate that the traditional view of females was incorrect. Beginning about 1970, experimental studies of reactions to erotica at the Institute for Sex Research in Hamburg and by the United States Commission on Obscenity and Pornography reported for the first time that females are as aroused by erotic stimuli as males. Also, survey data began to show that women now were behaving sexually more and more like men. These very rapid sexual changes constitute a remarkable new fact of life in our society, one to which both males and females must now learn to adjust.

LOVE AND MARRIAGE

Even though sexual attitudes and sexual practices are rapidly changing and even though sexual permissiveness is greater than anyone would even have imagined a few decades back, most people are found to have some very "old-fashioned" goals with respect to finding someone to love and with whom to establish a permanent relationship.[27] Most of us value such relationships, and most would agree that sex in a loving context is infinitely better than impersonal sex. Perhaps the contrast is analogous to having your favorite home-cooked meal versus lunch at a fast-food franchise; even though both can totally satisfy one's hunger, the two experiences differ in many other ways. It appears that loving and being loved are extremely important. But how do any of us go about finding an appropriate partner? We will briefly describe some aspects of the process.

From Acquaintanceship to Love

In recent years, social psychologists have directed a great deal of research toward an understanding of the process whereby people meet, become acquainted, and develop friendships.[9] Even more recently, and despite the vocal criticism of one member of the U. S. Senate, they have extended their research to the question of how friendship between two members of the opposite sex develops into love.[5, 35] How can these findings be summarized? We will take an example of two individuals, a male and a female college student, and see how they might meet, become friends, and "fall in love."

Though it is obvious that two people must meet before they can become acquainted, it is not so obvious how the meeting takes place. Though we occasionally are introduced to someone by a mutual friend or make a deliberate effort to meet a particular stranger, most meetings are accidental. They are not random events, however, and some of the most powerful determinants of interpersonal contacts are embodied in the physical structure of our environment. It has been found over and over that such variables as the location of driveways between houses, the closeness of apartment units, the way in which sidewalks are laid out, the position of desks in an office, and even the arrangement of seats in a classroom determine who will meet whom.[3] If two college students live in residences that are located on the same sidewalk leading to the student union or if they are assigned adjoining seats in a classroom, they are very likely first to become aware of one another as familiar faces, then to speak when they encounter one another, and finally to engage in conversation.

Beyond the environmental factors that may bring a male and a female in close enough proximity to interact, there are numerous variables which determine whether they merely say, "Hi" or proceed to an actual conversation. Physical characteristics play a major role at this point, and males and females are especially concerned about the physical attractiveness of one another.[16] In addition, some people have learned to respond positively or negatively to such factors as skin color, accent, height, weight, etc. If the other person does not live up to one's minimal standards on all such observable features, the relationship is not likely to proceed. If the other person is seen as suitably attractive, however, the interaction is likely to roll right along. In addition, anything in the situation that enhances positive emotions increases the likelihood of a positive interaction, while negative emotions decrease the probability of pleasant interactions. For example, people respond to strangers more positively in a comfortable room rather than in a hot and humid one, after viewing an amusing movie rather than a sad one, and after hearing good news on the radio rather than bad news.[21, 22, 40] It is also true that individuals differ in their need for affiliation: the greater their desire to form a relationship, the more likely they are to interact.[8] In addition, those who are not currently involved in a relationship have a greater need to affiliate than those for whom such needs are being satisfied.

If all of the factors so far discussed are positive, our two college students can be expected to begin talking to one another. At this point, the content of the conversation is crucial. A great many investigations have shown that people respond most positively to those who are similar to themselves in attitudes, values, beliefs, interests, and even in many personality characteristics.[9] In fact, much of the early conversation of individuals who have just met, or who are having their first date, consists of a series of comparisons. People talk about their likes and dislikes with respect to movies, music, food, television programs, sports, politics, religion, and many other things as well. To the extent that they are alike, they respond positively to one another and are pleased at how much "they have in common." This sort of positive interaction leads to friendship and the expression of flattering evaluations of one another—"I like you," "You're interesting," "You're the smartest boy I know," "You're *so* funny," "I've never known a girl who knew so much about football," "You're beautiful." These evaluations are even more powerful than similarity in enhancing the relationship and in deepening the friendship. We all like to be liked and to have someone respond positively to us.[13]

For this friendship between a male and a female to develop into a relationship described as "love," a few other variables are important. Physical attractiveness (at least in one another's eyes) is crucial, and this tends to be strongly related to sexual attraction.[12] In addition, intense passionate love seems to occur if the individuals are emotionally aroused when they are together and if they interpret that arousal as love.[41] Because love is not a universal concept, we probably must learn to label the mixture of liking, sexual desire, and emotional arousal as love. It is likely that our songs, books, movies, and television shows perform this teaching function in that we are informed over and over again that a male and female who like each other very much and who desire each other sexually must inevitably "fall in love."[10] Passionate love consists of a highly aroused state in which the individual thinks primarily about the other person and has difficulty in going about the necessary routines of life such as studying, working, or even eating— "You're not sick, you're just in love." Luckily, this superheated level of emotion cannot last; one cannot stay forever in a state in which birds sing and bells ring. If the relationship is to function more realistically, it must simmer down to a very close friendship, with mutual sexual attraction, concern about one another's welfare, and mutual respect.[36] And, in our society, a male-female friendship of that type, a "meaningful relationship," generally leads to marriage or at least cohabitation. Two people who feel that they love one another want to be together, to live together, and to establish a relatively exclusive social and sexual bond.

Marriage:
Can a Loving Relationship Be Maintained?

Though people who fall in love and live together generally assume that a permanent step is being taken, it is obvious that the relationship very frequently disintegrates over time. Love can sour and turn to hate. Many couples are at least periodically unhappy, many feel trapped in a hopeless situation, many break up. As Paul Simon tells us, there must be at least 50 ways to leave your lover. A typical statistic appeared in a local newspaper. In Marion County (Indiana), during the first 3 months of 1976, 1821 couples filed for marriage licenses and 1678 couples filed for divorce.

Unfortunately, we know much less about the reasons for the failure of an interpersonal relationship than we know about what brings people together in the first place, but a few factors are apparent. People must be compatible to be able to live together in close proximity, and this is especially true of something as basic as their sexual interactions.[11] A male and female who do not agree about sexual matters will find it difficult or impossible to continue a positive relationship. In addition, similarity in life style, in deciding about the expenditure of money, in the desire to have or not have children are crucial—and often these things are not really explored prior to marriage. Even differences in seemingly minor things like planning meals, setting the thermostat, squeezing the toothpaste tube, or tossing one's clothes on the floor at night can mount up as major sources of discontent.

Even if two people are perfectly compatible, one or both can change in time, and if they do not change in the same direction, trouble arises. Changes in sexual attitudes on the part of just one member of a pair can create an enormous conflict, and changes in educational level, political beliefs, religious practices, or anything else of importance can be equally divisive. If children are born, the parents may find that offspring create more changes in their lives than was anticipated. Children can add to existing financial difficulties, they provide a whole series of things about which to disagree, and they can interfere with their parents' sex life. Surprisingly, when columnist Ann Landers surveyed her readers as to their feelings about being parents, 70% of those who responded said that they regretted having had children. One mother of two small youngsters wrote, "I was an attractive, fulfilled career woman before I had these kids. Now I'm an exhausted, shrieking, nervous wreck. I'm too tired for sex, conversation, or anything else." Another sort of change that occurs is in physical appearance. The cute young girl can become an overweight, middle-aged woman while the trim and handsome young boy can become a weary, balding older man with a beer belly. Thus, countless changes can alter the relationship to the extent that love and even basic friendship can disappear.

If this description sounds pessimistic, it is only because there are a great many failed relationships in our society. There are also many very successful ones. How can any couple boost the odds for success? People need to be realistic in choosing a mate and they need to know as much as possible about the other person and about themselves. Rather than taking one's partner for granted, people need to work hard at pleasing one another and at trying to keep up with one another sexually, intellectually, and in every other way. People need to have fun together whether it is in bed, on a tennis court, at a cookout in the backyard, on a vacation, or at the corner bar.

Considering the possible things that can go wrong in a loving relationship and the difficult work involved in maintaining positive interpersonal feelings over time, perhaps the failure rate is not all that surprising. Possibly what is surprising is that many people *are* able to live together, to find mutual enjoyment, and to maintain a friendship over several decades. It is not an easy accomplishment.

TWO NEGATIVE CONSEQUENCES OF SEX:
UNWANTED AND UNNEEDED CONCEPTION

Conception is the biological "goal" of sexual intercourse even if it is not necessarily the goal of the participants. It goes without saying that reproduction is necessary to maintain our species. In addition, each of us is indebted to our parents for engaging in the process, and many of us who have children are very pleased that we did so. Nevertheless, conception is not always desired or desirable. We will point out the two most general problems.

Accidental Babies: Unwanted Conception

In several articles in this book various authors have outlined the changes in sexual behavior that have been occurring in recent years. Premarital intercourse now occurs more frequently, it takes place at an earlier age, and more individuals are involved than in previous periods in our history. In January 1976, Planned Parenthood reported that a study of 421 urban boys found that half of them had sexual intercourse by the time they reached age 13. With teen-agers today relatively better educated than ever before and with contraceptive techniques more effective and more available, it would seem that sexual activity need not involve fears of unwanted pregnancies.

The fact is that the situation is a horrendous one in which contraception is practiced infrequently and irregularly. Increasing numbers of young couples are faced with age-old problems of embarrassment, pressures toward unwanted marriages, and painful decisions about the medical and moral issues involved in seeking an abortion. Despite forced marriages and the increased availability of abortions,[37] there were 418,000 illegitimate births in the United States in 1974, with blacks slightly outnumbering whites, according to the National Center for Health Statistics. Why are hundreds of thousands of unwanted infants conceived each year? It has been found that most teen-agers who engage in intercourse for the first time use either no contraception or an unreliable technique.[18] In some localities it is difficult or impossible to obtain the most effective forms of contraception without parental consent. As will be discussed in greater detail in a later article, there are also psychological reasons that sometimes prevent an individual from admitting that contraceptive precautions need to be taken and from taking the public steps necessary to obtain condoms, a diaphragm, the pill, or other contraceptive devices. It should be added that the conception of an unwanted child within a marriage can also be personally traumatic even though there is no public "shame" involved.

Unless the existing patterns of sexual behavior undergo an unexpected reversal and we enter a new period of sexual repression, it is crucial that we find ways to alter the present contraceptive practices (or nonpractices) of those who are enjoying the new sexual freedom. There are quite different views as to whether premarital sex should be condoned, tolerated, or condemned. There should be little disagreement, however, as to the belief that it is preferable *not* to conceive children who are not wanted by their parents. Children are too valuable to be created by accident and to be a source of unhappiness and shame rather than a source of joy.

Overpopulation: Unneeded Conception

Even when children are wanted by their parents and are purposely conceived, there is still a more general problem that transcends the concerns of the participating individuals. The specter of overpopulation may be seen as a causative or contributing factor in many of humankind's most pressing problems. It is difficult to argue against the fact that as the number of individuals in a given geographic area increases, there is a related increase in difficulties as diverse as the energy shortage, interpersonal disharmony, the shortage of food, and the crime rate.[24, 30, 33] Our dilemma is very bad at present (80 million additional people each year) and is getting worse at an accelerated rate. The figures are staggering. On a Sunday late in March 1976, the world population reached 4 billion. The worldwide growth rate is slightly more than 2% per year. That may sound small, but it means that the population will double in less than 35 years, and then double again in another 35 years.[19] Another 350 years at the present rate will give us a world population of more than 4 trillion individuals.[14] An infinite extension of our current contraceptive practices is not only unwise and irresponsible, it is impossible. Isaac Asimov[1] has calculated that at the present rate of population growth, the entire mass of the known universe will consist of human bodies in 6700 years. That will not happen, of course. The growth of population will halt, either through democratic educational efforts that bring about voluntary changes in behavior, through manipulation of behavior by means of positive incentives, through totalitarian measures that enforce new contraceptive practices, or through worldwide Malthusian disasters that reduce existing populations through genocidal wars, starvation, and pestilence.[25, 35] India's minister of health and family planning said in January 1976 that family planning depends on discipline which, if not self-inspired, must be imposed by the government; shortly afterward, a program was announced which demands sterilization of government employees once they have two children. Failure to comply leads to massive economic sanctions *(Time,* March 8, 1976) Similarly, Lee Kuan Yew, the prime minister of Singapore, has instituted a measure that excludes any family with more than three children from all welfare services *(Forum,* January 1975). The democratic-educational alternatives seem unmistakably preferable, but it is difficult to be optimistic about what, in fact, *will* happen.

Despite the looming catastrophe, there is differential awareness and differential concern about these issues among people in general; further, it is found that awareness of the problems of overpopulation is not affected by such familiar procedures as saturation of the mass media with appropriate factual information.[29] One aspect of the difficulty is that there is a tremendous conceptual gap between the abstract problem of an overpopulated world and the very concrete reality of one's own immediate sexual desire or one's beliefs about the satisfactions involved in having a large family.

There are many ideological barriers to family planning. For example, in the nations that could benefit most from a reduction in the birth rate (for example, the underdeveloped countries of the Third World), a rate of population growth exceeding 3% is not unusual.[33] The most rapidly growing nations (3.3% or more) are Algeria, Morocco, Rhodesia, Jordan, Kuwait, Syria, Pakistan, Philippines, Thailand, Vietnam, El Salvador, Dominican Republic, Colombia, Ecuador, Surinam, Venezuela, and Paraguay. Even in the economically developed nations such as the United States and the USSR, which are approaching a zero growth rate (2.1 children per family), actual growth in the population will continue for 50 or 60 years because of the large proportion of young people who have not yet reproduced.[19] In addition, there is still considerable variation among subgroups within each nation. Usually those who are least well off educationally and financially have the highest birthrate. The social implications of that fact with respect to unemployment, poverty, and crime are not hard to imagine. Even worse, there is evidence that our birth rate is likely to rise again in the near future.[38, 39]

Various national and ethnic groups argue strongly *against* population control for themselves. Rosenman[34] finds that blacks in the United States resist family planning programs for the black community because they distrust the motives of the white-dominated government. China's Ministry of Health denounced birth control as an imperialist plot against the underdeveloped countries (*Forum,* January 1975). A conservative rabbi in New York City has organized the Jewish Population Regeneration Unit which rejects the idea of zero population growth for Jews and recommends that each Jewish couple have four or five children *(Time,* July 14, 1975). The World Moslem League announced that "birth control was invented by the enemies of Islam" and succeeded in getting contraceptives banned in Saudi Arabia (*Forum,* October 1975). Few African nations perceive birth control as a problem,[26] and they joined the Communists and the Catholics at the 1974 World Population Conference at Bucharest in resisting any proposal to limit population growth.[2]

Beyond ideological concerns, effective birth control is dependent on technological advances in areas as unrelated as human physiology, surgery, and rubber manufacturing in conjunction with policy decisions at various levels within religious and governmental groups.[17] Ultimately, however, birth control and hence population control rests on the private sexual attitudes and practices of individuals.[6] It is, therefore, necessary that we learn as much as possible about the determinants of what people know about conception and contraception, what they believe about family size and parenthood, and what they do and fail to do in their sexual interactions to influence the fertilization process.

REFERENCES

1. Asimov, I. Colonizing the heavens. *Saturday Review,* 1975, **2** (20), 12–13, 15–17.
2. Astrachan, A. "People are the most precious." *Saturday Review/World,* 1974, **2** (3), 10, 58–59.
3. Baron, R. A., & Byrne, D. *Social psychology: Understanding human interaction.* Boston: Allyn & Bacon, 1977.
4. Bermant, G. Response latencies of female rats during sexual intercourse. *Science,* 1961, **133**, 1771–1773.

5. Berscheid, E., & Walster, E. A little bit about love. In T. L. Huston (Ed.), *Foundations of interpersonal attraction.* New York: Academic Press, 1974.

6. Blake, J. The teenage birth control dilemma and public opinion. *Science,* 1973, **180**, 708–712.

7. Broverman, I. K., Vogel, S. R., Broverman, D. M., Clarkson, F. E., & Rosenkrantz, P. S. Sex-role stereotypes: A current appraisal. *Journal of Social Issues,* 1972, **28**, 59–78.

8. Byrne, D. Response to attitude similarity-dissimilarity as a function of affiliation need. *Journal of Personality,* 1962, **30**, 164–177.

9. Byrne, D. *The attraction paradigm.* New York: Academic Press, 1971.

10. Byrne, D. Learning from Andy Hardy. *Sexual Behavior,* 1972, **2** (12), 34.

11. Byrne, D., Cherry, F., Lamberth, J., & Mitchell, H. E. Husband-wife similarity in response to erotic stimuli. *Journal of Personality,* 1973, **41**, 385–394.

12. Byrne, D., Ervin, C. R., & Lamberth, J. Continuity between the experimental study of attraction and real-life computer dating. *Journal of Personality and Social Psychology,* 1970, **16**, 157–165.

13. Byrne, D., & Rhamey, R. Magnitude of positive and negative reinforcements as a determinant of attraction. *Journal of Personality and Social Psychology,* 1965, **2**, 884–889.

14. Coale, A. J. The history of human population. *Scientific American,* 1974, **231** (3), 40–51.

15. Comfort, A. *The joy of sex.* New York: Crown, 1972.

16. Dion, K., Berscheid, E., & Walster, E. What is beautiful is good. *Journal of Personality and Social Psychology,* 1972, **24**, 285–290.

17. Djerassi, C. Birth control after 1984. *Science,* 1970, **169**, 941–951.

18. Eastman, W. F. First intercourse. *Sexual Behavior,* 1972, **2** (3), 22–27.

19. Freedman, R., & Berelson, B. The human population. *Scientific American,* 1974, **231** (3), 30–39.

20. Gordon, M., & Shankweiler, P. J. Different equals less: Female sexuality in recent marriage manuals. *Journal of Marriage and the Family,* 1971, **33**, 459–466.

21. Gouaux, C. Induced affective states and interpersonal attraction. *Journal of Personality and Social Psychology,* 1971, **20**, 37–43.

22. Griffitt, W. Environmental effects on interpersonal affective behavior: Ambient effective temperature and attraction. *Journal of Personality and Social Psychology,* 1970, **15**, 240–244.

23. Griffitt, W. Response to erotica and the projection of response to erotica in the opposite sex. *Journal of Experimental Research in Personality,* 1973, **6**, 330–338.

24. Griffitt, W., & Veitch, R. Hot and crowded: Influences of population density and temperature on interpersonal affective behavior. *Journal of Personality and Social Psychology,* 1971, **17**, 92–98.

25. Heilbroner, R. L. *An inquiry into the human prospect.* New York: Norton, 1974.

26. Holden, C. World population: U.N. on the move but grounds for optimism are scant. *Science,* 1974, **183**, 833–836.

27. Hunt, M. *Sexual behavior in the 1970's.* Chicago: Playboy Press, 1974.

28. Jazwinski, C., & Byrne, D. Watching a skin-flick: Sex differences in affect, evaluations, and attributions. Unpublished manuscript, Purdue University, 1976.

29. Jobes, P. An empirical study of short-term mass communication saturation and perception of population problems. *Journal of Sex Research,* 1973, **9**, 342–352.

30. Lamm, R. D. Urban growing pains: is bigger also better? *The New Republic,* 1971, **164** (23), 17–19.

31. Mead, M. *Sex and temperament in three primitive societies.* New York: Morrow, 1935.

32. Pierre, J. T., & Muttall, R. L. Self-paced sexual behavior in the female rat. *Journal of Comparative and Physiological Psychology,* 1961, **54**, 310–313.

33. Rosenfeld, S. S. What happened to "America the Beneficent"? *Saturday Review/World,* 1973, **1** (8), 14–19.

34. Rosenman, M. F. Resistance to family planning centers in the black community. *JSAS Catalogue of Selected Documents in Psychology,* 1973, 82, MS. No. 410.

35. Rothschild, E. Running out of food. *New York Review of Books,* 1974, **21** (14), 30–32.

36. Rubin, Z. From liking to loving: Patterns of attraction in dating relationships. In T. L. Huston (Ed.), *Foundations of interpersonal attraction.* New York: Academic Press, 1974.

37. Sklar, J., & Berkov, B. Abortion, illegitimacy, and the American birth rate. *Science,* 1974, **185**, 909–915.

38. Sklar, J., & Berkov, B. The American birth rate: Evidences of a coming rise. *Science,* 1975, **189**, 693–700.

39. Tyner, C. V. Birth rates rebound. *Not Man Apart,* 1975, **5** (11), 18.

40. Veitch, R., & Griffitt, W. Good news—bad news: Affective and interpersonal effects. *Journal of Applied Social Psychology,* 1976, **6**, 69–75.

41. Walster, E. Passionate love. In B. I. Murstein (Ed.), *Theories of attraction and love.* New York: Springer, 1971.

CHAPTER SIX

Male Sexuality and Female Sexuality

Lust, Latency and Love:
Simian Secrets of Successful Sex

As has been discussed earlier, much has happened to alter the traditional view that males and females are totally different creatures, especially in their sexual needs and interests. One difficulty with any such dramatic change in knowledge and opinion is that there tends to be an overcompensation as the pendulum swings too far. That is, there is currently the inclination to assert that there are *no* sex differences of any kind or—more dramatically—that females have much stronger sexual desires and much greater sexual capacity than males. Though you may see some of these new exaggerations from time to time even in this book, in calmer moments we all know that the truth probably lies somewhere inbetween the old notions of nonsexual females and the new notions of the sexually voracious superwomen.

One way to approach the reality of sex differences is by examining animal behavior. In the following article, the distinguished experimental psychologist Harry Harlow presents some fascinating insights into the developmental process as observed among the male and female monkeys in his laboratory. In addition to describing the way that primate sexual development occurs in the absence of cultural inhibitions, Professor Harlow also points out many aspects of Freud's psychosexual stages that are revealed among these animals, though not always in precisely the way that Freud reconstructed them in his theoretical writings. Finally, you will find that important data and meaningful theory can be presented in a very amusing way by one of the most erudite humorists of our profession.

Lust, Latency and Love:
Simian Secrets of Successful Sex

Harry F. Harlow

I would like to dedicate this presentation to Sigmund Freud, in spite of the fact that he believed love developed from sex when, actually, all of our work, and probably all the work of others, shows that successful sex develops from love, or rather from multiple forms of antecedent love.

Returning to Freud, I have long insisted that he was the greatest social scientist of the twentieth century. Furthermore, in view of the present pace of the progress of psychiatric research, Freud will undoubtedly also go down in history as the greatest psychiatric scientist in the twenty-first century.

Reprinted in an edited version from: Harlow, H. F. Lust, latency and love: Simian secrets of successful sex. *Journal of Sex Research*, 1975, **11**, 79–90.

One of Freud's many contributions was that of his developmental stages. Other scientists have contributed other developmental stages not nearly as earthy, but, much as I may disagree with Freud on many basic facts, I still feel that it is a shame he never observed monkeys. For instance, consider monkeys and Freud's first developmental stage—the oral. Infant monkeys are mighty, mobile, mouthing machines. Neonatal monkeys suck with incestuous ingenuity and aphrodisiacal propensity. All available engulfable structures are tested and tasted not only to the fullest, but even to the fulsome. Incidentally, my personal research discloses that only 1 out of every 50 persons accurately defines the word "fulsome." I do not know whether the real meaning was forgotten or repressed. Orality, or at least oral opportunity, is illustrated clearly in Figures 6-1 and 6-2, and I need not name the engulfable structures. Honest, honorable onanism is more masculine than feminine, but this may be an anatomical accident. Penile pride is omni-evident, whereas clitoral culmination is more cleverly concealed and does not lend itself as easily to accidental acceleration. However, the marvels of masturbation are not denied to either sex.

Primate boys and girls are anatomically different, but they differ just as much in their antics and acrobatics as in their anatomy. The antics

Figure 6-1.   Satisfying the oral need.

Figure 6-2. The marvels of masturbation.

and acrobatics are more easily observed than the anatomical. The conjunctive combination of both the oral and the phallic stages is shown in Figure 6-3 by a magnificently mechanically minded male monkey. This combination does not mean that the oral and phallic stages are not really separate. It probably just means that the monkeys have not read Freud.

Another bisexual infantile implementation is that of infant thrusting. This masturbatory machination is bisexual, although more common in the male than in the female. Furthermore, this behavior has been both observed and documented in infant man as well as infant monkey. Human mothers seem loathe to admit the existence of this behavior, but the monkey mothers suffer no sense of such sullen shame. The differential, developmental evidence of thrusting in male and female monkeys has indicated much more thrusting behavior among males than among females. Perhaps the male thrusts and the female trusts.

Freud's second stage was the anal stage, which I always assumed was a cultural rather than a biological stage. Eibl-Eibesfeldt long ago classified mammals as placers or spreaders, in terms of their personal fecal fielding proprieties. Cats and dogs and pigs are placers, but mon-

Figure 6-3.   The conjunctive combination of the oral and the phallic stage.

keys and children are spreaders. From this fact results the Freudian classification of analytic anal activities.

Before we analyze Freud's anal stage, it can be described as a special language where every little meaning has a movement all its own. It may also be described as a phase of sphincter thinking. Even in the subhuman form it may achieve elegance and excellence and may be the precursor of anal art, characterized by finger painting in both the monkey and the human child.

Freud emphasized anal aggression, a thesis in which he was anticipated about 20 million years earlier by chimpanzees who developed aggressive anal eroticism to a high degree. More recently, there is the story of the Yerkes chimpanzee, Nancy, who was a liberated female. Endowed with female finesse, Nancy spent many of her creative hours huddled in the back of her cage manufacturing and collecting ammunition, which she stored in her right and righteous hand. Nancy's greatest achievement in feral finger painting came when eight girls from a local convent school visited the Yerkes laboratory all dressed up in their most fetching organdy gowns. Nancy patiently waited until the girls lined up in perilous proximity in front of her cage. It was a massacre. No dress and no girl escaped, and Nancy retired to the back of her cage self-satisfied, uttering the inarticulate laugh of a happy chimpanzee.

As our monkeys approached and achieved this anal stage, which might be called the frightening, fecal foundation stage, we observed an interesting phenomenon. The infants that were raised with real living mothers never soiled the ventral surface of the mother's body. The infants raised on cloth surrogates did not differentiate between the mother and the bathroom. Surrogate surface laundering became a major project as the anal stage developed. Fortunately this stage passed as the infants gradually left the surrogate to seek solace with age-mate companions.

Don't soil a mother
Instead choose some other,
For mothers are faultless and pure.
Though anal expression
Is not a transgression,
The feces have limited lure.

Freud's third stage was the phallic stage, and he divided this into male and female form as the basis of this breathtaking discovery that the reproductive organs of the male and the female are structurally different. Freud, and especially Freud's followers, emphasized the pleasurable sensations to be derived from stimulation of these differentiated genital parts. Simian studies do not support the separation and timing of Freud's oral, anal, and phallic stages. Monkey masturbation, for instance, makes its early entrance along with the oral stage and continues from beginning to end.

Of even more importance is the fact that Freud did not discover that the very basic behavior patterns of the male and female differed significantly and statistically from early infancy onward. These differentiated male-female behavior patterns are sex-determined patterns, whether or not they are primary sexual patterns. These patterns were not discovered by us during any study of sex. The maturation of basic behaviors was the theme of our studies and sex differences were a fringe benefit, perhaps one of the finest fringe benefits ever to be uncovered.

We are now in a position to discuss freely and frankly the biological basis of the latency period without resort to whether or not Freud's beautiful beatitudes are true or false. We describe the latency period in terms of facts, rather than feelings, and find it unnecessary to formulate such tenuous constructs as the Oedipus complex, Electra complex, castration anxiety, penis envy, and castration fear. Of course it is possible that man has all of these problems, whether or not they really exist.

The latency period, during which each sex cleaves to its own and avoids the opposite sex, probably is present in more definitive form in monkeys than in man. This fact would bother Freud, because the monkey latency period cannot possibly be ascribed to genital jealousy or father fear. Monkey fathers are unwept, unhonored, unsung, and practically unknown to the infant monkeys. There is no Electra mechanism, since female monkeys cannot be emotionally attached to fathers they have never seen.

It should be perfectly clear that the latency stage is not a form of psychic pathology but, or instead, a guarantee of psychic perpetuity. Sexual secrets and sexual surcease are the heritage of birth. From then onward the sexes pursue different roads, and, at the proper times, the sexes pursue each other.

Three sex-distinguishing behaviors will be described and illustrated. A female pattern of passivity is essentially complete by 2 months of age. Another female pattern is that of rigidity, where the female retreats from the male, assumes a rigid posture, and waits for the turn of events. It illustrates the maxim, "They also serve who only stand and wait." A male pattern, that of threat, is sexually differentiating by 3 months of age. Threat is a basic male pattern underlying many other masculine behavioral forms. Now we have had occasional female monkeys that threaten males, just as there are occasional atypical human females that threaten males.

More complex sex distinctive activities subsequently develop. Later maturing sex behaviors are almost always appropriate to biological sex and become progressively more appropriate with advancing age. This is one of the few fringe benefits of love. Grooming is a female behavior in monkeys and the human analogues are obvious. Of the greatest social importance is the gradual sex differentiation of play. Both males and females increase in play behavior over time, with males showing more of such activity, but the striking data are those contrasting the development of rough-and-tumble play in the two sexes. This sexual separation is not a function of castration anxiety or penis envy. As we have already emphasized, the male becomes progressively rougher and the female more passive with increasing maturational age, and play capability and compatibility is sexually separated.

Sexually differentiating biological behaviors separate the girls from the boys in both monkeys and man. Although threatening is a masculine trait, we have occasionally observed threatening in some atypical female monkeys. As we have said, no doubt the same phenomenon is found in the human species, but fortunately most threatening females become cultural anthropologists and seldom pose difficult problems. These behaviors might be thought of as characterizing not only the latency period but also Freud's phallic stage. In deference to the importance of play as an antecedent to heterosexual success, however, the stage should be called the frolic, not the phallic.

Since play is the primary age-mate bonding mechanism and little boys and girls do play apart because they prefer to play differently, females and males grow apart and live separate lives until a mysterious mechanism called sex rears its ugly head or buttocks or both. It may be enhanced or hidden by cultural concomitants, but it cannot be forsaken. If Freud had possessed the same data, I am sure he would have been the first to agree. Freud liked biological data even if they could not be achieved by way of introspection or free association.

Early faltering and fitful erotic explorations may be more wistful than wanton, but even these early behaviors tend to be appropriately sex coded. The sexlike responses of the very immature male are masculine in form and the sexlike responses of the immature female are feminine in form, if not in function.

The basic heterosexual heritage of socially inexperienced or socially isolated infant monkeys are often appropriate in intent, though hopeless in achievement. This is demonstrated by a male in Figure 6-4 who was a

Figure 6-4.   Sexual approach by a socially inexperienced infant monkey.

charter member of our head start program. When this foil failed, he mounted the female laterally and thrust sidewise, a posture which left him totally at cross purposes with reality. At least the motions were made, even if the behavior was meaningless. In complementary fashion, Figure 6-5 shows a socially isolated female inadequately responding to a determined male. Unfortunately, throughout the affair, she looked lovingly into the male's eyes while sitting flat on the floor. This was a posture in which only her heart was in the right place, but at least it was a feminine heart. Thus it is perfectly obvious that even immature and abnormal sex patterns may differentiate the two sexes. Pubertal probing characterizes the males, even though the results are totally inadequate and immature. Contrariwise, early sex behaviors of female infants are caricatures of adult female functions. Furthermore, it is obvious that the females are doing better than the males—a phenomenon not entirely surprising.

Figure 6-5. The inadequate response of a loving but inexperienced female.

I have often been asked if monkey data generalize to man. It is impossible to prove this is true and equally impossible to prove that it is not true. The best I can do is let you make your own judgments. For comparative purposes I offer you Figure 6-6, which illustrates that human boys should not go to dancing school too long.

Once significant bisexual signposts have been biologically achieved, they tend to be formalized and accentuated by cultural variables. Biology, however, is always first and culture is always second.

Figure 6-6. Significant biological signposts tend to be accentuated by cultural variables.

Responses to Reading Erotic Stories: Male-Female Differences

Decades of survey research and centuries of prevailing wisdom have taught us that males and females are very different in their sexual needs, in the kinds of stimuli that elicit sexual arousal, and in their arousability. During the past few years, as the experimental study of male and female sexuality has gradually become respectable, laboratory findings such as those in the following article consistently indicate that the two sexes are remarkably similar. The cultural norms have been such that it was unacceptable for females freely to express their sexuality or even to reveal a frank interest in erotic books or movies. These norms are changing, and the following investigation demonstrates that young males and females are equally aroused by reading a sexual story, as evidenced both verbally and physiologically. In fact, one of the few sex differences reported by these investigators was that the female subjects reported a *greater* increase in sexual activity, sexual tension, and sexual desire in the 24 hours after reading the story than was true for the males. Among the other myths about sex differences is the supposed female requirement for affection and tenderness in erotica in order to become aroused; in this study, a purely sexual story and an affectionate sexual story had almost identical effects on both males and females.

Responses to Reading Erotic Stories: Male-Female Differences

Gunter Schmidt, Volkmar Sigusch,
and Siegrid Schäfer

In two earlier experiments,[13,16] we examined sex differences in the emotional and sexual responses to slides, slide series, and films, explicitly sexual in content. This article presents the results of a third experiment which was basically designed parallel to the first two and in which we utilized erotic stories as stimuli. We were interested in testing whether or not we could find the same results with narrative stimuli as we had previously gained with pictorial stimuli. In addition, we sought an answer to the question of whether the extent of sex differences in response to erotic materials is dependent on the degree of affection expressed in the stimuli.

Reprinted in an edited version from: Schmidt, G., Sigusch, V., & Schäfer, S. Responses to reading erotic stories: Male-female differences. *Archives of Sexual Behavior*, 1973, **2**, 181–199.

METHOD

The sample was composed of 120 male and 120 female students of the University of Hamburg who volunteered to participate in an experiment involving "psychosexual stimulation." Most of the subjects were single, had had coital experience, were members of Protestant faiths, and were in their early 20s. The male and female samples were highly comparable with respect to age, marital status, denomination, and coital experience.

Stimuli

As stimuli, two stories with sexual themes were utilized which we had prepared for this experiment and in which we used excerpts from the writings of John Cleland, D. H. Lawrence, Mary McCarthy, Henry Miller, and Hubert Selby as well as sections from lesser-known sex literature.

In both stories, sexual experience between a young couple was

Table 6-1
Text Samples of the Stories Used as Stimuli

Story I (without affection)	Story II (with affection)
1. They walked for a long time in silence. Then he took her in his arms, and she pressed her body against his, so that they couldn't move anymore. . . . "You're pretty great, he said . . . "You don't want anybody to stare into your eyes and say a lot of deep and fine things about love. You're hot for me and I'm hot for you! That's all."	1. They walked for a long time in silence. Neither of them seemed to notice where. He took her into his arms. She cuddled up to him, pressed herself against his body. Now he wrapped his arms about her tightly, so tightly that they couldn't move at all. His tongue ran tenderly across her lips. . . . "I like you," he said. . . . "You don't want anybody to stare into your eyes and say a lot of deep and fine things. You just love me and I love you and that's all."
2. He shoved his cock into her. He felt his sperm spurting into her hot cunt, he arched his back, shuddered groaning, and lay down on her breathing heavily and exhausted. When he pulled it out and slid down beside her, the two glowing, sweat-covered bodies glued to each other separated. It was warm in the room, and the sweat still lay on his forehead. She lay there stretched out with her hand on his cock. . . . Both of them yielded to their limpness and passivity.	2. He thrust his member into her. He felt his sperm flow into her hot vagina, he arched his back, shuddered moaning, and lay down on her breathing heavily and exhausted. Tenderly he kissed her and stroked her arms. When he slid from her slowly and softly, two glowing, sweat-covered bodies glued to each other separated. It was warm in the room, and the sweat still lay on his forehead. After they had lain there for a while in silence he asked her softly how it had been, and she answered that it was the most delightful and beautiful thing there was.

described. Flirting, petting, and foreplay including oral-genital stimulation, coitus in various positions, orgasm, and postcoital behavior were described in detail. In preparing the texts, we were careful to make sure that, in contrast to much of pornographic literature, in both stories the man and the woman displayed sexual initiative and activity, pleasure, and satisfaction to the same degree.

The two stories did not differ in the actual plot or in the description of specific sexual activities. They did, however, differ in the degree to which any affection was expressed. Story I (without affection) made it completely clear that the partners are bound together solely by their common sexual experience. This was emphasized by the use of four-letter words, which tend to create the impression of sexuality isolated from affection. Story II (with affection) described a closer integration of sexual and affectionate desires. To demonstrate the differences between the two stories, we have provided corresponding samples of the two texts in Table 6-1. It is clear from these samples that it was *not* a ques-

---

Table 6-1 (continued)
Text Samples of the Stories Used as Stimuli

	Thus they lay there silently, enchanted by one another, with their hands on each other's genitals. Their limbs locked together, they gazed at one another, caressing each other with their eyes. From time to time he kissed her mouth, her throat, her breasts. . . . Both of them yielded to the pleasantness of their limpness and passivity.
3. Exhausted and completely satisfied, they fell apart. He turned over and reached for a cigarette. That was a good fuck, he thought.	3. After the orgasm which caused both of them to shudder, they lay there completely satisfied, happily exhausted. Although he knew, he asked her again how it had been. "It was good, it was so good," she whispered tenderly. That made him happy, but he said nothing, only kissed her softly, lay down next to her, and pulled her close to himself. She laid her head on his shoulder, wrapped her leg around his leg, and then she fell silent, devoid of thoughts. And he was still with her, lying there next to her in the same silence.

Two stories were prepared so that subjects read either a purely sexual theme or a story that combined sex and affection. The first example is taken from the first part of the stories, the second example is taken from the middle of the stories, and the last example constitutes the last paragraph of the respective stories. Examples represent parts of the two stories where there were especially marked differences.

tion of a hard-core sex story on the one hand and a love story on the other hand. On the contrary, both stories centered around sexual activities and differed only to the degree with which sexuality is practiced with affection.

Procedure

The experiments were carried out in two stages:

1. The subject was provided with one of the stories in an individual session. Half of the subjects read Story I, the other half read Story II. Subjects were asked to read the story "in leisure." While reading the story, the subjects rated their own sexual arousal and their favorable-unfavorable reaction to the story. They then evaluated their "present feelings" on a semantic differential. (The subjects had previously filled out the same semantic differential prior to reading the story.) The rating scales and the semantic differential were given to the subjects at the beginning of the experiment so that they could judge their reactions immediately after reading without any added intervention on the part of the experimenter.

2. At the end of the first stage of the experiment, subjects were given a sealed envelope containing a questionnaire. They were asked to fill out the questionnaire 24 hours after having read the story. The importance of keeping to this interval was stressed. The questionnaire contained the same questions regarding sexual behavior and sexual reactions during the 24 hours after reading the stories and during the 24 hours before reading the stories. In addition, the subjects stated their emotional reactions while reading the stories. Finally, the questionnaire gathered data concerning personal background and sexual history of the subjects.

For the female subjects, a woman carried out the experiments, and a male experimenter was used for the men. The anonymity of all answers was guaranteed.

RESULTS

Ratings of sexual arousal and favorable-unfavorable response

Immediately upon having read the story, subjects evaluated on 9-point scales how strongly they were stimulated and whether the story had created a favorable response.

The mean stimulation ratings for men and women varied between 5.2 and 6.0 (Table 6-2); thus the subjects described their own sexual arousal as somewhat greater than "moderate."

The variable "affection-without affection" in the stories had roughly the same significance for sexual arousal for both sexes.

The mean favorable-unfavorable ratings varied between 3.6 and

Table 6-2
Mean Ratings of Sexual Arousal

Group	Males	Females	Total
Story I (without affection)	5.4	5.2	5.3
Story II (with affection)	6.0	5.4	5.7
Total	5.7	5.4	

On a 9-point scale, subjects indicated how sexually aroused they felt value, high sexual arousal. Males and females were equally aroused after reading the story. Low value indicates low sexual arousal; high by the sexual story without affection and the sexual story involving affection. The values in the table indicate self-ratings somewhat greater than "moderate."

5.4 (Table 6-3), i.e., ranged between "neutral" and "somewhat favorable." Both sex and type of story significantly influenced the ratings: men evaluated the stories more positively than women; the story "with affection" was evaluated more positively than the story "without affection" by both the men and women. Yet the type of story affected the ratings to a greater degree than did sex. The differences for both sexes were roughly the same and were not dependent on whether the story was affectionate.

Emotional reactions while reading the stories

Using a semantic differential containing a total of 24 items, the subjects were asked to describe their "present feelings" both before reading the story and immediately upon finishing it. A comparison of the answers

Table 6-3
Mean Ratings of Favorable-Unfavorable Response

Group	Males	Females	Total
Story I (without affection)	5.0	5.4	5.2
Story II (with affection)	3.6	4.3	4.0
Total	4.3	4.9	

On a 9-point scale, subjects indicated how favorably or unfavorably they responded to the story. Low value indicates favorable response; high value, unfavorable response. Males liked the stories slightly more than females. Both sexes liked the story with affection better than the story containing only sex. The values in the table indicate "somewhat favorable" ratings for the affection story and "neutral" ratings for the story without affection.

before the experiment and immediately after provides us with information on the spontaneous reactions generated through confrontation with
the stimuli.

After reading either Story I or Story II, both the men and the
women were *more emotionally activated and agitated* (more excited,
aggressive, cheerful, impulsive, wild, emotional, and less inhibited) and
revealed *greater emotional instability and emotional tension* (more in-
nerly agitated, more quarrelsome, shocked, jumpier, irritated, driven,
numbed), and to a lesser degree they also revealed *emotional avoidance
reactions* (more repelled, disgusted).

We calculated the difference between the "before" and "after" ratings, and found sex differences for 8 of the 24 items: the women were
more strongly repelled after reading the story, more disgusted, more
shocked, more quarrelsome, and more irritated than men. Men, on the
other hand, after reading the story became more gregarious, more
driven, and more impulsive. Within the total pattern of activation-
instability-avoidance, the women revealed a greater tendency toward
avoidance reactions, and to a lesser degree increased emotional instability, whereas the men revealed a greater tendency toward activation.

For the main effect of *type of story*, we came up with significant
results for only 1 of the 24 items, this being that the subjects were more
strongly repelled by Story I (without affection) than by Story II. Thus
in general, the type of story had only a slight influence if any at all on
the emotional reactions of the subjects, as tested by the semantic differential.

For none of the 24 items was there any significant *interaction* between sex and type of story. This means that the differences in emotional reactions to sex stories were not influenced by the fact that the
stories did or did not contain affectional components.

Physiological-sexual reactions while reading the stories

Tables 6-4 and 6-5 summarize the data provided by the subjects concerning physiological-sexual reactions experienced during the experiment. For obvious reasons, we had to limit our questions to those
reactions that the subjects themselves could easily and reliably detect.

Roughly 90% of the men registered at least slight or moderate erections during the reading of the stories; one-fourth of them had a full
erection. One-sixth of the male subjects reported a preejaculatory emission. Two of the 120 subjects experienced ejaculation; one instance was
spontaneous, the other was masturbation induced. Statistically, the type
of story did not have a significant influence on the sexual-physiological
reactions experienced while reading the story.

Among the women, the most common type of physiological-sexual
reaction while reading the story was genital sensations, with four-fifth
of the women reporting such sensations. One-fourth of the women

Table 6-4
Male Physiological-Sexual Reactions while Reading the Stories

	Story I (without affection) (%)	Story II (with affection) (%)	Total (%)
1. Preejaculatory emission			
Don't know	15	23	19
No	73	57	65
Yes	12	20	16
2. Erection			
None	12	7	9
Slight, moderate	65	67	66
Full	23	27	25
3. Ejaculation			
No	97	100	98
Yes	3	0	2

Most of the male subjects reported some degree of erection while reading the stories, one-sixth reported a preejaculatory emission, and two experienced ejaculation. These response patterns were similar for the two types of sexual stories.

Table 6-5
Female Physiological-Sexual Reactions while Reading the Stories

	Story I (without affection) (%)	Story II (with affection) (%)	Total (%)
1. Vaginal lubrication			
Don't know	13	18	16
No	60	52	57
Yes	27	28	28
2. Genital sensations of warmth, pulsation, or itching			
Don't know	2	7	4
No	17	15	16
Yes	82	78	80
3. Sensations in the breasts			
Don't know	8	7	8
No	83	85	84
Yes	8	8	8
4. Orgasm			
No	98	100	99
Yes	2	0	1

Most of the female subjects reported genital sensations while reading the stories, over one-fourth reported vaginal lubrication, less than 10% indicated sensations in the breast, and one subject masturbated to orgasm. As with males, response patterns were similar for the two types of sexual stories.

experienced vaginal lubrication; one-tenth experienced sensations in the breasts. One of the 120 female subjects had an orgasm while reading the story which was masturbation induced. Statistically, the type of story appeared to have no significant influence for the female subjects either. The sexual-physiological reactions among the women, as was the case among the men, while reading the story without affection were as great as they were while reading the story with affection.

The observed sexual-physiological reactions among the men and women are not directly comparable because of the differing anatomical substrates. Thus it is not possible to provide an exact analysis of sex differences for this area. However, it is significant and important for the discussion of sex differences in psychosexual stimulation to note the fact that the *overwhelming majority* of both the women and the men registered physical correlates of sexual arousal while reading the stories.

Masturbatory activity while reading the stories

Masturbatory activity was defined as "stimulation of the genitals, for example, by touching them through or beneath the clothing, by pressure from the thighs, by pressing the genitals against objects." Roughly between one-sixth and one-fifth of the men and women reported such activity. Sex differences and differences between the stories were no significant. The same number of men and women tended to transfer the sexual arousal induced by reading the stories to active genital stimulation, and both the story with and the story without affection instigated this activity to the same extent.

Obviously, in most cases masturbatory activity was only transient and not particularly intensive, because only one male and one female subject achieved a masturbation-induced orgasm.

Sexual behavior in the 24-hour period
after reading the stories

On the day after the experiment, we asked the subjects about their sexual behavior and sexual reactions in the 24 hours after the experiment and in the 24 hours before the experiment. By comparing these data, we can estimate whether and to what extent reading the stories influenced sexual behavior.

There was no statistically significant difference between the two stories. Thus the affectionate and the nonaffectionate stories did not have differing influence on the type and degree of sexual behavior changes in the 24 hours after reading the stories.

Thus, to simplify the matter, we can limit the description of our results to the aggregate data for Stories I and II. According to this, there were significant changes among the female subjects for 8 of the 11 items: they revealed an increase in coital activity in the 24 hours after

he experiment as compared to the 24 hours before the experiment, and
he same applied to the number of orgasms, sexual fantasy activity,
arousability through external stimuli, number of talks about sex, and
tendency to look at texts, pictures, and/or films that are sexual in content. In addition, sexual tensions and the wish for sexual activity increased significantly. Only with respect to masturbation, sexual dreams,
and attendance at discotheques in the 24 hours after narrative stimulation were no significant changes found in the behavior.

For the male subjects there were significant differences for only 5
of the 11 items. There were measurable changes in their behavior in the
24-hour period following the experiment with respect to activation and/
or an increase of sexual fantasy, talks about sex, reading and/or watching books, films, and pictures with sexual content, attendance at discotheques and/or bars in quest of sexual activity.

Thus reading the stories evoked a general activation of sexual behavior in the 24-hour period after the experiment (significant only for
the women) and, to a greater extent, an activation of sexual fantasy and
sexual drive. The changes, however, were only slight (behavior) to
moderate (fantasy, drive) and observable only among a minority of the
subjects.

In analyzing the sex differences, we checked the ratio of increase/
decrease in a certain type of behavior during the 24 hours following the
reading of the story as compared to the 24 hours before. Here we found
significant changes for three items: there was a greater increase in sexual
activity, in sexual tension, and in the wish for sexual activity among the
women than among the men on the day following the experiment. Thus
the sexual activity of females appeared to be more highly activated in
the 24-hour period following narrative activation than was that of the
male subjects.

DISCUSSION

Our experiment on the emotional and sexual responses to erotic stories
by men and women generally corroborates the results obtained in two
previous experiments[13,16] using pictorial stimuli:

1. Narrative sexual stimuli, like pictorial stimuli, generate sexual
   arousal which is rated on average as "moderate," and physical correlates of this arousal are consciously perceived by the majority of
   the subjects. In the 24 hours following the confrontation with the
   stimuli, a slight to moderate activation of sexual behavior, sexual
   fantasy, and sexual appetency results among both men and women.
   The nonsexual emotional responses of both the men and women
   consist basically of a general emotional activation and increased
   emotional instability and emotional avoidance reactions.
2. The above-mentioned responses are roughly the same for both men

and women whether subjected to narrative or pictorial stimuli. Where significant sex differences do arise, they represent only specific accentuations within a general pattern. In this vein, the male emotional response to sexual materials is more characterized by activation, that of the women is characterized more by instability and avoidance. The subjective evaluation of sexual arousal is slightly higher among males (however, this is not significant for narrative stimuli), whereas the females are slightly more sexually activated than the men during the 24 hours following the experiment (this is particularly true for the narrative stimuli).

The slight differences in the responses of men and women to narrative and pictorial stimuli have also been recorded in a number of experiments conducted among American students and married couples as well as married Danish students. According to these data, the average ratings of sexual arousal are only slightly higher among males than among females,[8,9,10,11] equally high among men and women *on the whole*, differing only for *special* topics[1,4,5,6] or indeed higher for women than for men.[6] Both the majority of males and females register physiological sexual reactions upon confrontation with sexual stimuli.[8,9,10] None of the experiments record differing sex-specific effects of sexual stimuli with respect to sexual behavior, sexual fantasy, or sexual drive on the day following the experiment.[8,9,10] The sex differences in emotional responses to stimuli are slight;[1] where differences are found, relatively stronger activation and approach tendencies are recorded for males[10]— much the same as in our experiment—and relatively stronger negative and avoidance reactions are recorded for females.[4,9,10,11]

In contrast to the findings of Kinsey et al.,[7] which assume major sex differences in the arousability by explicitly sexual pictorial and narrative stimuli on the basis of retrospective data provided by their interviewees, more recent experiments in the United States and Europe reveal only slight differences in the sexual and emotional responses to such stimuli. We have previously subjected this discrepancy between older results and more recent ones to a relatively detailed discussion.[13] Here we prefer to comment briefly on the significance of the variable "affection" with respect to responses to narrative stimuli.

It is generally assumed, and surveys on sexual behavior unanimously corroborate,[2,3,14,15] that the sexuality of women in Western societies is more dependent on affection than is that of men. This could lead to the assumption that the degree of sex differences in reactions to narrative (or pictorial) stimuli is dependent on the extent to which affection is expressed in such stimuli. According to our findings, this is not the case: the sex differences are equally slight for stories with and without expressions of affection; the stories with and without affection do not have a significantly differing effect on men or women.

It is possible to argue that the stories which we used did not differ sufficiently with respect to "affection." Our attempt to provide stories with the same content and approximately the same length necessarily limited the variation open to us with respect to the dimension "affectional-nonaffectional." In interpreting our results, it is important to keep in mind that neither of the two stories was a "love story" or "romantic story"; on the contrary, both stories contained detailed descriptions of a sexual experience, and they differed only in that in one of them more tenderness is expressed during sexual activity. Thus we cannot exclude the possibility of achieving greater differentiation in sex-specific responses using stories in which the emotional and social relationships of a couple are described in the same detail as sexual activities.

While it is true that our experiments do not provide any information about sex differences for stories which have a greater affectional component than ours, our data do permit another conclusion: affection is not a necessary precondition for women to react sexually to sexual stimuli in the same manner as men. Even for stories that describe sexual relations in detail excluding and avoiding any expressions of tenderness and affection (Story I), sexual arousal and sexual activation among females are as great as among males. This finding tends to refute the claim that female sexuality is basically more dependent on affection than male sexuality.

REFERENCES

1. Byrne, D., & Lamberth, J. The effect of erotic stimuli on sex arousal, evaluative responses, and subsequent behavior. In *Technical report of the Commission on Obscenity and Pornography*. Vol. 8. Washington, D. C.: U. S. Government Printing Office, 1971.

2. Christensen, H .T. Scandinavian and American sex norms: Some comparisons with sociological implications. *Journal of Social Issues*, 1966, **22**, 60–75.

3. Ehrmann, W. W. *Premarital dating behavior*. New York: Holt, Rinehart & Winston, 1959.

4. Griffitt, W. Response to erotica and the projection of response to erotica in the opposite sex. *Journal of Experimental Research in Personality*, 1973, **6**, 330–338.

5. Griffitt, W., Veitch, R., & Littlepage, G. Erotic arousal and interpersonal behavior: Influences on interpersonal attraction. Kansas State University, Manhattan (mimeographed).

6. Jakobovits, L. A. Evaluational reactions to erotic literature. *Psychological Reports*, 1966, **16**, 985–994.

7. Kinsey, A. C., Pomeroy, W. B., Martin, C. E., & Gebhard, P. H.

Sexual behavior in the human female. Philadelphia: Saunders, 1953.

8. Kutschinsky, B. The effect of pornography—an experiment on perception, attitudes, and behavior. In *Technical report of the Commission on Obscenity and Pornography.* Vol. 8. Washington, D. C.: U. S. Government Printing Office, 1971.

9. Mann, J., Sidman, J., & Starr, S. Effects of erotic films on sexual behaviors of married couples. In *Technical report of the Commission on Obscenity and Pornography.* Vol. 8. Washington, D. C.: U. S. Government Printing Office, 1971.

10. Mosher, D. L. Psychological reactions to pornographic films. In *Technical report of the Commission on Obscenity and Pornography.* Vol. 8. Washington, D. C.: U. S. Government Printing Office, 1971.

11. Mosher, D. L. Sex-guilt and reactions to pornographic films. University of Connecticut, Storrs (mimeographed).

12. Schmidt, G., & Sigusch, V. Sex differences in responses to psychosexual stimulation by films and slides. *Journal of Sex Research,* 1970, *6,* 268–283.

13. Schmidt, G., & Sigusch, V. Woman's sexual arousal. In J. Money & J. Zubin (Eds.), *Contemporary sexual behavior: Critical issues in the 1970's.* Baltimore: The Johns Hopkins Press, 1973.

14. Schofield, M. *The sexual behaviour of young people.* London: Longmans, 1965.

15. Sigusch, V., & Schmidt, G. Lower-class sexuality: Some emotional and social aspects in West German males and females. *Archives of Sexual Behavior,* 1971, *1,* 29–44.

16. Sigusch, V., Schmidt, G., Reinfeld, A., & Wiedemann-Sutor, I. Psychosexual stimulation: Sex differences. *Journal of Sex Research,* 1970, *6,* 10–24.

Male-Female Sexual Variations:
Functions of Biology or Culture?

Several phenomena have caused investigators in many different fields to reexamine the question of whether or not males and females are fundamentally different in their sexual attitudes and behavior. One such phenomenon has been the "sexual revolution." As was noted at the beginning of this book, people have been raising the possibility of widespread changes in sexual behavior at least since the end of World War II. It was pointed out that the evidence is unequivocal that standards of sexual permissiveness in books, movies, and magazines have changed rapidly and radically over these past few decades.

Actual changes in sexual behavior present a more crucial question, however, and most of the interest has been focused on female behavior. That is, males have traditionally been freer to express their sexual needs, and data on masturbation, premarital intercourse, the consumption of pornography, etc., seem to confirm the differences between the sexes. Any real sexual revolution must be spearheaded by observable changes in the behavior of females. An inescapable barrier to change would be the existence of fundamental biological differences between the sexes. As sociologist Robert Staples points out in the following article, cross-cultural anthropological data have long been available to document the fact that vast differences in "typical" male and female behavior are quite possible. These findings strongly suggest that human sexuality is overwhelmingly influenced by learning and thus it would potentially be quite possible for females in our culture to learn to behave sexually in the same fashion that males do.

Despite the increasing tolerance of society and the rhetoric of revolution, survey data for some time continued to dampen the hopes of those who wanted freely expressed sexuality, and to comfort those in the older generation who wanted their offspring (especially their female offspring) to be chaste prior to marriage. The general conclusion during the 1950s and early 1960s was that adolescents talk much more freely about sex than their parents did, but that they behave no differently than those who lived in past eras. Then, about 1965, the data began to tell a different story, and the revolution suddenly was reflected in deeds as well as words.

Male-Female Sexual Variations:
Functions of Biology or Culture?

Robert Staples

Male-female disparities in sexual attitudes and behavior are so obvious, and pervade all strata of the society, that it would be easy to assume that this is the natural order of things. However, any historical or cross-

Reprinted in an edited version from: Staples, R. Male-female sexual variations: Functions of biology or culture? *Journal of Sex Research*, 1973, **9**, 11–20.

cultural analysis would challenge many notions concerning innate difference among males and females in sexual attitudes, desire, or behavior. From both an historical and cross-cultural perspective, societies and epochs may vary greatly as to the kinds of behavior approved for different sex-role groupings. These variations reflect the fact that while male and female are biological entities, they appear to be social roles as well.[14]

According to some nineteenth-century anthropologists,[1,16] ancient societies allowed free sexual relations to prevail and the fathers of the children were unknown. Within certain tribal groupings, every woman belonged to every man, and there was unrestricted sexual intercourse between brother and sister, parent and child. In these primitive societies, there was absolute sexual equality between males and females. It was only after the emergence of private property that sexual freedom was restricted for either sex. As part of the evolution of civilization, man had to secure the faithfulness of wives in order to ensure reliability of paternal lineage. This was required because the children would later on inherit the fortunes of their fathers. Not only did this stage of civilization mark the beginning of monogamous marriages but the double standard of sexual conduct as well. Only women were expected to be strictly faithful and adultery on their part was cruelly punished.[5]

These theories and many similar ones have only historical interest today. For the most part they are now recognized as undocumented metaphysics. As Leslie[12] notes, the proposition that families everywhere have passed through similar stages or that there is any unilinear trend toward the monogamous family has long since been rendered implausible by more sophisticated anthropological study. In essence, he says, the question of family origins is lost in prehistory, and social scientists have stopped investigating a problem upon which data can never be brought to bear.

A contrasting view held by a contemporary historian[25] is that female sexual freedom has varied throughout certain periods. In pre-Christian England, for example, virginity was considered shameful, women were free to take lovers, and marriage was usually a temporary affair. During the Victorian age repression of sex reached the point where even piano legs had to be covered. As late as 1857 a law was introduced to make adultery punishable by death.

It was the thesis of this particular historian that the various changes and contrasts in European sexual behavior could be accounted for in terms of sex-role identifications. At certain periods there was a predominating tendency for male children to model themselves on their father and so to produce an authoritarian and restrictive attitude in society as a whole. This was known as the "patrist" era. In the other era, labeled "matrist," there was a tendency to model on the mother, producing a permissive attitude toward sex, freedom for women, and a high status for females in a society where sex differences were mini-mized.[25]

The historical evidence used to document the Taylor hypothesis relating to sex-role differences in sexual behavior is rather fragile. Not only is any supporting evidence lacking but Taylor's theory contains some weaknesses. One might question, for instance, how identification is relevant to sex-role differences in sexual behavior. If one identifies with a father who is nonauthoritarian and nonrestrictive, why should the individual become patrist? Additionally, identification is very akin to saying that a society has a normative structure.

We get a more credible view on the infinite possibilities of sex-role variations in sexual behavior by examining cross-cultural data. In her findings on sex temperament in three preliterate societies of New Guinea, Margaret Mead[15] concluded that "all of the personality traits which we label masculine or feminine are as lightly linked to sex as are the clothing, the manners and the form of head-dress that a society at a given period assigns to either sex [p. 191]." In essence, the differences between individuals within a culture are almost entirely attributable to differences in socialization, especially during early childhood, and the form of this socialization is culturally determined.

As an example of these culturally determined sex-role differences, Mead[15] cites her observation in the Arapesh culture:

We found no idea that sex was a powerfully driving force for men or women. In marked contrast to these attitudes, we found among the Mundugumor that both men and women developed as ruthless, aggres-sive, positively sexed individuals, with the maternal cherishing aspects of personality at a minimum. Both men and women approximated to a per-sonality type that we in our culture would find only in an undisciplined and very violent male. . . . In the third tribe, the Tchambuli, we found a genuine reversal of the sex attitudes of our own culture, with the woman the dominant, impersonal managing partner, the man the less responsible and the emotionally dependent person [p. 190].

While standardized sexual differences between the sexes may be largely cultural creations, there remains the question of the origin of these culturally determined differences. Bernard[3] suggests that women are assigned the task of supporting the existing sexual norms because of their greater sexual plasticity. She notes that a point not often con-sidered in sex differences is the greater cultural susceptibility of the female than of the male body to sexual restraints. Parenthetically, she refers to the historical documents on the relations between the sexes in Western society. Her assumption is that since female sexual responses have ranged from frigidity to lust, their bodies are more capable of adapt-ing to different norms of sexual behavior. The belief that women can tolerate sexual abstinence better than men is not proven. Reiss[19] points out that the belief that males need sex more than females has little factual basis. More likely it is due to men not trying as hard to control their sexual behavior.

In an interesting study of psychosexual development, Simon and Gagnon[23] observe that female sexual development during adolescence is so similar in all classes that it is easy to suspect that it is solely determined by biology. Nevertheless they recognize that girls in our society are not encouraged to be sexual—in fact, they may be strongly discouraged from being so. Consequently, they suggest that the protracted period of relative sexual inactivity among girls may come from repression of an elemental drive or simply from a failure to learn how to be sexual. This learning approach appeals to the authors because it defines female sexuality in terms that seem less like a projection of male sexuality. The learning answer suggests that women create or invent a capacity for sexual behavior, learning how and when to be aroused and how and when to respond.

Male-female differences in sexual attitudes and behavior, then, may be accounted for by the greater constraints and controls placed upon the female in her relationships with males and in particular upon her sexual expression. Females, to a greater degree than males, are oriented in their environment toward marriage and parenthood. They are instilled with the idea that their self-respect and the respect of others for them are contingent upon their use of restraint and discretion in sex matters. However, the culture condones, and even encourages, the expression of the male libido. Moreover, males are less specifically oriented toward marriage, parenthood, or any need for restraints in sexual behavior.[7]

These differences in the conditioning of males and females in early childhood lead to marked distinctions in sexual attitudes and behavior. In general, females are inclined to be more conservative in their attitudes and more passive in their behavior. They are more conservative and males are more liberal in their judgment as to the propriety of sexual activity for themselves and for the opposite sex.[6] Females are less likely to have engaged in premarital or extramarital sex than males. When they do engage in premarital sexual activity, they are more inclined to demand affection as a basis for their participation.[20]

Probably one of the most significant aspects of female sexuality is their slower sexual maturation rate in comparison to males. The Kinsey Institute reported that the orgasmic capacity of males reaches its peak within 3 or 4 years after the beginning of their adolescence period. In contrast, the maximum incidence of sexually responding women is not approached until some time in their late 20s and in the 30s.[11]

However, the etiological basis of this difference may be more social than biological. Sherfey[22] has noted that:

Less than one hundred years ago, and in many places today, women regularly had their third or fourth child by the time they were eighteen or nineteen, and the life span was no more than thirty-five to forty years. It could well be that the natural synchronization of the peak periods for sexual expression in men and women have been destroyed only in recent years [pp. 118–119].

Some of the sex-role differences we find are related to class values. In the lower classes, the expression of masculinity receives a great deal of emphasis. The lower-class male, for example, is distinguished from the middle-class male in that he moves sooner into heterosexual relationships.[10] In the lower-class environments, distinctions between masculinity and femininity are sharply drawn. The male frequently sees sexual conquest as a strong sign of his masculinity. In many cases, the sexual act is defined as satisfying only the male, thereby providing him with an activity considered exclusively male. The double standard of sexual conduct is much stronger in the lower-class group.[26] Both sexual rights and sexual pleasure are perceived as male prerogatives. In most cases where a double standard of sex conduct prevails, males have more sexual freedom than females.[8]

It appears as if among females fewer sex-role differences are determined by class. One difference, however, is very salient to this discussion—the age of first intercourse. In general, the higher the class, the later the age of initial coitus—a relationship that is also true of first marriages. This fact often is attributed to the greater propensity of middle-class females to use substitutes of dreams and masturbation for intercourse.[23] After the age of 20, however, middle-class girls are more likely than lower-class girls to have premarital relations, probably because of the earlier date of marriage for lower-class girls. It is assumed that the longer a female remains unmarried (up until a certain age), the greater are the chances that she will engage in premarital coitus. Consequently, the overall premarital sex rate of lower-class females is reduced by their earlier age at marriage.

It was in the past decade that a revolution in sexual attitudes and behavior seemed to be taking place. The advent of the birth control pill freed women from the fear of pregnancy resulting from premarital sex relations. Many agencies and institutions supplied this contraceptive to women on demand—no questions asked. Laws prohibiting abortion were either abolished or liberalized in some states. More sexual candor in movies, uncensored literature, the sexually enticing clothes of women, all seemed to augur a significant change in American sexual attitudes and behavior.[24]

For a long time, however, most observers of human sex conduct argued that no significant change had taken place in premarital coitus. The Kinsey[11] group found that the most marked increase in premarital sexual behavior occurred in females born after the turn of the century.

After that time any increase had been negligible. Most researchers on sexual behavior confirmed the Kinsey findings.

In his classical study of worldwide changes in family patterns, Goode[9] asked the question: Has there indeed been a change in sexual attitudes and behavior in the direction of greater premarital freedom? In looking at the available data on sexual behavior for many Western countries, his cautious answer was: "We cannot assume that these data prove any great change from the past. With respect to sexual relations with the future spouse alone, it is not clear that any change has occurred [p. 37]." With similar reservations, Reiss[21] states that the popular notion that America is undergoing a sexual revolution is a myth. What has happened, he asserts, is that young people have been taking more responsibility for their own sexual standards and behavior. More reliable data on sexual behavior would rectify these myths, he states.

Upon examining the available data on sexual behavior after World War II, Pope and Knudsen[18] concluded that there has not been a mass retreat from chastity standards among the advantaged groups. The only change they noted was the allowance of increased permissiveness for women under certain conditions—those conditions being strong affection or love. Countervailing forces in the society, such as the need to maintain family lines and status, they report, will prevent any significant changes in sexual behavior among this group.

There was no complete unanimity of agreement on the lack of any significant change in American sexual behavior. Leslie,[12] for instance, investigated this problem by classifying chronologically most of the studies which had reported on premarital coitus rates, beginning with 1915 and ending with 1965. He found that, for both males and females, the percentage engaging in premarital sex had increased in the more recent studies. In a similar analysis Packard,[17] in examining more than 40 studies, observed that while the coital experience of United States college males seemed comparable to that of males 15 or 20 years ago, the college females reported a quite significantly higher rate of experience.

It is in the data on sexual behavior reported since 1965 that the significant changes taking place begin to emerge. In one such study, Luckey and Nass[13] report that 43.2% of their college female sample had engaged in premarital coitus, a marked increase over the percentages reported for earlier periods. This study also reported on sexual behavior among college students in Canada, England, Germany, and Norway. Similar increments in the premarital coitus rate for females were noted. In another study of the sexual behavior of college women in 1967, a distinct contrast was found between pre-1962 study findings and those of the researchers. Their female sample reported a rate of 41%—a figure twice as high as that which has been traditionally reported at other universities.

To further corroborate that permissive sexual behavior is gaining ascendancy for females, the findings of Davis,[4] who reviewed all the published and some unpublished studies of college student sexual behavior in which the data were collected in the 1960s are germane:

> In my examination of the data I find only two substantial carefully executed studies . . . which showed a non-virgin rate below 30 percent for college women and most of the studies yield figures in the 40 percent to 55 percent range . . . overall, it is clear that there are several schools with rates considerably higher than the classic 25 percent figure, and that the weight of the data suggests a marked change in the number of college women who experience premarital coitus.[4]

Some of these studies may be challenged on the basis of the incomparability of the samples and methods of recent studies with older studies. Thus, the recently published study by Bell and Chaskes[2] has certain advantages over others in that it studied the sexual behavior of college students in the same institution, with the same measuring instruments, at two different points in time. In a limited fashion, this study more adequately assessed the trend toward increased premarital sexual behavior on the part of college females.

The Bell and Chaskes[2] study revealed that the premarital coital rate increased in a decade from 10% to 23% during the dating relationship, from 15% to 28% during the going-steady relationship, and from 31% to 39% during the engagement relationship. According to Bell and Chaskes, large numbers of college youths are rejecting many aspects of the major institutions in American society. It is expected, then, that the younger generation would view with skepticism the institution concerned with marriage and sexual behavior. It is this increasing rejection of normative sexual values plus other factors that led to the significant changes that are occurring in the premarital sexual experiences of female college students since the mid-1960s. These more recent studies reveal significant increments in the number of premarital sexual liaisons. This increase in premarital coital activity may be largely attributed to two factors: the increasing freedom of women and the American dating system.

In the United States the dating activity of young people is largely unchaperoned. Consequently, the adherence to the society's moral standards is mostly a matter of individual discretion and the availability of appropriate settings. Commitment to the sexual mores has to be internalized when restraint in sexual activity is internally imposed and not externally controlled. Since the double standard of sexual conduct condones, and even encourages, male premarital sexual relations, the female must frequently set the limit on the degree of sexual intimacy in which she will engage. As the constraints on female premarital sexual expression have diminished, there has been a corresponding increase in pre-marital coital activity.[21]

The relaxation of societal restraints on the expression of female sexuality forebodes a greater symmetry in heterosexual relations in this society. In the past when her status depended on sexual repression, the female either abstained from any overt expression of sexual satisfaction and sought to employ the enticement of sex relations with a man for whatever emotional or material gains she could obtain. To a greater extent today her sexual activity may be enjoyed more nearly for its own sake without promiscuity and loss of status. Women do not have to see themselves any longer as sex objects, as commodities governed by market relations. Sexual relations are no longer something to withhold for exchange purposes but an act to be mutually enjoyed.

REFERENCES

1. Bachofen, J. A. *Das Mutternecht*. Stuttgart, 1861.

2. Bell, R., & Chaskes, J. B. Pre-marital sexual experience among coeds, 1958 and 1968. *Journal of Marriage and the Family*, 1970, **22**, 81–84.

3. Bernard, J. The fourth revolution. *Journal of Social Issues*, 1966, **22**, 76–87.

4. Davis, K. E. Sex on campus: Is there a revolution? *Medical Aspects of Human Sexuality*, 1972.

5. Engels, F. *The origin of the family, private property and the state.* Chicago: Charles H. Kerr, 1902.

6. Ehrmann, W. *Premarital dating behavior.* New York: Holt, Rinehart & Winston, 1959.

7. Ehrmann, W. Marital and non-marital sexual behavior. In *Handbook of marriage and the family.* Skokie, Ill.: Rand McNally, 1964.

8. Ford, C. S., & Beach, F. A. *Patterns of sexual behavior.* New York: Harper & Row, 1951.

9. Goode, W. *World revolution and family patterns.* New York: Free Press, 1963.

10. Kinsey, A. C., Pomeroy, W. B., & Martin, C. E. *Sexual behavior in the human male.* Philadelphia: Saunders, 1948.

11. Kinsey, A. C., Pomeroy, W. B., Martin, C. E., & Gebhard, P. H. *Sexual behavior in the human female.* Philadelphia: Saunders, 1953.

12. Leslie, G. *The family in social context.* New York: Oxford, 1967.

13. Luckey, E. B., & Nass, G. D. A comparison of sexual attitudes and behavior in an international sample. *Journal of Marriage and the Family*, 1969, **31**, 364–379.

14. Maccoby E. (Ed.) *The development of sex differences.* Stanford, Calif.: Stanford University Press, 1966.

15. Mead, M. *Sex and temperament in three primitive societies.* New York: Morrow, 1935.

16. Morgan, L. H. *Ancient society.* New York: Holt, 1877.

17. Packard, V. *The sexual wilderness.* New York: McKay, 1969.

18. Pope, H., & Knudsen, D. D. Premarital sexual norms, the family and social change. *Journal of Marriage and the Family,* 1965, **27,** 314–323.

19. Reiss, I. *Premarital sexual standards in America.* New York: Free Press, 1961.

20. Reiss, I. Premarital sexual permissiveness among Negroes and whites. *American Sociological Review,* 1964, **29,** 688–698.

21. Reiss, I. How and why America's sexual standards are changing. *Transaction,* 1968, **5,** 26–32.

22. Sherfey, M. J. The evolution and nature of female sexuality in relation to psychoanalytic theory. *Journal of the American Psychoanalytic Association,* 1966, **14,** 28–127.

23. Simon, W., & Gagnon, J. Psychosexual development. *Transaction,* 1969, **6,** 9–17.

24. Staples, R. Sexual morality and the crisis in human relations. *Sexology,* 1970, **37,** 3–6.

25. Taylor, G. R. *Sex in history.* New York: Ballantine, 1954.

26. Whyte, W. A slum sex code. *American Journal of Sociology,* 1943, **48,** 24–31.

Convergence toward a Single Sexual Standard?

The increase in female sexual activity which has been reported since about the middle of the 1960s has continued at a rapid pace. As psychologist James Curran suggests in the next article, the two sexes are now remarkably alike—at least on a college campus. Most of these students, both males and females, reported that they had engaged in heavy petting with manual manipulation of the breasts and genitals. Less than half had had intercourse or engaged in oral sex, but again the two sexes are very similar with the females equaling or exceeding the males in their sexual behavior.

Such investigations provide still further evidence of the basic similarity between males and females in their sexual needs and sexual responsiveness. Because the recognition of this similarity is a new concept in our culture, it represents a potential source of threat to those who have accepted the more traditional notions of the sexually active male and the sexually passive female. Equality in sexuality can be a source of liberation for both men and women, but negative possibilities must be recognized. For example, the female who has successfully learned to suppress her sexual desires can suffer a blow to her self-esteem when she learns that other females are sexually active and enjoying multiorgasmic experiences. Analogously, the traditional male who has successfully learned that the initiation and total enjoyment of sexual interactions is a masculine prerogative can suffer an equal blow when he learns that females can be as sexually active and aggressive as he. Perhaps in the postrevolutionary phase, we can each learn to accept one another as sexual persons and to free ourselves of some of the culturally imposed restraints on femininity and masculinity.

Convergence toward a Single Sexual Standard?

James P. Curran

Although many psychological theories have stressed the importance of sexuality as a major determinant of human behavior, there exists a scarcity of data regarding the interrelationships between sexual behavior and other aspects of personality functioning. Evidence is beginning to accumulate that the frequency of sexual behavior and the types of sexual encounters experienced are related to a wide variety of factors. Among these are degree of religiosity,[5,10,16] liberal attitudes,[5,6] personality variables,[7] female career orientation,[6] marital happiness,[15] marital orgasm,[13] physical attractiveness,[5] and dating experience.[5,14] This study was undertaken, in part, to explore the relationship between college students'

Reprinted in an edited version from: Curran, J. P. Convergence toward a single sexual standard? *Social Behavior and Personality,* in press.

sexual experiences and certain attitudinal, experiential, and somatic factors.

In the last decade, Americans have experienced great changes in their sexual mores. Recently, Hunt[9] has confirmed the widely held belief that, since the time of Kinsey[12] and his co-workers' surveys, "there have been dramatic increases in the frequencies with which most Americans engage in various sexual activities and in the number of persons who include formerly forbidden techniques in their sexual repertoire [p. 85]." This increase in sexual behavior appears to be especially true for females[9] who are reaching closer parity with males with regard to certain sexual behaviors such as premarital sex, oral sex, etc.

Interestingly, there are some data[5] to indicate close similarity in percentages of male and female participation in "more advanced" types of sexual behavior such as ventral-dorsal intercourse* and oral sex to orgasm. However, for "less advanced" forms of sexual behavior such as manual and oral manipulation of the female's breast, significantly more males than females reported experiencing these activities. Curran et al.[5] offered a "commitment" hypothesis to explain these data. There is some evidence[14] to indicate that females are more willing to engage in sexual behavior if they are in love, while males are less sexually aggressive if they are in love. Perhaps most women are willing to cross a "certain line" with regard to sexual behavior only with a steady partner; hence, the concordance for the "more advanced" sexual behaviors. The reported greater percentage of males engaging in the "less advanced" forms of sexual behavior might be a function of their selection of females who will participate in those behaviors on a less intimate basis. If, indeed, females are experiencing a sexual liberation, and commitment is of lesser importance to females than a decade ago as suggested by Bell and Chaskes,[1] then one would expect to find greater concordance between the sexes for even the "less advanced" types of sexual behavior. The exploration of this hypothesis was the second goal of this study.

METHOD

The subjects consisted of 88 male and 76 female students from a large, relatively conservative midwestern university. All the subjects had originally participated in a "computer dating" study, and had volunteered after the study to complete a questionnaire regarding their sexual experiences. The Heterosexual Behavior Scale[2,3] was used to assess a subject's degree of sexual experience. These scales consist of 21 items which are answered either yes or no, and have been shown to possess high internal consistency and certain Guttman[8] scale properties. A subject's degree of sexual experience is computed on the Heterosexual Behavior

---

* Illustration of basic coital positions on p. 133.

Scale by summing the number of yes responses. Bentler's data on his scales indicate that sexual experiences are cumulative and that they possess a fixed pattern. That is, it appears that few males or females have experienced actual coitus` without first experiencing the stages of light and heavy petting.

The attitudinal, experiential, and somatic variables were obtained during the process of the "computer dating" study. As part of the procedure for the "computer dating" study, subjects were administered a questionnaire devised by the author. This questionnaire consisted of general attitudinal items on moral and political issues, as well as items regarding a subject's previous dating experiences. Subjects' responses to this questionnaire were factor analyzed, and items with high loadings on attitudinal issues and dating experiences were utilized in the computation of a subject's scores on those variables.

While the subjects were applying for the computer dating study, six undergraduates unobtrusively rated each subject on a 5-point scale for physical attractiveness. The mean of the judges' ratings was taken as a measure of each subject's "objective" physical attractiveness. In addition to these ratings, each subject rated himself (herself) during the application period, and his or her dating partner after the date, on the same 5-point scale for physical attractiveness.

Subjects were matched for their computer date on the basis of height, age, and physical attractiveness. Approximately 2 to 3 weeks after the initial application, subjects were notified of their date's name, address, and phone number. It was the male's responsibility to arrange for the date, and no restrictions were placed by the experimenter on the type of date that occurred. After the date, subjects completed a Date Evaluation Scale which attempted to assess several dimensions of the dating experience including the amount of interpersonal attraction experienced toward the dating partner. The interpersonal attraction factor possesses good factorial and construct validity.[4] A subject's attraction score was derived by summing the multiple-choice responses of his or her dating partner.

RESULTS AND DISCUSSION

The amount of interpersonal attraction a male felt for his date was significantly related to her degree of sexual experience. Significant relationships were found for both males and females between degree of sexual experience and various indicators of their physical attractiveness. Dating experience, dating anxiety, attitudes toward alcohol consumption, religious and moral issues, and politics (female only) also correlated significantly with degree of sexual experience. In general, the more sexually experienced subjects may be characterized as better liked by their dating partner, better looking, having more dating experience, and feeling more comfortable about dating. In addition, they were more liberal on topics concerning alcohol, religion, and moral and political issues than the less sexually experienced subjects.

Table 6-6 contains the percentage of males and females who answered "yes" to the 21 items on the Heterosexual Behavior Scale. The percentages of affirmative responses for each item were ranked in order to determine if the pattern of sexual behavior experienced in this sample corresponded to Bentler's[2,3] original sample. The degree of association between this sample's rank ordering and Bentler's rank ordering showed good agreement for both the male and female rank orderings, with only a few minor reversals.

An examination of Table 6-6 reveals some interesting differences

Table 6-6
Percentage of Yes Responses
to Heterosexual Behavior Scale

Have you ever engaged in the following behavior with a member of the opposite sex?	Percentage of Males Saying "Yes"	Percentage of Females Saying "Yes"
1. One minute of continuous kissing on the lips?	86.4	89.2
2. Manual manipulation of clothed female breasts?	82.7	71.1
3. Manual manipulation of bare female breasts?	75.5	66.3
4. Manual manipulation of clothed female genitals?	76.4	67.5
5. Kissing nipples of female breast?	65.5	59.0
6. Manual manipulation of bare female genitals?	64.4	60.2
7. Manual manipulation of clothed male genitals?	57.3	51.8
8. Mutual manipulation of genitals?	55.5	50.6
9. Manual manipulation of bare male genitals?	50.0	51.8
10. Manual manipulation of female genitals until there were massive secretions?	49.1	50.6
11. Sexual intercourse, face to face?	43.6	37.3
12. Manual manipulation of male genitals to ejaculation?	37.3	41.0
13. Oral contact with female genitals?	31.8	42.2
14. Oral contact with male genitals?	30.9	42.2
15. Mutual manual manipulation of genitals to mutual orgasm?	30.9	26.5
16. Oral manipulation of male genitals?	30.0	38.6
17. Oral manipulation of female genitals?	30.0	41.0
18. Mutual oral-genital manipulation?	20.9	28.9
19. Sexual intercourse, entry from the rear?	14.5	22.9
20. Oral manipulation of male genitals to ejaculation?	22.7	26.5
21. Mutual oral manipulation of genitals to mutual orgasm?	13.6	12.0

When asked about their sexual experiences, male and female undergraduates in the 1970s tend to give quite similar responses. An interesting finding is that males are more likely than females to report having the milder or "less advanced" experiences, while this pattern reverses with respect to the stronger or "more advanced" types of sexual activity.

between males and females in their order of sexual experiences. These differences are found on items 11 (intercourse ventral-ventral), 14 (fellatio), 15 (mutual manual manipulation to orgasm), and 17 (cunnilingus). Male subjects indicated that they experienced coitus and mutual orgasm by manual manipulation earlier in their pattern of sexual experiences than did the females. Females, however, indicated that they had practiced fellatio and experienced cunnilingus earlier in their pattern of sexual experiences than did the male subjects. In fact, the pattern for females seems to indicate that they experience cunnilingus and fellatio before experiencing coitus while for males the pattern is reversed. Similar patterns were found in studies conducted by Bentler[2,3] and Curran et al.[5] This pattern of sexual behavior by females might represent an attempt by them to enjoy mutual sexual satisfaction while technically remaining virgins.

Inspection of the data indicates a greater percentage of males than females experienced the "less advanced" forms of sexual behavior. However, beginning with item 9, an approximately equal or even greater number of females than males indicated that they had experienced the types of sexual behavior represented. As mentioned above, Curran et al.[5] have shown concordance between males and females for the "more advanced" types of sexual behavior measured by the Heterosexual Behavior Scale. However, this parity was not reached until item 17 in the earlier study. The data from the present study then would appear to support a hypothesis that with the waning of the "double standard," commitment to a relationship is becoming of less importance for females in deciding whether to engage in sexual activities. Wagner, Fujita, and Pion[17] have also presented some suggestive evidence that the sexual revolution has resulted in a convergence for males and females toward a single behavioral standard.

An alternate hypothesis to this interpretation is that the data may have been biased by the sampling procedures utilized. The subjects had previously participated in a "computer dating" study and had volunteered to complete the Heterosexual Behavior Scale after the study. Volunteers might be more sexually experienced than nonvolunteers. A study by Kaats and Davis[11] however has demonstrated that, while there were differences between volunteers and nonvolunteers with regard to both their attitudes concerning sexual behavior and their experiences with "less advanced" types of sexual behavior such as necking and petting, there were no differences between volunteers and nonvolunteers with respect to the more advanced types of sexual behavior such as coitus. The parity between male and female sexual behavior demonstrated in this study was largely for the "more advanced" types of sexual behavior and would, therefore, be more likely to be due to a real convergence toward a single sexual standard than to a volunteer sampling bias.

CONCLUSION

The data supported the hypothesis that male and female sexual experiences are cumulative and follow a fixed pattern. However, the sequence of sexual experience differs for males and females. Females are more apt than males to experience oral-genital activities before they experience coitus with the reverse being true for males. The widely held belief that the sexual revolution has had its greatest impact on female sexual activity also received some support. The percentage of females who had participated in the "more advanced" and "moderate" types of sexual behavior equaled and sometimes exceeded the percentage of males who had participated in such activities. The degree of a subject's sexual experience was also found to be related to interpersonal attraction, physical attractiveness, dating experience, and attitudes regarding religious, moral, and political issues.

REFERENCES

1. Bell, R. R., & Chaskes, J. B. Premarital sexual experience among coeds, 1958 and 1968. *Journal of Marriage and the Family*, 1970, **32**, 81–84.

2. Bentler, P. M. Heterosexual behavior assessment-I. Males. *Behavior Research and Therapy*, 1968, **6**, 21–25. (a)

3. Bentler, P. M. Heterosexual behavior assessment-II. Females. *Behavior Research and Therapy*, 1968, **6**, 27–30. (b)

4. Curran, J. P. Examination of various interpersonal attraction principles in the dating dyad. *Journal of Experimental Research in Personality*, 1973, **6**, 347–356.

5. Curran, J. P., Neff, S., & Lippold, S. Correlates of sexual experience among university students. *Journal of Sex Research*, 1973, **9**, 124–131.

6. DeYoung, G. E., Cattel, R. B., Gaborit, G., & Barton, K. A. Causal model of effects of personality and marital role factors upon diary reported sexual behavior. *Proceedings of the 81st Annual Convention of the American Psychological Association*, Montreal, Canada, 1973, **8**, 357–358.

7. Eysenck, H. J. Hysterical personality and sexual adjustment, attitudes and behavior. *Journal of Sex Research*, 1971, **7**, 274–281.

8. Guttman, L. The basis of scalogram analysis. In S. A. Stouffer, L. Guttman, E. A. Sachman, P. F. Lazerfield, S. A. Stone, & J. A. Clausen (Eds.), *Measurement and prediction*. Princeton, N.J.: Princeton University Press, 1950.

9. Hunt, M. *Sexual behavior in the 1970's*. Chicago: Playboy Press, 1974.

10. Jackson, E. D., & Potday, C. R. Precollege influences on sexual experience of coeds. *Journal of Sex Research*, 1973, **9**, 143–149.

11. Kaats, G. R., & Davis, K. E. Effects of volunteer biases in studies of sexual behavior and attitudes. *Journal of Sex Research*, 1971, **7**, 26–34.

12. Kinsey, A. C., Pomeroy, W. B., & Martin, C. E. *Sexual behavior in the human male.* Philadelphia: Saunders, 1948.

13. Kinsey, A. C., Pomeroy, W. B., Martin, C. E., & Gebhard, P. H. *Sexual behavior in the human female.* Philadelphia: Saunders, 1953.

14. Lewis, R. A. Parents and peers: Socialization agents in the coital behavior of young adults. *Journal of Sex Research*, 1973, **9**, 156–170.

15. Reevy, W. R. Petting experience and marital success: A review and statement. *Journal of Sex Research*, 1972, **8**, 48–60.

16. Sutker, P., & Kilpatrick, D. G. Personality, biographical and racial correlates of sexual attitudes and behavior. *Proceedings of the 81st Annual Convention of the American Psychological Association,* Montreal, Canada, 1973, **8**, 261–262.

17. Wagner, N. N., Fujita, B. N., & Pion, R. Sexual behavior in high school: Data on a small sample. *Journal of Sex Research*, 1973, **9**, 150–155.

Written Descriptions of Orgasm:
A Study of Sex Differences

Before you read any further, please turn to page 207 and complete the Sex of Orgasm Questionnaire according to the instructions.

As with other aspects of sexual behavior, the similarities and differences between males and females can be viewed from many different perspectives. We have looked at responses to erotic stories, at sexual behavior in other cultures, and at surveys dealing with sexual practices. In the following article, an attempt is made to examine the subjective experience of sexual pleasure and to determine whether this experience is different for males and females.

It is, of course, not possible to make a direct comparison of what different people perceive or feel. There is no way to know if Tom and Mary experience the same sensations when they see the color red, taste an olive, smell a rose, or have an orgasm. All we can know is that they identify the same stimulus event by the same verbal label. The approach of psychologists Vance and Wagner is somewhat different, however, in that they ask individuals to describe in words what an orgasm feels like. Do you think men and women are likely to describe a sexual climax in the same way or very differently? When you examined these descriptions, yourself, did you feel that some were almost certainly written by men and others by women? As you will see, even in the realm of the subjective description of orgasm, males and females do not seem to differ in any measurable fashion.

Written Descriptions of Orgasm:
A Study of Sex Differences

Ellen Belle Vance and Nathaniel N. Wagner

Kinsey et al.[7] noted the remarkable similarity of male and female sexual response, but there was little interest in the topic of orgasm prior to the publication of Masters and Johnson's[8] research on the physiology of sexual response. Since 1966 there has been considerable discussion in the literature about female orgasm. Especially through the vocal efforts of the woman's liberation movement, orgasm during coitus has come to be considered a woman's due, just as it is her partner's.

An important difference in male and female orgasm is the relationship to reproductive function. Orgasm for the male because of its association with ejaculation is closely linked to effective conception. The male who does not have an orgasm and does not ejaculate has little

Reprinted in an edited version from: Vance, E. B., & Wagner, N. N. Written descriptions of orgasm: A study of sex differences. *Archives of Sexual Behavior*, 1976, **5**, 87–98.

possibility of impregnating a female. The nonorgasmic female, however, may be quite fertile. There appears to be no relationship between orgasmic capacity in the female and her fecundity.

The work of Masters and Johnson on the psychological and physiological aspects of orgasm in 1966 raised serious issues for persons working in the area of sexual behavior. The heretofore widely accepted psychoanalytic belief in two kinds of female orgasm, the clitoral and the more "mature" vaginal orgasm, was disputed. Masters and Johnson found that all orgasms were the same physiologically regardless of where stimulation had occurred.

Singer and Singer[12] dispute this finding and argue for a broader definition of orgasm which incorporates emotional satisfaction as well as physiological changes. Also in favor of a broader definition, Glenn and Kaplan[4] suggest defining female orgasm not only by the location of stimulation but also by the location of orgastic experience. They feel a need for further research on the anatomical and physiological changes that take place during orgasm and would like to see researchers look for the differences among orgasms as defined by their method. Heiman[5] proposes another tack; although he applauds the work of Masters and Johnson on the anatomy of orgasm, he discusses a need for going beyond their work and examining the psychological factors in orgasm. Female sexuality and the role of orgasm must be reexamined within the context of the total life experience of women living in a particular culture and society. Robertiello[10] also argues for psychologically differentiated orgasms. While orgasms are physiologically the same, he believes that there are two distinct and easily distinguishable kinds of orgasm experienced subjectively. He also argues against equating having orgasms with the degree of pleasure and satisfaction a women finds in sex.

Wallin and Clark's 1963 study[13] was designed with this issue in mind. They questioned the assumption that orgasm is necessary for a woman's enjoyment of intercourse. They found a marked positive correlation between frequency of orgasm and enjoyment of coitus but orgasm was not necessary for this enjoyment: 17% of the women in their sample enjoyed coitus very much but experienced orgasm infrequently or not at all. Little difference in marital happiness or sexual adjustment between orgastic and nonorgastic nonvirgins was also found by Shope and Broderick.[11] In yet another correlational study, Gebhard[2] found that greater marital happiness was associated with higher percentages of coitus resulting in orgasm for the woman but this was so only in the extreme categories of very happy marriage and very unhappy marriage. Gebhard also found that the percentage of orgasm during coitus rose steadily with the length of the marriage but that differences were not great. He found a positive correlation between length of sex play prior to coitus and the rate of orgasm for the woman and a tendency for higher rates of orgasm to be associated with prolonged intromission.

The work of Masters and Johnson created much discussion among psychoanalytic practitioners. Freud differentiated between a clitoral and a vaginal orgasm, conceptualizing the latter as more mature. Gillespie[3] concludes from Masters and Johnson's research that it is impossible to distinguish clitoral from vaginal orgasm as demanded by psychoanalytic theory. Moore,[9] however, attempts to reconcile the apparent discrepancies between the observations of Masters and Johnson and psychoanalytic theory. A preference for vaginally induced orgasms is the result of maturation of the ego and contributes to a woman's feminine identity. Focusing on a different aspect of sexual activity, including orgasm, Barnett[1] reexamines the Oedipal conflict within a psychoanalytic framework. Yet another focus of the literature on orgasm is the influence of various hormonal levels on a woman's desire for sex and capacity for orgasm.[6]

It is apparent that most of the recent literature on orgasm has been either a discussion of the work of Masters and Johnson and its implications or of a correlational nature. Except for the work of Masters and Johnson, there has been no experimental research in the area. In addition, the attention of these studies has been almost exclusively on female orgasm.

The present study was designed to expand upon the experimental work in the area of orgasm, both male and female. It has been assumed for a long time that there are basic differences between a male's and a female's experience of orgasm. What these differences are has not been made particularly clear, but, in the opinion of the authors, it has generally been agreed that a male orgasm is more sudden and explosive in nature while a female orgasm is more prolonged and less violent.

In order to discover whether such differences are reported, professional judges were employed to identify the sex of 48 written descriptions of orgasm. Three professional groups were represented: obstetricians-gynecologists, clinical psychologists, and medical students. There were 8 females and 62 males represented. The question of the ability of these professional and sex groups to sex-identify these written descriptions was also examined.

PROCEDURE

Students in a college introductory course on the psychology of sexual behavior were asked to write a description of orgasm. Their instructor gave them the following instructions:

> Write a brief statement indicating what an orgasm feels like. If you have never had an orgasm, please describe how you think it would feel.

Do not sign your name, but indicate your sex and whether your description of an orgasm is real or imagined by putting an R or an I on the paper. Limit your comments to at most one side of the paper.

On the other side of the paper, describe what it feels like when you have eaten too much. If you have never eaten too much, describe how you think it would feel. Put R for real and I for imagined. An explanation for this second description will be given later.

From the approximately 300 students present in the class, 246 responses were obtained, 121 male and 125 female. Of these, the 26 imaginary descriptions of orgasm were eliminated from the sample; 3 were male and 23 were female. Another 42 responses were eliminated either because they consisted of 10 words or less or because they were unalterably male or female. Descriptions that were unalterably male or female were those that were clearly sex-identifiable (feelings in the penis were described, for example) and could not be altered with the substitution of a few sex-neutral words. It was also decided to eliminate orgasm descriptions of 10 words or less because such descriptions would be so concise as to allow very little basis for sex identification. After these deletions 178 responses remained, 85 of them male and 93 of them female.

The descriptions of overeating were obtained as part of a control for sex differences in the use of descriptive language. It may be that certain males and females can be sex-typed simply on the basis of the flavor they impart to their language—in this case, written language. To rule out sexually stereotyped stylistic differences, five naive individuals (three females and two males) were asked to classify the 178 descriptions of overeating as either male or female. On a purely chance basis, the descriptions should have been correctly sex-identified by two and one-half individuals. If a description was correctly classified by four or five of the individuals, therefore, there was reason to believe that the language of the description was sex-typed in some way. The descriptions of orgasm paired with these sex-typed descriptions of overeating were eliminated from the sample. Fifty-four such descriptions were eliminated this way.

Of the 124 descriptions of orgasm that remained, 48 (24 male and 24 female) were randomly selected for use in this study. The 48 descriptions were assigned, using the table of random numbers, to one of three groups. Group A contained 11 female descriptions and 5 male descriptions. Group B contained 8 female and 8 male descriptions. Group C contained 5 female and 11 male descriptions. The setting up of groups in this manner was done to make the task of sex-identification more difficult for the judges and, it was hoped, to reduce the possibility of lucky guessing. The judges were not told the number of male and female descriptions in each group.

The 48 descriptions of orgasm were examined and slightly altered where it was necessary to eliminate wording that was positively sex-identifying. "Partner" was substituted for "wife," "husband," or "boy-friend," etc.; "genitals" was substituted for "penis," "vagina," etc.

Questionnaires were submitted to groups of medical students, obstetrician-gynecologists, and clinical psychologists (graduate students and faculty). The judges were asked simply to go over each description and to classify it as male or female depending on whether they thought it was written by a man or a woman. Questionnaires then were scored; the score was the number of correct classifications.

Statistical tests were performed on the data in order to discover whether any of the three professional groups could sex-identify the descriptions of orgasm better than any of the other groups. The judges were further separated into sex groups in order to discover whether members of either sex could better sex-identify the descriptions than members of the other sex.

Tests were also performed to ascertain whether the individuals with the most correct classifications and the least correct classifications from each group had performed significantly better or worse than chance. If this was true, it would then be determined if other individuals had also performed significantly better or worse than chance.

RESULTS AND DISCUSSION

A frequency distribution of correct classifications obtained on the sex of orgasm questionnaire was made. The highest possible score on the questionnaire is 48; a score of 24 would be expected by chance alone. Analysis indicates that the judges in our sample could not correctly identify the sex of the person having an orgasm on the basis of written descriptions of orgasm alone. In only one case, the best-performing medical student, are the results statistically significant. This student, with a score of 33 out of a possible 48, performed significantly better than chance. Among the other two groups, the highest- and lowest-scoring individuals did not perform significantly better or worse than chance on the sex-identification of written reports of orgasm.

An analysis of the items on the questionnaire revealed that item 8 in Group A was perceived correctly as having been written by a female more often than would be expected by chance alone (65 of the 70 individuals). This description was the only one that dealt with multiple orgasms ("And then if the lovemaking is continued it repeats again and again"), a phenomenon which appears predominantly female.

CONCLUSIONS

From the results of this study, it would appear that individuals are unable to distinguish the sex of a person from that person's written description of his or her orgasm. Neither psychologists, medical students, nor obstetrician-gynecologists had significant success in this task. Furthermore, neither sex was more adept at recognizing characteristics in descriptions of orgasm that would serve as a basis for sex differentiation, if, indeed, there are factors in such descriptions which can be differentiated.

These results raise questions about the assumption that orgasm as experienced by males is something different from orgasm as experienced by females. The two have long been considered to be qualitatively different. The only difference consistently noticed by the sample of professionals in this study was the report of multiple orgasms in a single female subject. This suggests that the experience of orgasm for males and females is subjectively the same, except that women appear able to have multiple orgasms.

It may be that only in written descriptions of orgasm are there no differences. Perhaps our written language is insufficient to handle the differences that may exist. It is possible also that differences do exist but these professionals were unable to recognize them.

It seems more parsimonious, however, without contrary data, to view the results of this study as indicating no absolute differences in male and female orgasm other than the occurrence of multiple orgasms with women. Until there is empirical evidence to the contrary, it is reasonable to assume that the experience of orgasm for males and females is essentially the same.

Further research should attempt to discover (1) what professionals believe to be the differences between male and female orgasm, and (2) whether these differences are borne out by experimental findings.

REFERENCES

1.   Barnett, M. C. "I can't" versus "he won't": Further considerations of the psychic consequences of the anatomic and physiological differences between the sexes. *Journal of American Psychoanalytic Association*, 1968, **16**, 588–600.

2.   Gebhard, P. H. Factors in marital orgasm. *Journal of Social Issues*, 1966, **22**, 88–95.

3.   Gillespie, W. H. Concepts of vaginal orgasm. *International Journal of Psychoanalysis*, 1969, **50**, 495–497.

4.   Glenn, J., & Kaplan, E. H. Types of orgasm in women: A critical review and re-definition. *Journal of American Psychoanalytic Association*, 1968, **16**, 549–564.

5.   Heiman, M. Female sexuality. *Journal of American Psychoanalytic Association*, 1968, **16**, 565–568.

6. Kane, F. J., Lipton, M. A., & Ewing, J. A. Hormonal influences in female sexual response. *Archives of General Psychiatry*, 1969, **20**, 202–209.

7. Kinsey, A. C., Pomeroy, W. B., Martin, C. E., & Gebhard, P. H. *Sexual behavior in the human female.* Philadelphia: Saunders, 1953.

8. Masters, W. H., & Johnson, V. E. *Human sexual response.* Boston: Little, Brown, 1966.

9. Moore, B. E. Psychoanalytic reflections on the implications of recent physiological studies of female orgasm. *Journal of American Psychoanalytic Association*, 1968, **16**, 569–587.

10. Robertiello, R. C. The "clitoral versus vaginal orgasm" controversy and some of its ramifications. *Journal of Sex Research*, 1970, **6**, 307–311.

11. Shope, D. F., & Broderick, C. B. Level of sexual experience and predicted adjustment in marriage. *Journal of Marriage and the Family*, 1967, **29**, 424–427.

12. Singer, J., & Singer, I. Types of female orgasm. *Journal of Sex Research*, 1972, **8**, 255–267.

13. Wallin, P., & Clark, A. L. A study of orgasm as a condition of women's enjoyment of coitus in the middle years of marriage. *Human Biology*, 1963, **2**, 131–139.

SEX OF ORGASM QUESTIONNAIRE

The following three groups of statements are replies by both men and women to a request to describe what an orgasm feels like. For each group please indicate in the blank spaces provided whether you think the statement was written by a male or a female. Put an M for male and an F for female.

Group A

1._____ A sudden feeling of lightheadedness followed by an intense feeling of relief and elation. A rush. Intense muscular spasms of the whole body. Sense of euphoria followed by deep peace and relaxation.

2._____ Feels like tension building up until you think it can't build up any more, then release. The orgasm is both the highest point of tension and the release almost at the same time. Also feeling contractions in the genitals. Tingling all over.

3._____ I often see spots in front of my eyes during orgasm. The feeling itself is *so* difficult to describe other than the most pleasurable of all sensory impressions. I suppose the words "fluttering sensation" describe the physical feeling I get. All nerve endings sort of burst and quiver.

4._____ There is a great release of tensions that have built up in the prior stages of sexual activity. This release is extremely pleasurable and exciting. The feeling seems to be centered in the genital region. It is extremely intense and exhilarating. There is a loss of muscular control as the pleasure mounts and you almost cannot go on. You almost don't want to go on. This is followed by the climax and refractory states!

5._____ An orgasm feels extremely pleasurable, yet it can be so violent that the feeling of uncontrol is frightening. It also is hard to describe because it is as if I am in limbo—only conscious of release.

6._____ To me an orgasmic experience is the most satisfying *pleasure* that I have experienced in relation to any other type of satisfaction or pleasure that I've had which were nonsexually oriented.

7._____ The period when the orgasm takes place—a loss of a real feeling for the surroundings except for the other person. The movements are spontaneous and intense.

8._____ They vary a great deal depending on circumstances. If it's just a physical need or release it's OK, but it takes more effort to "get there." If you're really very much in love (at least in my case) it's so close at hand that the least physical expression by your partner, or slightest touch on the genitals brings it on. And then if the lovemaking is continued it repeats again and again. It's about 90% cortical or emotional and the rest physical. But one has to have the emotion or (in my case) I don't even want to begin or try.

9._____ Obviously, *we* can't explain what it feels "like" because it feels "like" nothing else in human experience. A poetic description may well describe the emotions that go with it, but the physical "feeling" can only be described with very weak mechanical terminology. It is a release that occurs after a period of manipulation has sufficiently enabled internal, highly involuntary spasms that are pleasurable due to your complete involuntary control (no control).

10._____ It's like shooting junk on a sunny day in a big, green, open field.

11._____ It is like turning a water faucet on. You notice the oncoming flow but it can be turned on or off when desired. You feel the valves open and close and the fluid flow. An orgasm makes your head and body tingle.

12._____ An orgasm . . . located (originating) in the genital area, capable of spreading out further . . . legs, abdomen. A sort of pulsating feeling—very nice if it can extend itself beyond the immediate genital area.

13._____ A build-up of tension which starts to pulsate very fast, and there is a sudden release from the tension and desire to sleep.

14._____ Begins with tensing and tingling in anticipation, rectal contractions starting series of chills up spine. Tingling and buzzing sensations grow suddenly to explosion in genital area, some sensation of dizzying and weakening—almost loss of conscious sensation, but not really. Explosion sort of flowers out to varying distance from genital area, depending on intensity.

15._____ A heightened feeling of excitement with severe muscular tension especially through the back and legs, rigid straightening of the entire body for about 5 seconds, and a strong and general relaxation and very tired relieved feeling.

16._____ A tremendous release of built-up tension all at once lasting around 5–10 seconds where a particular "pulsing" feeling is felt throughout my body along with a kind of tickling and tingling feeling.

Group B

1._____ I really think it defies description by words. Combination of waves of very pleasurable sensations and mounting of tensions culminating in a fantastic sensation and release of tension.

2._____ Physical tension and excitement climaxing and then a feeling of sighing, a release of tensionlike feelings.

3._____ It is a pleasant, tension-relieving muscular contraction. It relieves physical tension and mental anticipation.

4._____ It is a very pleasurable sensation. All my tensions have really built to a peak and are suddenly released. It feels like a great upheaval; like all of the organs in the stomach area have turned over. It is extremely pleasurable.

5._____ Orgasm gives me a feeling of unobstructed intensity of satisfaction. Accompanied with the emotional feeling and love one has for another, the reality of the sex drive, and our culturally conditioned status on sex, an orgasm is the only experience that sends my whole body and mind into a state of beautiful oblivion.

6._____ Tension builds to an extremely high level—muscles are tense, etc. There is a sudden expanding feeling in the pelvis and muscle spasms throughout the body followed by release of tension. Muscles relax and consciousness returns.

7._____ A release of a very high level of tension, but ordinarily tension is unpleasant whereas the tension before orgasm is far from unpleasant.

8._____ Basically it's an enormous build-up of tension, anxiety, strain followed by a period of total oblivion to sensation then a tremendous expulsion of the build-up with a feeling of wonderfulness and relief.

9._____ Intense excitement of entire body. Vibrations in stomach—mind can consider only your own desires at the moment of climax. After, you feel like you're floating—a sense of joyful tiredness.

10._____ It is a great release of tension followed by a sense of electriclike tingling which takes over all control of your senses.

11._____ A building up of tensions—like getting ready for takeoff from a launching pad, then a sudden blossoming relief that extends all over the body.

12._____ The feeling of orgasm in my opinion is feeling of utmost relief of any type of tension. It is the most fulfilling experience I have ever had of enjoyment. The feeling is exuberant and the *most enjoyable* feeling I have ever experienced.

13._____ I think that there are a variety of orgasms that I experience. I have noted a shallow "orgasm" which consists of a brief period which is characterized by an urge to thrust but which passes quickly. On the other hand, I have also experienced what I call a hard climax, characterized by a mounting, building tension and strong thrusting movements which increase in strength and frequency until the tension is relieved.

14._____ An orgasm is a very quick release of sexual tension which results in a kind of flash of pleasure.

15._____ An orgasm is a great release of tension with spasmodic reaction at the peak. This is exactly how it feels to me.

16._____ A building of tension, sometimes, and frustration until the climax. A *tightening* inside, palpitating rhythm, explosion, and warmth and peace.

Group C

1._____ An orgasm feels like heaven in the heat of hell; a tremendous build-up within of pleasure that makes the tremendous work of releasing that pleasure worthwhile.

2._____There is a building up of "tension" (poor description) to a very high stage. There is then a surging release which is exhilarating, leaving me in a totally relaxed, exhausted state.

3._____ Spasm of the abdominal and groin area, tingling sensation in limbs, and throbbing at the temples on each side of my head.

4._____ Experience of a build-up of tension, uncoordination of movement—to a few seconds of amazing feeling, to a release of tension and a period of satisfaction and relaxation.

5._____ Often loss of contact with reality. All senses acute. Sight becomes patterns of color, but often very difficult to explain because words were made to fit in the real world.

6.———— A feeling where nothing much else enters the mind other than that which relates to the present, oh sooo enjoyable and fulfilling sensation. It's like jumping into a cool swimming pool after hours of sweating turmoil. "Ahh Relief!" What a great feeling it was, so ecstatically wild and alright!

7.———— A feeling of intense physical and mental satisfaction. The height of a sexual encounter. Words can hardly describe a feeling so great.

8.———— Stomach muscles get "nervous" causing a thrusting movement with hips or pelvis. Muscular contraction all over the body.

9.———— Building of tenseness to a peak where it seems as if everything is going to drain out of you. It's almost like a complete physical drain.

10.———— Starts with hot-cold tingles up in the back of the thighs. What happens from there depends on the strength of the stimulation. Usually, shuddery contractions and the same sort of hot-cold feeling only in the genital area. Sometimes, with really strong stimulation, there's more of a blackout of complete mental awareness of what's happening, then a gradual letting down.

11.———— An orgasm is a heightening relief of tension wherein the muscles are flexing and a great deal of tension is relieved in an extremely short period. It's a feeling of incurring climax and enjoyment due to the acute sensual nerve feelings and consciousness (kind of two opposing dialectics).

12.———— Building up of a good type of tension. With the release of all this build-up in one great rush that makes your whole body tingle and feel very pleasurable. Feeling is weakening and is great. Just want to stay still for a long time.

13.———— Has a build-up of pressure in genitals with involuntary thrusting of hips and twitching of thigh muscles. Also contracting and releasing of the genital muscles. The pressure becomes quite intense—like there is something underneath the skin of the genitals pushing out. Then there is a sudden release of the tension with contraction of genitals with a feeling of release and relaxation.

14.———— I have had orgasm at times under certain conditions. I also have had it during intercourse. It is more relaxing with less mental duress during intercourse. It is a tensing of the whole body and a bright sensual feeling of release after.

15.———— Orgasm amounts to a build-up of muscle tension accompanied by an increase in respiration rate. A sudden release of the build-up constitutes an orgasm. All in all, a highly pleasurable physical sensation.

16._____ A complete relief of all tensions. Very powerful and filled with ecstasy. Contraction of stomach and back muscles.

Answer key for Sex of Orgasm Questionnaire

Group A: 1-F, 2-F, 3-F, 4-M, 5-F, 6-M, 7-F, 8-F, 9-M, 10-F, 11-F, 12-F, 13-F, 14-M, 15-F, 16-M

Group B: 1-M, 2-M, 3-M, 4-F, 5-M, 6-F, 7-M, 8-M, 9-F, 10-F, 11-F, 12-F, 13-F, 14-M, 15-M, 16-F

Group C: 1-M, 2-M, 3-M, 4-F, 5-M, 6-M, 7-F, 8-M, 9-M, 10-F, 11-M, 12-M, 13-F, 14-M, 15-F, 16-M

CHAPTER SEVEN

Sexual Attraction and Love

Continuity between the Experimental Study of Attraction and Real-Life Computer Dating

There are two aspects of the next article that are of primary concern in the study of human sexual behavior. First, there is the notion that the laboratory investigation of such complex phenomena as friendship, love, and sexual attraction is a necessary step in gaining enough knowledge to be able to seek practical applications. It is suggested that laboratory findings cannot be instantly generalized to the more complex outside world nor should they be dismissed as artificial and irrelevant; rather, applied research must bridge the gap between the laboratory and the real world. In this particular study of a brief computer dating interaction, it is shown that laboratory-established variables such as attitude similarity, personality similarity, and physical appearance can be used to predict the attraction of pairs of college students who meet for the first time.

Second, this study is one of many which have shown very clearly the overwhelming importance of physical appearance in determining interpersonal attraction and especially in influencing evaluations of an individual as a date, a sexual object, and a spouse. This emphasis on external attractiveness is true for both males and females in our culture. Regardless of one's own appearance, it is the most attractive member of the opposite sex who is desired. Other research has shown, not surprisingly, that actual dating and marriage choices tend to depart somewhat from this pattern, with less attractive individuals "settling for" someone relatively similar to themselves in physical appeal. The most disturbing aspect of all such findings is the fact that attractiveness is a poor predictor of behavior and hence an unrealistic criterion for choosing either a date or a mate. At some level, we know that "beauty is only skin deep" and "you can't tell a book by its cover," but we nevertheless make our most important interpersonal decisions partly on the basis of the most superficial aspects of those around us.

Continuity between the Experimental Study of Attraction and Real-Life Computer Dating

Donn Byrne, Charles R. Ervin, and John Lamberth

A familiar but never totally resolved problem with any experimental findings is the extent to which they may be generalized to the nonlaboratory situation. At least three viewpoints about the problem may be discerned. First, and perhaps most familiar, is instant generalization

Reprinted in an edited version from: Byrne, D., Ervin, C. R., & Lamberth, J. Continuity between the experimental study of attraction and real-life computer dating. *Journal of Personality and Social Psychology*, 1970, **16**, 157–165.

from the specific and often limited conditions of an experiment to any and all settings which are even remotely related. This tendency is most frequently seen at cocktail parties after the third martini and on television talk shows featuring those who popularize psychology. Second, and almost as familiar, is the notion that the laboratory is a necessary evil. It is seen as an adequate substitute for the real world only to the extent that it reproduces the world. For example, Aronson and Carlsmith[1] ask, "Why, then, do we bother with these pallid and contrived imitations of human interaction when there exist rather sophisticated techniques for studying the real thing [p. 4]?" They enumerate the advantages of experiments over field studies, but emphasize that good experiments must be realistic in order to involve the subject and have an "impact" on him. Concern with experimental realism often is expressed in the context of positing qualitative differences between the laboratory and the outside world; it is assumed that in moving from simplicity to complexity, new and different principles emerge. Third, and least familiar in personality and social psychology, is a view that is quite common in other fields. Laboratory research is seen not as a necessary evil but as an essential procedure which enables us to attain isolation and control of variables and thus makes possible the formulation of basic principles in a setting of reduced complexity. If experiments realistically reproduce the nonlaboratory complexities, they provide little advantage over the field study. Continuity is assumed between the laboratory and the outside world, and complexity is seen as quantitative and not qualitative. To move from a simple situation to a complex one requires detailed knowledge about the relevant variables and their interaction. Application and the attainment of a technology depend upon such an approach.

With respect to a specific psychological phenomenon, the problem of nonlaboratory generalization and application may be examined more concretely. The laboratory investigation of interpersonal attraction within a reinforcement paradigm[3] has followed a strategy in which the effect of a variety of stimulus variables on a single response variable was the primary focus of interest. A model has evolved which treats all relevant stimuli as positive or negative reinforcers of differential magnitude. Attraction toward any stimulus object (including another person) then is found to be a positive linear function of the proportion of weighted positive reinforcements associated with that object. Attitude statements have been the most frequently employed reinforcing stimuli, but other stimulus elements have included personality variables,[14] physical attractiveness,[12] economic variables,[6] race,[7] behavioral preferences,[16] personal evaluations,[13] room temperature,[15] and sexual arousal.[21]

Considering just one of those variables—attitude similarity-dissimilarity—why is it not reasonable to propose an immediate and direct parallel between laboratory and nonlaboratory responses? One reason is simple and quite obvious, but it seems often to be overlooked. Laboratory research is based on the isolation of variables so that one or a limited number of independent variables may be manipulated, while, if possible, all other stimulus variables are controlled. In the outside world, multiple uncontrolled stimuli are present. Thus, if all an experimental subject knows about a stranger is that he holds opinions similar to his own on six out of six political issues, the stranger will be liked.[4] We cannot, however, assume that any two interacting individuals who agree on these six issues will become fast friends because (a) they may never get around to discussing those six topics at all, and (b) even if these topics are discussed, six positive reinforcements may simply become an insignificant portion of a host of other positive and negative reinforcing elements in the interaction. Another problem lies in the nature of the relationship investigated. For a number of quite practical reasons, the laboratory study of attraction is limited in its time span and hence might legitimately be labeled the study of first impressions. Whether the determinants of first impressions are precisely the same as the determinants of a prolonged friendship, of love, or of marital happiness is an empirical question and one requiring a great deal of research.

In view of these barriers to extralaboratory application of experimental findings, how may one begin the engineering enterprise? The present research suggests one attempt to seek a solution. Specifically, a limited dating situation is created in which the barriers to application are minimized. Independent variables identified in the laboratory (attitude similarity, personality similarity, and physical attractiveness) are varied in a real-life situation, and an attempt is made to make the variables salient and to minimize the occurrence of other stimulus events. Even though similarity has been the focus of much of the experimental work on attraction, the findings with respect to physical attractiveness have consistently demonstrated the powerful influence of appearance on responses to those of the opposite sex and even of the same sex. Both field studies[18,20,23,24] and laboratory investigations[12,17,19] have shown that those who are physically attractive elicit more positive responses than do those who are unattractive. The paper-and-pencil response measure most often used in the laboratory was retained so that a common reference point was available, but additional response variables were also used in order to extend the generality and meaning of the attraction construct. Finally, in this experiment, the interaction was deliberately limited in time so that it remained close to a first-impression relationship. Given these deliberately limited conditions, it was proposed that the positive relationship between the proportion of positive reinforcements and attraction is directly applicable to a nonlaboratory interaction. Specifically, it was hypothesized that in a computer dating situation (1) attraction is a joint function of similarity and physical attractiveness, and (2) the greater the extent to which the specific elements of similarity are made salient, the greater is the relationship between similarity and attraction.

METHOD

Attitude-personality questionnaire

In order to provide a relatively broad base on which to match couples for the dating process, a 50-item questionnaire was constructed utilizing five variables. In previous research, a significant similarity effect has been found for authoritarianism,[22] repression-sensitization,[9,10] attitudes,[2,3] Edwards Personal Preference Schedule items,[11] and self-concept.[14] Each variable was represented by 10 items which were chosen to represent the fewest possible intercorrelations within dimensions; the rationale here was the desire to maximize the number of *independent* scale responses on which matching could be based.

Paper-and-pencil response measures

Dates were rated on an expanded version of the Interpersonal Judgment Scale, consisting of ten 7-point scales. The measure of attraction[3] consists of the sum of two scales: liking and desirability as a work partner. This attraction index ranges from 2 (most negative) to 14 (most positive). In addition, four buffer scales deal with evaluations of the other person's intelligence, knowledge of current events, morality, and adjustment. These variables are found to correlate positively with attraction, but they have somewhat different antecedents and are included in the analysis simply as supplemental information. Three new scales, added for the present study in order to explore various responses to the opposite sex, asked the subject to react to the other person as a potential date, as a marriage partner, and as to sexual attractiveness. Finally, a tenth scale was added in order to assess a stimulus variable: the physical attractiveness of the other person. In addition, the physical attractiveness of each subject was rated by the experimenter on the same 7-point scale on which the subjects rated one another.

Procedure

Selection of dating couples   The attitude-personality questionnaire was administered to a group of 420 introductory psychology students at the University of Texas. By means of a specially prepared computer program, the responses of each male were compared with those of each female; for any given couple, the number of possible matching responses could theoretically range from 0 to 50. The actual range was from 12 to 37. From these distributions of matches, male-female pairs were selected to represent either the greatest or the least number of matching responses. There was a further restriction that the male be as tall as or taller than the female. Of the resulting pairs, a few were eliminated (1) because one of the individuals was married, (2) because the resulting pair was racially mixed, or (3) because of a failure to keep the experimental appointment. The remaining 88 subjects formed 24 high-similar pairs and 20 low-similar pairs.

Levels of information saliency   The experiment was run with one of the selected couples at a time. In the experimental room, they were introduced to one another and told the following:

> In recent years, there has been a considerable amount of interest in the phenomenon of computer dating as a means for college students to meet one another. At the present time, we are attempting to learn as much as possible about the variables which influence the reactions of one individual to another.

In order to create differential levels of saliency with respect to the matching elements, subjects in the salient condition were told:

> Earlier this semester, one of the test forms you filled out was very much like those used by some of the computer dating organizations. In order to refresh your memory about this test and the answers you gave, we are going to ask you to spend a few minutes looking over the questions and your answers to them.

> The answers of several hundred students were placed on IBM cards and run through the computer to determine the number of matching answers among the 50 questions for all possible pairs of male and female students. According to the computer, the two of you gave the same answers on approximately 67% (high-similar pairs) [or 33% (low-similar pairs)] of those questions.

In the nonsalient condition, they were told:

> Imagine for the purposes of the experiment that you had applied to one of the computer dating organizations and filled out some of their information forms. Then, imagine that the two of you had been notified that, according to the computer, you match on approximately 67% (high-similar pairs) [or 33% (low-similar pairs)] of the factors considered important.

All subjects were then told:

> For our experiment, we would like to create a situation somewhat like that of a computer date. That is, you answered a series of questions, the computer indicated that you two gave the same responses on some of the

questions, and now we would like for you to spend a short time together getting acquainted. Specifically, we are asking you to spend the next 30 minutes together on a "coke date" at the Student Union. Here is 50¢ to spend on whatever you would like. We hope that you will learn as much as possible about each other in the next half hour because we will be asking you a number of questions about one another when you return.

Measures of attraction   When they returned from the date to receive their final instructions, an unobtrusive measure of attraction was obtained: the physical distance between the two subjects while standing together in front of the experimenter's desk. The distance was noted on a simple scale ranging from 0 (touching one another) to 5 (standing at opposite corners of the desk). The subjects were then separated and asked to evaluate their date on the Interpersonal Judgment Scale.

Follow-up measures   At the end of the semester (2–3 months after the date), it was possible to locate 74 of the 88 original subjects who were willing to answer five additional questions. Each was asked to write the name of his or her computer date and to indicate whether or not they had talked to one another since the experiment, dated since the experiment, and whether a date was desired or planned in the future. Finally, each was asked whether the evaluation of the date was influenced more by physical attractiveness or by attitudes.

RESULTS

Predicting attraction in the computer dating situation

The mean attraction responses for male and female subjects at two levels of information saliency and two levels of response similarity are shown in Table 7-1. Analysis indicated the only significant effect to be that of proportion of similar responses. The attempt to make the matching stimuli differentially salient did not affect attraction, and there were no sex differences.

The other variable which was expected to influence attraction was the physical attractiveness of the date. Two measures of attractiveness were available: ratings by the experimenter when the subjects first arrived and by each subject of his or her own date following their interaction. The correlation between these two measures was significant. As might be expected, the subject's own ratings proved to be better predictors than did the experimenter's ratings. The more physically attractive an individual rated his or her date, the greater the attraction toward the date and the more positively that person was rated as a potential date and as a marriage partner. The strongest relationship of all was between ratings of physical attractiveness and ratings of sexual attractiveness. Thus, the first hypothesis was clearly confirmed, but there was no support for the second hypothesis.

Table 7-1
Mean Attraction Responses[a] of Males and
Females toward Dates Low or High in Similarity
at Two Levels of Information Saliency

	Proportion of Similar Responses	
	Low	High
Male subjects		
Information salient	10.00	11.91
Information nonsalient	10.56	11.38
Female subjects		
Information salient	10.73	11.82
Information nonsalient	10.33	12.15

[a] Possible range is 2 (dislike very much) to 14 (like very much).
Attraction was found to be higher toward a highly similar computer
date than toward a relatively dissimilar one. Males and females
did not differ in their responses, and the manipulation of information saliency had no effect on liking.

With respect to the prediction of attraction, it seems likely that a
combination of the similarity and attractiveness variables would provide
the optimal information. In Table 7-2 are shown the mean attraction
responses toward attractive (ratings of 5–7) and unattractive (ratings of
1–4) dates at two levels of response similarity. For both sexes, each of
the two independent variables was found to affect attraction. The physical attractiveness variable was significant for both males and females.
The most positive response in each instance was toward similar attrac-

Table 7-2
Mean Attraction Responses[a] of Males and
Females toward Dates Low or High in Similarity
Who Are Relatively Attractive and Unattractive

	Proportion of Similar Responses	
	Low	High
Male subjects		
Attractive date	10.55	12.00
Unattractive date	9.89	10.43
Female subjects		
Attractive date	11.25	12.71
Unattractive date	9.50	11.00

[a] Possible range is 2 (dislike very much) to 14 (like very much).
Attraction was affected by the date's similarity and by his or her
physical attractiveness. For both males and females, the response
was most positive toward a highly similar attractive date and
least positive toward a relatively dissimilar unattractive date.

tive dates, and the least positive response was toward dissimilar unattractive dates. An additional analysis indicated no relationship between an individual's own physical attractiveness (as rated by the date) and response to the other person's physical attractiveness.

Other effects of similarity and attractiveness

On the additional items of the Interpersonal Judgment Scale, similarity was found to have a significant positive effect on ratings of the date's intelligence, desirability as a date, and desirability as a marriage partner.

The simplest and least obtrusive measure of attraction was the proximity of the two individuals after the date, while receiving their final instructions from the experimenter. If physical distance can be considered as an alternative index of attraction, these two dependent variables should be correlated; for both sexes, the greater the liking for the partner, the closer together they stood. Another way of evaluating the proximity variable is to determine whether it is influenced by the same independent variables as is the paper-and-pencil measure. For both sexes, physical separation was found to correlate with similarity. Thus, the more similar the couples, the closer they stood. Because similarity and proximity are necessarily identical for each member of a pair, it is not possible to determine whether the males, the females, or both are responsible for the similarity-proximity relationship. When the physical attractiveness measure was examined, however, there was indirect evidence that proximity in this situation was controlled more by the males than by the females. For females, there was no relationship between ratings of the male's appearance and physical separation. For males, the correlation was a significant one.

In the follow-up investigation at the end of the semester, 74 of the 88 original subjects were available and willing to participate. For this analysis, each subject was placed in one of three categories with respect to the two stimulus variables of similarity and attractiveness. On the basis of the same divisions used in the analysis in Table 7-2, subjects were either in a high-similarity condition with a physically attractive date, a low-similarity condition with a physically unattractive date, or in a mixed condition of high-low or low-high. In response to the question about the date's name, the more positive the stimulus conditions at the time of the date, the more likely was the subject to remember correctly the date's name. With respect to talking to the other individual during the period since the experiment, the relationship was again significant. The same effect was found with regard to whether the individual would like or not like to date the other person in the future. The only follow-up question which failed to show a significant effect for the experimental manipulation was that dealing with actual dating; even here, it might be noted that the only dates reported were by subjects in the high-similarity, high-attractiveness condition.

The only other question in the follow-up survey represented an attempt to find out whether the subjects could accurately verbalize the stimuli to which they had been found to respond. Of the 74 respondents, about one-third indicated that both attitudes and physical attractiveness determined their response to the partner, while about one-sixth of the subjects felt they had responded to neither variable. With the remaining half of the sample, an interesting sex difference emerged. Physical attractiveness was identified as the most important stimulus by 14 of the 18 males, while attitudes were seen as the most important stimulus by 16 of the 19 females. The present subjects seemed to have accepted Bertrand Russell's observation that "On the whole, women tend to love men for their character, while men tend to love women for their appearance." In contrast to these verbal sentiments, it might be noted that the date's physical attractiveness correlated much more strongly with attraction responses of female subjects than with attraction responses of male subjects. A further analysis compared the similarity-attraction effect and the attractiveness-attraction effect for those subjects who indicated one or the other stimulus variable as the more important. The similarity-attraction effect did not differ between the two groups. It has been reported previously that awareness of similarity is not a necessary component of the similarity effect.[9] There was, however, a difference in the attractiveness effect. For the subjects identifying attractiveness as the major determinant, physical attractiveness correlated very strongly with attraction responses; for the subjects identifying similarity as the major determinant, attractiveness was not related to attraction.

CONCLUSIONS

Perhaps the most important aspect of the present findings is the evidence indicating the continuity between the laboratory study of attraction and its manifestation under field conditions. At least as operationalized in the present investigation, variables such as physical attractiveness and similarity of attitudes and personality characteristics are found to influence attraction in a highly predictable manner.

The findings with respect to the physical distance measure are important in two respects. First, they provide further evidence that voluntary proximity is a useful and unobtrusive measure of interpersonal attraction. Second, the construct validity and generality of the paper-and-pencil measure of attraction provided by the Interpersonal Judgment Scale is greatly enhanced. The significant relationship between two such different response measures is comforting to users of either one. In addition, the follow-up procedure provided evidence of the lasting effect of the experimental manipulations and of the relation of the attraction measures to such diverse responses as remembering the other person's name and engaging in conversation in the weeks after the termination of the experiment.

The failure to confirm the second hypothesis is somewhat puzzling. It is possible that present procedures, designed to vary the saliency of the elements of similarity, were inadequate and ineffective, that the actual behavioral cues to similarity and dissimilarity were sufficiently powerful to negate the effects of the experimental manipulation, or that the hypothesis was simply incorrect. There is no basis within the present experiment on which to decide among these alternatives.

In conclusion, it must be emphasized that striking continuity has been demonstrated across experiments using paper-and-pencil materials to stimulate a stranger and to measure attraction,[2] more realistic audio and audiovisual presentations of the stimulus person,[5] elaborate dramatic confrontations in which a confederate portrays the stimulus person,[8] and a quasi-realistic experiment such as the present one, in which two genuine strangers interact and in which response measures include nonverbal behaviors. Such findings suggest that attempts to move back and forth between the controlled artificiality of the laboratory and the uncontrolled natural setting are both feasible and indicative of the potential applications of basic attraction research to a variety of interpersonal problems.

REFERENCES

1. Aronson, E., & Carlsmith, J. M. Experimentation in social psychology. In G. Lindzey & E. Aronson (Eds.), *The handbook of social psychology*. Vol. 2. (2d ed.) Reading, Mass.: Addison-Wesley, 1968.

2. Byrne, D. Interpersonal attraction and attitude similarity. *Journal of Abnormal and Social Psychology*, 1961, **62**, 713–715.

3. Byrne, D. Attitudes and attraction. In L. Berkowitz (Ed.), *Advances in experimental social psychology*. Vol. 4. New York: Academic Press, 1969.

4. Byrne, D., Bond, M. H., & Diamond, M. J. Response to political candidates as a function of attitude similarity-dissimilarity. *Human Relations*, 1969, **22**, 251–262.

5. Byrne, D., & Clore, G. L., Jr. Predicting interpersonal attraction toward strangers presented in three different stimulus modes. *Psychonomic Science*, 1966, **4**, 239–240.

6. Byrne, D., Clore, G. L., Jr., & Worchell, P. Effect of economic similarity-dissimilarity on interpersonal attraction. *Journal of Personality and Social Psychology*, 1966, **4**, 220–224.

7. Byrne, D., & Ervin, C. R. Attraction toward a Negro stranger as a function of prejudice, attitude similarity and the stranger's evaluation of the subject. *Human Relations*, 1969, **22**, 397–404.

8. Byrne, D., & Griffitt, W. Similarity versus liking: A clarification. *Psychonomic Science*, 1966, **6**, 295–296.

9. Byrne, D., & Griffitt, W. Similarity and awareness of similarity of personality characteristics as determinants of attraction. *Journal of Experimental Research in Personality*, 1969, **3**, 179–186.

10. Byrne, D., Griffitt, W., & Stefaniak, D. Attraction and similarity of personality characteristics. *Journal of Personality and Social Psychology*, 1967, **5**, 82–90.

11. Byrne, D., Lamberth, J., Mitchell, H. E., & Winslow, L. Sex differences in attraction: Response to the needs of the opposite sex. *Journal of Social and Economic Studies*, 1974, **2**, 79–86.

12. Byrne, D., London, O., & Reeves, K. The effects of physical attractiveness, sex, and attitude similarity on interpersonal attraction. *Journal of Personality*, 1968, **36**, 259–271.

13. Byrne, D., & Rhamey, R. Magnitude of positive and negative reinforcements as a determinant of attraction. *Journal of Personality and Social Psychology*, 1965, **2**, 884–889.

14. Griffitt, W. B. Interpersonal attraction as a function of self-concept and personality similarity-dissimilarity. *Journal of Personality and Social Psychology*, 1966, **4**, 581–584.

15. Griffitt, W. B. Environmental effects of interpersonal affective behavior: Ambient effective temperature and attraction. *Journal of Personality and Social Psychology*, 1970, **15**, 240–244.

16. Huffman, D. M. Interpersonal attraction as a function of behavioral similarity. Unpublished doctoral dissertation, University of Texas, 1969.

17. McWhirter, R. M., Jr. Interpersonal attraction in a dyad as a function of the physical attractiveness of its members. Unpublished doctoral dissertation, Texas Tech University, 1969.

18. Megargee, E. I. A study of the subjective aspects of group membership at Amherst. Unpublished manuscript, Amherst College, 1956.

19. Moss, M. K. Social desirability, physical attractiveness, and social choice. Unpublished doctoral dissertation, Kansas State University, 1969.

20. Perrin, F. A. C. Physical attractiveness and repulsiveness. *Journal of Experimental Psychology*, 1921, **4**, 203–217.

21. Picher, O. L. Attraction toward Negroes as a function of prejudice, emotional arousal, and the sex of the Negro. Unpublished doctoral dissertation, University of Texas, 1966.

22. Sheffield, J., & Byrne, D. Attitude similarity-dissimilarity, authoritarianism, and interpersonal attraction. *Journal of Social Psychology*, 1967, **71**, 117–123.

23. Taylor, M. J. Some objective criteria of social class membership. Unpublished manuscript, Amherst College, 1956.

24. Walster, E., Aronson, V., Abrahams, D., & Rottmann, L. Importance of physical attractiveness in dating behavior. *Journal of Personality and Social Psychology*, 1966, **4**, 508–516.

Some Evidence for Heightened Sexual Attraction under Conditions of High Anxiety

In the computer dating study we saw that both males and females seem to equate physical attractiveness with sexual attractiveness. In this article, psychologists Donald Dutton and Arthur Aron go another step and suggest that sexual attraction is increased further by the presence of any sort of emotional arousal. First, the external cues must be appropriate; for example, an individual is in the presence of an attractive member of the opposite sex. Second, any sort of arousal such as anxiety, anger, or elation will then be relabeled as sexual attraction. The two experiments to be described provide interesting evidence that supports this proposition.

Such findings give us a new perspective for evaluating the way in which people characteristically spend their time in a dating relationship. Though there are quiet dates and quiet interactions, consider the frequency with which couples deliberately seek some sort of emotional arousal. Dates very often include some sort of controlled fearfulness as with roller coaster rides, disaster or horror movies, or mildly dangerous illegal acts such as smoking pot or obtaining beer with fake identification. Other dates involve a general sense of excitement such as a football or basketball game, a motorcycle ride, or a speeding automobile. Even more generally, individuals on dates seek to have "fun," which seems to mean a search for emotional "highs" in the context of parties, music, entertainment, and other types of stimulation. In a way, the dating situation can be viewed as a relatively artificial one in which liking and sexual attraction become exaggerated and augmented by the misinterpretation of additional emotional states.

One sobering aspect of such phenomena is the realization that artificial excitement and emotionally based sexual attraction do not provide a very realistic basis for gauging one's basic interpersonal feelings or predicting one's future responses in the relatively less frantic setting of marriage.

Some Evidence for Heightened Sexual Attraction under Conditions of High Anxiety

Donald G. Dutton and Arthur P. Aron

There is a substantial body of indirect evidence suggesting that sexual attractions occur with increased frequency during states of strong emotion. For example, heterosexual love has been observed to be associated

Reprinted in an edited version from: Dutton, D. G., & Aron, A. P. Some evidence for heightened sexual attraction under conditions of high anxiety. *Journal of Personality and Social Psychology*, 1974, **30**, 510–517.

both with hate[15,24] and with pain.[11] A connection between "aggression" and sexual attraction is supported by Tinbergen's[25] observations of intermixed courting and aggression behaviors in various animal species, and a series of experiments conducted by Barclay have indicated the existence of a similar phenomenon in human behavior. In one study, Barclay and Haber[4] arranged for students in one class to be angered by having their professor viciously berate them for having done poorly on a recent test; another class served as a control. Subsequently, both groups were tested for aggressive feelings and for sexual arousal. A manipulation check was successful, and the angered group manifested significantly more sexual arousal than did controls as measured by explicit sexual content in stories written in response to Thematic Apperception Test (TAT)-like stimuli. Similar results were obtained in two further studies[23] in which fraternity and sorority members were angered by the experimenter. One study[3] employed a female experimenter, which demonstrated that the aggression-sexual arousal link was not specific to male aggression; the other study[2] provided additional support for the hypothesis by using a physiological measure of sexual arousal (acid phosphatase content in urine samples).

Barclay has explained his findings in terms of a special aggression-sexuality link and has cited as support for his position Freud's[13] argument that prehistoric man had to physically dominate his potential mates and also a study by Clark[8] in which increased sexual arousal produced by viewing slides of nudes yielded increased aggression in TAT responses. Aron,[1] however, argued that an aggression-sexuality link exists, but it is only a special case of a more general relationship between emotional arousal of all kinds and sexual attraction. To demonstrate this point, he designed a study in which, instead of anger, residual emotion from intense role playing was the independent variable. In this experiment, each of 40 male subjects role-played with the same attractive female confederate in either a highly emotional or a minimally emotional situation. Subjects enacting highly emotional roles included significantly more sexual imagery in stories written in response to TAT-like stimuli and indicated significantly more desire to kiss the confederate than did subjects in the control condition. One possible explanation is suggested by Schachter's theory of emotion.[22,23] He argued that environmental cues are used, in certain circumstances, to provide emotional labels for unexplained or ambiguous states of arousal. However, it is notable that much of the above-cited research indicates that a sexual attraction—strong emotion link may occur even when the emotions are unambiguous. Accordingly, taking into account both the Schachter position and findings from sexual attraction research in general, Aron[1] hypothesized that strong emotions are relabeled as sexual attraction whenever an acceptable object is present, and emotion-producing circumstances do not require the full attention of the individual.

The present experiments are designed to test the notion that an attractive female is seen as more attractive by males who encounter her while they experience a strong emotion (fear) than by males not experiencing a strong emotion. Experiment 1 is an attempt to verify this proposed emotion-sexual attraction link in a natural setting. Experiment 2 is a laboratory study which attempts to clarify the results of Experiment 1.

EXPERIMENT 1: METHOD

Subjects

Subjects were males visiting either of two bridge sites who fit the following criteria: (1) between 18 and 35 years old and (2) unaccompanied by a female companion. Only one member of any group of potential subjects was contacted. In all, 85 subjects were contacted by either a male or a female interviewer.

Site

The experiment was conducted on two bridges over the Capilano River in North Vancouver, British Columbia, Canada. The "experimental" bridge was the Capilano Canyon Suspension Bridge, a 5-ft wide, 450-ft ·long bridge constructed of wooden boards attached to wire cables that ran from one side to the other of the Capilano Canyon. The bridge has many arousal-inducing features such as (1) a tendency to tilt, sway, and wobble, creating the impression that one is about to fall over the side; (2) very low handrails of wire cable which contribute to this impression; and (3) a 230-ft drop to rocks and shallow rapids below the bridge. The "control" bridge was a solid wood bridge further upriver. Constructed of heavy cedar, this bridge was wider and firmer than the experimental bridge, was only 10 ft above a small, shallow rivulet which ran into the main river, had high handrails, and did not tilt or sway.

Procedure

As subjects crossed either the control or experimental bridge, they were approached by the interviewer.

Female interviewer   The interviewer explained that she was doing a project for her psychology class on the effects of exposure to scenic attractions on creative expression. She then asked potential subjects if they would fill out a short questionnaire. The questionnaire contained six filler items such as age, education, prior visits to bridge, etc., on the first page. On the second page, subjects were instructed to write a brief, dramatic story based upon a picture of a young woman covering her face with one hand and reaching with the other. The instructions and the picture employed were adapted from Murray's[18] *Thematic Apperception Test Manual*. A similar measure of sexual arousal has been employed in the Barclay studies,[2,3,4] and in other sex-related experiments.[1,8,16] The particular TAT item used in the present study was selected for its lack of obvious sexual content, since projective measures of sexual arousal based on explicit sexual stimuli tend to be highly sensitive to individual differences due to sexual defensiveness.[9,10,16,17] If the subject agreed, the questionnaire was filled out on the bridge.

Stories were later scored for manifest sexual content according to a slightly modified version of the procedure employed by Barclay and Haber.[4] Scores ranged from 0 (no sexual content) to 5 (high sexual content) according to the most sexual reference in the story. Thus, for example, a story with any mention of sexual intercourse received 5 points; but if the most sexual reference was "girl friend," it received a score of 2; "kiss" counted 3; and "lover," 4.

On completion of the questionnaire, the interviewer thanked the subject and offered to explain the experiment in more detail when she had more time. At this point, the interviewer tore the corner off a sheet of paper, wrote down her name and phone number, and invited each subject to call, if he wanted to talk further. Experimental subjects were told that the interviewer's name was Gloria and control subjects were told Donna, so that they could easily be classified when they called. On the assumption that curiosity about the experiment should be equal between control and experimental groups, it was felt that differential calling rates might reflect differential attraction to the interviewer.

Male interviewer   The procedure with the male interviewer was identical to that above. Subjects were again supplied with two fictitious names so that if they phoned the interviewer, they could be classified into control or experimental groups.

RESULTS

Check on arousal manipulation

Probably the most compelling evidence for arousal on the experimental bridge is to observe people crossing the bridge. Forty percent of subjects observed crossing the bridge walked very slowly and carefully, clasping onto the handrail before taking each step. A questionnaire was administered to 30 males who fit the same criteria as the experimental subjects. On the experimental bridge, 15 males were asked, "How fearful do you think the average person would be when he crossed this bridge?" The mean rating was 79 on a 100-point scale where 100 was equal to extremely fearful. On the control bridge, 15 males gave a mean rating of 18 on the same scale. In response to the question "How fearful were you while crossing the bridge?" experimental-bridge males gave a rating of

65 and control-bridge males gave a rating of 3. Hence, it can be concluded that most people are quite anxious on the experimental bridge but not on the control bridge. To prevent suspicion, no checks on the arousal of experimental subjects could be made.

Thematic apperception test responses

Female interviewer On the experimental bridge, 23 of 33 males who were approached by the female interviewer agreed to fill in the questionnaire. On the control bridge, 22 of 33 agreed. Of the 45 questionnaires completed, 7 were unusable because they were either incomplete or written in a foreign language. The remaining 38 questionnaires (20 experimental and 18 control) had their TAT stories scored for sexual imagery by two scorers who were experienced with TAT scoring. (Although both were familiar with the experimental hypothesis, questionnaires had been coded so that they were blind as to whether any given questionnaire was written by a control or experimental subject.)

Subjects in the experimental group obtained a mean sexual imagery score of 2.47 and those in the control group, a score of 1.41. Thus, the experimental hypothesis was verified by the imagery data.

Male interviewer Out of 51 subjects who were approached on the experimental bridge, 23 agreed to fill in the questionnaire. On the control bridge 22 out of 42 agreed. Five of these questionnaires were unusable, leaving 20 usable in both experimental and control groups. These were rated as above. Subjects in the experimental group obtained a mean sexual imagery score of .80; those in the control group obtained .61. Hence the pattern of results obtained by the female interviewer was not reproduced by the male interviewer.

Behavioral data

Female interviewer In the experimental group, 18 of the 23 subjects who agreed to the interview accepted the interviewer's phone number. In the control group, 16 out of 22 accepted (see Table 7-3). A second measure of sexual attraction was the number of subjects who called the interviewer. In the experimental group 9 out of 18 called, in the control group 2 out of 16 called. Taken in conjunction with the sexual imagery data, this finding suggests that subjects in the experimental group were more attracted to the interviewer.

Male interviewer In the experimental group, 7 out of 23 accepted the interviewer's phone number. In the control group, 6 out of 22 accepted. In the experimental group, 2 subjects called; in the control group, 1 subject called. Again, the pattern of results obtained by the female interviewer was not replicated by the male.

Table 7-3
Attraction and Sexuality on
Anxiety-Arousing Bridge and on Safe Bridge

	Percentage of Subjects Telephoning Interviewer (%)	Sexual Imagery Score[a] on TAT
Female interviewer		
Safe bridge	12.5	1.41
Anxiety-arousing bridge	50.0	2.47
Male interviewer		
Safe bridge	16.7	.61
Anxiety-arousing bridge	28.6	.80

[a] Possible range is 0 (no sexual content) to 5 (high sexual content).
When male subjects were interviewed by a female on an anxiety-arousing suspension bridge, they were more likely to telephone her afterward and more likely to write a story with sexual content than if the interview took place on a safe, solid bridge. Presumably, various sorts of arousal, such as anxiety, influence sexual arousal and enhance sexual attraction. When the interviewer was a male, these effects disappeared.

Although the results of this experiment provide prima facie support for an emotion-sexual attraction link, the experiment suffers from interpretative problems that often plague field experiments. The main problem with the study is the possibility of different subject populations on the two bridges. First, the well-advertised suspension bridge is a tourist attraction that may have attracted more out-of-town persons than did the nearby provincial park where the control bridge was located. This difference in subject populations may have affected the results in two ways. The experimental subjects may have been less able to phone the experimenter (if they were in town on a short-term tour) and less likely to hold out the possibility of further liaison with her. If this were the case, the resulting difference due to subject differences would have operated *against* the main hypothesis. Also, this difference in subject populations could not affect the sexual imagery scores unless one assumed the experimental bridge subjects to be more sexually deprived than controls. The results using the male interviewer yielded no significant differences in sexual imagery between experimental and control subjects; however, the possibility still exists that sexual deprivation could have interacted with the presence of the attractive female experimenter to produce the sexual imagery results obtained in this experiment. Second, differences could exist between experimental and control populations with respect to personality variables. The experimental population might be more predisposed to thrill seeking and therefore more willing to chance phoning a strange female to effect a liaison. Also, present knowledge of personality theory does not allow us to rule out the combination of thrill seeking and greater sexual imagery. Accordingly, a second experiment was carried out in an attempt to rule out any differential subject population explanation for the results of Experiment 1.

Some additional problems in the interpretation of the apparent anxiety-sexual attraction link require the superior control afforded by a laboratory setting.

First, although the female interviewer was blind to the experimental hypothesis and her behavior toward the subjects was closely monitored by the experimenter, the possibility of differential behavior occurring toward the subjects was not excluded. Distance of the interviewer from the subjects was controlled in Experiment 1, but more stable nonverbal forms of communication (such as eye contact) could not be controlled without cuing the female interviewer to the experimental hypothesis.

Second, even if the interviewer did not behave differentially in experimental and control conditions, she may have appeared differently in the two conditions. For example, the gestalt created by the experimental situation may have made the interviewer appear more helpless or frightened, virtually a "lady in distress." Such would not be the case in the control situation.

If this different gestalt led to differences in sexual attraction, the apparent emotion-sexual arousal link might prove artifactual. Accordingly, a laboratory experiment was run in which tighter control over these factors could be obtained. This experiment involved a design, where (a) the male subject expected either a painful or nonpainful shock (subject's emotion was manipulated) and (b) the female confederate also expected either a painful or nonpainful shock (the lady-in-distress gestalt was manipulated).

EXPERIMENT 2: METHOD

Subjects

Eighty male freshmen at the University of British Columbia took part in this experiment. All subjects were volunteers.

Much of the initial phase of the procedure was patterned after that used in Schachter's[21] anxiety and affiliation research. Subjects entered an experimental room containing an array of electrical equipment. The experimenter welcomed the subject and asked him if he had seen another person who looked like he was searching for the experimental room. The experimenter excused himself "to look for the other subject," leaving the subject some Xeroxed copies "of previous studies in the area we are investigating" to read. The articles discussed the effects of electric shock on learning and pain in general.

The experimenter reentered the room with the "other subject," who was an attractive female confederate. The confederate took off her coat and sat on a chair 3 ft to the side and slightly in front of the subject. The experimenter explained that the study involved the effects of electric shock on learning and delivered a short discourse on the value and importance of the research. At the end of this discourse, the experimenter asked if either subject wanted out of the experiment. As expected, no subject requested to leave.

The experimenter then mentioned that two levels of shock would be used in the experiment, describing one as quite painful and the other level as a "mere tingle, in fact some subjects describe it as enjoyable," and concluded by pointing out that the allocation of subjects to shock condition had to be "completely random so that personality variables won't affect the outcome." At this point, the experimenter asked both subjects to flip a coin to determine which shock level they would receive. Hence, the subject reported "heads/tails," the confederate reported "heads/tails," and the experimenter said, "Today heads receives the high shock level." The experimenter then described the way in which the shock series would take place, the method of hooking subjects into electrodes, etc.

The experimenter then asked if the subjects had any questions, answered any that arose, and then said:

> It will take me a few minutes to set up this equipment. While I'm doing it, I would like to get some information on your present feelings and reactions, since these often influence performance on the learning task. I'd like you to fill out a questionnaire to furnish us with this information. We have two separate cubicles down the hall where you can do this—you will be undisturbed and private, and I can get this equipment set up.

The confederate then got up, walked in front of the subject to her coat, which was hanging on the wall, rummaged around for a pencil, and returned to her chair. The experimenter then led the subject and the confederate to the cubicles, where they proceeded to fill out the questionnaires.

RESULTS

A three-part questionnaire constituted the dependent measure of this study. Part 1 (feelings about the experiment) included a check on the anxiety manipulation, Part 2 (feelings toward your co-subject) included two attraction questions found to be most sensitive in experimental situations of this sort,[1] and Part 3 included the TAT picture used in Experiment 1, which again was scored for sexual imagery.

Anxiety

Anxiety was measured by the question, "How do you feel about being shocked?"[21] to which subjects could respond on a 5-point scale where scores greater than 3 indicated dislike. (The greater the score, the greater the anxiety.) In conditions where the subject anticipated receiving a strong shock, subjects reported significantly more anxiety than in conditions where the subject anticipated receiving a weak shock. No significant differences in the subject's anxiety occurred as a function of the confederate receiving a strong versus a weak shock.

Attraction to confederate

Two questions assessed attraction to the confederate in this study: (1) How much would you like to ask her out for a date? (2) How much would you like to kiss her? Attraction ratings were established by taking the mean rating made by subjects on these two questions. Table 7-4 shows the results, by condition, of those ratings. Analysis revealed a significant mean effect for subjects anticipating strong shock to themselves on attraction ratings. Subjects' expectations of strong versus weak shock to the female confederate produced no significant increase in attraction. Hence, the lady-in-distress effect on attraction did not seem to appear in this study.

Thematic apperception test responses

Sexual imagery scores on the TAT questionnaire were obtained as in Experiment 1. In the present study, sexual imagery was higher when the subject expected strong shock but only when the female confederate also expected strong shock. When the female confederate expected weak shock, differences in sexual imagery scores as a function of strength of shock anticipated by the subject failed to achieve significance.

Table 7-4
Attraction[a] toward a Female Confederate
by Males Expecting to Receive a Strong or Weak Electric Shock

	Female Confederate To Get a Strong Shock	Female Confederate To Get a Weak Shock
Male expects to get a strong shock	3.7	3.4
Male expects to get a weak shock	2.9	2.7

[a] Possible range is 1 (very low attraction) to 5 (very high attraction).

Male subjects who were expecting to receive a strong electric shock (and hence were aroused) were more attracted to a female confederate than were male subjects who expected a weak shock. The shock level they thought the female would receive had no effect on their attraction toward her.

GENERAL DISCUSSION

The results of these studies would seem to provide a basis of support for an emotion-sexual attraction link. The Barclay studies[2,3,4] have already demonstrated such a link for aggression and sexual arousal, and the present findings seem to suggest that the link may hold for fear as well. Indeed, the present outcome would seem to be particularly satisfying in light of the very strong differences obtained from the relatively small subject populations, and because these results were obtained, in Experiment 1, outside of the laboratory in a setting in which real-world sexual attractions might be expected to occur.

The strong result of Experiment 2 supports the notion that strong emotion per se increases the subject's sexual attraction to the female confederate. Brehm, Gatz, Goethals, McCrimmon, and Ward[6] obtained results consistent with Experiment 2 in a similar study.

The theoretical implications of these results are twofold. In the first place, they provide additional support in favor of the theoretical positions from which the original hypothesis was derived: the Schachter and Singer[23] tradition of cognitive labeling of emotions and the Aron[1] conceptual framework for sexual attraction processes. In the second place, these data seem to be inconsistent with (or at least unpredictable by) standard theories of interpersonal attraction. Both the reinforcement[7] and the cognitive consistency[12,14] points of view would seem to predict that a negative emotional state associated with the object would *decrease* her attractiveness; and neither theory would seem to be easily capable of explaining the arousal of a greater sexual emotion in the experimental condition of the present experiments.

Although the present data support the cognitive relabeling approach in general, they are consistent with more than one interpretation of the mechanics of the process. The attribution notions of Nisbett and Valins,[19] self-perception theory,[5] and role theory[20] can all provide possible explanations for the anxiety-sexuality link. A further possible explanation is that heightened emotion, instead of being relabeled as sexual, serves merely to disinhibit the expression of preexistent sexual feelings. It is known that inhibition and sexual defensiveness influence sexual content in TAT stories,[8] and this alternative cannot be ruled out by the present data. Yet another alternative suggested by Barclay is that the aggression-sexuality and anxiety-sexuality links may be independent phenomena and not necessarily subcases of a general emotion-sexuality link.

Some evidence for the mechanics of the anxiety-sexual arousal link in the current research may be obtained from the fear ratings made by subjects in Experiment 2. When subjects anticipated receiving a strong shock and the female confederate was present during the anxiety manipulation, subjects reported significantly less fear than when no potential sexual object was present. Since the questionnaires were filled out in private in both groups, it is unlikely that subjects' reporting merely reflects appropriate behavior in the presence of the opposite or same sex. One possible explanation for this result is that, having relabeled anxiety as sexual arousal, the subject is less likely to feel anxious. A more conclusive explanation of the mechanics of the anxiety-sexual arousal link must await the conclusion of present laboratory studies designed specifically to investigate this problem. However, regardless of the interpretation of the mechanics of this link, the present research presents the clearest demonstration to date of its existence.

REFERENCES

1. Aron, A. Relationship variables in human heterosexual attraction. Unpublished doctoral dissertation, University of Toronto, 1970.

2. Barclay, A. M. The effect of hostility on physiological and fantasy responses. *Journal of Personality*, 1969, **37**, 651–667.

3. Barclay, A. M. The effect of female aggressiveness on aggressive and sexual fantasies. *Journal of Projective Techniques and Personality Assessment*, 1970, **34**, 19–26.

4. Barclay, A. M., & Haber, R. N. The relation of aggressive to sexual motivation. *Journal of Personality*, 1965, **33**, 462–475.

5. Bem, D. Self-perception theory. In L. Berkowitz (Ed.), *Advances in experimental social psychology*. Vol. 6. New York: Academic Press, 1972.

6. Brehm, J. W., Gatz, M., Goethals, G., McCrimmon, J., & Ward, L. Psychological arousal and interpersonal attraction. Unpublished manuscript, Duke University, 1967.

7. Byrne, D. Attitudes and attraction. In L. Berkowitz (Ed.), *Advances in experimental social psychology*. Vol. 4. New York: Academic Press, 1969.

8. Clark, R. A. The projective measurement of experimentally induced levels of sexual motivation. *Journal of Experimental Psychology*, 1952, **44**, 391–399.

9. Clark, R. A., & Sensibar, M. R. The relationship between symbolic manifest projections of sexuality with some incidental correlates. *Journal of Abnormal Social Psychology*, 1955, **50**, 327–334.

10. Eisler, R. M. Thematic expression of sexual conflict under varying stimulus conditions. *Journal of Consulting and Clinical Psychology*, 1968, **32**, 216–220.

11. Ellis, H. *Studies in the psychology of sex*. New York: Random House, 1936.

12. Festinger, L. *A theory of cognitive dissonance*. New York: Harper & Row, 1957.

13. Freud, S. *Basic writings*. New York: Modern Library, 1938.

14. Heider, F. *The psychology of interpersonal relations*. New York: Wiley, 1958.

15. James, W. *The principles of psychology*. Vol. 2. New York: Holt, 1910.

16. Leiman, A. H., & Epstein, S. Thematic sexual responses as related to sexual drive and guilt. *Journal of Abnormal and Social Psychology*, 1961, **63**, 169–175.

17. Lubin, B. Some effects of set and stimulus properties on T.A.T. stories. *Journal of Projective Techniques*, 1960, **24**, 11–16.

18. Murray, H. A. *Thematic Apperception Test manual*. Cambridge, Mass.: Harvard University Press, 1943.

19. Nisbett, R., & Valins, S. *Perceiving the causes of one's own behavior*. Morristown, N.J.: General Learning Press, 1972.

20. Sarbin, T. R., & Allen, V. L. *Role theory: Handbook of social psychology*. Reading, Mass.: Addison-Wesley, 1968.

21. Schachter, S. *The psychology of affiliation*. Stanford, Calif.: Stanford University Press, 1959.

22. Schachter, S. The interaction of cognitive and physiological determinants of emotional state. In L. Berkowitz (Ed.), *Advances in experimental social psychology*. Vol. 1. New York: Academic Press, 1964.

23. Schachter, S., & Singer, J. E. Cognitive, social and physiological components of the emotional state. *Psychological Review*, 1962, **69**, 379–399.

24. Suttie, I. D. *The origins of love and hate*. London: Routledge & Kegan Paul, 1935.

25. Tinbergen, N. The origin and evolution of courtship and threat display. In J. S. Huxley, A. C. Hardy, & E. B. Ford (Eds.), *Evolution as a process*. London: Allen & Unwin, 1954.

A Little Bit about Love

As may be seen in the following article, there are four quite different approaches to understanding love, and these are just now beginning to be united in a single formulation. Historically, novelists and poets were the only ones to deal with this topic, and we have many literary descriptions of the phenomenon as well as insightful hints as to the variables affecting love. Next came the psychological essays, mostly by psychoanalysts and clinical psychologists, who attempted to explain love in ways that were compatible with existing theories of personality dynamics. Then, and with an almost shy reluctance, the sex researchers occasionally began to deal with feelings and relationships as well as with the variety and frequency of sexual acts. The last to arrive on the scene were experimental social psychologists who became interested in extending current knowledge about interpersonal attraction and about emotional responses to encompass the hitherto taboo concept of love.

Two landmarks in the social psychological involvement in love research should be noted. First, Zick Rubin devoted his 1969 doctoral dissertation at the University of Michigan to "The Social Psychology of Romantic Love" in which, among other things, he described the development of a scale to measure the degree to which individuals are in love. Second, Elaine Walster delivered a talk in 1970 on "Passionate Love" at a symposium at Connecticut College, presenting the general outlines of a theoretical schema developed in collaboration with Ellen Berscheid. These very important new theoretical ideas led to a variety of experiments in both laboratory and field settings. In the following article, the old and the new approaches to love are described by Berscheid and Walster. In part because of this current work, love has now become at least as respectable as sex as a topic for scientific research.

A Little Bit about Love

Ellen Berscheid and Elaine Walster

Many who have tried to understand the nature of love have concluded in despair that it is impossible to specify in advance who will inspire love, under what conditions, or why. They have resonated to Durrell's[9] poetic definition of love:

> It may be defined as a cancerous growth of unknown origin which may take up its site anywhere without the subject knowing or wishing it. How often have you tried to love the "right" person in vain even when

Reprinted in an edited version from: Berscheid, E., & Walster, E. A little bit about love. In T. L. Huston (Ed.), *Foundations of interpersonal attraction*. New York: Academic Press, 1974. Pp. 355–381.

your heart knows it has found him after so much seeking? No, an eyelash, a perfume, a haunting walk, a strawberry on the neck, the smell of almonds on the breath—these are the accomplices the spirit seeks out to plan your overthrow [p. 106].

LIKING AND LOVING

Passionate love can be perceived as a variety of *interpersonal attraction.* Interpersonal attraction has been defined by a number of researchers[14,22] as a positive attitude toward another, evidenced by a tendency to approach and interact with him.

Research on interpersonal attraction began early (1884), as may be seen in Figure 7-1, and has continued at a prodigious rate. Attraction theorists have generally agreed upon the genesis of interpersonal attraction: We are attracted to persons who reward us. The more reward they provide, the more attractive we find them. Reward has been conceived to have so predictable an impact on attraction that Byrne[5] has even proposed an exact correspondence.

Although a good deal of evidence has been marshalled to support

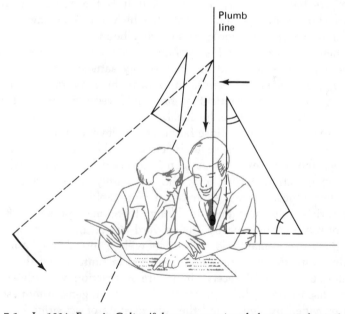

Figure 7-1. In 1884, Francis Galton[48] became convinced that metaphorical expressions often mirror physical reality. He proceeded to investigate "the inclination of one person toward another [p. 151]." On the basis of his observations of people seated next to each other at dinner, Galton concluded that the more attracted dinner partners were toward one another, the more they leaned toward one another. Galton evidently believed that insults could be discreetly traded in an upright position, but that sweeter words are usually spoken at an angle of less than 90°.

the reinforcement formulation of attraction, almost all of these data (a well as most data gathered to illuminate the antecedents of attraction are concerned with one variety of interpersonal attraction—liking. De spite the almost exclusive focus upon this one type, attraction theorist recognize that there are many other varieties. Byrne[5] has noted, for exam ple, that in addition to liking, interpersonal attraction is composed of number of other specific response components—such as friendship, pa rental love, romantic love, sexual attraction, and we would add, com panionate, or marital, love. Byrne also warns that the antecedents o these various subcategories of attraction may not be identical.

We agree that "passionate love" (in Byrne's terminology, romanti *and* sexual attraction) is a very special variety of interpersonal attractio and as such is entitled to independent attention. Furthermore, since th antecedents of passionate love seem to differ from liking in severa important ways, the prediction of romantic love may demand specia knowledge. Some of the ways in which these two phenomena appear t differ are outlined below.

The importance of fantasy

Researchers have generally assumed that it is the actual rewards ex changed during interpersonal contact which create liking. It seem doubtful, however, that people are so reality-bound.

When the lover closes his eyes and daydreams, he can summon up a flawless partner—one who instantaneously satisfies all his unspoken conflicting, and fleeting desires. In fantasy he may receive unlimite reward or he may *anticipate* that he would receive unlimited rewar were he ever to actually meet his ideal.

Compared to our grandiose fantasies, the level of reward we receiv in our real interactions is severely circumscribed. As a consequence sometimes the most extreme passion is aroused by partners who exis only in imagination or partners who are barely known. Reactions t real-life love objects often seem to be far more tepid.

Theorists interested only in *liking*, then, may possibly afford t focus entirely on the impact actual reward has on liking. In contrast, i seems likely that romantic-love theorists will be forced to take into con sideration both the rewards a lover receives in fantasy and the reward he fantasizes he might receive in future interaction with the partner (Further discussion of the importance of fantasy in generating passionat love is provided by Reik,[24] and the current state of scientific knowledg of fantasy is reviewed by Klinger.[19])

The effect of time on passion

Passionate love also seems to differ from liking in its fragility. One o the laws of liking, expressed by Homans,[15] is that "other things equal

he more a man interacts with another, the more he likes him [p. 203]."
n stark contrast to this statement is the observation that "The history
f a love affair is the drama of its fight against time." Authors of mariage and family texts tend to agree. Williamson,[38] for example, warns
hat romantic love is a temporary phenomenon and cautions that al-
hough intense passion may be a prerequisite for marriage, it is bound
o dwindle after lengthy interaction. Reik,[24] too, warns that the very
est one can hope for after several years of marriage is an "afterglow."

Over time, then, one's feelings toward another are probably
ffected less by the infinite rewards one fantasizes he will receive from
is ideal, more by the lesser rewards one can receive from an ordinary
ortal. Thus to the extent that the passionate lover is aroused more by
antasy than fact, the reality information about another, which time
sually provides, may erode passionate love. To the extent that liking
s based on more realistic grounds, it should not be as vulnerable with
ontinued interaction with the partner.

Liking is associated with positive reinforcements: passion is associated with a hodgepodge of conflicting emotions

iking seems to be a sensible phenomenon. From Aristotle onward,
heorists are in agreement: We like those who reward us and dislike
hose who thwart our desires. Unfortunately, that exotic variety of
ttraction, passionate love, does not seem to fit as neatly into the rein-
orcement paradigm. It is true that some practical people manage to fall
assionately in love with beautiful, wise, entertaining, and wealthy peo-
le who bring them unending affection and material rewards. Other
eople, however, with unfailing accuracy, seem to fall passionately in
ove with people who are almost guaranteed to bring them suffering and
aterial deprivation.

Observers disagree, passionately, about the nature of the emo-
ional states which are most conducive to passion. Some insist that
assionate love is inexorably entwined with fulfillment and the anticipa-
ion of fulfillment. Others insist that passionate love is virtually synon-
mous with agony. (Indeed, the original meaning of passion was
agony"—as in "Christ's Passion.") College students evidently share the
heorists' confusion as to whether passionate love is a joyous state or a
ainful one. Students at several universities were allowed to ask psy-
hologists one question about romantic love. Among the most frequent
uestions was: "Can you love and hate someone at the same time?"

A TENTATIVE THEORY OF PASSIONATE LOVE

t can be argued, then, that passionate love differs from liking in several
mportant ways and that a special approach to this particular variety of
nterpersonal attraction may be needed. Walster and Berscheid[33] pro-

posed a tentative theoretical framework to facilitate investigation o romantic love. Following Schachter's[27] general theory of emotion, it wa suggested that individuals will experience passionate love whenever tw conditions coexist: (1) They are intensely aroused physiologically; (2 situational cues indicate that "passionate love" is the appropriate labe for their intense feelings.

Schachter's two-component theory of emotion

In 1964, Schachter proposed a new paradigm for understanding huma emotional response. Schachter argued that two factors must coexist i a person is to experience emotion: (1) The person must be aroused phys iologically; (2) it must be appropriate for him to interpret his stirred-u state in emotional terms. Schachter argued that neither physiologica arousal nor appropriate emotional cognitions would, by themselves, b sufficient to produce an emotional experience for the individual.

To test the hypothesis that physiological arousal and appropriat cognitions are separate and indispensable components of a true emo tional experience, Schachter had to find a technique for separatel manipulating arousal and cognition. In their classic study, Schachter an Singer[28] conceived a way to do just that.

The data supported their hypothesis and provided support for th contention that *both* physiological arousal and appropriate cognition are indispensable components of a true emotional experience; neithe component alone appears to create the experiencing of an emotion.

The two-component theory and passionate love

Walster and Berscheid[33] speculated that perhaps the two-componen theory would be a more useful blueprint than the reinforcement para digm for assembling the apparent jumble of redundant, inconsisten and implausible pieces of the passionate love puzzle. Certain puzzl pieces which do not fit into the reinforcement framework seem less awk ward in the two-component framework. There is, for example, no longe the problem of explaining why both intensely positive and intensel negative (and presumably unrewarding) experiences can be conducive t love. Both types of experiences may produce physiological arousa Stimuli that produce "aesthetic appreciation," "sexual arousal," "grati tude," "rejection," "jealousy," or "total confusion" generally produc states of intense physiological arousal. Thus, these positive *and* negativ experiences may all have the potential for deepening an individual' passion for another.

What may be important in determining how the individual feel about the person who is apparently generating these intense feelings i how he *labels* his reaction. If the situation is arranged so that it is rea sonable for him to attribute this agitated state to "passionate love," h should experience love. As soon as he ceases to attribute his arousal to passionate love, or the arousal itself ceases, love should die.

Does any compelling experimental evidence exist to support the contention that under conditions of physiological arousal, a wide variety of stimuli, properly labeled, may deepen passion? No. Studies have not yet been conducted to test this hypothesis. There are, however, a few investigations designed to test other hypotheses that provide tangential support for the two-component theory of passionate love.

GENERATING PHYSIOLOGICAL AROUSAL: THE FIRST STEP IN GENERATING PASSIONATE LOVE

Unpleasant emotional experiences: facilitators of passion?

Negative reinforcements produce arousal in all animals.[29] For human beings there is some evidence that under certain conditions such un-pleasant—but arousing—states as fear, rejection, and frustration may enhance romantic passion.

Fear   When a person is frightened, he becomes intensely physiologically aroused for a substantial period of time.[1,26,40] An intriguing study by Brehm, Gatz, Goethals, McCrimmon, and Ward[4] suggests that fear can contribute to a man's attraction to a woman. Brehm and co-workers tested the hypothesis that a person's attraction to another would be multiplied by prior arousal from an irrelevant event. To test this hypothesis, one group of men was led to believe that they would soon receive three "pretty stiff" electrical shocks. Half of the men in this group ("threat" subjects) were allowed to retain this erroneous expectation throughout the experiment. The other half ("threat-relief" subjects) were frightened, but then were later reassured that the experimenter had made an error; they had been assigned to the control group and would receive no shock. The remainder of the men were told at the start that they had been assigned to the control group; the experimenter did not even mention the possibility that they might receive shock. All of the men then were introduced to a young female college student and asked how much they liked her.

The men in the three groups should vary in how physiologically aroused they were at the time they met the girl. The threat subjects should be quite frightened. The threat-relief subjects should be experiencing both residual fear reactions and vast relief. Both groups of men should be more aroused than the men in the control group. The investigators predicted, as we would, that both threat and threat-relief subjects would like the girl more than would control subjects. These expectations were confirmed. (Threat and threat-relief men did not differ in their liking for the girl.) A frightening event, then, may facilitate attraction.

Rejection   Rejection is always disturbing. When a person is rejected, he generally experiences a strong emotional reaction. Usually one labels his reaction embarrassment, pain, anger, or hatred. It should also be possible, however, under certain conditions, for a rejected individual to label his emotional response as "love."

Some suggestive evidence that love or hate may spring from rejection comes from several laboratory experiments designed to test other hypotheses.[7,16,31] Let us consider one of these experiments and the way a Schachterian might reinterpret it.

Jacobs and co-workers attempted to determine how changes in the self-esteem of college men affected their receptivity to affection expressed by a female college student. First, the experimenter gave the men a number of personality tests (the MMPI, Rorschach, etc.). A few weeks later he returned a false analysis of their personalities. Half of the men were given a flattering report, stressing their sensitivity, honesty, originality, and freedom of outlook. The other half received an insulting personality report. The report stressed their immaturity, weak personality, conventionality, and lack of leadership ability. This critical report naturally disturbed most of the men.

Soon after receiving their analyses, each man was made acquainted with a young female college student, who actually was an experimental confederate. Half of the time the girl responded to the man with a warm, affectionate, and accepting evaluation. The investigators found that the men who had received the critical personality evaluation were *more attracted* to the girl than were their more confident counterparts. Half of the time the girl was cool and rejecting. Under these conditions, a dramatic reversal occurred. The previously rejected men *disliked* the girl more than did their more confident counterparts. Under these conditions, the previously insulted individual's agitation was presumably transformed to enmity. A preceding painful event, then, may heighten the emotional response we feel toward another's expression of affection or disapproval.

Frustration and challenge   Khrushchev,[13] depicting the Russian character, said:

> When the aristocrats first discovered that potatoes were a cheap way of feeding the peasants, they had no success in getting the peasants to eat them. But they knew their people. They fenced the potatoes in with high fences. The peasants then stole the potatoes and soon acquired a taste for them [p. 110].

Theorists seem to agree that the obstacles a lover encounters in his attempt to possess another intensify love.

Sexual inhibition is often said to be the foundation of romantic feelings. For example, Freud[12] argued: "Some obstacle is necessary to swell the tide of libido to its height; and at all periods of history whenever natural barriers in the way of satisfaction have not sufficed, mankind has erected conventional ones in order to enjoy love [p. 213]." Presumably, when sexual energy is bottled up, it will be sublimated and expressed as romantic, rather than sexual, longing.

Experimental evidence concerning the impact of other kinds of obstacles to love on the intensity of the lovers' romantic feelings comes from Walster, Walster, Piliavin, and Schmidt[36] and from Driscoll, Davis, and Lipitz.[8]

Socrates, Ovid, the *Kamasutra*, and "Dear Abby" are in agreement about one thing: A girl who is hard to get inspires more passion than does a girl who "throws herself" at a man.

Socrates[41] advises Theodota, a *hetaera*:

. . . They will appreciate your favors most highly if you wait till they ask for them. The sweetest meats, you see, if served before they are wanted seem sour, and to those who had enough they are positively nauseating; but even poor fare is very welcome when offered to a hungry man. [Theodota inquires] And how can I make them hunger for my fare? [Socrates' reply] Why, in the first place, you must not offer it to them when they have had enough—by a show of reluctance to yield, and by holding back until they are as keen as can be for them the same gifts are much more to the recipient than when they are offered before they are desired [p. 247].

Ovid[23] remarks:

Fool, if you feel no need to guard your girl for her own sake, see that you guard her for mine, so I may want her the more. Easy things nobody wants, but what is forbidden is tempting. . . . Anyone who can love the wife of an indolent cuckold, I should suppose, would steal buckets of sand from the shore [pp. 65, 66].

Bertrand Russell[18] argues:

The belief in the immense value of the lady is a psychological effect of the difficulty of obtaining her, and I think it may be laid down that when a man has no difficulty in obtaining a woman, his feeling toward her does not take the form of romantic love [pp. 10–11].

To find authors in such rare accord on an aspect of passionate love is refreshing. Better yet, their observation seems to provide support for the two-component theory. Unfortunately for the theory (but fortunately for easy-to-get men and women), the data suggest that hard-to-get men and women do not inspire especially intense liking in their suitors.[34,35]

Walster et al.[34] report several experiments designed to demonstrate that a challenging girl will be a more dazzling conquest than a readily available girl. All experiments secured negative results.

In the first set of experiments, college males were recruited for a computer date-match program. The program was ostensibly designed to evaluate and improve current computer matching programs. In an initial interview, men filled out a lengthy questionnaire. They were informed that the computer would *either* provide them with the name of a girl especially matched to their requirements, *or* with the name of a girl randomly selected from the date-match pool. (Presumably, only by comparing men's reactions to matched versus randomly selected girls could it be judged whether or not the matching procedure was effective.)

Two weeks later the men reported to collect the name and telephone number of their date-match. They were asked to telephone her and to arrange a date from the laboratory, so that after the call their first impressions of the date could be assessed. Actually, each man was provided with the telephone number of the same girl—an experimental confederate.

In the *easy-to-get* condition, the girl was delighted to receive his telephone call and grateful to be asked out. In the *hard-to-get* condition, the girl accepted a coffee date with some reluctance. She obviously had many other dates, and was not sure whether or not she really wanted to get involved with someone new.

The results of this and other similar experiments failed to support the "hard-to-get" hypothesis; it was found that boys had an equally high opinion of the hard-to-get and the easy-to-get girls.

A further study—a field experiment—also failed to support the hypothesis. In this study, a prostitute serving as the experimenter delivered the experimental communication while she was mixing drinks for her clients. Half the time she played hard to get. She indicated that she could only see a limited number of clients, and thus, she had to be very selective about whom she could accept as a customer. Half of the time (in the easy-to-get condition) she did not deliver this communication, but allowed the clients to assume that she would accept all customers. She then had sexual intercourse with the clients.

The client's liking for the prostitute was assessed in three ways: (1) the prostitute estimated the client's liking for her; (2) she recorded how much he paid for the 50-min hour; and (3) she recorded how soon he called her for a second appointment.

The hard-to-get hypothesis was *not* supported. Clients appeared to like the selective and unselective prostitute equally well, regardless of the measure of liking used.

Faced with this shower of evidence that a hard-to-get date does *not* seem to inspire more passion than the easy-to-get one, Walster and co-workers reconsidered their hypothesis. First, they systematically considered the advantages and disadvantages a suitor might anticipate from a generally hard-to-get or a generally easy-to-get girl. For example, an "easy-to-get" girl, while perhaps desperate for company because she is unattractive, might be a friendly and relaxing date; a "hard-to-get" girl, while having the advantage of being a challenge, might be unfriendly and ego crushing. In previous research, each girl's advantages and disadvantages may have balanced one another out. The girls—whether easy or hard to get—had potentially attractive assets and potentially dangerous liabilities. What would the perfect date be like? What kind of a girl would possess most of the advantages, but few of the disadvantages, of both the hard-to-get and the easy-to-get girls? A girl who is crazy about you (she is easy for *you* to get) but is hard for anyone else to get should be maximally rewarding.

Walster and co-workers then tested the hypothesis that the selectively hard-to-get girl would be preferred to a generally hard-to-get girl, to a generally easy-to-get girl, or to a control girl (a person whose general hard-to-getness or easy-to-getness was unknown) in the following way: Men were again recruited for a computer date-match program. They filled out questionnaires, and then waited several weeks for the computer to match them with potential dates. When they reported to the lab for the name of their date, they were told that five girls had been selected by the computer. The men examined biographies of these girls so that they could choose which one they wanted to date. The girls' biographies described their backgrounds, interests, attitudes, etc. Attached to the biography was each girl's evaluation of the dates that had been assigned to her. Each subject, who knew his own code numbers, could thus discover how each girl had rated him and the four other men with whom the computer had matched her. (Presumably, her evaluations were based on the biographies she had been shown.)

These ratings constituted the experimental manipulation. One girl made it evident that she was *generally easy to get*. She indicated that she was "very eager" to date every fellow the computer had assigned to her. A second girl made it evident that she was *generally hard to get*. She indicated that she was willing, but not particularly eager to date the five fellows assigned to her. One of the girls made it evident that she was *selectively hard to get*. Although she was very eager to date the subject, she was reluctant to date any of his rivals. Two of the potential dates were *control* girls. (The experimenter said that they had not yet stopped in to evaluate their computer matches, and, thus, no information was available concerning their preferences.)

These data provided strong support for the revised hypothesis. Men liked the generally hard to get, the generally easy to get, and control dates equally. The selectively hard-to-get girl, however, was uniformly the most popular girl, liked far more than her competitors.

Driscoll, Davis, and Lipitz[8] proposed that parental interference in a love relationship intensifies the feelings of romantic love between members of the couple. The authors begin their delightful article by surveying the extent to which parental opposition and intense love have been pitted against one another. They remind readers that Romeo and Juliet's short but intense love affair took place against the background of total opposition from the two feuding families. The difficulties and separations which the family conflict created appear to have intensified the lovers' feelings for each other.

Finally, the authors remind us that DeRougement,[6] in his historical analysis of romantic love, emphasized the persistent association of obstacles or grave difficulties with intense passion. They conclude that an affair consummated without major difficulty apparently lacks zest.

The authors distinguish between romantic love (for example, infatuation, passionate love) and conjugal love. They point out that romantic love is associated with uncertainty and challenge in contrast to the trust and genuine understanding of conjugal love. Conjugal love is said to evolve gradually out of mutually satisfying interactions and from increasing confidence in one's personal security in the relationship.

The authors tested their hypothesis that parental opposition would deepen romantic love (as opposed to conjugal love) in the following way: 91 married couples and 49 dating couples (18 of whom were living together) were recruited to participate in a marital relations project. Some of these couples were happily matched; others were not. The typical married couples had been married 4 years.

All of the 49 couples were seriously committed to one another; most of them had been going together for about 8 months.

During an initial interview, all the couples filled out three scales:

Assessment of Parental Interferences: This scale measured the extent to which the couple's parents interfered and caused difficulties in their relationship. Participants were asked whether or not they had ever complained to their mate that her (his) parents interfere in their relationship, are a bad influence, are hurting the relationship, take advantage of her (him), don't accept him (her), or try to make him (her) look bad.

Conjugal Love Scale: This scale measured the extent to which participants loved, felt they cared about and needed their partner, and felt that the relationship was more important than anything else.

Romantic Love Scale: The researchers rescored the Conjugal Love Scale in order to obtain "a purified index of Romantic Love." (This index was constructed by partialing out of the Love Scale that portion of variance which could be counted for by trust—a characteristic the authors felt more typical of conjugal love than of passionate love.)

The authors found that parental interference and passion were related, as they expected them to be. Parental interference and romantic love were correlated for both the unmarried sample and for the married sample. However, parental interference and conjugal love were also correlated for the unmarried sample, although not for the married sample. Parental interference and romantic love did seem to be positively and significantly related.

Next, the authors investigated whether *increasing* parental interference would provoke increased passion; 6–10 months after the initial interview, the authors invited all of the couples back for a second interview. During this second interview, the participants once again completed Parental Interference, Conjugal Love, and Romantic Love scales. By comparing subjects' initial interview responses with their later ones, the authors could calculate whether the participants' parents had become more or less interfering in the relationship, and how these changes in parental interference had affected the couples' affair. The authors found that as parents began to interfere more in a relationship, the couple appeared to fall more deeply in love. If the parents had become resigned to the relationship, and had begun to interfere less, the couples began to feel less intensely about one another.

Data indicating that parental interference breeds passion are fascinating. When parents interfere in an "unsuitable" match, they interfere with the intent of destroying the relationship, not of strengthening it. Yet, these data warn that parental interference is likely to boomerang if the relationship survives. It may foster desire rather than divisiveness.

The preceding data lend some credence to the argument that the juxtaposition of agony and ecstasy in passionate love may not be entirely accidental. Although most people assume that agony follows love, it may be that it precedes it and provides the ground in which it can flourish. Loneliness, deprivation, frustration, hatred, and insecurity all appear capable—under certain conditions—of supplementing a person's romantic feelings. Passion demands physiological arousal, and unpleasant experiences are arousing.

Pleasant emotional experiences: facilitators of passion?

Sexual gratification We previously noted that Freud and others assumed the arousal associated with inhibited sexuality to be the foundation of romantic feelings. Yet both inhibited sexuality and gratified sexuality should be arousing. According to Masters and Johnson,[21] sexual intercourse induces hyperventilation, tachycardia, and marked increases in blood pressure. According to Zuckerman,[42] during the initial, or excitement, phase of sexual arousal, the physiological reactions exhibited are "not specific to sexual arousal, but may reflect orienting to novelty, or emotions other than sexual arousal [p. 297]." In fact, many of the physiological responses typical of this phase are also characteristic of fear and anger. Zuckerman argued that, "In general, only tumescence, vasodilation, genital secretions, and rhythmic muscular movements are characteristic of sexual arousal alone [p. 300]."

In brief, sexual experiences and the anticipation of such experiences are generally arousing. And religious advisors, school counselors, and psychoanalysts to the contrary, sexual gratification has probably incited as much passionate love as has sexual frustration.

Valins[30] has demonstrated that even the erroneous belief that a woman has excited a man sexually can facilitate his attraction to her. Valins recruited male college students ostensibly to determine how males react physiologically to sexual stimuli. The men were told that their heart rate would be amplified and recorded while they viewed 10 semi-nude *Playboy* photographs. The feedback the men received was experimentally controlled. They were led to believe that when they examined slides picturing some of the *Playboy* bunnies, their heart rate altered markedly; when they examined others, they had no reaction. (Valins assumed that men would interpret an alteration in heart rate as enthusiasm for the bunny and no change in heart rate as disinterest.)

The men's liking for the "arousing" and "nonarousing" slides was assessed in three ways: (1) they were asked to rate how "attractive or appealing" each pinup was; (2) they were offered a photo of a pinup in remuneration for participating in the experiment; and (3) they were interviewed a month later (in a totally different context) and were asked to rank the attractiveness of the pinups. Regardless of the measure of attraction used, men markedly preferred the pinups they thought had aroused them to those they thought had not.

Need satisfaction   Psychologists have tended to focus almost exclusively on the contribution that sex makes to love, but other rewards are also important. People have a wide variety of needs, and, at any stage of life, many of their needs must remain unsatisfied. When a potential love object meets an important, unsatisfied need, the suitor is likely to have a strong emotional response. Such positive emotional responses should be able to provide the fuel needed for passion.

Excitement   Dangerous experiences are arousing. For some peculiar reason, psychologists almost inevitably assume that the arousal one experiences in dangerous settings is entirely negative. Thus, they typically label the physiological reactions which are provoked by dangerous experiences as "fear," "stress," or "pain." They then focus upon ways individuals can learn to foresee and avoid actual danger, or to overcome unrealistic fears. (They almost seem to equate "excitement seeking" with wickedness. For example, in *Human Sexual Response*, Masters and Johnson[21] reassured readers that "mere thrill seekers" were scrupulously prohibited from participating in their research. Presumably, one has to be properly respectful about sex before he is entitled to assist in scientific discovery.)

Almost never do psychologists acknowledge that it is sometimes fun to be frightened; that it is enjoyable to have a strong emotional response; that reactions to danger can be labeled in positive, as well as in negative, ways; that excitement is an antidote to boredom. One pioneer, Berlyne,[2] has recognized that "danger and delight grow on one stalk," and has systematically explored the conditions under which novelty and excitement are especially attractive to people.

Nonscientists appear to believe that arousal can be fun. Parachuting, skiing, and sports car racing are valued by sports enthusiasts for the danger they provide. Passionate affairs are valued by many for their excitement. The individual who realizes that he is on dangerous ground may label the rush of passion that he experiences as "love," as well as "anxiety."

We have proposed a two-factor theory of passionate love. The preceding discussion has focused almost exclusively on one factor. We have discussed the idea that physiological arousal is a crucial component of passionate love, and that the stimuli often associated with fear, pain, and frustration, as well as those often associated with more positive experiences, may contribute to passionate love. Let us now consider the circumstances that help push individuals to label their tumultuous feelings as "passionate love."

THE SECOND STEP IN GENERATING
PASSIONATE LOVE: LABELING

What determines how an aroused individual will label his tumultuous feelings? The reinforcement paradigm helps us to pinpoint some of the factors that should affect the way individuals interpret the arousal.

Children are taught how to label their feelings

An anarchic array of stimuli constantly impinge on a child. The child learns how to categorize these stimuli, to discriminate "important" categories of stimuli from "unimportant" ones. He also learns what reactions different categories of stimuli produce in a person.

Envision, for example, a little boy who is playing with a truck while his mother greets a newly arrived neighbor and her infant daughter. He is rubbing his eyes; he has missed his nap. Soon it will be dinner time; he experiences vague hunger pangs. While absorbed in the visitor's movements, he accidently runs his truck over his hand; it hurts. He watches his mother talking and gesturing to the visitor and her little girl. Her voice seems unusually high and animated. They all look at him. His nose tickles.

In response to this *complex* of factors, the boy becomes momentarily overwrought. He hides his face in his mother's skirt for a few seconds; and then peers out. What caused him to hide his face? What emotion is he feeling? Is he jealous of the little girl? Is he afraid of strangers? Is he playing a game? Is he angry because the truck hurt his hand? Is he trying to get attention?

His mother provides an answer for him. She says, "Don't be shy, John. Susan won't hurt you. Come out and meet her." His mother reduces a chaotic jumble of stimuli to manageable size. She instructs him that it is Susan's appearance that has caused his emotional agitation. She informs him that when one has an emotional reaction in the presence of strangers it is called "shyness." She also communicates that the other stimuli, his sore hand for example, are not responsible for his aroused state.

By the time the child reaches adolescence, he has learned cultural norms concerning categories of stimuli (situations) that produce specific emotions. He has been painstakingly taught what the common emotions "feel" like. He may base his identification on: (1) the perception that he is generally aroused *plus* his knowledge of the situation, or (2) the perception that he is *generally* aroused *plus* his knowledge of the situation *plus* the perception that he is physiologically aroused in a *special* way. (Physiologists have not yet identified the extent to which each emotion is associated with unique and readily recognized physiological cues.) In any case, by adolescence, individuals are well trained in what stimuli go with what emotions.

Some emotions are better articulated than others

Children undoubtedly have clear perceptions as to what hate, embarrassment, jealousy, and joy are supposed to feel like. They get little practice in learning to discriminate more esoteric emotions, such as bliss, loathing, and contempt.

"Passionate love" is undoubtedly a poorly articulated emotion. Children receive little instruction as to the conditions under which "passionate love" is an appropriate label for one's feelings versus the conditions under which the passionate love label is inappropriate. Most parents assume that children are incapable of experiencing passionate love; they consider passion to be an adolescent phenomenon.

The fact that children are given only glimmerings of information as to the situations conducive to passion, and what passion is supposed to feel like, probably accounts at least in part for the fact that so many teen-agers seem confused about the nature of love. "Dear Abby" frequently receives concerned letters asking, "How can I tell if I'm really in love?" Inevitably, she fails to provide an answer. Her stock reply is,

"When you're in love, you'll know it; you won't have to ask." Perhaps "Dear Abby" does not know either.

Popular songs provide some instructions to teen-agers concerning what love should feel like: "When your heart goes bumpety, bump . . . that's love, love, love" they are informed. (The notion that love can be identified by the presence of physiological arousal, at least as evidenced by a quickened heart rate, or even, in severe cases, by cardiac arrest, is common in folklore—if new to social science.) The fact that adolescents often have only very general and somewhat vague notions about how to identify love suggests that situational factors should have a profound impact on whether they label a wide variety of states of generalized arousal as love or as something else.

Sometimes individuals experience a mixture of emotions

People sometimes have difficulty labeling their feelings because a number of potential labels could reasonably describe their aroused state. Consider, for example, the soldier who reports that when he received his first mail from home, he became extremely agitated. He is at a loss to explain just why the package had upset him. Was he feeling homesick? Perhaps the package was upsetting because it was a tangible reminder of how much he longed to be back home. Was he feeling lonesome? His girl friend had sent the package; perhaps he hadn't realized how much he missed her. Was he feeling resentful? The package reminded him that people back home were free while he was stuck in foreign combat. Or was he worried? His girl friend's accompanying letter mentioned problems with his car and with his application for admission to college. When a myriad of labels are potentially appropriate for one's feelings, we might again expect social influences to have an unusually great impact on one's choice of label.

Everyone loves a lover: the cultural encouragement of love

In our culture it is expected that almost everyone eventually will fall in love. Individuals are strongly encouraged to interpret a wide range of confused feelings as love. Linton[20] made this point in a harsh observation:

> All societies recognize that there are occasional violent emotional attachments between persons of the opposite sex, but our present American culture is practically the only one which has attempted to capitalize on these and make them the basis for marriage. The hero of the modern American movie is always a romantic lover, just as the hero of an old Arab epic is always an epileptic. A cynic may suspect that in any ordinary population the percentage of individuals with capacity for romantic love of the Hollywood type was about as large as that of persons able to throw genuine epileptic fits [p. 175].

Cultural norms specify whom it is reasonable to love

I took one look at you and then my heart stood still   Firestone[11] says, "It's not true that only the external appearance of a woman matters. The underwear is also important [p. 134]." In our culture, people assume that passionate fantasies are inspired only by attractive human beings. If one admits that he is sexually attracted to a hunchback, an octogenarian, or a man with no nose, he is branded as sick or perverse.

The evidence suggests that most individuals docilely accept the prescription that beauty and sexual and romantic passion are inexorably linked. The best evidence we have suggests that teen-agers and young adults are more enamored by the physical attractiveness of their dating partners than by the partners' intelligence, personality, or similarity.

In a typical study, Berscheid, Dion, Walster, and Walster[3] took Polaroid snapshots of college males and females. Judges categorized each photo as attractive or unattractive. The experimenters then secured a dating history from the student. The physical attractiveness of female subjects was strongly related to their actual dating popularity. Attractive females had more dates within the past year, the past month, and the past week. There was slight (but insignificant) relationship between the males' physical attractiveness and his dating frequency.

Walster, Aronson, Abrahams, and Rottmann[32] assessed the physical attractiveness of 752 college freshmen. (A panel of college sophomores rated them; they had only 5 sec or so in which to rate the freshmen's attractiveness.) A good deal of data concerning the freshmen's intelligence, personality, and attitudes were also assembled in subsequent university-wide testing. Freshmen were then randomly assigned a date for a large computer dance. During intermission, the freshmen were asked to say how satisfied they were with their computer date. The authors discovered that the sole determinant of how much students liked their date, how eager they were to date their partner again, and how often they subsequently asked their partner out for a date (it was determined later) was simply the physical attractiveness of the partner. The more physically attractive the date, the more he or she was liked and the more he or she was pursued. Efforts to find additional factors that would influence attraction failed. For example, students with exceptional social skills and intelligence levels were not liked any better than were students less fortunate in this regard. It seems, then, that it is helpful to be beautiful if you wish to inspire passion in your contemporaries.

Love and marriage . . . go together like a horse and carriage   Winch[39] has also argued that one's culture dictates whom one can or cannot love. He maintains that cultural norms legislate that for each person only a strictly prescribed subsample of the population is lovable or "marriageable." This acceptable group is called "the field of eligibles." Young,

unmarried adults soon learn that if they fall in love with the right person—someone in their field of eligibles—they can marry and merit social
approval. If they should fall in love with the wrong person, they must
expect to encounter stinging social disapproval. In American culture,
the "field of eligibles" consists of partners who are of the opposite sex,
who are single, who are similar to oneself in age (marriages between
elderly women and young boys are subject to more disdain than marriages between elderly men and young girls, however), similar in other
social background variables, who have known one another for some
time, and who desire one another sexually.

Cultural influences are generally effective in determining whom
one should love. If parents try to impose additional restrictions on their
children's choices, they may not be effective in guiding their children's
selections. We recall that "unjustified" parental interference was found
by Driscoll et al.[8] not to deter the formation of romantic bonds.

Infatuation versus love In a poll conducted at three universities, college students were asked what one thing they most wished they knew
about romantic love. A surprisingly frequent question was: "What is
the difference between infatuation and love? How will I know when I
am really in love and not just infatuated?" We have become increasingly
skeptical that infatuation and passionate love differ in any way—*at the
time one is experiencing them.* Data provided by Ellis and Harper,[10] for
example, suggest that the difference between infatuation and romantic
love is merely semantic. Ellis reported that young adults use the term
"romantic love" to describe relationships with the opposite sex that are
characterized by strong positive affect and that *are still in progress.*
They use the term "infatuation" to describe relationships with the opposite sex that were characterized by strong positive affect and that, for a
variety of reasons, *were terminated.*

It appears, then, that it may be possible to tell infatuation from
romantic love only in retrospect. If a relationship flowers, one continues
to believe he is experiencing true love; if a relationship dies, one concludes that he was merely infatuated. We need not assume, then, that at
the time one experiences the feeling, "true love" differs in any way
from the supposed "counterfeit," infatuation.

If an individual relabels his feelings as infatuation, rather than love,
it may have important consequences for his subsequent behavior. In our
culture, "romantic love" tends to be the *sine qua non* for marriage.
Kephart[17] found that in his sample, 65% of the college men would *not*
marry a woman they did not love—even though she possessed every
other characteristic they desired in a wife. (Women did not associate
"love" with "marriage" to the same extent as did men. Only 24% of the
women said that they would *not* marry a desirable man simply because
they did not love him.)

Since romantic love is likely to lead to marriage in our culture, parents are eager to ensure that young people label their feelings as "love" only if they are directed toward "right" people. When their children are attracted to the wrong sort—to someone outside their field of eligibles—the parents may try to persuade their children to label their attraction as "infatuation" and thereby decrease the likelihood that the children will marry unsuitable partners.

Cultural reinforcements determine appropriate labels   When an individual is experiencing arousal which he can reasonably label in a variety of ways, we speculated earlier that he will prefer to label his feelings in whatever way he anticipates will be most rewarded by others and will avoid labeling his feelings in ways that he can anticipate will provoke punishment. When one systematically applies such reinforcement principles to predicting how individuals will label their reactions there are some interesting ramifications. For example, at one period in American history (and perhaps even today), the "double standard" for sexual behavior was commonly accepted.[25] This standard insisted that "nice" girls must not have sexual intercourse before marriage. If, however, they were "in love," especially if they were engaged, and particularly if they married soon after, transgression was forgivable. These restrictions did not apply to men. Men were supposed to have some sexual experience before marriage. In fact, in many circles a man who had many sexual conquests was held in high regard.

How would we expect these inconsistent sex-specific, social norms to affect the way men and women labeled sexual arousal? Cost considerations would predispose men and women to choose quite different labels for precisely the same type of physiological reaction. When a man became aroused in a sexual context, he could afford to frankly label his reaction as "sexual excitement." A woman could not. She had most to gain from convincing herself that passion equaled love since such a label allowed her to have both sexual relations and self-respect. Given such a reward structure, it is not surprising that people soon came to believe that men are sexier than women, and that women are the romantics.

REFERENCES

1. Ax, A. F. Fear and anger in humans. *Psychosomatic Medicine*, 1953, **15**, 433–442.

2. Berlyne, D. E. *Conflict, arousal and curiosity*. New York: McGraw-Hill, 1960.

3. Berscheid, E., Dion, K., Walster, E., & Walster, G. W. Physical attractiveness and dating choice: A test of the matching hypothesis. *Journal of Experimental Social Psychology*, 1971, **7**, 173–189.

4. Brehm, J. W., Gatz, M., Goethals, G., McCrimmon, J., & Ward, L.

Psychological arousal and interpersonal attraction. Mimeo. Available from authors, 1970.

5. Byrne, D. *The attraction paradigm.* New York: Academic Press, 1971.

6. DeRougemont, D. *Love in the western world.* (Translated by M. Belgion.) New York: Harcourt Brace Jovanovich, 1940.

7. Dittes, J. E. Attractiveness of group as function of self-esteem and acceptance by group. *Journal of Abnormal and Social Psychology,* 1959, **59**, 77–82.

8. Driscoll, R., Davis, K. E., & Lipitz, M. E. Parental interference and romantic love: The Romeo and Juliet effect. *Journal of Personality and Social Psychology,* 1972, **24**, 1–10.

9. Durrell, L. *Clea.* New York: Dutton, 1961.

10. Ellis, A., & Harper, A. *Creative marriage.* New York: Lyle Stuart, 1961.

11. Firestone, S. *The dialectic of sex.* New York: Bantam, 1971.

12. Freud, S. *Group psychology and the analysis of the ego.* (Translated by J. Strachey.) New York: International Psychoanalytic Press, 1922.

13. Galbraith, J. K. *The ambassador's journal.* Boston: Houghton Mifflin, 1969.

14. Homans, G. C. *The human group.* New York: Harcourt Brace Jovanovich, 1950.

15. Homans, G. C. *Social behavior: Its elementary forms.* New York: Harcourt Brace Jovanovich, 1961.

16. Jacobs, L., Berscheid, E., & Walster, E. Self-esteem and attraction. *Journal of Personality and Social Psychology,* 1971, **17**, 84–91.

17. Kephart, W. M. Some correlates of romantic love. *Journal of Marriage and the Family,* 1967, **29**, 470–474.

18. Kirch, A. M. (Ed.). *The anatomy of love.* New York: Dell, 1960.

19. Klinger, E. *Structure and functions of fantasy.* New York: Wiley, 1971.

20. Linton, R. *The study of man.* New York: Appleton, 1936.

21. Masters, W. H., & Johnson, V. E. *Human sexual response.* Boston: Little, Brown, 1966.

22. Newcomb, T. M. *The acquaintance process.* New York: Holt, Rinehart & Winston, 1961.

23. Ovid. *The art of love.* (Translated by Rolfe Humphries.) Bloomington: University of Indiana Press, 1962.

24. Reik, T. *A psychologist looks at love.* New York: Holt, Rinehart & Winston, 1944.

25. Reiss, L. *Premarital sexual standards in America.* New York: Free Press, 1960.

26. Schachter, S. Pain, fear and anger in hypertensives and normotensives: A psycho-physiological study. *Psychosomatic Medicine,* 1957, **19**, 17–24.

27. Schachter, S. The interaction of cognitive and physiological determinants of emotional state. In L. Berkowitz (Ed.), *Advances in experimental social psychology.* Vol. 1. New York: Academic Press, 1964.

28. Schachter, S., & Singer, J. F. Cognitive, social and physiological determinants of emotional state. *Psychological Review,* 1962, **69**, 379–399.

29. Skinner, B. F. *The behavior of organisms: An experimental analysis.* New York: Appleton, 1938.

30. Valins, S. Cognitive effects of false heart-rate feedback. *Journal of Personality and Social Psychology,* 1966, **4**, 400–408.

31. Walster, E. The effect of self-esteem on romantic liking. *Journal of Experimental Social Psychology,* 1965, **1**, 184–197.

32. Walster, E., Aronson, V., Abrahams, D., & Rottmann, L. The importance of physical attractiveness in dating behavior. *Journal of Personality and Social Psychology,* 1966, **4**, 508–516.

33. Walster, E., & Berscheid, E. Adrenaline makes the heart grow fonder. *Psychology Today,* 1971, **5**, 47–62.

34. Walster, E., Berscheid, E., & Walster, G. New directions in equity research. *Journal of Personality and Social Psychology,* 1973, **25**, 151–176.

35. Walster, E., Walster, G., & Berscheid, E. The efficacy of playing hard-to-get. *Journal of Experimental Education,* 1971, **39**, 73–77.

36. Walster, E., Walster, G., Piliavin, J., & Schmidt, L. "Playing hard-to-get": Understanding an elusive phenomenon. *Journal of Personality and Social Psychology,* 1973, **26**, 113–121.

37. Webb, E. J., Campbell, D. T., Schwartz, R. D., & Secrest, L. *Unobtrusive measures: Nonreactive research in the social sciences.* Skokie, Ill.: Rand McNally, 1966.

38. Williamson, R. C. *Marriage and family relations.* New York: Wiley, 1966.

39. Winch, R. F. *The modern family.* New York: Holt, Rinehart & Winston, 1952.

40. Wolf, S., & Wolff, H. G. *Human gastric function.* (2d ed.) New York: Oxford University Press, 1947.

41. Xenophon. *Memorabilia III.* (Translated by E. C. Marchant.) London: Heinemann, 1923.

42. Zuckerman, M. Physiological measures of sexual response in the human. *Psychological Bulletin,* 1971, **75**, 297–329.

CHApter Eight

Marital
Sexuality

Premarital Sexual Experience:
A Longitudinal Study

It has been noted several times in previous chapters that premarital inter-course is occurring with increasing frequency, especially between individuals who feel that they are in love and who plan to marry. Beyond the issue of morality, one question which is inevitably raised about such statistics has to do with the effect of this sexual intimacy on the subsequent marriage.

At the level of speculation, there are arguments for either a negative or a positive effect. Those who feel that marriage benefits from premarital sex argue that it makes little sense for a couple to enter into a lifetime sexual partnership without first getting to know one another sexually as well as socially. In addition, it is said that the traditional image of two virgins fumbling awkwardly at one another on the wedding night places too great an emo-tional and psychological strain on what should be simply a happy and comfortable new stage in a close relationship.

Alternatively, it has been suggested that premarital sex most often in-volves negative elements in which the individuals must hide their behavior from disapproving parents. Hurried, nervous encounters in a parked auto-mobile or down the hallway from sleeping parents are not recommended as the ideal way to begin a sexual relationship. In addition, however permissive we may have become as a society, many individuals still feel strongly that sexual purity is superior to sexual experience in one's bride or bridegroom; if they have premarital relations, they afterward may feel disapproving of their partner and guilty about their own behavior.

In the following article, psychologist Ben Ard presents data which sug-gest that, in effect, it does not matter. That is, the overwhelming majority of married couples who had had premarital intercourse felt that it either helped their marriage or had no effect, *and* the overwhelming majority of the couples who refrained from premarital intercourse thought the same thing. It seems that most individuals are relatively pleased with what they themselves chose to do premaritally and that there is no reason to believe that one's sexual activity or inactivity with a future spouse should have a negative effect on the later relationship.

Premarital Sexual Experience:
A Longitudinal Study

Ben N. Ard, Jr.

The premarital sexual experience of men and women today seems to be changing from that of previous generations. Terman[12] found that there has been a steady increase in premarital intercourse among persons born

Reprinted in an edited version from: Ard, B. N., Jr. Premarital sexual experience: A longitudinal study. *Journal of Sex Research*, 1974, **10**, 32–39.

in 4 successive decades (before 1890, and through 1910), and that these trends were proceeding with such extraordinary rapidity that he predicted intercourse with one's future spouse before marriage will become universal among persons born in 1950–1955.

Kinsey and co-workers[8] found that the double standard is being resolved by the development of a single standard in which premarital coital activities have become extended among females to levels which are more nearly comparable to those in the male. Kinsey et al.[7] also reported that a very high proportion of those having premarital intercourse did not regret having such experience, nor did they feel the premarital intercourse had caused any trouble in their subsequent marital adjustments.

Ehrmann[4] presented a summary of previous studies on the incidence of premarital intercourse. All of these previous studies were cross-sectional and were done by various investigators over a period from 1929 to 1959. For females, the incidence ranged from 2% to 47%, with a median of 20%. For males, the incidence ranged from 32% to 73%, with a median of 54%.

Christensen[3] studied premarital sex norms in Utah, Indiana, and Denmark, and found that fewer negative psychological consequences resulted from premarital intercourse in the most permissive culture, i.e., Denmark.

Green[5] has documented the exploitative views of premarital sex in certain subcultures in America. Blood[2] raised the question of whether romance and premarital intercourse are incompatibles. Kirkendall[9] discussed the problems of premarital sexual relations and its implications. Kirkendall[10] also published a book on premarital intercourse and interpersonal relationships wherein he sees premarital intercourse largely as exploitative promiscuity, more likely to occur among "casual" interpersonal relationships than among closer, more involved relationships. However, Reiss[11] studied premarital sexual standards in America and stated that a new, more permissive and equalitarian sex code is evolving.

In the present study (part of a larger longitudinal study of the sexual behavior and attitudes of marital partners,[1]) an attempt has been made to shed some light on this complex matter of premarital sexual experience, with particular emphasis (because of the unique aspects of this longitudinal study) upon the long-term effects of premarital sexual experience.

QUESTIONS AND "HYPOTHESES"

In the present study, answers have been sought to the following empirical questions:

1. What is the effect of premarital sexual experience (i.e., intercourse) on subsequent marriage?

2. Does the degree of premarital intimacy make any difference in the subsequent marriage?

3. How do couples with premarital sexual experience (intercourse) evaluate it after 20 years of marriage?

In addition to seeking answers to the above empirical questions, this phase of the present study was planned to provide some evidence for or against the following "hypotheses":

1. Premarital intercourse will adversely affect later marriage.
2. Increasing degrees of premarital intimacy will have increasingly detrimental effects upon later marriage.
3. A high percentage of the respondents will see no reason to regret their premarital coitus.

SAMPLE CHARACTERISTICS AND METHODOLOGY

The present study is based on a sample originally studied by Kelly.[6] During 1935–1938, Kelly enlisted the cooperation of 600 individuals in the New England area who volunteered to participate in a longitudinal study of marriage. This total original sample was made up of 300 couples engaged to be married to each other at that time. Each of these 600 individuals was assessed with an elaborate battery of techniques. The mean age of the men at the time of the original testing was 26.7 and that of the women 24.7, with nearly 9 out of 10 of the subjects being between the ages of 21 and 30.

An annual follow-up questionnaire was obtained on the anniversary of each marriage, and thus followed until 1941. In 1954–1955 a full-scale follow-up was completed, reporting in detail on the marriage between the research partners and on other intervening life experiences.

After nearly 20 years, 454 of the original persons were still living as husband and wife in 227 marriages. Completed follow-up forms were returned in 1954–1955 by 446 of the 521 individuals contacted, or 86%.

The sample turned out to be superior to the general population in education and intelligence. Regarding religious affiliation, 82% of the males and 89% of the females indicated membership in some church. Approximately 11% of the sample indicated a preference for the Catholic faith and 8% for the Jewish faith. The sample studied was characterized by wide individual differences with respect to the roughly 200 variables on which the subjects were assessed. Except for education and intelligence, the resulting distributions on the other variables were very similar to those of normative samples.

The overall basic data on which the present study is based consist of the responses of 161 couples (still married to each other after 20 years) on 42 variables having to do with their sexual behavior and attitudes.[1] At the present time only the data on premarital sexual experience will be presented.

RESULTS

In the personal history obtained from each respondent in this study, the following question regarding premarital sexual experience was asked: "Which of the following most nearly describes the extent of your physical relationship with the following members of the opposite sex until the end of your engagement?" The answers were check marks in the following degrees of premarital intimacy:

1.   Frequent intercourse
2.   Intercourse once or a few times
3.   Considerable physical intimacy, stopping short of intercourse
4.   A little physical intimacy
5.   Hugging and kissing
6.   Holding hands and good-night kiss
7.   Very little physical contact

Each respondent was asked to state the degree of physical intimacy with each of three different sorts of premarital relationships:

1.   Your research partner
2.   Other persons for whom you felt considerable affection
3.   Others (casual dates, acquaintances, etc.)

The results indicated that 45% of the men and 39% of the women reported having had premarital intercourse with their future spouse.

The men reported that they had premarital intercourse with others for whom they felt considerable affection in 32% of the present sample. For the women, 9% reported premarital intercourse with others for whom they felt considerable affection. While only 1% of the women reported any premarital intercourse with anyone else (i.e., casual dates, acquaintances, etc.), 20% of the men said they had such premarital intercourse.

The next question to be considered is what effect did the premarital experience of these couples have on their later marriages? Each respondent was asked: "Would you say that your marriage was affected in any way by your sexual experiences before marriage or by the lack of them? Please consider both favorable and unfavorable effects." The answers to this "open-ended" question were categorized into the following possibilities:

1.   Favorable effect
2.   No or mixed effect
3.   Unfavorable effect

The hypothesis that premarital sexual experience will have an adverse effect on later marriage receives little support from these data. However, to provide a clearer test of the above hypothesis, the evaluations of those *having* premarital intercourse were separated from those *not* having such experience, and the results are shown in Table 8-1.

The actual frequencies of persons falling in each category reveal that those rating their experience as having a *favorable* effect outnumber those saying such experience had an unfavorable effect. The same is true for those having no premarital intercourse: more rate this as having a favorable effect than an unfavorable effect. The present study cannot determine in a definitive manner which of the above patterns of behavior is "better," but the evidence here does *not* support the hypothesis that premarital intercourse will have an adverse effect on later marriage.

Our findings show no evidence to support the hypothesis that increasing degrees of premarital intimacy will have increasingly detrimental effects upon later marriage. While the percentages of those premaritally experienced marital partners reporting favorable effect over unfavorable offers no support for the adverse effect hypothesis, those who were premaritally chaste also claim this has no adverse effect (most of the time).

The findings reported in this study are unique in showing the degree of premarital intimacy with a variety of kinds of partners. Subjects reported *decreasing* degree of premarital intimacy as one moves from the research partner (or future spouse), through contacts with others for whom there was considerable affection, to casual dates, acquaintances, etc. This result goes against Kirkendall's[10] finding of less premarital intercourse as the interpersonal relationships ranged from casual to more involved relationships. However, his findings were based on a study of 200 college-level men between the ages of 17 and 28, who were unmarried. Premarital intercourse among such a sample certainly can be exploitative and promiscuous, as Kirkendall claims. But that is not the whole story about premarital intercourse, as the present findings

---

Table 8-1
Percentage of Husbands and Wives Reporting Various Effects of Premarital Sexual Experience on Their Marriages

	Individuals Who Had Premarital Intercourse with Spouse		Individuals Who Did Not Have Premarital Intercourse with Spouse	
	Husbands	Wives	Husbands	Wives
Favorable effect	22	19	27	50
No effect or mixed effect	63	70	64	45
Unfavorable effect	15	11	8	5

After 20 years of marriage, husbands and wives were asked to evaluate the effect of their premarital sexual experiences on their relationship. The vast majority of both those who had had premarital intercourse and those who had not felt that their premarital activity had a favorable effect or no effect on their marriages.

indicate. Before definitive conclusions are reached about "premarital intercourse" in general, more studies of samples of mature individuals must be included.

The present findings are in line, however, with those of Reiss,[11] who found that the premarital sexual standards in America are changing in the direction of more permissiveness with affection, which links sex and love. As he noted, women are now given a chance for a third choice; that is, it is no longer the choice of being a "pleasure-woman" *or* a wife; women can now choose to accept premarital sexual behavior, not as prostitutes or mere pleasure seekers, but as lovers. This, evidently, is what happened in a significant proportion of the present sample.

REFERENCES

1. Ard, B. N., Jr. Sexual behavior and attitudes of arital partners. Unpublished doctoral dissertation, University of Michigan, 1962.

2. Blood, R. O., Jr. Romance and premarital intercourse—incompatibles? *Marriage and Family Living*, 1952, **14**, 105–108.

3. Christensen, H. T. Cultural relativism and premarital sex norms. *American Sociological Review*, 1960, **25**, 31–39.

4. Ehrmann, W. *Premarital dating behavior*. New York: Holt, Rinehart & Winston, 1959.

5. Green, A. W. The "cult of personality" and sexual relations. *Psychiatry*, 1941, **4**, 344–348.

6. Kelly, E. L. Consistency of the adult personality. *American Psychologist*, 1955, **10**, 659–681.

7. Kinsey, A. C., Pomeroy, W. B., & Martin, C. E. *Sexual behavior in the human male*. Philadelphia: Saunders, 1948.

8. Kinsey, A. C., Pomeroy, W. B., Martin, C. E., & Gebhard, P. H. *Sexual behavior in the human female*. Philadelphia: Saunders, 1953.

9. Kirkendall, L. A. Premarital sex relations: The problem and its implications. *Pastoral Psychology*, 1956, **7**, 46–53.

10. Kirkendall, L. A. *Premarital intercourse and interpersonal relationships*. New York: Julian Press, 1961.

11. Reiss, I. L. *Premarital sexual standards in America*. New York: Free Press, 1960.

12. Terman, L. M. *Psychological factors in marital happiness*. New York: McGraw-Hill, 1938.

Can Students View Parents as Sexual Beings?

In the first chapter of this book, we presented some of the findings of Morton Hunt which indicated that sexual attitudes have become increasingly permissive and that various types of sexual behavior occur more frequently than in previous generations. There is one setting, however, in which nonpermissive sexual attitudes, lack of open communication, and misperception still occur, and that is within one's family.

The difficulties involved in communicating about sex across the generation gap between parents and their children are formidable. Much has been written about the uptightness and the lack of candor characteristic of parents. A classic comedy scene is the embarrassed father trying to explain the facts of life to a relaxed and knowledgeable son. Similarly, it is easy to laugh at a red-faced mother who stumbles through euphemisms trying to prepare her experienced and sophisticated daughter for the mysteries to be unfolded on the honeymoon. Beyond embarrassment, parents are believed to communicate only one other sexual message to their sons and daughters—*don't do it!*

In the following article, Ollie Pocs and Annette Godow point out that the barriers between generations are erected by both sides. College students were found to be quite upset at the prospect of even thinking about the sex life of their parents; they greatly underestimated the sexual practices of their mothers and fathers and the frequency with which they had sexual relations. As a female friend recently confided to us, she reached adulthood and was married before she could accept the idea that her parents actually had intercourse more than three times in their lives (she has one brother and one sister). It appears that neither parents nor their offspring want to deal with one another's sexual realities. Each generation hides its own sexuality from the other, and each seems to feel more comfortable in considering the other as relatively nonsexual.

Can Students View Parents as Sexual Beings?

Ollie Pocs and Annette G. Godow

"The gulf between parent and child is to a large extent probably inevitable, with its roots perhaps lying in the difficulty that children have in accepting their parents as sexual beings."[12] This statement represents quite a different perspective from the common statements made regarding sex and the so-called generation gap. It is a common complaint of high school and college students that their parents cannot deal with their sexuality as legitimate and natural. But can youth view their par-

Reprinted in an edited version from: Pocs, O., & Godow, A. G. Can students view parents as sexual beings? *Family Coordinator*, in press.

ents as sexual beings? It was the authors' prediction that this would be a difficult perception for college students to make. The authors hypothesized that when forced to estimate their parents' past and present sexual behavior, college students would predict *far less frequent and less varied* sexual behavior than one would expect of married males and females as based upon the research findings of Kinsey. It was predicted that many students would view their parents as essentially nonsexual. The authors were also interested in investigating the possible differential effects of certain demographic variables upon the student estimates of parental sexual behavior, namely, the variables of sex, age, year in school, hometown background, and socioeconomic level.

RESEARCH PROCEDURES

A questionnaire was designed to investigate students' views of their parents' sexuality by asking them to estimate the past and present sexual behaviors of their mothers and fathers. The sexual behaviors included premarital petting; premarital coitus; extramarital coitus; oral-genital contact, now and ever; masturbation, now and ever; and the present frequency of marital coitus. Demographic background information was also requested for both the students and their parents.

Questionnaire data from 646 college students (239 males and 407 females) were analyzed in this study. The original sample included 810 questionnaire responses from several general education undergraduate classes at a midwestern state university. This sample was not strictly a random one, but the classes from which the data were collected were ones taken by a wide variety of students. The questionnaire was distributed on a voluntary and anonymous basis. Only the white student population was included in the present analysis, since research studies have demonstrated that sexual attitudes and behavior vary significantly across racial lines.[10] The complete sample did not include enough black students to provide for a statistically sound black-white analysis. Also eliminated, for obvious reasons, were data from those students whose parents were separated, divorced, widowed, or both deceased. Thus, the sample used for this research analysis included 646 white students whose parents were presently living together.

In analyzing how accurate the students' estimates were, the authors compared these estimates with Kinsey's data[7,8] on self-reported sexual behavior of parent-age populations. Since it was impossible to obtain responses from the students' parents themselves, Kinsey's data were used as representative of a comprehensive sample of sexual behavior in our society. Given the gradual sexual liberalization in our society over the past several years, it was assumed that Kinsey's figures would be conservative if any consistent error existed in applying these data. This simply means that the authors were making it more difficult to obtain significant differences between student estimates and actual research findings since they expected the students to err in a conservative direction. If one utilizes the most conservative comparison data available and still obtains significant differences, then one can be even more confident that real differences do exist.

Estimates from male and female students were analyzed separately since the authors expected that some male-female differences would be present. Clearly, males and females exhibit different sexual attitudes and behaviors, and therefore, might be expected to exhibit differential perceptions of their parents' sexual behavior. In addition to testing the major hypothesis of this study, the authors also conducted statistical tests to examine the possible differential effects of the following student variables—sex, age, year in school, home town background, and socio-economic status—upon the estimates of parental sexual behavior.

RESULTS

Table 8-2 presents students' perceptions of parental sexual activity as compared to Kinsey's findings. Upon inspection of this table, it is clear that across the board, both daughters' and sons' estimates were significantly lower than Kinsey's data. For all behaviors—premarital petting, premarital coitus, extramarital coitus, oral-genital contact ever, and masturbation ever—the differences were significant. Particularly striking differences were found for premarital and extramarital coitus, for both mothers and fathers. The results for present parental masturbatory activity and oral-genital contact were similar to the above findings: students dramatically underestimated these activities for both their mothers and fathers.

All of the sexual behaviors considered above are societally prohibited activities, at least to some extent. What about coitus which is clearly a culturally expected and sanctioned sexual activity? Table 8-3 presents the students' estimates of their parents' present coital frequency as compared to Kinsey's married sample by age categories. Upon inspection of this table, one finds that Kinsey's figures are usually more than twice the student estimates. If one looks at the modal age group for this study's sample (41–45 for mothers and 46–50 for fathers), the student estimate is 2.8 times per month whereas Kinsey found a frequency of about 7.0 times per month. Clearly, the results are in the predicted direction with student estimates appearing to be dramatically lower than actual frequencies found by Kinsey.

Looking at students' estimates of parental coital frequency and combining appropriate frequency categories, the authors found that as many as 41% of daughters and 36% of sons estimated that their parents engaged in sexual intercourse with a frequency of a few times a year to never. Combining more categories, it was found that 57% of

Table 8-2
Offsprings' Perceptions of Their Parents' Sexual Activities Compared to Kinsey's Data

Percentage of Individuals Engaging in Activity

Sexual Activity	Mothers as Perceived by Their Daughters	Mothers as Perceived by Their Sons	Kinsey's Female Sample	Fathers as Perceived by Their Daughters	Fathers as Perceived by Their Sons	Kinsey's Male Sample
Premarital petting	63	69	99	80	81	89
Premarital coitus	10	22	50	33	45	92
Extramarital coitus	2	2	26	7	12	50
Oral-genital sex	25	30	49	29	34	59
Masturbation	31	49	62	62	73	93

When college students were asked to make estimates regarding the sexual activity of their parents, they tended to underestimate their parents' sexual experiences, judging by comparisons with the survey data of Kinsey. Males tended to assume more sexuality among their parents than did females, but their guesses were still lower than national norms would indicate.

Table 8-3
Offsprings' Estimates of the Frequency
with which Their Parents Engage in Sexual Intercourse

Coital Frequency	Daughters' Estimates (%)	Sons' Estimates (%)
Never or less than once a year	25	22
Few times a year	16	14
About one time a month	16	16
Two to three times a month	15	21
One to two times a week	23	22
Three to four times a week	4	4
More than four times a week	0	0

When college students were asked to estimate the frequency with which their parents had intercourse, their estimates were much lower than survey data would indicate. Over half of these students felt that their mothers and fathers had sexual relations only once a month or less.

daughters and 52% of sons estimated a coital frequency of once a month or less. At the same time, over 90% of the students characterized their parents' marriage as ranging from somewhat happy to very happy, with over 80% falling within the happy to very happy range. Yet, for over half of these students, a happy marriage includes a barely active sexual life.

Analyses of the effects of the student demographic variables—sex, age, year in school, home town background, and socioeconomic status—upon students' estimates revealed only few significant differences. Regarding the variable of sex, the authors hypothesized that males would give higher estimates than females. Given that society allows and even encourages males to be more "liberated" sexually, both in terms of attitudes and behavior, it was assumed that they would find it easier to imagine their parents as sexual. Analysis of the sex variable revealed significant differences in the predicted direction for the estimates of premarital coitus for both mothers and fathers, and of masturbation, ever, for mothers; for the estimates of present oral-genital contact, for both mothers and fathers, and of masturbation, ever, and extramarital coitus for fathers. Thus, the hypothesis regarding male-female differences was moderately supported but not universally so. It should be remembered, nevertheless, that even in cases where male estimates were higher than those of females, they were still significantly lower than Kinsey's data.

Regarding the variables of age and year in school, the authors hypothesized that as students' age and year in school increased, estimates of parental sexual activity would also increase since students generally become more sophisticated sexually as they become older and progress through school. This hypothesis was only mildly supported—estimates of some sexual behaviors for fathers, namely, premarital petting, premarital coitus, and masturbation, ever, did increase significantly across age and year in school. Regarding the variables of home town background and socioeconomic class, no significant differences were found.

POSSIBLE EXPLANATIONS

The results of this study clearly demonstrate that students tend to view their parents as significantly less sexual than one would expect them to be based on Kinsey's findings. Several explanations of this phenomenon seem plausible. One explanation is related to the fairly strong cultural expectation or myth that as people get older, sexual expression becomes unimportant, irrelevant, and even inappropriate. In a research study[5] assessing youth's attitudes toward old people conducted at Brandeis University, students were asked to complete the following sentence: "Sex for most old people . . . ." Nearly all of the experimental subjects considered sex to be "negligible, unimportant" for old people. "In fact, subjects made no mention of the possibility that sex may evoke pleasant reminiscences, though on another item . . . subjects consider reminiscing one of the great pleasures of old people [p. 357]." Insofar as college students view their parents as "older" and are influenced by the fairly pervasive myth of the sexless old years, one might expect them to underestimate their parents' sexual activity, especially present behavior.

A second possible explanation for students' apparent tendency to deny their parents' sexuality is related to the incest taboo.[9,11] Given the very strong societal prohibition against incestuous relations, children might suppress thoughts of parents as sexual beings since such a perspective could easily lead to anxiety-producing thoughts of parents as potential sexual partners. Several students expressed strongly defensive responses to completing the questionnaire: "Who ever thinks about their parents' sexual relations—except perverts." "I'm not always under my parents' asses, especially not in bed." "Why didn't you send it to them, I don't sleep in the same bed with them." These comments include not only disapproval of thoughts about parental sexuality, but they also imply strong denial and disapproval of incestuous activities as well. Student denial of parental sexuality can be conceptualized as a form of perceptual defense,[4] which is perhaps employed by both parent and child to aid them in avoiding the anxiety associated with incestuous thoughts and feelings.

A third explanation concerns the requirements of the parental role in the socialization of children in our society. In the role of parent, adults are expected to transmit to their children the generally nonpermissive sexual standards advocated by our society.[13] In so doing, they may foster a similarly restrictive view of their own sexual behavior. For example, if a student's mother professes the importance of premarital virginity, it is reasonable for the student to assume that the mother did not engage in this forbidden activity herself. In fact, mothers who themselves had participated in premarital coitus without regret will often teach their daughters the importance of virginity.[2,8] It appears that when women adopt the role of mother, they may also adopt the traditional societal stance concerning premarital coitus regardless of their individual feelings or history.

In addition, many parents may appear to be nonsexual because they hesitate to discuss the topic of sexuality in any way with their children[1] or because they are not inclined to exhibit loving, affectionate responses, let alone sexual behavior, in the presence of their children. Applying a symbolic interactionism perspective,[3] children often have no frame of reference based upon parent-child interactions within which to conceptualize their parents as sexual. When they do learn about sexuality, it is usually from their peers and usually in terms of "street" talk, i.e., dirty words. Subsequently, the child may have difficulty conceptualizing his or her parents in relation to these derogatory terms. For example, it must seem quite illegitimate for youth to imagine their parents as "fuckers." In other words, youth may not have at their disposal appropriate symbolic tools with which to think of their parents as sexual. The absence of a mutually shared, socially appropriate language may be one of the major inhibitors of parent-child discussion of sexuality.[6] In addition to misperceiving their parents' sexual activity, the above situation might also lead one to expect a misperception of parental attitudes as well. Some evidence to support this was obtained in Walsh's[13] study of sexual attitudes of college freshmen and their parents. In general, he found that children tend to view their parents as having more conservative attitudes than the parents report themselves as holding.

A final and very simple explanation of the research findings is the possibility that students have no reasonable way of knowing about their parents' sexuality. If their parents have never told them about their sexual behavior and if they have not heard or read about the statistics concerning the sexual behavior of people their parents' age, then one cannot expect the students to accurately estimate this behavior. Of course, they could have erred in the direction of overestimation rather than underestimation. Thus, this explanation alone cannot account for the research results.

IMPLICATIONS

Comments from a few students who participated in the study revealed insight into what was actually found—"I can't even imagine what type of sex life my parents have!" "Let's face it, very few people can actually imagine their parents copulating at all, let alone figure out the small details." It appears that students have little understanding or insight into one important aspect of their parents' lives. As parents get older, these students may influence their parents in a similarly destructive fashion as they had been influenced as children. They may communicate the expectation that sexual expression for their "older" parents is no longer legitimate or appropriate and, subsequently, contribute to its actual suppression. Thinking of parents as nonsexual also entails an unnecessarily pessimistic view of middle and old age, since sex is viewed as fairly unimportant at these times and as a pleasure mainly for the "young." This view perpetuates our culture's overemphasis upon the virtues of youth.

It is the authors' opinion that an important component of the so-called generation gap between parent and child concerning sexuality is related to the mutual denial of the other's sexuality. The "gap" seems to be a "two-way street" with students as closed to their parents' sexuality as their parents are restrictive of theirs. This situation seems to preclude any kind of real communication between parent and student in the important area of sexuality. It is the authors' contention that if both sides could view the other's sexuality more realistically and as a legitimate aspect of the other's life, both sides might be more communicative with the other, more understanding of the other, and perhaps more helpful in affirming the other's sexuality as a healthy and positive force.

REFERENCES

1. Bell, R. R. Parent-child conflict in sexual values. *Journal of Social Issues*, 1966, **22**, 34–44.

2. Burgess, E. W., & Wallin, P. *Engagement and marriage.* Philadelphia: Lippincott, 1953.

3. Eshleman, J. R. *The family: An introduction.* Boston: Allyn & Bacon, 1974.

4. Forgus, R. H. *Perception.* New York: McGraw-Hill, 1966.

5. Golde, P. G., & Kogan, R. A sentence completion procedure for assessing attitudes toward old people. *Journal of Gerontology*, 1959, **14**, 355–363.

6. Johnson, W. R. The language barrier. *Journal of the American College Health Association*, 1966, **15**, 72–76.

7. Kinsey, A. C., Pomeroy, W. B., & Martin, C. E. *Sexual behavior in the human male.* Philadelphia: Saunders, 1948.

8. Kinsey, A. C., Pomeroy, W. B., Martin, C. E., & Gebhard, P. H. *Sexual behavior in the human female.* Philadelphia: Saunders, 1953.

9. Murdock, G. P. *Social structure.* New York: Macmillan, 1949.

10.   Reiss, I. L. *The social context of premarital sexual permissiveness.* New York: Holt, Rinehart & Winston, 1967.

11.   Reiss, I. L. *Heterosexual relationships inside and outside of marriage.* Morristown, N.J.: General Learning Press, 1973.

12.   SEICUS. *Sexuality and man.* New York: Scribner, 1970.

13.   Walsh, R. H. The generation gap in sexual beliefs. *Sexual Behavior,* 1972, **2**, 4–10.

Group Sex among the Mid-Americans

Perhaps the most startling current phenomenon with respect to marital sexuality is the practice of swinging or mate swapping. It has long been suggested that one of the most difficult problems for a husband and wife to overcome is that of sexual boredom after interacting with the same partner over a long period of time. A solution throughout history has been the secret extramarital affair carried out by the husband, the wife, or both. A very different solution that apparently appeals to several million individuals at the present time is for the couple to embark on extramarital sex together as a social activity.

Though some fictional accounts leave the impression that everyone on the block but you is engaged in nightly swinging, research data indicate that only a very small proportion of Americans has had even *one* experience with group sex. What is not known, however, is whether swinging represents a passing fad that will go the way of the hula hoop, a permanent new aspect of sexual behavior for a minute segment of the population, or the wave of the future that will eventually become a familiar addition to married life. One could imagine, in a few years, little invitations being mailed out all over the country with messages such as, "You are cordially invited to a Group Sex Party at our place next Saturday around eightish. Informal. B.Y.O.B."

Whatever the future of mate swapping and whatever its long-range effects on the traditional marriage relationship, it is currently a very real part of the lives of a great many people. In the next article, anthropologist Gilbert Bartell describes several aspects of the group sex scene and the solid citizens who participate in it.

Group Sex among the Mid-Americans

Gilbert D. Bartell

Our data were collected from a selected sample of midwestern and southwestern white, suburban and exurban couples, and single individuals engaged in what they call swinging. We contacted and interviewed approximately 350 informants during the 2 years of our research, using data from 280 interviewees who fit into the above category.

These informants define the term "swinging" as having sexual relations (as a couple) with at least one other individual. Since more than a simple dyadic relationship exists whether the sexual activity involved takes place together or apart, the fact remains that more than two people had to enter into an agreement to have sexual experiences together. We therefore conclude that this must be considered group sex.

Reprinted in an edited version from: Bartell, G. D. Group sex among the mid-Americans. *Journal of Sex Research*, 1970, **6**, 113–130.

We were interested in the growth and development of the broad spectrum of activities associated with organized swinging, but we wished to concentrate specifically upon those individuals belonging to some form of sodality or swinging organization. We attempted to ascertain to what extent American cultural patterns would be transferred to this relatively new phenomenon. Since white middle-class, non-inner city people constitute the majority in the United States, and we assume they are the major actors within the cultural system, our sample is restricted to these informants.

Interviews lasted anywhere from 2 to 8 hours. We eliminated individuals from the inner city, blacks, and Latin couples to keep our sample restricted. We did not misrepresent ourselves, but told them that we were anthropologists interested in knowing more about swinging. We did not use a tape recorder or questionnaires, as these people were frequently too frightened to even give their right names, let alone fill out questionnaires or speak into a recorder. We were also able to attend many parties and large-scale group sexual activities.

Our basic method of interviewing was the anthropological one of participant observer. Due to the etiquette and social mores of swinging as we shall detail below, we were able to observe and only act as though we were willing to participate.

Evidently the interest in swinging (or wife swapping, mate swapping, or group sex) came about as the result of an article in *Mr. Magazine* in 1956. Since then it has received a great deal of attention from the semipornographic press. However, despite the fact that there are an estimated 1 to 10 million people involved in mate exchange, it has received practically no attention from the scientific community. We do not have any reliable figures on how many people are involved in swinging, but a club in a midwestern city published a list with names and addresses of 3500 couples in the metropolitan area and its suburbs who are actively engaged in mate exchange.

The impetus toward swinging usually comes from the male, but it is the contention of a number of sophisticated swingers that it is often promoted by the female who lets the male take the aggressive role in suggesting that they become involved in the swapping situation.

Within the area of investigation, there are primarily four methods of acquiring similarly minded partners for sexual exchange: (1) most prevalent is the utilization of an advertisement in one or more of the various magazine/tabloids catering to these specialized interests; (2) an introduction to another couple at a bar, set up exclusively for this purpose or through one of the swingers' sodalities; (3) personal reference from one couple to another; (4) personal recruitment, seduction, or proselytizing.

In the first method an advertisement is placed in one of the sensational tabloids such as the *National Informer*. This might read, for example:

Athens, Georgia marrieds. Attractive, college, married, white, want to hear from other marrieds. She, 36, 5'7", 35–22–36, 135. He, 40, 6'2", 190. Photo and phone a must. Discretion. Box #.

or

Florida Marrieds. Attractive, refined, professional marrieds would like to hear from similar liberal-minded marrieds. Complete discretion required and assured. Can travel southern states. Photo and phone please. Box #.

Alternatively, the couple may respond to such an ad. This method is the least expensive and time consuming as the *National Informer* sells for 25¢ and is printed and distributed on a weekly basis. The couple has to pay for an ad or a fee plus postage for their letter to be forwarded to an advertisee. Exactly the same method is used if the couple selects one of the large slick paged magazines, such as *Swinger's Life* or *Kindred Spirits*. The major difference between tabloids and slick magazines is that the magazines offer membership in a sodality and cater exclusively to swingers. Examples of such ads would be:

Baltimore, D. C., 60 mile radius, luscious, upper thirties, attractives, seeking couples, females to 40 for exotic French Culture, etc. She, 35–27–35, 5'6". He, husky, muscular, but gentle. Let's trade pictures and telephone and addresses.

or

New Orleans, young couple, 28 and 32. She, a luscious redhead, 5'7", 36–26–38. He, 5'9", 175, well built. Enjoy all cultures. Attractive couples main interest, but will consider extremely attractive single girls and men. Photo required for reply.

Please note the difference in the tenor and construction of the advertisements, remembering that the magazine sells for $3.00 per copy. Additionally these magazines offer instruction on what kinds of letters to write to attract the highest results. Initial contacts are made through letters with descriptions formulated in such a way as to stimulate the interest in making a personal contact with the other couple. These would almost universally include a nude or seminude photograph of the female, and sometimes, but much less frequently, a photograph of the male. These photographs are considered very important. Physical dimensions, particularly of the female, usually somewhat overly abundant in the mammary zone, are frequently included. Ages are given and usually minimized. The written answer usually states that the couple is fun loving, vivacious, friendly, and extremely talented sexually. This leads, hopefully, to a telephone contact with the other couple and from there to a first meeting, which is by agreement social in nature with no obligations to swing on the part of anyone. If successful, this first meeting leads to an invitation to swing, either open or closed (see below) or an invitation to a party. If unsuccessful, it may lead only to a referral to another couple or to some club.

The second method of meeting other couples, the bar or sodality, can be the result of reference from another couple. In a few cases, the club or bar may advertise openly in either a swinging magazine or a tabloid. These units or sodalities break down into three categories. The very common, but least imminent, is the large-scale semiannual party social, advertised in one of the national swingers' magazines. The magazine advertises where the social will be held, and the cost for dinner, dance, and drinks. The organizer most commonly will be some local couple who agree to do the actual work. Usually these meetings, or socials, are held at a motel. The swingers bar is one which is open on certain nights of the week only to couples, and it is known to everyone that all couples present are either active or interested in becoming swingers. The bars can be run by either an individual who has an interest in promulgating swinging or an organizer who will contract with the bar owner offering a guarantee for the use of the bar for the particular night involved. Occasionally some interested couple or couples may institute a club which charges a membership fee and rents a hall or bar one or two nights a month at which times known swingers congregate. These clubs are frequently chartered, operating as social organizations much like ski clubs. Inducements are offered to the members for recruiting new members. The club may, for example, sponsor "Bring another couple night," and only charge half price for entrance. A number of clubs seek to go beyond the purely sexual by organizing hay rides, beach parties, and picnics. Several attempts have been made within our area to organize a group tour of swingers to the Caribbean and to Las Vegas. These efforts have not been successful. In general, swinging does not take place on the premises of these bars or clubs, but instead the couples make their alliances or organize private parties and leave the bar in groups.

A third method of meeting other compatible swingers is a simple reference from another couple. If a couple has made a few contacts either by one of the two methods mentioned above or sometimes purely by accident, they can meet a number of other couples by this reference method. A knowledgeable couple who have been swinging for some time will recommend other known swingers to the new couple. This in turn, of course, can lead to other contacts without ever having to write letters, join a club, or go to a bar.

The fourth method of contacting new swingers appears with the least degree of frequency in our sample. Many swingers, either due to the zeal of the convert or personal stimulus, attempt to seduce (that is, convert) other couples to what they call the "swinging life." We have reports of this occasionally occurring in nudist camps or with couples that have known each other on a social basis for some time. In a few cases, couples who had been bridge partners or dance partners have mutually consented to exchange.

The neophytes coming onto the "swinging scene," as it is referred to, are faced with a number of dilemmas. They must find out, with a certain degree of care, exactly what actions are appropriate to allow them to participate in this venture which is somewhat surrounded by mystery. The various books and magazines purporting to open the door and guide the novice through the intricacies of swinging, universally exaggerate its ecstasies. In fact, what swingers do is relatively prosaic. For example, one responds to an ad with a letter. This letter gives one's interests and includes a picture. The purpose of the letter is to present oneself in such a manner as to elicit further response in the form of a telephone call. Then, usually using only first names, such as Joe and Ruth, a meeting is arranged.

This first meeting we call the Mating Dance (taken directly from ethologists). The couple goes through a patterned ritual behavior. In effect what they are doing is testing each other. If one couple is baby swingers—baby swinger meaning one who has never been involved in a swinging situation before—of necessity they must permit themselves to be seduced. This role also allows one to ask questions which the experienced couple are more than pleased to answer. In most cases this is the role we took. It is also advantageous in that you have to learn the secret vocabulary of swinging in order to interview effectively. These people do have a definite secret language, or at least they think it is secret. Terms most often used are TV (transvestite), S & M (sadomasochist), A-C D-C (homosexual and heterosexual), bisexual (enjoying both males and females, usually applied to women only), ambisexual (the correct term, yet less frequently used for the preceding two terms), gay (homosexual or lesbian), B & D (bondage and discipline), French culture (cunnilingus and fellatio), Roman culture (orgies), and Greek culture (anal intercourse).

This first meeting is the equivalent of the dating coffee date or coke date. The general etiquette dictates that this first contact is without sexual involvement. Should it be decided that the foursome wants to get together they will meet later either at a motel or at the house of one of the couples.

Once this decision to participate has been made by all four people, we arrive at the three typologies of swinging: (1) open and closed swinging; (2) open and closed large-scale parties; and (3) three-way parties. As defined locally, closed swinging means that the two couples exchange partners and then go off separately to a private area to engage in what amounts to straight, uncomplicated sexual intercourse. Then after an agreed-upon time, all four return back to the central meeting place. Sexual behavior under these circumstances is relatively ritualized. It almost always includes fellatio, cunnilingus, and coitus, with the male either dorsal or ventral. In the vast majority of cases, fellatio does not lead to orgasm. Every attempt is made by the male to bring the female to climax by cunnilingus. Climax by the male after prolonged delay occurs most frequently during coitus with the female supine.

In contrast, open swinging in a foursome means that the couples at some time during the evening engage in sexual activity together, either in the same room, on the same bed, or as a four-way participatory activity. In 75% of our cases, this will generally include the two females engaging in some form of cunnilingal activity, although in approximately 15% of the cases one of the female partners will be passive. Less than 1% of the cases reported that any male homosexual activity takes place. We have only two or three reports of males performing fellatio, and in six or seven cases the male informant was passive, permitting another male to fellate him. We have no reports of anal intercourse taking place between either male or female in a swinging scene. Sometimes references are made to this fact, but we have no verification. Occasionally a foursome of the open variety may result in everyone devoting their attention to one person, three on one in effect—again, most frequently, this means two males and one female devoting their attention to the female. The only other variety is the so-called daisy chain, which is alternately fellatio, cunnilingus in a circle.

The second type of swinging is the party, which can be organized in several different ways, and can be run as an open or closed party. Certain individuals are known in this area as organizers. These individuals devote a great deal of their time to the organization and promulgation of swinging activities. They may organize nothing more than social events in which people meet to make future contacts, or they may organize a party at which sexual activity will take place. These parties are frequently held in a private home. Couples are invited by the organizer, who may or may not be the owner of the home. Frequently each couple invited is asked to bring another couple who are known to be swingers. Although not always true, there is an implication that no one is required to swing. At other parties, no swinging activity takes place until after a certain time, such as 10:30. Any couple still there past 10:30 is expected to participate. In contrast to the swingers' self-image, they are not nudists and they are still relatively inhibited, hesitating to initiate any positive action. Therefore, the organizer or the host or some less patient swingers may initiate a game, the object of which, obviously, is the removal of everyone's clothing.

Parties in suburbia include evenly numbered couples only. In the area of our research, singles, male or female, are discriminated against. Blacks are universally excluded. If the party is a closed party, there are rules, very definitely established and generally reinforced by the organizer as well as other swingers. These rules may even include clothing restrictions, "baby dolls" for the women and for the men, swinger's shorts (abbreviated boxer type). Or there may be a regulation that one couple may occupy a bedroom at a time or that they may stay only so long or that no one must appear nude in the central gathering area. Most parties are "bring your own bottle" parties, although in a few cases the host supplies the liquor. Food is often prepared by the hostess, but seldom consumed. Stag films are generally not shown. Music is low key fox trot, not infrequently Glen Miller, and lighting is definitely not psychedelic, usually making use of nothing more than a few red or blue light bulbs. Marijuana and speed are not permitted.

The same generalized format is true for the open party, the difference being that the party is less structured. Nudity is permitted in any part of the house and couples are free to form large groups of up to 10 or 12 people in large sexual participating masses. Voyeurism is open and not objected to by the majority of the participants. Parties generally begin around 9 o'clock in the evening and frequently continue until 9 o'clock the following morning in contrast to closed parties, which generally terminate around 1 A.M. It is not infrequent that as the party proceeds and the males become progressively more exhausted, the females continue to party without males. Open parties in suburban groups appear infrequently and when they do, they are held by the younger swingers between the ages 20 and 35, who have begun swinging in the last year and a half. Culturally this younger group resembles the older closed group with the exception that they have never been under the influence of the organizers. They have no ideas as to what is considered appropriate party behavior, as does the older group. This younger group apparently either is more innovative or is learning from the now-frequent popular writings on swinging. Some of the older swingers who are now participating in open parties state that when they began swinging they "didn't know there was any other way to do it." Although most couples state an interest in the taking of Polaroid pictures during sexual exchanges, in practice, this is very infrequent. Among other reasons it points out the extreme caution and fear with which the majority of our informants react to the possibility of their identities being revealed.

The third type of swinging is in a threesome, which can hardly be called *ménage à trois*, which implies a prolonged triadic relationship. Analysis of advertisements in swingers' magazines indicates that the vast majority of swingers, whether potential or experienced, advertise for either a couple or a female. Although the majority of threesomes constitute a couple and an alternate single female, 30% of our informants indicate that they have participated as a threesome with an alternate single male. (Cross-checking of informants cause our own figures to be revised upward as high as 60%.) The males report that they enjoy the voyeuristic qualities of watching their partner engaging in sexual activity with another male. Most commonly, threesomes with two females include ambisexual behavior of mutual cunnilungus between the females. Although in the majority of our cases the triad is of relatively short duration, 12 couples report triadic relationships of longer duration ranging from a low of 2 or 3 weeks to a high of as long as 10 years. In three of the cases the extra woman lived in the household on a more or less permanent basis. In two cases the male was a boarder, and in one case the male lived in the household for 10 years, for 7 of which he had been involved in *ménage à trois*.

Few other variations of sexual activity had been reported. We have in our entire sample only two reports of bondage and/or discipline. Transvestitism has never been reported. We have observed one case of bestiality. Obviously from the preceding, homosexual males are not welcome. In three cases, we have reports of a lesbian participating at a large party, however she was not discriminated against. It should be noted that to accuse a woman of being "straight-gay" is considered pejorative. Clothes fetishists are uncommon. Bizarre costume is not considered proper and clothing is decidedly not "mod," but rather very middle class.

THE INFORMANTS

Of our informants, 95% were white. We included Latin Americans in this category as well. Of our Latin Americans, 10 individuals in all, each swung with a white partner. The predominant ethnic division was German. In fact, of all foreign-born informants, Germans constituted the single largest group, comprising 12 couples in our sample. We have only 5 black couples, none of whom live in the suburbs. The ages of our informants ranged from 18 to the mid-40s for the women, and from 21 to 70 for the males; median age for women was 28–31, for males, 29–34. All couples, based on our knowledge of certain societal factors, tended to minimize their age, except for the very young (21–30) age group. In general we believe the men gave younger ages when they were married to younger women. Age plays an extremely important role in acceptance or rejection for swinging. Although informants almost universally verbalize that age is unimportant, in reality they tend to reject couples who are more than 10 years older than themselves. Invitations to parties are generally along age lines also. With the emphasis on youth in our culture today, it is important to appear young and our interviewees were reluctant to give exact ages.

Of the women in our sample, 90% remain in the home as housewives. We have no exact figures as to how many worked prior to marriage. In cases where this was their first marriage, they had married between the ages of 17 and 21. Several were married as young as 15 to 17. There were 17 female teachers in our sample. Those who had advanced schooling, both males and females, had attended small colleges and junior colleges. About 25% of our males had some college. Of the men, 40% to 50% could be classified as salesmen of one sort or another. Our interviewees also included one doctor, one dentist, three university professors, three high school teachers, and several owners of small service-oriented businesses. A number of swingers in this group are truck drivers and some are employed in factory work. Lawyers made up the largest professional group. Earnings were extremely difficult to ascertain. We based our estimate on life style, houses, and occupations. The range of income extends from $6000 to a probable high of $75,000.

Religion was seldom discussed. These people would not admit to atheism or agnosticism. They would say that they were Protestant, Catholic, or Jewish. The majority are Protestant and the proportion of Jews is the same as in the general population. The proportion of Catholics is a little higher. The majority did not attend church regularly.

Universally, they were extremely cautious with regard to their children, phone calls, and visits from other swinging couples. The majority of couples would not swing if their children were in the house, and some made elaborate arrangements to have children visit friends or relatives on the nights when they were entertaining. All couples took precautions so that their children did not find letters from other swinging couples, pictures, or swinging magazines. We found few instances of couples merely socializing and bringing their children together, although the children might be of the same ages, and have the same interests. Only a few in our sample said that they would raise their children with the same degree of sexual libertarianism they themselves espouse, or that they would give the girls the pill at a very early age.

In interviewing these respondents, we found that they have no outside activities or interests or hobbies. In contrast, the suburbanite is usually involved in community affairs, numerous sports, and family-centered activities. These people do nothing other than swing and watch television. About 10% are regular nudists and attend some nudist camps in the area during the summer. Their reading is restricted to newspapers, *occasional* news magazines, and women's magazines with the outstanding exception that 99% of the males read *Playboy*. An occasional couple owns a power boat and spends a few summer weekends boating. A striking contradiction is the fact that in their letters they list their interests as travel, sports, movies, dancing, going out to dinner, theater, etc. In reality they do none of these things. Therefore all conversational topics are related to swinging and swingers as well as television programs. Background is usually rural or fringe areas, not inner city.

Due to the exclusion in the Midwest of singles from the swinging scene, we find that approximately one-third of the swinging couple interviewed admitted they were not married. However, to be include in parties and to avoid pressures and criticism from married couples they introduced themselves as man and wife. We were unable to com pile exact statistics of the frequency or cause of divorce in the swinging scene. At least one partner and sometimes both had been married be fore. Frequently they have children from a previous marriage. We hav only hearsay evidence that couples have broken up because of swinging However, we feel in general that the divorce rate is about that of an comparable group of people in the country. As we have not followe up any couples who have dropped out of swinging, these findings ar susceptible to change.

As much of the interviewing took place during the 1968 nationa presidential campaign, we had occasion to hear political views. Normall politics is never discussed. There were many Republicans and bette than 60% of the respondents were Wallaceites (partially due to chang from blue-collar to white-collar jobs). These people were anti-Negro They were less antagonistic to Puerto Ricans and Mexicans. They wer strongly against hippies. They were also against the use of any and al drugs, and would not allow in their homes marijuana or people wh use it, if they had knowledge of it.

Based on overt statements in letters and advertisements, such a "white only" and from the fact that blacks are seldom, if ever, invited t parties, it is safe to say that a strong antiblack prejudice exists. In socia conversation antagonism, although veiled, often is expressed.

Informants overall reflect generalized white suburban attitudes a outlined in almost any beginning sociology text. Their deviation exist mainly or primarily in the area of sex. And even this has imposed upo it middle-class mores and attitudes. For example, some men have been paying prostitutes to pose as their swinging partners. In the few cases in which this occurred and became general knowledge, a large outcry from both males and females was heard. The same attitudes prevai toward couples who are not married as well as singles, male or female The reason is less the sanctity of marriage than the idea that the single individual or the prostitute has nothing to lose. They are absolutely terrified, even though they think of themselves as liberated sexually, by the thought of involvement. If you swing with a couple only one time you are obviously not very involved. It is taboo to call another man's wife or girl friend afterward, or to make dates on the side.

The consumption of alcohol, sometimes in large quantities, is per missible. Current fashions (at the time, mini skirts and bell-bottom trousers for men) and beards are seldom seen except among the young est of the swingers.

ANALYSIS

As stated originally, we were particularly interested in swinging as a cultural phenomenon. We feel convinced that it reflects very much the culture of the individuals interviewed and observed. They represent white middle-class suburbia. They do not represent a high order of deviance. In fact, this is the single area of deviation from the norms of contemporary society, and there may be some question whether they really represent the acting out of an ideal image in our society rather than an attempt to be innovative. They represent an attempt to act out the cult of youth, the "in scene." They are, in their own minds, the avant garde, the leaders in a new sexual revolution. They see swinging as a "way of life." They refer, like the hippie, like the ghettoite, to the non-swinger as being "straight." In contrast to their own conceptualization of themselves, the majority of swingers are very "straight" indeed. The mores, the fears, that plague our generation are evidenced as strongly in swingers as in any other random sampling from suburbia. It has been said that our data reflect a mid-American bias; however, the same phenomena can be found in suburbs on both the East and West coasts. What we find in these couples consistently is a boredom with marriage. Much of this problem stems from diffuse role expectations in the society. Americans have imposed upon themselves a number of possible roles, both ideal and real, which one may assume. We believe the action of the media to be crucial in the self-perception of ideological roles. Most of the male swingers want to see themselves as—and many groups actually call themselves—international jet setters, the cosmopolitans, the travelers, the beautiful people. Instead, they have become a consequence of suburban life. They sit in silence and look at television. The woman who feels restricted to the household environment believes she should be out doing things, being a career women, but she has her obligations. The man wants to be a swinger, and to be in on the "scene" and know "where it's really at."

Within the psychosocio-sexual context of contemporary American culture, we would like to present those positive and negative effects of swinging for the individuals involved. Please note that we have been unable to interview more than a few dropouts from swinging. Therefore, our information is based solely on those who are participants. Our interviews with people who have discontinued swinging, about six or seven couples, reflect what we shall call the negative aspects of swinging. But first, we should like to summarize what we believe to be the positive aspects of swinging. Among these, there is an increased sexual interest in the mate or partner. All of our respondents report that due to swinging they now have a better relationship, both socially and sexually. These people are replaying a mating game. They can relive their youth and for many it is advantageous. They can get dressed up, go out together, and attempt a seduction. It is a form of togetherness that they never had before. There is the desire of each partner to reinforce in the other the idea that they are better sexually than any swinger they have encountered. There is a general increase in sexual excitation of both partners due to the possibilities of new types of sexual experiences and increase in thought and discussion of actual sexual experiences. The woman receives a great deal of positive reinforcement if she is seen as the least bit desirable. She is actively committing men to her. A 50-year old man can "make it" with a 22-year-old girl without any legal repercussions, and his wife will be equally guilty. It must be a tremendous satisfaction. Women uniformly report that they have been able to shed sexual inhibitions with which they were raised. And our society certainly has an overabundance of sexual inhibitions, mainly because we impose different standards on different members of the society. The Raquel Welches of our world can perform in one fashion, but the good little housewife must perform in another. How does one adjust to this conflict between one's model and one's own activities? The female respondents state that one way to resolve this conflict is to swing.

The partners now share an interest, which can be explored, observed, and discussed between themselves and among their new "friends." Both partners can indulge in voyeurism at parties, and thereby utilize the learning experience in their own relationship. Due to the fact that most of these people have had few, if any, opportunities throughout their lives for actually observing or learning by observation how to act and respond to sexual stimuli, the swinging scene may be an experience which could not be provided in any other way.

Swinging may be extremely exciting inasmuch as it carries certain elements of danger. Swingers may feel very avant garde in the breaking of cultural taboos or of legal codes. There is also a certain implied danger and possibility of losing the love of one's partner; however, this is usually offset by the mutual reinforcement mentioned previously. There can be a great deal of sexual excitement provided by the stimulus of profane versus sacred love. Both partners can now become conspirators in writing and hiding advertisements and letters and evidence of their new interest from children, relatives, "straight friends," and business colleagues. We feel that one of the greatest advantages in the relationship comes from the fact that the couple may now spend more time together searching for new contacts and pursuing leads for parties, bars, and other compatible couples. They may now plan weekend trips and vacations together to other parts of the country to meet swingers. They feel that now they have broadened their social horizon, and acquired new interests or hobbies as a by-product of their swinging contacts. Swingers seem to derive a great deal of satisfaction out of merely meeting and gossiping with other swingers, which gives them the dual role of also proselytizing. For the first time in many years, due to the restriction of early marriage, suburban environment, and the social and economic restraints of raising children, they may now have the opportunity to dress up, make dinner dates, plan for parties, acquire a full social calendar, and be extremely busy with telephone conversations, letter writing, picture taking. If they do prove to be a fairly "popular" couple and are in demand, they can now feel that they are both attractive and desirable. They see themselves and each other in a new light. They may now feel that they are doing what the "in" people are doing and living up to their "playboy" image. Most swingers report unsatisfactory sexual relationships prior to swinging. Now, due to the necessity of operating as a pair on the swinging scene, they may find that they actually have an increase in perception, awareness, and appreciation, sexual and otherwise, of each other.

One of the most important negative aspects, as we see it, is the inability to live up to one's own psychosexual myth and self-illusions. This is particularly disadvantageous in the case of the male. They read about sexual behavior in the outer world, and they realize they are not participating in this elaborate sexual life. Since the demise of the houses of prostitution, many early sexual contacts by males became hit-and-miss propositions. Boys usually begin by masturbating; to masturbate, one must fantasize.[1] Most males have an elaborate fantasy world in their internalized sexual lives. One of the fantasies is that of having access to many females. He sees himself as being capable of satisfying any and all of them. He now goes to a party, particularly a younger group party, and he has all these naked women running around in front of him. He experiences the anxiety of being incapable of performing up to his own expectations. This very anxiety may defeat him. In American society, the male is expected to be a tremendous performer sexually, and he must live up to his own publicity. This is extraordinarily difficult. He may find he cannot maintain an erection, he cannot perform. He finds himself envying younger men who are physically more attractive and his anxiety and fears increase. For the woman, such self-doubts are less in evidence, although beyond a doubt all females upon initiation to the swinging scene go through a stage of comparison of their own physical appearance and sexual performance with that of the other females. Should the couple be both older and less attractive than the majority of swingers encountered, they may regard the whole swinging scene as a failure, and withdraw immediately. For those who remain, other negative aspects include sexual jealousy. The male may find after a number of parties that his opportunity for satisfaction is limited, while he sees the women around him engaging in homosexual activities and continuing to satisfy each other over and over again for the duration of the evening. He may feel, and this is verbalized, that the "women have the best time," that the swinging scene is "unfair to men." We find that less than 25% of the men "turn on" regularly at large-scale open parties. In contrast to this, many men report that they "turn on" much more frequently at small-scale parties or in small groups of threesomes. This is the major deterrent to the swinging situation. If one keeps experiencing failure, and continuously worries about this failure, one will keep failing. This is a complete feedback situation. In an attempt to "turn themselves on," the males push their women into having ambisexual relations with another girl. Most of them got the idea from either books or porno-graphic movies. Again, the male experiences disaster. Why? Of the female respondents, 65% admit to enjoying their homosexual relation-ships with other females and liking it to the point where they would rather "turn on" to the female than to males.

For a couple who are relatively insecure with each other and with themselves, swinging may invoke a great deal of personal jealousy. The man who finds he is occasionally rejected or easily tired physically may resent his wife's responsiveness to other men. She, in turn, may feel that her partner is enjoying other women more or to a different degree than he enjoys her. These personal jealousies frequently erupt under the pressure of alcohol and the ensuing scene evolves into an event which makes all parties present uncomfortable if not antagonistic to the cou-ple. This causes them to be excluded from future invitations and branded as "troublemakers."

Another less common negativism in swinging is the "bad experi-ence." A couple may encounter another couple who have sexual "hang-ups," habits, or attitudes that are repulsive or objectionable to the initiating couple. If they encounter two or three consecutive "bad" couples, they may decide that it is not worth taking the risk of such exposure.

Some of our respondents report that in the past there have been incidences of venereal disease that were introduced into a swinging group by one couple; for all concerned, this provoked a great deal of fear and embarrassment due to the necessity of seeking medical aid from sources that would not report to health authorities. Fear of disease is always present, and is discussed frequently.

For many swingers a constant negative aspect of swinging is the perpetual hazard of discovery. To professional people and to those who work for a state or national government or for very conservative busi-ness firms, there is a strong possibility of status diminution or loss of occupational position if they are discovered. All respondents consist-ently insist upon all possible discretion and some go so far as to not give out addresses, correct last names, and place of employment. The majority of swingers keep unlisted telephones. The upwardly mobile feel that their "life would be ruined" if the world knew they were swingers.

Although our findings are inconclusive on this last negative aspect we feel it is important and perhaps the primary reason for the dropout among the more sensitive intellectual group of people who enter swinging. These people seem to feel that swinging in general is much too mechanistic, that there is a loss of identity and absence of commitment and a total noninvolvement that is the antithesis of sexual pleasure and satisfaction. Some explicitly say that the inconsistencies between the stated objectives and the actual performance are too great to overcome. Although a couple initially report that they want new friends, interests, and activities in addition to pure sexual contact, in reality this is not so. As proof of this we offer the fact that most couples will see another couple only once, and even on those occasions when they have relationships with the other couple, their social relationship is minimal even when their sexual relationship is maximal. In much the same light their self-image of avant-garde/sexual freedomists suffers when one considers their worries vis-à-vis jealousy.

Since many people have asked us where we think swinging is leading we should like to make some comments on our personal attitudes toward the future of the swingers. We feel that those individuals interviewed in our sample are not really benefiting themselves because the ideals that led them into swinging have not been fully realized. They may very well be acting out and getting positive reinforcement, psychologically and physically from their activities. However, their human relationships outside of the diad are not good. Their activities with other couples reflect mechanical interaction rather than an intimacy of relationships. As a cultural anthropologist one cannot doubt that this reflects the impersonalization as well as the depersonalization of human relationships in our culture. One would suppose that the next generation will carry a duality of purpose rather than a single-minded interest in sexual performance. We would like to see a freedom of sexuality, but one more concerned with human relationships; then these human relationships rather than the sexual relationships can become the primary goal.

REFERENCE

Simon, W., & Gagnon, J. Psycho-sexual development. *Transaction,* 1969, **6** (3), 9–18.

CHAPTER NINE

Contraception
and
Family
Planning

Contraception

The individual who wishes to engage in sexual intercourse but does not wish to become a parent logically should seek authoritative information about appropriate contraceptive techniques. Even when such information is readily available, it is not easy for most of us to assimilate.

There is a series of variables to be considered in evaluating each method. The ideal contraceptive would be 100% effective, absolutely free of side effects, inexpensive, aesthetically pleasing, easy to use, and it would in no way interfere with the spontaneity or pleasure of sexual interactions. Such a technique or device does not exist. As physicians Robert Glass and Nathan Kase suggest in the following article, each existing type of contraception is a mixture of positive and negative features.

The two approaches that are completely reliable in preventing conception (the pill and sterilization) also present some of the most difficult negative features. These authors suggest that the birth control pill may be associated with a variety of major and minor side effects that range from annoyances such as skin discoloration to very serious problems such as the increased probability of developing potentially fatal physiological disorders. Sterilization for either males or females presents all of the possible hazards associated with any surgical procedure plus the fact that an irreversible decision is being made about the possibility of future conception.

Finally, with respect to all means of contraception, there are specific psychological responses by individuals which may outweigh all of the factual data about effectiveness, safety, etc. That is, some individuals seem never to feel quite normal while taking the pill, some find the insertion of a diaphragm to be unpleasant and unsexual, some feel that condoms are unattractive and unnatural, some decide that withdrawal (coitus interruptus) spoils their sexual pleasure, and some (especially males) respond psychologically to sterilization with at least partial loss of sexual desire and/or of ability to perform sexually. The perfect contraceptive of the future should therefore be designed to avoid all such individualistic negative reactions. Fortunately, intensive research efforts are under way in various parts of the world in an attempt to solve such problems.

Contraception

Robert H. Glass and Nathan G. Kase

Pregnancy may be intentionally prevented in a variety of ways. These possibilities include the elimination of ovulation, interference with the egg's passage through the fallopian tube, the prevention of implantation

Reprinted in an edited version from: Glass, R. H., & Kase, N. G. *Woman's choice: A guide to contraception, fertility, abortion, and menopause.* New York: Basic Books, 1970. Chap. 3.

in the womb after fertilization, the prevention of the early development of the egg, and the prevention of the sperm's entry to the womb. Contraceptives employing each of these mechanisms are currently available. Their usefulness, however, is modified by such factors as effectiveness, safety, simplicity, and reversibility of action. Furthermore, to be useful, a method must provide contraceptive assurance in a manner acceptable to the individual. Unfortunately, there is no current contraceptive method that is completely suitable to all women in all these respects. The purpose of this article is to provide the individual woman with the basis for choosing a contraceptive that best answers her own needs.

HORMONAL TECHNIQUES

The birth control pill, a hormonal prevention of ovulation, is the only method which, if used properly, provides almost 100% contraceptive efficiency. A natural precedent exists for this type of contraception. During pregnancy ovulation cannot occur. The combined high levels of estrogen and progesterone at this time shut down the pituitary centers, resulting in elimination of the ovulation messenger. The pill, administered as combined progestin and estrogen, creates a condition similar to pregnancy and duplicates the natural contraception of pregnancy. Ovulation is eliminated and not merely delayed. No ovarian nests are stimulated. As a result, no ovarian hormones are produced and all the sex hormone needs of the woman are provided by the contents of the pill.

Such therapy by substitution raises some of the most important and controversial issues surrounding hormonal contraception. The duration of contraception imposed by pregnancy is limited by the 9-month length of pregnancy itself. With pills artificial pregnancy may be prolonged for years. Furthermore, one of the hormones of pregnancy, progesterone, is not suitable for use as a contraceptive pill because it is inactive when taken by mouth. This limitation is overcome by the availability of progesteronelike materials, the progestins, which are orally active. However, they are not chemically exactly like progesterone. What are the liabilities of this prolonged and imperfect substitution? To be sure, these hormones share many effects that are contraceptively advantageous, including changes in the uterine lining and cervical mucus. The basal body temperature rises in response to both types of hormone. But despite these fundamental biological duplications, there are detectable differences in activity between the parent compound and its synthetic imitators. It is not that the response of any given tissue is different when exposed to a progestin or progesterone. Rather, it is the magnitude of the induced response that may be dissimilar. Undoubtedly this fine but important distinction applies equally to the synthetic estrogen component of these pills. As shall be seen, the liabilities of these differences will be reflected in the side effects of this therapy. Lastly, pills alone do not substitute for the presence of a baby and placenta. In true pregnancy these may compensate for the high levels of hormones. Without such compensation hormones alone may produce unpleasant reactions. In summary these three issues—the prolongation of pseudo-pregnancy beyond 9 months, the biologically imperfect hormonal duplication, and the lack of compensatory factors made available only by true pregnancy—raise questions concerning the effects and safety of hormonal contraception. Because the pills are so effective and simple to use, great efforts have been applied to find the right answers. It is now known, for example, that dosage changes can diminish or eliminate the untoward reactions of pseudo-pregnancy. Over the past decade the evolution of contraceptive pills has centered on alterations in hormone composition.

Side effects

In order to make an intelligent choice among various contraceptives, it is essential that a woman understand each potential side effect—its nature and implications for her continued good health. The problems associated with birth control pills may be divided into three categories: those that disappear spontaneously or can be treated simply by switching products; those that require specific treatment; and those that are a threat to well-being. In the first case it is unnecessary to stop the pills; in the second it is optional; in the third it is imperative.

Included in the group of unpleasant but nonhazardous reactions that will gradually disappear or simply require change of drug are nausea and vomiting. Very often these symptoms can be alleviated by the simple expedient of taking pills at bedtime so that much of the effect is dissipated during sleep. Depending on the dosage and the medication, as many as 20% of the users will experience nausea during the first few cycles. However, these rates decline to minimal levels after 3 or 4 months. Even in persistent cases, its occurrence is intermittent. Therefore, attempts should be made to bear with moderate degrees of nausea in the anticipation that it will disappear with time.

Breasts are extremely sensitive to hormone stimulation, and therefore it is not surprising that contraceptive pills often cause breast enlargement and tenderness. These symptoms may require changes in the type of medication used. Only in exceptional cases is this problem sufficient to cause discontinuation of medication. The use of contraceptive pills in nursing mothers does present some difficulties. If given too early after delivery, the supply of milk may be diminished. Also, hormones do pass into the milk and may affect the infant. In rare cases, the pills cause spontaneous passage of breast milk in nonpregnant women, a symptom that should be reported to the prescribing physician.

Complaints of periodic bloating, water retention, and weight gain also fall in this group of nonhazardous symptoms. If these occur, relief can be obtained by eating low-salt, low-calorie foods. Unfortunately, women who tend to gain weight anyway will find this problem accentuated by the pill. Continuation of hormonal medication demands of them an even more rigorous and persistent diet. The anxiety generated may reach a point where the value of the drug is not worth these difficulties and should be discontinued.

Lastly, some users report an apparent increase in hair loss similar to that found in pregnancy. This loss is not final and is replaced by new hair growth.

The description of any side effect as minor or nonhazardous can represent only a consensus of professional views. In accordance with her own needs, an individual woman may feel that any of these problems is sufficient cause to discontinue medication.

Special problems

Other side effects require specific treatment. Possibly the most unpleasant and irritating problem associated with these pills is the fairly common presence of augmented vaginal discharge. This symptom can represent three types of vaginal change. A clear, moist, sometimes copious discharge beginning early in the cycle is often found with sequential pills. The "mucorrhea" is simply cervical mucus stimulated by estrogen. It may be so abundant as to require the use of a tampon or napkin. The woman may mistake this excess discharge for leakage of urine or complain of loss of sexual sensation because of the increased lubrication. However benign and natural, the abundance of this showing may require switching to combined agents in which a daily dose of progestin will markedly reduce mucus production. Unfortunately, combined pills may lead to the development of other types of vaginal discharge. It is worth remembering that some amount of vaginal discharge is normal in almost all women and is a natural expression of the self-cleansing capability of this organ. The contraceptive pills increase the cellular debris which in some women may reach unpleasant proportions of cloudy, sometimes staining discharge. Simple douching usually controls this problem.

The occurrence of monilia vaginitis, a yeast overgrowth of the vagina, which causes annoying irritation and itching, is increased by these pills as well as by pregnancy, and also often by the use of antibiotics. The manner in which the yeast arises in the vagina is not known. Certainly there is a probability that it may be introduced during sexual relations, but infection without intercourse also occurs. It is important to emphasize that this is not a venereal disease, such as gonorrhea or syphilis. Aside from the annoyance created, it has no general health importance. The yeast infections are easily treated with a variety of medications but may just as easily return. Two forms of local vaginal treatment are most often prescribed. The first is the use of gentian violet. The other is a specific antiyeast medication available in either tablet or ointment form. In difficult and recurring cases a switch from combination to sequential pills may be helpful. Sometimes this infection becomes chronic, and as a result it may be necessary to stop birth control pills entirely.

As with monilia, many of the side effects of contraceptives are similar to those found in pregnancy. Some women will be disconcerted to find that they have developed a fine gray-brown pigmentation of the skin over the forehead and cheeks. This change, chloasma, is better known as the mask of pregnancy. About 1 out of every 10 or 15 women on pills has this problem. It is usually mild and easily covered with ordinary cosmetics. It may be particularly aggravated by prolonged exposure to sun. If it is severe, skin blanching agents can be used under the direction of a physician. Such agents are not always successful; often the change fades only slowly, and in some cases not at all. Severe early problems with chloasma require discontinuation of contraceptive pills.

A woman's menstrual flow may be variably altered while she is using hormonal contraception. Sometimes her period is excessive, but usually it is far less than previously experienced. A not uncommon effect —and for obvious reasons one that may cause concern—is the disappearance of the monthly flow while on pills. Absence of one period or a heavy flow for one period can be ignored. If either occurs a second time, medical consultation is necessary. The absence of flow for two consecutive cycles requires reassurance that pregnancy has not occurred. In the case of excessive bleeding, it may be that gynecologic conditions unrelated to the pill need attention.

Far more frequent is the appearance of unexpected (breakthrough) bleeding while the woman is still taking some of her 21 pills. Many physicians suggest that the woman double her dose and take two pills a day for the remainder of the cycle. In the following cycle, treatment returns to one pill a day. If this type of bleeding is persistent, switching to another drug may prove helpful.

Regular medical checkups

All judgments concerning the importance of the variety of side effects which have been discussed assume that a woman has made periodic visits every 6 months to her physician while on medication. Examinations at these times must include, at a minimum, a check on her blood pressure, eyes, breasts, and internal pelvic organs. In addition, a urine analysis and a Pap smear for cancer detection should be done. In the Pap test, a wooden stick is used to scrape some cells free from the cervix. After treatment with proper fixative solutions and stains, these cells are examined microscopically. Their size, shape, and staining characteristics will distinguish normal cells from those that are suspected of being cancerous. Since cancer in the cervical area develops slowly, changes in the cells give warning of impending danger. The object of taking a Pap smear is to pick up these early changes and to treat the disease at this stage when the cure rate is 100%. If all women had even a yearly Pap smear, it is estimated that almost all cases of incurable cervical cancer would be eliminated. As will be discussed later, there is no evidence that contraceptive pills increase the risk of cervical cancer.

Serious side effects

The physical examination and the patient's medical history may uncover evidence of disorders which preclude starting on the pills or demand their discontinuation. Serious medical problems which prohibit the use of hormonal contraception include cancer of the breast, cancer of the pelvic organs, and heart disease of such severity that it would also make pregnancy too great a risk. Similarly, chronic liver ailments associated with jaundice do not permit use of these medications. In these instances, the basis for prohibition is clear. However, in several disorders the data are less certain. Here it is probably unwise to begin therapy in view of the possibility of severe reactions. Included in this group are epilepsy, migraine headaches, and asthma.

Women with a history of thrombophlebitis (blood clots in the veins of the legs associated with local pain and swelling) should not be started on the pills. There is a growing feeling among many physicians, now substantiated by statistical surveys, that the development of thrombophlebitis may occur as a result of contraceptive medication. One study comes from England. In this series of reports it is claimed that 1 out of 2000 pill users will need hospitalization for thrombophlebitis yearly as opposed to 1 in 20,000 women not taking the pills. Serious complications of thrombophlebitis are rare, but when these do occur they may be lethal. The English study points out that in women between the ages of 20 and 34 years there will be 1.5 deaths yearly in 100,000 pill users due to complications of thrombophlebitis. This compares with the lower rate in nonusers of .2 deaths per 100,000 women. To put these risks in perspective, women of the same age group experience an annual death rate from cancer of 13.7 per 100,000 and from auto accidents of 4.9 per 100,000. Of the overall death rate of 60.0 per 100,000 women of this age, 22.8 (better than one-third of all yearly deaths) are due to complications arising from pregnancy, delivery, and the immediate postdelivery period. Of great interest is that a portion of these pregnancy-related deaths are due to thrombophlebitis. The lethal risk of phlebitis after true pregnancy was 1.3 per 100,000 annually. These data closely resemble the risk (1.5) claimed for women on the pill.

This series of English reports concludes that pill users have a 9–10 times greater risk of thrombophlebitis than nonusers and, as a result, a 7 times greater than expected risk of dying in a year of pill usage. Neither the type nor duration of therapy was incriminated in this report. However, in a recent American study where the complication rate for thrombophlebitis was 4.4 times higher in pill users, there was a suggestion that sequential pills were more hazardous.

One recent report suggested that women with blood group O who were on contraceptives had far less thrombophlebitis than women with other blood groups. Hence a predisposing factor, other than the pill, must be involved.

There is a small but definite risk of thrombophlebitis and its rare attendant complications with the use of these drugs. This risk does not constitute a basis on which to prohibit their use except in women with a positive history. The normal patient should not approach these drugs with undue trepidation.

Long-term use

Menopause is not delayed by the pill; postponement and prolongation of the fertile age do not occur. Babies born following contraceptive use are as normal as the general population. With rare exceptions, fertility promptly returns following discontinuation of the pill. Just as there may be a delay in the resumption of periods following a 9-month pregnancy so there may be—for as long as 6 months—following pseudopregnancy. In the few instances where lack of flow and involuntary infertility occur, these are easily reversed by ovulation-inducing medication.

Some symptoms may appear that require discontinuation of the pill and are an important reason for periodic medical checkups while on medication. Persistent or recurrent severe headaches and blurring or double vision are each indicative of possible changes in the blood vessels of the brain and the eye. These rare complications also appeared more frequently in pill users in England. Should these symptoms occur, immediate consultation is advised. An even rarer effect is rising blood pressure that returns to normal when the pills are discontinued.

There are changes in body chemistry associated with contraceptive pills that raise some questions concerning their effects on the long-term health of the users. Women taking oral contraceptives have for the first few months a diminished capacity to metabolize extra sugar. The significance of this change, which often returns to normal despite continuing contraceptive use, is unknown. If a woman is destined to become diabetic, it may be that the use of contraceptive pills will bring on the diabetes earlier in her life. There is no proof for this at the moment. If the urine contains no sugar at the 6-month check, there is no need for concern. In a woman with a family history of the disease, more frequent urine and blood sugar studies while on the pill are a wise precaution.

Some women show changes in the pattern of fatty substances circulating in their blood while on the pill and develop a pattern similar to that found in normal males. This is disturbing because males have a higher incidence of coronary artery disease than do females and there is some suspicion that these blood-borne fatty substances contribute to this problem. For the moment, the evidence is not strong enough to warrant adverse conclusions about the long-range impact of the pills. This is another area where further investigation and evaluation are needed.

The psychology of the pill

Far more common than these rare but potentially hazardous complications are the almost infinite variety of psychological difficulties attributed to pill usage. These include fatigue, irritability, depression, and loss of sexual desire. The majority of such complications seem to be related to the hormones, although there is no doubt that some of the symptoms are related to extraneous influences and would appear regardless of drug intake. The decision to switch or discontinue therapy depends on the severity of these symptoms, the degree to which they disrupt life patterns, and the acceptability of other contraceptives.

Unfortunately, in many women, these psychological side effects occur regardless of the type of contraceptive technique employed. They represent a reaction to contraception itself and not to the method utilized. Although the decision to postpone pregnancy may have good practical reasons, such as money, career, or family planning, thwarted subconscious desires for pregnancy may magnify psychological difficulties. Probably an equal number of women, however, have found that the release from the fear of pregnancy can result in a better adjustment to life and even increased sexual desire.

It is difficult to measure the effect of oral contraception on sexual desire. Certainly women taking this medication do report changes in desire. However, it is interesting that some women report an increased desire for sexual activity while others report decreased receptivity. Are these effects of the hormones themselves or do they reflect subtle psychological reactions to the use of contraception? Does the woman, now sure of contraception, feel freer to enjoy her sexual life? Are there women who enjoy sexual activity only when it involves a chance of pregnancy, and do these women lose their desire when they know that this possibility is eliminated? Hormones do directly affect sexual performance in animals. Female rabbits given progestin will not mate. An analogous effect has not been demonstrated in the human female. However, if loss of desire is a complaint while on birth control pills, it would be wise to discontinue their use.

Schedules

The task of remembering to take a pill each night for 20 or 21 days often proves difficult and anxiety-provoking for many women. Two questions that always arise are, "If I miss a pill (or two), will I still be protected against pregnancy?" and "If I forget a pill shall I take two the next day?" Protection becomes less assured if pills are missed, especially if this occurs during the early part of the cycle. With the combination pills, after the first 7 to 10 have been taken, changes in the cervical mucus and endometrium will *probably* provide adequate contraceptive effect even if 1 or 2 pills are missed. This chance must not be taken. With the sequential contraceptive drugs omitting even one pill may prove disastrous. Here, the cervical mucus is easily penetrable by sperm so that if ovulation occurs due to a decreased hormone level, pregnancy becomes quite possible. Doubling the dose the following day does not compensate for missing the previous day's pill. Certainly, a missed pill should be taken as early as possible after it is remembered that a scheduled one has been forgotten. If there is any doubt of pill intake, the couple should employ some form of mechanical contraception until the cycle in question is completed.

Individual dosage schedules should be reviewed with the prescribing physician; usually they call for the use of one pill a day for 20 or 21 days starting on the fifth day of the menstrual cycle. The first day of flow is counted as day 1. All currently approved regimens allow an interval between month-long contraception for a menstrual flow. In some formulations, as an aid to the forgetful woman, seven inactive nonhormonal pills are taken in the week between the active pills. In this approach the ease of "a pill a day every day" is realized. The user is almost habituated to the contraceptive technique and is relieved of the necessity for counting days, marking calendars, or using other memory devices.

There has been some thought among public health theoreticians that the requirement for scheduled pill-taking precludes the use of contraceptive pills among illiterate people. However, work in India by our colleague Rama Vaidya has shown that careful explanation and proper motivation provide even illiterate women with all the equipment they need to use the pills successfully for contraception. In fact, these women were often as skillful in using this medication as women educated at leading universities.

What if a baby finds the pills and swallows a number of them? The only danger is to the mother if she does not realize she is short of pills. The baby is unlikely to suffer any ill effects except transient nausea.

Cancer

There is no indication that hormonal contraception can cause cervical cancer. However, cancer of the lining of the uterus as opposed to that of the cervix may even be made less likely by the use of contraceptive pills. During the past decade, many cases of uterine-lining cancer have been treated with high doses of progestins and in some cases the extent of the cancer has been lessened. It is felt by many physicians that progestins given as contraceptive pills may in the long run provide considerable protection against the development of this type of cancer.

Lastly, there is absolutely no evidence that pill usage predisposes in any way to cancer of the breast.

Before leaving the hormonal techniques of contraception, it is important to emphasize that while attention has been directed to the numerous difficulties associated with the pill, this should not obscure the fact that this medication remains the most effective and acceptable contraceptive currently available. The pill provides complete protection without requiring any action at the time of intercourse.

MECHANICAL TECHNIQUES

Intrauterine devices

Theoretically, the pill answers all needs, particularly in offering 100% effectiveness. However, some women find daily pill-taking an insupportable burden. A few women cannot take the pills for medical reasons. Many others are intolerant of the side effects accompanying hormonal contraception and seek other means of family planning. In recent years, intrauterine devices (IUDs) have been applied with great success. For thousands of years, Arabian camel drivers have prevented pregnancy in their camels by inserting stones into the uterus. Earlier in this century, the practice was extended to women, but instead of stones, silver rings and devices of silk were used. For reasons that are not quite clear, use of these intrauterine devices fell into disfavor and it was not until the 1960s that large-scale use of IUDs (ring, coil, loop, bow) became commonplace. Extensive research has been performed in many animal species in an effort to understand the mechanism by which these devices prevent pregnancy. In sheep there is interference with sperm progression through the womb as well as a depression of the activity of the corpus luteum. In rabbits, eggs are fertilized but implantation is faulty. As yet, there is no convincing explanation for the contraceptive activity of IUDs in women. Among the many theories advanced to explain their action, the three most likely effects are a change in the structure of the endometrium; a chronic low-grade inflammation of the endometrium; and a change in the muscular activity of the uterus.

Notwithstanding our relative ignorance of how this contraceptive method works, the IUD has been applied with great success. Although offering somewhat less than complete protection (92–98%), these devices free the woman from the necessity of remembering her daily pill. An important advantage is that the woman's hormone cycle continues unaltered, and the general body effects of hormone therapy are eliminated.

Recently a woman sought help from her gynecologist because of

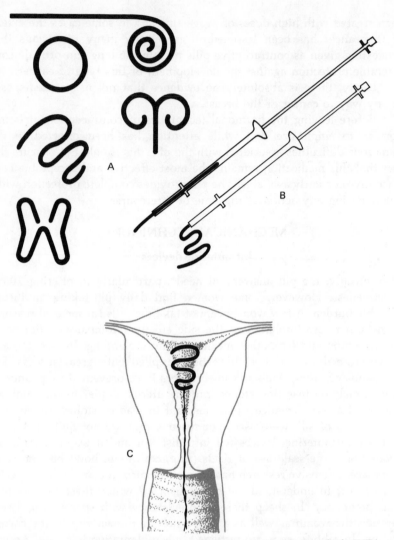

Figure 9-1.   The IUD (A) A few of the common shapes in which IUD's are manufactured. (B) An IUD pulled into a device used for insertion (top) and expelled (bottom). (C) The IUD in place inside the uterus. Note nylon string passing through cervix.

infertility. Investigation disclosed the presence of an IUD in the uterus which had been placed there many years earlier for contraceptive purposes but had been forgotten by the patient. This would seem to be the ultimate compliment for the device. It had remained such a silent and innocuous guardian that its presence was completely erased from memory. Unfortunately, this experience is not universal. In addition to the incomplete contraception offered by these devices, it is recognized that troublesome side effects, such as pain and bleeding, occur which often require removal of the IUD.

The IUD may be expelled unnoticed, leaving the woman unprotected, and pregnancy may occur. It has been estimated that one-third of pregnancies with IUDs are due to expulsion of the device. In an effort to eliminate undetected expulsion, most devices have fine nylon strings attached to them which protrude through the mouth of the womb into the vagina. The user should frequently check to confirm that these strings are still in place. If the IUD is expelled, a second placement may be more successful. Unfortunately, even though the IUD remains in the womb, pregnancies may occur. Although a high spontaneous abortion rate is associated with these latter pregnancies, there is no evidence that those pregnancies which are retained produce abnormal offspring. On most occasions, the device remains in the uterus throughout the pregnancy and then is expelled with the placenta.

Unfortunately, as we have noted, the devices are not without local side effects which require its removal. Approximately 15% are removed in the first year of use due to cramping pelvic pains, discharge, or persistent bleeding. Even in the second year as many as 10% require removal for these reasons.

As with contraceptive pills, side effects have stimulated the search for and production of new types of devices. The original ring form has been largely supplanted by other designs. At the moment, the Lippe's loop and its variants appear to be the most satisfactory. A recently introduced springlike device which unfolds in the uterus is an interesting modification, but any advantage over the loop is not yet apparent.

There are only a few reasons in a woman's medical history that would rule out trying IUDs provided she can face some risk of pregnancy. Women who have not delivered a baby, for example, face substantially higher expulsion and side-effect rates. In addition, women with anatomical distortion of the cavity of the womb caused by fibroids and women with pelvic infections are not good candidates for an IUD.

There is no evidence that prolonged placement of these devices will lead to cancer of the pelvic organs. However, as in all matters pertaining to health, women with IUDs should be checked yearly. There is no need to remove or change the device periodically because of prolonged wear. Actually, it is wise to reduce manipulation to a minimum, as it is claimed that once in every 2500 insertions a womb is perforated. This is a potentially serious complication that may require surgical treatment. Lastly, following removal of the device, uterine function and subsequent fertility return to normal. Ninety percent of the women using IUDs who then try to become pregnant succeed within 1 year after removal of the device.

Because of the uncertainty surrounding its effectiveness, the IUD has been reserved for second place in the contraceptive choice of American women. Those unhappy with the pill may turn with relative assurance to these devices. Perhaps more important than styles of usage or claims of clinical effectiveness are the individual woman's instincts and personal appraisal of contraceptives. For example, if she fears her own lack of motivation to maintain careful and continuous attention to pill use, then an IUD may be preferable. The drawbacks of the device are few, and the difficulties they impose are not cumulative. For these reasons the IUD deserves widespread and confident use.

Other mechanical methods

Even with the availability of the pill and IUD, many women still prefer to use the more simple mechanical methods that deny sperm entry to the womb: the diaphragm, vaginal foams, creams, jellies, and the condom or rubber. Despite the stringent demands these methods make on the motivation of the couple employing them, their lack of major side effects has obvious appeal. Minor side effects include diminished sexual sensation with the condom, messiness with creams, and the annoyance of need prior to intercourse to insert the diaphragm and any spermicidal medications. In addition, the decreased effectiveness of these methods may place some psychological strain on the couple. There are conflicting data on the success and failure of contraception with these methods, but overall they are less certain than either the pill or IUDs. However, a well-motivated couple may expect to use any of these techniques with a good deal of confidence.

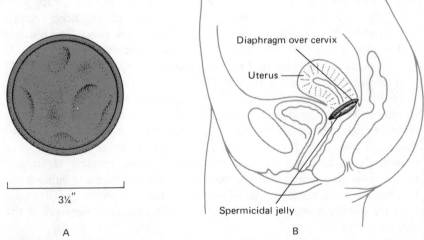

Figure 9-2. The diaphragm. (A) External view. (B) Diaphragm inserted, with a coating of spermicidal jelly.

If 100 fertile women have intercourse at regular and frequent intervals for 1 year, approximately 80 of them will become pregnant. Clearly any method of contraception is more effective than none. Withdrawal of the penis just prior to ejaculation is a time-honored and, for *highly practiced couples*, a reasonably reliable method of contraception. It has been the mainstay, along with abortion, in limiting families in some largely Catholic countries. Certainly withdrawal detracts from the pleasure of the sexual act, but the question of whether it can cause emotional or physiological problems remains pure speculation.

RHYTHM

A substantial portion of women are limited by religious belief to methods based on sexual abstinence. Users of the rhythm method attempt to estimate a woman's short fertile phase when she can conceive, usually from a year's records of menstrual cycles. The fertility phase is usually about 14 days before the next menstruation. It is reasoned that sperm may be able to fertilize for 48 hours after intercourse, and that the egg may last 24 hours after ovulation. Thus, a 3-day danger interval before and after ovulation is defined; in fact, because of errors of estimation a much longer interval must be set aside for abstention. Based on menstrual records, the time of abstention extends from 18 days before the earliest likely menstruation up to and including 11 days before the onset of the latest recorded menstruation. In a woman with a 28-to-31-day cycle, this continent period would be day 10 (28 minus 18) through day 20 (31 minus 11). A more variable cycle (26 to 40 days) would lead to abstinence from 8 through day 29. An alternate method relies on daily basal body temperatures. At ovulation, the temperature rises and stays up until the next period. Abstinence is required throughout the first half of the cycle until 2 to 3 days after the temperature rises.

Aside from severely testing the motivation of the couple, these methods are often too complicated for safe application. The requirements for the "perfect" contraceptive have not been met. Research continues in an effort to uncover remedies for the defects of current methods.

SURGICAL METHODS

Permanent contraception or, more appropriately, sterilization can be achieved by surgical ligation of the fallopian tubes or by hysterectomy. The use of these methods will depend not only on the woman's preference but also on the judgment of her physician and the accepted medical standards for sterilization within her community. It should be emphasized that neither of these surgical methods interferes with sexual satisfaction. Equally unwarranted is the fear that hysterectomy may trigger excessive weight gain.

Surgical methods of abortion are widely used as an alternative to contraception in many countries. Ideally, these procedures should be resorted to only if conventional contraception fails.

Other possible sterilization approaches include surgical tying of the vas deferens in the male. This operation prevents the sperm from reaching the penis but does not interfere with sexual performance or ejaculation. Semen is produced but it does not contain sperm. If the male later changes his mind and desires more children, an attempt can be made to reestablish continuity of the vas. Unfortunately, in a fair proportion of cases, this is unsuccessful. Therefore, the tying of the vas should be viewed as a permanent procedure.

THE FUTURE

In an effort to reduce dependence on daily intake, once-a-month pills and injectable hormones with prolonged activity are under study. Another variant of this method is the implantation beneath the skin of plastic devices impregnated with a hormone that is slowly released over a number of months. A major problem with all these methods is the unpredictable occurrence of vaginal bleeding. In addition, after discontinuation of hormone injections the contraceptive effect may persist for many months. Therefore, the return of fertility may be delayed for as long as a year.

In an effort to reduce dosages below side-effect thresholds, small-dose "mini" progestin pills without estrogen have been developed. Ovulation may occur at times. The contraceptive effect then depends in part upon a change in the cervical mucus to make sperm entry more difficult and upon changes in the womb lining that, in some cases, make it less receptive to implantation of a fertilized egg. While most other side effects are low with this medication, there is a 25% incidence of abnormal uterine bleeding. There is also a pregnancy rate of 2.5%.

Estrogen in high doses may be used as a contraceptive when intercourse has occurred near ovulation. A 5-day treatment with a synthetic estrogen, stilbestrol, has been effective in preventing pregnancy in cases of rape and as an aid to girls who have had a single episode of unprotected sexual intercourse. This "morning after" method was pioneered by John McLean Morris and Gertrude Van Wagenen of Yale University Medical School. It can produce strong side effects of nausea and vomiting and requires a physician's direction. Medical help is necessary not simply to modify the side effects but also to direct the timing of medication, which is critical for effectiveness. This is not a feasible contraceptive for women having intercourse a number of times a month.

Early pregnancies in animals can be aborted by injections of antibodies directed against the hormones of the pituitary or against those associated with pregnancy. This has not been developed for human use because of the adverse reactions that might accompany the use of these materials. Similarly, certain drugs that interfere with metabolism may cause abortion. However, they are so powerful that, in addition to inducing abortion, they may suppress the body's ability to fight infection and therefore expose the aborting woman to potentially life-threatening illnesses. However, if smaller doses are used to avoid this complication, the drug may fail to cause abortion. Yet damage to the unaborted pregnancy may have occurred, so that the child will be born with multiple defects. For these reasons antimetabolite drugs are not, at the moment, feasible for human use. This does not rule out the possibility that newer drugs of this type may overcome these problems.

The male pill

There has been much speculation concerning the possibility of a male pill for contraception. At this time no such pill is available. Should this medication be developed, then males will join their mates in experiencing psychological uncertainties and fears of bodily harm as part of contraception. It would be of interest to see whether males would accept a systemic contraceptive as readily as women accepted the pills.

On the Psychology of Adolescents' Use of Contraceptives

Among those who do not wish to have children but who do wish to engage in sexual intercourse, it is obvious that some contraceptive precautions must be taken. The elementary logic in that statement is saved from banality by one simple and startling fact—hundreds of thousands of unmarried American teen-agers are sexually active and contraceptively inactive. Why?

Psychologist George Cvetkovich and his research associates present the available data on unwanted teen-age pregnancies in terms of statistics concerning babies born to unwed mothers, hasty and unsuccessful marriages with pregnant brides, and the attendant problems which include such diverse tragedies as suicide, inadequate prenatal care, and child abuse. These investigators also suggest a number of reasons for teen-age neglect of contraception in terms of stages of cognitive development and a naive acceptance of several erroneous beliefs.

This description of teen-agers was brought to mind recently in a non-sexual context as we drove onto the campus at Purdue just as there was a break between classes. As at every campus with which we are familiar, student pedestrians and student bicyclists suddenly swarmed in all directions seemingly oblivious to the movement of cars, trucks, and buses and seemingly uninterested in such mundane matters as crosswalks, stop lights, and the unpleasantness involved in colliding with several tons of motorized steel. In a familiar but always amazing miracle, the moving vehicles slowed and the individuals who failed to take such primitive precautions as observing their surroundings were once again spared. The idea then occurred to us that if society has not been successful in conveying to very bright college students the wisdom of thinking, looking, and otherwise trying to avoid the possibility of immediate pain and a bloody demise before crossing the street, our failure to teach high school students to think about the abstract mystery of conception while seeking enjoyable genital stimulation should scarcely come as a surprise. As suggested in the following article, the real question is whether we can develop effective educational procedures that will change these current behavior patterns.

On the Psychology of Adolescents' Use of Contraceptives

George Cvetkovich, Barbara Grote,
Ann Bjorseth, and Julia Sarkissian

According to the report of the U. S. Commission on Population Growth and the American Future in 1968, over 600,000 infants were born to

Reprinted in an edited version from: Cvetkovich, G., Grote, B., Bjorseth, A., & Sarkissian, J. On the psychology of adolescents' use of contraceptives. *Journal of Sex Research*, 1975, **11**, 256–270.

women under 20 years of age. This figure accounted for 17% of all births that year. A large portion of these teen-age pregnancies were undoubtedly unwanted. The commission reported that 160,000 of those children were born to unwed teen-age mothers. Based on figures from the U.S. Census Bureau, Fugita, Wagner, and Pion[13] reported that 1 out of every 11 children is born out of wedlock, and that 40% of females who bear children out of wedlock are teen-agers. The figures on out-of-wedlock births are, of course, very conservative indices of the proportions of the problem of unwanted teen-age pregnancies, since they do not consider the teen-ager marital status at the time of conception. Based on figures from the National Center for Health Statistics, Wagner, Perthou, Fugita, and Pion[36] reported that one out of every six women gives birth within 8 months after her first marriage.

Tillack, Tyler, Pacquette, and Jones[31] found that 73% of the 16-year-olds in one county who married in 1968 were pregnant. This was also true of 55% of the 17-year-olds, 26% of the 18-year-olds, but only 10% of the 22-year-olds. Evidently premarital pregnancy is a major reason for teen-age marriages. But these marriages bring with them problems of their own. Teen-age girls are still developing emotionally and many are not ready to accept the long-term commitment to a child or a husband. This may explain why 50% of teen-age marriages end in divorce within the first 4 years.[29]

According to the Population Commission report, pregnant teen-agers, especially those in their early teens, are more likely to experience serious health, social, and psychological difficulties. The commission also reports that teen-age mothers have a suicide rate 10 times that of the general population.

An out-of-wedlock pregnancy may introduce further difficulties. The pregnant teen-ager may be denied further public education or, at best, have her education seriously disrupted.[2] One county school study, reported in Moore and Slesnik,[23] found that one-half of the women who dropped out of high school during the 1969–1970 school year did so because they were pregnant. Compared to married mothers, unwed mothers are less likely to have adequate prenatal care. Children born out of wedlock are more likely to be born prematurely and to have health problems.[2] There is some evidence that out-of-wedlock children, especially those of very young mothers, are more likely to be subjected to inadequate or even abusive mothering.[18] Even as the child grows up, he is likely to face difficulties related to inferior social and, in some states, legal status. By even the most conservative estimates, teen-age illegitimacy represents a manifestly important social problem.

It is a frequent conclusion that the problem of premarital conception can be solved by increasing sexual and contraceptive information. The Population Commission succinctly summed up the thinking of many when it stated, "One characteristic American response to social issues is to propose educational programs and this Commission is no exception

[The Commission on Population Growth and the American Future, *Population and the American Future*, 1972, p. 123]." While the presentation of accurate contraceptive information is important, it is not in itself sufficient to deal with the problem of premarital pregnancy. The illegitimacy statistics sufficiently demonstrate that more and better education is needed. They may also indicate that education along conventional lines will not be adequate. As will be discussed later, one of the most striking characteristics of teen-age illegitimacy is that many adolescents who have the benefit of the best sex education and have available contraceptive materials do not use contraception. Clearly, new directions are called for that can offer suggestions for improving existing programs.

This discussion, therefore, has been designed with the purpose of answering two general questions: (1) Why does contraceptive and sexual knowledge go unused? (2) How can educational programs be developed to ensure maximum contraceptive use among sexually active teen-agers?

To address these two questions, this article presents a conceptual scheme that diverges from the pattern common to most research on the psychology of contraceptive use. To date, research has predominantly followed an attitude-survey model. While this approach has provided much useful information, the information has been inherently limited. There does not now exist an adequate comprehensive theory of contraception behavior; nor will such a theory be developed until research moves beyond the descriptive level. Back[1] has recently commented along similar lines. In an address before the American Psychological Association he proposed that psychological research on population take on new directions leading to a more theoretical orientation. Among his specific suggestions is that studies be conducted examining the individual's activities in a variety of situations and over an extended period of time —a far cry from the one-shot approach of many contraceptive-attitude studies. This article is in line with Back's suggestion. It is an attempt to account for contraceptive-use patterns during the first years of sexual activity by applying existing psychological theory.

CONTRACEPTIVE-USE RESEARCH

The most striking characteristic of adolescent contraceptive use is its apparent irrationality. To cite some selected examples: Nearly 6 in 10 women interviewed by Kantner and Zelnick[17] did not use contraception at last intercourse. These women report that they failed to do so because they believed either they could not become pregnant, they were too young, they had sex too infrequently, or they had intercourse at the wrong time of the month. Goldsmith and associates[14] report that "Guilt about sex and denial of risk are evident in the reasons given by many respondents for not using birth control, 'pregnancy would never happen to me' and 'I'd feel that I shouldn't have intercourse at all, so I wouldn't plan ahead to do it or to use birth control' [p. 35]." In their advice to medical contraception counselors, Sandberg and Jacobs[28] summarize the state of affairs in the following way:

> A physician who accepts proffered statements for the whole truth is soon confounded by the apparent irrational action of some patients in their misuse or rejection of the prescribed contraceptives and by the unreasonable and inconsistent explanations as to why none of the various methods are utilizable. It is obvious that behavior in contraceptive use does not always conform to apparently rational, externally voiced attitudes and that conflicted psychological forces, consciously and unconsciously, are extremely influential [p. 35].

Given the apparent pervasiveness of adolescent "irrationality," surprisingly little research has conceptualized contraceptive use in these terms. The dominant model in past research has been a search for a one-to-one relationship between expressed attitudes and contraceptive behavior.[16, 19] Sample survey research does indicate the importance of dealing with the problem from the subjective viewpoint of the adolescent. Seemingly of great importance is the adolescent's evolving self-concept of his sexuality. This is precisely what Goldsmith and associates[14] conclude from the results of their opinion survey of girls coming to two Bay Area teen centers: "The findings in this study suggest that an attitude accepting one's own sexuality is a more important correlate with contraceptive use than such other factors as exposure to sex education, knowledge of sex and contraception or religious background [p. 36]." Similarly, results of a national sample survey of 4611 young women 15–19 years of age[17] found a strong relationship between contraceptive use and self-perception. In this study, evaluation of one's own fecundity was found to be particularly important. Those who thought they were highly susceptible to conception were much more likely to use contraception. Nearly 56% of the women who did not use contraception at last intercourse believed that they could not conceive. While sample studies are valuable for pointing to the problem and possible psychological antecedents, they are not able to provide in-depth information about the subjective viewpoint of the adolescent. Three further general shortcomings of prior research may be briefly noted.

Prior research has most often been concerned with a point-in-time analysis of the adolescent's attitudes. Given, however, the apparent episodic nature of teen-age sexual activity,[3,17,28] and the rapidly evolving adolescent self-concept, longitudinal study is needed. As Sandberg and Jacobs[28] remind us, "A great many of these forces [relating to contraceptive use] appear to be changeable in type and strength and vary with time, age, situation, partner, etc. This leads to the necessity for repeated decision-making ... [p. 35]."

A second shortcoming is the dearth of studies on males. While a review of the literature has found several studies dealing with husbands and college males,[3, 13] we have not uncovered a single in-depth analysis of male adolescents regarding contraception.

Finally, a third shortcoming of prior research may be noted. Most studies, particularly those that have attempted a more in-depth analysis of contraceptive use, have dealt with special populations. Notably, persons who are easily identifiable and readily available have been heavily studied. For example, women who appear at population clinics for either contraceptive materials or pregnancy tests have been common targets of research. Similarly, research has more heavily studied the sexually active than the inactive. For a fuller understanding of contraceptive use, studies are clearly needed which investigate nonclinical populations of both the sexually active and the (as yet) sexually inactive.

THE PSYCHOLOGY OF ADOLESCENCE

The major cognitive task of the adolescent years is the mastery of thought.[10, 12, 22, 25] The manner in which the adolescent grapples with this problem is directly relevant to the understanding of sexual activity and use of contraceptives. Particularly important for the understanding of adolescence is the transition necessitated near the end of childhood at approximately 11 years of age. Later childhood is characterized by concrete cognitive operations. The problem at this time is that the child cannot adequately differentiate between perceptual givens and his own mental products. The child is, to use the Piagetian term, egocentric. The school-age child believes that the conclusions he has arrived at are not only true, but are the only conclusions that could have been reached. His judgments and hypotheses have, to him, a logical necessity. Thus, Peel[24] found that when 7- to 10-year-olds were given information that contradicted their previously made conclusions, they interpreted the new information to fit their conclusions.

Adolescence (approximately 13 to 18 years of age) is marked by the emergence of formal operational thought. The adolescent begins to discover the arbitrariness of his mental products and to separate them from perceptual phenomena. He begins to think in logical propositional terms and to gain the ability to analyze complex multivariable problems in a systematic way. The advantages of these developments are twofold: (1) the adolescent can think about his own thinking and the thinking of other persons, and (2) he gains the ability to recognize possibilities as well as actualities. As in previous stages of development, these new cognitive powers which extricate the adolescent from one form of egocentrism entangle him in another form.

The adolescent can think about his own thinking and the thinking of others; but, he fails to differentiate the object of his own thought from the object of others' thought. Thus, he assumes that other persons are thinking about the same things that occupy his thinking. One particularly important object of the adolescent's thought is, of course, himself. This is understandable because of the rapid body changes that the adolescent is experiencing. Teen-age concerns about clothes, cosmetics, hair, and other adornments may be understood in these terms.

Two particular aspects of adolescent egocentrism[10] relate to contraceptive use: (1) the imaginary audience, and (2) the personal fable.

The imaginary audience

Elkind[10] suggests that the adolescent's failure to differentiate thought-objects is manifested in the widespread belief in an imaginary audience. This audience consists of the adolescent's anticipations of the reactions of others to him. It is imaginary because the adolescent assumes that others are as preoccupied with him as he is with himself. This, of course, is seldom true.

The imaginary audience aspect of egocentrism may relate to sexual activity. The adolescent is as yet uncertain of his ability to live up to the demands of adult sexuality. Indeed, there are some who are probably uncertain that they want anything to do with the whole business of sex. Use of contraceptives requires not only a certain amount of premeditation and objective thinking, but also application of the analytic process to one's own case. The adolescent may not be ready, cognitively or emotionally, to accept his sexuality to the degree that allows premeditated sex. To prepare for sex by using contraception is to admit to self and the imaginary audience a willingness to accept adult sexuality. As Wagner[34] suggests, there may be many adolescents who believe that they "are not that kind of girl"—at least not yet.

A young woman interviewed by Sorenson[30] puts her retrospective analysis of this situation in more forceful terms:

> Pills? That's what I should have taken. But I didn't want to take them because that's like coming right out and admitting, "I AM FUCKING," you know. I didn't want to admit that to myself . . . I was trying so hard to think I wasn't fucking that the thought I might get pregnant never entered my mind [p. 324].

Sorenson also reports that 71% of all nonvirgin adolescents he interviewed agree, "If a girl uses birth control pills or other methods of contraception, it makes it seem as if she were planning to have sex."

National sample surveys[3, 30] have shown that 50–60% of the teen-agers studied were not protected by contraception at the time of first intercourse. About 40% of those sexually active were found to have never used contraception. About 75% of the men and 89% of the women reported that their first sexual encounter was not planned. Additionally, teen-agers generally describe the nature of their sexual activities as being episodic.[17] These findings are characteristic of individuals who have not as yet come to fully accept the nature of their sexuality.

The exact constituency of the imaginary audience has never been specified. For the young adolescent it could be expected to be composed of idealized images of parents and other important adults. Later, same-age peers, and still later, potential sexual partners, are likely to become especially important. The relationship between the adolescent and his parents, particularly during the early stages of adolescence, might be an important determinant of acceptance of sexuality. Contrary to expectation perhaps, the results of one study suggest that the more independent the adolescent is of parental influence, the more likely he is to use contraceptives. Kantner and Zelnik[17] found that in their national sample young women who were living alone, who were in households not headed by a father, or who reported a low degree of confidence sharing with parents were *more* likely to use contraceptives than women with the opposite characteristics. They conclude that "living in what is generally presumed to be the most stable and supportive family group does not appear to elicit a level of contraceptive practice satisfactory for prevention of unwanted pregnancy [p. 24]." These findings no doubt indicate a complex relationship between contraceptive use, living arrangements, and relationship with parents. Girls living at home, for example, may not use contraceptives because of fear of having them discovered. From the theoretical view developed here, it could also be argued that a certain amount of individual differentiation is needed for effective contraceptive activity. At least one previous study has found that women who have more individual control over their lives are more likely to use contraceptives. Goldsmith and associates[14] concluded that: "Greater scholastic and vocational interests of the contraceptive group confirms our impression that girls in this group were more apt to plan their lives and were more achievement oriented than girls in the pregnancy group [p. 33]." Seemingly, a necessary component of premeditated sex is that the adolescent is well on the way to developing an identity as a person separate from his parents. As one male contraceptive user put it,[30] "Sex is my own business and not that of my parents."

The personal fable

If the adolescent fails to differentiate self concerns from the concerns of others, he also tends to commit a complementary error. He tends to over-differentiate the uniqueness of his emotions and affect. Elkind[10] suggests that affective overdifferentiation often is manifested in the form of a personal fable. For instance, many adolescents evidently believe that they are immune to death. Long, Elkind, and Spilka[21] report that adolescents often believe that they have a special relationship with God. In this relationship they look to God for guidance and support as one would to a personal confidant rather than asking for special favors and privileges. Keeping personal diaries, a widespread practice among adolescents, also reflects a personal fable. Such journals are often kept with the express belief that their content will have universal significance to posterity.

Many adolescent women evidently hold the notion that they cannot become pregnant. It would seem to be very important to be able to specify the origins of this personal fable. As noted earlier, those who believe they cannot get pregnant are least likely to use contraceptives. Interviews[7, 8] indicate that substantial numbers of women and men conclude that they are sterile after one, or at the most several, sexual encounters that do not result in pregnancy. Many did not know at the time that there is a probabilistic relationship between intercourse and becoming pregnant. This may be due to the difficulty that young adolescents have in thinking in probabilistic terms. This problem is compounded by the fact that there is actually a lag between the age of menarche and the onset of fecundity. The confusion may be fostered in this instance by overzealous parents and teachers who emphasize the risks of pregnancy. They thereby present the picture that pregnancy following intercourse is a near certainty.

The personal fable of sterility seems to be an example of a situation where a person fails to apply the laws of probability to his own case. Tversky and Kahneman[32] have concluded that people in general are very poor in taking into account base rate information. On the basis of a few personal experiences, the men and women we have interviewed are willing to conclude that they are uniquely different in a manifestly important way. An adolescent may fail to apply, or be unaware of, the actual low probability that he or she is sterile. The adolescent's preoccupation with self may explain his failure to consider the other possible source of infertility, the sexual partner.

In contrast to the personal fable of sterility, many young people evidently believe that they cannot get pregnant because "we only did it a few times." This seemingly is another example of how the laws of probability are applied in a lopsided manner. It is an example of the classical gambler's fallacy—the chances of getting pregnant are considered to be cumulative across incidents of intercourse rather than being independent. Thus, one is safe if a certain degree of abstinence is practiced. The research available,[2, 30] although limited, indicates that this fallacy may be an important reason why contraceptives are not used. At this point, it is not known how the two myths—the fable of sterility and the gambler's fallacy of intercourse—are related. It might be that the fable of sterility precedes the gambler's fallacy. The adolescent may first believe that intercourse and pregnancy are determinantly related. Later the concept of probability is applied, but incorrectly.

Much research is needed on such subjectively held beliefs, particularly on how they are sustained by firsthand experience and how fallacious thinking is overcome. Elkind[10] has concluded that egocentrism diminishes by the time the adolescent is 15–16 years old. As the adolesment begins to apply the operations of formal logic to himself (i.e., to think about himself objectively), first the imaginary audience and then the personal fable begin to recede as important considerations. As he tests against reality the hypotheses he has about others' reactions, he gradually learns to discriminate the difference between his own preoccupations and the concerns of others.

The personal fable probably lasts longer than does the imaginary audience. Elkind in fact suggests that it may never entirely disappear. He goes on to state that the personal fable is reduced by the establishment of close relationships with others.[10] The personal fable is probably overcome by:

> the gradual establishment of what Erickson[11] has called "intimacy." Once the young person sees himself in a more realistic light as a function of having adjusted his imaginary audience to a real one, he can establish true rather than self-interest interpersonal relations. Once relations of mutuality are established and confidences are shared, the young person discovers that others have feelings similar to his own and have suffered and been enraptured in the same way [p. 1033].

Flavell[12] conceptualizes the reduction of egocentrism in similar terms:

> Social interaction is the principal liberating factor, particularly social interaction with peers. In the course of his contacts (and especially his conflicts and arguments) with other children, the child increasingly finds himself forced to reexamine his own precepts and concepts in the light of those of others and by so doing gradually rids himself of cognitive egocentrism [p. 279].

Egocentrism and sexuality

While the ages given by Elkind for the reduction of egocentrism may be generally true, application of decentered thinking to sexuality may be an exception. It has been found that the cognitive operations which a person achieves are not always universally applied to all domains of thinking. Recent research, particularly that comparing children from different cultures,[9] has shown that "horizontal *décalages*" occur in cognitive development. These *décalages* represent the application of an acquired cognitive structure to one content area but not to others. For example, Price-Williams, Gordon, and Ramirez[26] have found that potters' children in Mexico acquire the concept of conservation of volume of solids earlier than do European and North American children. One common daily activity of these children is the manipulation of clay in preparing it for their fathers. However, tests on other conservation problems—e.g., the conservation of liquids—show that the accelerated cognitive ability is specific to the conservation of solids.

Sexuality may well represent an area where a *décalage* in the application of formal operational thinking occurs. Sex is generally a hidden, undiscussed aspect of life in American culture. Precisely those aspects of sexuality that the child needs to know most remain undiscussed. Parents, for example, are more concerned with maintaining the sexual status quo than in answering their children's personal questions.[27] Sex education, likewise, often fails to concern itself with the subjective perspective of the child. Teaching sex education as a solely academic subject means that answers are given to questions that the adolescent has not asked. The questions which, from the adolescent's viewpoint, are the most important, may go unanswered because in an academic setting they may seem "dumb" or embarrassing. The failure of sex education to address the personal aspects of sex knowledge may be the reason why studies have failed to find a difference in amount of formal sex education between contraceptive seekers and women who are premaritally pregnant.[8, 14] These studies do show that these groups of women are equally ignorant of some of the more basic facts of sex. For example, Goldsmith and associates[14] found that about one-third of all the girls they interviewed had sex education courses in school; another third had discussed sexual topics in other classes; two-thirds had discussed birth control; and 7 in 10 had discussed sexual intercourse, pregnancy, and reproduction in the classroom. Despite this, they found there was considerable ignorance of and false notions about sexual matters and birth control on the part of all of these sexually active girls. A surprisingly large number of adolescents are unaware of such important sexual facts as the physical and psychological effects of masturbation. Even the questions that are covered in sex education, such as the point in the menstrual cycle at which pregnancy is most likely to occur, may not be learned because of the way they are presented in the academic environment. Not getting answers to personal sex questions from parents or school, the adolescent may turn to unorthodox sources. For example, many young women each year write letters to the Kotex Company because it is the only source of information they know that might answer their questions.[4]

Adolescents are being required to make a decision about contraceptive use at a time when they are sexually undifferentiated and perhaps unprepared for such analytical thinking about themselves. The problem is made more difficult by evident biological changes lowering the age of onset of fecundity.[5, 6] It is not known exactly how adolescents normally are liberated from egocentric thinking about sexuality. It has been speculated here that social interaction is particularly critical in this respect. / with other aspects of egocentrism, the details of how the adolescen/

liberated from egocentric thinking remain obscure. It is clear that cognitive changes do occur; the aspects described earlier are not found in the thinking of most adults. We tend to expect that the nature of decision making about contraceptive use differs for adults. We do not, however, disregard the possibility that aspects of egocentrism may be involved in contraceptive nonuse even for adults. An in-depth longitudinal research strategy which follows male and female adolescents from sexual inactivity and early sexual activity to young adulthood seems necessary to obtain answers to these questions.

PRACTICAL IMPLICATIONS

Three general practical steps for the improvement of sex-related education are suggested by the theoretical framework presented here.

Personalized discussion

Sex education must be made personal in order to be effective. One means of accomplishing this is the extensive use of classroom discussion. Students, in their discussions, lay bare their egocentrism to themselves. The act of stating an idea, in a very special sense, makes it concrete. As Vygotsky[33] says, "Language is thought made real." Once a concept has been stated, it can be examined by the adolescent and by others. Class discussion has a further advantage in that by gauging the level of egocentrism of discussion the teacher can determine the informational needs of each individual student. Needless to say, effective group discussion requires a teacher who is not only well versed in the technical knowledge of the subject matter but also sensitive to the psychological aspects of adolescence.

Cross-aged tutors

The above suggestion implies that the sex education teacher's task can be effectively supplemented by the students themselves. This suggestion can be taken a step further by having older adolescents serve as instructor/counselors to younger adolescents. Such arrangements have been found to be effective in counseling[20] and education.[36] The older student, having recently mastered the problem the younger is struggling with, can serve as a valuable and sensitive guide. His information and suggestions are, therefore, all the more credible.

Aesthetics of contraceptives

Little is as yet known about why people select particular contraceptives. Yet this information should be critical in helping persons find a form of contraception that they like, and would presumably continue to use. In a recent study[7] sexually active male and female college students (ages 19 to 24) were asked to evaluate forms of contraception on five dimensions: (1) effectiveness, (2) convenience, (3) availability, (4) possibility of side effects, and (5) aesthetics. Ratings of personal use and how much they liked each form of contraceptive were also made. A different pattern of evaluation was found for each contraceptive. For instance, liking for foam was more strongly related to its perceived effectiveness than to its perceived convenience. Liking for the diaphragm, however, was more strongly related to its convenience than to its effectiveness. Personal use was found to bear a complex relationship to both liking and other evaluations. This may reflect large differences among the respondents in the amount and kind of personal experience, as well as in the nature of secondhand information they had. Analysis of supplemental interviews conducted with the respondents is now being made in an attempt to untangle some of these relationships. One finding, however, stands out for its consistency. For almost all contraceptive evaluations, perceived aesthetics is highly related to both assessed liking and to personal use. This would seem to have implications for improving birth-planning counseling. Rather than providing only technical information such as effectiveness statistics, a more personal approach is warranted. One approach that might be effective would explore with the prospective user his own feelings and the reasons for those feelings about different contraceptives.[15] It is our impression that this is often a *sub rosa* aspect of the contraceptive selection process.

REFERENCES

1. Back, K. W. Neglected psychological issues in population. *American Psychologist*, 1973, **28**, 567–572.

2. Baizerman, M., Sheehan, C., Ellison, D. B., & Schlessinger, E. R. *Pregnant adolescents: A review of literature with abstracts 1960–1970*. Washington, D.C.; Consortium on early childbearing and childrearing research utilization and sharing project, 1971.

3. Bauman, K. E. Selected aspects of the contraceptive practices of unmarried university students. *American Journal of Obstetrics and Gynecology*, 1970, **108**, 203.

4. Block, J. L. What school girls want to know about sex. *Good Housekeeping*, 1971.

5. Cowgill, U. M. Changes in the fertility span of man. *Perspectives in Biology and Medicine*, 1971, 141–146.

6. Cutright, P. The teenage sexual revolution and the myth of an abstinent past. *Family Planning Perspectives*, 1972, **4** (1), 24–31.

7. Cvetkovich, G., & Bjorseth, A. Evaluation of contraceptive methods by college students. 1974 (in progress).

8. Cvetkovich, G., & Sarkissian, J. Sex-knowledge and fear of pregnancy. 1974 (in progress).

9. Dasen, P. R. Cross-cultural Piagetian research: A summary. *Journal of Cross-Cultural Psychology*, 1972, **3**, 23–39.

10. Elkind, D. Egocentrism in adolescence. *Child Development*, 1967, **38**, 1025–1034.

11. Erickson, E. H. Identity and the life cycles. *Psychological Issues*, 1959, **1** (1), Monograph 1.

12. Flavell, J. H. *The developmental psychology of Jean Piaget*. New York: Van Nostrand, 1963.

13. Fugita, B., Wagner, N. N., & Pion, R. J. Contraceptive use among single college students. *American Journal of Obstetrics and Gynecology*, 1971, **109**, 787–793.

14. Goldsmith, S., Gabrielson, M. O., Gabrielson, I., Mathews, V., & Potts, L. Teenagers, sex and contraception. *Family Planning Perspectives*, 1972, **4** (1), 32–38.

15. Hawkins, C. H. The erotic significance of contraceptive methods. *Journal of Sex Research*, 1970, **6**, 143–157.

16. Jaccard, J. J., & Davidson, A. R. Toward an understanding of family planning behaviors: An initial investigation. *Journal of Applied Psychology*, 1972, **2**, 228–235.

17. Kantner, J. F., & Zelnik, M. Contraception and pregnancy: Experiences of young unmarried women in the United States. *Family Planning Perspectives*, 1973, **5** (1), 21–35.

18. Kempe, R. R., & Helfer, C. H. *The battered child*. Chicago: University of Chicago Press, 1968.

19. Kothandapani, V. Validation of feeling, belief and intention to act as three components of attitude and their contribution to prediction of contraceptive behavior. *Journal of Personality and Social Psychology*, 1971, **19**, 321–333.

20. Lippitt, R., & Lippitt, P. Cross age helpers. *National Education Association Journal*, March 1968, 24–26.

21. Long, D., Elkind, D., & Spilka, B. The child's conception of prayer. *Journal of the Scientific Study of Religion*, 1967, **6**, 101–109.

22. Looft, W. R. Egocentrism and social interaction across the life span. *Psychological Bulletin*, 1972, **78**, 73–92.

23. Moore, J. S., & Slesnik, I. L. Unplanned pregnancies. *Washington Education*, May–June 1972.

24. Peel, E. A. Experimental examination of some of Piaget's schemata concerning children's perception and thinking, and a discussion of their educational significance. *British Journal of Educational Psychology*, 1959, **29**, 89–103.

25. Piaget, J. *Six psychological studies.* New York: Random House, 1967.

26. Price-Williams, D. R., Gordon, W., & Ramirez, M. Skills in conservation. *Developmental Psychology,* 1969, **1**, 769.

27. Rubin, I., & Kirkendall, L. A. *Sex in the adolescent years: New directions in guiding and teaching youth.* New York: Association Press, 1968.

28. Sandberg, S. C., & Jacobs, R. I. Psychology of the misuse and rejection of contraception. *American Journal of Obstetrics and Gynecology,* 1971, **110**, 34–67.

29. Semmens, J. P. Marital sexual problems of teen-agers. In J. P. Semmens & K. E. Krants (Eds.), *The adolescent experience.* New York: Macmillan, 1970.

30. Sorenson, R. C. *Adolescent sexuality in contemporary America.* New York: World Publishing, 1973.

31. Tillack, W. S., Tyler, C. W., Paquette, R., & Jones, P. H. A study of premarital pregnancies. *American Journal of Public Health,* 1972, **62**, 676–679.

32. Tversky, A., & Kahneman, D. Availability: A heuristic for judging frequency and probability. *Cognitive Psychology,* 1973, **5**, 207–232.

33. Vygotsky, L. S. *Thought and language.* Cambridge, Mass.: M.I.T. Press, 1962.

34. Wagner, N. "I am not that kind of a girl." Article written for Planned Parenthood Center of Seattle, January 1971.

35. Wagner, N., Perthou, N., Fugita, B., & Pion, R. Sexual behavior of adolescents. *Postgraduate Medicine,* 1969, **46** (4), 68.

36. Werth, T. G. An assessment of the reciprocal effect of high school senior low achievers tutoring freshman low achievers in English classes. Education Department dissertation, Oregon State University, 1968.

Beyond Sowing and Growing: The Relationship of Sex Typing to Socialization, Family Plans, and Future Orientation

A married couple we know decided some years ago never to become parents; at a dinner party one evening they raised the question, "Why would *anyone* want to have children?" In the first place, given an overpopulated and uncertain world, it may not be either kind or logical to bring additional human beings into existence. They then listed the negative personal discomforts, which included morning sickness, the pain of childbirth, the messiness and demandingness of infants, the succession of problems that arise at every age level, the financial burden, the interference with one's life style, the loss of privacy, the problems of having others totally dependent upon you, and the difficulty for a woman to be a mother and simultaneously to pursue a career. Besides, the kids themselves often are a total disappointment as we noted earlier in describing Ann Landers' survey.

The reasons *for* having offspring are somehow less numerous and include such historical reasons as ignorance, economic necessity, lack of effective contraceptive technology, and religious injunctions. Sometimes babies are conceived in the vain hope of saving an unhappy marriage. For other individuals there is the egocentric desire to attain vicarious success through the accomplishments of the next generation or to achieve a kind of immortality by passing on one's genes. It is also possible to have children because one truly enjoys them and feels that he or she has the talent to be a good parent. There is still another reason, however, which seems to cut across all of these.

It can be said in many different ways, but the general idea is that in the natural order of things, our basic function is to fulfill the roles of mother and father. "That's what we're here for." Women, especially, have traditionally been taught that their main purpose in life is to attract a husband, maintain a home, bear children, and raise a fine family. Any alternative plans such as childlessness or the pursuit of a career were seen as aberrations and decidedly unfeminine. Since these traditional ideas of the roles to be played by each sex are presently in a state of flux, psychologist Elizabeth Allgeier decided to determine whether those individuals who do not fit into the traditional male and female roles would be different from the usual sex-typed individuals in such things as their notions about the size of the ideal family. The results are described in the following article.

Beyond Sowing and Growing: The Relationship of Sex Typing to Socialization, Family Plans, and Future Orientation

Elizabeth Rice Allgeier

Mirroring the alarm over the population explosion expressed by Ehrlich,[8,9] Ward and Dubos,[22] and numerous others, Heilbroner[14] depicted world population growth as proceeding unhindered along its fatal course, with a virtual certainty of an 80–100% increase in numbers by the year 2000. To compound the problem, the fastest growing nations are characterized by age distributions in which almost half the population is under childbearing age. Therefore, Heilbroner pointed out, "even if drastic measures manage to limit families to a maximum of two children within a single generation, the steady advance of larger and larger numbers of individuals into their fertile years brings with it a potential increase in numbers [p. 22]." Efforts to provide food for famine-ridden areas are already inadequate; and, ultimately, as Ward and Dubos[22] stated, the world's population must be stabilized.

Amid the pessimistic present statistics and future projections of catastrophe, however, a positive shift has occurred within some segments of American society. The birth rate of the United States dropped below replacement level in 1973 for the first time. The U.S. Census Bureau reported (Associated Press, May 30, 1974) that although the nation had a net gain of 1.5 million people the previous year, for a total of 211,-210,000, three population parameters declined, including the crude birth rate, general fertility, and the total fertility rate. If the 1973 patterns continued, families would produce an average of 1.9 children per couple, a rate below the population replacement level of 2.1 children. Although it was suggested[12,13] that coercive measures (e.g., involuntary sterilization) might be necessary to save the species, the American shift in family-size patterns occurred in the absence of any coercion. Identification of the factors responsible for this shift may provide us with practical knowledge for helping those countries (as well as the overpopulating segments of United States society) that are requesting aid in dealing with geometric population increase.

A factor frequently associated with family-size desires in the birth-planning literature has been that of sex-role norms.[4,5,11,15,16,18] Specifically, it has been inferred, on the basis of case histories and correlational evidence for both sexes, that the degree of identification with traditional sex-role norms is positively associated with actual and desired family

Reprinted in an edited version from: Allgeier, E. R. Beyond sowing and growing: The relationship of sex typing to socialization, family plans, and future orientation. *Journal of Applied Social Psychology*, 1975, *5*, 217–226.

size. Russo,[20] advancing the sex-role stereotyping/overpopulation hypothesis, summarized some of the available support for this relationship, as follows. Working women desire and have fewer children than nonworking women,[17,19] people with high educational and career achievement prefer to delay marriage and childbearing;[21] and career-oriented female graduate students desire smaller families than noncareer-oriented female graduate students.[10] In addition, Catholic women who express relatively masculine self-concepts have smaller completed families than Catholic women who express more stereotypically feminine self-concepts.[3]

The speculation is that a variety of attitudes and behaviors including professional choices (particularly for women) and family-size desires are mediated by the extent to which one is identified with traditional sex-role norms. Previously, however, a direct test of this hypothesis has been hampered by a methodological limitation, that is, the nonavailability of a measure of the extent of sex-role identification. As Bem[1] notes in her description of the Bem Sex Role Inventory (BSRI), earlier sex-role inventories assumed that identification with male traits was the opposite of identification with female traits. For instance, a person was either passive (female) or active (male). On the recently developed BSRI, however, maleness and femaleness (in terms of self-endorsement of stereotypically sex-typed traits) are treated as independent dimensions. Bem's scoring system permits individuals to be characterized as sex-typed males, sex-typed females, sex-reversed, or androgynous. An androgyn is someone who gives equally high endorsement to traits that are male and traits that are female. Bem[1] suggested that "whereas a narrowly masculine self-concept might inhibit behaviors that are stereotyped as feminine, and a narrowly feminine self-concept might inhibit behaviors that are stereotyped as masculine, a mixed, or androgynous, self-concept might allow an individual to freely engage in both 'masculine' and 'feminine' behaviors [p. 155]."

The BSRI thus provides a measure of the extent of sex-role identification that permits a direct investigation of the relationship between this factor and a number of other variables heretofore only presumed relevant to the search for solutions to the population explosion. Although the main goal of the present research was to test the relationship between the sex-typing dimension and desired family size, it was expected that sex-typed and androgynous persons might differ on a number of other variables potentially relevant to changes in population growth patterns, including childhood socialization, personal plans, and future orientation.

Socialization   It has been suggested[20] that the kind of role models available during childhood provide a powerful influence on the development of adult sex roles. Thus, it was hypothesized that a sample of highly sex-typed people would be more likely to have been raised by mothers of traditional occupational status (e.g., housewives) than would a sample of androgyns. In addition, one might expect that androgyns would have experienced a greater variety of models, life styles, and attitudes than sex-typed individuals. Accordingly, it was hypothesized that during childhood, androgyns would have lived in larger communities and would have been more likely to have moved frequently than sex-typed individuals.

Personal plans   Bem[1] suggested that androgyns may be more responsive to situational contingencies than sex-typed individuals. In an agrarian and/or underpopulated environment, reproduction is a highly valuable activity. However, given our industrialized and crowded society, with its greater range of roles and life styles for both sexes, it was hypothesized that androgyns would desire higher educational degrees, higher occupational status, and fewer children than would sex-typed persons.

Future orientation   An area in which extent of sex typing might be expected to influence attitudes, particularly of females, is that of the importance attached to various future activities. When asked to indicate the value they placed on the achievement of particular goals within 10 years, it was hypothesized that female androgyns would rank being competent at work higher in importance than would sex-typed females. In contrast, it would not be expected that several family-centered activities (e.g., being a good spouse and a good parent) would be differentially ranked by sex-typed and androgynous females.

METHOD

Subjects

The subjects (20 males and 20 females) were selected on the basis of their scores on the BSRI administered to introductory psychology students at the beginning of the semester. Experimental participation was in partial fulfillment of the requirements for the introductory psychology course at Purdue University.

Bem Sex Role Inventory (BSRI)

In responding to Bem's[1] scale, subjects were instructed to indicate on a 7-point scale ranging from "never or almost never" to "always or almost always" the extent to which each of 60 traits was self-descriptive. Of these trait words or phrases, 20 were scored as male sex typed (e.g., athletic, self-reliant) and 20 as female sex typed (e.g., yielding, affectionate). In addition, 20 were included as a correction for social desirability (e.g., helpful, theatrical). On the basis of his or her responses, each person received a masculinity, femininity, and androgyny score. The androgyny score involves the difference between a person's masculine and feminine self-endorsement. Those persons whose endorsement of masculine attributes differed sufficiently from their endorsement of feminine attributes were classified as significantly sex typed, whereas those who did not differ in their endorsement of masculine and feminine items were classified as androgynous. In the present study, four subgroups were identified (sex-typed or androgynous males or females) following administration of the BSRI.

Procedure

Ten subjects from each subgroup were contacted by telephone and offered a half hour of experimental credit for completion of a survey of college students' future plans. When each subject arrived at the research lab, the experimenter said, "We're conducting a survey of students' future plans. I realize that it's sometimes difficult to know what you're going to do in the future, but do the best you can," and handed him or her the Allgeier Future Projection Inventory. After completion of the inventory, each subject was debriefed and dismissed.

Dependent measures

The Allgeier Future Projection Inventory contained the dependent measures of interest plus a number of other items. The inventory began with demographic (sex, age, etc.) and socialization items, including parents' occupations, which were coded according to Edwards'[7] sixfold classification system from 1 (unskilled) to 6 (professional). Subjects were also asked to check a box if they had moved frequently during childhood and to indicate the size of the community in which they were raised by checking one of five categories ranging from "5000 or under" to "100,000 or over."

With respect to educational objectives, subjects were asked to check one of four categories ranging from 1 ("stop prior to obtaining a B.A.") to 4 ("obtain a degree beyond the M.A."). They were asked to indicate their occupational plans, and as with parents' occupations, these were coded according to Edwards.[7] Subjects responded to one of two alternatives regarding children, 1 ("I would prefer not to have children at all") or 2 ("Ideally, I would like to begin having children at about age ——") and the number of boys and girls they considered ideal.

Finally for the future orientation hypotheses, subjects were asked to rank each of 13 alternative values in terms of the importance they attached to the achievement of each within 10 years.

RESULTS

Males

Sex typing produced no significant differences on any of the variables except for the importance attached to being an influential member of the community, with androgynous males placing more importance on this value than did sex-typed males.

Females

Socialization   In support of the hypotheses, androgynous females, as compared to sex-typed females, were reared in larger communities and had greater mobility as children. In addition, androgynous females were raised by fathers and mothers of higher occupational status than were sex-typed females.

Personal plans   Androgynous females tended toward higher educational aspirations and desired fewer children than did sex-typed females. However, contrary to the hypothesis that androgyns would have higher occupational aspirations, there was no significant difference between the two groups.

Future orientation   Androgynous females placed more importance on being competent at work than did sex-typed females. There were marginally significant effects on recognition for work and sexually fulfilling marriage with androgynous females placing more importance on the former and less importance on the latter than did sex-typed females. Androgynous and sex-typed females did not differ in the importance they attached to being a good spouse or a good parent.

DISCUSSION

The hypotheses concerning differences between sex-typed and androgynous females in socialization, family-size desires, and future orientation were generally supported. Androgynous females, in contrast to sex-typed females, lived in larger communities, moved frequently, and were raised by parents of higher occupational status. They tended to have higher educational aspirations, wanted fewer children, and placed more value on achieving competence at work.

The extent of sex typing among males, however, was not generally related to the variables under investigation. The differential effects of the sex-typing variable on the family and future plans of the two genders may be partially due to some real-world constraints. As Farley[10] has pointed out, for females it may be more difficult to produce and mother a large family and attain high professional competence, whereas a male may marry, produce a large family, and devote the major portion of his time to career advancement while his spouse takes care of their children. The finding in the present study that sex typing was significantly related to family-size desires and to the importance attached to achieving competence at work for females, but not for males, was consistent with Farley's suggestion.

However, considering the strength of the obtained relationship between sex typing and the socialization variables for females, the absence of this relationship for males is quite surprising. In the male sample, only one socialization variable approached significance; that is, fathers of androgynous males had higher occupational status than fathers of sex-typed males. Differences in the means for community size and mobility were in the expected direction, but did not approach significance. The available evidence from the present study and from Bem's[2] study of the relationship of the extent of sex typing of several stereotypically sex-typed behaviors (conformity and kitten playing) suggested that although extent of sex typing makes a difference, this factor manifests itself differently in males and females.

The most important finding in the present study, of course, was that androgynous females desire fewer children than do sex-typed females. In a recently published and closely related study, Eagly and Anderson[6] tested the sex-role/family-size desires relationship using a methodology different from that used in the present study. In their study, subjects were asked to evaluate each of 20 adult activities (earning money, caring for baby, etc.) on a 5-point scale ranging from "appropriate only for males" through "equally appropriate for both sexes" to "appropriate only for females." Congruent with results from the present study, Eagly and Anderson found that persons approving of a relatively equivalent pattern of sex roles desired smaller families than did persons approving of less equivalent sex roles. The findings from the present study and from Eagly and Anderson are quite consistent with the indirect correlational evidence reviewed in the introduction on the relationship between desired family size and female educational achievement and career orientation. It was from these kinds of relationships that previous writers[20] inferred the relationship between sex-role norms and desired family size. However, with the use of the BSRI to measure extent of sex typing, in the present study we have found a direct link between extent of sex-role identification and desired family size. The mean for androgynous females desired family size was precisely at replacement level, 2.1, whereas sex-typed females desired a mean of 3.1 children. Although national norms with regard to the distribution of sex-typed and androgynous individuals in our society are not yet available, Bem[1] presented distributions from two college student samples, indicating that between 62% and 70% of her sample was significantly sex typed. It is probably safe to assume that these proportions would be much higher in cultures where strong sex-role norms are still extant, and where the problems of overpopulation pose a much greater threat than they do in the United States. If the pattern of results with respect to the relationship between socialization, sex-role norms, and desired family size for females obtained in the present study and in Eagly and Anderson[6] are borne out by further research, particularly in underdeveloped areas, efforts at reduction of extreme sex-role norms may be warranted.

REFERENCES

1. Bem, S. L. The measurement of psychological androgyny. *Journal of Consulting and Clinical Psychology*, 1974, **42**, 155–162.

2. Bem, S. L. Sex-role adaptability: One consequence of psychological androgyny. *Journal of Personality and Social Psychology*, 1975, **31**, 634–643.

3. Clarkson, F. E., Vogel, S. R., Broverman, I. K., Broverman, D. M., & Rosenkrantz, P. S. Family size and sex role stereotypes. *Science*, 1970, **167**, 390–392.

4. Davis, K. Institutional patterns favoring high fertility in under-developed areas. *Eugenics Quarterly*, 1955, **2**, 33–39.

5. Davis, K. Population policy: Will current programs succeed? *Science*, 1967, **158**, 730–739.

6. Eagly, A. H., & Anderson, P. Sex role and attitudinal correlates of desired family size. *Journal of Applied Social Psychology*, 1974, **4**, 151–164.

7. Edwards, A. M. *Comparative occupational statistics for the United States. 1870–1940.* Washington, D. C.: U. S. Government Printing Office, 1943.

8. Ehrlich, P. *The population bomb.* Stanford, Calif.: Sierra Club, 1968.

9. Ehrlich, P., & Ehrlich, A. *Population, resources, environment.* San Francisco: Freeman, 1972.

10. Farley, J. Graduate women: Career aspirations and desired family size. *American Psychologist*, 1970, **25**, 1099–1100.

11. Fawcett, J. T. *Psychology and population: Behavioral research issues in fertility and family planning.* New York: Population Council, 1970.

12. Hardin, G. The tragedy of the commons. *Science*, 1968, **162**, 1243–1248.

13. Hardin, G. Parenthood: Right or privilege? *Science*, 1970, **169**, 472.

14. Heilbroner, R. The human prospect. *The New York Review of Books*, 1974, **20**, 21–34.

15. Hoffman, L., & Wyatt, F. Social change and motivations for having larger families: Some theoretical considerations. *Merrill-Palmer Quarterly*, 1960, **6**, 235–244.

16. Pohlman, E. H. *Psychology of birth planning.* Cambridge, Mass.: Schenkman, 1969.

17. Pratt, L., & Whelpton, P. K. Extra-familial participation of wives in relation to interest in the liking for children, fertility planning, and actual and desired family size. In P. K. Whelpton & C. V. Kiser (Eds.), *Social and psychological factors affecting fertility.* Vol. 5. New York: Milbank Memorial Fund, 1958.

18. Rainwater, L. *And the poor get children.* Chicago: Quadrangle, 1960.

19. Ridley, J. Number of children expected in relation to nonfamilial activities of the wife. *Milbank Memorial Fund Quarterly,* 1959, *37,* 277–296.

20. Russo, N. F. Sex role stereotyping. *Equilibrium,* 1974, *2,* 12–16.

21. Russo, N. F., & Brackbill, Y. Population and youth. In J. Fawcett (Ed.), *Psychological perspectives on population.* New York: Basic Books, 1973.

22. Ward, B., & Dubos, R. *Only one earth.* New York: Norton, 1972.

Negative Sexual Attitudes and Contraception

Some friends of ours had a family of seven children. Because having that many offspring is relatively unusual today, people who met them for the first time frequently asked if they were Catholics. Their standard reply was, "No—we're just passionate Protestants." That self-characterization was probably accurate in their case, and it fits well with a cultural stereotype that those who have a great many children must be strongly interested in sex and must engage in intercourse as often as possible.

In reality, of course, it is obvious that sexual intercourse may occur joylessly and infrequently and yet result in numerous babies. For example, a female with superb timing could have nonorgasmic sex once a year for 15 years and end up with an enormous family. In the following article, the authors reject the traditional notion that positive attitudes toward sexuality are associated with conception. Instead it is proposed that sexual anxieties and a negative orientation toward sex actually are related to a negative orientation toward contraception; thus, those who feel least positively toward sex should have the most offspring.

Though the point is made in the article itself, it should be emphasized that anything as complex as contraceptive attitudes and behaviors may be expected to have multiple determinants. The effect of sexual attitudes is only one of many possible determinants, and, for that reason, is not conceptualized as a perfect predictor of either contraceptive practices or family size. Rather, it is one element in the mosaic of determining factors.

Negative Sexual Attitudes and Contraception

Donn Byrne, Christine Jazwinski,
John A. DeNinno, and William A. Fisher

Any individual's attitudes and practices concerning contraception rest on a series of learning experiences which involve both informational and emotional components. Presumably, these components operate singly and in combination to determine each person's emotional responses and beliefs and ultimately what he or she actually does with respect to contraceptive practices. We will briefly describe some of the factors that seem to be relevant.

DETERMINANTS OF CONTRACEPTIVE PRACTICES

Learning about contraception

Once a given contraceptive technology has been developed, its existence and the details of its use must be disseminated. Because of existing taboos on anything involving sex, because of beliefs that information about contraception serves to encourage sexual promiscuity, and because of religious objections, there have been severe limitations as to how each individual receives a contraceptive education. Unlike other products, contraceptive advertising has been circumscribed and circumspect. For example, only since 1973 have there been ads in general circulation magazines promoting condoms, and the very first television commercial for such a product (Trojans) was broadcast in San Jose, California, in July 1975.

Whether in the general press, in advertising, or even in sex education courses, what is specifically communicated about each type of contraceptive technique tends to be relatively abstract and nonpersonal. Precise details such as how to insert a diaphragm or how to put on a condom are very often omitted. In addition, the factual knowledge about different contraceptive techniques is somewhat confusing because it consists of multiple bits of information involving differential effectiveness, differential cost, differential intrusiveness with respect to the sexual act, and differential side effects. For example, birth control pills are essentially 100% effective in preventing pregnancy and they are not even associated in any direct way with intercourse, but they are relatively expensive and their possible side effects range from nausea and weight gain to increased blood clotting and hence risk of stroke. Sterilization for either sex is also essentially a perfectly effective and nonintrusive contraceptive method, but the operation is expensive, and any surgical technique carries some risk of complications. In addition, there can be negative psychological reactions, and there is no sure way to reverse the procedure if the individual later wants children. Reasonably effective techniques with no side effects such as diaphragms for women and condoms for men involve a continuing moderate expense, and they bother some people because they must be utilized just prior to coitus. The rhythm method involves no expense, but it requires careful monitoring of the menstrual cycle and the daily calendar; the major side effect is an occasional baby, because it is not a very effective method of contraception. Because such multiple factors must be considered and because each involves certain probability statements, there really is no simple way to impart the necessary facts about contraception.

Even if an individual has mastered the information about the various "artificial" means of birth control, it is then necessary actually to obtain the appropriate materials. Family-planning agencies and government-sponsored clinics can be very helpful in this respect, and research shows that when condoms are distributed without cost to inner city adolescent males, they are very likely to be used.[2] In addition, current developments include the possibility of ordering condoms by mail, the open display of contraceptive products on drugstore shelves in many states, and the work of Zero Population Growth in opening "contraceptive boutiques" such as The Rubber Tree in Seattle, Washington, which attempts to make the purchase of contraceptives as relaxed and pleasant as the purchase of phonograph records.

Beliefs and emotions may influence contraceptive practices

We have earlier discussed the way in which an individual's beliefs may be incompatible with effective contraception. Many adolescents have erroneous notions about their chances of conceiving a baby,[7] and females who adhere to traditional sex roles desire more children than androgynous females.[1] It was also pointed out that many groups espouse an ideology that renounces birth control, at least for themselves —for example, Arabs, Jews, Catholics, communists, and blacks both in Africa and in the United States. In this article, however, we will examine a very different type of barrier to contraception: negative attitudes about sex.

In much of the research on individual differences in sexuality, it has been shown that people tend to fall along a positive-negative continuum that has been identified by different investigators as consisting of sex guilt,[18] positive and negative affect,[5] and sexual liberalism and conservatism.[23] For some individuals ("erotophiles"), sexual cues seem to be associated primarily with positive emotions, pleasure, and approach tendencies. For others ("erotophobes"), the same cues are associated with negative emotions, guilt, and avoidance tendencies as well as with pleasure. These reactions are hypothesized to be quite general, and they are assumed to be reflected in responses to erotic stimuli, in personal sexual activities, and in attitudes about the sexual practices of others.

It has been found that negative attitudes about sexuality can actually interfere with the process of learning and retaining information about birth control.[22] In the present research, we hoped to demonstrate that erotophobic and erotophilic orientations have additional important implications for contraceptive attitudes and practices. The reasoning behind this hypothesized relationship goes as follows. In order to take effective action to avoid pregnancy, four steps are involved; each is related to sexuality and hence should be influenced by an individual's positive or negative feelings in this realm. The four steps will now be described.

Planning to engage in intercourse   In order to be able to avoid conception, an individual must know in advance that he or she is going to have intercourse or is at least likely to do so. Thus, the person must think about his or her forthcoming sexual acts. For the erotophile, such anticipation should be a positive experience and even a source of added excitement, as in the punch line of an old joke, "Tonight's the night!" For the erotophobe, however, any such thoughts should be at least partially a negative experience and a source of guilt, shame, and anxiety. One way to avoid the unpleasant feelings associated with anticipatory sexual thoughts and nevertheless to engage in intercourse is to experience sex as a spontaneous, unplanned act.[14] Planned sex and hence sex for which the individual is responsible is not necessary if one is carried away by love or by uncontrollable passion or if one is under the influence of alcohol or some other drug. Under such circumstances, contraceptive devices are obviously much less likely to be involved because sex is "accidental."

Publicly acknowledging one's sexual intentions   For most contraceptive techniques, an individual must take some public action to acquire the necessary product or service and in effect announce that he or she is planning to become sexually active. Thus, a female must see a physician to obtain a prescription for pills, to be fitted for a diaphragm, to have an IUD inserted, or to arrange for a sterilization procedure. A male must do the same thing to arrange a vasectomy. For many contraceptive methods it is necessary to go to a drugstore to obtain pills, foam, condoms, contraceptive jelly, and so forth. In all such public interactions, the individual is letting someone else (most often, a stranger) know something about his or her sexual activity. Most people are at least somewhat concerned about the attributions that are being made about their behavior, their morals, or whatever. Some of these interactions and perceived attributions are embarrassing to almost everyone, married or single. For the erotophobe, the negative feelings should be extreme and would lead the individual to avoid such situations if at all possible.

Communicating with one's partner about sex and contraception   Two individuals who are going to engage in intercourse must communicate to one another in some way about their sexual interaction. Little is really known about the various ways in which this is actually done by either married or unmarried couples. Anecdotal evidence, letters to columnists, and fictional presentations suggest that coital communication includes detailed erotic descriptions of upcoming activities (e.g., the letters of James Joyce to his wife), euphemistic indications of desire (e.g., in *Diary of a Mad Housewife*, the husband regularly asks his wife if she wants "a little roll in de hay"), and nonverbal understandings in which silent partners undress in the dark and then wordlessly copulate. It seems reasonable to suppose that erotophobes would be less likely to communicate about sex than would erotophiles and that the lack of communication would extend to inquiries about contraception. Such direct questions as, "Are you taking the pill?"; "Do you have any rubbers?"; or "Have you put in your diaphragm?" should be much too painful for the erotophobe to ask. As a result, lack of communication would be expected to lead to misunderstandings and miscalculations about one another's contraceptive plans and hence to unprotected intercourse.

Practicing the contraceptive technique   Finally, the individual who uses a particular technique must actually proceed with the necessary activity. Some of these activities occur only once, as with sterilization, and some occur infrequently, as with the placement of an IUD. The taking of a pill is a daily occurrence, which requires that the person at least think about sexually related activities regularly even though contraception is usually removed from a sexual context. Other devices such as diaphragms, condoms, or foam require some contact with the genitals in close temporal proximity to the sexual act itself. While all such activities should be more difficult for the erotophobe than for the erotophile, the techniques requiring genital contact are more personal and more directly sexual and would seem to be especially anxiety evoking to erotophobic individuals.

It must be stressed that the present emphasis on the erotophobic-erotophilic determinants of contraceptive behavior should not be taken to mean that there are no other determinants of such behavior. In fact, there are probably multiple determinants at each step.[16] For example, effective planning should be hampered by low intelligence or by the belief that one's fate is not in one's own hands.[3,13] Whether or not public acknowledgment of sexual intentions is anxiety evoking is in part a function of such situational constraints as the age and sex of the drugstore clerk who is dispensing contraceptives.[12] Communicating with one's partner about sex and contraception would seem to be made more difficult by our cultural emphasis on the male as the sexual exploiter who is not likely to ruin a good seduction by talking about the possibility of pregnancy[14,19] and by the fact that females have historically been taught that the only acceptable label for their arousal in such a situation is "love";[4] our society provides no models and no encouragement for a romantic couple discussing condoms by candlelight. Finally, the actual practice of any contraceptive techniques would seem more likely to occur if the educational process stressed the specific application of each method rather than abstract facts. It would also help if the use of contraceptives were depicted realistically in novels, television programs, movies, and even in pornography—one of the rare exceptions to this tendency to ignore contraception in erotica appeared unexpectedly in a story in SMUT:[24]

> "Bitte?" she asked all of a sudden, and out of nowhere she had a rubber. A rubber? I thought, and then yeah, it makes sense, I guess . . .
>
> So she slipped it on me, which was a thrill in itself, unrolling it down the sides of my cock and then smoothing it up and down between her palms. The hair rose on the back of my balls, man. Shivery sensation. And you wouldn't even know the rubber was there, they make them so good these days [p. 18].

In any event, if the analysis of the erotophobic-erotophilic determinants of contraceptive behavior is correct, it would be expected that individuals who hold positive or negative views about sexuality would also be characterized by a positive or negative orientation to birth control. Thus, such seemingly unrelated concerns as evaluations of pornography, attitudes about censorship, and the use of contraception should be related to one another. Our first step, then, was to discover whether or not these and other sexual beliefs and attitudes are, in fact, associated in the hypothesized fashion.

STUDY I: SEXUAL AND CONTRACEPTIVE ATTITUDES

Method

The Sex Information Questionnaire consists of a series of items dealing with a variety of sexual attitudes and practices, including contraception. This survey was administered to 120 unmarried male and female undergraduates at Purdue University.

Results and discussion

Factor analysis revealed two primary response dimensions among the test items, and each of these seems to involve the kind of prosex and antisex orientation that we have described. In addition, each dimension contains some evidence indicating that sexual attitudes are related to contraceptive attitudes in the expected way. The first dimension consists of sexual experience and attitudes associated with sexuality, erotica, and contraception. The second dimension deals primarily with attitudes about masturbation and will not be discussed here. The first dimension is summarized in Table 9-1, and the items are arranged in order from the strongest to the weakest in terms of their association with this factor.

These results are somewhat encouraging in their support of the general idea that one's orientation to sexuality includes reactions to erotica, sexual behavior, and contraception. This sample of unmarried students contains many sexually inexperienced individuals, however, and it might be argued that attitudes about sex and birth control could be quite different in a sample of married couples who had established a regular, legally and morally sanctioned sexual relationship. Further, such individuals would have to deal more explicitly with the problems of family planning.[6,8,10,11,17] For this reason, we conducted a second study using a group of husbands and wives.

Another consideration was taken into account in this second study. A number of psychological theories predict that individuals try to maintain self-consistency with respect to their beliefs and their behaviors.[9,15,20] In addition, it has been proposed that people do not generally attribute emotional causes to their beliefs and behavior—rather, they attempt to justify themselves on "more rational" and intellectual grounds.[5] Therefore, we would not expect erotophobes to say that, "Sex makes me anxious, and therefore I avoid contraception and will acciden-

Table 9-1
Factor Defining Erotophobic-Erotophilic
Attitudes and Practices

Responses of Erotophobes	Responses of Erotophiles
There *should be* stricter censorship of erotic movies and books.	There *should not be* stricter censorship of erotic movies and books.
My response in general to erotic or pornographic material is a *certain degree* of disgust.	My response in general to erotic or pornographic material is *no* disgust.
College clinics should *possibly* make artificial means of birth control available to college students regardless of their marital status.	College clinics should *definitely* make artificial means of birth control available to college students regardless of their marital status.
It would be *highly unlikely* for me to volunteer for an experiment in which I engaged in sexual acts.	It would be *moderately likely* for me to volunteer for an experiment in which I engaged in sexual acts.
My response in general to erotic or pornographic material is a *certain degree* of arousal.	My response in general to erotic or pornographic material is *great* arousal.
I have *once or twice* voluntarily obtained or seen erotic or pornographic books, movies, magazines, etc.	I have *sometimes* voluntarily obtained or seen erotic or pornographic books, movies, magazines, etc.
Increased sexual activity among today's college students *does not necessarily* indicate that they are badly adjusted.	Increased sexual activity among today's college students *definitely* does not indicate that they are badly adjusted.
I *have not* engaged in sexual intercourse.	I *have* engaged in sexual intercourse.
I rate myself as *less* experienced sexually than my age group.	I rate myself as *more* experienced sexually than my age group.
Pornography *should be* kept out of the hands of people younger than eighteen years of age.	Pornography *should not be* kept out of the hands of people younger than eighteen years of age.
Sexuality is *perhaps* one of the most important factors in a satisfactory marriage.	Sexuality is *definitely* one of the most important factors in a satisfactory marriage.

When unmarried college students were asked to respond to a Sex Information Questionnaire, their responses were found to fall along a positive-negative dimension with respect to pornography and erotica, censorship, sexual behavior, and relative support for making birth control available to undergraduates. It should be noted that there were, in addition, male-female differences on some of these items. Compared to males, females tended to favor censorship, to find pornography disgusting, to be unwilling to volunteer for a sex experiment, to say that pornography is un-arousing, to have obtained or seen erotica less frequently, and to feel that pornography should not be made available to those younger than eighteen.

tally have a great many children." Instead, they should convince themselves that their sexual and contraceptive values have a moral and factual basis and that they genuinely desire to have a large family. "Why would I be having intercourse without contraception unless that were the proper and intelligent thing to do?" Analogously, erotophiles should find equally moral and factual bases to justify their enjoyment

Table 9-2
The Relationship between Desired Family Size
and Sexual and Contraceptive Attitudes and Beliefs

Opinions of Those Wanting a Large Family	Opinions of Those Wanting a Small Family
Personal Sexuality	
My response to erotic books, movies, magazines, etc., is *mixed arousal and disgust.*	My response to erotic books, movies, magazines, etc., is *sexual arousal.*
Social disapproval *has* prevented me from freely expressing my sexuality.[a]	Social disapproval *has not* prevented me from freely expressing my sexuality.[a]
Compared to the average person, my own sexual attitudes are *moderate.*	Compared to the average person, my own sexual attitudes are *somewhat liberal.*
Sexual intercourse without love is *not* enjoyable.	Love greatly enriches sexual relations, but it is *not necessary for enjoyment.*
Premarital sexual intercourse is all right for *couples who are in love.*	Premarital sexual intercourse is all right for *consenting adults.*
I have *no feelings* about having engaged in premarital intercourse.	I'm *very glad* I engaged in premarital intercourse.
Extramarital sexual intercourse is *allowable under very special circumstances,* e.g., partner sick, invalid, or absent.	Extramarital sexual intercourse is *all right* for either partner as long as he/she doesn't talk about it.
Marital Sexuality	
I would rate my sex life as *somewhat satisfactory.*	I would rate my sex life as *satisfactory.*
Sexual problems have been *somewhat important* in my marriage.	There have been *no* significant sexual problems in my marriage.

of sex and their employment of contraception, and they should espouse equally logical reasons for having a small family or no children at all. Such an analysis suggests that desired family size should be related to sexual and contraceptive attitudes.

STUDY II: SEXUAL ATTITUDES AND FAMILY PLANNING

Method

In response to a request for volunteers, 36 married couples agreed to participate in a study of sexuality. These 72 individuals were seen in small groups, and they filled out several questionnaires, viewed an erotic movie, and gave their reactions to it.

Results and discussion

One of the key questions asked of each subject was the number of children he or she hoped to have. Even though this question was answered

Table 9-2 (continued)

Compared to the average person, my spouse's sexual attitudes are *somewhat conservative.*[a]	Compared to the average person, my spouse's sexual attitudes are *somewhat liberal.*[a]
My spouse experiences sexual intercourse as *occasionally pleasant.*[a]	My spouse experiences sexual intercourse as *mostly pleasant.*[a]
I *am not* now using contraception.	I *am* presently using contraception.
I *have not* used spermicidal agents as a contraceptive technique.	I *have* used spermicidal agents as a contraceptive technique.

The Sexuality of Others

Erotic material *should not be* made freely available to adolescents.	Erotic material *should be* made freely available to adolescents.
I *slightly agree* that the law has no business regulating sexual relations between consenting adults.	I *strongly agree* that the law has no business regulating sexual relations between consenting adults.
I *slightly agree* that religious groups should not attempt to impose their standards of sexual behavior on others[a]	I *strongly agree* that religious groups should not attempt to impose their standards of sexual behavior on others.[a]
An unwanted child *is not* a valid reason for an abortion.[a]	An unwanted child *is* a valid reason for an abortion.[a]

[a] This difference was significant only for male subjects.

When young married couples were asked to state the number of children they plan to have, the size of their desired family was found to be related to their sexual and contraceptive attitudes. The greater the number of desired children the more negative, conservative, and restrictive they tended to be with respect to their personal sexuality, their marital sexuality, and their attitudes about the sexuality of others. Again, several sex differences were found. Compared to males, females were likely to report that pornography was not a source of sex education (10% versus 35%), that their spouse is sexually liberal, that they are less aroused by erotica, and that they had fewer premarital sex partners.

individually, husbands and wives tended to give very similar responses, which suggests that most couples communicate about this topic and reach a relatively high degree of agreement. On the basis of their responses, we divided the subjects into three groups with respect to desired family size. Consistent with previous investigations,[21] within this sample 22% of the couples wanted either no children or just one, 57% wanted to have two children, and 21% wanted to have three or more offspring. These three groups may be seen to have family goals that represent population decrease, zero population growth, and population increase.

Statistical analyses were carried out to compare these three groups with respect to their attitudes about sex and contraception. If the general theoretical propositions presented thus far are correct, the greater the number of desired children, the more negative should be the attitudes about sex and contraception.

The significant relationships presented in Table 9-2 are true for both sexes unless otherwise noted. It may be seen that those who desire the most children tend to have relatively negative personal attitudes about sex, are relatively less satisfied with their marital sex life, and are relatively restrictive about the sex life of others in the community. In addition, these individuals tend not to be using contraceptives, and they tend to be negative toward pornography and (for the men at least) abortion.

Additional background data on these individuals provide a few hints as to the antecedents of these differential attitudes about sex and about family size. Those subjects who desired the most children reported that they had been raised in communities of 10,000 to 25,000 population whereas those desiring a small family indicated that they came from larger towns and cities. Desire for several children was also associated with a home environment in which sex was seldom discussed within the family and in which most of their initial information about sex was provided by friends of the same age. Those wanting the most offspring describe their political views as moderate to conservative while those wanting small families describe themselves as liberal. The personality trait of authoritarianism is also positively related to the number of children desired. In summary, then, those desiring the largest families are characterized by a small-town background, a sexually restrained home atmosphere, political conservatism, and an authoritarian personality.

IMPLICATIONS

There are two major aspects of the present findings that should be considered in future research.

First, the evidence presented here provides at least tentative support for the hypothesis that many feelings and attitudes about sexual matters tend to be associated with one another along roughly positive-negative dimensions. Thus, there are relationships among responses to such diverse topics as pornography, censorship, sexual adjustment, and premarital intercourse. More important, in the present context, such responses are found to be related to evaluative responses regarding contraception and family planning. Such findings suggest that individual differences in learned emotional responses to sexuality are widely generalized in evaluative reactions. Inferences about cause and effect or directional influences must, of course, be tested in research designs quite different from the present correlational ones.

Second, the data suggest that the practical goal of altering contraceptive attitudes and behaviors such that the incidence of unwanted and unneeded pregnancies can be reduced may possibly be reached through an alteration in negative emotional responses to erotic cues. Thus, an approach to child rearing, sex education, or psychotherapy which stressed a positive effective response to sexuality might, in turn, result in changes in contraceptive behavior at each of the four behavioral steps outlined earlier in this article. In the most general sense, it is proposed that a sexually free and erotically nonanxious society would be characterized by responsible contraceptive behavior. Again, research is badly needed to verify such a proposal.

REFERENCES

1. Allgeier, E. R. Beyond sowing and growing: The relationship of sex typing to socialization, family plans, and future orientation. *Journal of Applied Social Psychology*, 1975, **5**, 217–226.

2. Arnold, C. B. The sexual behavior of inner city adolescent condom users. *Journal of Sex Research*, 1972, **8**, 298–309.

3. Bauman, K. E., & Udry, J. R. Powerlessness and regularity of contraception in an urban Negro male sample: A research note. *Journal of Marriage and the Family*, 1972, **34**, 112–114.

4. Berscheid, E., & Walster, E. A little bit about love. In T. L. Huston (Ed.), *Foundations of interpersonal attraction*. New York: Academic Press, 1974.

5. Byrne, D., Fisher, J. D., Lamberth, J., & Mitchell, H. E. Evaluations of erotica: Facts or feelings? *Journal of Personality and Social Psychology*, 1974, **79**, 111–116.

6. Crawford, T. J. Beliefs about birth control: A consistency theory analysis. *Representative Research in Social Psychology*, 1973, **4**, 53–65.

7. Cvetkovich, G., Grote, B., Bjorseth, A., & Sarkissian, J. On the psychology of adolescents' use of contraceptives. *Journal of Sex Research*, 1975, **11**, 256–270.

8. Davidson, A. R., & Jaccard, J. J. Population psychology: A new look at an old problem. *Journal of Personality and Social Psychology*, 1975, **31**, 1073–1082.

9. Festinger, L. *A theory of cognitive dissonance*. New York: Harper & Row, 1957.

10. Fishbein, M. Toward an understanding of family planning behaviors. *Journal of Applied Social Psychology*, 1972, **2**, 214–227.

11. Fishbein, M., & Jaccard, J. J. Theoretical and methodological considerations in the prediction of family planning intentions and behavior. *Representative Research in Social Psychology*, 1973, **4**, 37–51.

12. Fisher, W. A., Fisher, J. D., & Byrne, D. Consumer reactions to contraceptive purchasing. *Personality and Social Psychology Bulletin*, in press.

13. Groat, H. T., & Neal, A. G. Social psychological correlates of urban fertility. *American Sociological Review*, 1967, **32**, 945–959.

14. Gross, A. E., & Bellew-Smith, M. Some factors which may increase "pregnancy risk" and some possible remedies. Paper presented at the meeting of the Association for Women in Psychology, Knoxville, February 1976.

15. Heider, F. *The psychology of interpersonal relations.* New York: Wiley, 1958.

16. Jaccard, J. J., & Davidson, A. R. Toward an understanding of family planning behaviors: An initial investigation. *Journal of Applied Social Psychology*, 1972, **2**, 228–235.

17. Kothandapani, V. Validation of feeling, belief, and intention to act as three components of attitude and their contribution to prediction of contraceptive behavior. *Journal of Personality and Social Psychology*, 1971, **19**, 321–333.

18. Mosher, D. L. The development and multitrait-multimethod matrix analysis of three measures of three aspects of guilt. *Journal of Consulting Psychology*, 1966, **30**, 25–29.

19. Mosher, D. L. Sex callousness toward women. In *Technical report of the Commission on Obscenity and Pornography.* Vol. VIII. Washington, D. C.: U. S. Government Printing Office, 1971.

20. Newcomb, T. M. Interpersonal balance. In R. P. Abelson, E. Aronson, W. J. McGuire, T. M. Newcomb, M. J. Rosenberg, & P. H. Tannenbaum (Eds.), *Theories of cognitive consistency: A sourcebook.* Skokie, Ill.: Rand McNally, 1968.

21. Scarlett, J. A. Undergraduate attitudes towards birth control: New perspectives. *Journal of Marriage and the Family*, 1972, **34**, 312–314.

22. Schwartz, S. Effects of sex guilt and sexual arousal on the retention of birth control information. *Journal of Consulting and Clinical Psychology*, 1973, **41**, 61–64.

23. Wallace, D. H., & Wehmer, G. Evaluation of visual erotica by sexual liberals and conservatives. *Journal of Sex Research*, 1972, **8**, 147–153.

24. Webster, A. Dog days in Deutschland. *SMUT*, 1973, **1** (2), 18–20.

PART FOUR

Society
and
Sexuality

An Overview:
Public Aspects of a Private Activity

Throughout most of this book, sexuality has been considered from the viewpoint of the individual with respect to its anatomical, physiological, intellectual, emotional, behavioral, and interpersonal components. In addition, there is a public aspect of sex in that the expression of sexual needs is regulated by laws and customs in every society. Such societal concerns about the sexual behavior of its citizens involve three distinct topics: abnormal sexual expression, censorship of pornography, and political ideology. In examining those topics, we will touch on three basic questions: What is sexual abnormality? What are the effects of erotic stimuli on behavior? Are sexual freedom and political freedom related? Though each of these questions has been emphatically answered from time to time and though these answers have often been translated into laws that can affect each of us, it appears that the questions are still open to debate and that new and different answers might be appropriate.

WHAT IS SEXUAL ABNORMALITY?

Generally, people define as normal whatever behavior is practiced by the majority. There have been several quite distinct ways of explaining and dealing with any behavior that is different from that norm. Prevailing theories of mental and physical abnormality tend to be applied to non-normative sexual behavior as well as to other deviations from the majority. Thus, when the supernatural model of deviancy held sway, those whose sexual behavior was not in the mainstream were assumed to be possessed by demons or to have signed a pact with the devil. Literally, "the devil made them do it." The association of witchcraft and demonic possession with bizarre sexual rites and unbridled passion is still in our consciousness as can be seen in novels and movies such as *Rosemary's Baby* and *The Exorcist.* On the basis of this supernatural theory of abnormality, those who deviated sexually became the responsibility of religious authorities who sought in sometimes humane and sometimes cruel ways to rid the victim's body of its unearthly invaders. Then came the medical model and the notion that abnormality was an illness requiring treatment by a physician. As we shall see in the next chapter, pervasively negative beliefs about sexuality were readily assimilated within the medical model, and diagnostic categories were created to cover all forms of unacceptable sexual behavior. With this approach, medical terminology was applied to sexual deviations: the *patients* were given *therapy* in an attempt to *cure* their *pathological* condition. Next came the psychological model in which personality theories blended with theories of learning to explain abnormality on the basis of early experiences and the rewards and punishments associated with particular behaviors. With the advent of such diverse theoretical approaches as client-centered therapy and behavior modification, the medical model began to be abandoned by psychology, and clients are now helped in various ways to alter their response patterns.

Currently, and especially with respect to sexual behavior, there remains a degree of confusion and a somewhat inappropriate residue of the medical model. One who deviated sexually used to be called a "psychopathic personality with pathologic sexuality." Today, any sexual deviation is classified psychiatrically as one of the conduct disorders along with antisocial behavior, addiction, and dyssocial reactions. The trouble, of course, is that changes in our values, our behavior, and our laws about sex mean that yesterday's conduct disorder may be today's normality.

How, then, can sexual deviations be defined? One of the most inclusive definitions that we have encountered[19] states, "The sexual deviations include all sexual behaviors in which gratification of sexual impulses is obtained by practices other than intercourse with a genitally mature person of the opposite sex who has reached the legal age of consent [p. 311]." Thus, any sexual behaviors involving some other act or some other object choice would be classified as deviant behavior. Because this definition includes such widely practiced "deviations" as masturbation, fellatio, and cunnilingus, it seems illogical to accept this specification of what is abnormal.

If we were to shift to a definition that took into account what the majority of individuals in our society actually do, it would mean that behaviors that are currently practiced by a minority of the population (for example, anal intercourse, homosexual acts, mate swapping, and prostitution) would automatically be labeled abnormal. Is that a reasonable approach? Should we take annual polls to determine when sexual practices shift from abnormal to normal or vice versa in a kind of popularity contest? There might even be advertising campaigns and bumper stickers to promote the cause of one's favorite "perversion."

Personally, we prefer a very different type of definition which remains constant over time and which involves an affective-interpersonal approach to the concept to abnormality. From this viewpoint, *abnormal sexuality consists of any sex-related behavior that causes psychological distress or unwanted physical pain for the individual engaging in the act and/or for an unwitting or unwilling participant.* According to this definition, any sexual act that causes unhappiness or discomfort to anyone is abnormal, and any sexual act that brings pleasure is normal, so long as all participants are acting voluntarily and knowingly. Thus, any violence or threat of violence or any force applied to coerce an unwilling victim are unacceptable. Any sexual act that takes advantage of another's weakness, fear, poverty, inexperience, ignorance, or state of consciousness is unacceptable—therefore, sex with animals, or children, or someone who is mentally incompetent is not acceptable. Equally abnormal is sex with someone who is drugged, not in contact with reality, unconscious, or dead. Any sexual act that is unpleasant, anxiety evoking, or guilt inducing is unacceptable. Any sexual act that results in delayed negative consequences such as venereal disease or an unwanted pregnancy is unacceptable.

It may be seen, then, that no sexual act can in itself constitute abnormality. Abnormality rests on the *reasons* for engaging in the act, on the *feelings* engendered by the act, and on the *outcome* of the act. This definition leads to novel ways of conceptualizing normal and abnormal sexuality. Knowledgeable, consenting adults who wish to engage in any sort of sexual interaction that brings them mutual pleasure and that has no negative consequences could not be defined as behaving abnormally. If someone enjoys bondage, sadism, group sex, a partner of one's own sex, incest, masturbating with a vibrator or a watermelon, dressing in the clothes of the opposite sex, working as a prostitute, becoming the customer of a prostitute, being urinated on, employing an unusual fetish object, or engaging in heterosexual intercourse in the missionary position, he or she is behaving normally so long as all of the conditions of the definition are met.

Abnormality includes any sexual act with someone who is unwilling, including white slavery, rape, torture, bondage, or sadism. Also abnormal is the implied threat when sex is demanded from someone who is financially or otherwise dependent on one's good will such as one's student, a job applicant, or an employee. Voyeurism is abnormal if those being watched are unaware of their audience and would not like to be observed; reading a pornographic novel, viewing an X-rated movie, or watching a striptease are normal. Inflicting oneself on an involuntary audience (such as exposing one's genitals to a passing stranger in the park, sending an obscene letter, or making an obscene telephone call) is abnormal. In contrast, exposing one's body to a willing audience, writing obscene letters or saying sexual words on the telephone to a receptive partner would be perfectly normal. Once again, it is not the act itself, but the social and emotional context in which it occurs, which determines abnormality.

WHAT ARE THE EFFECTS OF EROTIC STIMULI ON BEHAVIOR?

Why should there be any concern about individuals being exposed to words and pictures that involve explicit sexual fiction or even explicit sexual facts? Why should many parents be against the establishment of sex education courses in the school system, and why should the vast powers of church and state frequently be exercised in the enforcement of sexual censorship?

One answer is the widespread assumption that behavior will be affected by exposure to erotic material, even educational material that relates to sexuality. One parent expressed this belief[16] as follows:

> I try to keep them from knowing too much; I approach it the same as my parents did. My parents did not tell me about it. I don't discuss it either. I think sex education corrupts the minds of 15–16 year olds! There is absolutely *no* communication between parents and kids about sex. Kids know too much already. I just tell them to behave and keep their eyes open [p. 233].

The effects of traditional sex education courses on subsequent sexual attitudes and sexual behavior have received only limited research attention. At the college level and beyond, however, there have been several studies examining the proliferation of courses and special programs that combine the presentation of factual material, exposure to erotic stimuli, and group discussions that attempt to explore personal feelings about sexuality. One finding is that the individuals who voluntarily take such courses tend to have more permissive sexual attitudes and to be more sexually experienced than comparable control groups.[21] In addition, these courses are found to have measurable effects on those who take them. In the University of Minnesota program on human sexuality, for example, it has been found that students show an increase in knowledge about sex and an increase in permissive attitudes after completing the course.[10] After taking the course individuals are more likely to agree or strongly agree that homosexuality is a way of life rather than an illness, that masturbation is a healthy practice, that oral sex is an acceptable form of erotic play, and that contraceptive materials should be freely available to anyone who is engaging in intercourse. In addition, the attitudinal changes are found to persist a year later, even though some of the factual material is forgotten.[11]

Whether such courses affect sexual *behavior* is another question. Following a course on human sexuality at the University of Delaware, Zuckerman, Tushup, and Finner[21] found more permissive sexual attitudes among both male and female students, but only males indicated a change in behavior. Compared to a control group, undergraduate males taking the sex course reported a greater increase in masturbation, sexual intercourse, and other orgasmic experiences; female students did not report these behavioral changes. It should be noted, however, that except for six males who reported having their first homosexual experiences, the increases tended to involve those who had already had similar experiences previously—only two males and no females reported having their first coital experience during the course. The authors suggested that even the homosexual acts might not represent something really new but rather a willingness to admit a socially unacceptable activity after the course that the students were not willing to talk about beforehand. It should be noted, of course, that changes in the direction of more permissive attitudes and increased sexual activity can be viewed as positive evidence of the liberating value of education or as scientific confirmation of the worst fears of those who oppose sex education.

Beyond the academic sphere, there is the world of erotica and pornography in books, magazines, and movies. What effects might repeated exposure to such stimuli have on attitudes and behavior? Here, beliefs about the possible consequences of exposure to erotica are found to be related to one's age. The younger an individual is, the greater the tendency to attribute desirable effects to erotica, while older individuals attribute negative effects to such exposure.[17] Thus, those under 40 are likely to see sexual materials as providing entertainment, acting as an outlet for bottled up impulses, giving relief to those with sex problems, improving marital sex, and providing sex information. Those over 40 suggest that erotica makes people sex crazy, leads to a breakdown in morals, and induces men to lose respect for women and to commit rape.

The negative beliefs and attributions were largely responsible for the appointment by President Johnson of the Commission on Obscenity and Pornography[8] in January 1968. One of its four tasks assigned by Congress in Public Law 90-100 was "to study the effect of obscenity and pornography upon the public, and particularly minors, and its relationship to crime and other antisocial behavior [p. 1]." It was quickly discovered that knowledge about such effects was virtually nonexistent,[4, 5] and steps were taken to contract a variety of research projects in an attempt to document precisely how behavior might be affected when individuals are exposed to erotica.

In Chapter 12, we will present representative samples of the type of research that was conducted. The overall conclusions can be quickly summarized, however. Because the unrestricted production and sale of erotica in Denmark beginning in 1969 led to a *decrease* rather than an increase in sexual crimes in that country and because sex criminals report no more contact with nor different reactions to erotica than is true for normal individuals, the supposed causal relationship between pornography and sex crime seems not to exist. Further, the effects of erotica on other types of sexual behavior were found to be severely limited—even though subjects are sexually and emotionally aroused by erotica, this arousal tends to have only a small and temporary influence on their sexual activity, any posterotica sexual acts seem to involve each individual's familiar repertoire rather than something they learned from the erotic presentation, and the effect of erotica appears to diminish with repeated exposure to such material.

Despite these findings, there are additional considerations which suggest that perhaps there *are* long-range effects of erotica on behavior. In addition, the attitudinal changes reported in the sex education studies might also apply to erotica. Elsewhere, Byrne[2] has suggested the way in which such changes might occur over a period of time even though there is no direct evidence in existing research:

> Let us take as an example a female who has never engaged in fellatio, is made somewhat anxious by even thinking of it, and has no desire to alter her attitudes or behavior. Leaving aside the question of the prudence of her views, we can simply say that in a sexually restrictive society, there would be little or no reason to expect this behavior to change. She could easily avoid thinking about the topic, and external representations of fellatio would seldom if ever be thrust upon her. In many parts of the world in recent years, such an individual would find it very difficult to avoid verbal and pictorial fantasies involving oral stimulation of the penis. In movies, books, and popular magazines, she would be repeatedly exposed to the idea that fellation is an acceptable, expected, pleasurable aspect of heterosexual relationships. It is proposed that such exposure results in a progressive series of changes in the sequence described below.

Step I. Attitude Change
via Familiarization and Desensitization

The therapeutic use of desensitization indicates that repeated exposure to an anxiety-evoking stimulus leads to decreased anxiety. More generally, Zajonc[20] has proposed that repeated exposure to any stimulus results in more favorable evaluations of that stimulus. Over a period of months or years, our hypothetical female is exposed directly or indirectly to material contained in such books as *Portnoy's Complaint*, such movies as *Deep Throat*, and such plays as *Let My People Come*. Each time that the topic of fellatio arises, there should be less and less anxiety. The expected result is a more favorable evaluation of fellatio. It is hypothesized that exposure to sexual images tends to bring about changes in evaluative responses such that attitudes toward the depicted sexual activity are gradually changed from negative to neutral to mildly positive.

Step II. Tolerance
and Imaginative Rehearsal

Once there has been an attitudinal shift, the individual is able to think about the activity in question without being blocked by anxiety and the necessity to vindicate the negative feelings by means of negative attributions. For example, it would now be possible for our female more easily to tolerate the idea that others are engaging in fellatio without condemning them for it. Hunt[13] describes many instances in which there is increased tolerance in the United States for various sexual practices such as anal intercourse even among those who have never engaged in such acts. The ability to think about a given sexual activity without anxiety also means that such thoughts can occur during masturbation or coitus. There is evidence that erotic stimuli, especially pictorial stimuli, directly influence the masturbatory and coital fantasies of both males and females.[18] In effect, the individual becomes involved in an active conditioning procedure much like the guided masturbation technique used in therapy. The end result is that a previously forbidden act such as fellatio may become a stimulus for arousal, sexual pleasure, and orgasm.

Step III. Behavioral Change

It is proposed that the new associations which the individual learns are apt to be followed by changes in overt behavior. For example, if the idea of fellatio has become an exciting and pleasurable one, the inclination is to try it out in real life. In this way, the erotic images prevalent in the culture become transferred to private erotic images which are later translated into overt behavior.

It should be added that this three-step process is not inevitable because of numerous possible disruptions and that each progressive step has a lower probability of occurrence than the previous one. Thus, more people change their attitudes as a result of repeated exposure than become actively enaged in imaginative rehearsal, and fewer still try out the imagined scene in overt behavior. For the population as a whole, however, the net long-range result of sexual explicitness should be (1) more favorable attitudes toward the depicted activities, (2) an increase in tolerance for the activities and in private fantasies about the activities, and (3) an increase in the frequency of the activities themselves. Because of the very nature of the process being described, no single experiment can pinpoint the effects very convincingly, but changes in the explicitness of erotic images in our society have obviously occurred concomitantly with changes in sexual attitudes, tolerance, and overt practices.

The kinds of effects attributed to sexually explicit material may be interpreted by many of us as beneficial in that increasing numbers of people may be learning to be less anxious about many aspects of their sexual lives and to obtain more joy from engaging in a variety of sexual practices. A word of caution is in order, however. In the example, changes were described with respect to fellatio. The example could just as easily have been rape, flagellation, or pederasty. Though we as citizens may disagree about which sexual acts are acceptable and which are detrimental to society, we can all agree that at least *some* erotic activities should not be encouraged. If our present knowledge and theorizing about the effects of erotic images on human behavior prove to be generally correct, even the most permissive and tolerant among us may reluctantly have to consider the wisdom of selective censorship.

ARE SEXUAL FREEDOM AND POLITICAL FREEDOM RELATED?

In various places in this book, there have been contrasts between prosex and antisex orientations—in examining divergent cultures, in assessing the attitudes and beliefs of individuals, and in determining the very different emotional responses that can be elicited by erotic stimulation. Now we come to perhaps the most important consideration of all —the implications of these differing sexual orientations for the broader aspects of our society. Let it be said initially that the evidence is primarily of an indirect nature and open to multiple interpretations. Nevertheless, our conclusion is that sexual freedom is associated with political freedom whereas sexual restrictiveness is associated with political tyranny.

This is not, of course, the first time that anyone has proposed such a relationship. Black novelist James Baldwin[6] suggested in an interview the reason for societal pressures against homosexuality and against sexual love in general:

> The idea that you would like to be in somebody's arms is anathema to a Christian-Commercial civilization because if you can make a man scared of where he lives, you've got him. The whole idea is not to make you stop fucking. It is to stop you making love.
>
> If you can make love, then maybe you won't listen to the president. If you can be free where you live, nobody can tell you what to do. The way to tell a man what to do is to make him scared of what he's got between his legs. Make him guilty about it [p. 16].

A compatible view is expressed in a recent book by Alex Comfort:[7]

> The antisexualism of authoritarian societies and the people who run them doesn't spring from conviction (they themselves have sex) but from the vague perception that freedom here might lead to a liking for freedom elsewhere. People who have eroticized their experience of themselves and the world are, on the one hand, inconveniently unwarlike . . . and, on the other, violently combative in resisting goons, political salesmen, racists and "garbage" people generally who threaten the personal freedom they've attained and want to see others share.

When one considers totalitarian states whether of the political left or political right, they are united by certain commonalities. What is similar about such past political entities as Nazi Germany, Franco's Spain, and Greece when it was ruled by the cabal of colonels and what do they share with such present countries as The People's Republic of China, Chile, the USSR, and Saudi Arabia? First, there is governmental control of information through censorship, propaganda, and careful monitoring of education, and there is governmental control of behavior through restrictive laws and fearful punishments for any unsanctioned act. It sounds like a shopworn cliche because of overrepetition, but the people living in such societies are not free to talk, write, behave, or (the leaders hope) think in ways that deviate from what is officially prescribed. Second, there is a special concomitant of this lack of freedom, and it is the zeal with which such governments attack sexual expression in the name of "morality" whether that morality is expressed in terms of racial purity, the good of the socialist state, or in religious terms. Erotica is not tolerated, and contraception is taboo. Books are banned, skirts are lowered and hair is shortened by decree, and the populace is expected to work unceasingly for the good of the nation, be ready to engage mindlessly in war for the defense of the glorious homeland, and to engage in sex only in order to increase the population and not, horrible though the thought may be, for personal pleasure.

There are many examples of sexual repressiveness in these societies, such as the description of China by Dr. William T. Liu[15] of Notre Dame:

> To say that the sex instinct does not exist in The People's Republic is absurd. The Chinese do not deny that they have sexual drives, but they have done a splendid job of controlling their feelings. No courtship or romance is permitted or even tacitly approved in school, including the university level. Boys and girls are not exactly segregated during the adolescent years, but the emphasis is on party participation and not on personal relationships. Unisex uniforms, and the absence of feminine makeup have helped to "de-sex" gender differences. Premarital sex is considered not only immoral but unpatriotic [p. 34].

Examples of societies at the opposite extreme of political and sexual freedom are more difficult to find, perhaps because total freedom in both spheres has not yet been instituted anywhere in the world. Nevertheless, in contrast to the nations just named, consider the relative amount of democracy currently practiced in such countries as Sweden, Denmark, and Great Britain and also the relative amount of sexual permissiveness there. We know of Swedish erotica, Danish sex films, and swinging English females in provocative clothing. Can you even conjure an image of Russian erotica, Chinese sex films, or sexy attire on the streets of Riyadh?

At the individual level, there are numerous research findings that have established a link between negative and repressive sexual attitudes and an acceptance of fascistic ideology as indicated by studies using the California F-Scale.[1, 3, 9, 12, 14] Those who are high in authoritarianism tend to favor the suppression of sexual freedom, the imposition of censorship, and the punishment of those who deviate from whatever sexual behavior they define as normal.

If no society has yet been totally free, no one can say with any certainty what such a society would be like, but some imaginative possibilities are presented in Chapter 13. One might envision a place in which everyone simply enjoys all aspects of sexuality as a source of pleasure and recreation and not merely as a way to satisfy a biological need or to fulfill a marital duty. Sex would not cause fear, guilt, or anxiety, and no one would engage in abnormal sexuality that caused psychological distress or unwanted physical pain to anyone.

What would be the effects of such a sexual atmosphere? Again, no one can really answer the question. Perhaps, as conservative columnist Jeffrey Hart has proposed, unrestrained sexuality would lower the barriers for other kinds of unrestrained acts—murder, anarchy, theft, and so forth. Perhaps he is right that the basis of civilization is restraint, beginning with sexual restraint. In addition, perhaps people would be less willing to man the assembly lines or serve in the armed forces. Perhaps people would work less hard and have less desire to achieve. Perhaps the Gross National Product would plummet.

It is also possible that sexual freedom would result in happy, contented human beings who would live together harmoniously, feel satisfied with their lives, and actually find pleasure in working harder and more creatively. Maybe sexually contented people would be less willing to exploit and be exploited and less willing to hurt and be hurt. We have seen numerous examples of the opposite kind of society, and we have seen the results which run the gamut from political corruption to genocide. With luck, the time may be coming when a very different and, we hope, a better society can be created.

REFERENCES

1. Adorno, T. W., Frenkel-Brunswick, E., Levinson, D. J., & Sanford, R. N. *The authoritarian personality.* New York: Harper & Row, 1950.

2. Byrne, D. Sexual imagery. In J. Money & H. Musaph (Eds.), *Handbook of sexology.* Amsterdam: Excerpta Medica, 1976.

3. Byrne, D., & Lamberth, J. The effect of erotic stimuli on sex arousal, evaluative responses, and subsequent behavior. In *Technical report of the Commission on Obscenity and Pornography.* Vol. VIII. Washington, D. C.: U. S. Government Printing Office, 1971.

4. Cairns, R. B., Paul, J. C. N., & Wishner, J. Sex censorship: The assumptions of anti-obscenity laws and the empirical evidence. *Minnesota Law Review*, 1962, **46**, 1009–1041.

5. Cairns, R. B., Paul, J. C. N., & Wishner, J. Psychological assumptions in sex censorship: An evaluative review of recent research (1961–1968). In *Technical report of the Commission on Obscenity and Pornography.* Vol. I. Washington, D. C.: U. S. Government Printing Office, 1971.

6. Carre, A. James Baldwin talks. *Forum*, 1975, **4** (6), 14–19.

7. Comfort, A. *More joy. A lovemaking companion to the joy of sex.* New York: Crown, 1975.

8. Commission on Obscenity and Pornography. *The report of the Commission on Obscenity and Pornography.* Washington, D. C.: U. S. Government Printing Office, 1970.

9. Eliasberg, W. G., & Stuart, I. R. Authoritarian personality and the obscenity threshold. *Journal of Social Psychology*, 1961, **55**, 143–151.

10. Garrard, J., Vaitkus, A., & Chilgren, R. A. Evaluation of a course in human sexuality. *Journal of Medical Education*, 1972, **47**, 772–778.

11. Garrard, J., Vaitkus, A., Held, J., & Chilgren, R. A. Follow-up of effects of a medical school course in human sexuality. *Archives of Sexual Behavior*, 1976, **5**, 331–340.

12. Griffitt, W. Response to erotica and the projection of response to erotica in the opposite sex. *Journal of Experimental Research in Personality*, 1973, **6**, 330–338.

13. Hunt, M. *Sexual behavior in the 1970s.* Chicago: Playboy Press, 1974.

14. Kogan, N. Authoritarianism and repression. *Journal of Abnormal and Social Psychology*, 1956, **53**, 34–37.

15. Landers, A. Sex behind the bamboo curtain. *The Saturday Evening Post,* September 1975, 32–34, 36, 80–81.

16. Libby, R. W., & Nass, G. D. Parental views on teenage sexual behavior. *Journal of Sex Research*, 1971, **7**, 226–236.

17. Merritt, C. G., Gerstl, J. E., & LoSciuto, L. A. Age and perceived effects of erotica-pornography: A national sample study. *Archives of Sexual Behavior*, 1975, **4**, 605–621.

18. Schmidt, G., & Sigusch, V. Women's sexual arousal. In J. Zubin & J. Money (Eds.), *Contemporary sexual behavior: Critical issues in the 1970's.* Baltimore: Johns Hopkins University Press, 1973.

19. Suinn, R. M. *Fundamentals of behavior pathology.* New York: Wiley, 1970.

20. Zajonc, R. B. Attitudinal effects of mere exposure. *Journal of Personality and Social Psychology Monograph Supplement*, 1968, **9**, 1–27.

21. Zuckerman, M., Tushup, R., & Finner, S. Sexual attitudes and experience: Attitude and personality correlates and changes produced by a course in sexuality. *Journal of Consulting and Clinical Psychology*, 1976, **44**, 7–19.

CHAPTER TEN

"Abnormal"
Patterns
of
Sexual
Behavior

Sex Offenders: An Analysis of Types

When one person compels another to engage in a sexual act by means of force or verbal threats, the behavior is clearly abnormal by our definition. The most common and most fearful such act is rape. As anthropologist Paul Gebhard and his distinguished colleagues at the "Kinsey Institute" point out, there are at least five distinct types of individuals who commit rape. Some men are hostile and assaultive, some are amoral delinquents, some commit rape only as part of a drunken episode, some suddenly and surprisingly engage in an explosive attack, and some are the double-standard rapists who only force themselves on "the kind of girls who are really asking for it anyway."

In addition to these personality types among rapists, it should probably be noted that situational factors can also have a powerful influence on such behavior. Whenever males find themselves in a position of total power with respect to females—invading soldiers in contact with unarmed civilians being the most obvious example—rape becomes likely. Sexual assaults by a conquering army are not limited to any single nationality or race or to a deviant segment of the male population. This universal phenomenon has led some observers to suggest that all males are potential rapists, held tenuously in check by the restraints of civilized society. That may be going a step too far, but the role that rape plays in private fantasies plus the titillation afforded by both fictional and nonfictional accounts of the rape experience suggest its importance in our conceptualizations of male-female sexual interactions. Of course, much the same statements could be made with respect to murder, so perhaps one can only conclude that violent behavior of every variety represents the darkest aspects of our human heritage—aspects that are still much too familiar a part of twentieth-century behavior.

In the following article, two other sexual offenses are also discussed—incest and peeping Tomism. Once again, abnormality is involved in that there is the use of force (e.g., father forces daughter to have intercourse) or an intrusion on the privacy of an unwilling victim (e.g., a stranger peers through a bedroom window to watch someone undress). With respect to each type of sex offender described here, it might be noted that these acts are overwhelmingly committed by males. Though there are numerous sexual similarities between males and females as was discussed earlier, keep in mind that sexual offensiveness seems to be an undeniably masculine characteristic.

Sex Offenders: An Analysis of Types

Paul H. Gebhard, John H. Gagnon, Wardell B. Pomeroy,
and Cornelia V. Christenson

HETEROSEXUAL AGGRESSORS AGAINST ADULTS

Examination of heterosexual aggressors against adults leads us to feel that the majority can be classified into seven varieties, and that the classification is scientifically and clinically useful.

The most common variety, accounting for between one-quarter and one-third of our sample, we have labeled the assaultive variety. These are men whose behavior includes unnecessary violence; it seems that sexual activity alone is insufficient and that in order for it to be maximally gratifying it must be accompanied by physical violence or by serious threat. In brief, there is a strong sadistic element in these men and they often feel pronounced hostility to women (and possibly to men also) at a conscious or unconscious level. They generally do not know their victims; they usually commit the offense alone, without accomplices; preliminary attempts at seduction are either absent or extremely brief and crude; the use of weapons is common; the man usually has a past history of violence; he seemingly selects his victim with less than normal regard for her age, appearance, and deportment. Lastly, there is a tendency for the offense to be accompanied by bizarre behavior including unnecessary and trivial theft. Aside from the drunken variety of aggressor, the assaultive type has more cases involving erectile impotence than do the others. In some instances the violence seems to substitute for coitus or at least render the need for it less. In other cases there appears to have been a conflict between sexual desire and hostility resulting in some measure of erectile (less often ejaculatory) impotence.

The assaultive aggressor who seemingly requires violence for his gratification is exemplified by a semiskilled laborer with two marriages and seven prison sentences behind him when he was interviewed in his late 40s. While no conscious sadism appeared in his dreams, fantasies, or reactions to stories of brutality, all or nearly all his four rapes or attempted rapes were marked by unnecessary violence. The first rape, committed when he was in his early 20s, was a case of two young men picking up two women, one of whom fled when the men refused to take them home. While it seems clear that the other woman could have been easily subdued and restrained by the two sturdy males, the subject felt it necessary to beat her and, after placing her on the ground, to kick her in the mouth before having coitus. Data are incomplete regarding his

Reprinted in an edited version from: Gebhard, P. H., Gagnon, J. H., Pomeroy, W. B., & Christenson, C. V. *Sex offenders: An analysis of types.* New York: Harper-Hoeber, 1965.

second rape when he was in his late 20s, but he entered the bedroom of a sleeping woman and attempted to have coitus with her. His third rape was committed, when he was in his 30s, upon his mother-in-law, who was nearly 20 years his senior. He raped her twice and in the process beat her so severely that she was hospitalized for a month. He evaded prosecution by fleeing the state. His fourth rape, when he was in his late 30s, consisted of forcing a woman into his motel cabin and threatening her with a knife. When she tried to escape he struck her with a bottle and beat her up. Before coitus was accomplished, she did manage to run, nearly nude, from the cabin to seek help. The man solaced himself by taking her purse before he fled, but made the error of returning to salvage a bottle of whiskey which he had forgotten to take with him. After serving some years for this offense he was paroled but extradited to another state to stand trial for having raped his former mother-in-law.

The second most common variety of aggressors against adults is the amoral delinquents. These men pay little heed to social controls and operate on a level of disorganized egocentric hedonism, and consequently have numerous brushes with the law. They are not sadistic—they simply want to have coitus and the females' wishes are of no particular consequence. They are not hostile toward females, but look upon them solely as sexual objects whose role in life is to provide sexual pleasure. If a woman is recalcitrant and will not fulfill her role, a man may have to use force, threat, weapons, or anything else at his disposal. The amoral delinquent may or may not have previously known his victim, but this too is a minor point to someone who regards women as mere pleasantly shaped masses of protoplasm for sexual use. It appears that one-eighth to one-sixth of the aggressors against adults may be classed as amoral delinquents.

One case is that of a semiskilled man of 22 with a tenth-grade education. The descriptions of him contain terms such as "lazy," "drifter," "reckless," "restless," and "a chronic nuisance in his area." Almost half of his brief army career was spent in the stockade for having been absent without leave. About 2 years later, by which time he was tattooed and running with local gangs, he and two companions picked up two women and, instead of giving them the promised ride to their destination, took them to a rural area where they forced sexual activity by threatening the women with a knife. After serving slightly more than a year for this offense, the young man was released on parole. Shortly thereafter he was arrested along with a large group of males and females who were engaged in some sort of street fight. He was also suspected of encouraging a woman to write bad checks. In the year he came of age his parole was revoked when he and a friend broke a window and stole several hundred dollars' worth of tools.

An example of an older amoral delinquent is a 37-year-old in our sample. There was nothing unusual about his life until impending fatherhood forced his marriage at age 19. He made his living through semiskilled labor and also got into the entertainment world. His first marriage ended in divorce after 3 years and his second marriage, when he was in his early 20s, lasted only a year. His wife, complaining of his too frequent sexual demands, made the following highly significant remark: "He treated me as though I were a child," i.e., not as a real person, but as an inferior of use only as a sexual object. Soon after the collapse of this second marriage the man held up a number of stores, in one of which he found a young saleswoman and opportunistically forced her to undress and have coitus. These acts resulted in a long prison term. He was paroled in his early 30s and within about a year was back in prison for petty theft. Paroled again, he supported himself by managing an eating place staffed by waitresses who doubled as prostitutes while he served as the pimp. This remunerative situation came to an end when his attempts to persuade a woman to have coitus resulted in some sort of struggle during which the woman fell, or was pushed, down a flight of stairs, at least partially forced coitus occurred, and the man was injured in his left eye. In any event, he returned to prison on a charge of assault with intent to commit rape.

About as common as the amoral delinquent variety of aggressor is the drunken variety. The student of sex offenders soon comes to realize that drunks are omnipresent, appearing in all offense categories to a greater or lesser degree. The drunk's aggression ranges from uncoordinated grapplings and pawings, which he construes as efforts at seduction, to hostile and truly vicious behavior released by intoxication.

The simplest and least aggressive sort of drunken offense is exemplified by a 19-year-old farm laborer of borderline intelligence. The case is summed up in the words of the prison psychologist: "The subject is a dull boy of nineteen. . . . While drunk, he tried to force the young wife of his former employer into a bedroom in an attempt to have sexual intercourse. She resisted and later told her husband. . . ." This resulted in a 90-day sentence for assault and battery. The boy was under the impression that the wife was more amenable than she actually was.

A more bizarre, but still relatively harmless, case is one of a 42-year-old, previously married man of average intelligence who was living in a motel and was feeling sexually deprived. He had in the past once forced coitus on a girl friend with whom he had had a mutually voluntary coital relationship and also had once forced coitus on his ex-wife. Both women had resisted, wrestling ensued, and both had finally yielded in order to get it over with and get rid of him. It seems probable that the man looked upon the use of minor force as both effective and safe. He became intoxicated and recalled that a young, unmarried woman lived in a motel cabin nearby. He decided to peep in her window to see if she was with a man, his logic being that if she were with a man this would be evidence that she was sexually loose and, hence, worth cultivating. He peered in and saw her alone asleep in bed and at this moment conceived the idea of having coitus with her then and there. He cut the window screen and then with drunken logic recalled that he was not properly clothed for bed, so he returned to his own cabin and changed into his pajamas. Thus properly dressed, he went back to the woman's cabin, removed the cut screen, opened the window, and crawled inside. He tiptoed to the bed, turned off the bed lamp which had been left on, and tried to slip unobtrusively into the bed. The woman awoke and screamed. The man, frightened, clapped his hand over her mouth and the woman became quiet and immobile—possibly fainting. He then crawled on top of her and removed his hand from her mouth in order to kiss her. The woman, galvanized into action, screamed and scratched. The man was severely scratched before he managed to get out of bed and stumble out the door into the grasp of a man attracted by the screams.

In contrast to these two examples, which involved no physical harm of any consequence and which were not without some humorous aspects, the cases where intoxication releases a violent pathological response are extremely serious. One of the best illustrations is the case of a young man who up to the time of this offense seemed in no way unusual except for his above-average intelligence, his hatred for his abusive father, and a tendency to want to bite his sexual partners as he reached orgasm. Following graduation from high school he enlisted in military service where he served well; he had just reenlisted before his offense. He had gone on a drunken binge and was frequenting bars in order to pick up women. He finally found one; they drank and left together. They went into an alley and began petting. According to the man, while they were deep-kissing she suddenly bit his tongue severely, and subsequent medical examination disclosed a deep cut nearly halfway through his tongue. This intense pain coming on top of erotic arousal and extreme intoxication precipitated a sadistic assault in which he not only beat the woman but repeatedly bit her face, breasts, and genitals. Portions of flesh were actually bitten off. He claimed only vague memory of this and had no memory of taking the woman's wristwatch and dental plate when he left her. The psychologists and psychiatrists who examined him reported deep underlying hostile impulses which were released during intoxication.

The next commonest variety of aggressor, constituting perhaps 10–15% of the aggressors against adults, might be termed the explosive variety. These are men whose prior lives offer no surface indications of what is to come. Sometimes they are average, law-abiding citizens, sometimes they are criminals, but their aggression appears suddenly and, at the time, inexplicably. As one would expect in situations where individuals snap under hidden emotional stresses, there are often psychotic elements in their behavior. The stereotype of this variety of aggressor is the mild, straight-A high school student who suddenly rapes and kills. For total unexpectedness, one of our cases is equally dramatic. A small, physically delicate, devoutly religious 18-year-old had been reared by his mother, who seems to have dominated him. While heterosexually oriented, he never developed sociosexually with girls of his own age; instead, on rare occasions he engaged female children in what would be called childhood sex play had he been preadolescent rather than 15 or older. He was never able to achieve coitus, but usually ejaculated when the children struggled or when his penis touched their genital area. This behavior resulted in his being sent to a juvenile institution for about a year. On his return home and only a few days after his eighteenth birthday, during his mother's absence he asked a neighbor woman to come into the kitchen and light the oven for him. When she entered he struck her on the head with a hammer, hoping to knock her unconscious so that he could have coitus. She was not rendered unconscious by the blow and succeeded in escaping.

While the above case is unusual in that the subject was so sociosexually underdeveloped, in the following case the man's sexual history was normal. He was a hard-working, semiskilled laborer described by the prison psychologist as having "many fine traits, . . . deep respect for authority, family pride, sense of personal responsibility, a knowledge of right and wrong and a willingness to abide by the same, . . ., etc." His dossier contained numerous and various letters attesting to his good character and respectability. The only negative note was his wife's statement that he tended to worry excessively and became emotionally upset easily. This statement is biased by the fact that the behavior of the wife and her relatives directly led to the sex offense. This conservative and respectable man had made the error of marrying a woman from a very low socioeconomic stratum who brought with her to marriage not only an unborn child, but a number of shiftless, drunken, parasitic relatives. The resultant bitter arguments essentially destroyed the marriage, and the man decided to make the best of a bad situation by having extramarital coitus with some of his promiscuous female in-laws. He chose his mother-in-law, having interpreted her behavior toward him as provocative; the psychologists say that this choice also was unconsciously motivated by a desire for revenge against his wife and all her relatives. In any case, coitus occurred and the woman was at least partly forced.

The next variety of aggressor against adults, and one accounting for perhaps as much as 10% of the group, is the double-standard variety. The males so classified divide females into good females whom one treats with some respect and bad females who are not entitled to consideration if they become obstinate. While one would not ordinarily think of maltreating a good girl, any girl one can pick up easily has in essence agreed to coitus and can legitimately be forced to keep her promise. These double-standard aggressors are somewhat like the amoral delinquents in attitude, but differ from them in being less criminal, in resorting to force only after persuasion fails, and in not being so generally asocial. In brief, the double-standard variety may be described as rather average males of lower socioeconomic background who feel that with provocation the use of moderate threat or force is justifiable when applied to females judged to be sexually lax or promiscuous. These double-standard males share with the amoral delinquents a penchant for group activity, the logical result when several males cruise about looking for female pickups. This trend may include a sort of man-to-man generosity, the female being shared much as men would share food or liquor, and with about the same emotional affect. Indeed, we have one case in which the man left a pickup and his friend in his car to go to a nearby parked car containing three other men and suggested sharing the woman in exchange for a gallon of wine. Yet this man strongly desired to marry a virgin and had refrained from coitus with his fiancée.

Another man of limited intellect and education who had a clear record, except for juvenile car theft (not uncommon behavior in his social milieu), helped a woman get her stalled auto started, mistook her appreciation and offer of a lift for an indication of sexual willingness and then threatened and struck her when she refused coitus. The prison report is illuminating: "[The subject has] habitually a naive expression . . . anxious to have everyone understand that he was neither brutal nor violent with his victim . . . admits that when he could not persuade her in friendly fashion he uttered threats . . . Frank to admit he sees nothing wrong with what he did for the victim was not harmed in any way and it was nothing more than what he has done on many occasions in the past to other girls . . . ."

The rationalization of a double-standard aggressor might often be in the following vein, to quote one of them: "Man, these dumb broads don't know what they want. They get you worked up and then they try to chicken out. You let 'em get away with stuff like that and the next thing you know they'll be walking all over you."

After subtracting the above five varieties, nearly one-third of the aggressors against adults remain. A few of them may be recognized as clear cases of mental defectives and a few others as unquestionable psychotics, but the others strike one as being mixtures of the varieties described.

INCEST OFFENDERS AGAINST ADULTS

Incest offenders against adults are adult males who have had sexual contact with their daughters or stepdaughters who were aged 16 or older at the time. As in the other incest groups, the use of force will not be a separate category. When a female is 16 or older, the presence or absence of threat or force is more easily determined than when she is younger; both parental authority and the disparity in physical strength are less and, to be effective, physical force or threat must ordinarily be so extreme as to be easily identified.

All the elements that served as real or fancied mitigating factors in the case of incest offenders against minors are intensified in the incest offenders against adults. The females were all physically mature and would be considered appropriate sexual partners by most men. The "child molesting" element of the other incest offenders no longer exists. Bluntly speaking, society tells the father or stepfather of a female aged 16 or over, "You must live on rather intimate terms with a female who is old enough for sex and who is sexually attractive, but you must not allow yourself to take advantage of this situation." To the average person this dictate seems a reasonable law and one easy to obey. However, in certain circumstances even the most conservative person must admit that obedience to the law requires an iron will. For example, there are cases where a man marries a woman who has a full-grown daughter perhaps far more attractive than her mother; here the man may find himself sharing a home with a female with whom he could have a socially acceptable sexual relationship were it not for the fact that he married her mother. To view this female, whom he can scarcely look upon as a true daughter, in provocative dishabille without any thought of sex entering his mind is a virtual impossibility. The daughter, looking upon him not as a father but merely as her mother's husband, may make the situation more acute by applying to him the semisexual behaviorisms that have proved useful in obtaining her way with other males.

Many a father who would rather commit suicide than have sexual contact with his daughter has guiltily repressed incestuous thoughts that come unbidden to his mind. It is hard to recognize sexual attractiveness without being sexually attracted.

At the other extreme one sometimes finds cases that bring to mind the primate families or European peasant families of the past, where the wife and nubile daughters were regarded as the personal property of the male to do with as he pleased. Even today in some nations incest is looked upon as a family problem rather than a matter calling for legal action by society. In these cases the male's basic attitude is a simple and not illogical one: "I've reared them, fed them, and protected them for years; by rights I should have sexual access to them in recompense." Vestiges of this old pattern remain in some of our culturally "backward" communities and urban slums. These vestiges are not only recognized but expected by the persons involved—"Pop's drinking again tonight, Sis; you'd better go over and stay with Aunt Jennie." Such a situation, accepted as one of life's hazards by the participant, is enough to send the college-educated social worker running for the nearest policeman.

The overall impression is of a group of impoverished, uneducated farmers or ranchers of less than average intelligence. This impression is substantiated by the facts: 14 of the 25 grew to adulthood in rural surroundings, another 3 were rural for a large proportion of their formative years, 11 were well below average in intelligence, and only 5 were above average. Four families could rival the Jukes and Kallikaks.

As one would judge from all this, the most common incest offender against adults was of the subculture variety. Such an offender was a member of a Tobacco Road type of milieu wherein incest was regarded as unfortunate but not unexpected. A few were of the amoral delinquent variety. An amoral delinquent in a subculture situation can be recognized chiefly by his greater tendency toward serious crime, marital instability, and aggressiveness, but differentiation is admittedly difficult in some instances.

One example of a subculture offender is a male, aged about 40 at conviction, who had been born and reared in rural Oklahoma until he was 18, and thereafter lived a nomadic life in the western states doing unskilled and semiskilled labor. He did not go beyond the eighth grade and was rated as "dull-normal" in intelligence. At 15 he had his first coitus with a divorcee more than twice his age; 4 years later he married a woman of his own age who was pregnant by her uncle. The marriage broke up after 5 years and they did not see one another for about 15 years, when they met by accident at a carnival where the woman (still legally married to the subject) and her common-law husband were employed. Through their conversation at this chance meeting the wife learned enough to find him later, and she and the 19-year-old daughter, who was already a mother and divorcee, appeared and took up residence with him. He was not particularly interested in a reconciliation, and his wife was in the terminal stages of a pregnancy by her common-law husband. His daughter (actually his stepdaughter), however, was sexually attractive, and since he had not seen her since her early childhood it "seemed just like being with a strange woman." Flirtation developed into petting and finally coitus. The wife caught them and in the ensuing quarrel the man told her to leave the house, which she did. The incestuous arrangement continued (and resulted in pregnancy) until the father and daughter had a fight, the police were called, and the daughter, in a fury, told about the incest. The officials recognized this as a subculture case, the probation officer stating, "The girl of 19 appears to be mentally and morally below average—no force or threats were probably necessary." The district attorney stated, "In view of the low intellectual and moral conditions surrounding all the members of this family it is the recommendation of this office that the defendant be given a short sentence"; and the prison psychologist remarked that the man's actions were "mostly explained by the social and cultural patterns of a primitively organized family group and his behavior is not uncommon in his native locale."

Aside from the subculture and amoral delinquent varieties, the remaining offenders who could be classified were a motley group; two senile deteriorates, two situational cases, and several other varieties represented by only one or two men each.

One important aspect of the incest offenders against adults was obvious during the reading of each case history in our search for varieties of offenders. This is their ability to be religious, moralistic, intolerant, and sexually inhibited, and at the same time to live a life of disorganization, drunkenness, violence, and sexual activity opposed to their religious tenets. This incongruence usually occasions no psychological stress, or at least none that cannot be relieved by periodic open repentance. The incest offenders against adults were the "most religious" of any offenders, nearly half being classed as devout. Nearly all of these devout men were members of Pentecostal sects or were "hard-shell" Baptists and Methodists.

A second and more important aspect of the incest offenders against adults is that most were behaviorally but not legally offenders against minors: of the 21 cases with sufficient data for determining the age of the daughter when the incestuous behavior began, in 13 the initial contact took place when the daughter was aged 12 to 15. In three cases she was under 12 and in only five cases was she 16 or more. The general rule seems to be that in the eyes of these offenders puberty renders a female eligible for sexual exploitation. One might very well regard the incest offenders against adults as chiefly incest offenders against minors who were not found out until later. Why were they belatedly apprehended? Probably because their familial and social milieu (their subculture) was such that the incest came to the attention of the authorities only through unlikely chance.

This likeness between the incest offenders against adults and the incest offenders against minors explains why the two groups are so frequently similar in various measurements.

The five men who began their incest after their daughters were 16 were all rural in their formative years, all had moderate to restrained sexual histories (none had extramarital coitus except with a daughter, and only three had premarital coitus), at least four of the five did not rate better than dull-normal in intelligence, and only one of the five was devoutly religious. None had more than a grammar school education. Aside from their lack of devoutness, these five men look much like the other incest offenders against adults.

PEEPERS

Peepers are adult males who, for their own sexual gratification, looked into some private domicile or into some area or room reserved exclusively for females with the hope of seeing females nude or partially nude, the observation being made without the consent of the females concerned. The term "peeper," as thus defined, is not quite synonymous with the term "voyeur," which is broader. A voyeur is a person who, according to the dictionary, "attains sexual gratification by looking at sexual objects or situations." Thus, a lounger on the street watching passing women, or a person watching a striptease act could qualify as a voyeur, and so could the peruser of "cheesecake" magazines. One might say the peeper is a voyeur who has no legal right to be at the location whence he observes, but even this definition is imperfect since a man has a right to be on a public street at night, but is liable to arrest if he stands on the sidewalk looking into the window of the adjacent apartment house.

We prefer to limit our classification to the stereotype of the "Peeping Tom," the man who looks at females through some opening in a building. Such limitation excludes only a very few cases and, frankly, these cases should be excluded. Whereas the basic motivation may be the same, there is great psychologic and personality difference between the ordinary surreptitious peeper and the man who, let us say, persuades or hires a female to undress before him. The peeper in our sense of the word seldom desires any prearrangement with the person or persons observed; he wants to see them behaving in presumed privacy; he prefers the authentic to the contrived. True, on rare occasions the peeper may believe (sometimes rightly) that the female has become aware of his presence and is "putting on a show," and this he finds contributes more to his sexual excitement. However, in these rare circumstances we are no longer dealing with pure peeping; an unsolicited element of deliberate feminine seductiveness, an erotic stimulus under any circumstances, has been added. A few peepers deliberately draw attention to themselves by, for example, tapping on the window or slipping a note under a door, but here again this represents an extraneous element: a desire to frighten or embarrass, or a desire to elicit a reciprocal interest —motivations usually associated with exhibitionists. The vast majority of peepers try to avoid detection.

One of the complications in studying peeping is the fact that virtually all males have voyeuristic and peeping tendencies. No one is apt to quarrel with this generalization even though we do not have statistical data to substantiate it.[1] The differentiation between the average man and the peeper is not one of seeking visual stimuli, but of willingness to assume risks in obtaining the stimuli. To cite a simple example, the average man may slow his step as he passes a window with the shade up, but he is unwilling to cross the lawn and press his nose against the pane. Unfortunately, for our analyses, the hypothetical average man may yield to temptation a few times in his life (especially when younger) and thereby become a part of our category of convicted peepers. Thus this category is a mixture of "real" peepers who have a long-standing and rather compulsive pattern of peeping, and individuals who have simply yielded to impulse once or twice and had the misfortune to be caught.

Still another, though minor, complication is constituted by the prowler, the opportunistic amateur burglar. Such a person roves about, usually by night, on the lookout for anything of value. If in the course of his prowling he has the opportunity to see nudity or sexual activity, he avails himself of it as an unexpected bit of luck. If he is arrested as a peeper, he is not apt to state that he was in actuality looking for something to steal; in fact, if he has a prior record of larceny, he may be happy to plead guilty to a peeping charge.

Like all men, the peepers have preferences and standards of sexual attractiveness; the simple act of peeping is not sufficient gratification—the person observed must be aesthetically acceptable. Virtually all peepers are looking for adult females with at least a modicum of physical attractiveness. The ideal, of course, is to see an attractive female engaged in some sort of sexual activity. As a group, peepers are persevering optimists. In this way they remind one of ardent fishermen, undaunted by failure and always hoping that the next time their luck will be better. Just as the fisherman will wait patiently for hours, so will the peeper wait patiently for a female to finish some interminable minor chores before going to bed—and then, like as not, she may turn off the light before undressing. Again like the fisherman who keeps a list of areas where fishing is especially good, the peeper not infrequently has in mind a number of particularly likely places to which he returns.

In childhood and youth peeping is commonly a joint venture involving two or more persons, but in adult life it is always a solitary activity. There seem to be two major reasons for this. First of all, it is difficult to find another adult male willing to admit that he is a peeper and willing to share the risks of peeping expeditions. One can scarcely take a census of one's friends and acquaintances in a search for possible peeping partners without disclosing one's own proclivities and incurring censure. Second, the presence of a witness almost necessarily inhibits one's sexual response. A substantial number of peepers masturbate while watching, and in our culture to be seen masturbating, as an adult, is an extreme embarrassment. The masturbating peeper would be doubly vulnerable to ribald remarks and derogatory jests.

One characteristic of the peeper is that he almost never watches females whom he knows well. This is not a precaution against being recognized; he simply does not find in known females the satisfaction he seeks.

Acquaintanceship does not necessarily disqualify a woman, but it is extremely rare to find adults peeping at a "girl friend," relative, or spouse. All the peepers who were questioned on this point expressed a definite preference for females who were strangers. The human, and especially masculine, interest in novelty and diversity is doubtless an important factor here.

The most common variety of peepers is the sociosexually under-developed: nearly one-third of the peepers fit this description. They have much less heterosexual experience than is customary for their age and socioeconomic status, they are shy with females, and have strong feelings of inferiority. Intelligence does not seem a significant variable; these men range from dull to superior. As we have said, marriage does not remove a man from this category—it is no cure for peeping.

Among the sociosexually underdeveloped, peeping often becomes a repetitive and important part of sexual life, frequently substituting for masturbation fantasy. The linkage between masturbation and peeping is mutually reinforcing, and for some men peeping-plus-masturbation becomes a truly compulsive activity carried on over lengthy periods of time.

A classic example is a man who was in his mid-20s when we inter-viewed him. He had begun petting at 14 and had petted with a modest number of females, but had gone beyond above-the-waist stimulation with only two girls. When he was 17 he had coitus three times with one girl and none thereafter. Timidity and an overwhelming fear of being rejected kept him from seeking more heterosexual activity which he strongly desired. His fear of rejection began, insofar as he knows, with a traumatic event shortly after he reached puberty and was experi-encing the usual quick and intense sexual arousal at that period of life. Circumstances forced him to share a bed with his married sister and he became extremely aroused and desirous of coitus. Unable to express his wish, he simply showed her his erect penis. She rejected him violently and harangued him at length on how vile he was. Ever since then he had felt extremely awkward and hesitant about approaching females sexually, and every rebuff was excruciating.

He began peeping regularly, first at his sister through a keyhole, and later at other women through windows, usually masturbating while doing so and reaching orgasm. The peeping became a compulsion which he was unable to resist despite repeated arrests. Heterosexual petting—in which he engaged to a mild degree—did not satisfy his sexual or emo-tional needs, and his sensitivity about being rejected was so great that he ceased trying for coitus after four rebuffs. He found the idea of coitus with a prostitute unappealing and, moreover, he was strongly afraid of catching a venereal disease.

Of the five peepers who exhibited fetishistic behavior (in every case female lingerie was the fetish), three belonged to the sociosexually underdeveloped variety.

Another variety, constituting perhaps 1 peeper in 10, is the drunk. In essence, these are men who would not, and did not, peep while sober, but when their control was weakened by alcohol they either deliberately

set out to peep or else took advantage of an unexpected opportunity t(
do so. Of the six men whom we classed as of the drunken variety, three
were chronic vagrants and one was a professional criminal.

About one-fifth of the peepers may be regarded as the situational
variety—men who availed themselves, while sober or reasonably sober,
of the opportunity to peep. This variety runs a wide gamut. At one end
of the range is a virgin college freshman who had never seen a nude
woman and who stopped to peep into a room where a woman was
undressing. At the opposite end is a married man with a grammar school
education, in his 30s, who had spent nearly half of his life in juvenile
homes, jails, and prisons, who evidently combined pleasure (peeping)
with business (burglary) when the opportunity presented itself.

Perhaps one-eighth of the peepers owed their trouble with the law
to their mental deficiency. These men could not control their impulses
adequately nor could they peep discreetly enough to avoid being caught.
Many of these mental defectives tend to blend with the situational and
drunken varieties of peepers, but the root of their trouble was their low
intelligence rather than circumstances or alcohol.

After subtracting these four varieties, we are still left with about
one-quarter of the peepers unclassified. These men were neither drunken
nor mentally deficient, their sociosexual behavior was generally within
normal limits, and their peeping was not an opportunistic offense. Upon
closer examination it was found that 10 of these 14 men had been convicted of rape and 3 of exhibitionism. In the case of five rapists the
peeping antedated the rape: these are the men who generate the popular notion that peepers become, in time, rapists. While it is true that an
occasional peeper of one of our four varieties may rape, the use of force
is generally uncommon—it happened in only three cases (all of the sociosexually underdeveloped variety).

We cannot determine from our data what behaviorisms differentiate the harmless peeper from the peeper who will subsequently rape,
but we do have the impression that peepers who enter homes or other
buildings in order to peep, and peepers who deliberately attract the
female's attention (tapping on windows, leaving notes, etc.) are more
likely to become rapists than are the others.

REFERENCE

1. Hamilton, G. V. *A research in marriage.* New York: Boni, 1929.

Fetishism and Sadomasochism

When we move away from blatantly abnormal sexuality such as rape, it becomes clear why there is confusion about definitions and classifications. In the following article, Paul Gebhard describes fetishism and sadomasochism and touches on such phenomena as transvestism and bondage. Though many professionals would disagree, none of these behaviors would be labeled as abnormal according to our definition—except under very specific circumstances. That is, if the behavior caused the person himself (or herself) guilt or anguish, if it brought shame and unhappiness to the person's immediate family, and/or if it involved the use of force on unwilling participants, then and only then would we be willing to speak of abnormality.

In the cases to be described, it is pointed out that both fetishism and sadomasochism represent extreme examples of characteristics shared by most individuals. Dr. Gebhard mentions a male who is sexually aroused only by females with red hair. If such an individual were able to attract a redheaded mate, what reason would anyone have to be upset by this preference? To take more unusual instances, what if someone wants a stuffed teddy bear on the bed during intercourse, or likes his or her partner to wear a metallic belt, or enjoys being spanked as part of foreplay, or is excited by a Lone Ranger mask or recordings of John Philip Sousa marches? So long as such proclivities contribute only to happiness and sexual pleasure, no one need condemn the person in question to a psychiatric-diagnostic category nor strive to alter the behavior in order to make the individual conform to an arbitrary standard of "normality." The only real problem for someone strongly oriented toward any sexual specialty is to locate a partner who enthusiastically shares or at least contentedly tolerates the behavior in question.

Fetishism and Sadomasochism

Paul H. Gebhard

It is appropriate to consider these two phenomena together since they frequently intermingle. Sadomasochism very often incorporates fetishistic elements, and one may with justification regard much of the sadomasochistic paraphernalia as fetish objects since the sight or touch of these devices can engender sexual arousal. Fetishism, however, is less dependent on sadomasochism: one type of fetishism is almost devoid of it. The two phenomena do share certain relationships. In mild and often unconscious form they are both moderately common in the general population; they occur in both heterosexuality and homosexuality;

Reprinted in an edited version from: Gebhard, P. H. Fetishism and sadomasochism. *Science and Psychoanalysis*, 1969, **15**, 71–80.

and in more extreme form they are true paraphilias with neurotic compulsive elements.

While there exists a substantial literature on both fetishism and sadomasochism, virtually all of it is based on the more extreme forms which have come to clinical or legal attention. The milder forms have largely escaped attention except for speculative essays or for passing observations appended to a study of some other phenomenon such as violence. Those fetishists and sadomasochists who have not run afoul of the law or who have not encountered clinical scrutiny remain an unknown majority.

In their milder forms—such as the opinion that high heels add to feminine allure or the impulse to pinch a well-rounded buttock—these phenomena involve millions of United States males. Even the more extreme manifestations may be found in thousands rather than hundreds of individuals. These quantitative aspects fully justify giving more attention to fetishism and sadomasochism, especially in a social era marked by increasing concern about mental health and violence. Even beyond this, studies of these phenomena can elucidate much of the etiology and function of normal sexuality, just as study of a malfunctioning or atypical organ of the body can show us something about the function of the normal organ.

In our present state of knowledge the Institute for Sex Research cannot offer any reasoned theories buttressed by factual data. We can, however, present some findings and ideas which should prove useful and suggest future lines of investigation.

FETISHISM

The initial stumbling block in sexual studies is generally a lack of reasonably precise definition, and my first task is to describe what I consider fetishism. Freud and most psychiatrists and analysts use substitution as the basic criterion: the fetish functions much as a substitute for the "normal sexual object."[1] This criterion at once gives rise to vexing questions. Must the substitution be total or partial? What if the putative fetish is not a substitute, but a highly desirable adjunct to sexual activity? Or, to push the matter to the boundary of absurdity, is a sexstarved shepherd a victim of ewe fetishism? Obviously supplementary criteria are required. Phyllis Greenacre[6] attempted to fulfill this need with a more rigorous definition: "We may define fetishism as the obligatory use of some non-genital object as a part of the sexual act without which gratification cannot be obtained. The object may be some other body part or some article of clothing and less frequently some more impersonal object." Even this definition has deficiencies. The word "obligatory" rules out too many cases, and the "non-genital object" which may be a "body part" implies that use of the mouth or hand could constitute fetishism.

Rather than become involved in a definition of Talmudic intricacy I wish to present an operational definition which has proved satisfactory in dealing with fetishism in overt form or at a conscious level. I envision the whole matter of fetishism as a gradated phenomenon. At one end of the range is slight preference; next is strong preference; next is the point where the fetish item is a necessity to sexual activity; and at the terminal end of the range the fetish item substitutes for a living sexual partner. Nearly all humans have preferences as to the physical or sartorial attributes of their sexual partners. Hence I feel that statistical normality ends and fetishism begins somewhere at the level of strong preference. This is nicely exemplified by one man who had his first recognition of his own fetishism when he realized he had ignored a beautiful girl to court a plain girl with a particular hair style. The next stage, that of necessity, would be the case of a man who is impotent unless his partner wears a certain type of shoe. The ultimate stage is the man who habitually dispenses with the female and achieves orgasm with only the shoe.

As more speculation than information, I suggest that there seems to be escalation of degree of fetishism only when the individual suffers from some other sexual maladjustment. A youth who has not yet established a satisfactory sociosexual life may experience an upsurge of fetishism (often female lingerie) which declines when he later develops heterosexual or homosexual liaisons. An old man may also experience an escalation of fetishism as problems of impotence appear—here the fetish is employed as a crutch upon which he may increasingly depend. If age or poor health radically diminishes the sexual drive the fetishism tends to die out before the basic sexuality is extinguished. This same gerontological denouement is seen equally often in cases of sadomasochism. Some fairly substantial amount of sexual drive seems necessary to maintain a paraphilia. Several middle-aged men have told me that obtaining sexual partners is difficult enough without the additional burden of finding one with, or tolerant of, the paraphilia. An aging person cannot afford to be particular lest he doom himself to involuntary celibacy. In some respects the decline of paraphilia reminds one of the "burning out" seen in aging narcotic addicts.

One can divide fetishism into two major classes: In one the fetish in its purer—or at least more distinctive—form is an inanimate object; in the other the fetish is some physical attribute of the sexual partner, aptly labeled "partialism."[3] The latter blends with normality so inextricably that it can be differentiated only in certain extreme forms. Thus we would not call a man a breast fetishist because he insisted his female partners had at least vestigial mammae, but we would label as a hair fetishist a man who could have coitus only with redheads. Because of this difficulty of differentiating and because in partialism the stage of substitution cannot be attained (except for hair fetishists) short of necrophilic amputation, I shall confine the remainder of this discussion of fetishism to the class of inanimate objects.

We have divided inanimate fetishism into two types: media and form. Fetish items are often a combination of both, but in such instances one type is considered more important by the individual than the other. Also, a person may have several fetishes, some of one type and some of the other, but generally one is dominant. A media fetish is one where the substance rather than the form of the object is the important aspect. Leather fetishism is an excellent example: the person responds to leather and whether it be a coat, glove, or shoe is less consequential. A form fetish is one where the form of the object is more important than the material of which it is constituted. Shoe fetishism is a good example of this.

Media fetishism can be usefully subdivided into two subtypes. Without intending any humor I have labeled these "hard" and "soft." Hard fetish objects are generally smooth, slick, and with a hard metallic sheen. Leather, rubber, and lately plastics, exemplify this. Hard fetish items are often tight constricting garments or shoes, usually black. Note that in our culture a tight black shiny dress is regarded as the trademark of the *femme fatale*. Hard media fetishism very frequently is associated with sadomasochism. In other cases the hard media fetishist in his or her tight garb feels secure and armored against the world, much like a matron who feels soft and vulnerable without her corset, or the military officer who feels ineffectual out of uniform.

Soft media fetish objects are fluffy, frilly, or soft in texture. Fur and lingerie are common examples. There is no emphasis on constriction or tightness. Color is generally less important, although black is a favorite. Soft media fetishism, despite Sacher-Masoch, is not usually associated with sadomasochism. Effective combinations of hard and soft media fetishism are commonly exploited in burlesque and floor shows.

Form fetishism is potentially limitless, but the most common items are clothing and foot gear. Shoe fetishism nearly always involves high heels which in our society symbolize adulthood and sexuality. High heels often are associated with sadomasochism: to be stepped upon by a female with long sharp heels on her shoes is a classic masochistic theme. Conversely, extremely high heels functionally cripple a female and turn her into a sexual object incapable of flight and hence appeal to the bondage enthusiast or sadist. Boot fetishism is almost totally affiliated with sadomasochism. Until the recent fashion for them, high boots were the trademark of prostitutes specializing in sadomasochism.

Lingerie fetishism is the extreme form of an interest common to many males. Every Christmas the stores sell large quantities of black or red lingerie and the purchasers are predominately males buying these sexually enhancing garments for their wives or girl friends. Clothesline thefts of lingerie are a common police problem.

Garter fetishism has undergone a metamorphosis. The garter has been associated with sex for centuries. Note, for example, its role in Jewish weddings and the inevitable garter on chorus girls from cancan dancer days to recent times. However, in the past 15 years the garter as a fetish item has been largely replaced by the garter belt, which has become almost a standard fixture in pornographic photographs and films.

Stockings, especially black mesh hose, have a strong fetishistic value, but at the preference level. True stocking fetishists are quite rare. The same is true of glove fetishism, but the glove seems to be suffering a decline since it plays a lesser part in current feminine dress. Black opera length gloves nevertheless remain a part of sadomasochistic costume.

Corset fetishism was once prevalent and certain corsetry shops sold space at peepholes whereby men could glimpse customers trying on corsets. As the corset declined in popularity and became a symbol of stout matrons rather than of beauties such as Lillian Russell, it rapidly declined as a fetish item. Corset fetishism now survives as an adjunct to bondage and sadomasochism.

Other form fetishes are numerically less important. Interestingly enough, some items of dress seem unsuited for fetishism. Hats are one example. One might reasonably expect that brassieres would be almost as popular as underpants, but inexplicably they are seldom fetish items despite our cultural emphasis on breasts as sexual centers of interest.

At this juncture it must be noted that transvestism is related to fetishism, but not synonymous with it. Many transvestites report no conscious sexual arousal from wearing clothing of the opposite sex and do not fixate on any special piece of clothing. In a questionnaire distributed by Virginia Prince to 390 transvestites only 13% reported any fetishistic feelings. Two-thirds of the males said they felt they had a feminine component which was seeking expression through transvestism. The remaining 11% were transsexuals who felt they were women trapped in male bodies.[7]

The various theories as to the etiology of fetishism all suffer from fatal flaws. Freud's hypothesis that the fetish substitutes for the male genitals and hence protests against castration fear seems corroborated by the rarity of fetishism among females, but it does not stand up under scientific scrutiny. Michael Balint suggests the fetishist's entire body is phallic and hence the fetishist inserts it into hollow objects such as shoes, gloves, and clothing—all being symbols of female genitalia.[2] Phyllis Greenacre thinks fetishism arises from a disturbance of body image in early life.[6] Caprio regards it as symbolic masturbation.[4] Allen says it is an attempt to return to mother.[1] Frankly, I find all these and other theories grossly inadequate. Actually the only important elements of fetishism now known are these: (1) It is confined to well-developed civilizations, especially European-American cultures. It is essentially nonexistent in preliterate cultures. (2) It is far rarer in females than in males. (3) It is usually associated with the body, clothing, or body by-products. (4) It seems almost wholly a sexual phenomenon. Aside from the fixation of some children on their blankets or particular toys, and an occasional adult's dependence on some lucky piece, it is difficult to think of nonsexual analogies. (5) It generally manifests itself in puberty or adolescence, but can be induced even in adult life by some trauma or powerful experience.

I agree with psychoanalysts that fetishism is basically a matter of symbolism. Physical attributes or objects assume a sexual symbolic value through association. The process stops here with the average person, but the fetishist falls victim to what Whitehead called "the fallacy of misplaced concreteness": the symbol is given all the power and reality of the actual thing and the person responds to the symbol just as he would to the thing. Due to the greater sexual responsiveness of the male he is more liable to such sexual association than the average female, and he is especially vulnerable in puberty and adolescence when sexuality becomes powerful and when he has been exposed to the symbols of sex before experiencing the actuality of sociosexual gratification. Perhaps the seeming absence of fetishism in preliterate cultures is due to the frequent tolerance of childhood sex play and early knowledge of coitus. If this be true, a study of a prudish preliterate society should unearth cases of fetishism. On the other hand perhaps fetishism can develop only in a literate civilization wherein there is from infancy on a great use of and dependence on a multiplicity of verbal, written, and other symbols. This seemingly feeble idea is reinforced by the fact that fetishism seems largely confined to literate people taught to be imaginative and to make extensive use of symbolism in verbal and written communication and hence in their thought processes. This theory does not explain why some people become fetishists and others in the same culture do not, but it at least is in agreement with what little we know about fetishism.

SADOMASOCHISM

Sadomasochism may be operationally defined as obtaining sexual arousal through receiving or giving physical or mental pain. Unlike fetishism, analogues are common among other mammalian species wherein coitus is preceded by behavior which under other circumstances would be interpreted as combative. Temporary phases of actual fighting may be interspersed in such precoital activity. In some species, such as mink, sexual activity not infrequently results in considerable wounds. This precoital activity has definite neurophysiological value in establishing, or reinforcing, many of the physiological concomitants of sexual arousal such as increased pulse and blood pressure, hyperventilation, and muscular tension. Indeed one may elicit sexual behavior in some animals by exciting them with nonsexual stimuli. This may explain why sadomasochism is used as a crutch by aging men in our society who require some extra impetus to achieve arousal. From a phylogenetic viewpoint it is no surprise to find sadomasochism in human beings.

Sadomasochism is embedded in our culture, which operates on the basis of dominance-submission relationships. Aggression is socially valued. Even our gender relationships have been formulated in a framework conducive to sadomasochism: the male is supposed to be dominant and aggressive sexually while the female is reluctant or submissive. Violence and sex are commingled to make a profitable package to sell through the mass media. This is no innovation—for centuries the masochistic damsel in distress has been victimized by the evil sadist who is finally defeated by the hero through violent means.

Relatively few sadomasochists are exclusively sadists or exclusively masochists; there is generally a mixture with one aspect predominant. This mixing sometimes is necessitated by circumstances: sexual partners are extremely difficult to find and consequently, for example, if two masochists meet they are obliged to take turns at the sadist role. This role trading is made easier by ability to project. The masochist playing the sadist may fantasy himself receiving the pain he is inflicting.

Sadists are far rarer than masochists, and female sadists are so highly prized that masochists will travel hundreds of miles to meet them. I postulate that this imbalance between sadists and masochists is a product of our culture wherein physical violence, particularly to someone of the opposite gender, is taboo and productive of intense guilt. To strike is sin; to be struck is guiltless or even virtuous in a martyrdom sense. Even more psychodynamically important is masochism as an expiation for the sin of sexuality. During childhood, puberty, and part of adolescence sexual behavior is punished and it is easy to form an association between sexual pleasure and punishment. The masochist has a nice guilt-relieving system—he gets his punishment simultaneously with his sexual pleasure or else is entitled to his pleasure by first enduring the punishment.

It is important to realize that pain per se is not attractive to the masochist, and generally not to the sadist, unless it occurs in an arranged situation. Accidental pain is not perceived as pleasurable or sexual. The average sadomasochistic session usually is scripted: the masochist must allegedly have done something meriting punishment, there must be threats and suspense before the punishment is meted out, etc. Often the phenomenon reminds one of a planned ritual or theatrical production. Indeed, sadomasochistic prostitutes often report their clients give them specialized instructions to follow. Genet's *Balcony* is true to life. When one appreciates this, one realizes that often in the relationship the sadist is not truly in charge—the sadist is merely servicing the masochist. The sadist must develop an extraordinary perceptiveness to know when to continue, despite cries and protests, and when to cease. A sadist who goes too far or stops prematurely may find his ineptitude has cost him a sexual partner. Not infrequently sadomasochistic activity is interspersed with loving and tenderness. This alternation makes the process far more powerful. Police and brainwashers use the same technique of alternate brutality and sympathy to break their subjects.

Sadomasochism is extremely complex. Some achieve orgasm during the pain; in other cases the sadomasochism only constitutes the foreplay and the session culminates in conventional sexual behavior. Some masochists dislike the pain while it is being inflicted, but obtain gratification by anticipation of the pain or by thinking about it after it has ceased. Lastly, there are the bondage people who do not enjoy pain but are stimulated by constraint, mild discomfort, and a sense of helplessness. Bondage has both sadistic and masochistic aspects. The sadist has the pleasure of rendering his partner helpless and at his mercy—a favorite sexual theme in mythology, literature, and fantasy. The masochist bondage enthusiast enjoys not only the restraint itself but the guilt-relieving knowledge that if anything sexual occurs it is not his or her fault. Also as Dr. Douglas Alcorn points out, some persons derive a sense of comfort and security from physical constraint. Lastly the hood, often used in bondage, offers the advantage of depersonalization and heightens the helplessness through interfering with sight, hearing, and vocalization.

Both sadomasochism and bondage are often replete with fetish items including specialized clothing and restraint or torture devices. All this offers the devotee substantial additional gratification. The average heterosexual or homosexual has relatively little paraphernalia for supplementary pleasure and it offers scant opportunity for ingenuity or creativity.

The prevalence of unconscious sadomasochism is impossible to ascertain, but it must be large if one can make inferences from book and magazine sales and from box office reports. We do know that consciously recognized sexual arousal from sadomasochistic stimuli is not rare. The Institute for Sex Research found that about one in eight females and one in five males were aroused by sadomasochistic stories, and roughly half of both sexes were aroused by being bitten.

The etiology of sadomasochism, while the subject of much writing especially in the form of interminable German books, is not well understood. In individual cases the genesis may be clear as psychoanalysis and psychiatry amply demonstrate, but these individualistic explanations do not suffice for the phenomenon as a whole. After all, the supply of English headmasters and Austrian girl friends is limited. We must turn to broad hypotheses, and I will offer a rather simplistic one.

First, we may assume on the basis of mammalian studies and history that we humans have built-in aggressive tendencies. Second, it is equally clear that males are on the whole more aggressive than females.

Experiments indicate this is in large part an endocrine matter: androgens elicit or enhance aggression. Third, animal and human social organization is generally based on a dominance-submissiveness relationship, a peck-order. Fourth, when one couples the difficulties of sexual gratification with the problems involved in living in a peck-order society, one has an endless source of frustration which lends itself to expression in pathological combinations of sex and violence. Note that in our own culture when we wish to say that someone was badly victimized we use sexual terms such as, "he got screwed." From a rational viewpoint we should apply the words "he got screwed" to someone who has had a pleasurable experience, but we have unfortunately mixed sex with dominance-submissiveness behavior.

This using sex as a symbol brings up the puzzle as to why explicitly sexual sadomasochism, like fetishism, seems the monopoly of well-developed civilizations. One never hears of an aged Polynesian having to be flogged to obtain an erection, and for all their torture and bloodshed there seem to have been no de Sades among the Plains Indians or Aztecs. While it is true that in various preliterate societies sexual activity often involves moderate scratching and biting, well-developed sadomasochism as a life style is conspicuous by its absence. It may be that a society must be extremely complex and heavily reliant upon symbolism before the inescapable repressions and frustrations of life in such a society can be expressed symbolically in sadomasochism. Sadomasochism is beautifully suited to symbolism: what better proof of power and status is there than inflicting humiliation or pain upon someone who does not retaliate? And what better proof of love is there than enduring or even seeking such treatment?

REFERENCES

1. Allen, C. *The sexual perversions and abnormalities.* New York: Oxford University Press, 1949.

2. Balint, M. A contribution of fetishism. *International Journal of Psychoanalysis,* 1935, **16,** 481–483.

3. Caprio, F. *Variations in sexual behavior.* New York: Citadel Press, 1955.

4. Caprio, F. Fetishism. In A. Ellis and A. Abarbanel (Eds.), *Encyclopedia of sexual behavior.* 1961.

5. Freud, S. *Collected papers.* Vol. 5. London: Hogarth, 1950.

6. Greenacre, P. Certain relationships between fetishism and faulty development of the body image. *Psychoanalytic Study of the Child,* 1953, **8,** 79–98.

7. Prince, V. *A survey of 390 cases of transvestism.* Los Angeles, privately printed, 1965.

Sex and the Medical Model

In view of current relatively permissive sexual attitudes and relatively varied sexual practices, we can look back in wonder at the fact that some of today's most widely practiced sexual acts have been repeatedly denounced as immoral, unhealthful, maladjusted, and illegal. How could such ideas have originated and how could they remain at least partially operative today?

Historian Vern Bullough traces the development of these erotophobic formulations across more than 2 centuries of medical thought which contained a pervasively antisex bias. Sex was equated with illness and weakness, and hence was to be avoided except for the necessities of procreation. Sexual acts that could not possibly lead to conception—masturbation, oral sex, anal sex, and so forth—were sufficiently horrifying as to require harsh legal sanctions against anyone so depraved as to "defy the laws of nature." Some of the older quotations are amusing in their antisexual hysteria buttressed by erroneous beliefs, and yet they provided the historical framework for many current laws against various sexual practices. And, lest we think that all this lies buried in the restrictive history of our culture, it should be remembered that many bright college students today still believe that masturbation causes mental and emotional harm, that prostitutes are still being arrested regularly all across the nation, and that the U. S. Supreme Court in 1976 ruled, in effect, that a state such as Virginia was within its constitutional rights to prosecute anyone who committed an oral or anal sex act.

The precise statute that was upheld appears in the *Code of Virginia,* Section 18.1-212, Crimes against nature, and it states:

> If a person shall carnally know in any manner any brute animal, or carnally know any male or female by the anus or by or with the mouth, or voluntarily submit to such carnal knowledge, he or she shall be guilty of a felony and shall be confined in the penitentiary for not less than one year nor more than three years.

There is another aspect of the medical model of "abnormal" sexuality that should be mentioned. Even where the most virulent sexual prejudices have died down, moral condemnation and legal punishment of an individual's sexual preferences tend to be replaced by psychiatric and psychological concepts of psychopathology. Thus, if society does not imprison the sexually deviant person, it can seek treatment for him or her and thus attempt to cure the illness. Psychotherapy is infinitely more humane than legal harassment, but it still has all too often rested on shifting quasi-moralistic definitions of what should and should not be done sexually. When psychiatrists declassified homosexuality as an illness in 1974, the medical profession took a giant step away from its antisexual past.

Sex and the Medical Model

Vern L. Bullough

In 1974 the American Psychiatric Association removed homosexuality from the category of a pathological illness. The removal raises two sorts of questions which I would like to examine—first, how a behavior can be classed as pathological one day and not the next, and second, what continuing effect the original erroneous classification has upon our society. Since I am a historian I would like to put these ideas into a historical context and project some implications for society today.

Definitions of what constitutes dangerous sexual behavior for the past 100 years or so have been in terms of what might be called the medical model. Instead of using the reference to sin or to evil or to unnaturalness which was once applied to certain forms of sexual behavior, the medical community defined certain activities as pathological, and by implication they then became an illness. The medical model had the advantage over the previous religious definitions of being changeable; that is, when new findings appeared they could be incorporated into the model and ultimately, as in the case of homosexuality, new definitions could be developed. It had the disadvantage of validating certain unproven assumptions, of giving a sort of scientific *imprimatur* to past prejudices, and this has proven to be disastrous in the field of sexuality—so disastrous in fact, that I would like to argue that it is not enough for the American Psychiatric Association to say that their previous categories of sexual pathology are inoperative, but they also must take cognizance of the damage they had done by their own erroneous assumptions, which in light of other scientific findings should long ago have been discarded. This is because stereotypes about sexual behavior, once established in the medical model, prove very difficult to remove because of the vested interest of the status quo.

Most of our vested medical interests in sexuality were formed in the nineteenth century and are associated with Victorianism. Victorianism was not the last vestige of religious ideology, as is sometimes explained, but rather a new confidence in ideas based upon scientific proof. Sigmund Freud, for example, was very much a Victorian, so was Krafft-Ebing, and so was Cesare Lombroso. What had happened is that a new age of science had given its *imprimatur* to explanations that tended to reconfirm the old religious truths. Though there were some challenges to the old religious beliefs, as in the field of Darwinian evolution, usually there were no such conflicts. Moreover, when science and religion did conflict, it was the scientific evidence that was accepted. But

Reprinted in an edited version from: Bullough, V. L. Sex and the medical model. *Journal of Sex Research*, 1975, **11**, 291–303.

science did not investigate all areas of behavior and in fact tended to accept old religious assumptions without much evidence and then erected these into scientific proofs.

Part of the explanation for this is that the religious model seemed to be so adaptable to the eighteenth-century system builders in medicine, the very time when the foundation of the medical model of sexuality was established. Although the historian can always be accused of tracing ideas backward in time until they are lost in the mists of antiquity, the key transition figure seems to be Hermann Boerhaave (1668–1738), who attempted to build a new system of medicine. In his *Institutiones medicae* Boerhaave[5] wrote that the "rash expenditure of semen" brought on a "lassitude, a feebleness, a weakening of motion, fits, wasting, dryness, fevers, aching of the cerebral membranes," obscuring of the sense, a decay of the spinal cord, "a fatuity, and other like evils." Probably, Boerhaave went from the small observable truths that an orgasm does bring on a degree of lassitude, to a whole theory of orgasm, but the effect was to incorporate traditional Christian prejudice about sex into a system of medicine.

Boerhaave was not alone in this respect and other system builders of the eighteenth century such as Georg Ernest Stahl (1660–1734), Frederick Hoffman (1660–1742), and John Brown (1735–1788) all managed to equate sexuality with illness. Without going into each one of these, Brown might be taken as an example. Basic to Brown's system was the notion of excitability, the seat of which lay in the nervous system. All bodily states were explained by the relationship between excitability and lack of excitability. Too little stimulation was bad, but excessive stimulation could be worse because it could lead to debility by exhausting the excitability. A favorite simile of the Brunonists, as his movement was called, was with fire. Insufficient excitement was compared to a lack of air which would cause the fire to smoulder and go out while too much excitement was like a forced draft which would cause the fire to burn excessively, become exhausted, and go out. Thus there were two kinds of diseases, those arising from excessive excitement and those from deficient excitement. Mutual contact of the sexes as occurred in kissing or close intimate contact gave an impetuosity to the nerves while intercourse could give temporary relief, *providing* it was not engaged in excessively. Too frequent orgasm would release too much energy and excessive loss of semen was to be avoided.[9]

The man who provided the ultimate argument about the dangers of sex was Samuel Tissot (1723–1787), who published his monograph on the dangers of masturbation in 1758. Tissot[24] believed that physical bodies suffered a continual waste, and unless the losses suffered in this process were replaced, death would result. Much of this wastage could be restored through nutrition, but even with an adequate diet, the body could still waste away through diarrhea, loss of blood, and most importantly for our purposes, through seminal emission. Seminal emission in males was particularly dangerous. Some indication of the importance of seminal emission was indicated by the fact that a castrated male tended not to grow a beard and his muscle tone degenerated. Obviously semen was a precious substance, and the loss of it under any condition imposed dangers. Some loss was necessary for purposes of procreation or otherwise the human race would die out, but the male had to carefully husband his semen making absolutely certain that any loss went into procreation. Frequent intercourse in itself was dangerous but the most dangerous activity that men could engage in was the loss of semen from practices not aimed at procreation. Though Tissot used the term "masturbation" to describe such activity, masturbation for him included everything that previously had been included in the Christian concept of sin against nature by the ecclesiastical writers, namely all nonprocreative sex. Loss of semen resulted in or would lead to (1) cloudiness of ideas to the point of madness, (2) decay of bodily powers eventually resulting in coughs, fevers, and consumption (i.e., tuberculosis), (3) acute pain in the head, rheumatic pains, and an aching numbness, (4) pimples on the face, suppurating blisters upon the nose, breast, and thighs as well as painful itching, (5) eventual weakness of the power of generation as indicated by impotence, premature ejaculation, gonorrhea, priapism, tumors in the bladder, and (6) disorders of the intestines, constipation, hemorrhoids, and so forth.

Females who engaged in nonprocreative sex were affected in much the same ways as males but in addition suffered from hysterical fits, incurable jaundice, violent cramps in the stomach, pain in the nose, ulceration of the cervix, and the uterine tremors which deprived them of decency and reason, lowered them to the level of the most lascivious brutes, and caused them to love women more than men. Onanism (a term also used) was far more pernicious than an excess in marital or premarital fornication and if engaged in by young people would ultimately destroy the mental faculties by putting too much strain upon the nervous system.

It was upon this foundation that the nineteenth-century physician built his attitude toward sex. Since I have written upon this subject elsewhere in some detail,[7] it is necessary only to summarize these ideas here. Among the writers who impressed upon the public the dangers of sexuality were Sylvester Graham, Claude-François Lallemand, William Acton, John Harvey Kellogg, George M. Beard, Paul Moreau, Richard von Krafft-Ebing, and even Sigmund Freud, all from much the same theoretical basis advanced by Tissot. In fact each new scientific discovery was seemingly seized upon to inculcate greater fears of sexuality. Critics of the new propagators of the dangers of sexuality wondered why, if sex was so dangerous, civilization had not died out. George M. Beard[2] answered such critics by responding that "modern" civilization had put such increased stress upon mankind that larger and larger numbers of people were suffering from nervous exhaustion. Such exhaustion, he held, was particularly great among the educated brain workers in society who represented a higher stage on the evolutionary scale than the less advanced social classes, and thus as man advanced, it became more and more necessary to save his nervous energy. According to Beard the human body was a reservoir of "force constantly escaping, constantly being renewed [pp. 58, 134–207]," but frequently in danger of imbalance. One of the chief causes of nervous exhaustion was sexual orgasm, and unless the nervous energy which went into it could be carefully regulated and controlled, nervous exhaustion would result.

All developments seemed to document the dangers of sexuality. Cesare Lombroso,[16] for example, held that man represented an advanced stage of animal life and had progressed from a hermaphroditic or self-fertilizing stage to a higher heterosexual phase. In the process of evolution some degenerate forms of man had been left at the levels of bisexuality, since the higher man progressed, the less his sex drives became. Lombroso believed that the life cycle of each individual went through the same as society as a whole, ontogeny recapitulates phylogeny, and that those who were unable to achieve the higher standards of today were pathological cases, perverts, morally insane, and so forth.

As the importance of heredity came to be recognized, this too was seized upon to explain why overt sexuality was pathological. The Frenchman Paul Moreau,[17] for example, held that mankind not only had the traditional five senses of seeing, hearing, smelling, tasting, and feeling, but a sixth sense, a genital sense, which inborn like the others, could also be injured psychically and physically. Usually such injury resulted from a hereditary taint, a sort of predisposition to perversion, but it might be further invoked by certain environmental conditions.

Not infrequently, under the influence of some vice of organism, generally of heredity, the moral faculties may undergo alterations. If these do not actually destroy the social relations of the individual, as happens in cases of declared insanity, they modify them to a remarkable degree, and certainly demand to be taken into account when we have to estimate the morality of these acts.

Nonprocreative sex was looked upon as a contagious disease which, if left untreated, "would lead to the patient practicing more and more [pp. 113–115]" perversions.[13] Cunnilingus and fellatio were said to cause cancer,[3] and if per chance anyone who engaged in "perverted" sex had offspring, the child itself would be born with "perverted instincts."[21] William Acton[1] wrote that the emission of semen imposed such a great drain on the nervous system that the only way a male could avoid damage was to engage in sex infrequently and then without prolonging the sex act. Acton held that males had been able to limit the emission of the semen because God had created females as indifferent to sex; this heavenly act served to prevent the male's vital sexual energy from being overly expended. Only out of fear that their husbands would desert them for courtesans or prostitutes did most women waive their own inclinations and submit to the ardent embraces of their husbands. Even then, there were preservative factors since women's reluctance forced their husbands to perform the necessary biological duty of reproduction in as expeditious a way as possible, thus avoiding severe damage to the nervous system. Still there were dangers if the act was repeated too frequently and any kind of seminal emission, even that aimed at procreation, posed dangers.

Perhaps the ultimate in the absurd was reached by the physician who regarded menstruation as pathological. As evidence for this statement, A. F. A. King,[15] in the *American Journal of Obstetrics*, cited the well-known "fact" that conception was most likely when intercourse occurred during the female's monthly flow, but intercourse at such times was dangerous and forbidden because the menstrual blood was the source of male gonorrhea. Since menstruation, therefore, stood in the way of fruitful coitus, it obviously had not been ordained by nature. This particular bit of misinformation was based upon some actual studies by the German E. F. W. Pfluger,[19] who had demonstrated that menstruation did not take place in women whose ovaries had been removed. This led him to conclude that there was a mechanical stimulus of nerves by the growing follicle in the ovary which was responsible for congestion and menstrual bleeding, and that menstruation and ovulation occurred simultaneously.

Obviously there were investigators who disagreed with the general trend towards classifying most sexual activity as a pathological illness, but their influence was less than it might otherwise have been because of the growing nineteenth-century concern over venereal disease, particularly syphilis. Syphilis is a disease of several stages, not all of which appear obvious, and in fact it was not until the nineteenth century that the full course of the disease was understood, particularly its third stage. The first suspicion that syphilis might have a third stage occurred to an American-born French physician, Philip Ricord,[20] but conclusive evidence had to wait the discovery of microorganisms as a causative agent of disease. This came about through the research of Louis Pasteur. Following Pasteur's discovery, the various disease-carrying organisms were isolated. Albert Neisser in 1879 observed the gonococcus that caused gonorrhea. In 1889 Augusto Ducrey found that soft chancre was caused by a bacillus which he isolated, and in 1905 Fritz Shaudinn and Eric Hoffman found the treponema pallidum, a spirochete, the cause of syphilis. Even this discovery did not give the full story since syphilis proved to be a confusing disease because spirochetes were not found in all patients or in all stages of the disease. Diagnosis, however, was further assisted by the blood-testing method worked out in 1906 by the Berlin bacteriologist August von Wasserman.

Once the organism had been isolated, remedies were sought to deal with it, and the medical model received verification. Here the key investigator was Paul Ehrlich who, with the help of his Japanese assistant, Sahachiro Hata, experimented with a number of compounds which would kill the spirochete yet keep the patient alive. His six hundred and sixth compound, an arsenic derivate which he named salvarsan, proved successful in both respects. Salvarsan, however, was difficult to use, and at times it seemed a race as to whether the spirochete or the patient would be killed first. Ehrlich continued to experiment until, with his nine hundred and fourteenth compound, he isolated a substance which was less dangerous to man but equally dangerous to the spirochete, new salvarsan. Obviously the medical model had proved its effectiveness and if it could cure syphilis, it could also cure sexual "perversions." By implication, and in the minds of many, venereal disease was proof positive of the pathological nature of most sexual activity.

What were the results of the adoption of the concept that all non-procreative sex was basically pathological? A short paper is not the place to develop all of the ramifications, but let me illustrate by looking at three areas briefly: menstruation, prostitution, and homosexuality. Based upon the existing theories about menstruation, a physician, Edward H. Clarke,[10] professor of materia medica at Harvard, in 1874 published an influential book arguing that women were incapable of being educated to the level of man. He stated that males developed steadily and gradually from birth to manhood, while the female underwent a sudden and unique spurt of growth at puberty. From this he concluded that the female between 12 and 20 had to concentrate all her energies on developing her reproductive system and, since this was associated with the development of her nervous system, she could not also indulge in the development of her brain. If a female insisted on developing her brain power by going to school and trying to compete intellectually with males, she would overload the switchboard and the signals from the developing organs of reproduction would be ignored in favor of those coming from the overactive brain. Even after puberty, females were not to exercise their minds without restriction because of their monthly cycles. In fact, so dangerous was intellectual activity during the menstrual period, that Clarke held any mental activity would interfere with ovulation. Women who chose to ignore his advice (and that of other physicians) by intensively studying during their teens, underwent mental changes or suffered nervous breakdowns. He published several case histories of women whose study pushed them into mental illness, and argued that if, per chance, there were women who did not become ill, it was because they were so successful in their studies that they repressed their "maternal instincts" and became sexless humans analogous to eunuchs.

Though there was an immediate unfavorable reaction to Clarke's thesis, it still became widely accepted. His critics pointed out that he had done no scientific study of the matter, that he generalized from a few clinical cases in his own practice, and that much of what he wrote about was simply untrue,[11] but the popularity of his message is indicated by the fact that within 13 years his book went through some 17 editions. One disciple warned that if women continued to be educated, developing their brains at the expense of their reproductive organs, their pelvis would not develop and their increased brain activity would lead them to produce larger-headed children. The result would be a vast increase in maternal mortality from cephalo-pelvic disproportion, so that if women continued on their present path, few American women would be able to bear children.[25]

Eventually, the silliness of Clarke's ideas was exposed and ultimately rejected, in large part because of the growing agitation of women themselves. How deep his ideas penetrated, however, was recalled in 1908 by Martha Carey Thomas, president of Bryn Mawr College. She wrote[23] that as a student she had been "terror-struck lest I, and every other woman with me, were doomed to live as pathological invalids in a universe merciless to women as a sex." She added that she now knew that the superstition she was taught was put out by men who themselves were pathological, "blinded by neurotic mists of sex, unable to see that women" formed one-half of the race of normal, "healthy human creatures in the world [p. 168]." Remnants of such ideas appear in the works of Freud and others. Freud,[12] for example, believed that woman's undeveloped feminine intellect was due to her sexuality which inhibited all other mental effort. Since woman's thirst for knowledge might lead to society regarding this desire as a sign of immoral tendencies, women could only inhibit, repress, sublimating their mental effort and repressing their knowledge. The overtones of such erroneous assumptions as those made by Clarke continue to influence our dialogue, and in part the woman's movement today is an effort to remove some of the remaining hangovers. Although no reputable scientist today would regard menstruation as pathological, the ideas originally based upon such a belief still have influence.[8]

Similarly, the medical community, at least in America and England, entered into an effort to abolish prostitution. The ostensible reason for the entry of the medical profession into the field was an effort to expose and publicize the dangers both of venereal disease and of excessive sexuality. The first organized medical group to begin campaigning against prostitution in this country was organized in February 1905 by some 25 physicians who attended a meeting called by Prince A. Morrow at the New York Academy of Medicine. The original society called itself the

American Society of Sanitary and Moral Prophylaxis, and most of the charter members were physicians. As the movement grew, it changed its name into the American Federation for Sex Hygiene and, after a merger with the American Vigilance Committee, it became the American Social Hygiene Association.[18] Though there had been moral reform groups working on the abolition of prostitution since the middle of the nineteenth century, the appearance of the organized medical community emphasizing the dangers of prostitution on the basis of their own intimate sex knowledge made the situation unique. So rapidly did change come, that by 1920 most of the tolerated districts for prostitution had been closed down, and prostitution in America had gone underground.[6]

The area where the long-term effects of the early erroneous assumptions of the medical model still hold the greatest influence is in the field of law. During the early part of the nineteenth century, American legal attitudes toward sex were a holdover of attitudes expressed in the English common law. Influencing enforcement of these laws were the works of various legal commentators, most notably William Blackstone, whose four volume *Commentaries on the Laws of England* (1765–1769), was conceived as providing a rationale for the common law in history, logic, and "natural laws." Blackstone[4] included several sex-oriented crimes in his discussion, including mayhem, forcible abduction, rape, and the crime against nature.

> What has been here observed, especially with regard to manner of proof, which ought to be the more clear in proportion as the crime is the more detestable, may be applied to another offence, of a still deeper malignity; the infamous *crime against nature*, committed either with man or beast. A crime which ought to be strictly and impartially proved, and then as strictly and impartially punished. But it is an offence of so dark a nature, so easily charged, and the negative so difficult to be proved that the accusations should be clearly made out: for, if false, it deserves a punishment inferior only to that of the crime itself.
>
> I will not act so disagreeable a part, to my readers as well as myself, as to dwell any longer upon a subject, the very mention of which is a disgrace to human nature. It will be more eligible to imitate in this respect the delicacy of our English law, which treats it, in its very indictments, as a crime not fit to be named [Book 4, p. 215].

When the common-law attitudes were enacted into statutory law in the American states, several things happened. It was ruled that oral-genital contacts, even where children were involved, were excluded from the category of crimes against nature.[27] Mere solicitation to commit an act was not an offense, and just exactly what was included in the crime against nature was never quite clear. State courts made all kinds of contradictory decisions. In two early cases, the Texas courts held that since the Texas code did not describe or define what constituted the

"Crime against nature," they were at a loss to determine what was meant. Sodomy, therefore, was found not to be punishable. In 1883 the supreme court of Texas held that it was no longer necessary that an offense be expressly defined and that sodomy could be regarded as a punishable offense under the penal code. In 1893, the Texas court held that since common law did not classify copulation by mouth as sodomy, this could not be regarded as a crime under the Texas sodomy statute. In 1896 and 1905, however, the court ruled that copulation with a woman *per anum* was sodomy and should be so punished. Texas' difficulties with enforcement continued until 1943 when the state code was revised to cover almost every sexual act.[22,26]

Texas offers a rich mine of court cases, but every state has its own treasure trove. In Iowa, for example, in 1860 the courts held that, though sodomy was punishable at common law, it was not a crime in Iowa because it was not included and specified by name in the Iowa criminal code. If definition proved difficult, enforcement was even more troublesome. All this began to change in the last part of the nineteenth century as the organized medical and scientific communities threw their support and assistance to the various state legislatures to make harsher sex laws. In fact, most of the repressive state sex legislation dates from the last part of the nineteenth century, with England showing the way. Homosexual solicitation as well as homosexual activities were outlawed in England in 1886.[14] As the public became more aware of the medical "dangers" of sexuality they were willing to put more limits on sexual expression and most states enacted penal codes designed to curtail sexual activity. In California, for example, penal code 287 was enacted which defined the crime against nature to include "any sexual penetration, however slight," and in 1915 the state added prohibitions against fellatio and cunnilingus[28] and most states adopted similar specific laws, usually with the advice of the medical and scientific community.

Of course, the public was educated to receive these new laws by manuals teaching the dangers of masturbation and excessive sexuality (masturbatory insanity), by devices designed to prevent involuntary seminal emissions, by antimasturbatory girdles, by horror stories of homosexuality, mostly put out with medical acknowledgment. The point to emphasize in this rather long digression is that it is not enough for the psychiatric community to say something is no longer pathological. The damage has been done and the medical and scientific communities contributed to the damage and they have to adopt more positive steps to correct the results of their action.

Today the medical model of sexuality has begun to change, but it should be phased out altogether. Change comes much too slowly to undo the effects of generations of inculcated hostility or to eliminate the bad laws which once had strong medical backing. Obviously, the medical and scientific community should lobby for changes, but the basis for these changes should be the new models of sexual behavior drawn from the social and behavioral sciences. These new norms will not be a panacea and there is the danger that in undoing the bad caused by the medical model, we might well construct the basis for a more serious future misuse. When this has been said, however, I think a social and behavior science model is still far more valid for dealing with sexual behavior than the medical model. It eliminates the stigma of a pathology and overcomes the problem of illness. The problem is to avoid making any model a dogma. All of us have a responsibility to develop new modalities and in the process to be tolerant of findings that differ from ours. All we need is to keep reminding ourselves of some of the nineteenth- and twentieth-century figures who felt they had the ultimate answer in the field of sex.

REFERENCES

1. Acton, W. *The functions and disorders of the reproductive organs in childhood, youth, adult age, and advanced life considered in their physiological, social, and moral relations.* (5th ed.) London: J. & A. Churchill, 1871.

2. Beard, G. M. *Sexual neurasthenia, its hygiene, causes, symptoms, and treatment with a chapter on diet for the nervous.* (Edited by A. D. Rockwell.) New York: E. B. Treat, 1884.

3. Bergeret, L. F. E. *The preventive obstacle or conjugal onanism.* New York: Turner and Mignard, 1898.

4. Blackstone, W. *Commentaries on the laws of England.* New edition with notes by J. F. Archibold, 1811, **4**, 215. London: William Reed.

5. Boerhaave, H. Institutiones medicae. *Opera Medica Universa.* Geneva: Fratres de Tournes, 1728.

6. Bullough, V. L. *History of prostitution.* Secaucus, N.J.: University Books, 1964.

7. Bullough, V. L. Homosexuality and the medical model. *Journal of Homosexuality I.* 1975.

8. Bullough, V., & Voght, M. Women, menstruation, and nineteenth-century medicine. *Bulletin of the History of Medicine,* 1974, **47**, 66–82.

9. Brown, J. *The elements of medicine.* (Revised by T. Beddoes.) Portsmouth, N. H.: William and Daniel Treadwell, 1803.

10. Clarke, E. H. *Sex in education: Or a fair chance for girls.* Boston: James R. Osgood & Company, 1874.

11. Comfort, G. F., & Comfort, A. M. *Woman's education and woman's health.* Syracuse; N. Y.: Thomas W. Durston & Company, 1874.

12. Freud, S. Civilized sexual morality and modern nervousness. *Collected Papers*. (Translated by Joan Riviere.) New York: Basic Books, 1959.

13. Howe, J. *Excessive venery, masturbation and continence*. New York: E. B. Treat, 1889.

14. Hyde, H. M. *The love that dared not speak its name*. Boston: Little, Brown, 1970.

15. King, A. F. A. A new basis for uterine pathology. *American Journal of Obstetrics*, 1875–1876, 7, 242–243.

16. Lombroso, C. *Criminal man*. New Jersey: Patterson Smith, 1972.

17. Moreau, P. *Des aberrations du sens génétique*. Paris: Asselin & Houzeau, 1887.

18. Morrow, P. A. Report of progress. *Social Disease*, 1912, 3, 1–2.

19. Pfluger, E. F. W. Ueber die eierstocke der saugethiere und des menschen. Leipzig: Englemann, 1863.

20. Ricord, P. *Letters on syphilis*. Philadelphia: Blanchard and Lea, 1854.

21. Scott, J. F. *The sexual instinct*. New York: E. B. Treat, 1899.

22. Texas Criminal Reports. *Charlie Prindle* v. *State*, 31 *Texas Criminal Reports*, **551**, 1893; *Alex Lewis* v. *State*, 36 *Texas Criminal Reports*, **37**, 1896; *Algie Adams* v. *State*, 48 *Texas Criminal Reports*, **90**, 1905.

23. Thomas, M. C. Present tendencies in women's college and university education. In W. O'Neill (Ed.), *The woman movement: Feminism in the United States and England*. Chicago: Quadrangle, 1969.

24. Tissot, S. A. D. *Onanism: Or, a treatise upon the disorders of masturbation*. London: J. Pridden, 1766.

25. Van Dyke, F. W. Higher education a cause of physical decay in women. *Medical Records*, 1905, **67**, 296–298.

26. *Vernon's Penal Code of the State of Texas*. Kansas City: Vernon Law Books Company, 1.

27. Wharton, F. A treatise on the criminal law of the U. S. Philadelphia: Kay and Brothers, 1857.

28. *West's Annotated California Codes, Penal Code Sections 211 to 446*. St. Paul, Minn.: West Publishing Company, 1970.

The Homosexual Role

There is an unfortunate tendency among human beings to transform verbal labels that define some aspect of one another into an inclusive description of a *type of person.* All of those assigned to a given typological group by the label are then assumed to behave in a certain uniform manner. These stereotypes have been applied to almost every aspect of appearance, ethnic identity, and behavior. What are the typical characteristics of redheaded women, Italians, lawyers, black teen-agers, middle-aged Texans, blond surfers, fat men, Jewish bankers, boys with long hair, Japanese tourists, or California nudists? The chances are you would be able to express some of the accepted beliefs about each of these groups—even if you know intellectually that the stereotype is ridiculously untrue—because such ideas are expressed with sufficient frequency that we have each absorbed them. The problem, of course, is that such groupings of people are not really homogeneous; the stereotypes are more often wrong than right. Thus, they lead us to make incorrect assumptions and incorrect predictions about the behavior of one another. Sometimes the stereotype is so pervasive and we believe in its truth so strongly that we genuinely expect the stereotyped individuals to live up to it. Strangely enough, they may actually feel compelled to do so at times.

This tendency to label, categorize, and stereotype becomes even more peculiar and more disturbing when it occurs with respect to sexual behavior. Let us say that some people masturbate with the left hand exclusively, some with the right hand exclusively, and that some alternate between hands. We could even take the third category and divide it into such groupings as largely left-handed but with incidental history of right-handed masturbation, equal use of right and left hand, etc. Research could then be directed at seeking the causes of each type in hormonal factors, in genetic predisposition, in childhood experiences, etc. More importantly, if we began using such a labeling system and if people accepted it as referring to basic subgroups of human beings, we would quickly develop stereotypes to go with the labels. Further, if we decided that left-handed masturbators were a minority group and hence deviant, we could discriminate against them, make jokes about their peculiarities, worry about being latently left-handed ourselves, make such activities illegal, and seek to alter the maladaptive behavior through therapeutic techniques.

Though all of that may seem absurd, sociologist Mary McIntosh proposes that we have done much the same thing in the progression from *defining* certain sexual interactions as homosexual to saying that engaging in such behavior indicates the *condition* of homosexuality to identifying those who engage in the behavior as *being* homosexuals. Once the categorization was made, stereotypes and certain role expectations also came into being. The ironic thing is that the notion of homosexuality as a fixed either/or state is accepted most readily by those who reject homosexuals as unacceptable deviants *and* by those engaging in homosexual acts. Many of the latter individuals have decided that they must be constitutionally different and hence have no choice in the matter. Somehow the idea that sexual behavior can take many forms and that different people have had different experiences and hence have learned different forms is threatening. The threat apparently is reduced if one can assume that the condition is built in: that way, neither the homosexual nor the heterosexual need worry about the possibility of changing roles. We have reached the point where we should recognize that there is no such thing as homosexuality or homosexuals, bisexuality or bisexuals, heterosexuality or heterosexuals. To categorize oneself or others on the basis of one's preferences in sexual partners is as meaningless as categorizing on the basis of preferences in eating, buying automobiles, or attending movies.

The Homosexual Role

Mary McIntosh

Recent advances in the sociology of deviant behavior have not yet affected the study of homosexuality, which is still commonly seen as a condition characterizing certain persons in the way that birthplace or deformity might characterize them. The limitations of this view can best be understood if we examine some of its implications. In the first place, if homosexuality is a condition, then people either have it or do not have it. Many scientists and ordinary people assume that there are two kinds of people in the world: homosexuals and heterosexuals. Some of them recognize that homosexual feelings and behavior are not confined to the persons they would like to call "homosexuals" and that some of these persons do not actually engage in homosexual behavior. This should pose a crucial problem, but they evade the crux by retaining their assumption and puzzling over the question of how to tell whether someone is "really" homosexual or not. Lay people too will discuss whether a certain person is "queer" in much the same way as they might question whether a certain pain indicated cancer. And in much the same way they will often turn to scientists or to medical men for a surer diagnosis. The scientists, for their part, feel it incumbent on them to seek criteria for diagnosis.

Thus one psychiatrist,[1] discussing the definitions of homosexuality, has written:

> . . . I do not diagnose patients as homosexual unless they have engaged in overt homosexual behavior. Those who also engage in heterosexual activity are diagnosed as bisexual. An isolated experience may not warrant the diagnosis, but repetitive homosexual behavior in adulthood, whether sporadic or continuous, designates a homosexual [p. 248].

Along with many other writers, he introduces the notion of a third

Reprinted in an edited version from: McIntosh, M. The homosexual role. *Social Problems*, 1968, **16**, 182–192.

type of person, the "bisexual," to handle the fact that behavior patterns cannot be conveniently dichotomized into heterosexual and homosexual. But this does not solve the conceptual problem, since bisexuality too is seen as a condition (unless as a passing response to unusual situations such as confinement in a one-sex prison). In any case there is no extended discussion of bisexuality; the topic is usually given a brief mention in order to clear the ground for the consideration of "true homosexuality."

To cover the cases where the symptoms of behavior or of felt attractions do not match the diagnosis, other writers have referred to an adolescent homosexual phase or have used such terms as "latent homosexual" or "pseudo homosexual." Indeed one of the earliest studies of the subject, by Krafft-Ebing, was concerned with making a distinction between the "invert" who is congenitally homosexual and others who, although they behave in the same way, are not true inverts.[11]

A second result of the conceptualization of homosexuality as a condition is that the major research task has been seen as the study of its etiology. There has been much debate as to whether the condition is innate or acquired. The first step in such research has commonly been to find a sample of "homosexuals" in the same way that a medical researcher might find a sample of diabetics in order to study that disease. Yet, after a long history of such studies, the results are sadly inconclusive and the answer is still as much a matter of opinion as it was when Havelock Ellis[5] published *Sexual Inversion* 70 years ago. The failure of research to answer the question has not been due to lack of scientific rigor or to any inadequacy of the available evidence; it results rather from the fact that the wrong question has been asked. One might as well try to trace the etiology of "committee chairmanship" or "Seventh-Day Adventism" as of "homosexuality."

The vantage point of comparative sociology enables us to see that the conception of homosexuality as a condition is, in itself, a possible object of study. This conception and the behavior it supports operate as a form of social control in a society in which homosexuality is condemned. Furthermore, the uncritical acceptance of the conception by social scientists can be traced to their concern with homosexuality as a social problem. They have tended to accept the popular definition of what the problem is and then have been implicated in the process of social control.

The practice of the social labeling of persons as deviant operates in two ways as a mechanism of social control. First, it helps to provide a clear-cut, publicized, and recognizable threshold between permissible and impermissible behavior. This means that people cannot so easily drift into deviant behavior. Their first moves in a deviant direction immediately raise the question of a total move into a deviant role with all the sanctions that this is likely to elicit. Second, the labeling serves to segregate the deviants from others and this means that their deviant practices and their self-justifications for these practices are contained within a relatively narrow group. The creation of a specialized, despised, and punished role of homosexual keeps the bulk of society pure in rather the same way that the similar treatment of some kinds of criminals helps keep the rest of society law abiding.

However, the disadvantage of this practice as a technique of social control is that there may be a tendency for people to become fixed in their deviance once they have become labeled. This, too, is a process that has become well recognized in discussions of other forms of deviant behavior such as juvenile delinquency and drug taking and, indeed, of other kinds of social labeling such as streaming in schools and racial distinctions. One might expect social categorizations of this sort to be to some extent self-fulfilling prophecies: if the culture defines people as falling into distinct types—black and white, criminal and noncriminal, homosexual and normal—then these types will tend to become polarized, highly differentiated from each other. Below we will discuss whether this is so in the case of homosexuals and "normals" in the United States today.

It is interesting to notice that homosexuals themselves welcome and support the notion that homosexuality is a condition. For just as the rigid categorization deters people from drifting into deviancy, so it appears to foreclose the possibility of drifting back into normality and thus removes the element of anxious choice. It appears to justify the deviant behavior of the homosexual as being appropriate for him as a member of the homosexual category. The deviancy can thus be seen as legitimate for him and he can continue in it without rejecting the norms of the society.

The way in which people become labeled as homosexual can now be seen as a social process connected with mechanisms of social control. It is important, therefore, for sociologists to examine this process objectively and not lend themselves to participation in it, particularly since, as we have seen, psychologists and psychiatrists on the whole have not retained their objectivity but have become involved as diagnostic agents in the process of social labeling.

It is proposed that the homosexual should be seen as playing a social role rather than as having a condition. The role of "homosexual," however, does not simply describe a sexual behavior pattern. If it did, the idea of a role would be no more useful than that of a condition. The purpose of introducing the term "role" is to enable us to handle the fact that behavior in this sphere does not match popular beliefs; sexual behavior patterns cannot be dichotomized in the way that the social roles of homosexual and heterosexual can.

It may seem rather odd to distinguish in this way between role and behavior, but if we accept a definition of role in terms of expectations (which may or may not be fulfilled), then the distinction is both legitimate and useful. In modern societies where a separate homosexual role is recognized, the expectation, on behalf of those who play the role and of others, is that a homosexual will be exclusively or very predominantly homosexual in his feelings and behavior. In addition, there are other expectations that frequently exist, especially on the part of nonhomosexuals, but affecting the self-conception of anyone who sees himself as homosexual. These are the expectation that he will be effeminate in manner, personality, or preferred sexual activity; the expectation that sexuality will play a part of some kind in all his relations with other men; and the expectation that he will be attracted to boys and very young men and probably willing to seduce them. The existence of a social expectation, of course, commonly helps to produce its own fulfillment. But the question of how far it is fulfilled is a matter for empirical investigation rather than a priori pronouncement. Some of the empirical evidence about the chief expectation—that homosexuality precludes heterosexuality—in relation to the homosexual role in America is examined in the final section of this article.

In order to clarify the nature of the role and demonstrate that it exists only in certain societies, we shall present the cross-cultural and historical evidence available. This raises awkward problems of method because the material has hitherto usually been collected and analyzed in terms of culturally specific modern Western conceptions.

THE HOMOSEXUAL ROLE IN VARIOUS SOCIETIES

To study homosexuality in the past or other societies we usually have to rely on secondary evidence rather than on direct observation. The reliability and the validity of such evidence is open to question because what the original observers reported may have been distorted by their disapproval of homosexuality and by their definition of it, which may be different from the one we wish to adopt.

For example, Marc Daniel[3] tries to refute accusations of homosexuality against Pope Julian II by producing four arguments: the pope had many enemies who might wish to blacken his name; he and his supposed lover, Alidosi, both had mistresses; neither of them was at all effeminate; and the pope had other men friends about whom no similar accusations were made. In other words, Daniel is trying to fit an early sixteenth-century pope to the modern conception of the homosexual as effeminate, exclusively homosexual, and sexual in relation to all men. The fact that he does not fit is, of course, no evidence, as Daniel would have it, that his relationship with Alidosi was not a sexual one.

Anthropologists too can fall into this trap. Marvin Opler,[13] summarizing anthropological evidence on the subject, says: "Actually, no society, save perhaps Ancient Greece, pre-Meiji Japan, certain top echelons in Nazi Germany, and the scattered examples of such special status groups as the berdaches, Nata slaves, and one category of Chuck-chee shamans, has lent sanction in any real sense to homosexuality [p. 174]." Yet he goes on to discuss societies in which there are reports of sanctioned adolescent and other occasional "experimentation." Of the Cubeo of the North West Amazon, for instance, he says, "*true* homo-sexuality among the Cubeo is rare if not absent," giving as evidence the fact that no males with persistent homosexual patterns are reported.

Allowing for such weaknesses, the Human Relations Area Files are the best single source of comparative information. Their evidence on homosexuality has been summarized by Ford and Beach,[6] who identify two broad types of accepted patterns: the institutionalized homosexual role and the liaison between men or boys who are otherwise hetero-sexual.

The recognition of a distinct role of *berdache* or transvestite is, they say, "the commonest form of institutionalized homosexuality." This form shows a marked similarity to that in our own society, though in some ways it is even more extreme. The Mohave Indians of California and Arizona, for example,[4] recognized both an *alyha*—a male transves-tite who took the role of the woman in sexual intercourse—and a *hwame*—a female homosexual who took the role of the male. People were be-lieved to be born as *alyha* or *hwame*, hints of their future proclivities occurring in their mothers' dreams during pregnancy. If a young boy began to behave like a girl and take an interest in women's things in-stead of men's, there was an initiation ceremony in which he would become an *alyha*. After that he would dress and act like a woman, would be referred to as "she" and could take "husbands."

But the Mohave pattern differs from ours in that although the *alyha* was considered regrettable and amusing, he was not condemned and was given public recognition. The attitude was that "he was an *alyha*, he could not help it." But the "husband" of an *alyha* was an ordinary man who happened to have chosen an *alyha*, perhaps because they were good housekeepers or because they were believed to be "lucky in love," and he would be the butt of endless teasing and joking.

This radical distinction between the feminine passive homosexual and his masculine active partner is one that is not made very much in our own society, but which is very important in the Middle East. There, however, neither is thought of as being a "born" homosexual, although the passive partner, who demeans himself by his feminine submission, is despised and ridiculed, while the active one is not. In most of the ancient Middle East, including among the Jews until the return from the Babylonian exile, there were male temple prostitutes.[8,15] Thus even cul-tures that recognize a separate homosexual role may not define it in the same way as our culture does.

Many other societies accept or approve of homosexual liaisons as part of a variegated sexual pattern. Usually these are confined to a particular stage in the individual's life. Among the Aranda of Central Australia, for instance, there are long-standing relationships of several years' duration between unmarried men and young boys, starting at 10 to 12 years of age.[6] This is rather similar to the well-known situation in classical Greece, but there, of course, the older man could have a wife as well. Sometimes, however, as among the Siwans of North Africa,[6] all men and boys can and are expected to engage in homosexual activities, apparently at every stage of life. In all of these societies there may be much homosexual behavior, but there are no "homosexuals."

THE DEVELOPMENT OF THE HOMOSEXUAL
ROLE IN ENGLAND

The problem of method is even more acute in dealing with historical material than with anthropological, for history is usually concerned with "great events" rather than with recurrent patterns. There are some records of attempts to curb sodomy among minor churchmen during the medieval period,[12] which seem to indicate that it was common. At least they suggest that laymen feared on behalf of their sons that it was common. The term "catamite," meaning "boy kept for immoral purposes," was first used in 1593, again suggesting that this practice was common then. But most of the historical references to homosexuality relate either to great men or to great scandals. However, over the last 70 years or so various scholars have tried to trace the history of sex,[2,5,7,14] and it is possible to glean a good deal from what they have found and also from what they have failed to establish.

Their studies of English history before the seventeenth century consist usually of inconclusive speculation as to whether certain men, such as Edward II, Christopher Marlowe, William Shakespeare, were or were not homosexual. Yet the disputes are inconclusive not because of lack of evidence but because none of these men fits the modern stereotype of the homosexual.

It is not until the end of the seventeenth century that other kinds of information become available and it is possible to move from speculations about individuals to descriptions of homosexual life. At this period, references to homosexuals as a type and to a rudimentary homosexual subculture, mainly in London, begin to appear. But the earliest descriptions of homosexuals do not coincide exactly with the modern conception. There is much more stress on effeminacy and in particular on transvestism, to such an extent that there seems to be no distinction at first between transvestism and homosexuality. The terms emerging at this period to describe homosexuals—Molly, Nancy-boy, Madge-cull—emphasize effeminacy. In contrast the modern terms—like fag, queer, gay, bent—do not have this implication.

By the end of the seventeenth century, homosexual transvestites were a distinct enough group to be able to form their own clubs in London.[2] Edward Ward's *History of the London Clubs*, published in 1709, describes one called "The Mollies' Club" which met "in a certain tavern in the City" for "parties and regular gatherings." The members "adopt[ed] all the small vanities natural to the feminine sex to such an extent that they try to speak, walk, chatter, shriek and scold as women do, aping them as well in other respects [pp. 328–329]." The other respects apparently included the enactment of marriages and childbirth. The club was discovered and broken up by agents of the Reform Society.[2] There were a number of similar scandals during the course of the eighteenth century as various homosexual coteries were exposed.

A writer in 1729 describes the widespread homosexual life of the period:[15]

They also have their Walks and Appointments, to meet and pick up one another, and their particular Houses of Resort to go to, because they dare not trust themselves in an open Tavern. About twenty of these sort of Houses have been discovered, besides the Nocturnal Assemblies of great numbers of the like vile Persons, what they call the *Markets*, which are the Royal Exchange, Lincoln's Inn, Bog Houses, the south side of St James's Park, the Piazzas in Covent Garden, St. Clement's Churchyard, etc.

It would be a pretty scene to behold them in their clubs and cabals, how they assume the air and affect the name of Madam or Miss, Betty or Molly, with a chuck under the chin, and "Oh you bold pullet, I'll break your eggs," and then frisk and walk away [p. 142].

The notion of exclusive homosexuality became well established during this period. When "two Englishmen, Leith and Drew, were accused of paederasty . . . . The evidence given by the plaintiffs was, as was generally the case in these trials, very imperfect. On the other hand the defendants denied the accusation, and produced witnesses to prove their predilection for women. They were in consequence acquitted [p. 334]."[2] This could only have been an effective argument in a society that perceived homosexual behavior as incompatible with heterosexual tastes.

During the nineteenth century there are further reports of raided clubs and homosexual brothels. However, by this time the element of transvestism had diminished in importance. Even the male prostitutes are described as being of masculine build and there is more stress upon sexual license and less upon dressing up and play acting.

The homosexual role and homosexual behavior

Thus, a distinct, separate, specialized role of "homosexual" emerged in England at the end of the seventeenth century and the conception of homosexuality as a condition which characterizes certain individuals and not others is now firmly established in our society. The term "role" is, of course, a form of shorthand. It refers not only to a cultural conception or set of ideas but also to a complex of institutional arrangements which depend upon and reinforce these ideas. These arrangements include all the forms of heterosexual activity, courtship, and marriage as well as the labeling processes—gossip, ridicule, psychiatric diagnosis, criminal conviction—and the groups and networks of the homosexual subculture. For simplicity we shall simply say that a specialized role exists.

How does the existence of this social role affect actual behavior? And, in particular, does the behavior of individuals conform to the cultural conception in the sense that most people are either exclusively heterosexual or exclusively homosexual? It is difficult to answer these questions on the basis of available evidence because so many researchers have worked with the preconception that homosexuality is a condition, so that in order to study the behavior they have first found a group of people who could be identified as "homosexuals." Homosexual behavior should be studied independently of social roles, if the connection between the two is to be revealed.

This may not sound like a particularly novel program to those who are familiar with Kinsey's contribution to the field.[9,10] He, after all, set out to study "sexual behavior." Kinsey[9] rejected the assumptions of scientists and laymen:

> that there are persons who are "heterosexual" and persons who are "homosexual," that these two types represent antitheses in the sexual world and that there is only an insignificant class of "bisexuals" who occupy an intermediate position between the other groups . . . that every individual is innately—inherently—either heterosexual or homosexual . . . [and] that from the time of birth one is fated to be one thing or the other . . . [pp. 636–637].

But, although some of Kinsey's ideas are often referred to, particularly in polemical writings, surprisingly little use has been made of his actual data.

Most of Kinsey's chapter on the "Homosexual Outlet"[9] centers on his "heterosexual-homosexual rating scale." His subjects were rated on this scale according to the proportion of their "psychologic reactions and overt experience" that was homosexual in any given period of their lives. It is interesting, and unfortunate for our purposes, that this is one of the few places in the book where Kinsey abandons his behavioristic approach to some extent. However, "psychologic reactions" may well be expected to be affected by the existence of a social role in the same way as overt behavior. Another problem with using Kinsey's material is that although he gives very full information about sexual behavior, the other characteristics of the people he interviewed are only given in a very bald form. But Kinsey's study is undoubtedly the fullest description there is of sexual behavior in any society and as such it is the safest basis for generalizations to other Western societies.

The ideal way to trace the effects on behavior of the existence of a homosexual role would be to compare societies in which the role exists with societies in which it does not. But as there are no adequate descriptions of homosexual behavior in societies where there is no homosexual role, we shall have to substitute comparisons within American society.

Polarization If the existence of a social role were reflected in people's behavior, we should expect to find that relatively few people would engage in bisexual behavior. The problem about investigating this empirically is to know what is meant by "relatively few." The categories of Kinsey's rating scale are, of course, completely arbitrary. He has five bisexual categories, but he might just as well have had more or less, in which case the number falling into each would have been smaller or larger.

It is impossible to get direct evidence of a polarization between the homosexual and the heterosexual pattern, though we may note the suggestive evidence to the contrary that at every age far more men have bisexual than exclusively homosexual patterns. However, by making comparisons between one age group and another and between men and women, it should be possible to see some of the effects of the role.

Age comparison As they grow older, more and more men take up exclusively heterosexual patterns. *Each* of the bisexual and homosexual categories contains fewer men as time goes by after the age of 20. In everyday language, it seems that proportionately more "homosexuals" dabble in heterosexual activity than "heterosexuals" dabble in homosexual activity and such dabbling is particularly common in the younger age groups of 20 to 30. This indicates that the existence of the despised role operates at all ages to inhibit people from engaging in occasional homosexual behavior, but does not have the effect of making the behavior of many "homosexuals" exclusively homosexual.

However, the overall reduction in the amount of homosexual behavior with age can be attributed in part to the fact that more and more men get married. While the active incidence of homosexual behavior is high and increases with age among single men, among married men it is low and decreases only slightly with age. Unfortunately the Kinsey figures do not enable us to compare the incidence of homosexuality among single men who later marry and those who do not.

Comparison of men and women The notion of a separate homosexual role is much less well developed for women than it is for men and so too are the attendant techniques of social control and the deviant subculture and organization. So a comparison with women's sexual behavior should tell us something about the effects of the social role on men's behavior.

Fewer women than men engage in homosexual behavior. By the time they are 45, 26% of women have had *some* homosexual experience, whereas about 50% of men have. But this is probably a cause rather than an effect of the difference in the extent to which the homosexual role is crystallized, for women engage in less nonmarital sexual activity of any kind than do men. For instance, by the time they marry, 50% of women have had some premarital heterosexual experience to orgasm, whereas as many as 90% of men have had such experience.

The most revealing contrast is between the male and female distributions on the Kinsey rating scale. The distributions for women follow a smooth J-shaped pattern, while those for men are uneven with an increase in numbers at the exclusively homosexual end. The distributions for women are the shape that one would expect on the assumption that homosexual and heterosexual acts are randomly distributed in a ratio of 1 to 18. The men are relatively more concentrated in the exclusively homosexual category. This appears to confirm the hypothesis that the existence of the role is reflected in behavior.

Finally, it is interesting that although at the age of 20 far more men than women have homosexual and bisexual patterns (27% as against 11%), by the age of 35 the figures are both the same (13%). Women seem to broaden their sexual experience as they get older whereas men become narrower and more specialized.

None of this, however, should obscure the fact that in terms of behavior, the polarization between the heterosexual man and the homosexual man is far from complete in our society. Some polarization does seem to have occurred, but many men manage to follow patterns of sexual behavior that fall between the two, in spite of our cultural preconceptions and institutional arrangements.

CONCLUSION

This article has dealt with only one small aspect of the sociology of homosexuality. It is, nevertheless, a fundamental one. For it is not until he sees homosexuals as a social category, rather than a medical or psychiatric one, that the sociologist can begin to ask the right questions about the specific content of the homosexual role and about the organization and functions of homosexual groups. All that has been done here is to indicate that the role does not exist in many societies, that it emerged in England only toward the end of the seventeenth century, and that, although the existence of the role in modern America appears to have some effect on the distribution of homosexual behavior, such behavior is far from being monopolized by persons who play the role of homosexual.

REFERENCES

1. Bieber, I. Clinical aspects of male homosexuality. In J. Marmor (Ed.), *Sexual inversion*. New York: Basic Books, 1965.

2. Bloch, I. *Sexual life in England past and present*. London: Francis Aldor, 1938.

3. Daniel, M. Essai de méthodologie pour l'étude des aspects homosexuals de l'histoire. *Arcadie*, 1965, **133**, 31–37.

4. Devereux, G. Institutionalized homosexuality of the Mohave Indians. *Human Biology*, 1937, **9**, 498–527.

5. Ellis, H. *Sexual inversion*. London: Wilson and Macmillan, 1897.

6. Ford, C. S., & Beach, F. A. *Patterns of sexual behavior*. New York: Harper & Row, 1951.

7. Garde, N. I. *Jonathan to Gide: The homosexual in history*. New York: Vantage, 1964.

8. Henriques, F. *Prostitution and society*. Vol. 1. London: MacGibbon and Kee, 1962.

9. Kinsey, A. C., Pomeroy, W. B., & Martin, C. E. *Sexual behavior in the human male*. Philadelphia: Saunders, 1948.

10. Kinsey, A. C., Pomeroy, W. B., Martin, C. E., & Gebhard, P. H. *Sexual behavior in the human female*. Philadelphia: Saunders, 1953.

11. Krafft-Ebing, R. von. *Psychopathia sexualis*. 1889.

12. May, G. *Social control of sex expression*. London: Allen & Unwin, 1930.

13. Opler, M. Anthropological and cross-cultural aspects of homosexuality. In J. Marmor (Ed.), *Sexual inversion*. New York: Basic Books, 1965.

14. Taylor, G. R. *Sex in history*. London: Thames and Hudson, 1953.

15. Taylor, G. R. Historical and mythological aspects of homosexuality. In J. Marmor (Ed.), *Sexual inversion*. New York: Basic Books, 1965.

Massage Parlors and "Hand Whores": Some Sociological Observations

Commercialized sex has taken many forms over the centuries, but the current American variant of the "world's oldest profession" is one of the most curious. Newspaper ads throughout the nation (from New York to West Lafayette to Los Angeles) announce the business hours of massage parlors where girls are on duty to provide "total satisfaction." As with most business establishments, massage parlors range in style from bleak cubicles in back of shabby store-front offices to plush and richly decorated "clubs," complete with music and bar.

Who works in massage parlors? Who are the customers? What goes on behind the closed doors and drawn curtains? In the following article, sociologists Clifton Bryant and Eddie Palmer describe the employees, the clients, and the services provided in four different massage parlors in one American city.

One of the curious aspects of any form of paid sex is the relationship between the professional and the client. Various studies of call girls, streetwalkers, brothel prostitutes, and masseuses contain a common theme. The male customers who seek sexual services are very often motivated not only by lust or a need for variety but also by a desire for friendly companionship and conversation. The females, however, seem to be motivated entirely by the need for money, and their attitudes toward their clients range from indifference to disgust and hate. One cannot help but feel that this is not the happiest or most ideal type of sexual relationship, but both participants are there voluntarily and both receive some type of positive reinforcement from their interaction.

Massage Parlors and "Hand Whores": Some Sociological Observations

Clifton D. Bryant and C. Eddie Palmer

Recent years have seen the rise of a new form of service industry, ostensibly dedicated to the delivery of health and physical therapy, but in reality offering erotic fantasy and, in some instances, a continuum of sexual gratification services. The service-work system in question is the so-called executive massage parlor. This service industry has also spawned an essentially new and unique occupational specialty, socially deviant and marginally legitimate, in terms of legal ordinance and statute

Reprinted in an edited version from: Bryant, C. D., & Palmer, C. E. Massage parlors and "hand whores." Some sociological observations. *Journal of Sex Research*, 1975, **11**, 227–241.

—that of the "professional" masturbator. Interestingly enough, although the massage parlor and the attendant staff of sexual service operatives have been on the American scene for several years now, sociologists have only recently begun to take note of their existence and to document their ethnology.[1,7]

Many American men encountered female-administered massages firsthand as GIs in various of our wars. Massages, often with attendant sexual services, were particularly common in the Orient. In the Vietnam conflict, for example, many servicemen encountered the massage while on rest-and-recuperation leave. Armstrong[1] mentions one writer who reported that in Bangkok, Thailand (a popular R & R city) there were 7000 massage girls working in 152 massage parlors during the height of the war. In Vietnam, many soldiers used to speak of sauna bath and masturbation services as "steam and cream." Having become acclimated to such services, some have presumably continued to appreciate the erotic prospects of a female, particularly a scantily clad or topless female providing massage and other soothing ministrations.

THE MASSAGE PARLOR AS A DELIVERY SYSTEM FOR SEXUAL SERVICES

The massage parlor is clearly a ubiquitous service establishment on today's urban scene. Where only a mere handful of such establishments were to be identified in the larger cities a few years ago, today massage parlors are prominent in the larger metropolises and even aspiring cosmopolitan hamlets may boast a parlor or two in their general environs. In way of current census, a recent inspection of the yellow pages of various large cities reveals that San Diego, California, lists 50 such establishments, Seattle 44, Pittsburgh 28, Atlanta 13, Denver 12, New Orleans 11, Columbus, Ohio, 16, and Fort Worth 4, to name a few. Even in the interior provinces such sybaritic commercial amenities are appearing. Memphis, Tennessee, boasts 8, Roanoke, Virginia, 7, Richmond, Virginia, 8, and Knoxville, Tennessee, 2. Staid Springfield, Massachusetts, lists 4 massage parlors, while Greenville, South Carolina, has something of an innovation in possessing a "Dial-a-Massage" service which advertises, "ladies to serve you in your hotel or motel from 7 P.M.–3A.M., 7 days—" and further suggests "ask us about our escort dating service." Washington, D. C., advertises 66 massage parlors in its telephone directories, but New York surely holds the title of being the tense muscle center of the nation, inasmuch as Armstrong[1] says that in the summer of 1972, "there were at least 75 and perhaps as high as 100 massage parlors in Manhattan alone [p. 5]."

While no systematic content analysis of massage parlor names or advertisements has been attempted, it is safe to suggest that most bear (by accident or design) a name or logo suggestive of the exotic if not the erotic. Some bear the label of the fanciful and the halcyon such as

"Shangri-La," "Fantasia," "Golden Dawn" or "Ancient Palace of Lei-sure," while many simply rely on the foreign mystique (particularly the mysterious East) with such far horizon names as "Geisha House," "Pompeii," "Far East," or "Tiki-Tiki." Names redolent of France, Sweden, and other Scandinavian countries also seem to prevail. A few are bold in their suggestion of masculine elan with such names as "El Toro," while several are equally implicit in their connotation of feminine presence and service with such alluring logos as "La Femme Fatale," "Cleopatra," or "Yvette Chevette." A popular theme is the unabashed invitation to the sensate and the hedonistic with names like "Tender Touch," "Velvet Touch," and "Joy Massage," while others (perhaps catering to more varied tastes) call themselves "Apollo" and "Super-Boy." The vast majority emphasizes that their staff is "all girl" and "specially trained." Many advertise massages which "relieve tensions of the *entire* body" [italics ours] and offer a massage repertoire which may include vibrator and waterbed massages, massages in a "mirror" room or "his and her massages."

Massage parlors purport themselves to be legitimate enterprises, and in most localities are legal (at least, as long as massages are the only service offered). Some localities, however, have passed ordinances aimed at specifically outlawing massage parlors. Newport News, Virginia, for instance, passed such an ordinance and the Washington suburban area of Fairfax County, Virginia, urged the state to pass appropriate anti-massage legislation. Other towns and localities have had running legal battles with massage parlor owners, and often the owners of other types of businesses have been in the vanguard of the attack. The latter claim that massage parlors and other erotically oriented businesses such as store-front "peep shows" could pay "double and triple the rent that legitimate businesses can afford."[1] They also complain about how such establishments contribute to the deterioration of a neighborhood because of the disreputable clientele that they attract. In spite of social and legal pressures and harassment, massage parlors seem to be alive and well.

A TYPOLOGY OF MASSAGE PARLORS

Massage parlors may be articulated into four general varieties on the basis of services rendered and degree of misrepresentation intended. First there are the genuine massage parlors that exist as health clubs and service establishments to provide exercise and physical therapy. Often these are staffed by masseurs (or masseuses if the clientele is female), and in general they have some degree of expertise in their work. Many hotels and resorts either have massage facilities or trained personnel who can provide massage service in the guest's room. Such establishments are by no means new in this country and are legitimate in appearance and operation.

A second variety of massage parlor may best be described as a "rip-

off." The ads are seductive in their implicit promises of erotic fulfillment, but their staff is usually inept at providing a genuine massage and
adamant in its refusal to provide anything in the way of physical
sexual gratification (the customer is welcome to all the vicarious gratification he can generate). The "ripoff" parlors often go to considerable
lengths to create the illusion that the customer will be able to obtain
sexual services. Such efforts may include a scantily clad female staff,
likely in bikini or "harem" outfits, or even topless on occasion, suggestive ads and dialogue to greet the new customer, and sensuous theme
in the parlor decor and furnishings. The masseuse may provide friendly
conversation, a massage of mediocre quality, and little else.[5] The customer may importune, but to no avail. He will probably not return if
sexual service was his primary goal, but since parlors depend heavily
on transient clientele, the repeat customer is of little importance. These
kinds of parlors are not infrequently located in, or adjacent to, hotels
and motels, and at times in new shopping centers. Some customers do,
however, return under the impression that they simply did not have
the "right" masseuse, and hope for better success from their sexual
propositions the next time.

The massage parlors that perhaps contribute most significantly to
the negative image of such businesses are those establishments which
are little more than disguised brothels. This is a variation of the earlier
theme of "model studios," found in some parts of the country, where
ostensibly an individual could rent a model and a room in the studio
for photographic or painting purposes. The models frequently catered
to nonartistic tastes and requirements. Massage parlors of this variety
offer a full repertoire of sexual services—for an appropriate fee. Such
parlors, as Fortunato[3] phrased it, "are the places where anything goes
—from just good old-fashioned fornication to disciplinary enemas [p.
131]." Usually the client inquires about the "extras" and the masseuses
articulate services available and prices. Normally the house specials are
genital, oral, and manual sex, although more idiosyncratic sexual per-
suasions can usually be accommodated. In some cities there have been
concerted efforts by law enforcement agencies to eliminate this newly
emergent form of prostitution. In one such crackdown drive in New
York City in July 1971, some 1250 girls and 154 male clients were arrested. Of the clients arrested, more than 40% were given jail sentences. It would appear that such massage parlors offer little more dis-
creetness or protection from arrest than do conventional brothels. Law
enforcement officials, however, admit that massage parlors as cover-ups
for prostitution create special problems in detection, apprehension, and
conviction. Armstrong[1] mentions the supervisor of the Manhattan South
Public Morals Squad as viewing such massage parlors as the emergence
of a new form of prostitution, and quotes him as having commented

that, "These [massage parlors] are the more sophisticated operations and it takes a more sophisticated approach to cope with it [p. 8]."

The final variety of massage parlor which is suggested is the "massage and masturbation only" parlor. It may well be the most prevalent type of parlor and is the kind to which our observations in this article are primarily directed. In such establishments the masturbation service may be integral to the massage service, and tipping for such sexual service may be optional, as opposed to the parlors offering full prostitution services where everything in addition to (or in lieu of) the basic massage requires an extra fee or tip. In some massage and masturbation parlors, however, the masseuses may imply that the manual sex is only available for a tip, or even specify a particular fee for this service. Parlors of this variety may even advertise that they provide *complete* or *local* (italics theirs) massages, to indicate the availability of penis manipulation. They are enjoying a considerable trade and are popular with their clientele. In some areas, it is reported that their presence is making inroads into the local prostitution trade to the consternation of the prostitutes.[3] Clearly the M-and-M parlors are relatively successful in avoiding confrontation with the law, while affording convenient, albeit compromise sexual gratification to their clientele.

THE MASSAGE PARLORS OF MOUNTAIN CITY

In order to obtain more detailed data on massage parlors and masseuses, a series of visits (and revisits) to four massage parlors located in Mountain City were undertaken in the fall of 1973. Mountain City is a pseudonym for a medium-sized city in an Atlantic seaboard state. It is essentially a trade and distribution center, with some light industry and is moderately cosmopolitan in orientation. These visits afforded the opportunity for field observations, depth interviews with 10 masseuses, and several less formal taped group interviews with masseuses and massage parlor managers. The purpose of the visits was known by the women and, initially, cooperation was complete and enthusiastic. After several days, however, the masseuses and managers developed a degree of apprehension that the project might be some kind of law enforcement or crime commission probe, and further cooperation became difficult to obtain.

The massage parlors of Mountain City were located along several main commercial arteries and were convenient for both commuters and guests of nearby motels. The numerous vacant stores and old homes along such streets afforded inexpensive rent for the parlors and it appeared that minimum exterior remodeling had been undertaken. The outside appearance of the parlors suggested a modest financial outlay, but the lobbies of reception areas were relatively luxurious. Attractive furniture, deep carpets, bright colors, and imaginative lighting all combined to effect an atmosphere of modernity, semielegance, and respectability. The intended aim was clearly to present an image of a luxurious and accommodative service establishment, and thus to allay the anxieties of the new customer and to provide him reassurance that he was simply purchasing certain services rather than embarking on a possibly hazardous misadventure.

Beyond the reception areas were the actual massage areas, made up of small rooms or cubicles. These rooms are relatively spartan in comparison to the lobbies, and used exotic lighting to conceal the often shabby furnishings. Massage tables were frequently no more than wooden picnic tables covered with a slab of foam rubber and a white drop cloth. The lighting, no doubt, also had to make some contribution in terms of enhancing the appearance of the masseuses and the environment. The massage parlors usually had a back area or lounge, off limits to the clientele, where the masseuses could relax, eat, or even sleep when not giving a massage.

The individual client enters the reception room and makes his request for a massage. At this point, if there are several masseuses, they line up for the patron to make his selection. The masseuses in Mountain City referred to this line-up procedure as the "meat display." The client then selects the type of massage he desires. The variables may include length of massage; vibrator or hand administered; type of room in which it takes place, i. e., regular or mirrored; and whether the massage is totally administered by the masseuse or on the other hand, masseuse and client taking turns massaging each other—the so-called his and hers. In some cities the variations may also include whether the masseuse wears a total costume, is topless, or completely disrobes to give the massage. Massage parlors in some parts of the country offer even more variety including the opportunity to bathe with the masseuse. One article,[7] for example, reported a masseuse as saying, "It's $15 for an hour massage including a local. An extra $5 will get my top off and $5 more takes my bottom off. For $10 more he can bathe with me for a half hour [p. 70]." The customer may raise questions about the availability of sexual services, to which the girls, at this point, attempt to reassure him that they give "complete" massages. The individual is directed to a room and told to disrobe. In some parlors he may be given a towel and offered the opportunity to shower. The girl comes in and inquires as to his preference of massage compounds, i.e., powder, oil or lotion, or alcohol. She gives the massage, in some cases fends off sexual propositions and advances, and at some point either in response to the client or at her own initiative, asks if he would like her to "massage anything else" or some similar phrase. If he answers in the affirmative, the masseuse may further request that the patron take her hand and put it where he would like to have further massage. By utilizing such ploys, the girls can avoid the accusation that they are soliciting or offering prostitution services. If the customer were a vice-squad officer and had actually placed her hand on his penis, she could avoid conviction by claiming entrapment on the part of the officer. By assiduously refraining from genital sex (at least penetration), oral sex, discussions of fees and tips, explicit solicitation, and by taking the physical initiative in providing a "local" or "relief" massage, the masseuse remains on generally firm legal ground. If the customer receives the "local" before his full massage time is up, the massage session is terminated, inasmuch as the masturbation is considered to be the finale of the massage, regardless of when it is administered. The "his-and-hers" massages, as well as the topless and/or bottomless variations are also designed to speed up the processing of clientele. If such erotic stimuli help the customer achieve an erection faster, the masseuses are able to masturbate him sooner and get him out in order to receive the next patron. Efficiency and speed are clearly significant considerations in a volume service business. The general work posture of the massage parlors in Mountain City can be best summed up in the words of one masseuse interviewed, who revealed that at her place of work, their motto was, "get 'em in, get 'em up, get 'em off, and get 'em out."

THE MASSEUSES OF MOUNTAIN CITY

The masseuses interviewed were essentially the progeny of lower-middle- and middle-class parents. The fathers were primarily blue-collar and service workers whose education ranged from grammar school through 2 years of college, with some junior high or high school as the norm. Among the mothers, several were housewives, one was a cashier, and one was a school cook; two were waitresses or bartenders, while one was a secretary and one was a drugstore clerk. (One masseuse, when pressed, euphemistically conceded that her mother's vocation was "running around.") Educationally, the majority of the mothers ranged from tenth grade through high school graduates. With two exceptions the parents of the masseuses were married. There was one instance of a deceased father and only one set of divorced parents.

The majority of the masseuses were from Mountain City, either natives or residents there for several years. Some were from smaller towns in the vicinity. The masseuses were young—one was 30 and the rest were between the ages of 19 and 24, with 21 as the mean age. Two were presently married, one was divorced, and three were separated from their husbands. The remainder were single, although one was anticipating nuptials in the near future. Of the married, divorced, or separated women, four had children—one had two, one had three, one had four, and one had five children. Two of the masseuses had 1 year of college, one had attended school through the eighth grade, and the remainder had attended high school for a few years or were high school graduates.

They were a remarkably mobile group in terms of occupation and considering their youth. All admitted multiple jobs over the past 5 years, the number ranging from three to six with the average number of jobs being slightly over four. They had enjoyed a diversity of occupational experiences, such as retail salesclerk, factory operative, clerical worker, nurse's aid, waitress, teacher's aid, etc. Most of them had been masseuses for approximately 2 years on the average and had been in their present position for only a few weeks or months. They were presently earning inordinately high salaries considering their age and education. Even the lowest-paid masseuse reported $85 per week plus tips and one or two proudly confided salaries of $200 to $400 per week plus tips (the women with the higher salaries were likely to be managers). Tips amounted to approximately one-half of their salaries, averaging about $5 per customer. Thus the masseuses were averaging between $125 and $600 per week. A few heard of the job and applied through a newspaper ad, but the majority learned about openings through friends. A number of the girls mentioned that they knew other masseuses in town, and reported that they had known the other girls before they started working in massage parlors. One girl got her present job because she had given the owner a massage while working at another massage parlor.

Being a masseuse in most parlors requires little in the way of requisite skills and the girls readily admit this. In articulating the necessary qualifications the interviewees listed such items as "attractive," "personable," "good character," "level headed," "ability to work," and perhaps most important of all, "willing to massage nude men." Learning the technical skills was relatively simple and speedy. The girls received brief on-the-job training from other masseuses in the establishment, or from the boss. As some writers on the subject have observed, it is doubtful that many masseuses in such establishments ever develop massage expertise. One suggested, for example, that "[such] girls couldn't knead dough for a popover."[6]

In regard to the rendering of sexual services, a few of the girls reported that they did not know what they were getting into, until they were on the job and another masseuse enlightened them. The majority admitted, however, that they did know when they took up the vocation. One respondent confided that her friends had told her that as a masseuse she would be a "hand whore." One girl reported she had quit work at one time because she found it repulsive, but had later started back again. Although most said that the owner had given them no specific instructions, a few conceded that the owners had communicated various proscriptions which were patently designed to avoid legal entanglements. They were told that they were not to engage in prostitution, soliciting, or quoting prices, and there was to be no penetration of any body cavity, no oral sex, and no asking for tips. As a result, some of the girls developed a considerable sensitivity to the nuances of the law. As one put it, "We know what we can get away with."

When asked to list the occupations of their three closest friends, the majority mentioned other masseuses, and almost half listed other masseuses exclusively. The women reported that they knew 10 to 20 other masseuses in town. It would appear that they are essentially a clannish occupational group, perhaps because of the late or erratic hours that they work which tends to throw them together. The stigmatized nature of their jobs may also tend to engender group interaction, if not cohesion, in that it may be more comfortable and less ego threatening to interact only with others in the same line of work.

Some of the respondents volunteered the observation that many of the masseuses whom they knew were bisexual, and several admitted that they had had sexual relations with other masseuses.

The majority of the masseuses (with only two exceptions) admitted having previously been arrested. Among the reasons listed were drug charges, arrests for a variety of improper behavior such as disturbing the peace, assault, disorderly conduct, contributing to the delinquency of a minor, and reckless driving. Also mentioned were a bad check arrest and a "dog running loose." They had been fortunate in these arrests in either avoiding conviction or incarceration, or having spent only a few hours or a night in jail. One reported that she went to visit a boyfriend in jail, and got into an argument with the jailer and had been arrested and jailed herself.

THE CLIENTELE

The establishment names, the wording of the advertisement and the mode and location of the ads would seem to suggest that many massage parlors are patently aiming at a clientele that is (1) often transient, (2) temporarily separated from spouse or female companionship, (3) seeking diversion from sexual frustration, and probably (4) erotically curious. Likely prospects for such specifications would be the out-of-town traveling businessman who finds himself alone and bored in a strange town and motel, the conventioneer "out on the town" with "the gang," or even the indigenous businessman who seeks a new sensual experience appropriate to his existential appetite and financial affluence. In this connection, some of the masseuses spoke of regular customers who returned from week to week, often at the same general time of day, either on the way to or from work, or during a lunch or coffee break.

The masseuses of Mountain City when queried about their clientele provided composite descriptions of significant similarity. While the customers differed in age, the majority were depicted as mature adults or early middle-aged—35 to 40, or 35 "up" as the general norm. The customers were further consistently described as businessmen, traveling salesmen, or "upper middle" in occupational category. Only a very few instances of female customers seeking a massage were reported.

The masseuses told of encountering a variety of idiosyncratic sexual behavior and requests. One patron arrived with a whip, and several wanted the masseuses to yell at them. One insisted on being tied up, put in a closet and left for 1 hour. The masseuses obligingly complied. Another masseuse related an account of a man who would come in wearing what she described as a "Mr. Gay" outfit. His request, it turned out, was to have a girl watch him undress and then put on silk female underwear and a dress and to encourage him while he did. Another character was known as Flashlight Harry, because he always brought a flashlight and wanted to be massaged in the dark, while shining the flashlight beam on the masseuse. Nevertheless, most of the women expressed the opinion that they believed the great majority of their customers were "straight," and that they came to the massage parlor for sexual gratification as opposed to patronizing a call girl or house of prostitution because it was cleaner, safer, and "legal." They also suggested that the customers came because they had wives who were "pregnant" or "bitches," that they could not find a prostitute, they believed that in a massage parlor they "think they can get laid," or that they simply sought the opportunity for conversation and a sympathetic listener.

Most of the masseuses had a generally positive or at least nonnegative opinion of their patrons, although some took exception to what they perceived as the economic naiveté of the customer. As one masseuse went on to explain, "[it's] not worth it to pay a stranger to jerk you off." When asked about the type of client that they preferred, some indicated no particular choice or type, while one indicated that she liked "talkative persons who smiled a lot," because in such instances, she felt, the "massage goes faster." And another revealed a playful nature, in that, as she put it, "I like [to] talk—[to] joke and horse around." A few of the girls either preferred the kind of patrons "that just lay (sic) there and enjoy [the massage]," or "clients who come in get it over with and leave a good tip."

As in many work situations where the practitioners come into intimate contact with the clientele, the possibility of the practitioners becoming sexually aroused exists. This might appear to be an especially strong possibility where the practitioners attempt to sexually arouse the customers, and in doing so submit to being massaged or handled. When asked about this, all but one of the girls who responded said that they were not sexually aroused themselves. One or two attributed this to the fact that they had done it so much, or that they might lose their jobs if they did. Some revealed that self-control was not difficult since they found the clientele distasteful. For example, one suggested that she could always "think about the slobs I'm working on," as a defense, and another confided that she was, "disgusted [at the] idea of someone you don't know putting hands on you." Only one girl admitted that she was ever sexually aroused. To handle this, however, she would "stand up [presumably she had been getting massaged] look at him [the customer] [and] lose interest." Unlike the prostitutes described by Bryan[2] who had to be socialized to develop an interpersonal and unemotional response to sexual intimacies with their clientele, the masseuses of Mountain City apparently were able to do the same as a natural reaction to the nature of their work and their clientele.

The masseuses revealed that they most often give the reciprocal "his and hers" massage, and about half of the girls also reported that they prefer this type most. The reason, it appears, is that this type of massage may tend to sexually arouse the customer faster and they can more rapidly proceed to masturbate the client and get him out of the establishment faster. Again one made reference to the "in, up, off, out" orientation. A few mentioned other types of massages such as the vibrator massage which they like to give, again because it is quick. Some specified a preference for the Swedish "straight" massage since this was the only legitimate massage. Some girls, however, admitted that since they were the least expensive massages, they did not encourage them with customers, and in some instances, were rough with such a customer or even scratched him with their fingernails as punishment for being so "cheap."

COMMUNITY REACTION AND OCCUPATIONAL SELF-IMAGE

That massage parlors have been negatively labeled within the Mountain City community is evidenced by a running dialogue in articles and letters to the editor in the various newspapers of the area. One influential church leader openly protested to the City Council by declaring that his church had ended up in the middle of a "red-light district." Other citizens tried to have the parlors closed and subsequent efforts of public officials involved raising the licensing fee from the usual $60 business permit to a $5000 blanket fee.

The masseuses of Mountain City would seem to have no illusions about the community reaction to their occupational specialization and place of employment. While some said that they felt that the community in general did not object or did not object too much (evidenced, as they saw, it, by the fact that there were no ordinances specifically aimed at eliminating massage parlors), the majority admitted that the community did not like massage parlors, and felt that they were "whorehouses" and that the masseuses were "prostitutes," "sluts," and "white trash." They specifically mentioned women as not liking the existence of massage parlors, and "little old ladies and men" as "afraid to walk in [the] door." One related that she "gave up trying to impress neighbors."

In response to the negative community reaction to massage parlors, some of the masseuses made attempts to counter the label through their own devices, mostly through letters to the editor, proclaiming a number of defenses ranging from an appeal for a truly "open marketplace," to quoting biblical scriptures of the "judge not" variety and stating, "We don't drag our customers in; they come in on their own accord. I am sure some people appreciate us."

As to their own self-image, a few could not specify what they really considered themselves to be (occupationally speaking). Several mentioned therapeutic masseuse or provider of physical culture. One or two spoke of being an entertainer (providing "playboy" type of entertainment) or rendering a service to the public. One spoke of her work as being in a "class all its own." A number were frank in their negative assessment of their specialty, however, and spoke of themselves as "professional meat beaters" or, as one more eloquently put it, a "pecker checker and joint jerker." They variously spoke of providing different services for the community, including providing enjoyment, relieving sexual tension, and reducing rape, in addition to giving massages per se. Because they were rendering a sexual service, some were concerned about being labeled as prostitutes. As one massuse put it, "I guess I do worry about my reputation because I don't want to be known as a whore." Approximately one-half said they did not have guilt feelings about the nature of their job; the others, however, said they did have guilt feelings, at least at times. One even elaborated, and said, "I feel bad—[it makes me] lower myself."

The masseuses not only attempt to neutralize the public image of their work, but also make efforts to rationalize this work to themselves, as well as to others. One masseuse, for example, defended her job by asserting that the penis was a muscle just like any other muscle. Other writers[7] have reported a similar acceptance on the part of the masseuses to the exigent necessity of providing "locals." One account suggested that, "Well, like 99 out of 100 would! Not all of them would go beyond that, but almost any girl that came in would give a local without even batting an eye! [p. 63]"

Another means of coping with the negative self-image generated by the nature of their work involves adopting a high degree of impersonalization between the masseuse and the customer. Said one masseuse: "I imagine it's like a doctor or something—you just don't think about what you're doing. I think about something the kids did last week or something like that. You're not involved. What the heck. Get it over and it's finished."

In spite of the problem of a negative community reaction and an often unsatisfactory occupational self-image, when asked how they liked their present job, the majority expressed a favorable attitude with responses such as "love it," "fine," "O.K." or "like it," "[it's] different [and] sometimes exciting." A few were ambivalent and commented that they did not like it or disliked it. Several detailed some specific dislikes such as the late hours or the "grimy old men." A number of the girls, however, did qualify their responses with mention of the remunerative nature of the job.

A strong inducement and justification for the masseuse role is simply financial. One masseuse, who adamantly denied being a "prostitute," when asked why she did not become a clerk, waitress, or secretary, or have some other job that would pay approximately the same amount of money declared: "In Mountain City you can't make anywhere near the same amount of money that you can in a massage parlor. If you want to make any kind of money whatsoever and not live in one of these little $80 a month dumps, you work in a massage parlor."

When asked about the view of their husband or boyfriend, the majority of those with a boyfriend replied that he did not care or "thinks it neat." One or two mentioned that the boyfriend enjoyed some economic benefits as a result of their high salary and this may well have been a factor in their view of the work. One masseuse alluded to "steaks and cocktails" so as to suggest that she often treated her boyfriend.

The masseuses with husbands (even one who was separated from her husband) and one of the girls with a boyfriend spoke of the men not approving of their work, and in at least one instance being jealous (during an interview one masseuse was phoned twice by her husband who was checking up on her while she was at work). One mentioned that her boyfriend did not know about "locals." And several mentioned that they were dealing with the situation by not discussing their jobs with husband or boyfriend. It was mentioned that husbands were either not allowed or not welcome. All but one respondent interviewed used her name in her work.

Inasmuch as the girls cannot totally avoid or deny the label and self-image of prostitute, they create a new and less ego-threatening image for themselves by making a definite distinction between "whore" and "hand whore." One masseuse succinctly made this distinction when she emphatically stated that, "I'll hustle my hand but that's it." This relabeling as "hand whore" is similar to the process described by Glaser[4] when he suggests that: "A third alternative mode of reaction to labeling is that of equivocation and counter-labeling. . . . This defense against labeling consists of redefining the deviance to oneself and to others as conformity, or at least as not reflecting anything seriously objectionable [p. 45]." To the masseuses prostituting their hand is presumably not as seriously objectionable as prostituting the rest of their body. Thus anatomical compartmentalization facilitates rationalization, and the process of reconciling economic motives and rewards, self-image, and occupational exigencies becomes more manageable.

REFERENCES

1. Armstrong, E. G. The massage parlor phenomenon. Unpublished paper presented at the Forty-Sixth Annual Meetings of the Virginia Social Science Association, April 28, 1973.

2. Bryan, J. H. Apprenticeships in prostitution. *Social Forces*, 1965, **12**, 287–297.

3. Fortunato, F. Rubdub: The massage is the message. *Penthouse*, October 1973, 129–134.

4. Glaser, D. *Social deviance.* Skokie, Ill.: Rand McNally, 1971.

5. Irons, J. The massage is not the message. *Adam*, 1973, **10**, 5–7.

6. Mano, D. K. Aye, there's the rub. *National Review*, 1972, **24**, 963–964.

7. Velarde, A. J., & Warlick, M. Massage parlors: The sensuality business. *Society*, 1973, **2**, 56–61.

CHAPTER ELEVEN

Sexual Dysfunctions and Diseases

Secondary Orgasmic Dysfunction:
Case Study

Though the word "frigidity" still appears in our language from time to time, Masters and Johnson have given us a much more accurate terminology— *female orgasmic dysfunction*. Specifically, this refers to a situation in which a woman's sexual response involves the excitement and even the plateau phases, but somehow fails to reach the point of orgasm. An individual with this problem thus experiences the sexual act as frustrating and unsatisfying, and as a cause of lowered self-esteem. Because the inability to experience an orgasm is perceived as a failure on the part of the female and also threatens the male's feelings of sexual adequacy, a common response is to *pretend* that orgasm has occurred. Thus, unmarried girls who do not wish to frighten away their lovers, wives who do not wish to create marital disharmony, and bored prostitutes who wish to maintain the fiction of passion with their clients can all become adept at faking their climactic responses. Such performances may occur in erotic movies as well; Hedy Lamarr revealed that her seemingly orgasmic reactions in the film *Ecstasy* were produced by an unseen director sticking her with a pin.

There are two types of nonorgasmic women—those who have never experienced an orgasm (*primary orgasmic dysfunction*) and those who have had at least one but who do not now have them, at least not during intercourse (*secondary* or *situational orgasmic dysfunction*). Though there is the possibility of an organic cause such as a hormonal or neurological disorder, those instances are relatively rare. Interpersonal sources of the problem include a conscious or unconscious dislike of one's mate and/or a sexually clumsy mate who is not oriented toward tenderness, foreplay, or the importance of clitoral stimulation. Intrapersonal sources are perhaps the most commonly reported difficulty, because fear and anxiety can easily interfere with sexual responsiveness; the roots can be shame and guilt about sex, fear of pregnancy, anxieties about being overheard by others in the residence, fear of letting go and losing control of oneself at the moment of climax, and even worry over not being able to have a climax.

In the following article, a team of sex therapists, Arden Snyder, Leslie Lo Piccolo, and Joseph Lo Piccolo, describes one such case in which successful therapy involved both the teaching of sexual techniques *and* an attempt to deal with some of the emotional problems in the marital relationship.

Secondary Orgasmic Dysfunction:
Case Study

Arden Snyder, Leslie Lo Piccolo, and Joseph Lo Piccolo

McGovern and associates[9] indicate that cases of secondary orgasmic dysfunction tend to be associated with a disturbed marital relationship and narrow stimulus control over the occurrence of orgasm. These data also indicate that the usual sexual retraining program leads to marked increases in self-report measures of sexual satisfaction, compatibility, and happiness, but not to increases in the rate of orgasm in intercourse. Because of this failure to accomplish the most direct goal of therapy, and following their data analysis, McGovern, Stewart, and Lo Piccolo recommended two changes in the training program. In the past, the sexual therapy program involved focusing exclusively on sexual problems and avoiding intervention into nonsexual marital problems as much as possible. Thus the therapists would notice but not respond to nonsexual marital pathology except as was absolutely necessary to keep the clients following the sexual training program. Since it now appears that this procedure does not work with cases of secondary orgasmic dysfunction, a directive approach to marriage counseling was employed. The second focus of therapy in this case was an attempt to break the rigid and narrow stimulus control of orgasm that characterized the female client, as is typical in cases of secondary orgasmic dysfunction.

CASE HISTORY

The clients were a young couple in their early 20s, married for 6 months when first seen by the therapists. At intake Mrs. A. was able to reach orgasm while masturbating, but not during genital manipulation by her husband or in coitus. She masturbated digitally, in a rigidly constrained manner. Orgasm could be attained only during masturbation while standing, and the client had masturbated in this manner since early adolescence.

Mrs. A. had initially enjoyed intercourse with her husband, which they began 6 months prior to marriage. However, due to her subsequent inability to reach coital orgasm she gradually came to find all sexual activity aversive. The frequency of intercourse had dropped from three or four times a week prior to marriage to approximately two times a month on entering treatment.

Mrs. A.'s sexual history indicated no unusual or traumatic experiences in childhood. Her parents did make it clear they were against

Reprinted in an edited version from: Snyder, A., Lo Piccolo, L., & Lo Piccolo, J. Secondary orgasmic dysfunction: Case study. *Archives of Sexual Behavior*, 1975, **4**, 277–283.

premarital intercourse, and Mrs. A. did not engage in intercourse until she was in college and met Mr. A.

Mr. A.'s sexual history was relatively unremarkable. His previous sexual experiences included masturbation and petting; however, he did not engage in intercourse until meeting Mrs. A.

The couple began engaging in intercourse a few months after they met. Their first attempts were unpleasant experiences, due to the fear of parental discovery and pregnancy.

After several months of intercourse and concurrent with beginning oral contraceptives, Mrs. A. experienced a lessening in sexual responsiveness and mild depression. On advice of her gynecologist, the oral contraceptives were discontinued but her previous sexual responsiveness did not return.

At intake Mrs. A. reported that she thought she had been orgasmic on 40–50% of coital occasions prior to marriage, but had not experienced coital orgasm during the last several months. As treatment progressed, however, it became clear to the therapists that while Mrs. A. had been highly aroused, it was unlikely that she had ever experienced coital orgasm. She was unable to describe any of the physiological correlates of orgasm during coitus, although she was able to clearly describe these phenomena as occurring when she masturbated. This tendency to misperceive the orgasmic response is common in women with orgasmic difficulties.[9]

COURSE OF TREATMENT

The clients were seen together for 17 sessions over a 15-week period by a male-female cotherapy team. During history taking, it became clear to the therapists that, in addition to the couple's sexual dysfunction, there was also a good deal of marital disharmony. While this is consistent with the findings of McGovern and associates,[9] it was quite surprising in this case as both Mr. and Mrs. A.s' pretreatment scores on the Locke-Wallace Marital Adjustment Test[8] were well into the range considered to indicate satisfactory marital adjustment. On the basis of the clinical material, however, the therapists decided to focus treatment on three issues: (1) training in sexual technique, (2) breaking the narrow stimulus control of orgasm, and (3) dealing with the marital problems. Despite the fact that these were carried out more or less concurrently, they will be presented separately in the interest of clarity.

Sexual technique training

Treatment emphasized reduction of performance anxiety, increase in verbal feedback, and acquisition of more effective sexual techniques. Since the approach is well described elsewhere,[5,8] it will not be elaborated on here. Briefly, the clients were initially forbidden to engage in sexual intercourse. They were then given "homework" assignments each week. During the first week, only hugging, kissing, and body massage were permitted. This assignment allowed the couple to focus on sensual pleasure without anticipating, with anxiety, sexual intercourse. In subsequent weeks, the couple gradually moved toward intercourse by successively adding behaviors such as breast touching and genital stimulation by manual, oral, and electric vibrator means. Intercourse was introduced in a series of successive approximations starting with partial penile insertion with no movement, penile insertion with female movement, and finally full insertion with mutual pelvic thrusting and ejaculation. To eliminate performance anxiety, these behaviors were introduced only when both partners felt comfortable with the next step.

Breaking stimulus control of orgasm

Annon[1] has suggested that women who have narrow stimulus control over orgasm in their masturbation can learn new means of reaching orgasm by gradually switching from their restricted method to positions and techniques of masturbation which approximate coitus. Rather than follow this gradual stimulus generalization procedure in this case, the therapists decided to simply extinguish the stimulus-response link between standing masturbation and orgasm. Mrs. A. was forbidden to continue in her pattern of standing while masturbating. The therapists explained that discontinuing her current practice was necessary in order for her to learn to respond to a wider variety of sexual stimulation. She was therefore started on a nine-step program of masturbation designed to result in coital orgasm.[4] This program begins with visual and tactile exploration of the pelvic region, to locate sensitive areas; progresses to manipulation of these areas; and eventually (step 6) involves stimulation of the clitoral region with an electric vibrator. To break the previously established pattern of orgasm only while standing, the client was instructed to engage in each step of this program while lying down. Initially, while learning to masturbate in this new way, the client was not aroused, but she did eventually become orgasmic. Once orgasm in masturbation while lying down was well established, the final three steps of the masturbation program were used to transfer orgasmic response to coitus.[4] In subsequent weeks, Mrs. A. masturbated with her husband watching her, masturbated with her husband kissing, caressing, and embracing her, and then guided her husband's manipulation of her genitals. At this point, she began to experience orgasm during her husband's manipulation of her genitals with her vibrator. All that remained at this point was to instruct the clients to continue clitoral stimulation *during* coitus, and shortly Mrs. A. became orgasmic in intercourse.

Teaching a woman to switch, via successive approximation, her masturbation from the clitoris to the vaginal opening as Annon[1] advocates may be inefficient, given the Kinsey et al.[2] and the Masters and Johnson[7] data that clitoral stimulation is the focus for female orgasm. Annon's procedure, involving successive changes in masturbatory focus from the clitoral shaft to the mons area, to the vulva area, and to vaginal stimulation when orgasm is imminent may, furthermore, reinforce a client's erroneous belief in the now generally discredited concept of vaginal orgasm. It may be more effective to simply teach clients to have coital orgasms by maintaining active manual stimulation of the clitoris during intercourse, as was done in this case. Annon's procedure is, however, well thought out and is reported to have produced results with one client.[1]

Marital problems

After emphasizing to the couple the positive aspects of their relationship, the therapists pointed out that Mrs. A.'s dissatisfaction with her career prospects was having a negative influence on their sexual adjustment. The therapists shared their impression that Mrs. A. wanted either to attend graduate school or to secure employment in some field related to her art major, rather than take a menial job to support her husband and remain professionally stagnant for 4 years while he pursued his graduate career. The legitimacy of Mrs. A.'s discouragement over what she felt was expected of her was supported by the therapists, who openly indicated their belief that women should be permitted the same opportunity to develop their potential as men. Meanwhile, Mr. A.'s attentive listening and expressions of concern for his wife's feelings were mentioned and reinforced with praise. This strategy was aimed at minimizing his defensiveness and maintaining her esteem for him.

The therapists informed Mr. and Mrs. A. that they were convinced that until this issue was resolved the sexual problem would probably not be alleviated. It was suggested that they thoroughly talk out their thoughts and feelings about the issue and rate their conversations on a 1 to 10 scale along a "constructive-destructive" continuum. Mrs. A. was also encouraged to write out what she felt she "should do" and what she "wanted to do" in order to ensure that her value conflict would be clearly expressed in their discussions.

Several other marital problems emerged at this point: Mrs. A. felt negative about their spending too much time with their parents. She also resented the subtle pressure from Mr. A.'s mother to take a menial job to support Mr. A. She expressed dissatisfaction with Mr. A.'s constant compliance with his parents' wishes. In response to these issues, the therapists were directive and confrontive and informed the clients that satisfying sexual relations were dependent on redefining their family as the two of them. They were encouraged to ask "What is best for *us*?"

As the couple became more aware of the interrelatedness of their difficulties, it was recommended that they begin to identify the possible courses of action for their future and start constructing a branching tentative plan.[10] In subsequent interviews, the clients were assisted in exploring possibilities, constructing a plan, identifying choice points, and dealing with parental attitudes. As a result of this plan construction, they were able to disengage from their parents, and agree that Mrs. A. would pursue a graduate career in art.

OUTCOME DATA

Assessment data were collected from the couple before and after treatment and at 3 months following termination of therapy. A number of scores from this assessment battery are presented in Table 11-1. These data indicate that gains were made in all aspects of the sexual relationship. Additionally, at termination Mr. and Mrs. A. reported they were each initiating sexual intercourse about equally often, in marked contrast to their pretherapy pattern of Mr. A.'s usually doing the initiating. In response to the questionnaire item "Overall, how satisfactory to you is your sexual relationship?" both Mr. and Mrs. A. responded "extremely satisfactory" at the close of treatment in comparison to their responses of "slightly unsatisfactory" (Mr. A.) and "moderately unsatisfactory" (Mrs. A.) prior to treatment.

Mr. and Mrs. A. made significant gains in their sexual relationship as measured by scores on the Sexual Interaction Inventory.[6] For those scales that indicated the most pathology at intake, scores after treatment changed in the desired direction.

Scores on the Locke-Wallace Marital Adjustment Test[3] showed that the overall marital relationship improved following treatment.

Table 11-1
Changes in Sexual Behavior Following Treatment

	Before Treatment	After Treatment	Follow-up
Frequency of intercourse	once or twice a month	twice a week	twice a week
Duration of foreplay	15–30 min	30–60 min	16–30 min
Duration of intercourse	4–7 min	7–10 min	7–10 min
Percentage of female orgasm through genital stimulation by male	0%	100%	100%
Percentage of female orgasm in intercourse with concurrent clitoral stimulation	0%	50%	100%

A woman who had never had an orgasm during intercourse with her husband improved markedly after treatment. Intercourse occurred more frequently, lasted longer, and resulted in orgasm after successful sexual therapy.

DISCUSSION

In this case, a directive and confrontive marital therapy plus a direct, simplistic approach to breaking stimulus control of orgasm led to a successful treatment outcome. As reported by McGovern et al.,[9] the usual sex therapy program had previously failed to increase the orgasmic response in coitus of six successive secondary inorgasmic women. Two other couples with secondary orgasmic dysfunction have since been seen by other therapy teams, and in both cases following the procedures outlined in this article has led to regular coital orgasm. While treatment of only three cases clearly does not "prove" the effectiveness of a set of procedures, it is hoped that this report will lead other therapists to experiment with this therapeutic strategy.

REFERENCES

1. Annon, J. S. The therapeutic use of masturbation in the treatment of sexual disorders. Paper presented at the Fifth Annual Meeting of the Association for the Advancement of Behavior Therapy, Washington, D. C., 1971.

2. Kinsey, A. C., Pomeroy, W. B., Martin, C. E., & Gebhard, P. H. *Sexual behavior in the human female.* Philadelphia: Saunders, 1953.

3. Locke, H. J., & Wallace, K. M. Short marital adjustment and prediction tests: Their reliability and validity. *Marriage Family Living,* 1959, 21, 251–255.

4. Lo Piccolo, J., & Lobitz, W. C. The role of masturbation in the treatment of primary orgasmic dysfunction. *Archives of Sexual Behavior,* 1972, 2, 163–171.

5. Lo Piccolo, J., & Lobitz, W. C. Behavior therapy of sexual dysfunction. In L. A. Hammerlynck, L. C. Handy, & E. J. Mash (Eds.), *Behavior change: Methodology, concepts, and practice.* Champaign, Ill.: Research Press, 1974.

6. Lo Piccolo, J., & Steger, J. C. The Sexual Interaction Inventory: A new instrument for assessment of sexual dysfunction. *Archives of Sexual Behavior,* 1974, 3, 585–595.

7. Masters, W. H., & Johnson, V. E. *Human sexual response.* Boston: Little, Brown, 1966.

8. Masters, W. H., & Johnson, V. E. *Human sexual inadequacy.* Boston: Little, Brown, 1970.

9. McGovern, K. B., Stewart, R., & Lo Piccolo, J. Secondary orgasmic dysfunction. I. Analysis and strategies for treatment. *Archives of Sexual Behavior,* 1975, 4, 265–275.

10. Tyler, L. *The work of the counselor.* New York: Appleton, 1969.

The Hypnotherapeutic Approach
to Male Impotence

If the nonorgasmic female feels frustrated by and ashamed of her sexual difficulties and if her mate responds to the problem with a degree of self-blame, consider the plight of the impotent male—literally, the word means "powerless." An erection is both symbolically and practically the basic indicator of masculinity, and its absence is a source of humiliation. Not only is the individual frustrated and embarrassed, but there is no way to "fake" an erection so that the partner is always aware of the problem, equally frustrated sexually, and she can be either contemptuous of the weakling who "can't get it up" or consumed by her own failure to be adequately arousing.

Those who have never had an erection are said to be suffering from *primary impotence*; otherwise, the problem is termed *secondary impotence.* As with orgasmic dysfunction in the female, the male's impotence can stem from a physiological disorder, but such cases (*organic impotence*) are actually fairly unusual. More common is *functional impotence* which indicates that a normally functioning male has been rendered impotent by some physical cause. Perhaps the most familiar such barriers to erections are excessive alcohol or other drugs, fatigue, and old age. Most instances of lasting impotence, however, are psychological in origin, hence the term *psychogenic impotence*. As wtih females, males can be rendered sexually dysfunctional by anxieties, worries, and fears which may relate to sex or to extraneous problems such as finances or career. There is also a vicious-circle effect in that any episode of impotence can result in *that* becoming the focus of a male's sexual anxieties, which in turn interferes still further with the ability to obtain an erection. In some instances, a male may be able to masturbate with no erectile difficulties, but be unable to function with a partner because of social anxieties, fear of failure and rejection, and/or because of negative feelings associated with women in general or with a specific female.

In most therapy procedures for the treatment of impotence, the emphasis is on relaxation, learning to enjoy sexual pleasures without concentrating on performance, reassurance about the meaning of temporary impotence, learning to utilize fantasies as a source of arousal, and, often, on uncovering and dealing with unconscious emotional problems. In the following article, psychologist Hugo Beigel describes how hypnotism can be used as a means of facilitating such treatment.

The Hypnotherapeutic Approach to Male Impotence

Hugo G. Beigel

In 1955, Oscar Diethelm (*Treatment in Psychiatry*. Springfield, Ill.: Thomas, 1955) recommended the use of hypnosis in all those instances

Reprinted in an edited version from: Beigel, H. G. The hypnotherapeutic approach to male impotence. *Journal of Sex Research*, 1971, **7**, 168–176.

in which "impotence is related to lack of self-confidence, based on feelings of general inadequacy, or body overconcern, or where patients would be unable to deal with dynamic factors."

In the years that have passed since this book was published, hypnotic techniques have been so perfected that there is no subspecies of psychogenic impotence that cannot be successfully remedied by hypnotherapeutic treatment, excepting of course the instances in which the use of hypnosis is counterindicated for reasons inherent in the patient's personality structure. Hypnotherapy does not coincide with the television fan's image of a hypnotist commanding the bed-bound patient to rise (or whatever part of his should but does not seem to be capable of a similar effort). Rather the therapist employing this method addresses himself to the total personality of whose insufficiency in one or several respects non-organic impotence always is the expression.

The time in therapy, therefore, is divided between waking sessions and those in which hypnosis is used. The key to this division depends on the patient's ability to assist in getting at the causes of his trouble and his need to gain or regain confidence in his functioning. From the information received in the waking sessions the material is derived for situations to be suggested under hypnosis. The revelations made under hypnosis, however, are used for further probing in either the hypnotic or the waking state, for interpretations of expressed or illusioned experiences, and for the activation of the pertinent psychic dynamics.

Hypnosis itself serves in (1) the identification or confirmation of causative factors; (2) the elimination of mental block; (3) the emotional revivification of repressed or otherwise vague memories and the vivid imagining of desirable changes; (4) the planting of ideas essential to the change of attitudes toward the self, others, or specific objects, ideas, and circumstances; (5) the posthypnotic execution of tasks supporting the goal of the therapy; (6) the checking of his progress with regard to self-confidence and altered awareness; (7) the obtaining of material that has been withheld because the patient was unaware of its existence or considered it irrelevant or shameful.

Patients are rarely in doubt about the symptom itself. What has caused it, however, is not often known to them and must usually be concluded from their reports on their sexual experiences, concepts, thoughts, and fears. Since their statements are not necessarily complete or accurate, conclusions drawn from them do not always come even close to the bull's-eye.

Yet the correct diagnosis of the psychogenic process is the keystone of the therapeutic architecture. Whatever suspicion or doubt has been raised or whatever guess has to be made is therefore subjected to verification under hypnosis.

To give an example, Norman, 28 years old, had been married for 2 years. During the honeymoon the couple had had intercourse three times. Since then one time, and this one time more than a year before he sought therapy. The wife wanted a child. He did not really care either about a child or about intercourse. For, as he explained, when he came home from his job, he was dead tired and it merely annoyed him if she tried to interest him in sex relations. As a result, he rarely developed an erection of sufficient rigidity and if apparently he did, it collapsed during the fumbling attempts at intromission.

Reluctantly he confessed that he masturbated occasionally, allegedly without fantasies. He attributed his lack of interest in intercourse to his wife's prudish and ritualistic attitude that took all spontaneity out of sexual communication. In addition, he was disappointed in her. She did not share his interests as he had expected her to do and did not talk about anything except the immediate domestic needs and occurrences. Added to his own outspoken passive personality and an upbringing in the spirit of rigid religious sect, the disillusion could explain his difficulty.

To see whether it was really due to the man's aversion to or disinterest in the wife, the following imagery was suggested to him under hypnosis. "These are the Arabian Nights. You are an Arabian potentate. Half-naked women are dancing for you. Two of them are keeping close to you. One is Barbara (his wife). They are stripping. They are making seductive gestures at you. You are in the right mood. You like these girls, especially the one. You are reaching for her. You are pulling her to you on the cushions. You are kissing her . . . ."

At this point he was told to go on with the adventure and tell what was happening and how it ended.

The ending was, in fact, rather unexpected. He chose the other woman, not his wife. But as they rolled over each other, she turned into a man.

Confronted with the revelation of this happening Norman for the first time admitted homosexual leanings.

He had not lied when he said that he had had no sexual contacts with males after a short adolescent encounter. His religious beliefs had prevented him from indulging in overt homosexual acts, but they were unable to curb homosexual dreams, the feeling of being attracted by men, nor could they do away with his complete disinterest in women.

This finding dictated the course of the therapy: after much more probing, desensitization of homosexual feelings and sensitization to feminine attractiveness was attempted.

As in this case, in most others certain tendencies must be reduced and others intensified in order to assure restoration of sexual functioning. In one, for instance, the lessening of an aesthetically perceived revulsion at the sight or touch of the female genital had to be combined with the building up of a very wobbly self-confidence; in a second, anxieties aroused by past incest fantasies must be alleviated while at the same time thinking and feeling must be eroticized. In a third group of cases, a roaming sexual appetite must be balanced with all the tolerance to which a guilt-besieged conscience can be stretched.

Referring back to one of the possibilities just alluded to, we do not assume, of course, that nausea at the sight or touch of a vagina can be the only cause of a man's impotence. Such a trauma needs fertile ground to blossom to psychosomatic dimensions. Mere desensitization without probing more deeply, therefore, is not enough.

This technique is not new. Hypnotherapy however, has given it a new dimension. Under hypnosis the visual, tactile, oral, and genital contact is being related to pleasures which the patient has experienced, though more often than not at other than erotic occasions. The depiction of the originally repulsive content is not left entirely to imagination. The patient is exposed to pictures, first in the posthypnotic state after appropriate preparation under hypnosis. The pictures are of an erotic nature, growing in directness and naturalness. Art is a very effective bridge to live photos. Under hypnosis the patient is encouraged to put himself into situations suggested by such pictures. Later these pictures are scanned in the waking state and still later, wherever this is possible, the patient is supposed to transfer these hopeful imageries and fantasies into reality. The expectation, naturally, is that such situations either provoke what they would provoke in sexually unimpaired men, or, in different circumstances, no longer negatively affect the man. The time for reality testing has come when the feared situation is successfully presented in hypnotic imagery without any reference by the therapist to either fear or pleasure and a happy ending, preferably with actual sexual arousal, occurs during this procedure.

Experience has taught us that the results are more reliable if desensitization is preceded by conveying to the patient what circumstances accomplished the relation of two basically incongruous factors like stomach upset and the sight of a healthy female anatomy. To facilitate the search, the patient may be led under hypnosis either through experiences in which nudity in reality or in depiction or in talk or thoughts may have produced fear, punishment, guilt, or related emotions; or through situations in which past events produced nauseous feelings of similar intensity. In both processes, age regression may be helpful. The eventual finding is interpreted in terms that aid in undoing the undesirable connection. In the case alluded to, for instance, Gene and another boy, both about 8 years old, were invited by an older girl to look at her public hair and finger her vulva. The girl's mother surprised them at the game and slapped her daughter until the girl's nose bled. She did not beat the boys but she promised them an even more severe punishment from their fathers.

Gene was terribly afraid of his father. Anticipating untempered fury and brutality, he contemplated running away. Before he had come to a decision he was called to the supper table. The prevailing silence there did not ease his mind. After a few bites, the agitation affected his stomach and he could just make it to the bathroom before he vomited.

In reply to the routine question about the first failure in sexual functioning, he had previously reported an episode that had occurred when he was 17 years old. Under hypnosis this briefly mentioned episode was now revivified and explored in detail.

Somewhere "near a water" he had met a girl, "a tramp." Now, 12 years later, he described her as dirty and stinking. At the time she must have appeared rather exciting to him, for as she begged him for money and offered intercourse in return, he started pawing her. He was highly excited. But as she readied herself, she pulled some rags from between her legs. They were bloody. Gene's associations to the earlier experience caused his stomach to react. He did not actually throw up, but he was nauseated. He lost his erection, and he had had none since.

With these two episodes linked it was possible to show Gene the origin of his trouble and eventually to free him of it.

More difficult is the extirpation of ideological weed if the misconceptions are based on religious convictions or unquestioned authoritative training. If it becomes necessary to devalue such teachings because they are directly related to the man's impotence, hypnosis again is a very valuable tool. The complete relaxation makes the development of an indiscriminately rejecting attitude unlikely and argumentation unnecessary. In this passive state, a seed of doubt is planted, preferably concerning only the subjective interpretations and distortions of the pertinent teachings. The point to be made is repeated in varied form in subsequent hypnotic sessions. The effect is later tested in casual talk in the waking state after an open-end imagery has confirmed the emotional acceptance.

As has been indicated before, psychogenic sexual inadequacy never involves the genitals alone. It is always combined with other forms of insufficiency. As a rule, therefore, therapy must be extended to disorders directly or indirectly related to the symptom that brought the patient into therapy. Some of these men have immense feelings of inferiority either produced, or more often, intensified by genital impotence; some are incapable of forming human relationships; some are caught in magical concepts; and some are extremely inhibited. Whatever masks have been chosen to compensate for the shortcomings, they have to be broken if the patient is supposed to manage the stages that are considered preparatory to sexual intercourse.

This goes for married men as well as for the unmarried. Mutual concern and sexual interest in the marital union can be of great help in restoring normal functioning. Not only can all imagery be focused upon the mate, but guided posthypnotic nightdreams that have an arousing effect can be immediately translated into reality. Also the wife can be informed about the most and the least favorable approach to the man's problem and she can be persuaded to make concessions as long as the husband's confidence is still weak, or she can be told in which manner the husband may make his first try and be asked to tolerate whatever features in the beginning may not quite be to her own tastes. She may be induced to give up antisexual peculiarities (doing it only at night; in pajamas; in the dark; after a lengthy procedure of washing stockings, putting her hair in curlers, and the like) and to accept preferences of his that facilitate his functioning. Some wives are willing to cooperate but sometimes more elasticity is required than she can, or is willing to, muster.

Quite frequently, however, the man asking for therapy does not want his wife to participate or even to know of his decision. Some apparently feel that seeking therapy might indicate greater interest in the hedonistic business of sex than is legitimate, others obviously hope for extramarital pleasures but are afraid of failing in such adventures as they have been failing sexually with their wives. Is one instance, the man had regular but unsatisfactory intercourse with his wife; as a way out he sought extramarital liaisons, but in these attempts he proved to be impotent. So he asked for repair of this defect and, naturally, could not involve his wife.

Greater still than the number of such husbands is the number of men who are unmarried and also otherwise unattached. Many of them are extremely shy. Their feelings of inadequacy inhibit their approach to the opposite sex and any closer contact rouses the fear of seeing their defect exposed. Not only do they, therefore, come alone, but in addition to the therapy of the psychosomatic disorder a reeducational therapy concentrated on these shortcomings must accompany the one focusing on the main symptom.

In most instances, it can be ascertained that the symptom is of psychogenic origin by the fact that the patient can produce an erection by masturbation or upon direct hypnotic suggestion, or he reports more or less regularly appearing morning erections. If not, a urologist may confirm the absence of any detectable physiological or endocrinological cause. Neither of these factors, however, guarantees that the membrum will tumefy in the presence of an undressed girl or that the tumescence can be maintained when intromission into the female genital is attempted. While the origin of the disorder is established, partly on the grounds of conscious memory, partly in its deeper or repressed layers during hypnosis, sensitization or desensitization is introduced. By guided imagery with positive suggestions following, the man's desire is intensified, erotic dreams are suggested, and after occurrence analyzed. By these means the man is guided to develop a relationship with a female that may lead to sex relations. When such a relationship is established, he is neither pushed toward sexual communication nor slowed down in his eagerness to consummate them. Many of these men need basic information about how to approach a potential partner and how to keep a forming relationship alive. Often they have exaggerated standards of what a female whom they are seen with must look like. They are afraid that if she is not superperfect everybody would know why he had to content himself with the dregs. In part this is also a device to prevent an actual confrontation with both his clumsiness, inexperience, and the nuclear problem itself. This usually requires considerable work. Similarly, the usually lacking knowledge about sexual behavior itself must be gone into, preferable positions must be explained, the preliminaries be described, etc. He is warned not to rush, not to seek a test of his potency, not to "work" on bringing an erection about, but to surrender completely to the sensory pleasure that he has learned to enjoy and to provoke and, when the erection develops, to act in accordance with his feelings rather than the concepts of sexual politeness. These concepts are stressed in the waking state, suggested under hypnosis, reinforced in guided imagery depicting sexual situations, and eventually integrated in a posthypnotic suggestion if a specific date is likely to lead to greater intimacy than the previous ones. In most cases, this last step is not actually necessary, but it gives the patient a feeling of security and should therefore not be omitted. However, such posthypnotic suggestions are given only two times; thereafter they are replaced by a one-time general assurance that proper functioning is no longer in doubt. This limitation is necessary to demonstrate to the patient that he is no longer dependent on hypnosis.

This, of course, is only a schematic presentation of the hypnotherapeutic approach to impotence. Time does not allow the description of the variations by means of which the method is adjusted to the type of impotence from which the complainant suffers, the personality of the afflicted individual, the cause to which the disorder is traced, and the one which the patient ascribes to it. Evidently the converted homosexual, the male virgin, and the victim of a traumatic experience require different manners of handling the tools. So does the man whose potentia erigandi and ejaculandi appear to be normal except that he seems to have lost all capacity for pleasant sensations in the genitals and the erogenic zones; and, of course, the man who attributes his impotence to a curse or another magic cause.

I had two cases of this kind. One offers a unique example of the liability and vulnerability of the sexual apparatus. The man came to see me the first time when he was 45 years old. He felt that his sexual powers were draining from him as a result of some mystical involvement. When he was 20 and began to stay over night with practically every woman who offered him a bed, his mother warned him, "You are behaving like your father. And if you continue so, to you will happen what happened to him. He ceased being a man when he was 45 years old."

My client ridiculed this warning as he had then done when his mother had come out with it, but it must have had an effect on him, because at that time he made serious attempts to curb his sexual contacts. His rationalization was that sexual adventures impaired his creative power. Years later, when he had to admit to himself that he would never be the Verdi or Beethoven of his period, he regretted the time wasted without all the sexual pleasure he could have had and tried to catch up on his loss.

By now he was married and had a lady friend. But recently he had felt less appetite and experienced an occasional failure with her. This brought his mother's threat back to his mind. He was in his 40s. So had his father been when he "ceased to be a man." He was frightened. What he actually wanted was to counter the mystic power with another magic, hypnosis.

He came several times when he felt prone to failure and was—apparently successfully—reassured.

Eleven years later he reappeared admitting that possibly therapy was indicated. He was 56 years old, had buried his first wife and married a second one. They had, he said, a happy life together, but for the last 6 months he had been incapable of intercourse. He did not believe in the effect of the curse anymore but the terms "guilt" and "fear" also were unacceptable to him.

Yet, his second wife had a daughter from her first marriage. The girl, 23 years old, had several months ago come for a visit and had stayed in his and her mother's home for 2 weeks. A grateful guest, she had acceded to the stepfather's sexual wishes. Or had tried to. For he made two attempts to have intercourse with her but was unable to produce an erection. If this was bad, something worse followed; he also became impotent with his wife.

The repair took considerably longer this time. However, the man was a paradigm of suggestibility; virility was restored within a few months.

Unfortunately sexual potency does not last forever. The man looked me up again 14 years later. He was now 70 years old. Sexual functioning had first become more sporadic, then it ceased. He did not take it lightly as the philosophers say one should. He was sure hypnotherapy would restore his manly powers. I tried to convince him of the existence of insurmountable natural obstacles. We did use hypnosis again, but this time only to make submission to the inevitable easier for him and to teach him that the end of erection time need not mean the end of all sexual pleasure.

Group Treatment of Premature Ejaculation

The male's ejaculation response is not under direct conscious control any more than is the female's orgasm. In both sexes, such responses can occur during sleep or other types of unconsciousness, and the mechanism seems to involve signals from the brain via the spinal cord. There are two types of ejaculatory dysfunction. The less common problem is *ejaculatory incompetence* in which there is an erection and the ability to engage in intercourse, but there is no orgasmic response. This inability to ejaculate can sometimes occur after excessive alcohol ingestion (the sensitivity of the nerves is impaired, for one thing), but this problem spontaneously clears up when the alcohol is out of the man's system. A more serious difficulty is the inability to ejaculate during intercourse, even though the individual is able to masturbate successfully. A treatment procedure developed by Masters and Johnson involves a series of interactions with the sex partner in which she brings him to climax manually. After several such sessions she gradually proceeds to a combination of manual stimulation followed by insertion of the penis in the vagina at the moment of ejaculation. These interactions continue with increasingly greater portions of the time devoted to intercourse until normal functioning is restored.

A more common problem is that of *premature ejaculation* in which the male reaches a climax too rapidly to be able to satisfy his partner during intercourse. The definition of "too rapid" has been a problem, obviously. Kinsey and his associates defined premature ejaculation as a climax occurring within 1 min after the penis enters the vagina. In the following article by a Cornell medical team, the definition of Masters and Johnson is presented along with their own contributions. Their therapy procedure involves group treatment in which couples are instructed in the use of the now-famous "squeeze technique" and also are encouraged to discuss more general interpersonal problems that often contribute to the difficulty.

An alternative notion about the cause of premature ejaculation has been that it is the result of extreme sensitivity and excitability. Given that hypothesis, the obvious solution is to reduce feelings and excitement. Thus sensitivity can be reduced physiologically by overdrinking prior to intercourse or by the application of one of several nerve-deadening chemical preparations that promise to prolong, retard, or delay one's climax. Excitement can be reduced by masturbation to orgasm prior to intercourse or by attempting to dampen the imaginative response during intercourse by reciting the multiplication tables or thinking other nonsexual thoughts. Such approaches have been found to be unsatisfactory in that they are unreliable, provide no permanent solution to premature ejaculation, and, besides, they tend to decrease the male's sexual pleasure. The much more successful approach of current sex therapy strives to make the individual aware of and in control of his sexual sensations.

Group Treatment of Premature Ejaculation

Helen S. Kaplan, Richard N. Kohl,
Wardell B. Pomeroy, Avodah K. Offit, and Barbara Hogan

A pilot study of the group treatment of premature ejaculation is being undertaken as part of the Sex Therapy and Education Program of the Payne Whitney Psychiatric Clinic of the New York Hospital-Cornell Medical Center. The following is a report of the first group, which consisted of four couples. Premature ejaculation of the male was the chief complaint of each couple. The goal of the treatment was limited to the attainment of ejaculatory control.

DEFINITION OF PREMATURE EJACULATION

Premature ejaculation is probably the most common sexual dysfunction of American males, occurring in the psychiatrically healthy as well as in patients exhibiting various forms of psychopathology. It is a condition wherein a man reaches orgasm very quickly. Definitions of premature ejaculation have varied. They have been given in terms of length of coital time prior to ejaculation, number of strokes prior to ejaculation, and, by Masters and Johnson,[1] percentage of times in which the man reaches orgasm before the woman (more than 50% equals premature ejaculation). In contrast, at the Cornell Medical Center, we believe that the essential parameter of premature ejaculation consists of the failure of the man to attain control over the ejaculatory reflex once an intense level of sexual arousal has been attained, with the result that once excited he reaches orgasm rapidly. Hence, we define prematurity as the inability of a man to tolerate high (plateau) levels of sexual excitement without ejaculating reflexly.

TYPES OF TREATMENT

Various forms of therapy have been tried to cure prematurity with varying degrees of success. These have included psychoanalytic methods, "common sense" and behavioral approaches, and, more recently, a highly effective "sensory training" technique.

Psychoanalytic treatment is based on the premise that premature ejaculation is an expression of the unconscious conflicts regarding women which derive from developmental problems in the patient's childhood. The analytic methods have been employed to uncover and resolve the patient's postulated unconscious conflicts and hostilities toward

Reprinted in an edited version from: Kaplan, H. S., Kohl, R. N., Pomeroy, W. B., Offit, A. K., & Hogan, B. Group treatment of premature ejaculation. *Archives of Sexual Behavior*, 1974, **3**, 443–452.

females, with the expectation that such a resolution would be accompanied by an automatic improvement in sexual functioning. Although no systematic study has been performed, the general impression is that results of insight therapy alone, at least for the relief of premature ejaculation, have been disappointing.

The "common sense" approach, which is widely espoused by the medical profession and laity alike, is based on the supposition that premature ejaculation is caused by excessive erotic sensation and that the remedy lies in diminishing this sensation. Specific techniques prescribed by physicians include the use of condoms, anesthetic ointments applied to the penis, distraction from the sexual experience in progress by nonerotic imagery, and the use of alcohol, sedatives, and tranquilizers. All of these have been unsuccessful.

Behavioral approaches have also been applied to the therapy of prematurity. These have mainly employed desensitization, on the theory that anxiety is a cause of premature ejaculation. Behavioral treatment has not been very effective.

Various pharmacological treatments have also been tried. The use of tricyclic and hydrazine antidepressants has some success while the patient uses those drugs. However, when medication is discontinued, the man again is unable to exert voluntary control over ejaculation and reaches climax quickly.

Marital therapy treats prematurity by attempting to resolve the alleged transactional roots of the symptom. Again, to date there are no reports of success of this approach.

The most successful, however, and the foundation of the Masters and Johnson approach, was reported in 1956 by the urologist James Semans,[2] who based his treatment on "prolonging the localized neuromuscular reflex mechanism of ejaculation," which he felt was "extremely rapid" in premature ejaculation. His technique was exceedingly simple. It consisted of extravaginal stimulation of the man by his wife, until the sensation premonitory to ejaculation was attained, then interruption of the stimulation until the man could tolerate this stimulation indefinitely without ejaculating. At that point, in the eight patients who made up his study population prematurity was permanently relieved.

The Masters-Johnson approach is essentially the same. It differs primarily in substituting a "squeeze" of the penis (just below the rim of the glans) at the time of ejaculatory premonition, rather than a simple cessation of stimulation. The Masters-Johnson treatment also involves a complex, intensive format wherein the couple under treatment is seen every day for 2 weeks by a mixed-gender cotherapy team. In addition to the squeeze technique, various other exercises, including sensate focus, are included in the treatment regimen. A 98% success rate is reported by Masters and Johnson with this approach.

A WORKING CONCEPT OF PREMATURE EJACULATION

One implication of the success of the Semans type of approach is that an understanding of the original motivation roots of premature ejaculation is irrelevant for the purpose of treatment: the underlying dynamics do not have to be resolved in order for the patient to achieve ejaculatory control. Perhaps there are many remote factors that play a role in the etiology of prematurity. However, the multiple remote causes of the condition may be bypassed. It is only the immediate antecedents of the man's failure to acquire ejaculatory continence which have to be modified to cure the patient. What are these immediate antecedents? The final answer to this question is not clear. However, we postulate that for some reason, because of unconscious conflict or perhaps some other cause, the premature ejaculator has not focused his attention on the sensation of sexual arousal. He virtually does not perceive the sensations premonitory to orgasm and has therefore failed to learn control of his ejaculatory reflex. This is analogous to a child's failure to learn urinary continence because he has not perceived the sensations of a full bladder. The essential aim of treatment then becomes the clear-cut one of supplying previously deficient perceptual links to encourage the patient to be aware of and experience his sexual sensations.

APPROACH OF THE CORNELL PROGRAM

The approach to the therapy of prematurity in our program is based on these principles. As is true of the treatment of all sexual dysfunctions, the format employs exercises to be carried out by the patient and his wife in the privacy of their home which are integrated with conjoint psychotherapeutic sessions in the clinic. The primary aim of the exercises used in the therapy of prematurity is to help the man focus his attention and concentrate on, and fully experience, the sensations premonitory to orgasm. This experience must occur together with his partner because it is anxiety engendered by the sexual and marital transactions which often seem to distract the husband from abandoning himself to his sexual sensations.

Treatment begins with an evaluation session, attended by the couple, during which a detailed history is obtained of the sexual functioning of both partners. All motivated couples are accepted for treatment except those in which *either* partner exhibits active, severe psychopathology or in which the sexual symptom appears to be employed as a major defense against pathology.

The couple is given an explanation of the rationale behind the treatment, and it is made clear to the wife that, initially at least, there may be little reward for her. If she can defer her immediate gratification, a therapeutic "contract" is entered into with the couple, whereby they agree to cooperate in the recommended treatment. They are also made aware that they themselves are responsible for the success of the treatment. Finally, they are told that the prognosis for rapid relief is excellent, provided that they adhere to the treatment.

Couples are seen conjointly, usually once a week for 3–6 weeks, for a total of 6 to 12 times, and encouraged to telephone their therapist should questions arise. The exercises themselves, carried out in the home, follow a two-part sequence: extravaginal stimulation and stimulation during coitus. The exercises are based on the Semans approach. Initially, the man is stimulated manually by his wife, with four premonitory "ceases" prescribed before ejaculation is to be allowed. When improvement in control is seen, the exercises are repeated, with the penis first lubricated by vaseline, as this more closely simulates the vaginal environment. After three to six extravaginal sessions, sufficient improvement usually is attained to permit the beginning of intercourse. Intercourse is first attempted in the female-superior position, as being less stimulating to the man; with success, the lateral and then the male-superior position is attempted. The stop-short technique is used during the early intercourse sessions and is suggested for occasional use after treatment is terminated. As stated, the prognosis is excellent in that, if the couple follows the instructions and performs the exercises, the man will reach his goal of being able to choose when to ejaculate. In fact, we have treated 32 premature ejaculation couples with this approach, and of the couples who have completed therapy none has failed to attain ejaculatory continence. However, since these trials were not done under controlled conditions these promising results must be regarded with caution. Nonetheless, we were encouraged by this apparent success to hypothesize that the essential ingredients in the therapy of prematurity have been identified. Moreover, the therapy was exceedingly simple and might be more economically applied in a group setting in which several couples could be treated simultaneously.

GROUP TREATMENT

Our first group treatment for prematurely ejaculating men was undertaken with four couples, all having stable marriages, all without severe psychopathology in either partner, all previously screened and evaluated. Group sessions were 45 min long, and the group was seen once a week for 6 weeks. The group was directed by Drs. Kaplan, Pomeroy, Offit, and Mrs. Hogan as a task-oriented, theme-centered group, with the group process used to enhance the sex treatment. Specifically it was the objective of the group sessions to convey instructions for the exercises which the couples were to carry out at home and also deal with obstacles to sexual functioning and resistances to treatment which almost invariably emerge during the course of therapy. The group met once a week and the session began with the review of each couple's experiences during the previous week. The therapists worked with intrapsychic and transactional resistances to treatment as they emerged. As is usual in group therapy, the group dynamics were employed in the service of revealing and resolving conflicts. However, in this setting our objective was limited to the treatment of prematurity. Therefore, in contrast to the usual group therapy, where transactions between the members are employed to reveal and resolve all manner of problems, here interpretations were made only to implement sex therapy. For this reason, competition among couples was bypassed; emphasis was on mutual support and encouragement. Perhaps the group process can best be understood by describing the results obtained by each couple individually.

First couple

In Couple 1, the man, a 25-year-old carpenter, was married to a woman of the same age. They had been married to each other for 1½ years, and it was the second marriage for each. The wife had two children from her former marriage and was 4 months pregnant when the treatment began. She was attractive, intelligent, and easily multiorgastic. Her husband, whose early sexual experience had been with prostitutes, has been a premature ejaculator since he commenced sexual activity. On his first manual stop/start session, the husband twice successfully controlled his ejaculatory reflex. However, resistances emerged during the next session. He had had too much to drink, and when they began to exercise again he was unable to concentrate on his sensations and thus failed to stop in time, and ejaculated. The wife also presented obstacles. For the third exercise session, the couple did not practice the extravaginal sequence as recommended, but, with the wife's urging, the man proceeded directly to intercourse, in the female-superior position. Not surprisingly, he was unable to concentrate on the penile sensations and ejaculated immediately on insertion.

During a group discussion of these events, the wife of another couple pointed out that this man seemed to have a fear of failure that was distracting him from focusing on his sensations and that his wife also seemed fearful and was pressuring her husband. Clarification of the resistances of this couple helped the rest in getting in touch with their own previously unconscious fears of sexuality. The mutual discussion of this material was extremely helpful to all. However, the couple did not attend the third group session. They came to the fourth. A new resistance was revealed. Describing the exercises they had performed in the meantime, they reported waiting for the man's sexual sensation to cease completely before resuming manual stimulation, instead of resuming stimulation after a few seconds, per instructions. Again, resistances and anxieties were dealt with in the group. The man's sense of inadequacy and some of its roots were discussed during the session. In addition to psychodynamically oriented interpretations, it was pointed out that they were waiting too long and losing the benefit of experience with high plateau levels of excitement. It was suggested by the therapists that they have some additional extravaginal experience and then move to intravaginal stop/start. This was the couple's last session in the group. They canceled the final meeting and were rescheduled 4 months later for follow-up. Surprisingly, this resistant couple had a successful outcome. At the follow-up meeting, they reported having followed the recommended exercise sequence after they left the group, with the husband moving to the lateral and then the male-superior position with increasing success. The husband described a sense of control and awareness of his penile sensations. They declared that intercourse now lasted as long as they liked. She was multiorgastic on coitus, which was now a positive experience for both of them.

Second couple

In Couple 2, the man, a 44-year-old writer, had been married for 8 years to a 37-year-old woman, the second marriage for both. They were a sensitive, intelligent couple. The woman had been in analysis a number of years previously; she had great insight and freely communicated her knowledge and impressions to other group members in a helpful way. She was sexually responsive but coitally inorgastic. The man seemed to have an essentially normal history of sexual and psychological development. His prematurity had its onset with sexual activity. The couple had read Masters and Johnson and had tried, without success, to deal with the prematurity problem by themselves. Although the marriage was basically a healthy one, the man was obsessive and constantly worried about his inability to control his ejaculation and his wife's inability to have orgasm during coitus. For this couple, treatment proceeded without the dramatic resistances demonstrated by Couple 1.

The husband learned to concentrate on his sensations, which he had previously failed to do. He was very impressed with the sexual abandonment that was described by the multiorgastic wife of Couple 1. He compared this with his own constricted attitudes. He was delighted with the improvement of his sexual enjoyment and ejaculatory control, when he too was able to abandon himself "selfishly" to the sexual experience. The other women in the group vociferously confronted the husband with the pressure he was placing on his wife for coital orgasm. The couple discussed this openly between themselves in the group. Two sessions later, she reported that, free from having to worry about her husband's concern for her, she was able to concentrate on her own sexual feelings and was able to experience coital orgasm. He gained satisfactory ejaculatory continence by the fifth group session. The couple could not be reached for follow-up.

Third couple

Couple 3 had been married for 7 years and had one child. The man was a stockbroker, 35 years old; the woman was a teacher and social worker,

32 years old. This also appeared to be a good marriage. The man suffered from premature ejaculation. The wife, who had been in therapy for a short time, had been orgastic in the past, but not within a year of treatment. The man was suffering from a mild depression.

The treatment for this couple also progressed easily to a successful conclusion. The husband was able to participate in the exercises and concentrate on his sensations without resistance as soon as it became clear that his wife had no objections to such "selfishness." On the contrary, she was too eager to be generous. It was pointed out in group sessions that she was neglecting her own pleasures and that she too permitted overconcern for her partner to impair her sexual abandonment. During the sessions, it became clear that both partners were governed by unconscious fears that the other would abandon them. The more remote causes of this dynamic were not dealt with in the group sessions because it did not present direct obstacles to improved sexual functioning. This couple was seen 4 months later. At that time, they reported that success had continued; in addition, the wife had become orgastic again and was no longer worried about sex. The husband reported that his mild depression had lifted.

Fourth couple

Couple 4 were two college-educated people, married to each other for 20 years. The man was 47 years old, the woman 2 years his junior and easily orgastic. To find a cure for his premature ejaculation, the man had previously spent 10 years in therapy, going two or three times a week. Although he felt that he had benefited in general from the experience, his ejaculatory control had not improved. The goal that brought this couple to the clinic was not only increased ejaculatory control for the man but also an increase in the frequency of intercourse; at the time of treatment, they had intercourse about once every 3–4 weeks.

This couple began the Semans exercises along with the others. At first there was no difficulty. The man was easily aroused in his erotic feelings, approached the exercises eagerly, and experienced a number of initial successes. Then, quite suddenly, he began to have trouble achieving and maintaining an erection.

He revealed to the group that he had encountered this problem previously and that it had been related to a feeling of pressure to perform and consequent anxiety that he might fail. The treatment regimen was modified for this couple to accommodate for his erectile difficulty. They were advised that, if necessary, additional sessions could be scheduled with them in the fall but that in the meantime they should resume the exercises in a nondemand context, that is, at the husband's discretion, with no demand for coital stimulation.

During the group sessions, it became apparent that the wife was placing obstacles in the way of her husband's progress. As his functioning began to improve, her anxiety about losing control over him seemed to motivate her to place on him excessive demands for sexual performance. Not surprisingly, this vulnerable man began to experience erectile difficulties. His wife's demands, their destructive effects, and some of their underlying sources were discussed during group sessions. Consequently, she was able to control her behavior. Relieved of the demands for performance, the man was able to respond, to obtain an erection and carry through the start/stop sequences. Soon his ability to control ejaculations extravaginally improved, and a little later, when he proceeded to insertion, he also quickly attained intravaginal control. He discovered that he was capable of having intercourse two or three times a week, and even claimed that he had had more sexual experiences in the 6 weeks of group treatment than in the past 10 years.

The alleviation of this man's symptoms required more than the modification of the immediate obstacles to sexual functioning which sufficed to help the other couples. It was necessary to deal with some of the remote roots of the problem. Both transactional and intrapsychic determinants were dealt with in the group. It emerged that he was unconsciously continuing his struggle against a controlling "mother" (i.e., his wife) via the use of sex. He had already dealt with his relationship with his mother in his previous psychotherapy; however, he had heretofore failed to make the necessary connection between this genetic material and his current sexual functioning. This was done in the group. This couple was later rescheduled and seen in 4 months, by which time the man had achieved complete ejaculatory control. There were no further erectile problems, and frequency of sexual contact was once per week.

DISCUSSION

Our pilot experiment with the group treatment of premature ejaculation is gratifying on many levels. First, experience has supported our hypothesis that we have developed a useful working concept of the pathogenesis and essential treatment parameters of this condition. The hypothesis that the immediate obstacle to ejaculatory control lies in the man's failure, for multiple reasons, to perceive sensations premonitory to ejaculation requires experimental validation before it can be regarded as established. However, on an empirical level, the concept is useful. Similarly, it appears that the active ingredient of the successful therapy methods consists of overcoming the immediate obstacle to ejaculatory continence by inducing the man to experience the previously avoided perception of high levels of erotic arousal while he is with his sexual partner. This procedure may be thought of as supplying the perception necessary for learning ejaculatory continence.

From a technical standpoint, it seems that the group process can be employed to implement this treatment goal. Specifically, in the group sessions we gave directions for the stop/start exercises which are designed to overcome the alleged immediate cause of prematurity. In addition, the group process was employed to deal with obstacles and resistances which were motivated by deeper causes. How far we had to go to resolve these varied with each couple. Thus, in one instance, Couple 2, very little deeper transactional and intrapsychic material was interpreted. In contrast, the problems presented by Couple 4 necessitated explicit work with more complex marital interactions as well as with interpretation of the husband's unconscious conflicts and exploration of some of their genetic roots.

This treatment of premature ejaculation was based on a theme-centered, target-symptom-removal group. Success was defined as the husband's attainment of voluntary ejaculatory control with consequently prolonged coitus. The attainment of such control was indicated only if both spouses agreed that this had happened. According to this criterion, of the four couples in the pilot study, two were treated with success in the six group sessions, and the other two had gained ejaculatory continence successfully 2 months later. All four couples reported continued and improved sexual functioning at 4 months follow-up.

Results obtained in only one program involving only four couples cannot, of course, be definitive, but they are consonant with the results obtained with the single-couple treatment provided in the program, which is based on the same concept of pathogenesis and treatment. The group format seems well suited to implement the treatment procedure.

At the present time, we are seeing additional groups of premature ejaculators and their wives, using only single therapists, and the results continue to be excellent. It may be inferred that other types of sexual dysfunction may be similarly amenable to such treatment provided that the essential principles of treatment for these syndromes are also clearly delineated.

It is worth noting also that the actual amount of therapist time spent in helping four couples achieve success amounted to about 7 hr, or about 1½ hr per couple. This represents a significant reduction in therapist time from the already rapid treatment format for individual couples which is used at the Payne Whitney Clinic, where a couple is seen for an average of 7 hr. Four couples would thus have required 28 hr of therapist time.

REFERENCES

1.   Masters, W., & Johnson, V. E. *Human sexual inadequacy*. Boston: Little, Brown, 1970.
2.   Semans, J. Premature ejaculation: A new approach. *Southern Medical Journal*, 1956, **49**, 353–358.

Prevention of the Sexually Transmitted Diseases

Venereal is derived from the Latin word "venus" referring to love or lust, and thus *venereal disease* is any of several disorders that ordinarily can be contracted only during a sexual act. Most of these disease organisms thrive only in warm, moist environments and hence are transmitted during genital, oral, or anal intercourse. During childbirth, the infant can also become infected while passing through the vaginal canal. The possibility of catching such a "social disease" from a toilet seat or drinking cup is remote.

The best known and most feared of these diseases are *gonorrhea* (from a Greek word meaning flow of seed) and *syphilis* (from a sixteenth-century poem about a shepherd named Syphilis who had the "pox"). Gonorrhea causes more obvious symptoms in the male than in the female—there is an inflammation of the urethra, a thick and somewhat dark discharge from the penis, and pain during urination. Females can have the disease for some time and yet be totally unaware of it, but it may eventually lead to a vaginal discharge and painful urination. Untreated, gonorrhea can result in more serious problems and in chronic illness, but treatment with antibiotics is simple and effective. Syphilis is a more complicated and ultimately more threatening disease. This disease manifests itself first in a chancre or sore on the genitals, mouth, or anus. Treatment with penicillin can cure it at this stage. Untreated, the chancre disappears, but syphilis does not. After a few weeks or months, the disease erupts again in a rash (the pox) which may not even be particularly noticeable. Two years after the person is infected, the disease goes into a latent period when there are *no* symptoms. The organisms that cause syphilis (*spirochetes*) remain in the blood, however, and can manifest themselves as much as 3 decades later in any bodily organ, including the central nervous system. In addition to gonorrhea and syphilis, there are a variety of other diseases that can attack the genitals and can be spread by intercourse—they tend to be characterized by sores, itching, ulcerations, and blisters, and all can be cured by appropriate medical treatment.

The fact that venereal diseases *are* curable by modern medicine should mean that they are a problem of the past as when Columbus and his crew spread the disease between two continents. VD epidemics plagued various parts of the world throughout history, but one of the most curious such epidemics is that currently sweeping the United States. Syphilis, for example, increased in 1970 about 8% while gonorrhea is showing a 16% growth rate! The response to this problem has been of two varieties. Some take it as evidence of the moral decay of our society and as an excuse to try to prohibit sexual activity among young people—the failure of this crusade is obvious. A more sensible approach has been the attempt to provide information about the symptoms, free medical care to the victims, and the effort to trace and treat others who have had contact with the victim. This public health program in the United States and elsewhere along with such informative presentations as the television program "VD Blues" are commendable and helpful, and should be continued.

There is a third approach, however, which has been curiously neglected —prevention. Medical writer Edward Brecher describes in the following article a series of preventive measures (some of which are extremely simple) that have been known for a very long time by prostitutes, by the military, and by the medical profession. Public prudery has been such that it became acceptable to stress the treatment of VD (who can argue against curing a disease?) but not to stress preventive measures simply because the latter approach implies that nonmarital intercourse is condoned or at least tolerated. The article by Brecher may help to change these ostrichlike attitudes.

Prevention of the Sexually Transmitted Diseases

Edward M. Brecher

Control of venereal diseases in some countries depends solely on the treatment of symptomatic cases. Other countries also engage in the tracing and testing of the sexual contacts of those cases, and a few also screen various population groups for inapparent infections. The difficulty is that, even when all three methods of control are used, each 100 cases on the average give rise to slightly more than 100 fresh infections *before* diagnosis and treatment.

One way to interrupt this series of infections, and to curb the transmitted diseases, is through prophylaxis—here defined as measures taken before, during, or shortly after exposure to reduce the likelihood of disease transmission or to abort an incipient infection. Unlike the other forms of control, VD prophylaxis is effective before there is any opportunity for further transmission—and thus has a greater effect on curbing future incidence. Reviewed here are 11 methods of prophylaxis —all designed to reduce the likelihood that an infection will be passed along when a man has sexual relations with an infected woman or when a woman has sexual relations with an infected man. Several of these methods are usable for oral-genital and anal-genital as well as genital-genital contacts. Many of the methods are effective against monilial, trichomonal, and other infections as well as against syphilis and gonorrhea.

Like other medical procedures, none of these is 100% effective. Prophylaxis should therefore be considered along with, not in place of, case finding and treatment procedures described. Each method of prophylaxis, however, can contribute its mite to individual protection and thus to a downturn in the incidence and prevalence of VD.

Reprinted in an edited version from: Brecher, E. M. Prevention of the sexually transmitted diseases. *Journal of Sex Research*, 1975, **11**, 318–328.

PRECOITAL INSPECTION OF THE MALE GENITALIA

A skilled physician is able to spot infection during a "short-arm inspection" of the male genitalia, including a "milking" of the urethra for gonococcal exudate, in a high proportion of cases. Many prostitutes are at least equally skilled in making a short-arm inspection;[4,39] this no doubt explains the relatively low rate of infection in well-trained prostitutes as compared with untrained promiscuous amateurs, reported from various cities in various decades. Luys[22] summed up some of the evidence:

> Fournier's statistics show that this disease is far more common among kept women, actresses (138 out of 387), and working girls (126 out of 387), than amongst the regular prostitutes (12 out of 287). This discrepancy is no doubt due to the exquisite knowledge of venereal diseases which many prostitutes can boast of. They understand how to examine the man who is about to obtain their favors; they douche properly after each coitus, and resort to a series of other precautions which safeguard them [pp. 4–5].

The technique of the short-arm inspection can be easily taught to a woman, prostitute or not, if moralistic qualms do not intervene. If signs of infection are noted, a woman has her choice of refusing sexual relations or of agreeing to them but using one of the other modes of protection listed below. (The inspection of the female genitalia by the male can also be taught; but a much smaller proportion of infected women can be thus identified.)

DISINFECTION OF THE MALE PENIS PRIOR TO COITUS

Soap-and-water disinfection is simplest.[5,22,31,44] Whether use of a medicated soap increases effectiveness is not known but seems likely.[1] The douching of the female genitalia before coitus may also be a form of prophylaxis,[22] but effectiveness is likely to be quite limited.

THE CONDOM

The effectiveness of the condom for preventing venereal disease transmission is well established.[6,24,38]

Use of the condom is actively promoted by public health authorities in Sweden and a few other countries. In many cities and countries, however, its value for VD prophylaxis is still insufficiently known to the public. Indeed, some public health authorities seek to discredit the condom on the specious ground that it is less than 100% effective; and there are still legal restrictions on its availability in several countries (including some states in the United States). The chief drawback of the condom is its interference with male, and to a lesser extent female, sensory pleasure. Greatly improved condoms, less than one-third as thick as conventional models, and made of a plastic with good heat-transmission characteristics, have been developed in Japan and the United States, but have not as yet been generally marketed. If, as is likely, they prove more acceptable to male users and their partners than traditional condoms, they may contribute notably to a downturn in the VD incidence curve.

VAGINAL PROPHYLAXIS DURING COITUS

Neisser,[28] the discoverer of the gonococcus, reported that the introduction of petrolatum jelly into the vagina before coitus would provide a physical barrier to the transmission of disease agents in either direction; to increase the effectiveness of the barrier, Neisser proposed that suitable antiseptics be added to the petrolatum jelly. A variety of such products were subsequently marketed, based on petrolatum jelly or other viscous agents, but were used primarily by prostitutes. The effectiveness of at least one such product, Progonasyl, has been demonstrated under experimental conditions.[30] A recent field trial of Progonasyl in the United States[12] provided additional evidence of effectiveness.

Curiously enough, millions of women the world over have no doubt been unwittingly protected from VD by such products when used for contraception rather than prophylaxis. The effectiveness of the common contraceptive creams and jellies against the treponeme and gonococcus as well as against spermatozoa was understood by physicians in Britain, America, and no doubt other countries at least as early as the 1920s, but was kept a well-guarded secret from the public. Studies in the 1970s have confirmed what was known half a century earlier—that several of the agents used in vaginal contraceptive products to kill spermatozoa are also highly effective not only against syphilis and gonorrhea but also against several other sexually transmitted diseases. Field trials under way in Pittsburgh, Pennsylvania, in 1974 indicate a considerable degree of effectiveness for at least one brand of contraceptive cream in common use; for a list of other brands shown to be effective during *in vitro* tests, see Singh, Cutler, and Utidijian[34,35] and Bolch and Warren.[3] Cutler hopes to popularize vaginal creams, jellies, and foams as "pro-cons"— that is, preparations useful for both VD prophylaxis and contraception.

The recent switching of many millions of women in the Western countries from vaginal contraceptive agents (which are also prophylactic against VD) to the contraceptive pill and the intrauterine device (which are not) was no doubt one factor in the rise in VD in those countries. The switch from the condom to the newer forms of contraception may also have contributed—though some studies indicate that relatively few users of the contraceptive pill and IUD are drawn from former condom users.

The possibility of an intrauterine device (IUD) which is prophylactic against VD as well as contraceptive is, however, under study. The gonococcus and the treponeme are both exquisitely sensitive to very low concentrations of *copper*—concentrations of the magnitude found in the internal genitalia of women wearing IUDs made of copper. Observations are currently under way to determine whether women now wearing copper IUDs are in fact enjoying a lower VD rate than those wearing IUDs made of other substances.

POSTCOITAL URINATION

Urination by the male immediately after coitus has long been recommended by some authorities, including the U.S. Army, Navy, and Air Force.[7,24,38] The acidity of the urine provides an environment hostile to gonococci; and both they and other pathogens may be flushed out.

POSTCOITAL DISINFECTION FOR THE FEMALE

A medicated douche preparation for use after coitus, developed in the Venereal Disease Research Laboratory of the U. S. Public Health Service, proved quite effective during field trials in Guatemala;[15] other douche preparations have been shown *in vitro* to be effective against the treponeme, the gonococcus, and other vaginal infective agents.[34,35] Some prostitutes use the postcoital douche for VD prophylaxis as well as for cleanliness.[4,39] In some European countries the *bidet* takes the place of the douche;[14] some authorities attribute the remarkably low gonorrhea rate in France to prompt postcoital use of the bidet in most strata of French society. Males also can (and should) use the bidet before and after exposure.

Lacking bidets, some American prostitutes (and some other women as well) wash their outer and inner genitalia thoroughly while sitting over the washbowl after coitus. Promptness is probably as important as thoroughness in this procedure. This technique can be readily taught to women, whether or not they are prostitutes. Indeed, a public health official in Detroit is reported to have taught postcoital soap-and-water disinfection to 4000 women during the 1920s, with good results in terms of VD control.[8]

SIMPLE POSTCOITAL DISINFECTION OF THE MALE

Fallopius in the sixteenth century urged the thorough washing of the male genitals both before and after exposure. Thorough washing of the penis and surrounding area with water and soap (medicated or not) as soon as possible after exposure has long been recommended by those public health authorities not opposed to prophylaxis on moralistic grounds.[5,7,24,38]

TOPICAL PREPARATIONS FOR POSTCOITAL USE
BY THE MALE

During the late nineteenth century, at least a dozen European studies conclusively demonstrated that a simple ointment containing mercury is highly effective in preventing the transmission of syphilis if applied to the penis promptly after exposure.[18,23] This "secret" was known at least as early as 1733 by Agate and Desault.[18,33] Metchnikoff and Roux[25] at the Institut Pasteur in Paris, placed postcoital topical mercury on a scientific basis with a series of primate and human experiments demonstrating that a simple salve composed one-third of calomel is almost 100% effective in preventing genital syphilis in the male if it is thoroughly rubbed into the penis and surrounding areas within 1 hour after exposure; some protection is afforded even if the salve is used after several hours' delay.[23] Adopted by the armed forces of many countries as early as 1908, the "Metchnikoff ointment" proved its worth during countless military studies over a period of 50 years,[32,40,42,43] and remained in routine military use until the end of World War II; but moralistic considerations in most countries prevented its popularization for civilian use.[27,40]

Various silver compounds and other antiseptics were similarly used in military medicine for decades for the prophylaxis of gonorrhea in the male; the antiseptic in fluid or gel form was injected up the male urethra as soon as possible after exposure.[32] During World War II, United States government studies established the fact that drugs of the sulfanilimide group, introduced into the urethra shortly after coitus, were even more effective against gonorrhea and more acceptable to the exposed men; and "Pro-Kits" containing both calomel and a sulfa drug[40,41] were manufactured and distributed for use by American armed forces throughout the world—except those stationed in the United States, where moralistic hostility to prophylaxis prevailed. The chief drawback of all male postcoital methods of VD prophylaxis, however, is that they protect *only* the male. From the public health point of view as well as from the female point of view, protection of the female is even more important, since early diagnosis is so much more difficult and less likely in the female.

SYSTEMIC PREPARATIONS BEFORE PENICILLIN

Mercury was the treatment of choice for syphilis from the sixteenth through the nineteenth century. Some physicians and laymen knew at least as early as the eighteenth century that very small doses of mercury, administered systematically only once or a few times, could prevent a syphilitic infection which would require massive doses over a period of months or years if treatment was delayed until symptoms appeared. As various new agents for treating syphilis took the place of mercury, it was again and again discovered that very small systemic doses at the time of exposure can prevent hard-to-cure infections. Ehrlich's salvarsan (606), neosalvarsan, other arsenicals, bismuth, and other agents were each in turn found to be effective for syphilis prophylaxis;[11,18,19,26,27] but once again, their introduction was blocked except in some populations of prostitutes. Studies among these prostitutes showed a high degree of effectiveness.[21,37]

"PILLS TO PREVENT VD"

Shortly after it was discovered that small doses of penicillin will *cure* both syphilis and gonorrhea, it was similarly discovered that even smaller doses, taken orally at or shortly after the time of exposure, will *prevent* gonorrhea and probably syphilis.[10] The common view that small doses merely mask the symptoms of early syphilis was proved false.[2,45,47] Oral penicillin prophylaxis was widely used in the United States armed forces after World War II, and proved close to 100% effective in numerous studies, even with doses as low as 100,000 or 200,000 units.[2,9] Oral penicillin dosage needed to prevent gonorrhea today, with resistant strains prevalent, is unknown but no doubt remains lower than the dosage needed for cure. However, Smartt, Bograd, and Dorn[36] reported that a single 200-mg dose of doxycycline, taken orally shortly before or after exposure, provides effective prophylaxis. A research group drawn from the U. S. Navy Division of Preventive Medicine, the U. S. Center for Disease Control, and the U. S. Public Health Service-University of Washington Hospitals, in a double-blind field trial with placebo controls, found that the incidence of gonorrhea was significantly reduced following administration of 200-mg doses of minocycline reasonably soon after exposure—even in an area where highly resistant strains were prevalent.[17] The doses of doxycycline and minocycline used in these two field trials were modest fractions of the doses prescribed for treatment after symptoms appear.

LOCAL ANTIBIOTIC PROPHYLAXIS

The Japanese have developed a proprietary preparation, Penigin, composed of penicillin or some other antibiotic contained in an effervescing tablet, for introduction into the vagina before coitus. Field trials have shown a substantial degree of effectiveness.[29]

The prophylactic use of antibiotics and other potent chemotherapeutic agents to prevent rheumatic fever, malaria, tuberculosis, and gonococcal ophthalmitis of the newborn is almost universally accepted;[46] but the similar prophylactic use of such agents to prevent *sexually transmitted* infections still arouses great hostility in the medical and public health professions. One reason commonly given for this hostility to prophylaxis is that antibiotics and other chemotherapeutic agents produce adverse side effects. This objection will be considered below.

In addition to the readily available or potentially available methods of VD prophylaxis described above, several other methods have been proposed, such as vaccines for syphilis and gonorrhea. The relatively trivial scientific efforts to develop such vaccines—standing in stark contrast to the vast efforts invested in producing vaccines for infections which are not sexually transmitted—afford further evidence of tight moralistic curbs on the medical and scientific approach to the sexually transmitted infections. Recent work on vaccines for syphilis, gonorrhea, and genital herpes suggests the slow erosion of these curbs—though work on a genital herpes vaccine is motivated more by a concern with cancer of the cervix than by a desire to curb acute genital herpes.[16]

The *public health importance* of popularizing these or other forms of VD prophylaxis depends upon a fact of nature which is generally overlooked. Under stable conditions, each 100 venereal infections on the average give rise to 100 fresh cases before they are diagnosed and cured. If each 100 infections give rise to 101 fresh cases, the result is an epidemic in a remarkably short time. With gonorrhea, for example, the difference between 100 fresh cases and 101 fresh cases arising from each 100 preexisting cases can mean the difference between a stable incidence rate and a rate which rises by 15% or more per year—the kind of rise currently reported in several countries. Conversely, a rapidly falling incidence rate results if each 100 infections give rise to 98 or 99 fresh cases. Thus even a relatively ineffective form of prophylaxis, used by relatively few members of the population at risk, can mean the difference between a rising and a falling VD rate. Lee and associates have calculated that a method of gonorrhea prophylaxis which is only 50% effective can, even if used by only 20% of a population at risk, reduce the incidence of gonorrhea in that population by 90% in less than 2 years.[20]

A clinician who diagnoses and cures a symptomatic gonorrhea infection accomplishes very little toward curbing the disease; for on the average each patient has already infected one additional person prior to diagnosis and cure. The *prevention* of one infection, in contrast, also prevents all of the subsequent cases which would otherwise stem from that case through the years ahead. It is not unrealistic to estimate that the prevention of one gonorrhea infection today will also on the average prevent several hundred additional gonorrhea infections during the next 2 decades.

The current incidence of fresh gonorrhea cases in the United States is estimated at 2.5 million per year—50 million infections over the next 20 years, even if the rate does not continue to rise. Thus only a few hundred thousand cases need to be *prevented* in order to prevent the subsequent 50 million; for all 50 million future cases will stem from the few hundred thousand infectious cases present in the population on any given day.

In this perspective, the hazard of side effects from antibiotic prophylaxis can be evaluated. In the absence of prophylaxis, we can expect in the United States that massive doses of penicillin or other antibiotics will be needed to cure some 50 million gonorrheal infections over the next 20 years—and that gonorrhea will remain at least as prevalent at the end of that period as today. This is clearly a policy likely to perpetuate the need for antibiotics and the hazard of antibiotic side effects. Prophylaxis (including antibiotic prophylaxis) offers hope of curbing the disease and thus curbing the hazard of antibiotic side effects through the decades ahead.

CONCLUSION

The more effective the modes of VD prophylaxis made available to the public, and the more wholehearted the effort to popularize their use, the more rapidly the incidence curve is likely to fall. No other available method of control of the sexually transmitted diseases, especially gonorrhea, gives promise of accomplishing the same result.

REFERENCES

1. American Medical Association Council on Pharmacy and Chemistry. "Germicidal" soaps. *Journal of the American Medical Association*, 1944, **124**, 1195–1201.

2. Babione, R. W., Hedgecock, L. E., & Ray, J. P. Navy experience with the oral use of penicillin as a prophylaxis. *U. S. Armed Forces Medical Journal*, 1952, **3**, 973–990.

3. Bolch, O. H., & Warren, J. C. In vitro effects of Emko on Neisseria gonorrhoeae and Trichomonas vaginalis. *American Journal of Obstetrics and Gynecology*, 1973, **115**, 1145–1148.

4. Brecher, E. M. Women: Victims of the VD rip-off. *Viva*, October and November 1973 issues, **1**.

5. Buchan, W. *Domestic medicine: A treatise on the prevention and cure of diseases*. Boston: Printed by Joseph Bumstead for James White and Ebenezer Larkin, 1973.

6. Cautley, R., Beebe, G. W., & Dickinson, R. W. Rubber sheaths as venereal disease prophylactics. *American Journal of the Medical Sciences*, 1938, **195**, 155–163.

7. Department of the (U. S.) Army. Treatment and management of venereal disease. *Technical Bulletin Medical*, 1965, **230**.

8. Dickinson, R. L. *Control of conception.* (2d ed.) Baltimore: Williams & Wilkins, 1938.

9. Eagle, H., Gude, A. V., Beckman, G. E., Mast, G., & Sapero, J. J. Prevention of gonorrhea with penicillin tablets. *Journal of the American Medical Association,* 1949, **140**, 940–943.

10. Eagle, H., Gude, A. V., Beckmann, G. E., Mast, G., Sapero, J. J., & Shindledecker, J. B. Prevention of gonorrhea with penicillin tablets. *Public Health Reports,* 1948, **63**, 1411–1415.

11. Eagle, H., Hogen, R. B., & Fleischman, R. The local chemical prophylaxis of experimental syphilis with phenyl arsenoxides. *American Journal of Syphilis, Gonorrhea, and Venereal Diseases,* 1944, **28**, 661–681.

12. Edwards, W. M., & Fox, R. S. Progonasyl as an anti-V.D. prophylactic. Paper presented at the First National Conference in Methods of Venereal Disease Prevention, Chicago, 1974.

13. Forsyth, W. *A review of venereal disease.* London, 1785.

14. Fournier, A. *Treatment and prophylaxis of syphilis.* (Translated by C. F. Marshall.) London: Rebman, Ltd. 1906; New York: Rebman Co., 1907.

15. Funes, J. M., & Luz Aguilar, C. Mapharsen-Orvus solution in the prophylaxis of gonorrhea in women. *Bioletin de la Oficina Sanitaria Panamericana,* 1952, **33**, 121–125.

16. Hilleman, M. R. Human cancer virus vaccines. *Ca - A Cancer Journal for Clinicians,* 1974, **24**, 212–217.

17. Holmes, K. K. Advantages and hazards of antibiotic prophylaxis. Paper presented at First National Conference on Methods of Venereal Disease Prevention, Chicago, 1974.

18. Kilmer, J. A. *Chemotherapy, with special reference to treatment of syphilis.* Philadelphia: Saunders, 1926.

19. Kolmer, J. A., & Rule, A. M. Stovarsol in the prophylaxis and treatment of trypanosomiasis and syphilis. *American Journal of Syphilis,* 1932, **16**, 53–67.

20. Lee, T. Y., Utidijian, H. M. D., Singh, B., & Cutler, J. C. Potential impact of chemical prophylaxis on the incidence of gonorrhea. *British Journal of Venereal Diseases,* 1972, **48**, 376–380.

21. Levaditi, C. *Prophylaxie de la syphilis.* Paris: Librarie Maloine, 1936.

22. Luys, G. A. *Text-book on gonorrhea and its complications.* (2d ed.) New York: William Wood, 1917.

23. Maisonneuve, P. *The experimental prophylaxis of syphilis.* Paris: Shenheil, 1908.

24. *Medical Letter.* Treatment and prevention of syphilis and gonorrhea. *Medical Letter (on Drugs and Therapeutics),* 1971, **13**, 87.

25. Metchnikoff, E., & Roux, E. Experimental studies in syphilis. *Annals de l'Institut Pasteur,* 1907, **21**, 753–759.

26. Michel, L. L., & Goodman, H. Prophylaxis of syphilis with arsphenamin. *Journal of the American Medical Association,* 1920, **75**, 1768–1770.

27. Moore, J. E. Prophylaxis and treatment in the control of syphilis. *Southern Medical Journal,* 1926, **30**, 149–153.

28. Neisser, A. Is it really impossible to make prostitution harmless as far as infection is concerned? In W. J. Robinson (Ed.), *Sexual truths versus sexual lies, misconceptions and exaggerations.* New York: Eugenics, 1919.

29. Ohno, T., Kato, K., Nagata, M., Hattori, N., & Kanakawa, H. Prophylactic control of the spread of venereal disease through prostitutes in Japan. *Bulletin of the World Health Organization,* 1958, **19**, 575–579.

30. Porter, H. H., Witcher, R. B., & Knoblock, C. Social diseases at the crossroads. *Journal of the Oklahoma State Medical Association,* 1939, **32**, 54–61.

31. Reasoner, M. A. The effect of soap on treponema pallidum. *Journal of the American Medical Association,* 1917, **68**, 973–974.

32. Reid, Sir G. A. *The prevention of venereal disease.* London: Heinemann, 1920.

33. Schamberg, J. F., & Wright, C. S. Treatment of syphilis. In *Prophylaxis of Syphilis.* New York: Appleton, 1932.

34. Singh, B., Cutler, J. C., & Utidijian, H. M. D. Studies on the development of a vaginal preparation providing both prophylaxis against venereal disease and other genital infections and contraception. II-Effect *in vitro* of vaginal contraceptive and non-contraceptive preparations on treponema pallidum and neisseria gonorrhoeae. *British Journal of Venereal Diseases,* 1972, **48**, 57–64.

35. Singh, B., Cutler, J. C., & Utidijian, H. M. D. III. *In Vitro* effect of vaginal contraceptive and selected vaginal preparations in candida albicans and trichomonas vaginalis. *Contraception,* 1972, **5**, 401–411.

36. Smartt, W. H., Bograd, G., & Dorn, R. Prophylaxis of venereal disease with doxycycline. Paper presented at the First National Conference on Methods of Venereal Disease Prevention, Chicago, 1974.

37. Sonnenberg, E. Abstracted in *Venereal Disease Information,* 1935, **16**, 19–20.

38. Special Joint Committee Appointed by the American Social Hygiene Association and the United States Public Health Service. The chemical and mechanical prevention of syphilis and gonorrhea. *Venereal Disease Information*, 1940, **21**, 311–313.

39. Stein, M. L. *Friends, lovers, slaves.* New York: Putnam, 1974.

40. Sternberg, T. H., Howard, E. B., Dewey, L. A., & Pidget, P. Venereal disease. In U. S. Army Medical Department, *Preventive Medicine in World War II.* Vol. 5, *Communicable Diseases Transmitted Through Contact.* Washington, D. C.: Office of the Surgeon General, Department of the Army, 1960.

41. Sternberg, T. H., & Larrimore, G. W. Army contributions to postwar venereal disease control planning. *Journal of the American Medical Association*, 1945, **127**, 209–212.

42. Vedder, E. B. *Syphilis and public health.* Philadelphia: Lee & Febiger, 1918.

43. Walker, G. *Venereal disease in the American Expeditionary Forces.* Baltimore: Medical Standard Book Co., 1922.

44. Walker, J. E. The germicidal properties of soap. *Journal of Infectious Diseases*, 1926, **38**, 127–130.

45. Wilcox, R. R. Treatment before diagnosis in venereology. *British Journal of Venereal Diseases*, 1954, **30**, 7–18.

46. Willcox, R. R. Prophylaxis of non-venereal conditions. Paper presented at the First National Conference on Methods of Venereal Disease Prevention, Chicago, 1974.

47. Woodcock, J. R. Re-appraising the effect on incubating syphilis of treatment for gonorrhea. *British Journal of Venereal Diseases*, 1971, **47**, 95–101.

CHAPTER TWELVE

Effects of Erotic Stimulation on Behavior

Experience with Pornography:
Rapists, Pedophiles, Homosexuals, Transsexuals, and Controls

One of the most realistic fears about the possible consequences of uncensored pornography is the belief that teen-agers and adults will be *motivated* by such material to engage in sexual acts and *taught* by such material to engage in deviant or criminal sexuality. Newspaper stories of the apprehension of a rapist or child molester often contain information that the arresting officers discovered pornographic pictures and erotic magazines in the suspect's home. The implication is implicitly or explicitly drawn that the erotica was somehow the cause of the sex crime.

One sort of evidence that raises doubts about such effects is found in research dealing with the characteristics of those who are the biggest consumers of erotica. Most of the patrons of so-called adult movie theaters and bookstores are found to be adult white males who are in the middle or upper-middle class. Thus, the typical consumer is more likely to be a married businessman catching a skin flick during his lunch hour than an emotionally disturbed derelict who lurks with a fistful of sexual photos in dark alleys ready to force himself on passing victims.

One way to explore the possible role of erotica as a stimulus for sexual crimes or the adoption of an unusual life style is to compare the experiences, the reactions, and the behavior of a variety of people who differ in their criminality and their sexual preferences. In the following research, conducted for the Commission on Obscenity and Pornography, a team combining the skills of psychology, psychiatry, and the law made just such comparisons. Though these investigators present a considerable amount of data, two facts seem to stand out. First, there is no evidence that exposure to pornography or one's reactions to it are associated with committing a sex crime or adopting a particular sexual orientation. Second, the most common behavioral effect of erotica is masturbation. Though it is not yet prudent to conclude with certainty that erotica has *no* effect on acts of criminal sexuality, these data offer absolutely no support for the opposite conclusion.

Experience with Pornography: Rapists, Pedophiles, Homosexuals, Transsexuals, and Controls

Michael Goldstein, Harold Kant, Lewis Judd, Clinton Rice, and Richard Green

This article describes the second phase of a research project designed to assess whether relationships might exist between experience with por-

Reprinted in an edited version from: Goldstein, M., Kant, H., Judd, L., Rice, C., & Green, R. Experience with pornography: Rapists, pedophiles, homosexuals, transsexuals, and controls. *Archives of Sexual Behavior*, 1971, 1, 1–15.

nography and the development of normal or abnormal sexual behavior. The first phase of the research was concerned with developing a standardized clinical interview with which to survey both the qualitative and quantitative aspects of an individual's past and current uses of erotic materials. The first step was to develop a working model for the interview and this initial model served as a guide in the development of the questionnaire, which focused on the examination of factors antecedent to exposure to pornographic and obscene materials, the exposure itself, and the results or consequences of this exposure. The interview was designed as a series of modular sections such that it can be used in its entirety or in sections to fit specific research interests.

SAMPLE

The sample consists of a group of institutionalized male sex offenders comprised of rapists and pedophiles, two noninstitutionalized groups of sex deviants (male homosexuals and transsexuals), a group of noninstitutionalized heavy users of pornography, and control groups drawn from two ethnic backgrounds.

Institutionalized sex offender sample

The sample of male sex offenders was obtained with the generous cooperation of the research and psychology staffs at Atascadero State Hospital, a California institution for the "criminally insane." Any sex offender judged to be psychiatrically disturbed by a court having jurisdiction may be sent there for observation. If during a period of observation (typically 90 days) the patient is judged by the staff to be suitable for the program of rehabilitation and treatment provided by the hospital, he is permitted to stay.

From their total population of sex offenders, past their 90-day observation period, the research staff at Atascadero was asked to draw three groups of approximately 20 each of sex offenders for study: (1) aggressive sexual offenders, especially rapists or attempted rapists (hereinafter usually referred to simply as "rapists"); (2) pedophiles (child molesters) who selected *male* children as sexual objects and (3) pedophiles who selected *female* children as sexual objects.

Homosexual sample

This sample was drawn from the membership of a local homophile organization, One Incorporated.

Transsexual sample

Each person applying for a sex-change operation at UCLA is referred to the Gender Identity Clinic for psychiatric and psychological evaluation.

Those persons currently in the Los Angeles area as patients of the Gender Identity Clinic were asked to participate.

The users sample

This sample was designed to be drawn from those people who pay for or use erotic material. Subjects were obtained from people responding to flyers left in pornographic bookstores, "skin-flick" movie theaters, and an advertisement placed in an "underground" newspaper (*The Free Press*).

The black control samples

The black control subjects consisted of two groups: One group is composed of 22 males residing in the Los Angeles ghetto who are trainees in a job-training program for hard-core unemployed at the Community Skills Center, Gardena, California. The middle-class sample of 17 males was not systematically drawn from a known pool of subjects. Instead, the interviewers knowledgeable about the black community were instructed to locate persons satisfying an income definition of middle-class economic status.

The white control sample

In order to locate a sample of subjects with minimal chance of statistical bias in sampling, a subcontract was awarded to the UCLA Survey Research Center to locate respondents. They were given the age distribution and educational level distribution of the Atascadero samples and were told to locate a community sample matched on these parameters. This sample was white and Christian to match the Atascadero sample. The homosexuals, transsexuals, and users also were almost entirely white.

Demographic data

Subjects fell primarily in the 20–40 year age range with the homosexuals and pedophiles somewhat older than the controls. The match between controls and rapists on age, education, and socioeconomic status is very close. Educational levels are comparable for the controls, rapists, and pedophiles who prefer males, and, in turn, superior to the pedophiles who prefer females. The homosexuals and transsexuals have more formal education than the controls; the users and controls are comparable. There is no difference in the socioeconomic status of the controls, rapists, and pedophiles who prefer females. Compared to controls, the homosexuals and transsexuals have more professionals and fewer unskilled workers. The pedophiles who prefer males have more semiskilled and fewer clerical workers than the controls.

REPORTED FREQUENCY OF EXPOSURE TO
EROTIC STIMULI

In the course of the interview a respondent was asked to estimate the frequency of his exposure to stimuli representing various degrees of nudity and forms of sexual activity. In the section focusing upon adolescent experience, questions were asked about representations of sexual activity in a particular medium (photos, movies, or books). The questioning followed a systematic order starting with the most probable stimulus to be encountered, partial nudity, and ending with the least likely, sadomasochistic activity. As each type of stimulus was mentioned by the interviewer, the respondent was asked to recall the number of times that he encountered it during that period of his life. During the later section of the interview, designed to elicit material regarding the previous year's experience (or in the case of the institutionalized sex offenders, the year prior to hospitalization), the same questions were repeated and frequencies of exposure were elicited.

REPORTS OF ADOLESCENT EXPERIENCE

Sex offenders: rapists

The data were examined with respect to the percent of rapist respondents who report *never* being exposed during adolescence to various stimuli. While these data suggest a higher frequency of *never* reports for rapists when compared to controls, few significant differences are present for the total range of frequency estimates. The rapists report significantly less exposure to photos of partially and fully nude women and to books describing nudity and oral-genital relations.

Sex offenders: pedophiles who prefer male partners

There are sharper differences between pedophiles, male object, and controls than was the case for the rapists. Across all stimuli and media these pedophiles report a higher percent of never having encountered erotic stimuli as adolescents. Significant differences for the total range of frequencies reported are also more numerous for this contrast. They differ significantly for photos of partially and fully nude women, heterosexual intercourse, and sadomasochistic activity; movies of heterosexual intercourse; and books describing nudity, heterosexual intercourse, mouth-genital, and sadomasochistic activity. Those sex offenders who select young boys as sexual partners show a striking absence of reported exposure to representations of heterosexual intercourse across all media. This is the one type of stimulus for which significant comparisons are obtained on all three media. Whether this represented a deliberate avoidance of this class of stimuli (heterosexual intercourse) during adolescence by the pedophile who prefers males, or results from greater interest in other types of sexual stimuli, is impossible to determine from these data. The generally low levels of adolescent exposure reported by this group suggest that limited exposure to stimuli representing heterosexual intercourse is the extreme in a pattern of generally low exposure to erotica.

The smallest difference between this group comprised of persons who are homosexuals of a type and controls is for photos and books depicting homosexual activity. This suggests that their homosexual interest was already present during their adolescent years and influenced their choice of erotica.

Sex offenders: pedophiles who prefer female partners

As with the pedophile, male object, less exposure to erotica than controls is reported among pedophiles, female object. The significant differences for the total range of exposure occur for heterosexual intercourse, regardless of the media. There are also significant differences for photos representing oral-genital activities, movies portraying nude women, and sadomasochistic activity.

The two groups of sex offenders who prefer immature partners report a strikingly low degree of exposure to representations of mature sexual activity (heterosexual intercourse) during adolescence.

Homosexual sample

The percent of homosexuals reporting never being exposed to these stimuli was examined. The number of significant comparisons indicates that the marked difference between homosexuals and controls exists across all categories of exposure. During teen-age years, the homosexuals report significantly less exposure than controls to erotica. For a few stimuli they do not differ significantly from controls. These stimuli are partially and fully nude males, movies of homosexual acts, and books describing heterosexual intercourse. All but the latter are more likely to interest the homosexually inclined than the other stimuli. This suggests that these individuals may have sought out as adolescents, erotically tinged photos relevant to their emerging homosexual interest.

Transsexuals

The data from reports of adolescent exposure for the transsexual group were examined. In general, there is less exposure across all stimuli and all media. The most significant differences between male transsexuals and controls are found for photos of fully nude women, heterosexual intercourse, and oral-genital relations, and for books describing nudity or sex, heterosexual intercourse, and oral-genital relations. Male transsexuals apply for help at the Gender Identity Clinic because they believe themselves to be of the opposite sex and wish treatment to realize this opposite sex role. In their teen-age years, they report a strikingly low amount of exposure to stimuli in which the opposite sex is presented in some sexually provocative way. Thus, the curiosity and interest in taking on the role of the opposite sex did not appear to stimulate them to search out erotica likely to provide information about that sex. More often these respondents related that they found objects associated with the opposite sex (clothing particularly) to be far more erotic stimuli during adolescence than commercially produced pornography.

Users of pornography

People who are currently frequent buyers and consumers of commercially available pornography indicate a pattern of adolescent reports similar to the sex deviate samples. They report generally less exposure to erotica than controls and reveal significant differences for photos of fully nude women, fully nude males, and, as has been the case for the sex deviate groups, photos of sexual intercourse. In addition, they report a lower frequency for movies showing heterosexual intercourse and sadomasochistic content. The less frequent report of encountering sadomasochism in books represents the only significant difference in that category. Generally, the pornography user of today recalls strikingly little exposure to erotica as a teen-ager and as with all other previous samples the most consistent differences from the controls occur for stimuli representing heterosexual intercourse. It appears that sex deviates and users are noticeably lacking in experience, during their adolescent years, with stimuli representing our culture's definition of "the normal sex act."

Black and white control groups

The black ghetto control and white control groups do not differ significantly. Small differences exist between the black middle-class control and the white control groups. There are two significant differences, one for books describing nudity or sex, and one for books describing oralgenital activity. Overall, all three samples differ significantly from the samples selected on the basis of their deviate sexual activity.

REPORTS OF RECENT EXPERIENCE

In the interest of brevity, we will summarize the reports of frequency of exposure during the year prior to the interview. The institutionalized sex offenders (rapists and two pedophile groups) continue to report significantly less exposure to erotic stimuli than do controls. In fact, the differences are greater for recent than preadolescent estimates. The transsexuals also continue to report less exposure than controls. Two groups show a marked shift from the adolescent reports, the homosexuals and users. Each of these groups reported much less exposure to erotica as teen-agers than controls but significantly *greater* exposure during the previous year. The degree of exposure reported during the previous year is so much greater than controls as to suggest an obsessive interest in sexual stimuli in both groups.

REPORTED EFFECT OF EXPOSURE TO EROTIC STIMULI

Numerous questions were posed to the subjects in each group concerning detailed reaction following exposure to erotic materials. These questions were designed to elicit data which might explain the role that erotic materials play in people's lives, particularly the group selected as extensive users. These responses might also help to explain the function of erotica in individuals with deviant and normal sexual lives. The questions covered a broad spectrum of emotional reactions as well as actual activities. To date, only a small part of these data has been analyzed. The questioning was divided into two sections, the first analyzing reaction to erotic materials in general, and the second the reaction to that particular experience with erotic material which each subject selected as standing out most strongly in his mind. Questions dealt separately with experiences in adolescence and in the most recent year (the year prior to institutionalization for the Atascadero sample).

Reaction to erotic material in general

Table 12-1 shows that the sex offender and sex groups (other than the transsexuals) and the user group report a higher incidence of masturbation in response to erotic materials than the controls. However, these figures seem less impressive when compared to reports of incidence of masturbation when pornographic erotic material was not the stimulant; some of the groups actually show more masturbation without the pornographic erotic stimulant, the transsexuals being particularly striking in this regard. As adults, only the users show as much as 10% more of the subjects being stimulated to masturbate by erotic materials than would otherwise masturbate.

However, a striking comparison appears when the reports of excitement to masturbate by erotic materials in the past year are compared to the adolescent-based reports of being excited to masturbate by erotic materials. As adolescents, the white control group reports 87% were excited to masturbate by erotic materials, which is the highest report of any group other than the rapists, which were 90%. The black control groups each report about half the sample being excited to masturbate by erotic materials as adolescents. Each of these three groups show a sharp *decrease* in being so excited as adults. Compare this with the user group which shows only a small drop from 86% to 78% and to the

Table 12-1
Percentage of Subjects Reacting to Erotic Material in Specific Ways

	Heterosexual Control Subjects			Subjects with Varying Sexual Life Styles			Sex Criminals		
		Blacks							
	Whites	Ghetto	Middle Class	Pornography Users	Homosexuals	Transsexuals	Rapists	Pedophiles Attracted to Male Children	Pedophiles Attracted to Female Children
In adolescence Excited to the point of masturbation	87	46	50	86	69	36	90	65	60
In adulthood Excited to the point of masturbation	37	13	11	78	75	14	80	60	45
Look at erotic material while masturbating	11	4	7	46	39	14	35	25	10
Masturbate sometimes without erotic material	30	13	7	68	69	57	75	70	60
Excited to the point of having sexual relations	48	37	46	56	56	21	55	60	55
Think about erotic material while having sexual relations	19	4	10	28	19	7	20	30	30

Comparison of the reactions of several groups to erotica does not suggest striking differences between sex criminals and noncriminals in either adolescent or adult responsiveness.

homosexuals who actually show a small increase in masturbating in response to the erotic materials as adults. These data would suggest that erotic materials remain important to the user group in adult life as stimulants to masturbate.

This suggestion is consistent with the responses to a further question inquiring as to whether or not the erotic material was actually looked at while masturbating. Of the users, 46% so reported, while only 11% of the white controls and under 7% of each of the two black control groups so reported. The two homosexual groups (the homosexuals and the pedophiles, male object) and the rapists were higher than the controls but not as high as the users in this regard.

When asked how they felt when thoughts about the erotic material might come to mind at a later time, the controls were again low on reporting arousal, whereas the user and sex offender groups had about half reporting arousal or feeling good. The rapists again showed their strongly disturbed feelings with a substantial number, 20%, reporting feeling guilty when later thinking about these materials; they were the only group having a substantial number so reporting.

When asked whether thinking about the materials excited them to sexual relations other than masturbation, about half of all the groups except the transsexuals (only 21%) so reported. The users did not noticeably stand out from the controls in this regard, although they were slightly higher. Thus, it would seem that the erotic materials are much more significant in producing masturbatory reaction in the users compared with the controls than in inducing sexual relations.

When asked whether thoughts of the material appear during sexual relations, no group reported more than 30%. The users were higher than the controls but slightly lower than the two pedophile groups.

Reaction to peak experience as adult

After eliciting reports of frequency of exposure to erotic stimuli in all media in the most recent year, the subject was directed to select the one experience that stood out most in his mind. After that peak experience was specified, the subject was asked if there was anything viewed in that experience that the subject wished to try later. As shown in Table 12-2, 58% of the users reported affirmatively, while with the controls and other groups under 40% gave an affirmative answer.

When asked if the subject did in fact follow through with such sexual activity either immediately or shortly thereafter, all the reports dropped sharply. The users report only 22% imitating the act shown in the erotic stimuli while only 13% of the white controls so report. The other groups are about the same as the white controls, except that the pedophiles, female object (25%), and the black ghetto controls (21%) are somewhat higher. These data again tend to confirm that the use

Effects of the One Experience with Erotica that Stands Out Most in Subject's Mind

	Heterosexual Control Subjects			Subjects with Varying Sexual Life Styles			Sex Criminals		
		Blacks							
	Whites (%)	Ghetto (%)	Middle Class (%)	Pornography Users (%)	Homosexuals (%)	Transsexuals (%)	Rapists (%)	Pedophiles Attracted to Male Children (%)	Pedophiles Attracted to Female Children (%)
As a teen-ager									
Wished to try depicted act	48	63	54	66	39	29	80	65	40
Did try depicted act shortly afterward	28	38	28	30	14	14	30	25	20
Wished to try some other sexual act	63	71	50	72	51	50	75	70	55
Did try some other sexual act shortly afterward	22	4	0	52	28	21	25	40	25
As an adult									
Wished to try depicted act	30	29	4	58	33	14	35	35	25
Did try depicted act shortly afterward	13	21	4	22	6	7	15	15	25
Wished to try some other sexual act	65	37	29	66	61	28	40	60	45
Did try some other sexual act shortly afterward	35	29	10	32	36	0	20	40	15

Comparison of the effects of erotica on various groups does not suggest striking differences between sex criminals and noncriminals in the impact of erotica either as a teen-ager or as an adult.

made of the erotic material by the users is not direct or specific but tends more toward general arousal and masturbation. This seems to be generally true of the rapists as well.

When asked if the subject wished to engage in some sexual activity other than that represented in this pornographic stimulus, the groups do not reveal sharp differences between themselves. However, the rapists seem to be noticeably lower in reporting affirmatively. When asked if such activity was actually engaged in afterward, there is again a sharper drop in all groups in the number actually so engaging, with the rapists being low in this regard, and the user group being relatively high, although less so than the controls. The homosexually inclined groups seem to have the highest actual outlets for experience afterward.

As already noted, the rapists report relatively low actual activity either imitative, or of any kind, following stimulation by erotic materials. When the subjects were asked what the internal and external barriers were to actually engaging in sex activity, the only significant category of response for any group was the rapists' report of 15% "afraid of sex" and 15% having no available sex partner.

Reaction to peak experience as adolescent

Questions were also asked the subjects concerning the experience that most stood out in their minds as adolescents (Table 12-2). At this age, all of the groups showed greater interest than they did as adults in imagining a chance to imitate the behavior viewed in the erotic material. The rapists particularly stand out with 80% recalling having had a desire to do so. The figures also are much greater for wishing to try sex of any kind afterward with the rapists again having the highest report of 75%. The high reports of all groups to both these questions may be reflective of the higher generalized desire of sexual activity of adolescents as compared with adults, and it also might reflect greater stimulation because of the novelty of the experience of erotic material in adolescence as compared with the satiation effect evident later.

With respect to actual sexual activity, there seems to have been more imitative action initiated as adolescents than as adults, which also may be explained by the factors referred to above. The black ghetto control group reported the highest percentage, 38%, of actual imitation of the behavior viewed despite the group's very low reporting of general use of pornography. Most groups reported more general activity than specific imitative activity. The user group was much higher in general sexual activity than in imitating. The rapists were generally average or lower in any sexual activity afterward.

In the user group, arousal most frequently leads to masturbation as a drive reduction, with relatively little social sexual activity. This is quite characteristic of the person who develops a chronic dependency on pictures. The recurrence of thoughts of the erotic material leads to further masturbation. This pattern appears to continue into adulthood and becomes combined with the seeking of more erotic materials to induce arousal. The cycle of self-stimulation then continues. The users, more than the controls, reported thoughts about pictorial erotic material during intercourse, which may also be a type of self-stimulation necessary for them to complete the act of intercourse.

DISCUSSION

Generally, the reports of frequency during the adolescent years indicate that institutionalized sex offenders, homosexuals, transsexuals, and users of pornography report less frequent exposure than the control groups. The reports of frequency of exposure during the year previous to interview are consistent with retrospective adolescent data for the institutionalized sex offenders, transsexuals, and control samples in that the controls continue to show more exposure. The differences between institutionalized sex offenders and the controls are more marked for the recent than the retrospective adolescent data, although the trend of low exposure for sex offenders is present in both sets of data. In contrast, the homosexuals and pornography users show marked crossover relative to controls when adolescent and recent reports are compared. The lesser exposure during adolescence for these groups and the higher recent exposure differ at high levels of significance from control reports. It appears that both groups show a continuing interest in erotica, the homosexuals in homosexual erotica and the users in both heterosexual and homosexual erotica. Since our data on homosexuals are based upon a sample of homosexuals willing to join a homophile organization and to be publicly identified with this deviate sex role, it is difficult to know whether the trends found can be generalized to the majority of homosexuals not willing to be publicly identified. The data for the transsexuals suggest a marked difference between this group which requests sex change and homosexuals. Their reports of exposure to erotica suggest very limited experience both in adolescence and during the year prior to interview.

Comparison of the reports of exposure to erotica across all types of stimuli indicates that sex deviates report less average exposure than controls. This suggests that a reasonable exposure to erotica, particularly during adolescence, reflects a high degree of sexual interest and curiosity. This curiosity is correlated with an adult pattern of acceptable heterosexual interest and practice. Less than average adolescent exposure, as in the sex deviate sample, reflects either avoidance of heterosexual stimuli—witness the consistently low figures for stimuli representing heterosexual intercourse—or development in an extremely restrictive atmosphere in which contact with such stimuli is prohibited and punished. It appears that the degree of exposure to erotica is a surface manifestation of a total pattern of sexual development. If this pattern of sexual development proceeds along a deviant track, then in later life deviant sexual behavior is correlated with one of two extremes of a continuum of exposure to erotica, underexposure or obsessive interest in erotica.

The differences between controls and our comparison groups on demographic variables raise the question of whether the differences in reports of exposure to erotica reflect these socioeconomic, age-related, and educational factors.

The black middle-class control sample shows a very similar age distribution to the pedophiles, yet the blacks' exposure reports are identical to those of the white controls, suggesting that generational differences cannot fully account for differences in reported exposure. The pedophile and transsexuals represent markedly contrasting educational and occupational levels (transsexuals were better educated, had more professionals, and more unemployed) yet they share similar patterns of infrequent exposure to erotica. The homosexuals are high in educational level and their reports for adolescence parallel those of the pedophiles. It appears that all groups of sex deviates, with varying age distributions, educational levels, and occupational levels, share one common characteristic of low exposure to erotica during adolescence.

The present article deals primarily with reports of sex attitudes, practices, and frequency of exposure to erotic stimuli. However, frequency of contact with erotic stimuli does not tell the whole story. Certain experiences of a particularly vivid nature need only occur once or twice in order to produce significant effects on sexual attitudes and behavior. In the clinical interview, there are questions dealing with "peak" experiences with erotica suggested by the respondent. These questions deal with the nature of the experience and subsequent shifts in attitudes and behavior. While, to date, these data are only partially analyzed, the results, presented above, suggest that sexual arousal following exposure to erotica does not cue off any specific pattern of sexual action. The availability of a sex partner and internal attitudes and values concerning sexuality determine the mode of sexual expression. In adolescence, erotic materials suggest varieties of sexual behavior, but the behavior engaged in most typically is masturbation. In adult life, only the chronic pornography users and the sex offenders appear to continue this pattern of arousal and masturbation as their fearful sexual attitudes prevent the use of normal sexual outlets. It appears that unresolved sexual conflicts present in adolescence may relate to adult sexual patterns in which erotica is a necessary stimulus to gratification. In the other males, the adolescent use of erotica as an adjunct to sexual actions declines and the sexual partner becomes the primary source of arousal and gratification.

Satiation of the Transient Stimulating Effect
of Erotic Films

Even though there is no evidence to support the fear that pornography is a cause of sexual crimes, we would still expect it to have an effect on ordinary sexual behavior. Since it is well established that both males and females become sexually aroused while viewing erotic films, it seems very plausible to expect that this arousal would increase the probability of their engaging in a sexual act following the movie. One of the best ways to investigate these effects is within the confines of an established marital relationship. That is, it should be possible to determine if erotic stimulation has an effect on whether a husband and wife have sexual relations on a given day and, if they do so, whether the erotica affects the specific sexual behavior they choose.

The following article is based on data gathered in one of the experiments conducted for the Commission on Obscenity and Pornography. For 4 weeks, married couples were shown movies 1 night each week. They saw either erotic or nonerotic films and were asked to keep a record of their sexual activity during the experimental period. It was hypothesized that the erotic movies would have an effect on marital sexuality but that the effect would be limited to the actual night the movie was seen and that the effect would decrease over time as the couples became satiated in viewing filmed erotica. That was the general pattern of the findings to be reported, and there was no evidence that the subjects imitated or modeled the particular behaviors depicted on the screen. Thus, the erotic movies influenced *when* the viewers engaged in sex but not *what* they did.

Satiation of the Transient Stimulating Effect
of Erotic Films

Jay Mann, Leonard Berkowitz, Jack Sidman,
Sheldon Starr, and Stephen West

Most discussions of mass media influences have emphasized their long-term consequences to the comparative neglect of other, more short-lived effects.[1][2] Attention has focused primarily on such matters as the information that is transmitted, the learning that occurs, and the attitudes, interests, and values that are developed or changed. Relatively little consideration has been given to the transient behavioral reactions that are produced by the media with the possible exception of changes in

Reprinted in an edited version from: Mann, J., Berkowitz, L., Sidman, J., Starr, S., & West, S. Satiation of the transient stimulating effect of erotic films. *Journal of Personality and Social Psychology*, 1974, **30**, 729–735.

mood or general arousal. However, in a series of articles, Berkowitz[2,3,4,5] has suggested that, whatever else it does, the mass media can also stimulate socially significant behaviors.

Words, symbols, and pictures often serve as conditioned stimuli that evoke semantically associated reactions. Should an observer attribute a particular meaning to the media event (i.e., think of it in a certain way, say as an *aggressive* or a *sexual* occurrence), it stimulates reactions having the same meaning.[6] These elicited responses (ideas and often other related motor and autonomic reactions as well) are usually only covert and fairly weak but tend to facilitate overt behavior having the same meaning, especially if inhibitions against this particular action are weak at the time, the observer is already disposed to carry out the behavior, and he is also experiencing a strong general arousal. Thus, if an individual watches a fight when he is ready to attack someone and is not restrained against aggression, the witnessed violence might well evoke stronger aggressive reactions from him than he otherwise would have displayed if he had not seen the fight, particularly if he is also highly aroused on that occasion.[4,5]

There is another aspect of this stimulus-response analysis that is directly pertinent to the present report: the responses elicited by the media event are usually fairly transient. Even when the screen or printed page produces an observable reaction, this reaction typically subsides after a while as the individual enters other situations and comes under the influence of other environmental stimuli.

Although this conception grew out of experiments on movie violence, it is also supported by research on the effects of erotica. Studies have consistently shown that short-lived sexual activity often results from exposure to sexual materials.[13] In experiments carried out at the University of Hamburg[11] as an illustration, university men and women reported significant increases in the frequency of masturbation in the 24-hour period following exposure to erotic slides and motion pictures, while the women also reported a small but significant increase in the frequency of petting and sexual intercourse. Clearly documenting the typically brief influence of erotic movies, a study employing married couples in California found that sex films often promoted sexual activity on the movie night but caused no significant increase in this activity at other times.[9] Thus 77% of the males and 63% of the females seeing the erotic movies reported a greater frequency of sexual activity on the film-viewing nights than on the other nights, whereas this increase occurred in only 41% of the men and 35% of the women in the nonerotic-films control condition.

These data also highlight the one-sidedness of most modeling analyses of movie influences. Although Bandura's[1] discussion of modeling recognizes the possible stimulation effects, the usual reasoning generally emphasizes the information that is transmitted by the model's behavior and what the observer learns from seeing the model's action. However, in these erotic movie experiments, there is not much evidence of any new learning or even of a disinhibitory process arising from the information in the film. The subjects seeing the erotic films did become more favorably disposed toward erotic films in general. However, there were no indications that they had become less restrained in their own sexual activities or were more willing to carry out the less conventional sex acts they saw on the screen. The experimental subjects in both the Hamburg and California studies reported only previously practiced sexual activities and apparently did not carry out the relatively novel (for them) behaviors they saw on the screen.

Other findings obtained with erotic films are also consistent with Berkowitz's stimulus-response model: repeated exposure to sexual stimuli often weakens their impact, for a short period at least, as if satiation sets in.[13] As one example, when university men were given an opportunity to look at sexual material 90 min a day for 3 weeks, there was a gradual diminution of interest in this type of material and a corresponding reduction in physiological indicators of specific sexual reactions.[8] The sexual stimuli in the books and movies had temporarily lost their capacity to evoke sexual responses. This decreased responsivity to an environmental stimulus upon repeated presentation of the stimulus parallels the satiation effects noted in laboratory investigations of this phenomenon.[7]

This article reports a subsidiary analysis of the data from the California experiment conducted by Mann and associates.[9] We sought to determine if the married couples in this study also exhibited a satiation effect with repeated exposure to the erotic movies. The subjects had seen different films 1 night a week for 4 weeks. A decline in their rate of marital activity on the movie night over the course of the month would indicate that these films had become less and less effective elicitors of sexual responses as a consequence of the repeated viewings. In addition to supporting this general stimulus-response formulation, such a finding would also indicate that satiation processes govern the extent to which events portrayed in the mass media can evoke semantically associated reactions.

METHOD

Subjects

The original publication[9] contains a detailed description of the way the subjects were recruited and their background characteristics. Summarizing briefly, the subjects were recruited through advertisements and handbills soliciting volunteers for a study of "marital behavior." This notice said the volunteers would be paid for completing a very short checklist of their marital behavior every day for 12 weeks. A random sample of 66 couples provided the data for the present analysis.

The subjects were predominantly from the middle class, over 80% of the men in the total sample being from either white-collar or professional occupations. They were well educated (72% of the men and 41% of the women had at least a college degree) and moderately conservative in their sexual practices as well as in their political beliefs (according to their self-descriptions). They also generally thought they had a happy marriage (70% of the males and about 84% of the females rated their marriage as either very happy or happier than average) and over 60% rated their sex lives as either satisfactory or very satisfactory. The subjects in the total sample were between 30 and 64 years of age with a median age of 46 years for the men and 42 years for the women. Further, since the recruitment notices had stipulated a minimum of 10 years of marriage, their marriages had been long lasting, the median time being 17.5 years. Finally, we might also note the subjects' reported rate of sexual intercourse was generally consistent with the Kinsey norms for their age and education level, the mean frequency being "once or twice weekly."[9]

Experimental procedure

The original study was divided into three phases: (1) a month of daily reporting of sexual activity, (2) a month during which movies were seen once a week and the daily reports were made, and (3) a final month of the daily reporting only. Mann et al.[9] found that the experimental conditions did not produce any significant changes from the first to the third phases in either sexual attitudes or sexual behaviors, and we confine ourselves here to the data from the movie-viewing month.

We subdivided the subjects in terms of the order in which they had seen the erotic films. One condition began with 2 weeks of "conventional" sex movies depicting heterosexual couples engaged in various "standard" sexual activities together with a brief film showing a female masturbating. In the other condition, by contrast, the movies shown during the first 2 weeks depicted "less conventional" sexual practices including sexual acts by female and male homosexuals, two women and a man involved in oral-genital activity and anal play as well as coitus, and a male and female whipping each other as well as having intercourse. Then, in the final 2 weeks, the subjects saw the movies that had been presented earlier to the other group. As a result, we now have two erotic movie conditions—(1) conventional sex first, less conventional sex last; and (2) less conventional sex first, conventional sex last—and a third, control condition in which subjects were shown various nonerotic films (dealing with such topics as creativity, perception, and a day in the life of a teen-age expectant mother).

Sex data

Sexual activity measures The data used in this report were taken from the marital activities questionnaires sent in daily by each subject. The first part of this form described 22 different activities, including drug taking, alcohol drinking, and reading of erotic literature, as well as various sexual acts. For each one the subject was to indicate whether he or she performed the act, wanted to do so, or daydreamed about it, and in any of these cases, whether this was with the spouse, a same-sex partner or an opposite-sex partner other than the spouse.

The original investigators formed a number of scales out of the subjects' responses by combining various items. In general, however, the only measures yielding significant results had to do with the performance of fairly conventional sexual acts, largely because the frequencies for the other items were very low. We present the results for the two behavioral scales showing significant differences among the movie conditions. The scales are (1) intercourse with spouse based on two items, vaginal intercourse with spouse using usual position and vaginal intercourse with spouse using other than usual position, and (2) marital activity (other than intercourse) based on six items dealing with oral and manual stimulation of own and partner's genitals.

The scores on these scales were established for eight time periods: for each movie night as well as for the average nonmovie night during each of the 4 weeks of the movie-viewing month. In each period rate measures were computed for each subject by dividing the total number of acts reported by the number of 24-hour periods involved. For example, if a subject said he had performed four separate sexual acts listed in the scale over the five nonmovie nights for which he had sent in questionnaires during a given week, he would have a .80 rate score on that particular scale for the given week's nonmovie night. Since almost all of the subjects engaged in only their usual form of sexual intercourse, the scores on Scale 1 are typically based on only one of the two items. Thus, the mean rate of this scale in any one condition approximates the percentage of subjects in that group who had reported sexual intercourse with their spouses during the particular period.

In addition to listing various activities, the daily questionnaire also asked the subject about his feelings during the 24-hour period covered by the report. He was to indicate such things as how much energy he had, how much anxiety he experienced, and how much he enjoyed his spouse's company.

Agreement between spouses Not surprisingly, the husbands and wives tended to be in considerable agreement about their sexual activity. In the interest of brevity we report only the findings obtained with the male data. Although the male and female scores yielded virtually the same pattern of significant results, the indicated rate of sexual activity was slightly higher for the husbands, which suggests that the women may have been somewhat restrained in filling out the questionnaires.

RESULTS

Sexual reactions

The male scores on the two scales did not produce exactly the same findings. Nonetheless, the significant main effect for "night" indicates that, overall, there was a greater rate of sexual activity on movie nights than on the other nights of the week regardless of the nature of the films, although what significant differences there were *within any one week* occurred only in the sex-movie conditions. Evidently, there was something of a tendency for the couples to have been in a romantic mood when they had returned home from the movies, and they then tended to engage in sex. The findings with the attitude ratings on the daily questionnaires also point to this romantic mood. The men reported a reliably greater enjoyment of their spouse's company and also said they and their wives had been more affectionate toward each other on the movie nights than on the other nights of the week. (The female data yielded the same general results but also indicated a significantly greater closeness to their husbands on the movie night.)

The experimental conditions did affect the rate of coital activity in some weeks more than others. We delved further, since we had definitely expected (1) greater sexual activity on the movie than nonmovie nights and (2) a decline in this activity with the passage of time. The results of this closer examination are given in Table 12-3.

Here we note that the greatest difference between the movie and nonmovie nights occurred in the first week and that during this period, the men were significantly more likely to have sexual intercourse with their wives after they had returned from the erotic film than on the other nights of the week. This night difference declined in the following weeks, being significant later in the conventional-sex-first group only in Week 3 and in the less-conventional-sex-first group in Weeks 2 and 3 but not in the final week. Furthermore, as we had also anticipated, there also seemed to be a satiation effect, particularly in the less-conventional-sex-first group; the males in this latter condition reported a decrease in their rate of coitus on the movie nights from the beginning to the end of the month, as if the sexual stimuli on the screen had lost their ability to evoke sexual response. There was a significantly lower intercourse rate in this condition on the movie nights in Weeks 3 and 4 than in the first week. In the conventional-sex-first group, however, after a very high rate of intercourse in the first movie night (about two-thirds of the men reporting intercourse), there was a significant decline in the rate the following week and then a reliable jump the next time with the presentation of the first deviant sex films. It is as if the relatively novel

Table 12-3
Intercourse Rates Reported by Husbands on the Nights
They Were Shown a Movie and on Nonmovie Nights

	Week 1		Week 2		Week 3		Week 4	
	Movie Night	Nonmovie Nights	Movie Night	Nonmovie Nights	Movie Night	Nonmovie Nights	Movie Night	Nonmovie Nights
Conventional Sex Movies for 2 Weeks Followed by Unconventional Sex Movies for 2 Weeks	.67	.22	.24	.24	.58	.18	.36	.19
Unconventional Sex Movies for 2 Weeks Followed by Conventional Sex Movies for 2 Weeks	.64	.30	.48	.27	.44	.24	.28	.19
Nonerotic Movies for 4 Weeks	.25	.13	.40	.27	.25	.19	.34	.22

Married couples were shown one movie per week for 4 weeks. They were found to be more likely to have intercourse on the night they saw a movie than on nonmovie nights, and more likely to have intercourse after viewing a sexual movie than a nonsexual one. There was a tendency to become satiated by the weekly sexual movies (especially those subjects who saw unconventional movies first), so that the difference between movie nights and unmovie nights tended to decrease from the first week to the fourth one.

sex portrayed in these scenes had again "turned them on." The rate in this group was now significantly higher than the rate in the nonerotic films control condition but not significantly higher than the other sex movie group. Then, the coital rate again dropped on the fourth movie night, and there were no differences among the three experimental conditions.

The results are somewhat different for the other sexual-activity scale. Although the experimental conditions did not interact significantly with either the weeks or nights classifications, our a priori expectations again warranted a closer examination of the condition rates in each of the time periods. We found that the men in the two erotic films groups were more likely to engage in sexual activity with their spouses than were the controls on the first movie night, and the former groups' rates on this first night were reliably higher than on the nonmovie nights of the week. After this initial viewing, moreover, there tended to be a decreased rate of sexual activity so that both sex movie groups reported reliably less noncoital activity on the movie nights in the succeeding weeks than in Week 1. As with the intercourse measure, the men in the conventional-sex-first group reported a reliably higher rate of sexual activity than did the controls the first time they saw the novel, deviant sex films, but again, this significant difference disappeared the next week.

While this pattern bears a rough resemblance to the findings with the intercourse measure, other results suggest that the sex movies had affected noncoital and coital activity somewhat differently. Thus, where there had been a reliable difference in intercourse rates between movie and nonmovie nights during the second week only in the less-conventional-sex-first group, here the second-week significant difference existed only in the conventional-sex-first condition. It is not at all clear why these particular results arose.

Attitude reactions

Even though the erotic films had stimulated a considerable degree of sexual activity and the couples had also enjoyed going to the movies, participation in the erotic movie conditions was not sheer bliss. An examination of the subjects' attitudinal responses on the daily questionnaires revealed that the men in the conventional-sex-first group had some relatively unpleasant feelings as a result of their experience. They (and their wives as well) reported feeling significantly more anxious and more downhearted over the course of the movie-viewing month than did the people in the nonerotic film condition. The less-conventional-sex-first group had scores in between these two extremes. This pattern did not vary from movie to nonmovie nights or from one week to the next. We cannot say for sure why conventional-sex-first group had these negative reactions, but they might have thought that their own sexual experiences and/or sexual performances did not compare favorably with those on the screen. Some of the remarks made by the participants during the final debriefing are in line with this possibility. It is also worth noting, however, that the sex films had prompted many of the husbands and wives to discuss their own relationships, and this discussion conceivably might have contributed to the anxiety the men and women reported.

DISCUSSION

This study shows fairly clearly that (1) sexual stimuli on the screen can elicit relatively transient sexual reactions and (2) that repeated exposure to this type of stimulation often produces a satiation effect so that there is a reduced likelihood of a sexual response with each subsequent viewing. However, other data suggest that the satiation does not last; as time goes by, there is a reawakened interest in sex. In the experiment by Howard and associates[8] mentioned earlier, when the subjects again saw a sex film 2 months after the satiation period, they became physiologically aroused almost to the level that had existed at the start of the study. Also suggestive of such a recovery, a study of San Francisco erotica patrons sponsored by the U. S. Commission on Obscenity and Pornography[10] found that a coterie of them attended sex movies at least once a month. Satiation apparently wears off quite rapidly for these people. All this also suggests that the time interval between the successive exposures to erotic materials plays an important part in determining the degree to which satiation sets in. While the present subjects tended to become inured to the sex movies upon seeing them every week, they might have continued "getting a charge" out of these films if they had viewed them, say, only once every few months.

Our findings also indicate that the satiation effect may be somewhat specific to particular stimuli. The relatively novel deviant sex films were fairly effective stimuli for many of the men in the conventional-sex-first group the first time these movies were seen in the third week. Being different from the more commonplace sexual scenes the men had previously encountered, their sex-stimulating capacity was not significantly diminished on this first contact. But there, too, the novelty soon wore off, and the next exposure was much less effective. This specificity is also apparent in the results reported by Howard and his associates.[8] When the researchers introduced novel erotic material in the eleventh session, there was a sharply renewed sexual responsivity, although this diminished quickly in the next two sessions.

REFERENCES

1. Bandura, A. Vicarious processes: A case of no-trial learning. In L. Berkowitz (Ed.), *Advances in experimental social psychology*. Vol. 2. New York: Academic Press, 1965.

2. Berkowitz, L. Aggressive cues in aggressive behavior and hostility catharsis. *Psychological Review*, 1964, **71**, 104–122.

3. Berkowitz, L. The concept of aggressive drive: Some additional considerations. In L. Berkowitz (Ed.), *Advances in experimental social psychology*. Vol. 2. New York: Academic Press, 1965.

4. Berkowitz, L. The contagion of violence: An S-R mediational analysis of some effects of observed aggression. In W. Arnold & M. Page (Eds.), *Nebraska Symposium on Motivation: 1970*. Lincoln: University of Nebraska Press, 1971.

5. Berkowitz, L. Words and symbols as stimuli to aggressive responses. In J. F. Knutson (Ed.), *Control of aggression: Implications from basic research*. Chicago: Aldine, 1973.

6. Berkowitz, L., & Alioto, J. The meaning of an observed event as a determinant of its aggressive consequences. *Journal of Personality and Social Psychology*, 1973, **28**, 206–217.

7. Fowler, H. Satiation and curiosity. In K. W. Spence & J. T. Spence (Eds.), *Psychology of learning and motivation*. Vol. 1. New York: Academic Press, 1967.

8. Howard, J. L., Reiffler, C. B., & Liptzin, M. B. Effects of exposure to pornography. In *Technical report of the Commission on Obscenity and Pornography*. Vol. 8. Washington, D. C.: U. S. Government Printing Office, 1971.

9. Mann, J., Sidman, J., & Starr, S. Effects of erotic films on the sexual behavior of married couples. In *Technical report of the Commission on Obscenity and Pornography*. Vol. 8. Washington, D. C.: U. S. Government Printing Office, 1971.

10. Nawy, H. The San Francisco erotic marketplace. In *Technical report of the Commission on Obscenity and Pornography*. Vol. 4. Washington, D. C.: U. S. Government Printing Office, 1971.

11. Schmidt, G., & Sigusch, V. Sex differences in response to psychosexual stimulation by films and slides. *Journal of Sex Research*, 1970, **6**, 268–283.

12. Schramm, W., & Roberts, D. F. (Eds.) *The process and effects of mass communication*. (Rev. ed.) Urbana: University of Illinois Press, 1971.

13. U. S. Commission on Obscenity and Pornography. *The report of the Commission on Obscenity and Pornography*. New York: Bantam, 1970.

Effects of Heightened Sexual Arousal
on Physical Aggression

Though much of the concern about the behavioral effects of erotic stimulation has centered on sexual behavior, there is another possible effect: perhaps exposure to erotica increases *aggressive behavior.*

There are many lines of evidence, ranging from studies of animals to psychoanalytic theory, that suggest a link between sex and aggression. For many animal species and at least for some people, aggressive behavior often precedes and perhaps is a cue for sexual arousal. Whether one's image is two male animals fighting to determine which will be able to possess a waiting female, a lovers' quarrel that adds erotic spice to the subsequent sexual reconciliation, or the torturer who becomes aroused by inflicting pain, the notion that aggression can be sexually stimulating is a familiar one.

What about the reverse relationship? Can sexual arousal lead to aggression? Psychologists Robert Baron and Paul Bell point out theoretical reasons why such a relationship might be expected and refer to experimental evidence confirming that expectation. Their own research suggests a more complicated relationship in which mild sexual stimulation actually serves to inhibit aggressive responses whereas stronger stimulation enhances aggression. One of the key considerations, as they point out, may be whether or not erotica-produced excitement leads to a sexual act or to frustration. Thus, one would not expect aggression if an individual viewed an erotic film and afterward masturbated or engaged in intercourse. Sexual excitement that was left unsatisfied because of situational constraints, moral considerations, or emotional inhibitions might, however, be channeled into aggressive acts. Perhaps the slogan "Make love, not war" expresses not just the incompatibility of the two responses but the fact that, depending on the circumstances, excitement can produce either sexuality or hostility; thus, an individual must choose one of the behavioral modes.

Effects of Heightened Sexual Arousal
on Physical Aggression

Robert A. Baron and Paul A. Bell

It has frequently been contended that there is an intimate relationship between sexual and aggressive motives. For example, Freud[8] noted that desires to hurt or be hurt by one's lover form a normal part of heterosexual relations. Similarly, Berne[5] has suggested that the arousal of

Reprinted in an edited version from: Baron, R. A., & Bell, P. A. Effects of heightened sexual arousal on physical aggression. *Proceedings, Annual Convention, APA,* 1973, 171–172.

aggressive motives may often serve to increase sexual arousal and pleasure for both men and women. Actual evidence for the existence of a close link between sexual and aggressive motives has been obtained in several recent studies[1] which indicate that the arousal of one of these drives generally is associated with an increase in the other. In sum, it appears that sexual and aggressive motives are indeed closely related.

But what of the impact of heightened sexual arousal upon overt aggressive behavior? Are sexually aroused individuals actually more likely to engage in subsequent aggression than individuals who are not so aroused? Modern social psychological theory suggests that under some conditions at least, this may indeed be the case. In particular, Berkowitz[4] has recently suggested that any source of heightened arousal may serve to facilitate subsequent aggression under conditions where clearly defined aggressive stimuli are present in the environment. The results of two recent experiments[9,10] provide evidence that heightened sexual arousal may operate precisely in this manner. In both of these investigations, increments in sexual arousal (induced through exposure to erotic stimuli) were found to facilitate subsequent attacks against a victim who possessed a high level of aggressive cue value (a male confederate who had previously angered the subject).

But what of situations in which such aggressive cues are lacking or present only to a much lesser degree? Although Berkowitz[4] did not specifically address this problem, it seems reasonable to suggest that heightened sexual arousal will fail to facilitate subsequent aggression under these conditions. Indeed, since such arousal may serve to "energize" other responses, some of which could prove to be incompatible with the expression of overt aggressive acts (e.g., vivid sexual fantasies; vigorous love making), the frequency or intensity of such behavior might actually be reduced. The present study was designed to examine this possibility. More specifically, it sought to determine whether heightened sexual arousal would tend to facilitate subsequent aggression in the presence of aggressive cues, but fail to exert such effects or actually tend to inhibit overt aggression in their absence.

In order to examine this hypothesis, subjects in two groups were first exposed, respectively, to a series of erotic or neutral stimuli, and then permitted to aggress against either a male or female victim by means of electric shock. On the basis of previous findings,[7] it was anticipated that the male victim would possess a considerably higher level of aggressive cue value than the female victim. Thus, it was predicted that heightened sexual arousal, induced through exposure to the erotic stimuli, would tend to facilitate subsequent attacks against the victim when this person was a male, but would fail to exert such effects or actually tend to inhibit subsequent aggression when this individual was a female.

METHOD

Subjects and apparatus

Eighty undergraduate males enrolled in sections of introductory psychology at Purdue University participated in the experiment. The subjects took part in the study in order to satisfy a course requirement.

The apparatus consisted of a modified Buss[6] "aggression machine" identical to the one used in a number of previous investigations.[2]

Procedure

When subjects arrived for the experiment they were informed that they would be participating, along with another individual (actually a male or female confederate), in a study concerned with the effects of electric shock on physiological reactions.[3] They were then assigned the task of delivering a series of shocks to the confederate on occasions to be designated by the experimenter. This individual (i.e., the confederate) was then conducted by the experimenter to an adjoining room where shock and physiological recording electrodes were ostensibly attached to his/her arms and wrists. The experimenter then returned to the room where the subject was waiting and indicated that before beginning the shock trials, it would be necessary to wait for the confederate's physiological reactions to return to base levels. He/she further indicated that since this time was available, subjects would be asked to examine and rate a series of stimuli he/she was planning to use in another study. In the *aroused* condition, these stimuli consisted of 10 pictures of nude young women taken from back issues of *Playboy* magazine, and rated by a panel of three judges as highly attractive and quite sexually arousing. In the *nonaroused* condition, the stimuli consisted of 10 pictures of scenery, furniture, and abstract paintings judged to be completely nonarousing. The subjects were allowed a total of 5 min to examine the stimuli, during which time they were unobtrusively observed by the experimenter. These observations revealed no appreciable difference in the amount of time required by the subjects in the two groups to complete this task.

Following these procedures, the subjects were provided with detailed instructions regarding their task of shocking the confederate. They were informed that each time a red signal light was illuminated, they were to shock this individual by means of 1 to 10 buttons on the apparatus. It was further explained that the higher the number of the button they chose, the stronger the shock which would be delivered. In order to demonstrate the magnitude of the shocks which they could presumably employ, the experimenter then administered "samples" from Buttons 4 and 5. The shock delivered by Button 5 was stronger than that produced by Button 4, but both were generally judged to be moderately unpleasant by the subjects. In order to minimize the influence of demand characteristics, instructions emphasized the fact that the subjects should feel perfectly free to use any shock buttons they wished during the study. The shock signal was illuminated a total of 20 times.

RESULTS

Check on the manipulation of sexual arousal   A check on the manipulation of sexual arousal was obtained by means of a postexperimental questionnaire item on which subjects rated their degree of arousal while examining the pictures. As expected, subjects in the aroused group reported a significantly higher level of sexual arousal than those in the nonaroused condition. Thus, there was some evidence that the attempted manipulation of sexual arousal was successful.

Shock intensity   The major dependent measure of aggression was the intensity of the shocks directed by subjects against the confederate. An analysis of these data indicated that both the sex of the victim and the number of trials were significant. Thus, subjects delivered significantly weaker shocks to a female than a male victim, and the strength of their attacks against this person tended to increase over the course of the experiment. In addition, and of somewhat greater interest, subjects in the aroused group delivered weaker shocks to the victim than those in the nonaroused condition early in the experiment, but came to employ the same level of shock as the individuals in this latter group as the study progressed. Thus, it appeared that heightened sexual arousal tended to exert an initial inhibiting influence upon aggression which dissipated rapidly with the passage of time.

DISCUSSION

Consistent with the findings of previous research,[7] and Berkowitz's[4] contentions regarding the role of aggressive cues in the elicitations of aggressive behavior, subjects delivered significantly weaker shocks to a female than a male victim. However, the hypothesis that heightened sexual arousal would facilitate subsequent aggression against a male victim but inhibit attacks against a female target was not confirmed. Instead, exposure to erotic stimuli, and the resulting increments in sexual arousal so produced, seemed to inhibit aggression against victims of both sexes early in the experiment. This finding contrasts sharply with the results of previous studies[9,10] which have reported that increments in sexual arousal may enhance rather than inhibit subsequent attacks against others. One possible explanation for these contrasting patterns of findings may lie in the markedly different types of erotic stimuli employed in the previous and present investigations.

More specifically, subjects participating in both the Zillman[10] and Meyer[9] experiments were exposed to erotic stimuli which probably caused them to experience relatively high levels of sexual arousal (films of attractive young couples engaged in various acts of love making). Unfortunately, of course, they were then unable to satisfy the strong sexual urges they experienced. As a result, they may have felt irritated, annoyed, or frustrated, and so directed higher levels of shock against the victim than subjects who were not similarly aroused. In contrast, subjects in the present investigation were exposed to much milder erotic stimuli (pictures of attractive female nudes) which probably caused them to experience only moderate levels of sexual arousal. Comments during a postexperimental interview suggested that they found such arousal to be highly pleasurable, and it seems reasonable to suggest that such positive affective reactions may have caused them to lower the strength of their attacks against the victim, at least during early phases of the study while they persisted. In short, it is suggested that the impact of heightened sexual arousal upon subsequent aggression may depend, to an important degree, upon the magnitude of such arousal. When it is very high and cannot be immediately reduced, it may be irritating or annoying, and so lead to enhanced aggression by the individuals experiencing it. When it is relatively mild, however, it may be pleasurable, and so actually serve to inhibit such behavior. The validity of these suggestions may be readily examined in subsequent research by varying the level of sexual arousal induced among subjects in a systematic manner.

REFERENCES

1. Barclay, A. M. Linking sexual and aggressive motives: Contributions of "irrelevant" arousals. *Journal of Personality*, 1971, **39**, 481–492.

2. Baron, R. A. Aggression as a function of ambient temperature and prior anger arousal. *Journal of Personality and Social Psychology*, 1972, **21**, 183–189.

3. Baron, R. A., & Eggleston, R. J. Performance on the "aggression machine": Motivaion to help or harm? *Psychonomic Science*, 1972, **26**, 321–322.

4. Berkowitz, L. The contagion of violence: An S-R mediational analysis of some effects of observed aggression. In W. J. Arnold & M. M. Page (Eds.), *Nebraska symposium on motivation*. Lincoln: University of Nebraska Press, 1970.

5. Berne, E. *Games people play.* New York: Grove Press, 1964.

6. Buss, A. H. *The psychology of aggression.* New York: Wiley, 1961.

7. Buss, A. H. Aggression pays. In J. L. Singer (Ed.), *The control of aggression and violence.* New York: Academic Press, 1971.

8. Freud, S. *New introductory lectures on psycho-analysis.* New York: Norton, 1933.

9. Meyer, T. P. The effects of sexually arousing and violent films on aggressive behavior. *Journal of Sex Research,* 1972, **8**, 324–333.

10. Zillman, D. Excitation transfer in communication-mediated aggressive behavior. *Journal of Experimental Social Psychology,* 1971, **7**, 419–434.

Chapter Thirteen

Sex
and
a
Free
Society

Evaluation of Visual Erotica by
Sexual Liberals and Conservatives

Why is erotica threatening, anxiety evoking, and offensive to a great many individuals? Those who react in that negative way tend to stress the harmful effects of such material on behavior, especially on the behavior of other people. Psychologists who emphasize the importance of learning would suggest that these individuals probably underwent a continuing series of childhood experiences in which sexual cues were associated with negative emotions.

In the following article, psychologists Douglas Wallace and Gerald Wehmer touch on both of these explanations—the attributions made by those who dislike erotica and their possible socialization histories. Their major concern, however, is with personality differences which are related to attitudes and beliefs about threats to the stability of society. It is suggested that sexual conservatives interpret erotica as an affront to authority and hence as a danger to society itself. For them, an explicit sexual movie is as dangerous as an anarchist's bomb. At the opposite extreme, sexual liberals feel endangered not by erotica but by censorship. For them, a ban against pornography is an insult to each individual's intelligence and judgment, and it menaces his or her freedom. In a way, one group wishes to restrain individuals while the other wishes to restrain governmental authorities.

While we do not as yet have all of the answers as to how these various beliefs and attitudes are formed or all of the details about how they operate, one thing seems certain. There is a connection between one's reactions to sexuality and one's reactions to the relative priority that should be given to the individual versus the state. It is this connection that makes sexual attitudes a matter of potential political importance.

Evaluation of Visual Erotica by
Sexual Liberals and Conservatives

Douglas H. Wallace and Gerald Wehmer

The existence of graphic depictions of sexual behavior, commonly referred to as "obscenity" or "pornography," has long been considered to be an important social issue by many people in our society.[3] However, the level of concern evidenced by these laymen was not reflected in social science research until quite recently. In 1967, the Presidential Commission on Obscenity and Pornography was established by then

Reprinted in an edited version from: Wallace, D. H., & Wehmer, G. Evaluation of visual erotica by sexual liberals and conservatives. *Journal of Sex Research*, 1972, **8**, 147–153.

President Lyndon Johnson. In 1970, the commission issued its final report,[2] which contained, and has since stimulated, considerable empirical research on issues relating to visual erotica. The reception which has been given the report by the official government—its rejection by the U. S. Senate and by President Nixon—causes one to wonder whether the commission was guilty of an act of omission or commission, if in fact it was guilty of anything at all. It is the thesis of this article that a number of the same sociopolitical considerations which account for the differences between sexual "liberals" and "conservatives" in their evaluation of visual erotica should, in large measure, account for the government's reactions.

Morse Peckham, in his book *Art and Pornography: An Experiment in Explanation*,[4] presented a linguistic analysis of the various reactions to the existence of erotica in our society. He noted that the public appears to take one of two polar positions with respect to the issues of the existence of erotica and its availability. Those who regard the production and viewing of erotic materials as a legitimate means of expression were called "Intellectuals," while those who viewed the same activities as a violation of important social mores were labeled "Anti-Intellectuals." The author stated that the intellectual is commonly seen as defending the existence of erotica, even though he personally may find it distasteful or contemptuous. This is because he finds that any:

> attempt at legal control threatens his competency, his mastery, and his ability to be the final judge in verbal and non-verbal behavior, as in the non-verbal arts. If pornography is to be condemned, or even censored, it must be for *his* reasons.

The anti-intellectuals, however:

> condemn not only the objectionable and offensive presentations of sex facts and indecent and suggestive illustrations but also anything that smacks of "disrespect for authority." The condemnation of pornography and their mode of defining it, then, have their sources in political and social interests, in, as they always say, the stability of society [p. 11].

Thus the resultant conflict of positions may be seen as being of a social nature, with the focal sexual object(s) becoming lost in the battle. Because the intellectuals are interested in the competency and mastery of transgressing the rules of the social order in the name of progress, innovation, or social change; and because the anti-intellectuals are interested in the competency of obeying these social rules and in the mastery of making others follow their lead, there is little chance for an amiable settlement of their differences. The present study sought to obtain some empirical support for Peckham's analysis, and thereby to attempt a partial explanation for the official government's reaction to the report.

METHOD

Subjects

A total of 1083 self-selected, volunteer subjects were obtained from 38 intact groups during the course of a field study conducted in the Detroit metropolitan area. The groups ranged in size from 10 to 200. The mean age was 40 years. Males constituted 58% of the sample; females 42%. The study concerned the contemporary community standards of visual erotica, and was sponsored by the Commission on Obscenity and Pornography.[7]

Procedure

All subjects received and completed a questionnaire containing items relating to demographic characteristics, attitudes toward sexual behavior, and attitudes toward sexual materials. Following the questionnaire, the subjects rated 60 slides, which contained a number of different sexual themes. The themes ranged from fully clothed male and female models to acts of coitus and oral-genital behavior. Each slide was rated as to offensiveness, sexual arousal value, entertainment value, and acceptance. The subjects were instructed to respond to the scales in accordance with their own definitions of the end points, and not with what they thought others might believe.

RESULTS AND DISCUSSION

Thirty attitude items were scored by a group of clinical psychologists to reflect either a liberal or a conservative orientation toward human sexuality. Fifteen items were then selected, without knowledge of their scoring, to reflect Peckham's[4] description of the "Intellectuals" and the "Anti-Intellectuals." An average of these 15 items was computed for each subject and an overall average was obtained for the entire sample. The sample mean was used as a basis for dichotomizing the sample into "sexual liberals" ($N = 542$) and "sexual conservatives" ($N = 541$), which correspond, respectively, to Peckham's "Intellectuals" and "Anti-Intellectuals."

Significant differences between the two groups were found for several demographic variables: sex, age, and religion. The liberals were more likely to be male, of a younger age, and of the Jewish religion than were the conservatives. On three scales of general attitudinal orientation, the liberals were found to score significantly toward the liberal end of a general liberal-conservative orientation question; they reported themselves to be significantly less religious; and they held more liberal sex attitudes, though the difference between the two groups was not significant on this single item.

The results showed that the liberals obtained and/or viewed erotic materials more frequently than did the conservatives, and that they reacted with concomitant states of sexual arousal, whereas the conservatives reacted with mixed arousal and disgust states. In addition to their disgust reactions, the conservatives said that they were against the use of sex scenes in the movies; against any increased availability of sexual materials; and against any abolition of pornography laws, even if such materials have been demonstrated to have no harmful effects. Supporting these attitudes, the conservatives believed that recent Supreme Court decisions in obscenity cases have seriously threatened moral standards; that sexual materials lead to a decline in morals; and that sexual materials lead people to commit rape. The conservatives do agree with the liberals, however, that sexual materials might be entertaining for some people and that satiation of interest might occur after exposure to such materials. In general then, the attitudes of the conservatives are very similar to those which Peckham[4] advanced for his anti-intellectuals, while the liberals have attitudes which are close to those claimed for the intellectuals.

The analysis of the picture-rating responses found that despite the high level of agreement between the two subject categories on three of the four scales (all but entertainment), there were significant differences between the groups in their mean ratings of the pictures on each of the four scales. The liberals found the pictures to be significantly less offensive, less sexually arousing, more entertaining, and more acceptable. The same pattern of significant differences was obtained when the stimuli were categorized into "obscene" or "nonobscene" groups; obscenity being based on a criterion of hand-genital, genital-genital, or oral-genital contact. Thus the picture-rating results may be seen as being in accord with Peckham's theoretical presentation, with the exception of sexual arousal value, which was not treated in his analysis. The sexual arousal results are, however, discrepant with some previously reported results,[5] though it should be noted that these previous studies used other dimensions on which to obtain their liberal-conservative split (e.g., political or religious conservatism).

The intercorrelation of the picture-rating scales produced additional differences between the two subject groupings. The conservatives obtained a significant relationship between the offensiveness and sexual arousal scales, whereas the liberals produced a nonsignificant value. This result indicates that the conservatives find the pictures which are more offensive, as rated, to be more sexually arousing. Or, in the absence of additional evidence that might indicate the direction of causality, the more arousing pictures are found to be the most offensive.

Perhaps the most interesting correlations obtained were those between the sexual arousal and entertainment scales. For this relationship, the conservative's significant correlation was nearly as large as the one obtained for the liberals; however, it was in the opposite direction. The magnitude of the difference between the two values suggests that there is a major difference in the orientations of the two groups toward the entertainment value of sexual arousal. The results of the scale inter-correlations, when considered together, indicate that the conservatives find the more offensive pictures to be more sexually arousing; yet as the arousal value of the pictures increases, they find the pictures to be declining in entertainment value. The liberals, while not finding the offensive pictures more or less arousing than the nonoffensive ones, find increased entertainment value in those pictures that are rated as having sexual arousal value. As previously mentioned, the direction of causality cannot be inferred from the correlations presented. However, in the light of previous discussions in this area,[1,6] it may be suggested that the results indicate the existence of an unspecified amount of psychological defensiveness on the part of the conservatives—a defensiveness that manifests itself in the form of inconsistencies between different cognitions (e.g., belief statements), and in the form of a discrepancy between their public and private orientations toward sexual materials.

If the conservatives hold to the normative position that sexual arousal not in the service of reproduction is sinful, or at least not socially desirable, and if they view this position as being legitimated by the codification of these beliefs into law, then they can resolve the discrepancy between the intrinsic enjoyment of sexual arousal states[8] and their need to regulate the occurrence of such states in the interest of society. They can accomplish this by devaluing the amount of entertainment which they say that they derive from such states. This would make for an adequate explanation of the findings except for the fact that Peckham[4] has noted that some conservatives obtain considerable amounts of enjoyment from viewing erotic materials in private. The reconciliation of their public and private behavior and/or attitudes would appear to require the use of additional explanatory mechanisms. On an individual level, one such mechanism might be the isolation or compartmentaliza-tion of various cognitions. On a social level, the individual might choose to join an organization which is dedicated to the elimination of erotic materials from the public marketplace. He would thereby be permitted to view large quantities of erotic materials and, at the same time, be praised for his efforts which are being directed toward "public better-ment." In such a manner the conservative could make his public ex-pression of alarm about such materials, and yet privately enjoy them; albeit in a seeming contradiction to the gestalt principle that the whole society is made up of a sum of the parts. Some support for this explana-tion may be derived from a national survey of adults in which people were asked about the effects of viewing erotic materials. Most of the respondents believed that some harmful effects could arise from such viewing activity; however, when asked if they themselves had ever experienced such effects, the response rate was almost zero. It is the ubiquitous "they" who suffer all the ill effects.

In an attempt to explain the basis for the picture-rating differences between the two groups of subjects, four demographic variables were correlated with the four rating scales. The variables of age, education, religiosity, and general liberal-conservative orientation were all correlated significantly with the ratings of offensiveness and acceptance. Religiosity is the only variable to correlate meaningfully with the ratings of sexual arousal and entertainment value. The four demographic variables account for more of the variance on the offensiveness and acceptance scales than they do on the other two. Part of the reason for this could be the fact that sexual arousal and entertainment are more ideographic; i.e., they are less influenced by social norms than are the concepts of offensiveness and acceptance.

The younger, better-educated raters found the pictures to be less offensive and more acceptable. It will be recalled that the liberal category contained subjects who were significantly younger, better educated, and less religious than the conservatives. The basis for these results probably lies in the psychosexual socialization history of the individual raters, with this history being influenced by the prevailing social climate of the time. Because of the differences in the mean ages between the two groups, it might be said that the conservatives were socialized under a somewhat different set of prevailing social conditions which were more favorable to the development of their restrictive attitude toward sexual materials. However the fact that some of the liberals were also raised during this "older order" must not be lost. Differences in familial climate might account for the development of their more tolerant attitudes. Research into the developmental issues surrounding this differentiation process is just beginning. It is the opinion of this writer that the final verification or rejection of Peckham's theoretical ideas regarding the reactions to visual erotica by members of our society will be made on the basis of information obtained from research in this area.

REFERENCES

1. Byrne, D., & Shefield, J. Responses to sexually arousing stimuli as a function of repressing and sensitizing defenses. *Journal of Abnormal Psychology*, 1965, **70**, 114–118.

2. Commission on Obscenity and Pornography. *The report of the Commission on Obscenity and Pornography*. Washington, D. C.: U. S. Government Printing Office, 1970.

3. Gagnon, J., & Simon, W. Pornography—Raging menace or paper tiger. *Transaction*, July/August 1967, 41–48.

4. Peckham, M. *Art and pornography: An experiment in explanation.* New York: Basic Books, 1969.
5. Schmidt, G., & Sigusch, V. Psychosexual stimulation by films and slides. *Journal of Sex Research,* 1970, 6, 268–283.
6. Stuart, I., & Eliasberg, W. Personality structures which reject the human form in art. *Journal of Social Psychology,* 1966, 22, 395–403.
7. Wallace, D., Wehmer, G., & Podany, E. Contemporary community standards of visual erotica. *Technical report of the Commission on Obscenity and Pornography.* Vol. 7. Washington, D. C.: U. S. Government Printing Office, 1970.
8. Whalen, R. Sexual motivation. *Psychological Review,* 1966, 73, 151–163.

Nineteen Eighty-Four

The contrasting attitudes about sex and about society which have been discussed in this chapter are not just abstractions or points of theoretical interest. They also are expressed in overt behavioral acts. In the sexual realm, there are mate swappers, partners in open marriages, participants in nude encounter groups, individuals happily satisfying homosexual and bisexual desires, and lovingly monogamous couples, married and unmarried, enjoying totally sensuous heterosexual relationships. There are also vice squad officers busily harassing prostitutes and arresting homosexual "offenders," government prosecutors bringing charges against those involved in creating and distributing erotica, parents burning books in schoolyards, and even occasional judges sentencing individuals to prison for engaging in acts of oral sex. In the political realm, we all are aware of the difference between societies in which advocates of freedom are in control and those in which advocates of totalitarianism are in control. Thus, there exists a vital issue: Which of these sexual and political extremes represents the wave of the future for our society?

Science fiction serves many purposes, but one of its most noble functions is to take some aspects of our current world and project them into the future. This extrapolation allows us to see the logical consequences of continuing indefinitely along the particular pathway that we are presently traveling. The final two selections of this book consist of two such projections—the first a pessimistic and the second an optimistic prediction as to our sexual future. The first is by a novelist and political writer, the late George Orwell. In *Nineteen Eighty-Four* he describes a society in which the doomed hero, Winston, lives in one of the three authoritarian superstates into which the warring world has been divided. Here, he depicts what sex is like in 1984.

Nineteen Eighty-Four

George Orwell

The poorer quarters swarmed with women who were ready to sell themselves. Some could even be purchased for a bottle of gin, which the proles were not supposed to drink. Tacitly the Party was even inclined to encourage prostitution, as an outlet for instincts which could not be altogether suppressed. Mere debauchery did not matter very much, so long as it was furtive and joyless, and only involved the women of a submerged and despised class. The unforgivable crime was promiscuity between Party members. But—though this was one of the crimes that

Reprinted in an edited version from: Orwell, G. *Nineteen eighty-four.* New York: Harcourt Brace Jovanovich, 1949. Pp. 68–69.

the accused in the great purges invariably confessed to—it was difficult to imagine any such thing actually happening.

The aim of the Party was not merely to prevent men and women from forming loyalties which it might not be able to control. Its real, undeclared purpose was to remove all pleasure from the sexual act. Not love so much as eroticism was the enemy, inside marriage as well as outside it. All marriages between Party members had to be approved by a committee appointed for the purpose, and—though the principle was never clearly stated—permission was always refused if the couple concerned gave the impression of being physically attracted to one another. The only recognized purpose of marriage was to beget children for the service of the Party. Sexual intercourse was to be looked on as a slightly disgusting minor operation, like having an enema. This again was never put into plain words, but in an indirect way it was rubbed into every Party member from childhood onwards. There were even organizations such as the Junior Anti-Sex League which advocated complete celibacy for both sexes. All children were to be begotten by artificial insemination (*artsem*, it was called in Newspeak) and brought up in public institutions. This, Winston was aware, was not meant altogether seriously, but somehow it fitted in with the general ideology of the Party. The Party was trying to kill the sex instinct, or, if it could not be killed, then to distort it and dirty it. He did not know why this was so, but it seemed natural that it should be so. And so far as the women were concerned, the Party's efforts were largely successful.

Recreation—Not Procreation

The antisexual world of 1984 is one projection of where we are heading. On a particularly bad day, we can gloomily agree that Orwell may have been right about our political and sexual future. Happier predictions can be made, of course, and journalist Helen Colton paints just such a pleasant future world in the following article.

There is one remaining question: What will determine humankind's erotic future? A major consideration would seem to be how well we solve such interrelated problems as overpopulation, the energy shortage, the underproduction and maldistribution of food, and nationalistic enmities. In a crowded world with increasingly aggressive competition for dwindling resources, relaxed sexuality will probably be the first of many amenities of life to be lost. In a peaceful, stable, resourceful, and environmentally responsible world, people may have the time and the inclination to discover how to create a contented society that, among other things, is free of sexual conflicts and anxieties.

Perhaps the major uncertainty is whether any of us can do anything to help influence how our current problems are resolved and how our society evolves. Can individuals have an effect? What can you do?

Recreation—Not Procreation

Helen Colton

Where will our philosophy of sex for recreation and not procreation, our new ethic of existence which cares for quality not quantity of people, lead us? What will all this mean to humankind in the near future and, beyond that, to our descendants generations from now? Let us see what an historian of the future, say, 10 generations or about 300 years from today, might write about us. Or perhaps the report would be one written by a bright schoolchild as a history project, a boy or girl who was eugenically bred to be a creative, disease-free, nonviolent, cooperative humanist. What might our historian or our brilliant student write about the times and the traumas through which we are now passing? Let's take a look at ourselves in historical perspective and find out what history's verdict on our era might be. The report follows.

About halfway through the twentieth century on the planet Earth, the most revolutionary idea ever brought forth in humankind's existence exploded like an ideological atom bomb. This idea said that the sex act

Reprinted in an edited version from: Colton, H. Recreation—not procreation. *Forum*, 1975, **4** (11), 10–14.

for purposes of procreation was now about to end. Henceforth, sex would be acceptable mostly for pleasure.

This reversed everything humanity had ever been taught. Many of the "eternal verities"—the sacredness of motherhood, the desirability of large families, the acceptability of sex only in marriage—went sliding down the chute of time.

What sparked the ideological change was man's growing realization, at that point in time, that the planet whose interior decorator he had been was nothing but an overcrowded, dirty slum tenement.

I say "man" advisedly; woman had not up until then ever had any decision-making authority of great consequence.

Until that time, the theme of human sexual behavior had always been to be fruitful and to multiply, to fill up the Earth's empty spaces with more people. Societies needed more people to produce more population to produce more gross national product that would support a state's aggrandizement and expansion.

The sex act that resulted in pregnancy was lauded as pure; motherhood was woman's divine calling.

Because increased population was in the interest of the state, the state controlled people's sexual behavior through laws, social custom, folklore, mythology, and religious injunction.

Any sex act or human relationship or form of release from sexual tension—oral-genital sex, masturbation, male with male, female with female—which subverted the state's goal by denying the possibility of procreation, was declared to be illegal, immoral, and sinful.

Sex was approved only when it carried the possibility of socially sanctioned pregnancy.

A citizen's body belonged not to him but to his government. This was especially true in the social and legal position of the female. Woman was the chattel of the state and her husband. She had no rights whatever as to whether or not she wanted to bear and rear children.

For many centuries, woman wore the shackles of chauvinism around her body as she wore the symbol of her slavery—the wedding ring—around her finger. The ring had, in fact, derived from the custom of a master identifying his slaves through rings in their noses.

The laws of the world mostly approved of sex only when it encompassed these factors: man and woman face to face, the man above, with no contraception to interfere with nature's process. These were the factors most conducive to procreation.

Even a change in physical position—the woman above—was often illegal because that meant that the life-creating sperm could too easily flow back down out of the vaginal canal and thus would find more difficult its ordained task of fertilizing a female egg.

As the drawings on the ancient walls of Pompeii showed, men and women of all times ignored this law. The human need for variety of sources of pleasure has frequently taken precedence over the human wish for law and order.

In a perverse kind of human arithmetic practiced by that early man, the whole of a woman's body counted for much less than did the quarter-pound of skin, tissue, fiber and muscle dangling between a male's legs a couple of inches outside his torso.

That same half-century saw the ending of the sexual double standard and the introduction of equalism as a human standard. The words "male" and "female" were removed from statutes, legal forms, and job advertisements, to be replaced by the word "person" or "human."

The abbreviation Mrs., denoting a married woman, was declared discriminatory against women who chose not to marry and was replaced by the title of Ms., meaning Miss or Mrs.

The designation Mr. had never denoted marital status; now neither did Ms.

What many people had long suspected was confirmed at last. The former lack of creative output in music, art, poetry, literature, philosophy, and scholarship by the female, which man had long attributed to her intellectual inferiority, was due only to the fact that the female, busy with the demands of baby making and child rearing, had never before had time to devote to creative pursuits.

Freed at last from the primary use that had been made of her person as procreative apparatus, the female now began to be lauded for the first time more for her mentality than her mammaries.

In a complete reversal of all previous human experience, individuals who chose never to bear children, once looked upon as pariahs and social outcasts, now were hailed as ideal citizens.

Inspired by a college valedictorian who announced to the world in ringing tones that she chose not to bring children into the sick society, many now decided to forgo parenthood entirely.

Instead of nurturing their own biological offspring, they chose to nurture the many unwanted children born out of wedlock who might otherwise languish without loving.

As evolution brought our ancestors closer to the twenty-first century and the new freedom of sex for pleasure began to be incorporated into their behavior, they became the early ancestors of the Sensory Human we all are in this century.

Cadres of men and women became skin nutritionists in sensory groups, sometimes called touchy-feely groups, teaching people how to feed their skin hunger by stroking each other lovingly. People so pleasantly stroked found it hard to become angry and to make war on each other.

As industrial parks, office-residential edifices, and educational institutions like colleges were constructed, the law required them to include sandboxes, swings, seesaws, jungle gyms, and mud pits on their grounds for use by grown-ups, so that even adults, no matter what their ages, could swing high in the air, build sand castles, pat wet mud, and otherwise enjoy—guilt free—their physical beings and continue throughout life the sensual delights of their childhood.

These experiences in playpens for grown-ups and in feeding skin hunger so satisfied early Sensory Humans that they no longer needed chemicals, known as drugs, to enjoy the sensory experience they had long been deprived of by the Puritanism which said you were being sexually seductive if you touched other people in warmth and love and affection.

It was during this same era of which I write that humankind first learned to separate sensual need—for touching and stroking—from sexual need—for orgasm.

Folk dancing became the global pastime, providing one more way in which people could acceptably move and touch a wide variety of fellow humans in warmth and affection.

This was, of course, the origin of our annual Folk Dance Olympics, in which our winners come not from those who best each other but from those whose minicomputers, affixed to their bodies, reveal that they have touched in dancing the greatest numbers of fellow humans from the greatest numbers of countries throughout the globe.

It is with some amusement that we delve into historic archives and learn about the language customs of that era. Just how primitive and uncivilized that man of long ago was in his humanistic orientation can be judged by the language he chose to forbid.

Both law and custom said that words associated with the body processes of digestion, elimination, and procreation, popularly known as four-letter words, could not pass the lips of the refined and dignified.

When you stop and think about it, how illogical our ancestor was! Many words associated with the act of love he made ignominious while words associated with the act of hate he ennobled.

He would get whole armies to march and slay by exhorting the four-letter word "flag."

We wonder what he would think of our forbidden words of today —kill, maim, hurt, bomb, jail, war—which are becoming extinct in the human lexicon through disuse.

It was during the 1970s that a little-known philosopher, Irving Laucks, a scholar at the Center for the Study of Democratic Institutions in Santa Barbara, California, the Mount Olympus of twentieth-century thinkers, accurately forecast the future when he maintained that humankind was entering its third major stage of evolutionary development, which philosopher Laucks described as:

First evolutionary stage: Primeval Man

Second evolutionary stage: Acquiring Man

Third evolutionary stage: Cooperative Man

Dr. Jonas Salk, physician-inventor of a vaccine that had forever wiped out that dreaded ancient scourge, poliomyelitis, said much the same thing on November 3, 1970: "Mankind is in the midst of a transition from an epoch of competition to an epoch of cooperation. This new era is about three generations away."

As history confirms, these gentlemen were right. Man was indeed passing through in the stormy latter third of the twentieth century one more calibration on his evolutionary scale, en route to our present era.

The forward sweep of history selected that half century, from 1950 to 2000, as the time in which humankind would be forever freed from its sexual ignorance and prurience.

Many people suffered much as they fought for changes in laws and in human rights. Women marched to the sound of the drummer of freedom, demanding their rights to their own bodies.

Persons both male and female went to jail, fighting for the right of all to free access to contraceptives. Women throughout the world in order to force changes in repressive laws, courageously laid bare their illegal actions in having had abortions.

Many youth were freed from their age ghettos and allowed to become the masters of their own destiny, to seek a variety of medical help without having to ask parental approval.

A pioneer like Margaret Sanger, who began planned parenthood clinics in the early part of the twentieth century, was spat upon and physically beaten and jailed because she dared to gather women about her secretly in darkened living rooms to whisper the illegal tidings about how their worn-out bodies might achieve the spacing of their children.

The travail of such noble forebears did honor to all those who came after them. Ever since their time, humankind has maintained its right to do with its own body what it will. The sexual-civil-liberties code which began at that time, stating that no form of sexual expression may be legally proscribed unless it is done with force or violence, without the consent of both parties, to the mentally retarded, or to minors incapable of knowing the consequences of their actions, is now so ingrained a part of human existence that it is hard to imagine a time when there was no such sexual-right precept and human beings were made to feel shameful and fearful about the exercise of their sex drive.

It is because of such courageous forebears that we now lead the good life available to us on the planet Earth with space, air, water, and food for all. It is as a result of their efforts that we succeeded in amending the United States Constitution to insist that liberty and justice were not enough of an inalienable birthright; henceforth each person's birthright must also include space, air, water, and food.

The world has never known such flowering of human personality. The standard by which a person's worth is judged is not, as it once was in that long-ago time, how many babies he could turn out but how cooperative he can be in the human community.

We thank them for the freedoms they carved out for us.

An Epilogue:
Sexual Behavior and Sexual Values: Encouraging Tolerance for a Pluralistic Society

In the past several hundred pages, you have been exposed to dozens of articles that presented a wide variety of observations, research findings, opinions, and conclusions about many aspects of sexuality. You might be wondering whether all of this amounts to simply a hodgepodge of random material or whether these diverse elements can possibly be brought together into some kind of meaningful pattern. The answer is that the study of human sexuality adds up to more than unrelated bits and pieces, but that no one has yet combined this knowledge into a single theoretical framework on which there is general agreement. In the next few pages, we will present a brief version of one such way to organize and hence to think about human sexual functioning. There is no presumption that this represents a complete and polished theory of sexuality. Rather, it is a preliminary step and one which may prove helpful in our attempts to understand this rather complex aspect of human behavior.

Beyond this or any other conceptual schema lie other questions that are not answerable by scientific methods but which each of us must necessarily face in our own lives. As we have seen over and over again throughout this book, sexual behavior is intricately associated with emotions, values, moral codes, and legalities. Though people regularly must deal with issues such as masturbation, premarital intercourse, contraception, oral sex, extramarital sex, homosexuality, abortion, mate swapping, anal sex, rape, secret fantasies, pornography, and more besides, there obviously can be no scientific reply to questions of right and wrong, good and bad, moral and immoral. Rather than ignore these issues as though they were irrelevant, however, we would like to deal with them in two ways. First, it seems important that each of us be able to verbalize precisely what our sexual values are. We ourselves will attempt to make such a personal statement by summarizing a few of the points that have been made explicitly and implicitly in various parts of this book. Second, it must be recognized that people differ with respect to such values, and hence it is essential that we each find a way to accept the sexuality of others so long as their behavior does not infringe on anyone's individual rights.

THE SEXUAL BEHAVIOR SEQUENCE

To present a psychological theory of human sexuality, it would be best to start with a depiction of the proposed model as shown in Figure E-1. This tentative way of organizing what is known about human sexual

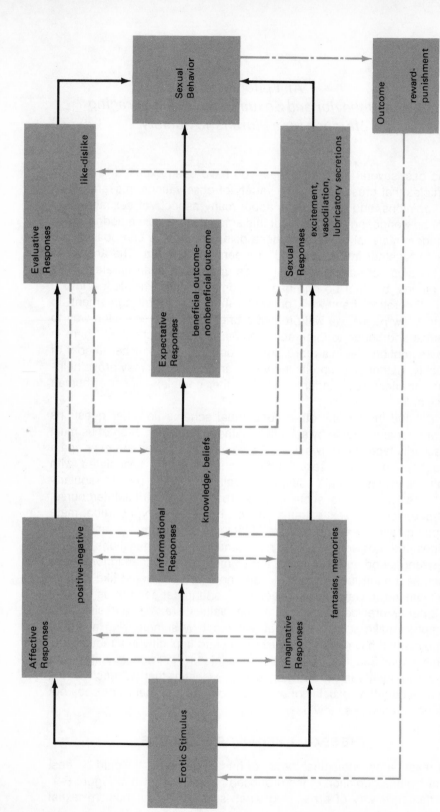

Figure E-1. The sexual behavior sequence. This model postulates sexual behavior as a function of three interactive response systems (affective-evaluative, informational-expectative, and imagery-excitement) which are evoked by an erotic stimulus. Rewarding and punishing behavioral outcomes feed back into the system, altering subsequent responses to erotic stimuli.

functioning grew from repeated attempts to make overall sense out of research findings such as those you have read in the preceding pages. Each enclosed box in the figure represents a basic theoretical construct and each solid arrow represents a proposed cause-and-effect relationship between variables. The dotted arrows represent secondary relationships and also indicate the way in which the various aspects of the sexual system are interdependent. The broken line represents the way in which rewards and punishments lead to alterations in the system. Though the figure does not include this aspect of the model, it should be pointed out that neutral stimuli can be associated with an erotic stimulus and, through conditioning, acquire the power to arouse positive and negative emotions[5] and to create sexual arousal.[11] As we saw in Chapter 3, sexuality can rather easily be taught to be as unashamed and free as in Arnhem Land or as repressed and circumscribed as in the Irish island of Inis Beag.

To describe how this theoretical framework may be used, we can trace one hypothetical sequence. As an arbitrary starting point, we will begin with the encounter between a sexually mature male or female and a visual erotic stimulus. An erotic stimulus is one which either is inherently arousing (for example, a gentle stroking of the genitals) or is arousing because of learned associations (for example, a motel bed). For the purposes of our example, let us say that a person opens a book and sees a color photograph depicting a heterosexual couple engaging in fellatio. As is indicated in the figure, such a stimulus is conceptualized as eliciting three partially independent response systems, each of which exerts an influence on subsequent sexual behavior.

The Affective-Evaluative System

The top row consists of the affective-evaluative system. As we saw in Chapter 5, erotic stimuli are clearly found to evoke very strong positive and/or negative feelings in both males and females. In part, these emotional responses are widely shared in a given cultural group; for example, heterosexual adults in the United States are found to respond positively to stimuli depicting kissing and petting and negatively to stimuli depicting sadism and homosexual anal intercourse.[3] In addition, there are powerful individual differences in responding to many erotic stimuli, probably based upon very different childhood learning experiences. Such concepts as sex guilt and erotophobia-erotophilia refer to ways of identifying how particular individuals have learned to respond emotionally to erotic stimulation.

In our example, fellatio would be expected to elicit a negative emotional response in an individual high in sex guilt and erotophobia and a positive emotional response in one low in sex guilt and high in erotophilia. Such emotional responses are conceptualized as determining evaluative responses.[2] That is, those who respond in an emotionally negative way to a stimulus will subsequently indicate a dislike for it; those who respond with positive emotions will say that they like it. For example, an individual who had negative feelings when looking at a fellatio photograph would be expected to dislike the picture, to describe it as pornographic, and to want to avoid further contact with it.

The final step in this affective-evaluative system is a behavioral act. The question is whether the person who views such a stimulus and responds to it emotionally will be more or less likely to make some overt sexual response afterward. Though only a limited amount of research has dealt with this specific question, it has been found that people who respond to erotica with positive affect are more likely to look at and sit near a member of the opposite sex than are individuals who respond with negative affect.[7] Also, those high in sex guilt tend to look at non-sexual rather than sexual magazines while sitting idly in a waiting room.[12] Logically, we would expect that an individual who felt positively when exposed to a fellatio photograph and who therefore liked it would be more likely to engage in a subsequent sexual act (for example, masturbation, intercourse, or especially fellatio) than would one who responded with negative affect. Whenever we speak of behavior being more likely to occur, this does not imply that those who are exposed to an erotic stimulus automatically dash off to experience a sexual act. We simply mean that there is an increased probability of such behavior occurring, all other things being equal, under the appropriate circumstances.

The Informational-Expectative System

The middle row of the figure outlines the informational-expectative response system. In the realm of sexual behavior, little research has been conducted to determine the way in which knowledge, beliefs, and expectancies influence behavior. In our example, the male or female who sees a photograph of fellatio would necessarily have to process that stimulus in relation to all that he or she knows or believes about what is depicted. Thus, the person will label the goings-on as "fellatio" (or some more common term), and that act will be classified on the basis of previous learning into such categories as normal-abnormal, moral-immoral, dirty-clean, healthful-unhealthful, safe-unsafe, and entertaining-dull.

Presumably, those whose belief system leads them to expect beneficial or pleasant consequences from engaging in a specific behavior will be more likely to engage in that behavior than those who expect harmful or unpleasant outcomes. For example, if someone believes that fellatio is a perversion that leads an individual to be rejected by all decent citizens of the community as abnormal, he or she would be unlikely to imitate what is seen in the photograph. However, if the person believes fellatio to be normal and to result in sexual pleasure, he or she should behave in a very different way.

In the preceding chapters, we have noted repeatedly that beliefs can have a strong effect on sexual behavior as with traditional notions about male-female differences (Chapter 6), the interpretation of strong emotions as sexual attraction and love (Chapter 7), the ideas an individual has about contraception and about the fulfillment of sexual roles (Chapter 9), concepts about "deviant" sexual patterns and practices (Chapter 10), convictions about the effects of pornography on behavior (Chapter 12), and the fact that there is an integral relationship between sexual and political beliefs (Chapter 13). In addition, a solidly held belief (such as the erroneous folklore proclaiming that sexual functioning naturally stops at age 40 or 50 or 60 or whenever) can directly dampen imaginative responses and thus prevent physiological arousal.

Note, too, that in the figure evaluative responses are shown to influence informational responses. That is, one's emotionally determined likes and dislikes exert an effect on what one learns, believes, and remembers. Thus, if the positive or negative affective responses are powerful enough, they can strongly influence the informational system. However, if the information one holds is powerful enough, it can influence emotional responses. If one were positive that fellatio led to bodily weakness and insanity in the male and to gastric distress and acne in the female, such beliefs could easily cause a negative emotional response to the stimulus.

The Imagery-Excitement System

In the bottom row of the figure is depicted the imagery-excitement response system. Actually, some erotic stimuli probably bypass the imaginative responses entirely and lead directly to the kinds of physiological activity described in Chapter 2. For example, when either the penis or the clitoris is stimulated manually or orally, the resultant excitement need not involve the individual's fantasies.

As we have seen in Chapter 4, however, human sexual arousal is characteristically associated with erotic thoughts. It may even be that a great many erotic stimuli fail to elicit physiological arousal *unless* imaginative activity takes place. It has been found that individuals can deliberately generate fantasies in order to excite themselves[1, 8] and that they can also deliberately interfere with the activation of fantasies in order to prevent themselves from becoming excited.[10] Part of imaginative activity seems to involve the evocation of memories of one's own past sexual acts, and arousal tends to be greatest in response to reminders of what the individual has personally experienced.[6] Thus, the person who sees a fellatio photograph will tend to think about personally engaging in that act and (if such experiences are included in the individual's past) will remember his or her own encounters with fellation. All such imaginative acts facilitate sexual arousal as indicated by genital responsiveness in each sex.

The behavioral effects of erotic fantasies and of sexual arousal are somewhat varied. As we saw in Chapter 10, sexual fantasies seem to play an important role in some types of abnormal sexual behavior, and we learned in Chapter 11 that imaginative activity can be crucial in alleviating such problems as orgasmic dysfunction in females and impotence in males. It was pointed out in Chapter 4 that sexual fantasies ordinarily accompany masturbation and intercourse and that they seem to ensure excitement, to enhance sexual pleasure, and to facilitate an orgasmic response. There is evidence, as discussed in Chapter 12, that the presentation of erotic fantasies in the form of pornography can not only elicit personal imagery and physiological arousal, but can also increase the likelihood of subsequent sexual activity. It has been established that the more aroused an individual feels in response to pictorial erotica, the greater the probability of engaging in subsequent sexual intercourse.[4]

Rewards and Punishments for Sexual Behavior

The three response systems are each activated by erotic stimuli, they affect one another, and they act in some joint fashion to determine what an individual will actually do sexually. If an erotic stimulus such as a fellatio photograph elicited positive emotions and evaluations, if it activated favorable information that led to the expectation of a beneficial outcome, and if it elicited rich erotic fantasies that resulted in a state of physiological arousal, the prediction would be that the individual would have an increased tendency to engage in an overt sexual act. In contrast, if such a stimulus elicited negative affect and evaluations, if it activated unfavorable information that led to the expectation of a harmful outcome, and if erotic fantasies and hence arousal were blocked, the prediction would be that no overt sexual act would be likely to follow. A great deal of research is needed to determine the precise way in which these three systems operate when there are inconsistencies among them. For example, what happens when an individual feels anxious about the fellatio photograph, believes that oral sex is only practiced by perverts, and also feels highly aroused by thoughts of engaging in such an act? We do not yet know how to predict sexual responsiveness under these and other conditions in which the three systems propel the individual in incompatible directions.

When anyone *does* engage in a sexual act, the outcome is likely to be reward or punishment, pleasure or pain, and the nature of that outcome feeds back into the system to affect future responses to erotic stimuli. The reinforcing power of an orgasm is, of course, obvious. Thus, if exposure to the fellatio photograph were followed by a sexual act that was entirely pleasurable, the person's next encounter with a similar stimulus should evoke positive affect and evaluations; should cause a strengthened belief that fellatio is a safe, normal, moral exercise that leads to a beneficial outcome; and should result in more vivid and detailed images of such sexually exciting experiences. Sexual activity can also involve a whole series of negative consequences ranging from guilt and fear (Chapter 5), to orgasmic failures and performance malfunctioning (Chapter 11), to venereal diseases and unwanted pregnancy (Chapters 9 and 11), and even to arrest and imprisonment (Chapter 10). Any such unpleasant outcomes should bring about negative changes in affect, information, and fantasy.

It should be pointed out that the sexual response sequence can be conceptualized chronologically; therefore, the succession of all such past sequences constitutes an individual's sexual socialization history up to the present time. Differences among individuals, across cultures, and between the sexes would seem to rest primarily on differential exposure to erotic stimuli and on differential outcomes following each sexual response sequence. You might want to think about the way in which permissive versus restrictive atmospheres in the home or in the total culture could provide very different opportunities for encountering erotic stimuli (including self-stimulation, hearing about sexual matters, reading about sexual acts, and viewing depictions of sexual interactions) and very different reactions to any overt acts in which the child engages (including touching the genitals, saying sexual words, expressing an interest in the genital area and its functions, playing "doctor" with a friend, or engaging in immature sexual movements in the manner of Harlow's monkeys). Reactions can range from outrage, shock, and anxiety to toleration, permissiveness, and acceptance to active encouragement, condonement, and instruction. What is the best way to respond to childhood sexuality? What is the ideal way to deal with an offspring's earliest sexual response sequences or even to arrange for their occurrence? We do not know, and neither does anyone else, but we will attempt to specify some of the possible goals that one might consider in his or her own approach to such issues.

SPECIFYING ONE'S SEXUAL VALUES AND TOLERATING THE VALUES OF OTHERS

With all aspects of one's behavior, it seems ideal to be able to specify what it is that one values, desires, and prefers. Such self-perception may rest within the context of a religious doctrine, a theory of personality, a philosophy of life, or a logical framework that makes sense for a particular individual.

At the risk of sounding banal to some and of offending others, we will suggest a few personal values as they might be reflected in the sexual behavior sequence. Such values are not meant as a prescription for others or as a newly discovered panacea for humankind. Rather, they are simply an expression of a few strongly held preferences. Perhaps the overriding value is that sexual stimulation and sexual expression are profoundly good and that joyous sexuality should be a continuing source of entertainment and satisfaction—an inalienable human right. Specifically, this means that people should be able to expose themselves to whatever erotic stimuli they find entertaining whenever they wish to do so. When such stimulation occurs, individuals should be able to feel positive emotions in which there are feelings of fun, curiosity, elation, and jubilant excitement rather than feelings of anxiety, shame, guilt, fear, disgust, despair, and anger. Thus, stimulation is best if it results in positive emotions and positive evaluations.

In the informational realm, our preference would be for truth and accuracy. The more knowledge that one has, the more freedom provided by that knowledge. We have seen in the articles just presented many instances in which myths and erroneous beliefs have interfered with human sexuality. We might also add that no one knows everything about human sexuality and that new information is being provided by scientific activity each year. We would hope that each person who reads this volume will realize that he or she can spend a lifetime learning more about sex and also unlearning some of yesterday's "truths." If nothing else, everyone who engages in sexual acts should know of the dangers of venereal diseases and how to take steps to prevent or cure them; it is of equal importance that everyone know the details of conception and of contraception.

With respect to imagination and fantasy, we believe that total freedom should prevail. That is, even though overt behavior must be limited by various restrictions, there is no reason to limit what goes on within one's own head. There can be no inherent evil in thinking about *anything* and no one need feel frightened or guilty about thoughts that include any sexual act, with any partner or partners, in any possible scenario. Fantasies should be free, fun, and exciting. They should lead to all of the miraculous bodily responses that prepare males and females for sexual activity. No one should be upset because blood congests in the genitals, breathing becomes more rapid, and lubricatory fluids begin to flow—it should not seem in the least shameful or unnatural for one's body to reach a state of sexual readiness.

Sexual behavior itself is the next step, and this should optimally be an integral part of one's life and a lasting means of giving and receiving pleasure. It is here, of course, that each person's freedom must be partly curtailed in order to ensure the comfort and well-being of all. Perhaps it would be useful to return to our definition of abnormal sexuality, and this may just as well also be considered the definition of bad sexuality and undesirable sexuality. We feel that society should prohibit *any sex-related behavior which causes psychological distress or unwanted physical pain for the individual engaging in the act and/or for an unwitting or unwilling participant.* All other sex is good, clean, moral, healthful, and desirable. The outcome of all sexual activity should be pleasure, usually including the intense pleasure of an orgasm (or orgasms) for all participants and the lingering pleasure of sexual satisfaction and contentment.

You might note that "good sex" is not defined as necessarily interpersonal (masturbation can also be very satisfying) nor as heterosexual (homosexual acts between consenting adults can undoubtedly be as positive as comparable heterosexual acts). Also, good interpersonal sex is not limited to partners who love one another. Sex can be casual, impersonal, and even professional and still be good. Sex that is part of an intense, loving relationship is almost always to be preferred, but there is no reason to pretend that all other sex is somehow a waste of time. A gourmet dinner with a loved one is infinitely better than a quick snack with strangers at a fast food franchise, but either one can be quite satisfying when you are hungry.

To return briefly to the problem of transmitting these (or other, quite different) values to another generation, the specifics for the optimal way to do so are not known. In the case of the values just enumerated, we would like to think that one's offspring should feel positively about sex, should be well informed, and should feel free to fantasize and to enjoy excitement and fulfillment. Nevertheless, the difficulties in communicating about such emotionally laden topics across generations are formidable. At what point and in what context children should be exposed to erotic stimuli or to sexual information and in what ways they should be allowed (or encouraged) to enjoy this bodily function are matters for each parent to decide. This may seem to be a cop-out, but it is a realistic one because no one knows just what consequences follow from particular types of childhood sexual experiences.

One problem in attempting to ascertain the effects of different methods of child rearing with respect to sexuality is that few people feel comfortable in even approaching such a topic. The way in which sexual hang-ups still operate in most of us can best be seen by contrasting our treatment of sex and our treatment of eating. Can you imagine agonizing over how to tell children about food, good nutrition, and table manners? Can you envision debates about the right age for a child to learn the correct words for chewing, for being exposed to a photograph of a steak, or for being encouraged to enjoy ice cream? We have yet to see parents march on the schools to protest the teaching of cooking skills in home economics, and no one seems concerned about the explicit words and pictures blatantly presented in cookbooks. Until or unless we can learn to feel as relaxed about sex as about food, it seems that psychological sexual liberation is not yet with us.

Finally, a word must be said about tolerance. There is a very real human tendency in all aspects of our lives to want others to believe as we believe, to do as we do, to value as we value. In the sexual realm, this tendency is all too apparent. Those who hate hard-core pornography want to prevent others from having access to it. Those who enjoy mate swapping want to spread the good word and enlist additional converts. Those who would not want to expose their bodies even in the marital bedroom want to close down nudist beaches where others are basking nakedly and unashamedly in the sunshine. Those who teach their children to be sexually free want to encourage their neighbors to teach their children the same thing.

Perhaps it is time to stress the most overriding value of all. We do not know where civilization is going sexually, but a safe bet is that it is probably going in a multitude of directions in a multitude of places. A century from now, there will probably still be advocates and practitioners of celibacy and orgiastic parties, sex in the missionary position and anal intercourse, heterosexual monogamy and homosexual promiscuity, and anything else you care to name. All of us in all our diversity would be happier, wiser, and nicer human beings if we could each learn to do our own thing sexually and to let others do their own thing.

REFERENCES

1. Barclay, A. M. Sexual fantasies in men and women. *Medical Aspects of Human Sexuality*, 1973, **7**, 205–216.

2. Byrne, D. *The attraction paradigm.* New York: Academic Press, 1971.

3. Byrne, D., & Lamberth, J. The effect of erotic stimuli on sex arousal, evaluative responses, and subsequent behavior. *Technical report of the Commission on Obscenity and Pornography.* Vol. 8. Washington, D. C.: U. S. Government Printing Office, 1971.

4. Cattell, R. B., Kawash, G. F., & De Young, G. E. Validation of objective measures of ergic tension: Response of the sex erg to visual stimulation. *Journal of Experimental Research in Personality*, 1972, **6**, 76–83.

5. Dean, S. J., Martin, R. B., & Streiner, D. L. The use of sexually arousing slides as unconditioned stimuli for the GSR in a discrimination paradigm. *Psychonomic Science*, 1968, **13**, 99–100.

6. Griffitt, W. Sexual experience and sexual responsiveness: Sex differences. *Archives of Sexual Behavior*, 1975, **4**, 529–540.

7. Griffitt, W., May, J., & Veitch, R. Sexual stimulation and interpersonal behavior: Heterosexual evaluative responses, visual behavior, and physical proximity. *Journal of Personality and Social Psychology*, 1974, **30**, 367–377.

8. Hariton, E. B., & Singer, J. L. Women's fantasies during sexual intercourse: Normative and theoretical implications. *Journal of Consulting and Clinical Psychology*, 1974, **42**, 313–322.

9. Laws, D. R., & Rubin, H. B. Instructional control of an autonomic sexual response. *Journal of Applied Behavior Analysis*, 1969, **2**, 93–99.

10. Rachman, S. Sexual fetishism: An experimental analogue. *Psychological Record*, 1966, **16**, 293–296.

11. Schill, T., & Chapin, J. Sex guilt and males' preference for reading erotic magazines. *Journal of Consulting and Clinical Psychology*, 1972, **39**, 516.

Sexual Glossary

Abnormal Sexuality Any sex-related behavior that causes psychological distress or unwanted physical pain for the individual engaging in the act and/or for an unwitting or unwilling participant.

Abortion Premature expulsion of the embryo from the uterus, either spontaneously or through surgical intervention.

AC-DC A colloquial term for bisexuality.

Adultery Sexual intercourse between a married individual and a partner who is not his or her spouse.

Ambisexuality Another term for bisexuality or engaging in sexual relations with both males and females.

Analingus Oral stimulation of the partner's anus.

Anal Intercourse Intercourse in which the penis is inserted in the partner's anus.

Anal Stage In psychoanalytic theory, the developmental stage involving the anus and learning to control bowel functions.

Androgen A male sex hormone secreted by the testes in the male, by the adrenal glands in both sexes, and in small amounts by the ovaries in the female.

Androgynous Individual One who has adopted the personality characteristics of both the traditional masculine and feminine roles.

Aphrodisiac Anything that arouses sexual desire.

Around the World Among prostitutes, a sexual interaction in which the female licks all portions of the customer's body, culminating in fellatio.

Artificial Insemination The injection of semen into the vagina or uterus by means of a syringe.

Attraction The extent to which one individual likes or feels positively about another individual.

Aureola The circular, darkened area around the nipple.

Autosexuality Any masturbatory interests or practices.

Balling Colloquial term for engaging in intercourse.

Balls Colloquial term for testicles.

Bartholin Gland Two small glands in the labia minora that produce a lubricating fluid during sexual excitement.

Beaver Colloquial term for the external genitalia of the female.

Bestiality Sexual interaction between a human being and a member of another animal species.

Bidet A low, basinlike bathroom fixture used to cleanse the genitals.

Birth Control Pill An oral contraceptive.

Bisexuality Engaging in sexual acts with members of both the opposite sex and of one's own sex.

Blow Job Colloquial term for fellatio.

Blue Balls Colloquial term for testicular pain caused by prolonged sexual stimulation that does not culminate in ejaculation.

Bondage and Discipline (B & D) Sexual practices in which the participants act out master and slave roles, with the slave eventually being bound and subjected to prolonged sexual tantalization.

Boobs Colloquial term for breasts.

Bordello A house of prostitution.

Breasts The two milk-secreting organs on the female's chest.

Brothel A house of prostitution.

Bugger Colloquial term for anal intercourse.

Bull Dyke A lesbian who dresses and behaves in a tough, masculine manner.

Bush Colloquial term for the external genitalia of the female.

Call Girl A prostitute, usually relatively expensive, with whom appointments can be arranged by telephone.

Call House A house or apartment at which call girls wait for telephone messages from customers.

Castration The removal of the testes.

Catamite A boy kept for homosexual purposes.

Cat House Colloquial term for a house of prostitution.

Celibacy Abstention from all sexual relations.

Cervical Cap A contraceptive device that fits over the cervix.

Cervix The tip or neck of the uterus which extends partially into the vaginal cavity.

Chastity Virginity.

Chastity Belt A locked device placed on women in the Middle Ages to prevent their having sexual intercourse.

Cherry Colloquial term for the hymen.

Chicken A homosexual slang term for a young male partner.

Circumcision An operation in which the foreskin is removed from the penis.

Clap Colloquial term for gonorrhea.

Climacteric The period during which the individual loses the ability to reproduce, culminating in the menopause among females.

Climax An orgasm, the culmination of the sexual act.

Clitoral Orgasm The mistaken notion that only some female orgasms are centered in the clitoris rather than in the vagina and indicate an immature stage of sexual development.

Clitoris The female sexual organ that is located in the vulva just above the urethral opening. The clitoris is an anatomical structure that is homologous to the male penis and is the center of the female's sexual sensitivity.

Closed Swinging When couples engaged in mate swapping go off separately to engage in sexual intercourse in private two-person interactions.

Closet Homosexual An individual who keeps his or her homosexual inclinations a secret.

Cock Colloquial term for the penis.

Cock-Sucking Colloquial term for fellatio.

Coitus Sexual intercourse.

Coitus Interruptus A contraceptive practice in which the male withdraws from his partner's vagina prior to ejaculation.

Come Colloquial term for reaching an orgasm (verb) or for semen (noun).

Coming Out Refers to a public announcement of one's homosexual inclinations; from the phrase "coming out of the closet."

Computer Date A date in which couples are matched on the basis of their responses to questionnaires.

Conception When the sperm enters the egg and fertilizes it, thus constituting the beginning of a new organism.

Concubine A woman who lives with and sexually interacts with a man to whom she is not married.

Condom A contraceptive device involving a rubber covering worn over the penis during intercourse.

Conjugal Pertaining to marriage.

Contraception Any method or device that prevents fertilization of the egg by a sperm.

Coprophagia The eating of feces.

Coprophilia Showing an extreme interest in feces.

Copulate Have sexual intercourse.

Corn Hole Colloquial term for anus (noun) or act of anal intercourse (verb).

Corona The rim of the glans of the penis.

Corpus Luteum A gland that develops within the ovary following ovulation.

Courtesan A prostitute, especially one who associates only with wealthy males.

Cream Colloquial term for ejaculation.

Crime against Nature An eighteenth-century term for what were considered abnormal sexual acts. Though it is vague and has been interpreted legally in various ways, most often it has been interpreted as meaning anal intercourse.

Cruise The homosexual term for the process of seeking a casual sexual partner in bars, parks, rest rooms, etc.

Cuckold A man whose wife is unfaithful to him.

Cunnilingus Oral stimulation of the female genitals.

Cunt Colloquial term for vagina or, in a derogatory sense, for a female.

Daisy Chain In group sex, an interconnected series of couples engaged in oral sex. Thus, a male performs cunnilingus on a female who performs fellatio on another male who performs cunnilingus on another female, etc.

Deep Throat Fellatio in which the penis is entirely engulfed, partially entering the partner's throat. The term was popularized by the movie of that name starring the orally talented Linda Lovelace.

Detumescence When the penis loses its swelling following an erection.

Diaphragm A contraceptive device made of latex which fits over the cervix and is used along with spermicidal jelly or cream.

Dick Colloquial term for penis.

Dildo An artificial device, often in the shape of a penis, which can be inserted in the vagina for masturbatory purposes.

Doggy Style Colloquial term for sexual intercourse in the rear-entry position, with the female on her hands and knees.

Dong Colloquial term for penis.

Dork Colloquial term for penis.

Dorsal-Ventral Intercourse Any intercourse position in which the male faces the back of the female.

Double-Entendre A word which has a double meaning, especially when one of the meanings has a sexual connotation.

Double Standard The traditional sexist view that different standards should be applied to the sexual behavior of males and females—with greater toleration for the male's activity. It also refers to the view that there are two types of females (good and bad), to whom different standards of conduct may be applied.

Douche The application of a stream of water into the vagina in order to cleanse it, protect against venereal disease, or (not very effectively) as an attempt at contraception.

Drag The wearing of female clothing by a male who is said to be "in drag."

Dyke A female homosexual, especially one who is masculine in appearance, clothing, or behavior.

Dysmenorrhea A disorder involving painful menstruation.

Eating Out Colloquial term for cunnilingus.

Ejaculate To expel semen from the penis at the point of orgasm.

Electra Complex In personality theory, the condition in which the female feels sexually attracted to her father while rejecting her mother.

Endometrium The membrane lining the uterus.

English Culture Colloquial term for sexual practices involving spanking or whipping.

Erection The swelling of the penis during sexual excitement as it becomes engorged with blood.

Erogenous Sexually sensitive or arousing.

Erotic Sexually arousing.

Erotica Literary or artistic productions that are sexually arousing.

Erotophile An individual for whom sexual cues elicit primarily positive emotions, pleasure, and approach tendencies.

Erotophobe An individual for whom sexual cues elicit both pleasure *and* negative emotions, guilt, and avoidance tendencies.

Estrogen Female sex hormone produced by the ovaries and adrenal glands.

Eunuch A male who has been castrated.

Exhibitionism The act of obtaining sexual stimulation or gratification by means of being observed in the nude or while engaging in sexual acts.

Extramarital Intercourse Intercourse with someone other than one's spouse.

Faggot A somewhat derogatory term for a homosexual.

Fallopian Tubes The tubes extending from the ovaries to the uterus through which the ova are transported and within which fertilization occurs.

Family Jewels Colloquial term for testes.

Family Planning The deliberate limitation on the size of one's family or on the spacing between offspring by means of contraception.

Fecundity Great fertility, the ability to produce offspring in abundance.

Fellatio Oral stimulation of the penis.

Femoral Coitus Intercourse in which the penis is rubbed between the closed thighs of the sexual partner.

Fetishism A strong preference for some nongenital object as part of the sexual act. In an extreme form, such an object may be necessary for sexual functioning or it may actually substitute for a sexual partner.

Finger Fuck Colloquial term for manual manipulation of the female genitals to orgasm.

Fist Fucking Colloquially, the insertion of the entire hand into the partner's vagina or anus.

Flaccid Soft and limp, such as a penis that is not erect.

Flagellation Whipping or lashing that may be used as part of a sadomasochistic interaction.

Flashing Exposing one's genitals to strangers, as when males throw open a raincoat to reveal their nakedness underneath.

Foam Contraceptive foam containing spermicidal agents which is injected into the vagina prior to intercourse.

Follicle A small pouch near the surface of the ovary that contains the developing ovum.

Follicle Stimulating Hormone (FSH) A hormone produced by the anterior pituitary gland. FSH stimulates the development of follicles in the ovaries and sperm in the testes.

Foreplay Sexually stimulating activities such as kissing and caressing that are a prelude to intercourse.

Foreskin The membrane that normally covers the glans of the penis, which is retracted during sexual intercourse. The foreskin is removed from the penis of many males through circumcision for religious or medical reasons.

Form Fetishism When the shape or form of the fetish object is the most important feature. Examples are shoes and garter belts.

Fornication Sexual intercourse between two individuals who are not married to one another.

French Culture Colloquialism for oral sex—fellatio or cunnilingus.

French Kiss To kiss with mouths open and the tongues making contact.

French Letter An old colloquial term for condom.

French Tickler A rubber device in various complex shapes, attached to a condom, which is designed to increase the sexual pleasure of the female during intercourse.

Frenulum The thin fold of skin on the penis that connects the lower surface of the glans with the foreskin.

Friccatrice A female who masturbates males to orgasm for a fee.

Frigidity The inability of a female to have a sexual orgasm.

Frotteurism Obtaining sexual excitement or gratification by rubbing one's clothed body against a stranger in a crowded public place.

Fuck Colloquial term for sexual intercourse.

Fundus The base of the uterus, the part opposite the cervix.

Gang Bang Colloquial term for rape or voluntary intercourse in which several males have sexual relations with one female.

Gash Colloquial term for female genitals.

Gay Homosexual.

Geisha A Japanese female who is trained to sing, dance, and serve as a companion to male customers.

Gender One's sex, male or female.

Genitalia The sexual organs, especially the external organs.

Genitals The sexual organs.

Gentian Violet A dye used in the medical treatment of some venereal diseases.

Gerontophilia Having a sexual preference for elderly individuals.

Gestation The period from conception to birth; pregnancy.

Ginseng Root An aromatic root of a plant grown in Asia and used as a medicine in China, Vietnam, Korea, and elsewhere. It is popularly believed to act as a sexual tonic or stimulant.

Giving Head Colloquial term for engaging in oral sex.

Glans The head of the penis.

Going Down Colloquial term for engaging in oral sex.

Golden Showers Colloquial term for sexual interactions involving the urination of at least one partner on the other.

Gonad A sex gland that produces the ova (females) or sperm (males). The female gonads are the ovaries, and the male gonads are the testes.

Gonococcus The bacterium that causes gonorrhea.

Gonorrhea A venereal disease caused by the bacterium gonococcus.

Goose Colloquial term for a poke between the buttocks.

Graafian Follicle The complete name for a *follicle* (a small pouch near the surface of the ovary that contains the developing ovum). Named for the Dutch anatomist Regnier de Graaf.

Greek Culture Colloquial term for anal intercourse.

Group Sex Any sexual practices involving the interaction of three or more individuals.

Gynecologist A physician specializing in female disorders, especially those of the reproductive system.

Half and Half Among prostitutes, a sexual interaction consisting of fellatio followed by intercourse.

Hand Job Colloquial term for masturbation of a client for a fee, popularized by massage parlors.

Hand Whore Colloquial term for a masseuse who only masturbates her clients.

Hard-Core Refers to explicit pornography. Though definitions change, hard-core pornography generally is identified as that which depicts erections, penetration of a bodily orifice, and/or external ejaculation.

Hard On Colloquial term for an erection.

Harem In an Oriental palace or house, the females or the part of the residence in which they live. Popularly used to refer to a group of live-in concubines.

Hermaphrodite An individual who has both male and female internal and external sexual organs.

Heterosexuality Having a preference for members of the opposite sex.

His and Her Massage In a massage parlor, when the customer is allowed to give a massage to the masseuse as well as to receive one.

Homophile One who prefers members of his or her own sex.

Homosexuality Having a preference for members of one's own sex.

Honey Pot Colloquial term for vestibule and vagina, especially when the female is in a state of sexual excitement.

Hormone A bodily secretion that has an effect on other specific bodily organs and tissues.

Horny Colloquial term for a state of strong sexual need.

Hung Colloquial term describing a male with large genital organs.

Hustler Among homosexuals, one who offers his body to customers for a fee.

Hymen A fold of membrane that partially covers the external opening of the vagina. Though the presence of the hymen traditionally has been taken as an indication of virginity, it is possible to lose the hymen in a variety of nonsexual ways and it is also possible to have sexual relations without entirely destroying the hymen.

Hypertrophy. Abnormal enlargement or growth of a bodily part.

Hypnotherapy Any psychotherapeutic technique that utilizes hypnosis as a procedure.

Impotence The inability of a male to have an erection. If the individual has never had an erection, the condition is termed **primary impotence**; if he has had an erection previously, the condition is called **secondary impotence.**

Impregnate To make a female pregnant.

Incest Sexual acts committed with a relative.

Incubus An imaginary male demon that was believed during the Middle Ages to descend on a sleeping woman to have intercourse with her.

Intercourse Sexual relations.

Interfemoral Intercourse Intercouse in which the penis is rubbed between the closed thighs of the sexual partner.

Intrauterine Device (IUD) A contraceptive device (a coil or loop designed in various shapes) that is inserted in the uterus.

Intromission In sexual terms, penetration of the vagina with the penis.

Inversion An outdated medical term for homosexuality.

Jack Off Colloquial term for masturbation.

Jerk Off Colloquial term for masturbation.

Jism Colloquial term for semen.

John Prostitute's term for a client.

Joy Button A colloquial term for the clitoris.

Jugs Colloquial term for breasts.

Kamasutra An ancient Hindu book that describes sexual practices.

Kinky Sex A colloquial term meaning very unusual sexual practices or interests.

Knockers Colloquial term for breasts.

Labia Majora The outer folds of skin of the external female genitals.

Labia Minora The inner folds of skin of the external female genitals.

Laparoscopic Sterilization A relatively simple means of sterilizing a female in which the surgeon makes a small incision in the abdomen in order to reach the Fallopian tubes. Often referred to as "band-aid" sterilization because the small incision can literally be bandaged in that fashion.

Lascivious Characterized by extreme interest in sex or something that arouses sexual desire.

Leather Trade Among homosexuals, those who are involved in bondage and discipline or sadomasochism. Particular clothing (leather jackets, boots) is worn as an indication of these inclinations.

Lesbianism Female homosexuality. Based on the reputed characteristics of the ancient inhabitants of the Greek island of Lesbos.

Lewd Characterized by lust, obscenity, or vulgarity.

Libido In psychoanalytic theory, the sexual instinct or sexual drive.

Local In massage parlor terms, a "hand job" or masturbation of the client.

Love A tender and passionate affection for another person.

Lucky Pierre In group homosexual activity, if three males are engaged in anal intercourse simultaneously, the one in the middle is known colloquially as Lucky Pierre. He is penetrating the anus of one participant and having his own anus penetrated by the other participant.

Luteinizing Hormone (LH) A hormone secreted by the anterior pituitary gland that, in the female, causes the Graafian follicle to rupture and release the egg. In the male, this hormone is involved in producing testosterone.

Madam A woman who owns or manages a house of prostitution.

Maidenhead A somewhat outdated term for the hymen.

Make Love Colloquial term for having sexual intercourse.

M and M Parlor A massage parlor that provides only massage and masturbation.

Manual Sex Any sexual activity (e.g., masturbation or petting) that involves hand-genital contact.

Mammary Glands The glands in the female breast that produce milk after the birth of a baby.

Masochism Being sexually aroused by receiving psychological or physical pain and humiliation. Named for von Sacher-Masoch, who described such practices in nineteenth-century novels and short stories.

Massage Parlor An establishment in which female employees offer massages to male clients. The services ordinarily include sexual acts ranging from masturbation to oral and genital sex.

Masturbation Sexual stimulation and gratification of oneself.

Mate Swapping When a married couple agrees to join at least one other couple for the purpose of engaging in mutually agreed upon extramarital sexual activity.

Media Fetishism When the substance of the fetish object is the most important feature. Examples are leather and rubber.

Ménage à Trois A sexual arrangement in which there are two members of one sex and one member of the other sex living together.

Menopause The period, usually at about age 45 to 50, when the female stops menstruating and is no longer able to reproduce.

Menstruation The periodic discharge of blood and the mucous lining of the uterus. This process occurs approximately each 28 days in females from puberty until menopause except during pregnancy.

Missionary Position Ventral-ventral intercourse with the female lying on her back and the male lying above her. The name is derived from the practice of European missionaries who sought to convert the natives in various lands to the prevailing sexual position of Western Europe, which was assumed to be the only natural and moral one.

Monilia A fungus disease that can occur in the genitals, mouth, and anus. The most familiar form occurs in the vagina and is known as thrush.

Monogamy Marriage in which there is one husband and one wife.

Mons Pubis The rounded abdominal area above the genitals that is covered with pubic hair.

Mons Veneris A special name for the mons pubis of females, "the mount of love."

Muff Diving Colloquial term for cunnilingus.

Multiorgasmic The capacity of some females under some conditions to experience a series of orgasms during one sexual interaction.

Myotonia Muscular tension, rigidity, or spasm.

Necrophilia Sexual interest in and sexual relations with a dead body.

Negative Population Growth A rate of growth lower than that needed to maintain a constant population, hence leading to a decrease in the population.

Nipple The protuberance on the breast from which, in the female, milk is available for infants. The nipples in both sexes are richly supplied with nerve endings and serve as secondary erogenous zones which swell when stimulated manually or orally.

Nocturnal Emission When ejaculation occurs during sleep as the culmination of a "wet dream."

Nuts Colloquial term for testes.

Nymphomania Medically, a condition in which a female engages in repeated sexual interactions in an unsuccessful attempt to receive satisfaction. Popularly and inaccurately applied to any female who is more sexually active and interested than the average.

Obscene Sexually offensive words, pictures, or actions that are perceived as disgusting.

Obstetrician A physician who specializes in pregnancy, childbirth, and postnatal care.

Oedipal Complex In psychoanalytic theory, the unresolved conflict between sexual desire for the mother and fear of retaliation from the father.

Onanism Masturbation. Taken from the biblical passage in which Onan ejaculated "on the ground" in what is now interpreted as an incidence of coitus interruptus rather than masturbation.

Open Swinging When couples engaged in mate swapping take part in sexual activity in full view of one another either as separate couples or in multiperson interactions.

Oral Contraception Contraceptive techniques that involve the oral administration of a pill.

Oral Sex Any sexual act that involves contact between mouth and genitals.

Oral Stage In psychoanalyic theory, the developmental stage involving the mouth and eating.

Orgasm The physical and emotional response that culminates a sexual act. In the male, orgasm ordinarily is associated with the ejaculation of semen.

Orgasmic Dysfunction The inability of a female to have a sexual orgasm. It is called *primary orgasmic dysfunction* when the individual has never experienced an orgasm and *secondary orgasmic dysfunction* when the individual has had at least one orgasm previously. The commonly used term is the somewhat inaccurate and derogatory one of "frigidity."

Orgy Group sex in which the participants interact in various combinations with multiple partners.

Orifice Any bodily opening, especially in sexual terms the vagina, mouth, and anus.

Ovaries The female gonads that produce the ova and sexual hormones.

Overpopulation The idea that there are excessive individuals on this planet.

Ovulation The expelling of an ovum from a follicle.

Ovum The egg produced in the ovary of females which, when united with a male sperm, can produce a new individual.

Pansy A derogatory colloquial term for a homosexual male.

Pap Smear The Papanicolaou test—a painless procedure in which a small sample of uterine cells is obtained in order to detect the presence of cancer.

Paraphilia A general term for any deviant or abnormal sexual preferences.

Partialism Fetishism in which the fetish object is some physical attribute of the sexual partner.

Passion Strong sexual desire and/or love.

Passionate Love An intense interpersonal emotional state involving a combination of interpersonal attraction, romantic feelings, and sexual desire.

Pecker Colloquial term for the penis.

Pederasty A homosexual act with a young boy.

Pedophilia Sexual preference for young children.

Peeping Tomism Engaging in voyeuristic activity when those being observed are unaware of the observer.

Penile Plethysmograph A scientific instrument used to measure changes in the circumference or volume of a penis. Thus, in experiments, sexual excitement can be determined objectively.

Penis The male sexual organ through which semen is ejaculated and urine is expelled.

Penis Envy In psychoanalytic theory, the assumption that females are envious of the "superior" external genitalia of males.

Perineum The area between the anus and the scrotum (males) or the base of the vulva (females).

Peritoneum The membrane lining the abdominal cavity and the viscera.

Perversion An inexact term that is applied to any sexual act or interest that is judged to be abnormal or deviant.

Peter A colloquial term for the penis.

Petting Fondling or caressing a sexual partner. *Light petting* generally refers to contacts made above the waist and *heavy petting* to below-the-waist contacts.

Phallic Stage In psychoanalytic theory, the developmental stage involving an interest in the clitoris or penis along with sexual urges toward the parent.

Phallus The penis (or clitoris) or an image of the male organ used in various religious ceremonies as a symbol of reproduction, fertility, and power.

Pheromone A hormonal substance the odor of which serves to attract and stimulate members of the opposite sex.

Pill Colloquially used to refer to the contraceptive pill or oral contraceptive.

Pimp A male who manages one or more prostitutes, solicits customers for them, and shares their income.

Placenta An organ that forms in the uterus during pregnancy from a combination of membranes from the uterine lining and the fetus. The placenta serves to transmit nourishment to and waste products from the fetus, and it is expelled at birth along with the infant.

Polyandry Marriage in which there is one wife and multiple husbands.

Polygamy Marriage in which there is one husband and multiple wives.

Popper A vial of amyl nitrite that is broken and inhaled at the moment of orgasm in order to intensify the subjective experience.

Population Control Any measures taken in an attempt to control the number of individuals conceived and born and thus to prevent overpopulation.

Population Explosion The concept that the growth rate is such that an already overpopulated planet is rapidly growing more and more crowded.

Pornography Originally the word meant writing about prostitutes. Formally, it means obscene literature, art, or photography that has no artistic merit. Because of legal and linguistic ambiguity, in practice it tends to mean that which a specific individual or group tends to dislike or find offensive.

Pounding One's Pud A colloquial term for male masturbation.

Pox An outdated, colloquial term for syphilis.

Preejaculatory Emission The lubricating fluid that is discharged from the penis when sexual excitement is sufficiently intense.

Pregnancy The period between conception and birth when the infant is developing within a female's body.

Premarital Intercourse Sexual intercourse that occurs prior to marriage.

Premature Ejaculation When ejaculation occurs very rapidly because the male cannot tolerate high levels of sexual excitement without reaching an immediate climax.

Priapism A pathological condition in which there is a continuous and often painful erection.

Prick A colloquial term for penis and, in a derogatory way, for a male.

Primal Scene In psychoanalytic theory, the memory or fantasy in which a child first observes his parents engaged in sexual intercourse.

Procreation Conception, or the creation of a new being.

Progesterone The hormone produced by the corpus luteum that prepares the uterus for the reception and development of a fertilized ovum.

Pro-kit Package of prophylactic materials issued to American servicemen to prevent venereal disease.

Promiscuity Having sexual relations indiscriminately with informal or casual partners.

Pronatalism An attitude in favor of large families and of males and females fulfilling their traditional sex roles as parents.

Prophylaxis The word means prevention and is applied to condoms or medications that act to protect the user from venereal disease.

Proposition To ask someone to engage in a sexual act, especially an illicit act.

Prostate Gland The muscular, glandular organ that surrounds the urethra of males at the base of the bladder. It produces the thin alkaline fluid that constitutes at least one-third of the semen. Its muscular tissues help eject the semen out of the penis during ejaculation.

Prostitute An individual, ordinarily a female, who engages in sexual acts for a monetary fee.

Prostitution The practice of engaging in sexual acts for a monetary fee.

Prurient Causing sexual excitement or tending to have sexual thoughts.

Pseudo-pregnancy A psychosomatic condition in which the female believes herself to be pregnant and exhibits many of the appropriate physiological characteristics such as cessation of menstruation, morning sickness, and swollen breasts.

Puberty The age period at which an individual first becomes capable of reproduction.

Pubic Any bodily part located in front of or near the pelvis. Thus, it tends to refer to the genital area.

Pussy Colloquial term for female genitals.

Queer Colloquial, derogatory term for a homosexual or homosexuality.

Rape Sexual intercourse with an unwilling participant who is coerced by force or threats of force.

Rear Entry Intercourse Intercourse position in which the male faces the female's back.

Refractory Period The temporary lack of response to sexual stimulation that follows orgasm in males.

Reproduction The act of creating a new member of one's species.

Rhythm Method The contraceptive technique that relies on the fact that the female is fertile only during a few days of her menstrual cycle; the couple abstains from intercourse during these days.

Rimming Colloquial term for analingus.

Roman Culture Colloquial term for orgies.

Rubber Colloquial term for condom.

Sadism Being sexually aroused by giving psychological or physical pain and humiliation. Named for the Count de Sade, who participated in and wrote about such practices in the eighteenth and early nineteenth centuries.

Sadomasochism (S & M) Obtaining

sexual arousal through receiving or giving physical or mental pain.

Satyriasis A condition in which a male has an abnormally strong and uncontrollable sexual desire.

Scatological Relating to excrement or an individual who is preoccupied with such bodily products.

Screw Colloquial term for sexual intercourse, used either as a verb or noun. Also, when spelled *SCREW*, the name of a weekly sexual publication.

Scrotum The pouch of skin below the penis that contains the testes.

Seduce To persuade or induce someone to have sexual intercourse.

Self-Abuse An outdated and derogatory term for masturbation.

Semen The whitish fluid ejaculated by males at orgasm. It consists of sperm plus secretions from the seminal vesicles, prostate gland, and Cowper's gland.

Seminal Vesicles The pair of male glands that produce at least two-thirds of the semen.

Sequential Pills Birth control pills that are designed to simulate the normal physiological secretions of the menstrual cycle, with estrogen during the first 15 days followed by a combination of estrogen and progestogen during the remaining 5 or 6 days.

Sex Education Formal school courses that are designed to teach the fundamental aspects of sexual anatomy, physiology, reproduction, and sexual behavior.

Sex Flush A rashlike reddening of the skin that may appear during sexual excitement, especially in the chest area.

Sex Guilt The expectancy of self-punishment whenever one violates his or her sexual standards or even anticipates violating them.

Sex Offender One who commits a sexual crime such as rape.

Sex Therapy Treatment of sexual dysfunctions.

Sex-Typed Individual One who has strongly adopted the traditional stereotyped personality characterisics of the masculine or feminine role.

Sexual Behavior Sequence A theoretical model in which sexual behavior is conceptualized as a function of three response systems (affective-evaluative, informational-expectative, and imagery-excitement) which are evoked by an erotic stimulus.

Sexual Dysfunction A disability that interferes with sexual performance or sexual pleasure.

Sexuality Anything relating to sexual interests, functioning, or activities.

Sheath A condom.

Shooting One's Wad Colloquial term for ejaculation.

Short-Arm Inspection Military colloquialism for an examination of the male genitalia for venereal disease.

SIECUS An organization devoted to promoting sexual education and sexual information for both young people and adults. The letters stand for Sex Information and Education Council of the United States.

Sixty-Nine Colloquial term for mutual and simultaneous oral-genital activity between two individuals.

Skin Flick Colloquial term for an erotic or pornographic movie.

Smegma A secretion of oil glands under the glans of the penis or clitoris. If the individual does not bathe regularly, smegma can accumulate (especially under the foreskin of an uncircumcised male) and develop an offensive odor.

Snatch Colloquial term for the female genitals.

Sodomy Usually means anal intercourse. It has been used to mean "abnormal" sex generally, especially anal and oral acts and bestiality. It refers to the behavior of the sinful residents of the biblical city of Sodom.

Soft-core Refers to mildly pornographic erotica, usually that in which bodily parts and sexual acts are not described in explicit detail (in writing) or in which erections, penetration, and external ejaculation are not shown (in pictorial form). Thus a movie that involved only female frontal nudity and simulated intercourse would be soft-core.

Soixante-Neuf The French word for sixty-nine.

Sperm The cells produced in the testes of males which, when united with a female ovum, can produce a new individual.

Spermicidal Agent A contraceptive material such as a cream or jelly that kills sperm.

Spirochete The corkscrew-shaped organism, *treponema pallidum*, that causes syphilis.

Splash Shot In pornographic films, a scene in which a male ejaculates externally, usually on some portion of his partner's body.

Spread Shot A photograph of a female's external genitals.

Squeeze Technique A procedure used to treat premature ejaculation in which the male is stimulated to the point of climax; then, the climax is stopped by having his partner squeeze the penis just below the rim the glans.

Stag Film An erotic or pornographic film that was designed to be shown at all-male gatherings.

Statutory Rape Sexual intercourse between a male and a consenting female who is below the legal age of consent (which varies from state to state in the United States).

Steam and Cream Colloquial description of massage parlor services in Southeast Asia involving a sauna bath and masturbation.

Sterilization Any procedure, usually an operation, that makes it impossible for the individual to reproduce.

Straight A colloquial term for heterosexuality. It can also refer to someone who is relatively conventional in his or her sexual practices.

Strain Gauge A research device used as part of a penile plethysmograph to detect increases in penis size during an experiment.

Streetwalker Generally, the lowest class and least expensive type of prostitute, who solicits customers on the street or sidewalk.

Stud Term for a sexually proficient or sexually active male.

Succubus An imaginary female demon that was believed during the Middle Ages to descend on a sleeping man to have intercourse with him.

Swinging Another term for mate swapping or exchanging spouses for sexual purposes.

Syphilis A very serious venereal disease that is caused by *spirochetes*, corkscrew-shaped organisms.

Tampon A device, ordinarily made of cotton, which can be inserted in the vagina during menstruation to absorb the discharged blood and cellular material.

Tea Room Homosexual colloquial term for a rest room in which random sexual interactions take place. Those who frequent a tea room are known as *tea room trade*.

Testes The two male gonads, glands located in the scrotum, that produce sperm and sex hormones. The singular is *testis*. Also known as testicles.

Testicles The testes or male gonads, located in the scrotum.

Testosterone The androgen, or male sex hormone, secreted by the testes.

Tijuana Bible A pornographic comic book, usually consisting of eight pages, in which the sexual exploits of familiar funny paper characters are depicted in graphic detail.

Transsexualism An individual's belief that he or she emotionally and psychologically is a member of the opposite sex. In recent years, transsexuals have been able to undergo hormone treatments and surgery to provide them with an approximation of the bodily structure of their preferred sex.

Transvestism (TV) The practice of dressing in the clothing of the opposite sex in order to become sexually aroused.

Treponeme A spirochete, the organism that causes syphilis.

Trick A prostitute's term for a customer or for a sexual interaction. "Turning a trick" refers to a completed and paid for sexual act.

Tubal Ligation A method of sterilizing the female in which the two Fallopian tubes are cut; the cut ends are then closed off.

Tumescence A swelling, most often used to refer to the state of an erect penis.

Unisex Clothing Clothes that are styled so as to be worn by either males or females and are thus not indicative of the individual's sex.

Ureter The tubes that convey urine from each kidney to the bladder.

Urethra The tube that conveys urine from the bladder to the urethral opening in the female and from the bladder through the penis in the male. The male's urethra also conveys semen when ejaculation occurs.

Urinary Acid Phosphatase A substance in the urine that has been found to increase in sexually aroused males.

Uterus The womb or feminine organ within which the fertilized ovum attaches itself and develops throughout pregnancy.

Vagina The female organ between the cervix and the vulva which receives the penis during intercourse and which serves as a passageway for the discharge during menstruation and for the infant during the birth process.

Vaginal Orgasm The mistaken notion that some female orgasms are centered in the vagina rather than in the clitoris and indicate a mature stage of sexual development.

Vaginal Plethysmograph A scientific instrument inserted in the vagina to measure changes in the blood supply

by means of a light source and its reflection on a light-sensitive device. Thus, in experiments, sexual excitement can be determined objectively.

Vas Deferens The sperm ducts which lead from the testes to the seminal vesicles.

Vasectomy A method of sterilizing the male in which the vas deferens is cut and tied off so that sperm from the testes cannot reach the seminal vesicle and hence are no longer included in the semen that is ejaculated.

Vasoconcentration The concentration of blood in a particular bodily part.

Vasoconstriction The constriction of blood vessels.

Venereal Disease (VD) A disease that ordinarily can be contracted only during a sexual act.

Ventral-Ventral Intercourse Intercourse in which the two participants are face to face.

Vestibule The region surrounding the opening of the vagina.

Vibrator A device, usually made of plastic, that is operated by batteries or an electric current. It can be used to provide sexual stimulation to the point of orgasm.

Vice An immoral act or practice.

Vice Squad A section of a police department whose purpose is to enforce laws against "vices" such as prostitution, homosexuality, and gambling.

Virgin An individual who has never engaged in sexual intercourse.

Voluptuous An individual who is characterized by an enjoyment of sensual pleasure.

Voyeurism The act of obtaining sexual stimulation or gratification from viewing the nudity or sexual interactions of others.

Vulva External sexual organs of the female.

Wasserman Test A diagnostic blood test which can detect the presence of syphilis. Named for August von Wasserman, a German physician and bacteriologist who lived in the last part of the nineteenth and first part of the twentieth century.

Water Sports Colloquial term for sexual practices involving the giving and/or receiving of an enema.

Wet Dream An orgasm that occurs while the individual is asleep.

Wet Shot In sexual movies, a scene in which the male ejaculates externally, usually on some portion of his partner's body.

White Slavery The practice of forcing women to become prostitutes and compelling them to continue working in this profession even though they are not willing to do so.

Whore A derogatory term for a prostitute.

Withdrawal The contraceptive procedure in which a male withdraws his penis from his partner's vagina prior to ejaculation.

Womb The uterus.

X-Rated Movie A movie not deemed suitable for viewers under the age of 18, usually because of its explicit sexual content.

Zero Population Growth (ZPG) A rate of growth that maintains a constant population because the annual number of births equals the annual number of deaths. It is generally found that an average of 2.1 children per family will achieve this rate.

Author Index

Subject Index